WHAT IS ART?

AESTHETIC THEORY FROM PLATO TO TOLSTOY

EDITED BY

ALEXANDER SESONSKE, *University of California*

New York · OXFORD UNIVERSITY PRESS

1965

TO SARAH AND SANDY

PREFACE

>>>>><<<<<

Before compiling this anthology I once dreamed of gathering in a single volume all of the major writings in Western aesthetics prior to the twentieth century. An impossible dream, of course; limitations of space, time, and ability have forced me to be content with the more modest volume now at hand. Though incomplete, it is, I hope, a rather comprehensive source book in the history of aesthetics.

I have long felt that the most useful book should include substantial portions of the most significant works rather than fragments representing the whole sweep of history. This, in conjunction with the fact that I read the history of aesthetics from the point of view of a twentieth-century English-speaking philosopher, has led to a not-quite-exclusive concentration on three historical periods—ancient Greece, eighteenth-century Britain, and nineteenth-century Germany. This has meant the omission of many interesting and historically influential writers, but has also made it possible to display the style and mode of thought of those included. Appropriately, I have given fullest treatment to the three giants of Western aesthetics: Plato and Aristotle, who are the major sources of the Western philosophic tradition in aesthetics as elsewhere, and Immanuel Kant, who provides both the consummation of eighteenth-century British thought and the foundations of nineteenth-century aesthetic theory. My most difficult problem of selection has been that of choosing among the wealth of eighteenth-century British writings in a period which shaped the fundamental notions of modern aesthetics. There are no giants in this period, but a score of able men, of quite

diverse interests, turned their attention to questions of "taste," "genius," "the beautiful and sublime"; read, wrote, and argued —and produced some of the most original and stimulating ideas in the history of aesthetics.

I have tried to use complete selections wherever possible, or at least relatively complete portions of larger works. But several major works defy such treatment; my only expedient here, e.g. with Burke, Kant, and Schopenhauer, has been an attempt to edit the work in a manner which preserves the most significant insight or view involved and retains what continuity is possible. However successful I have been at this, I hope the interested reader will be stimulated to consult the complete work—to see what it really says.

With one exception all of the writings collected here are well-known and have long been highly regarded. Most of them have had a considerable influence in shaping the thought of their own, or later, times. The one exception is Alexander Smith's "The Philosophy of Poetry," published anonymously in 1835 and unnoticed until recently rediscovered by M. H. Abrams and discussed in his book, *The Mirror and the Lamp*. This interesting paper anticipates some twentieth-century views and deserves a wider audience than it has had.

In compiling this volume I have had the encouragement of Monroe Beardsley, who also kindly permitted me to read the manuscript of his *Short History of Western Aesthetics* and to borrow, almost intact, the extensive bibliography he had prepared for that volume. I should also like to express my thanks to Sharon McKenna, Diana Axel-

son, Barbara Kuhn, Sally Sesonske, Sandra
Sesonske, Leslie Fingarette, and Noel Flem-
ing, who have each been of great assistance

at different stages in the preparation of the
manuscript.

Santa Barbara,   A. S.
October 1964

CONTENTS

>>>>>><<<<<

PART III   *Post-Kantian Aesthetics: Schiller to Tolstoy*

INTRODUCTION

➤➤➤➤➤◄◄◄◄◄

What is art? The question which forms the title of this volume, as well as of the essay from which the final selection was taken, was never asked by Socrates, though it has all the apparent simplicity and directness and the real difficulty of those Socratic questions that respectable Athenians found so disturbing: What is courage? What is piety? What is justice? Socrates does talk, of course, in Plato's dialogues, of music and poetry, painting and sculpture, but not of *art* as we understand the term. Neither his vocabulary nor Plato's contains a word which would have conveyed this idea. Not for many centuries was the concept of fine art to be clearly and explicitly formulated.

Once this concept is formulated and has become imbedded in our speech, the central problem of aesthetics seems finally to have taken clear shape. Now we can read the ancients and the moderns with an understanding eye, uncover the "theory of art" implicit in Plato or Augustine, and compare it with the explicit theories of Batteux or Hegel. Armed with our awareness of what the problem really is, we can see earlier writers groping toward a clear statement and solution of it, handicapped by the poverty of their language, yet dimly showing forth those fragmentary insights which make up the history of the subject before Baumgarten, or Dubos, or Vico, or Kant "spoke the first rational word on aesthetics" in the eighteenth century.

But if we take "What is art?" as a Socratic question, a request for definition, and read the history of aesthetics as a series of attempts to find the answer, we may well be dismayed by the diversity of these attempts. We may decide that the problem must be enormously difficult, since so many great minds have proposed such incompatible answers. Or we may, like Croce, knowing the answer, be unable to discover anything but deviations and errors in much of the historical material. Whatever we do, we shall probably not understand the things we read. The question which was to have clarified the field has become an impediment instead. We end, like Socrates, by being puzzled.

Socratic questions always lead to puzzlement if we accept them as being direct and simple, as they seem. As long as we seek merely an *answer,* we remain puzzled; only when we turn to examine the question itself shall we find the source of our perplexity.

What, then, shall we make of "What is art?" What *does* it ask? What sort of question is it? What would the *form* of a correct answer be? For example, would the key term of a correct answer be a noun or a verb? And what method could we use to establish its correctness? Think? Observe? Take a poll?—Observe what? Ask whom?

Prodded by such remarks, we may see that "What is art?" is not *a* question, but a whole cluster of questions disguised as one. It masquerades successfully as *the* problem of aesthetics only because it contains within itself all of the theoretical questions we ask about the arts. We shall read historical texts in aesthetics more perceptively if we begin by sorting out the cluster.

Here as elsewhere, theory follows practice in that theoretical questions initially arise in the context of some practical encounter in the world, some data of experience. The basic data in this field are the myriad occurrences of song, dance, painting, sculpture, architecture, poetry, drama—produced and responded to with a frequency, regularity, and insistence which marks a universal and fundamental aspect of human culture. Out of this pervasive data we can identify a typical "situation" with typical components. I shall call the typical situation the *aesthetic complex*. From a consideration of the complex and its components we can generate the theoretical questions which constitute the problems of aesthetics.

Browse through a museum, go to a film, play a record, read a poem—different as these events are, the structure of the situation remains constant: a human attending to a perceptible object which has been produced by humans and displayed, exhibited, or made available in some way. Of course many non-aesthetic situations have the same structure—a trip to the supermarket, for example. What is different about going to a museum? Well, we talk about it differently anyway. We call the object perceived a painting, a *work of art* or *art object*; and the person who produced it an *artist*. We who view it form an *audience*. These terms identify three of the components of the aesthetic complex: art object, artist, audience. The fourth component is perhaps not so readily noticed, since it is a constant condition of our lives, that is, the society or culture within which artist and audience move. All of the problems of aesthetics concern either the characteristics of these four components or the relations between them—and most of them seem plausible interpretations of the question "What is art?"

Though I have called this the aesthetic complex, its occurrence in no way depends upon the existence of anything that might be called *aesthetics*. For aesthetics involves only a theoretical concern with art, and there is little doubt that artists and audiences had existed for thousands of years before the first theoretical questions about art were asked. Doubtless, too, *criticism* preceded aesthetics. Perhaps the first critical remark occurred when a joyous artist hailed his busy brother, crying "Look what I have made!"—and the brother grunted "Why?"

or "What's so great about that?" We can ask such questions casually, but if we persist in trying to answer them we eventually must come to some general statement about what sorts of things are worth looking at, or what makes a thing "great." And when we seek to provide a rational justification of these general statements aesthetics has been born. But we can paint or sing or dance for a lifetime without coming to that.

It is important to notice that we can identify works of art, artist, and audience without being able to *say* just what it is that makes these terms apply. We do not need to define "work of art" before we can recognize one, any more than we need be able to define "beauty" before we can use the term to describe a sunset. Thus our assurance that we have correctly identified the components of the aesthetic complex in no way begs the theoretical questions we can ask only after we have done so. Having noted the components, our task now is to see what questions arise when we consider each.

(a) The work of art usually occupies the center of attention in the aesthetic complex. Thus it is perhaps natural that the most familiar theoretical questions concern it. In many fields theoretical questions have a common genesis; when we encounter any interesting sort of object the things we want to know are: What is it? What good is it? How can I tell a good one? Translated into more pedantic terms these questions achieve the status of theoretical problems: What is the true *nature* of the object? What is the *function* of the object? What are the *criteria* for evaluating objects of this kind? If the object in question is an art object we have then asked some of the fundamental aesthetic questions: 1. What are the characteristics common and peculiar to art objects—that is, what is the generic nature of a work of art? At one level this asks what qualities distinguish art objects from all other things and enable us to group them together in a class which includes *Hamlet*,

a Rembrandt painting, and a Bartok quartet, but excludes Aristotle's *Metaphysics,* Harlem, and the sound of my neighbor cutting his lawn. All the problems of *form* and *substance* are implicit here. At a different level, it is a question about the metaphysical status of the art object, its relation to the ultimate constituents of the universe. If, on the first level, we go on to ask what systematic distinctions we can make within the class of art objects we come to the problems of *genres* and *style*. If we are concerned with metaphysics, we may assert that distinctions of genre or style are meaningless.
2. How do aesthetic objects function? What role do they play in the lives of the individuals who produce and view them, or in the society in which they occur? Do they merely duplicate the functions performed by other sorts of things; if so, do they do it more or less effectively? Or is there some role or function that only art objects can perform, and which may then serve as an answer to the question "What is art?" 3. What are the bases of criticism? When we consider the relation of art objects to each other, or to us, what characteristics or considerations justify our willingness to rank them in some evaluative order or assert that one is good, or preferable to another?

(b) When we shift our attention from the object to the audience, a different group of questions appears. What constitutes a man as audience, or part of one, is that he has encountered an art object and is attentive to it. Thus the fundamental questions here are: What goes on in such an encounter? What makes such encounters worth having or seeking? In more technical, but still familiar terms: What is an *aesthetic experience?* How do aesthetic experiences resemble and differ from experiences of other kinds? Is there some unique and peculiar element that marks them off, such as an "aesthetic emotion"? Or some peculiar faculty or ability called into play, such as imagination, taste, or a "sense of beauty"? Is an aesthetic experience shaped primarily by the characteristics of the art object, or by the capacities, attitudes, or past experience of the viewer? Does the encounter with the object, the aesthetic experience, leave the viewer unaffected after it is over, or does it contribute to or detract from his character and personality, his knowledge or ability, his status or identity as a human being, his attitudes or value to society?

(c) The primary question about the artist, the third component of the complex, can be crudely stated as "What is he doing?" or what kind of activity is he engaged in? In the language of aesthetics this becomes "What is artistic creation?" or "What is the nature of the creative process?" "How does it resemble or differ from other human activities?" Answers to these questions range from discussions of technique to talk of genius and inspiration. Such terms as *intention* and *expression* seem appropriate here —each of them bearing its own cluster of difficulties, as do remarks about the role of reason, imagination, or emotion in the creative process. Some further questions concern the relation of artist to audience. Is an audience essential to the creative process, or merely accidental? Is communication at the core of the creative act—or simply an accidental by-product?

(d) The central questions here concern the relation of society to art and artists. A culture or society provides the context within which art objects are created and enjoyed, and in return art objects are often regarded as uniquely capable of revealing the character or inner nature of the culture. How does this occur? Do cultural forces inevitably determine the forms of art which are produced? Or are poets the true legislators of mankind, by their creative genius shaping not only individual art objects but the culture as well? Is art a unifying and constructive force within the community, or a danger to it? Is the artist properly subject to the same social rules and restrictions that apply to lesser men? May or must a society exercise some control over the form or content of particular works of art? How is art related to other elements within the culture? education? economics? political structure? religion? Why are some cultures or eras enormously fruitful in producing works of art, while others are relatively barren?

The questions which have come forth here do not, of course, exhaust the possibilities inherent in the aesthetic complex. They will, I hope, suggest the variety and complexity of the problems of aesthetics and serve as a warning against the belief that all the writers of the past must have been concerned with the same question, which we can now see more clearly than they.

In this introduction I have stated some of the problems of aesthetics, the questions that writers from Plato to Tolstoy, and beyond, have been concerned with. Perhaps if we could answer them all we would no longer think it necessary to ask "What is art?" And perhaps until we answer them all we will not feel that the question "What is art?" has been finally settled. In this sense we may say that all these questions were contained in the original one.

But if the history of aesthetics is not one long attempt to answer a single question, neither is it simply a series of attempts to answer all the questions we have found. For the questions were not all there, clearly posed, from the beginning, presenting a challenge to each thinker to choose among them those that suited his fancy and try to answer them. It is as much a history of the emergence of new questions as of the formulation of new answers. And here, as elsewhere, the greatest ferment often occurs when someone discovers a new question rather than merely answering an old one. Unfortunately the men who first uncover new questions often do not state them clearly, or at all—they simply start to give an answer, or announce a subject to be discussed, as Aristotle announces that he will talk of poetic art and the forms it takes.

Thus we often must gather from the discussion what question is at stake, and how this differs from questions previously asked. If we do this we shall perceive the direction in which history flowed at a given point. I am suggesting that we shall read historical writings in aesthetics with more perception and more understanding if we observe the rise and fall of questions as well as the ebb and flow of answers, and if we note how a shift of attention from one component of the aesthetic complex to another is reflected in the problems taken to be most important and the theories offered.

A few remarks about the history of aesthetics may illustrate this point. The importance of Plato in this history stems not merely from the fact that he is the first Western writer to discuss art objects and artists seriously, analytically, and in generic terms—questioning both the meaning of aesthetic terms in common use and common sense beliefs about the arts—but that in the half dozen or so dialogues in which he touches, briefly or at length, on aesthetic questions, he explores the whole field. He does not, of course, clearly formulate all, or even many, of the problems of aesthetics— but he suggests them all, as well as most of the answers which are to be elaborated through subsequent Western thought. But in all this exploration, what emerges as most important in traditional aesthetic thought is the basic concept which Plato formed and elaborated and which provided one of the two central terms in aesthetics for some 2000 years—the concept of *mimesis* or *imitation*. In his most important and influential passage on art, *Republic* X, Plato suggests, at least, a general theory about the nature of art objects—an art object is an imitation. The identification of imitation as the essential character of an art object is confirmed in Aristotle's *Poetics*, which is explicitly an examination of the nature of a particular class of art objects. This idea, that an art object is an imitation, forms the central conception of classical aesthetics. But stating this suggests that for classical thought, the central element in the aesthetic complex is the work of art. It stands as the focus of attention when theory begins to take shape, with artist and audience treated only as subordinate objects of concern. The second major classical term, *beauty,* confirms this view; for this seems overtly a term whose primary use is to describe a characteristic of *objects.* Thus, if we say that in the classical period the focal aesthetic question was "What is beauty?" then this also serves to describe the orientation of the classical world with regard to the aesthetic complex. We find talk of artists and audience, of course—much of it in Plato, who does not share this orientation—but usually it is secondary to the central inquiry.

In eighteenth-century England the orientation has changed. The change is clear in Addison's seminal essay on the "pleasures of imagination" at the beginning of the century. For Addison the pleasures of imagination are the pleasures of visual perception—the pleasures of the viewer, the audience. The term that recurs most frequently in the title of eighteenth-century essays is *taste*—referring again to audience rather than art object or artist. Even before Addison's essay Shaftesbury had formulated the concept which was to be the cornerstone of modern aesthetic theory, the concept of *disinterested pleasure.* Obviously the audience, the aesthetic observer, now holds the center of the stage and the development of theory mirrors this shift in view. Critics berate "imitation" as an inadequate aesthetic notion and "imagination" replaces it as the central theoretical term, reflecting further the extent to which the art object has become subordinate within the eighteenth-century view of the aesthetic complex. Attention focuses upon the experience and response of the viewer; the art object is treated as instrumental to this response.

Two secondary strands of thought run through eighteenth-century writings in aesthetics—the repeated discussions of "the beautiful and sublime" and a growing concern with the question of *genius.* Despite its appearance of continuing the classical concern with the qualities of the art object, the first of these strands is closely tied to the new orientation, regarding the aesthetic observer as central. For it is *our ideas* of the beautiful and sublime that are examined. Burke, who first makes the distinction clear, begins his treatise with a discussion of pain and pleasure, and finds the *origin* of our ideas of the sublime and beautiful not in differing characteristics of the object, but in a basic difference in the experience of the observer—the difference he marks by distinguishing between *pleasure* and *delight.* The discussions of genius, on the other hand, do constitute a departure from the general eighteenth-century orientation, for their concern is with the artist, not the audience.

The distinction of beautiful and sublime marks the beginning of a second significant shift of terminology. "Beauty," for so long *the* ultimate critical term, the term signifying the acme of aesthetic value, must now share this role with "sublime"—the pair soon to be joined by a third, "picturesque." But by then an ultimate critical term no longer exists, and the notion of a common property uniting all art objects has lost some of its plausibility. The decline of "beauty" as a fundamental aesthetic term is slow but inexorable—by mid-twentieth century it has nearly disappeared from discussions of the arts. And "sublime" fades back into a minor role almost as quickly as it had emerged. A new terminology which reunites the arts appears in late eighteenth-century writings, however—a terminology related to the third major strand of the eighteenth-century dialogue, the discussions of genius. The unifying term, "expression," has a major role in Alison's *Essays on the Nature and Principles of Taste,* but it is Kant's *Critique of Judgement* which sums up eighteenth-century thought and lays the basis for all nineteenth-century aesthetic theory. In the first large segment of *The Critique of Judge-*

ment, the *Analytic of the Beautiful,* Kant draws together the threads of the previous discussion of taste so completely as to nearly terminate all argument. But the discussion of genius runs through Kant, not merely to him, and Kant's formulation "genius shows itself in the expression of aesthetical ideas" might serve as a text upon which to expound the main currents of nineteenth-century thought.

The shift of orientation characteristic of this century is openly proclaimed by Nietzsche, perhaps with typical exaggeration: "In the whole of philosophy hitherto, the artist has been lacking." But no longer; nineteenth-century thinkers find the artist the most interesting component of the aesthetic complex and discussions of aesthetic questions now revolve around him. This orientation still persists to some degree. The Romantic poet or the alienated and suffering painter still symbolizes for us nineteenth-century art, and we have not yet fully disavowed the notion that the most illuminating criticism of the arts consists in a description of the life of the artist.

A second sort of reorientation also distinguishes the nineteenth from the eighteenth century. For most eighteenth-century thinkers, the problems of aesthetics are treated as empirical questions, to be settled by "experiment"—usually by an appeal to the experience of most men. But in the wake of Kant's *Critiques* the major nineteenth-century philosophers take aesthetic questions to be metaphysical. It is typical of the eighteenth-century that a work is entitled an "Inquiry" and concerns "our ideas" or "human understanding"—but one of the most significant nineteenth-century discussions of art occurs in a work entitled *The World as Will and Idea.*

I have put forth this brief sketch of some currents in the historical flow of theoretical thought about art in hope that it will aid the reader in understanding the essays collected in this volume. These are not the only currents in the flow—other writers describing the stream might do so quite differently. The only claim I make dogmatically is that the writings gathered here form a significant segment of the history of Western thought and that a reader who approaches them openly will emerge with a fuller understanding both of art and of the Western tradition.

A. S.

Part One

✦✦✦✦✦✦✦✦✦✦

THE CLASSICAL TRADITION

Plato to Augustine

>>>>><<<<<

Ion [530–542b]

Persons of the Dialogue

SOCRATES   ION

Socrates. Welcome, Ion. Are you from your native city of [530] Ephesus?

Ion. No, Socrates; but from Epidaurus, where I attended the festival of Aesculapius.

Soc. Indeed! Do the Epidaurians have a contest of rhapsodes in his honour?

Ion. O yes; and of other kinds of music.

Soc. And were you one of the competitors—and did you succeed?

Ion. I—we—obtained the first prize of all, Socrates.

Soc. Well done; now we must win another victory, at the Panathenaea.

Ion. It shall be so, please heaven.

Soc. I have often envied the profession of a rhapsode, Ion; for it is a part of your art to wear fine clothes and to look as beautiful as you can, while at the same time you are obliged to be continually in the company of many good poets, and especially of Homer, who is the best and most divine of them, and to understand his mind, and not merely learn his words by rote; all this is a thing greatly to be envied. I am sure that no man can become a good rhapsode who does not understand the meaning of the poet. For the rhapsode ought to interpret the mind of the poet to his hearers, but how can he interpret him well unless he knows what he means? All this is much to be envied, I repeat.

Ion. Very true, Socrates; interpretation

has certainly been the most laborious part of my art; and I believe myself able to speak about Homer better than any man; and that neither Metrodorus of Lampsacus, nor Stesimbrotus of Thasos, nor Glaucon, nor anyone else who ever was, had as good ideas about Homer as I have, or as many.

Soc. I am glad to hear you say so, Ion; I see that you will not refuse to acquaint me with them.

Ion. Certainly, Socrates; and you really ought to hear how exquisitely I display the beauties of Homer. I think that the Homeridae should give me a golden crown.[1]

Soc. I shall take an opportunity of hearing your embellishments [531] of him at some other time. But just now I should like to ask you a question: Does your art extend to Hesiod and Archilochus, or to Homer only?

Ion. To Homer only; he is in himself quite enough.

Soc. Are there any things about which Homer and Hesiod agree?

Ion. Yes; in my opinion there are a good many.

Soc. And can you interpret what Homer says about these matters better than what Hesiod says?

Ion. I can interpret them equally well, Socrates, where they agree.

Soc. But what about matters in which they do not agree? for example, about divination of which both Homer and Hesiod have something to say,—

Ion. Very true.

Soc. Would you or a good prophet be a better interpreter of what these two poets say about divination, not only when they agree, but when they disagree?

All selections from Plato are from *The Dialogues of Plato,* translated with analyses and introductions by B. Jowett (Oxford: Oxford University Press, 1953, 4th edition, revised by order of the Jowett Copyright Trustees; 1st edition, 1871). Reprinted by permission of the Clarendon Press, Oxford.

[1] [Or, "I think I have well deserved the golden crown given me by the Homeridae."]

Ion. A prophet.

Soc. And if you were a prophet, and could interpret them where they agree, would you not know how to interpret them also where they disagree?

Ion. Clearly.

Soc. But how did you come to have this skill about Homer only, and not about Hesiod or the other poets? Does not Homer speak of the same themes which all other poets handle? Is not war his great argument? and does he not speak of human society and of intercourse of men, good and bad, skilled and unskilled, and of the gods conversing with one another and with mankind, and about what happens in heaven and in the world below, and the generations of gods and heroes? Are not these the themes of which Homer sings?

Ion. Very true, Socrates.

Soc. And do not the other poets sing of the same?

Ion. Yes, Socrates; but not in the same way as Homer.

Soc. What, in a worse way?

Ion. Yes, in a far worse.

Soc. And Homer in a better way?

Ion. He is incomparably better.

Soc. And yet surely, my dear friend Ion, where many people are discussing numbers, and one speaks better than the rest, there is somebody who can judge which of them is the good speaker?

Ion. Yes.

Soc. And he who judges of the good will be the same as he who judges of the bad speakers?

Ion. The same.

Soc. One who knows the science of arithmetic?

Ion. Yes.

Soc. Or again, if many persons are discussing the wholesomeness of food, and one speaks better than the rest, will he who recognizes the better speaker be a different person from him who recognizes the worse, or the same?

Ion. Clearly the same.

Soc. And who is he, and what is his name?

Ion. The physician.

Soc. And speaking generally, in all discussions in which the subject is the same and many men are speaking, will not he who knows the good know the bad speaker also? For obviously [532] if he does not know the bad, neither will he know the good, when the same topic is being discussed.

Ion. True.

Soc. We find, in fact, that the same person is skilful in both?

Ion. Yes.

Soc. And you say that Homer and the other poets, such as Hesiod and Archilochus, speak of the same things, although not in the same way; but the one speaks well and the other not so well?

Ion. Yes; and I am right in saying so.

Soc. And if you know the good speaker, you ought also to know the inferior speakers to be inferior?

Ion. It would seem so.

Soc. Then, my dear friend, can I be mistaken in saying that Ion is equally skilled in Homer and in other poets, since he himself acknowledges that the same person will be a good judge of all those who speak of the same things; and that almost all poets do speak of the same things?

Ion. Why then, Socrates, do I lose attention and have absolutely no ideas of the least value and practically fall asleep when anyone speaks of any other poet; but when Homer is mentioned, I wake up at once and am all attention and have plenty to say?

Soc. The reason, my friend, is not hard to guess. No one can fail to see that you speak of Homer without any art or knowledge. If you were able to speak of him by rules of art, you would have been able to speak of all other poets; for poetry is a whole.

Ion. Yes.

Soc. And when anyone acquires any

other art as a whole, the same may be said of them. Would you like me to explain my meaning, Ion?

Ion. Yes, indeed, Socrates; I very much wish that you would: for I love to hear you wise men talk.

Soc. O that we were wise, Ion, and that you could truly call us so; but you rhapsodes and actors, and the poets whose verses you sing, are wise; whereas I am a common man, who only speak the truth. For consider what a very commonplace and trivial thing is this which I have said—a thing which any man might say: that when a man has acquired a knowledge of a whole art, the inquiry into good and bad is one and the same. Let us consider this matter; is not the art of painting a whole?

Ion. Yes.

Soc. And there are and have been many painters good and bad?

Ion. Yes.

Soc. And did you ever know anyone who was skilful in pointing out the excellences and defects of Polygnotus the son [533] of Aglaophon, but incapable of criticizing other painters; and when the work of any other painter was produced, went to sleep and was at a loss, and had no ideas; but when he had to give his opinion about Polygnotus, or whoever the painter might be, and about him only, woke up and was attentive and had plenty to say?

Ion. No indeed, I have never known such a person.

Soc. Or take sculpture—did you ever know of anyone who was skilful in expounding the merits of Daedalus the son of Metion, or of Epeius the son of Panopeus, or of Theodorus the Samian, or of any individual sculptor; but when the works of sculptors in general were produced, was at a loss and went to sleep and had nothing to say?

Ion. No indeed; no more than the other.

Soc. And if I am not mistaken, you never met with anyone among flute-players or harp-players or singers to the harp or rhapsodes who was able to discourse of Olympus or Thamyras or Orpheus, or Phemius the rhapsode of Ithaca, but was at a loss when he came to speak of Ion of Ephesus, and had no notion of his merits or defects?

Ion. I cannot deny what you say, Socrates. Nevertheless I am conscious in my own self, and the world agrees with me, that I do speak better and have more to say about Homer than any other man; but I do not speak equally well about others. After all, there must be some reason for this; what is it?

Soc. I see the reason, Ion; and I will proceed to explain to you what I imagine it to be. The gift which you possess of speaking excellently about Homer is not an art, but, as I was just saying, an inspiration; there is a divinity moving you, like that contained in the stone which Euripides calls a magnet, but which is commonly known as the stone of Heraclea. This stone not only attracts iron rings, but also imparts to them a similar power of attracting other rings; and sometimes you may see a number of pieces of iron and rings suspended from one another so as to form quite a long chain: and all of them derive their power of suspension from the original stone. In like manner the Muse first of all inspires men herself; and from these inspired persons a chain of other persons is suspended, who take the inspiration. For all good poets, epic as well as lyric, compose their beautiful poems not by art, but because they are inspired and possessed. And as the Corybantian revellers when they [534] dance are not in their right mind, so the lyric poets are not in their right mind when they are composing their beautiful strains: but when falling under the power of music and metre they are inspired and possessed; like Bacchic maidens who draw milk and honey from the rivers when they are under the influence of Dionysus but not when they are in their right mind. And the soul of the lyric poet does the same, as they themselves say; for they tell us that they bring songs from honeyed fountains, culling them out of the gardens and dells of the Muses; they, like the bees, winging their way from flower to flower. And this is true. For the poet is a light and winged and holy thing, and there is no invention in him until he has been inspired and is out of his senses, and reason is no longer in him: no man, while he retains that faculty, has the oracular gift of poetry.

Many are the noble words in which poets speak concerning the actions of men; but like yourself when speaking about Homer, they do not speak of them by any rules of art: they are simply inspired to utter that to which the Muse impels them, and that only; and when inspired, one of them will make dithyrambs, another hymns of praise, another choral strains, another epic or iambic verses, but not one of them is of any account in the other kinds. For not by art does the poet sing, but by power divine; had he learned by rules of art, he would have known how to speak not of one theme only, but of all; and therefore God takes away reason from poets, and uses them as his ministers, as he also uses the pronouncers of oracles and holy prophets, in order that we who hear them may know them to be speaking not of themselves, who utter these priceless words while bereft of reason, but that God himself is the speaker, and that through them he is addressing us. And Tynnichus the Chalcidian affords a striking instance of what I am saying: he wrote no poem that anyone would care to remember but the famous paean which is in everyone's mouth, one of the finest lyric poems ever written, simply an invention of the Muses, as he himself says. For in this way God would seem to demonstrate to us and not to allow us to doubt that these beautiful poems are not human, nor the work of man, but divine and the work of God; and that the poets are only the interpreters of the gods by whom they are severally possessed.

Was not this the lesson which God intended to teach when by the mouth of the worst [535] of poets he sang the best of songs? Am I not right, Ion?

Ion. Yes, indeed, Socrates, I feel that you are; for your words touch my soul, and I am persuaded that in these works the good poets, under divine inspiration, interpret to us the voice of the Gods.

Soc. And you rhapsodists are the interpreters of the poets?

Ion. There again you are right.

Soc. Then you are the interpreters of interpreters?

Ion. Precisely.

Soc. I wish you would frankly tell me, Ion, what I am going to ask of you: When you produce the greatest effect upon the audience in the recitation of some striking passage, such as the apparition of Odysseus leaping forth on the floor, recognized by the suitors and shaking out his arrows at his feet, or the description of Achilles springing upon Hector, or the sorrows of Andromache, Hecuba, or Priam,—are you in your right mind? Are you not carried out of yourself, and does not your soul in an ecstasy seem to be among the persons or places of which you are speaking, whether they are in Ithaca or in Troy or whatever may be the scene of the poem?

Ion. That proof strikes home to me, Socrates. For I must frankly confess that at the tale of pity my eyes are filled with tears, and when I speak of horrors, my hair stands on end and my heart throbs.

Soc. Well, Ion, and what are we to say of a man who at a sacrifice or festival, when he is dressed in an embroidered robe, and has golden crowns upon his head, of which nobody has robbed him, appears weeping or panic-stricken in the presence of more than twenty thousand friendly faces, when there is no one despoiling or wronging him;—is he in his right mind or is he not?

Ion. No indeed, Socrates, I must say that, strictly speaking, he is not in his right mind.

Soc. And are you aware that you produce

similar effects on most of the spectators?

Ion. Only too well; for I look down upon them from the stage, and behold the various emotions of pity, wonder, sternness, stamped upon their countenances when I am speaking: and I am obliged to give my very best attention to them; for if I make them cry I myself shall laugh, and if I make them laugh I myself shall cry, when the time of payment arrives.

Soc. Do you know that the spectator is the last of the rings which, as I am saying, receive the power of the original magnet from one another? The rhapsode like yourself and the actor are [536] intermediate links, and the poet himself is the first of them. Through all these God sways the souls of men in any direction which He pleases, causing each link to communicate the power to the next. Thus there is a vast chain of dancers and masters and undermasters of choruses, who are suspended, as if from the stone, at the side of the rings which hang down from the Muse. And every poet has some Muse from whom he is suspended, and by whom he is said to be possessed, which is nearly the same thing; for he is taken hold of. And from these first rings, which are the poets, depend others, some deriving their inspiration from Orpheus, others from Musaeus; but the greater number are possessed and held by Homer. Of whom, Ion, you are one, and are possessed by Homer; and when anyone repeats the words of another poet you go to sleep, and know not what to say; but when anyone recites a strain of Homer you wake up in a moment, and your soul leaps within you, and you have plenty to say; for not by art or knowledge about Homer do you say what you say, but by divine inspiration and by possession; just as the Corybantian revellers too have a quick perception of that strain only which is appropriated to the god by whom they are possessed, and have plenty of dances and words for that, but take no heed of any other. And you, Ion, when the name of Homer is mentioned have plenty to say, and have nothing to say of others. You ask, "Why is this?" The answer is that your skill in the praise of Homer comes not from art but from divine inspiration.

Ion. That is good, Socrates; and yet I doubt whether you will ever have eloquence enough to persuade me that I praise Homer only when I am mad and possessed; and if you could hear me speak of him I am sure you would never think this to be the case.

Soc. I should like very much to hear you, but not until you have answered a question which I have to ask. On what part of Homer do you speak well?—not surely about every part?

Ion. There is no part, Socrates, about which I do not speak well: of that I can assure you.

Soc. Surely not about things in Homer of which you have no knowledge?

Ion. And what is there in Homer of which I have no knowledge?

Soc. Why, does not Homer speak in many passages about [537] arts? For example, about driving; if I can only remember the lines I will repeat them.

Ion. I remember, and will repeat them.

Soc. Tell me then, what Nestor says to Antilochus, his son, where he bids him be careful of the turn at the horse-race in honour of Patroclus.

Ion. "Bend gently," he says, "in the polished chariot to the left of them, and urge the horse on the right hand with whip and voice; and slacken the rein. And when you are at the goal, let the left horse draw near, so that the nave of the well-wrought wheel may appear to graze the extremity; but have a care not to touch the stone."

Soc. Enough. Now, Ion, will the charioteer or the physician be the better judge of the propriety of these lines?

Ion. The charioteer, clearly.

Soc. And will the reason be that this is his art, or will there be any other reason?

Ion. No, that will be the reason.

Soc. And every art is appointed by God

to have knowledge of a certain work; for that which we know by the art of the pilot we shall not succeed in knowing also by the art of medicine?

Ion. Certainly not.

Soc. Nor shall we know by the art of the carpenter that which we know by the art of medicine?

Ion. Certainly not.

Soc. And this is true of all the arts;—that which we know with one art we shall not know with the other? But let me ask a prior question: You admit that there are differences of arts?

Ion. Yes.

Soc. You would argue, as I should, that if there are two kinds of knowledge, dealing with different things, these can be called different arts?

Ion. Yes.

Soc. Yes, surely; for if the object of knowledge were the same, there would be no meaning in saying that the arts were different,—since they both gave the same knowledge. For example, I know that here are five fingers, and you know the same. And if I were to ask whether I and you became acquainted with this fact by the help of the same art of arithmetic, you would acknowledge that we did?

Ion. Yes.

[538] *Soc.* Tell me, then, what I was intending to ask you,—whether in your opinion this holds universally? If two arts are the same, must not they necessarily have the same objects? And if one differs from another, must it not be because the object is different?

Ion. That is my opinion, Socrates.

Soc. Then he who has no knowledge of a particular art will have no right judgement of the precepts and practice of that art?

Ion. Very true.

Soc. Then which will be the better judge of the lines which you were reciting from Homer, you or the charioteer?

Ion. The charioteer.

Soc. Why, yes, because you are a rhapsode and not a charioteer.

Ion. Yes.

Soc. And the art of the rhapsode is different from that of the charioteer?

Ion. Yes.

Soc. And if a different knowledge, then a knowledge of different matters?

Ion. True.

Soc. You know the passage in which Hecamede, the concubine of Nestor, is described as giving to the wounded Machaon a posset, as he says,

Made with Pramnian wine; and she grated cheese of goat's milk with a grater of bronze, and at his side placed an onion which gives a relish to drink.[2]

Now would you say that the art of the rhapsode or the art of medicine was better able to judge of the propriety of these lines?

Ion. The art of medicine.

Soc. And when Homer says,

And she descended into the deep like a leaden plummet, which set in the horn of ox that ranges the fields, rushes along carrying death among the ravenous fishes.[3]

will the art of the fisherman or of the rhapsode be better able to judge what these lines mean, and whether they are accurate or not?

Ion. Clearly, Socrates, the art of the fisherman.

Soc. Come now, suppose that you were to say to me: "Since you, Socrates, are able to assign different passages in Homer to their corresponding arts, I wish that you would tell me what are the passages of which the excellence ought to be judged by the prophet and prophetic art"; and you will see how readily and truly I shall answer you. For there are many such passages, particularly in the Odyssey; as, for example, the passage in which Theoclymenus the

---

[2] *Iliad* xi. 639, 640.
[3] *Iliad* xxiv. 80.

prophet of the house of Melampus says to the suitors:

Wretched men! what is happening to you? Your heads and your [539] faces and your limbs underneath are shrouded in night; and the voice of lamentation bursts forth, and your cheeks are wet with tears. And the vestibule is full, and the court is full, of ghosts descending into the darkness of Erebus, and the sun has perished out of heaven, and an evil mist is spread abroad.[4]

And there are many such passages in the Iliad also; as for example in the description of the battle near the rampart, where he says:—

As they were eager to pass the ditch, there came to them an omen: a soaring eagle, skirting the people on his left, bore a huge blood-red dragon in his talons, still living and panting; nor had he yet resigned the strife, for he bent back and smote the bird which carried him on the breast by the neck, and he in pain let him fall from him to the ground into the midst of the multitude. And the eagle, with a cry, was borne afar on the wings of the wind.[5]

These are the sort of things which I should say that the prophet ought to consider and determine.

Ion. And you are quite right, Socrates, in saying so.

Soc. Yes, Ion, and you are right also. And as I have selected from the Iliad and Odyssey for you passages which describe the office of the prophet and the physician and the fisherman, do you, who know Homer so much better than I do, Ion, select for me passages which relate to the rhapsode and the rhapsode's art, and which the rhapsode ought to examine and judge of better than other men.

Ion. All passages, I should say, Socrates.

Soc. Not all, Ion, surely. Have you already forgotten what you were saying? A rhapsode ought to have a better memory.

[4] *Odyssey* xx. 351.
[5] *Iliad* xii. 200.

[540] *Ion.* Why, what am I forgetting?

Soc. Do you not remember that you declared the art of the rhapsode to be different from the art of the charioteer?

Ion. Yes, I remember.

Soc. And you admitted that being different they would know different objects?

Ion. Yes.

Soc. Then upon your own showing the rhapsode, and the art of the rhapsode, will not know everything?

Ion. I should exclude such things as you mention, Socrates.

Soc. You mean to say that you would exclude pretty much the subjects of the other arts. As he does not know all of them, which of them will he know?

Ion. He will know what a man and what a woman ought to say, and what a freeman and what a slave ought to say, and what a ruler and what a subject.

Soc. Do you mean that a rhapsode will know better than the pilot what the ruler of a sea-tossed vessel ought to say?

Ion. No; the pilot will know best.

Soc. Or will the rhapsode know better than the physician what the ruler of a sick man ought to say?

Ion. Again, no.

Soc. But he will know what a slave ought to say?

Ion. Yes.

Soc. Suppose the slave to be a cowherd; the rhapsode will know better than the cowherd what he ought to say in order to soothe infuriated cows?

Ion. No, he will not.

Soc. But he will know what a spinning-woman ought to say about the working of wool?

Ion. No.

Soc. At any rate he will know what a general ought to say when exhorting his soldiers?

Ion. Yes, that is the sort of thing which the rhapsode will be sure to know.

Soc. What! Is the art of the rhapsode the art of the general?

Ion. I am sure that I should know what a general ought to say.

Soc. Why, yes, Ion, because you may possibly have the knowledge of a general as well as that of a rhapsode; and you might also have a knowledge of horsemanship as well as of the lyre, and then you would know when horses were well or ill managed. But suppose I were to ask you: By the help of which art, Ion, do you know whether horses are well managed, by your skill as a horseman or as a performer on the lyre—what would you answer?

Ion. I should reply, by my skill as a horseman.

Soc. And if you judged of performers on the lyre, you would admit that you judged of them as a performer on the lyre, and not as a horseman?

Ion. Yes.

Soc. And in judging of the general's art, do you judge as a [541] general, or as a good rhapsode?

Ion. To me there appears to be no difference between them.

Soc. What do you mean? Do you mean to say that the art of the rhapsode and of the general is the same?

Ion. Yes, one and the same.

Soc. Then he who is a good rhapsode is also a good general?

Ion. Certainly, Socrates.

Soc. And he who is a good general is also a good rhapsode?

Ion. No; I do not agree to that.

Soc. But you do agree that he who is a good rhapsode is also a good general.

Ion. Certainly.

Soc. And you are the best of Hellenic rhapsodes?

Ion. Far the best, Socrates.

Soc. And are you also the best general, Ion?

Ion. To be sure, Socrates; and Homer was my master.

Soc. But then, Ion, why in the name of goodness do you, who are the best of generals as well as the best of rhapsodes in all Hellas, go about reciting rhapsodies when you might be a general? Do you think that the Hellenes are in grave need of a rhapsode with his golden crown, and have no need at all of a general?

Ion. Why, Socrates, the reason is that my countrymen, the Ephesians, are the servants and soldiers of Athens, and do not need a general; and that you and Sparta are not likely to appoint me, for you think that you have enough generals of your own.

Soc. My good Ion, did you never hear of Apollodorus of Cyzicus?

Ion. Who may he be?

Soc. One who, though a foreigner, has often been chosen their general by the Athenians: and there is Phanosthenes of Andros, and Heraclides of Clazomenae, whom they have also appointed to the command of their armies and to other offices, although aliens, after they had shown their merit. And will they not choose Ion the Ephesian to be their general, and honour him, if they deem him qualified? Were not the Ephesians originally Athenians, and Ephesus is no mean city? But, indeed, Ion, if you are correct in saying that by art and knowledge you are able to praise Homer, you do not deal fairly with me, and after all your professions of knowing many glorious things about Homer, and promises that you would exhibit them, you only deceive me, and so far from exhibiting the art of which you are a master, will not, even after my repeated entreaties, explain to me the nature of it. You literally assume as many forms as Proteus, twisting and turning up and down, until at last you slip away from me in the disguise of a general, in order [542] that you may escape exhibiting your Homeric lore. And if you have art, then, as I was saying, in falsifying your promise that you would exhibit Homer, you are not dealing fairly with me. But if, as I believe, you have no art, but speak all these beautiful words about Homer unconsciously under his inspiring influence, then I acquit you of dishonesty, and shall only say that you are inspired. Which do you prefer to be thought, dishonest or inspired?

Ion. There is a great difference, Socrates, between the two alternatives; and inspiration is by far the nobler.

Soc. Then, Ion, I shall assume the nobler alternative; and attribute to you in your praises of Homer inspiration, and not art.

Greater Hippias [286a to end]

Hippias. . . . what is more, Socrates, I have lately gained [286] much credit there by setting forth in detail the honourable and beautiful practices to which a young man ought to devote himself. On that subject I have composed a discourse, a beautiful work distinguished by a fine style among its other merits. Its setting and its exordium are like this. After the fall of Troy, Neoptolemus asks Nestor what are the honourable and beautiful practices to which a man should devote himself during his youth in order to win the highest distinction. Then it is Nestor's turn to speak, and he propounds to him a great number of excellent rules of life. This discourse I delivered in Sparta, and at the request of Eudicus, the son of Apemantus, am to deliver it here, as well as much else worth listening to, in the schoolroom of Pheidostratus, the day after tomorrow. Please be sure to come yourself, and bring with you other good critics of such dissertations.

Socrates. Certainly, Hippias, all being well. But now answer me a trifling question on the subject; you have reminded me of it in the nick of time. Quite lately, my noble friend, when I was condemning as ugly some things in certain compositions, and praising others as beautiful, somebody threw me into confusion by interrogating me in a most offensive manner, rather to this effect: "You, Socrates, pray how do you know what things are beautiful and what are ugly? Come now, can you tell me what

beauty is?" In my incompetence I was confounded, and could find no proper answer to give him; so leaving the company, I was filled with anger and reproaches against myself, and promised myself that the first time I met with one of you wise men, I would listen to him and learn, and when I had mastered my lesson thoroughly, I would go back to my questioner and join battle with him again. So you see that you have come at a beautifully appropriate moment, and I ask you to teach me properly what is beauty by itself, answering my question with the utmost precision you can attain; I do not want to be made to look a fool a second time, by another cross-examination. Of course you know perfectly, and it is only a scrap of your vast learning.

Hip. A scrap indeed, Socrates; and of no value, I may add.

Soc. Then I shall acquire it without trouble, and nobody will confound me again.

Hip. Nobody at all, if I am not a bungling amateur in my profession. [287]

Soc. Bravo, Hippias; how splendid, if we do defeat the adversary! Will it be a nuisance to you if I act as his understudy and fasten on your answers with my objections, so that you may put me through some vigorous practice? I have had a fair amount of experience of his objections. If, therefore, it makes no difference to you, I should like to play the critic; in this way I shall get a firmer grasp of what I learn.

Hip. Certainly; put in your criticisms. As I said just now, it is not a big question; I might teach you to answer much more difficult ones with such cogency that no human being would be able to confute you.

Soc. How magnificent! Well now, on your invitation let me assume his role to the best of my ability, and try to interrogate you. If you were to deliver to him the discourse to which you refer—the discourse about beautiful practices—he would hear you to the end; and when you stopped, the very first question he would put would be about beauty—it is a kind of habit with him;

he would say "Stranger from Elis, is it not by justice that the just are just?" Would you answer, Hippias, as if he were asking the question?

Hip. I shall answer that it is by justice.

Soc. "Then this, namely justice, is definitely something."

Hip. Certainly.

Soc. "Again, it is by wisdom that the wise are wise, and by goodness that all things are good?"

Hip. Undoubtedly.

Soc. "That is, by really existent things—one could scarcely say, 'by things which have no real existence'?"

Hip. Quite so.

Soc. "Then are not all beautiful things beautiful by beauty?"

Hip. Yes, by beauty.

Soc. "Which has a real existence?"

Hip. Yes, what else do you think?

Soc. "Then tell me, stranger," he would say, "what is this thing, beauty?"

Hip. By putting this question he just wants to find out what is beautiful?

Soc. I do not think so, Hippias; he wants to know what is beauty—the beautiful.

Hip. What is the difference between them?

Soc. You think there is none?

Hip. There is no difference.

Soc. Obviously you know best. Still, my good sir, look at it again; he asks you not what is beautiful, but what is beauty.

Hip. I understand, my good sir, and I will tell him what is beauty, defying anyone to refute me. I assure you, Socrates, if I must speak the truth, that a beautiful maiden is a beauty.

Soc. Upon my word, Hippias, a beautiful answer—very creditable. Then if I give that answer I shall have answered the question, and answered it correctly, and I can defy anyone to refute me? [288]

Hip. How can you be refuted when everyone thinks the same and everyone who hears you will testify that you are right?

Soc. Quite so. Now, Hippias, let me re-capitulate to myself what you say. That man will question me something like this: "Come, Socrates, give me an answer. Returning to your examples of beauty, tell me what must beauty by itself be in order to explain why we apply the word to them?" And you want me to reply that if a beautiful maiden is a beauty, we have found why they are entitled to that name?

Hip. Do you imagine that he will then try to refute you by proving that you have not mentioned a beautiful thing, or that if he does attempt it he will not look like a fool?

Soc. I am sure, my worthy friend, that he will try to refute me; the event will show whether the attempt will make him look a fool. But allow me to tell you what he will say.

Hip. Go on, then.

Soc. He will say, "How delicious you are, Socrates! Is not a beautiful mare a beauty—the god himself praised mares in his oracle?" How shall we reply, Hippias? Must we not say that the mare, too, or at least a beautiful one, is a beauty? We can hardly be so audacious as to deny that beauty is beautiful.

Hip. Quite right; I may add that the god, too, spoke quite correctly; the mares we breed in our country are very beautiful.

Soc. He will now say, "Very well; but what about a beautiful lyre? Is that not a beauty?" Are we to agree, Hippias?

Hip. Yes.

Soc. Judging from his character, I feel pretty sure that he will then go on, "What about a beautiful pot, my dear sir? Is not that a beauty?"

Hip. Who is this fellow? What a boor, to dare to introduce such vulgar examples into a grave discussion!

Soc. He is that sort of person, Hippias; not at all refined, a common fellow caring for nothing but the truth. Still, he must have his answer and I give my own first; if the pot is the work of a good potter, smooth and round and properly fired, like some very beautiful pots I have seen, the two-handled ones that hold six choes,—if he were to ask his question about a pot like that, we should have to admit that it is beautiful. How could we assert that what is a beautiful thing is not a beauty?

Hip. No, we could not.

Soc. "Then even a beautiful pot," he will say, "is a beauty?" Please answer.

Hip. Yes I suppose so. Even this utensil is beautiful when it is beautifully made, but generically it does not deserve to be judged beautiful in comparison with a mare or a maiden, or all the other things of beauty.

Soc. Very well. I understand, Hippias, that when he puts these questions [289] I should answer, "Sir, you do not grasp the truth of Heracleitus' saying that the most beautiful of apes is ugly compared with the human race; and the most beautiful of pots is ugly when compared with maidens—so says Hippias the wise"—that is correct?

Hip. Quite the right answer.

Soc. Now mark my words, I am sure that he will then say, "Yes, Socrates, but if maidens are grouped with gods, will not the result be the same as when pots were grouped with maidens? Will not the most beautiful maiden appear ugly? Does not Heracleitus, whom you adduce, employ these very words, 'The wisest of men, when compared to a god, will appear but an ape in wisdom and beauty and all else?'" Shall we admit, Hippias, that the most beautiful maiden is ugly in comparison with the race of gods?

Hip. That no one can deny, Socrates.

Soc. If then we make this admission, he will laugh and say, "Socrates, do you remember what you were asked?" "Yes," I shall answer. "I was asked what beauty by itself is." He will then rejoin, "Then when you are asked for beauty, do you offer in reply that which you yourself acknowledge to be no more beautiful than ugly?" "Apparently," I shall say; what do you advise me to reply?

Hip. As you do reply; for of course he will be right in saying that in comparison with gods the human race is not beautiful.

Soc. He will continue, "If I had asked you at the beginning what is both beautiful and ugly, and you had answered me as now, would not your answer have been correct? But do you still think that absolute beauty, by which all other things are ordered in loveliness, and appear beautiful when its form is added—do you think that that is a maiden, or a mare, or a lyre?"

Hip. But still, Socrates, if this is what he wants, it is the easiest thing in the world to tell him what is that beauty which orders all other things in loveliness and makes them appear beautiful when it is added to them. The fellow must be a perfect fool, knowing nothing about things of beauty; if you reply to him that this about which he is asking, beauty, is nothing else than gold, he will be at a loss and will not attempt to refute you. For I suppose we all know that if anything has gold added to it, it will appear beautiful when so adorned even though it appeared ugly before.

Soc. You do not know what a ruffian he is; he accepts nothing without making difficulties.

Hip. What do you mean? He must accept an accurate statement, on pain [290] of ridicule.

Soc. Well, my friend, this answer of yours he will not only refuse to accept, but he will even scoff at me viciously, saying, "You blockhead! Do you reckon Pheidias a bad artist?" I suppose I shall answer, "not in the least."

Hip. Quite right.

Soc. Yes, so I think. But when I agree that Pheidias is a good artist, he will say, "Then do you fancy that Pheidias was ignorant of this beauty of which you speak?" I shall reply, "What is the point?" and he will rejoin, "The point is that he did not give his Athena eyes of gold or use gold for the rest of her face, or for her hands, or for her feet, as he would have done if supreme beauty could be given to them only by the use of gold; he made them of ivory. Clearly he made this mistake through ignorance, not knowing that it is really gold that confers beauty on everything to which it is added." How are we to answer him then, Hippias?

Hip. Quite easy. We shall reply that Pheidias was artistically right; for ivory too is beautiful, I suppose.

Soc. "Why then," he will say, "did he not also make the eyeballs of ivory? He made them of stone, finding out stone as like as possible to ivory. Or is the stone that is beautiful itself a beauty?" Shall we say that it is?

Hip. Yes—it is beautiful, at least, whenever it is appropriate.

Soc. "But ugly when not appropriate?" Am I to agree?

Hip. Yes—when not appropriate.

Soc. He will then go on, "Well then, O man of wisdom, do not ivory and gold cause a thing to appear beautiful when they are appropriate, and ugly when they are not?" Shall we deny it or admit that he is right?

Hip. We shall at any rate admit that whatever is appropriate to a particular thing makes that thing beautiful.

Soc. He will continue, "Then when a man boils the pot of which we spoke, the beautiful pot full of boiling soup, which is the more appropriate to it—a ladle of gold or a ladle of fig-wood?"

Hip. Really, Socrates, what a creature! Please tell me who he is.

Soc. You would not know him if I told you his name.

Hip. I know enough about him at this moment to know that he is a dolt.

Soc. He is a terrible nuisance, Hippias; still, how shall we answer? Which of the two ladles are we to choose as appropriate to the soup and the pot? Obviously the one of fig-wood? For it gives the soup a better smell, I suppose; and moreover, my friend, it would not break our pot and spill the soup and put out the fire and deprive the

guests at our dinner of a truly noble dish, whereas that golden ladle would do all this; and therefore, if you do not object, I think we should say that the wooden [291] ladle is more appropriate than the golden.

Hip. Yes, it is more appropriate; but I should not myself go on talking with the fellow while he asks such questions.

Soc. Quite right, my friend. It would not be appropriate for you to be contaminated by such language, you who are so well dressed, and wear such good shoes, and are renowned for wisdom throughout the Greek world. But to me it does not matter if I am mixed up with that fellow; so fortify me with your instruction, and for my sake answer the questions. He will say, "If indeed the wooden ladle is more appropriate than the golden, will it not also be more beautiful, since you, Socrates, have admitted that the appropriate is more beautiful than the inappropriate?" Can we then avoid the admission that the wooden ladle is more beautiful than the golden?

Hip. Would you like me to give you a definition of beauty by which you can save yourself from prolonged discussion?

Soc. Certainly, but first tell me which of the two ladles I have just mentioned is appropriate, and the more beautiful?

Hip. Well, if you like, answer him that it is the one made of fig-wood.

Soc. Say now what a moment ago you were proposing to say; for following your answer, if I take the line that beauty is gold, I shall apparently have to face the fact that gold is more beautiful than fig-wood. Now, once more, what according to you is beauty?

Hip. You shall have you answer. You are looking, I think, for a reply ascribing to beauty such a nature that it will never appear ugly to anyone?

Soc. Exactly; you catch my meaning admirably.

Hip. Now please attend; if anyone can find fault with what I say, I give you full leave to call me an imbecile.

Soc. I am on tenterhooks.

Hip. Then I maintain that always, every-where, and for everyman it is most beauti-ful to be rich, healthy, honoured by the Greeks, to reach old age and, after burying his parents nobly, himself to be borne to the tomb with solemn ceremony by his own children.

Soc. Bravo, bravo, Hippias; those are words wonderful, sublime, worthy of you, and you have my grateful admiration for your kindness in bringing all your ability to my assistance. Still, our shafts are not hit-ting our man, and I warn you that he will now deride us more than ever.

Hip. A poor sort of derision, Socrates, for in deriding us when he can find no objec-tion to our view, he will be deriding him-self and will be derided by the company.
[292]

Soc. Perhaps so; perhaps, however, when he has the answer you suggest he may not be content just to laugh at me. So I fore-bode.

Hip. What do you mean?

Soc. If he happens to have a stick with him, he will attempt to get at me very for-cibly, unless I escape by running away.

Hip. What? Is the fellow somehow your lord and master? Surely he will be arrested and punished for such behavior? Or has Athens no system of justice, that she allows her citizens to commit wrongful assaults on one another?

Soc. She forbids it absolutely.

Hip. Then he will be punished for his wrongful assaults.

Soc. I do not think so, Hippias—emphati-cally not, if that were the answer I gave him; I think his assault would be justified.

Hip. Since that is your own opinion, well, I think so too.

Soc. But may I go on to explain why, in my own opinion, that answer would justify an assault upon me? Or will you too assault me without trial, refusing me a hearing?

Hip. No: such a refusal would be mon-strous. But what have you to say?

Soc. I will continue on the same plan as a moment ago, pretending to be that fellow but not using to you the kind of offensive and grotesque words he would use to me. He will say, I feel sure, "Do you not think, Socrates, that you deserve a thrashing after chanting so badly out of tune a dithyramb so long and so irrelevant to the question you were asked?" "What do you mean?" I shall say. "What do I mean? Are you incapable of remembering that I asked about beauty itself, that which gives the property of be-ing beautiful to everything to which it is added—to stone and wood, and man, and god, and every action and every branch of learning? I am asking, Sir, what is beauty itself, and for all my shouting I cannot make you hear me; you might be a stone sitting beside me, a real millstone with neither ears nor brain." Would not you, Hippias, be indignant if in terror I were to answer him, "But this is what Hippias de-clared beauty to be, although I kept on ask-ing him, exactly as you do me, for that which is beautiful always and for every-one." Frankly, will not that answer make you indignant?

Hip. I am quite sure, Socrates, that what I specified is beautiful to all, and will so appear to all.

Soc. He will reply, "And will be so in the future? For beauty, I take it, is always beautiful?"

Hip. Certainly.

Soc. "And it was beautiful, too, in the past?"

Hip. It was.

Soc. Then he will go on, "So, this stran-ger from Elis asserted that it would have been beautiful for Achilles to be buried after his parents, and similarly for his grandfather Aeacus, and for the other chil-dren of gods, and for the gods themselves?"
[293]

Hip. What is this? Tell him to go to—glory! These questions of his are irreverent, Socrates.

Soc. Surely it is not exactly irreverent to

say that these things are so, when someone else has asked the question?

Hip. Well, presumably not.

Soc. Presumably he will then say, "It is you who affirm that it is beautiful always and for everyone to bury his parents and be buried by his children. Does not 'everyone' include Heracles and all the others we mentioned a moment ago?"

Hip. I did not mean to include the gods.

Soc. "Nor the heroes either, apparently."

Hip. Not if they were the children of gods.

Soc. "But if they were not?"

Hip. Certainly.

Soc. "Then from your own argument, it now appears that the fate which is terrible and impious and shameful for Tantalus and Dardanus and Zethus is beautiful for Pelops and the other heroes of similar parentage?"

Hip. I think so.

Soc. He will go on, "Then you think, contrary to what you said just now, that to bury one's parents and be buried by one's children is sometimes, and for some persons, shameful; and it looks more than ever impossible that it should become, or be, beautiful to everyone. So this definition meets the same fate as those we discussed earlier—the maiden and the pot; it is an even more ludicrous failure, offering us that which is beautiful to some men, and not to others. And to this very day, Socrates, you cannot answer the question you were asked—beauty, what is it?" These and other like reproaches he will hurl at me with some justice, if I give him this answer. For the most part he talks to me something after this fashion; but sometimes, as if in pity for my inexperience and lack of education, he himself proffers a question, and asks whether I think beauty is such and such; or it may be on some other subject—whatever he happens to be thinking about, and we are discussing.

Hip. What do you mean, Socrates?

Soc. I will explain. "My worthy Socra-

tes," he says, "don't give answers of that kind, and in that way—they are silly, easily torn to rags; but consider this suggestion. In one of our answers a little while ago we got hold of, and expressed, the idea that gold is beautiful or not beautiful according as it is placed in an appropriate setting; and similarly with everything else to which this qualification can be added. Now consider this appropriateness, and reflect on the general nature of the appropriate, and see whether it might not be beauty." Myself, I am in the habit of invariably agreeing to such surmises, for I can never think of anything to say; but you, do you think that the appropriate is beautiful?

Hip. Certainly, Socrates.

Soc. Let us consider, and make sure that there is no deception.

Hip. So we ought.

Soc. Come on then. Do we define the appropriate as that which by its presence causes the things in which it becomes present to appear beautiful, [294] or causes them to be beautiful, or neither?

Hip. In my own opinion that which causes things to appear beautiful; for example, a man may be a figure of fun, but when he wears clothes or shoes that fit him well he does seem a finer man.

Soc. But then if the appropriate really makes things more beautiful than they are, the appropriate is a kind of fraud in relation to beauty, and would not be that for which we are looking, would it? We were looking, I think, for that by which all beautiful things are beautiful—corresponding to that by which all great things are great, namely, excess; by this all great things are great, and great they must certainly be if they exceed, even though they do not appear so: similarly we ask about beauty, by which all beautiful things are beautiful whether they appear so or not, and try to define it; this is what we are looking for, if we are looking for beauty.

Hip. But, Socrates, the appropriate causes things both to be and to appear beautiful, when it is present.

Soc. Then it is impossible for things that are in fact beautiful not to appear beautiful, since by hypothesis that which makes them appear beautiful is present in them?

Hip. It is impossible.

Soc. Then is it our conclusion, Hippias, that all established usages and all practices which are in reality beautiful are regarded as beautiful by all men, and always appear so to them? Or do we think the exact opposite, that ignorance of them is prevalent, and that these are the chief objects of contention and fighting, both between individuals and between states?

Hip. The latter, I think; ignorance prevails.

Soc. It would not, if the appearance of beauty were but added to them; and it would be added if the appropriate were beautiful and moreover caused them to appear as well as be beautiful. It follows that if the appropriate is that which causes things to be in fact beautiful, then it would be that beauty for which we are looking, but still it would not be that which causes them to appear beautiful; if, on the other hand, that which causes things to appear beautiful is the appropriate, it is not that beauty for which we are looking. That for which we are looking makes things beautiful, but the same cause never could make things both appear and be either beautiful or anything else. We have then these alternatives; is the appropriate that which causes things to appear beautiful, or that which causes them to be so?

Hip. To appear, I think.

Soc. Oh dear! Then the chance of finding out what the beautiful really is has slipped through our fingers and vanished, since the appropriate has proved to be something other than beautiful.

Hip. Upon my word, Socrates, I should never have thought it!

Soc. But still, my friend, do not let us give up yet; I have still [295] a sort of hope that the nature of beauty will reveal itself.

Hip. Yes indeed, it is not hard to discover. I am sure that if I were to retire into solitude for a little while and reflect by myself, I should define it for you with superlative precision.

Soc. Hippias, Hippias, don't boast. You know what trouble it has already given us, and I am afraid it may get angry with us and run away more resolutely than ever. But what nonsense I am talking; for you, I suppose, will easily discover it when once you are alone. Still, I beg you most earnestly to discover it with me here; or if you please, let us look for it together as we are now doing. If we find it, well and good; if not, I imagine I shall resign myself to my fate, and you will go away and discover it easily. Of course, if we find it now, you will not be annoyed by inquiries from me about the nature of your private discovery: so please look at your conception of beauty by itself. I define it as—pray give me your whole attention and stop me if I talk nonsense—well, let us assume that whatever is useful is beautiful. My ground for the proposition is as follows: we do not say that eyes are beautiful when they appear to be without the faculty of sight; we do when they have that faculty and so are useful for seeing. Is that correct?

Hip. Yes.

Soc. Similarly we say that the whole body is beautifully made, sometimes for running, sometimes for wrestling; and we speak in the same way of all animals. A beautiful horse, or cock, or quail, and all utensils, and means of transport both on land and on sea, merchant vessels and ships of war, and all instruments of music and of the arts generally, and, if you like, practices and laws—we apply the word "beautiful" to practically all these in the same manner; in each case we take as our criterion the natural constitution or the workmanship or the form of enactment, and whatever is useful we call beautiful, and beautiful in that respect in which it is useful and for the purpose for which and at the time at which it is useful; and we call ugly that which is useless in all these respects. Is not this your view also, Hippias?

Hip. Yes, it is.

Soc. Then we are now right in affirming that the useful is pre-eminently beautiful.

Hip. We are.

Soc. And that which has the power to achieve its specific purpose is useful for the purpose which it has the power to achieve, and that which is without that power is useless?

Hip. Certainly.

Soc. Then power is a beautiful thing, and the lack of it ugly?

Hip. Very much so. We have evidence of that fact from public life, among other sources; for in political affairs generally, and also within [296] a man's own city, power is the most beautiful of things, and lack of it the most ugly and shameful.

Soc. Good! Does it then follow—a momentous consequence—that wisdom is the most beautiful, and ignorance the most shameful of all things?

Hip. What do you think, Socrates?

Soc. A moment's quiet, my dear friend; I have misgivings about the line we are taking now.

Hip. Why these misgivings again? This time your argument has proceeded magnificently.

Soc. I could wish it were so; but let us consider together this point. Could a man do something which he had neither the knowledge nor the least atom of power to do?

Hip. Of course not; how could he do what he had not the power to do?

Soc. Then those who by reason of some error contrive and work evil involuntarily —surely they would never do such things if they were without the power to do them?

Hip. Obviously not.

Soc. And those who have the power to do a thing do it through power, not of course by being powerless?

Hip. Certainly not.

Soc. Those who do what they do, all have the power to do it?

Hip. Yes.

Soc. And evil is done much more abundantly than good by all men from childhood upwards, erring involuntarily?

Hip. That is so.

Soc. Well then, are we to say that this power, and these useful things—I mean any things useful for working some evil— are we to say that these are beautiful, or that they are far from being so?

Hip. Far from it, in my opinion.

Soc. Then the powerful and the useful are not, it appears, the beauty we want.

Hip. They are, Socrates, if they are powerful for good and are useful for such purposes.

Soc. Still the theory that that which is powerful and useful without qualification is beautiful has vanished away. Do you think, however, that what we really had in mind to say was that beauty is that which is both useful and powerful for some good purpose?

Hip. I think so.

Soc. But this is equivalent to "beneficial," is it not?

Hip. Certainly.

Soc. So we reach the conclusion that beautiful bodies, and beautiful rules of life, and wisdom, and all the things we mentioned just now, are beautiful because they are beneficial?

Hip. Evidently.

Soc. Then it looks as if beauty is the beneficial, Hippias.

Hip. Undoubtedly.

Soc. Now the beneficial is that which produces good?

Hip. Yes.

Soc. And that which produces is identical with the cause?

Hip. That is so.

Soc. Then the beneficial is the cause of the good?

Hip. It is. [297]

Soc. But surely, Hippias, the cause and that of which it is the cause are different; for the cause could scarcely be the cause of the cause. Look at it in this way. The cause was defined as something that produces, was it not?

Hip. Certainly.

Soc. And that which produces produces only that which is coming into existence; it does not produce that which produces.

Hip. That is so.

Soc. And that which is coming into existence, and that which produces it, are two different things?

Hip. Yes.

Soc. Then the cause is not the cause of the cause, but of that which is coming into existence through it?

Hip. Certainly.

Soc. If then beauty is the cause of good, then the good would be brought into existence by beauty; and it would appear that we devote ourselves to the pursuit of wisdom and of all other beautiful things for the reason that their product and offspring, the good, is worthy of devotion; and from our explorations it looks as though beauty is metaphorically a kind of father of the good.

Hip. Certainly; you say well, Socrates.

Soc. Do I not say this also well, that the father is not his son, nor the son his father?

Hip. Quite well.

Soc. And that the cause is not that which it brings into existence, nor vice versa?

Hip. True.

Soc. Then most certainly, my good sir, beauty is not good nor the good beautiful. Do you think that possible after our discussion?

Hip. No, I most certainly do not.

Soc. Then does it please us, and should we be willing to say, that the beautiful is not good, nor the good beautiful?

Hip. Most certainly not; it does not please me at all.

Soc. Most certainly I agree, Hippias; it

pleases me least of any of the theories we have discussed.

Hip. Very likely.

Soc. Then it looks as if the view which a little while ago we thought the finest result of our discussions, the view that the beneficial, and the useful, and the power to produce something good, is beautiful, is in fact wrong; but it is, if possible, more open to ridicule than those first definitions according to which the maiden was the beautiful, and so was a succession of other things.

Hip. Apparently.

Soc. For myself, Hippias, I don't know where to turn, and am completly at a loss; have you anything to say?

Hip. Not at the moment; but as I said a little while ago, I feel sure I shall find a way out after some reflection.

Soc. But I do not feel that I can wait for the issue of your reflection, I am so eager for this knowledge; and indeed, I fancy I have just hit on something. Come now: if we were to say that whatever we enjoy—I do not mean to include all pleasures, but only what we enjoy through our senses of hearing and sight—if we were to say that this is beautiful, how should we fare in our struggle? Surely beautiful human beings, [298] and all decorative work, and pictures, and plastic art, delight us when we see them if they are beautiful; and beautiful sounds, and music as a whole, and discourses, and tales of imagination, have the same effect; so that if we were to reply to that blustering fellow: "My worthy sir, beauty is the pleasant which comes through the senses of hearing and sight," do you not think that we should stop his bluster?

Hip. At last, Socrates, I think we have a good definition of beauty.

Soc. Well, but are we then to say that those practices which are beautiful, and the laws, are beautiful as giving pleasure through our senses of sight or hearing, or that they are in some other category?

Hip. Perhaps these cases might escape our man.

Soc. No, Hippias, they would certainly not escape the man by whom I should be most ashamed to be caught talking pretentious nonsense.

Hip. Whom do you mean?

Soc. The son of Sophroniscus, who would no more allow me to hazard these assertions while they are unexplored than to assert what I do not know as though I knew it.

Hip. Well, now you have raised the point, I must say that I too think this question about the laws is on a different footing.

Soc. Gently, Hippias; we may quite well be imagining that we see our way clearly, when we have really fallen into the same difficulty about beauty as that in which we were caught a moment ago.

Hip. What do you mean, Socrates?

Soc. This is what strikes me—there may be something in it. These matters of law and practice might perhaps prove after all to be within the range of the perceptions of hearing and sight; however, let us hold fast to the statement that the pleasant which comes through these senses is beautiful, leaving the question of the laws altogether on one side. But if we were asked by the person to whom I refer, or by anyone else: "Why, Hippias and Socrates, have you picked out within the class of the pleasant that which is pleasant in the way you affirm to be beautiful, while you deny the designation 'beautiful' to that which is pleasant according to the other senses, that is, the senses which have to do with food, and drink, and sexual intercourse, and all such things? Or do you deny that these are pleasant, and claim that in such things there is no pleasure whatever, or in anything except seeing and hearing?" What shall we reply?

Hip. Obviously we shall reply that these other things also offer very great pleasures.

Soc. "Why then," he will say, "do you take away this designation and refuse to allow them beauty when they are pleasures no less than the others?" We shall answer: "Because everyone would laugh at us if we [299] said that it is not pleasant to eat, but beautiful; or that a pleasant smell is not pleasant, but beautiful; and as to sexual intercourse, everyone would contend against us that it is most pleasant, while admitting that it ought to be enjoyed only where there is none to see because it is a disgraceful and repulsive sight." When we say this, Hippias, he would probably rejoin: "I too understand that you are and have been ashamed to say that these pleasures are beautiful, because that is not the common view; but my question was, what is beautiful, not what the mass of men think it to be." I imagine we shall restate our original proposition. "In our view that part of the pleasant which comes by sight and hearing is beautiful." However, can you suggest any other way of dealing with the question, or any addition to that reply?

Hip. As the argument now stands, we are bound to give that answer, and that only.

Soc. "Admirable," he will reply. "If then the pleasant which comes by sight and hearing is beautiful, is it not obvious that any pleasant thing outside that category could not be beautiful?" Shall we agree?

Hip. Yes.

Soc. He will go on: "Then is that which is pleasant through sight, pleasant through sight and through hearing, or is that which is pleasant through hearing, pleasant through hearing and through sight?" We shall reply: "By no means; the pleasant which comes by either sense would certainly not be pleasant through both—that seems to be your meaning; our statement was that either of these pleasant things would be beautiful just by itself, and also both of them together." Shall that be our answer?

Hip. Certainly.

Soc. "Well, then," he will say, "does any pleasant thing whatever differ from any other pleasant thing in respect of its pleasantness? The question is not whether a particular pleasure is greater or smaller, or exists in a higher or lower degree, but whether there can be a difference between pleasures in this particular respect, that one is, and another is not, a pleasure?" We do not think so, do we?

Hip. No.

Soc. He will continue: "It follows that you chose out these from among the other pleasures for some other reason than that they are pleasures. Since there is some difference between them and the others, you saw in both of them some quality capable of providing a criterion by which you judge them to be beautiful; for the pleasure that comes through sight, I take it, is not beautiful just because it comes through sight. If that were the reason why it is beautiful, the other pleasure, the one which comes through hearing, would never be beautiful; it is emphatically not pleasure through sight." Shall we reply that his reasoning is correct?

Hip. Yes.

Soc. "Nor again is the pleasure that comes through hearing beautiful [300] because it is through hearing; for again, in that case the pleasure through sight would never be beautiful since it is emphatically not pleasure through hearing." Shall we agree that he argues correctly?

Hip. He does.

Soc. "But yet both are beautiful, you affirm?" We do affirm it?

Hip. Yes.

Soc. "Then they have something identical which makes them to be beautiful, a common quality which appertains to both of them in common and to each singly; otherwise they could not, I take it, both of them be beautiful as a pair, and also each separately?" Answer me as though you were answering him.

Hip. I answer that what you say is my opinion also.

Soc. If then these pleasures are both of them as a pair conditioned in some way, but neither singly is so conditioned, they could not be beautiful by reason of this particular condition?

Hip. And how is it possible, Socrates, that when neither of them singly has been conditioned in some way—any way you like to think of—yet both as a pair should be conditioned in the way in which neither singly has been conditioned?

Soc. You think it is impossible?

Hip. I do: not being entirely unacquainted either with the nature of the subject, or with the terminology of our present discussion.

Soc. Very nice, Hippias. But still I fancy perchance I see an example of what you say to be impossible, though really I may see nothing.

Hip. It is not a case of "perchance"; you see wrong, of good set purpose.

Soc. Indeed, many such examples rise up before my mind's eye; but I distrust them because they are visible to me, who never earned a penny by wisdom, while they do not appear to you who have earned more in that way than anyone else alive; and, my friend, I am pondering whether you are not playing with me and deceiving me on purpose, so clearly and in such numbers do I see them.

Hip. Nobody will know better than you whether I am playing with you or not, when you start to describe these visions of yours; your description of them will be plain nonsense. You will never find both of us together conditioned in a way in which neither has been conditioned separately.

Soc. What's that Hippias? You may be talking sense and I do not grasp it, but please let me explain more clearly what I mean. It appears to me there are attributes which cannot, and do not, now, belong to either of us singly, but can belong to both together; and, conversely, that there are attributes of which both together are capable, but neither singly.

Hip. Here indeed, Socrates, are absurdities even more monstrous than those of your answer a little while ago. Only consider; if we are both just men, is not each of us individually just? if each of us is unjust, are not both so? If both are well, is not each of us well also? Or if each [301] of us were tired, or were wounded, or struck, or conditioned in any other way, then should we not both of us as a pair be conditioned in that way? Similarly, if both of us were made of gold, or silver, or ivory, or if you prefer it, were noble or wise or honoured, or, for that matter, old men or young, or had any other human attribute you like to mention, must it not follow inevitably that each of us singly is that same?

Soc. Most certainly.

Hip. You see, Socrates, the fact is that you yourself do not consider things as a whole, nor do those with whom you habitually converse; you test beauty and each general concept by taking it separately and mentally dissecting it, with the result that you fail to perceive the magnitude and continuity of the substances of which reality is composed. And now this failure has gone so far that you imagine that there is something, an attribute or substantive nature, which appertains to two of them together but not to each singly, or conversely to each singly but not to the two together; that is the state of mind to which you and your friends are reduced—how unreasoning and superficial, and stupid, and uncomprehending!

Soc. Such is the lot of us mortals, Hippias—a man does what he can, not what he wishes, according to the oft-quoted proverb; however, your constant admonitions are a great help. Just now, before your admonition of our stupidity in these matters, I had some further thoughts about them which perhaps I might explain to you—or shall I refrain?

Hip. I know what you are going to say, Socrates; I know the mind of every school of dialecticians. But say your say, if you prefer it.

Soc. Well, I do prefer it. Before you said what you did, my honoured friend, we were so uninstructed as to hold the opinion that each of us two, you and myself, is one, but that, taken together, we cannot be that which each of us is singly—for we are two and not one: such was our folly. Now, however, we have been taught by you that if together we are two, each of us singly must be two, and if each is one, so must we both be; for on the continuous theory of reality according to Hippias it cannot be otherwise—whatever two entities are together, each is singly, and whatever each is, both are. Here I sit, fixed by you in this belief. But first, Hippias, remind me; are you and I both one, or you two, and I two?

Hip. What do you mean, Socrates?

Soc. Exactly what I say; you frighten me out of plain speech, because you get angry with me whenever you think that you have made a good point. [302] Still, let me ask you this further question; is not each of us two one, possessing the attribute of being one?

Hip. Certainly.

Soc. Then if each of us is one, each is also an odd number; you hold that one is an odd number, do you not?

Hip. I do.

Soc. Are we both then together an odd number, being two?

Hip. Impossible.

Soc. Both together would be an even number?

Hip. Assuredly.

Soc. Since then both together are even, does it follow that each of us singly is even?

Hip. Certainly not.

Soc. It is not then absolutely inevitable that, as you said just now, each individual should be what both are together, and that both should be what each is?

Hip. Not in such cases, but it is inevitable in the kind of case I mentioned earlier.

Soc. That suffices, Hippias; even that reply is to be accepted, as it is an acknowledgement that sometimes it is so, and sometimes not. If you recall the starting-point of our discussion, you will remember that I was arguing that the pleasures which come through sight and hearing are beautiful not because each of them was so conditioned as to be beautiful but not both together, nor because both of them together were similarly conditioned but not each singly; they were beautiful by virtue of something which conditions both together and also each singly, and so you agreed that both together were beautiful and each singly. Accordingly I thought that if both together are beautiful, they must be beautiful because of an essential character belonging to both and not of a character which is lacking in one or other; and I still think so. But start again as from the beginning. If pleasure through sight and pleasure through hearing are beautiful both together and each singly, does not that which makes them beautiful belong to both together and to each singly?

Hip. Certainly.

Soc. Then can they be beautiful because each singly and both together are pleasures? On this reasoning, would not all other pleasures be beautiful just as much, for, if you remember, they were acknowledged to be just as much pleasures?

Hip. Yes, I remember.

Soc. These particular ones, however, were stated to be beautiful because they came through sight and hearing.

Hip. Yes, that was the statement.

Soc. Now consider whether I am right on this point. According to my recollection, it was said that part of the category of the pleasant was beautiful—not every "pleasant," but that which comes through sight and hearing.

Hip. That is correct.

Soc. And this quality belongs to both together but not to each singly, does it not? As we said earlier, each of them singly does not come through both senses; both together come through both but not each singly. Is that so?

Hip. Yes.

Soc. Then each of them singly is not beautiful by that which does not belong to each (for that which is of both does not belong to each); and it follows that while from our agreed propositions we may rightly say that both together are beautiful, we may not say it of each singly. Is not this the necessary conclusion?

Hip. It appears so. [303]

Soc. Are we to say then that both together are beautiful, but not each?

Hip. I see no objections.

Soc. I do, my friend. We certainly had examples of attributes appertaining to individual entities in such a way that if they appertained to two together they appertained also to each singly, and if to each, then to both—all the attributes which were specified by you.

Hip. Yes.

Soc. But on the other hand those which I specified did not; and among those were the concept "each," and the concept "both." Is that right?

Hip. Yes.

Soc. To which category, Hippias, do you think the beautiful belongs? To the category of those you mentioned? If I am strong and you are too, we are both strong, and if I am just and you too, we are both just, and if both, then each singly; in the same way, if I am beautiful and you too, are we also both beautiful and if both, then each accordingly? Or may the same principle apply as in mathematics, when for instance the two components of even numbers may severally be odd, but may also be even; and, again, when quantities which are irrational if taken singly may be either rational or irrational if taken together; and there are innumerable other such examples, as indeed I told you occurred to my mind? In which category do you place beauty? Do you take the same view of it as I do? To me it seems a gross absurdity to hold that while both of us together are beautiful, neither is so singly, or that each singly is beautiful but not both together, or anything else of that kind?

Do you choose my alternative, or the other?

Hip. Yours.

Soc. Quite right, if we wish to be spared further inquiry; for if this category included beauty, it can no longer be maintained that the pleasant which comes through sight and hearing is beautiful; the description "which comes through sight and hearing" makes both together beautiful but not each singly —which was impossible, as I think, and you too.

Hip. Yes, we think the same.

Soc. Then it is impossible for the pleasant which comes through sight and hearing to be beautiful, since when we equate it with beauty an impossible result is produced.

Hip. Quite so.

Soc. My questioner will say: "Now start again from the beginning since you have missed the mark this time. What according to you is this 'beautiful' which appertains to both these pleasures, and by reason of which you have honoured them above the others and called them beautiful?" I think, Hippias, we are bound to reply that these are the most harmless of pleasures and the best, both taken together and taken singly. Can you suggest any other reason why they are superior to the others?

Hip. None; they really are the best.

Soc. "This then," he will say, "is your definition of beauty; beneficial pleasure." "Apparently," I shall reply; and you?

Hip. I too.

Soc. He will go on: "Well then, is not the beneficial that which produces the good, and that which produces and that which is produced were shown a little while ago to be different, and so our discussion has ended up in the old discussion, has it not? For the good cannot be beautiful, nor beauty good, if the two are not identical with one another." [304] "Nothing is more certain," we shall reply, if we are honest; there can be no justification for demurring to truth.

Hip. But I must ask you, Socrates, what do you suppose is the upshot of all this? As I said a little while ago, it is the scrapings and shavings of argument, cut up into little bits; and what is both beautiful and most precious is the ability to produce an eloquent and beautiful speech to a law-court or a council meeting or any other official body whom you are addressing, to convince your audience, and to depart with the greatest of all prizes, your own salvation and that of your friends and property. These then are the things to which a man should hold fast, abandoning these pettifogging arguments of yours, unless he wishes to be accounted a complete fool because he occupies himself, as we are now doing, with trumpery nonsense.

Soc. You, my dear Hippias, are blissfully fortunate because you know what way of life a man ought to follow, and moreover have followed it with success—so you tell me. I, however, am subject to what appears to be some supernatural ill fortune. I wander about in unending perplexity, and when I lay my perplexity before you wise men, you turn on me and batter me with abuse as soon as I have explained my plight. You all say just what you, Hippias, are now saying, how foolish and petty and worthless are the matters with which I occupy myself; but when in turn I am convinced by you and repeat exactly what you tell me, that the height of excellence is the ability to produce an eloquent and beautiful speech and win the day in a law-court or any other assembly, I am called every kind of a bad name by some of the audience, including especially that man who is always cross-questioning me. He is a very close relative of mine and lives in the same house, and when I go home and he hears me give utterance to these opinions he asks me whether I am not ashamed of my audacity in talking about a beautiful way of life, when questioning makes it evident that I do not even know the meaning of the word "beauty." "And yet," he goes on, "how can you know whose speech is beautiful or the reverse (and the same applies to any action whatsoever) when you have no knowledge of beauty? And so long as you are what you are, don't you think that you might as well be dead?" It is my lot, you see, to be reviled and abused alike by you gentlemen, and by him. However, I suppose this all must be endured; I may get some good from it—stranger things have happened. And indeed, Hippias, I do think I have got some good out of my conversation with the two of you; I think now I appreciate the true meaning of the proverb, "All that is beautiful is difficult."

Republic: Book III [392c–402d]

Enough of the subjects of poetry: let us now speak of the style; and when this has been considered, both matter and manner will have been completely treated.

I do not understand what you mean, said Adeimantus.

[392] Then I must make you understand; and perhaps I may be more intelligible if I put the matter in this way. You are aware, I suppose, that all mythology and poetry is a narration of events, either past, present, or to come?

Certainly, he replied.

And narration may be either simple narration, or imitation, or a union of the two?

That again, he said, I do not quite understand.

I fear that I must be an absurdly vague teacher. Like a bad speaker, therefore, I will not take the whole of the subject, but will break a piece off in illustration of my meaning. You know the first lines of the Iliad, in which the poet says that Chryses prayed Agamemnon to release his daughter, and that Agamemnon flew into a passion with him; whereupon Chryses, failing of his object, invoked the anger of the god against the [393] Achaeans. Now as far as these lines,

"And he prayed all the Greeks, but especially the two sons of Atreus, the chiefs of the people,"

the poet is speaking in his own person; he never even tries to distract us by assuming another character. But in what follows he takes the person of Chryses, and then he does all that he can to make us believe that the speaker is not Homer, but the aged priest himself. And in this double form he has cast the entire narrative of the events which occurred at Troy and in Ithaca and throughout the Odyssey.

Yes.

And a narrative it remains both in the speeches which the poet recites from time to time and in the intermediate passages?

Quite true.

But when the poet speaks in the person of another, may we not say that he assimilates his style to that of the person who, as he informs you, is going to speak?

Certainly we may.

And this assimilation of himself to another, either by the use of voice or gesture, is the imitation of the person whose character he assumes?

Of course.

Then in this case the narrative of the poet, whether Homer or another, may be said to proceed by way of imitation?

. . .

You have conceived my meaning perfectly; and I think I can now make clear what you failed to apprehend before, that some poetry and mythology are wholly imitative (and, as you say, I mean tragedy and comedy); there is likewise the opposite style, in which the poet is the only speaker —of this the dithyramb affords the best example; and the combination of both is found in epic, and in several other styles of poetry. Do I take you with me?

Yes, he said; I see now what you meant.

I will ask you to remember also what I began by saying, that we had done with the subject and might proceed to the style.

Yes, I remember.

In saying this, I intended to imply that we must come to an understanding about the mimetic art,—whether the poets, in narrating their stories, are to be allowed by us to imitate, and if so, whether in whole or in part, and if the latter, in what parts; or should all imitation be prohibited?

You mean, I suspect, to ask whether tragedy and comedy shall be admitted into our State?

Perhaps, I said; but there may be more than this in question: I really do not know as yet, but whither the argument may blow, thither we go.

And go we will, he said.

Then, Adeimantus, let me ask you to consider whether our guardians should or should not be fond of imitation; or rather, has not this question been decided by the rule already laid down that one man can only do one thing well, and not many; and that one who grasps at many will altogether fail of gaining much reputation in any?

Certainly.

And this is equally true of imitation; no one man can imitate many things as well as he would imitate a single one?

He cannot.

Then the same person will hardly be able to play a serious [395] part in life, and at the same time to be an imitator and imitate many other parts as well; for even when two species of imitation are nearly allied, the same persons cannot succeed in both, as, for example, the writers of tragedy and comedy—did you not just now call them imitations?

Yes, I did; and you are right in thinking that the same persons cannot succeed in both.

Any more than they can be rhapsodists and actors at once?

True.

Neither do comic and tragic writers employ the same actors; yet all these things are imitations.

They are so.

And human nature, Adeimantus, appears to have been coined into yet smaller pieces, and to be as incapable of imitating many things well, as of performing well the actions of which the imitations are copies.

Quite true, he replied.

If then we adhere to our original notion and bear in mind that our guardians, released from every other business, are to dedicate themselves wholly to the maintenance of the freedom of the State, making this their craft and engaging in no work which does not bear on this end, then they ought not to practice or even imitate anything else; if they imitate at all, they should imitate from youth upward only those characters which are suitable to their profession—the courageous, temperate, holy, free, and the like; but they should not depict or be skilful at imitating any kind of illiberality or baseness, lest the fruit of imitation should be reality. Did you never observe how imitations, beginning in early youth and continuing far into life, at length grow into habits and become a second nature, affecting body, voice, and mind?

. . .

I answered: Of the harmonies I know nothing, but would have you leave me one which can render the note or accent which a brave man utters in warlike action and in stern resolves; and when his cause is failing, and he is going to wounds or [399] death or is overtaken by disaster in some other form, at every such crisis he meets the blows of fortune with firm step and a determination to endure; and an opposite kind for times of peace and freedom of action, when there is no pressure of necessity, and he is seeking to persuade God by prayer, or man by instruction and admonition, or when on the other hand he is expressing his willingness to yield to the persuasion or entreaty or admonition of others. And when in this manner he has attained his end, I would have the music show him not carried away by his success, but acting moderately and wisely in all circumstances, and acquiescing in the event. These two harmonies I ask you to leave; the strain of necessity and the strain of freedom, the strain of the unfortunate and the strain of the fortunate, the strain of courage and the strain of temperance; these, I say, leave. . . .

Then let us now finish the purgation, I said. Next in order to harmonies, rhythms will naturally follow, and they should be subject to the same rules, for we ought not to seek out complex systems of metre, and a variety of feet, but rather to discover what rhythms are the expressions of a courageous and harmonious life; and when we have found them, we shall adapt [400] the foot and the melody to words having a like spirit, not the words to the foot and melody. To say what these rhythms are will be your duty—you must teach me them, as you have already taught me the harmonies.

But, indeed, he replied, I cannot tell you. I know from observation that there are some three principles of rhythm out of which metrical systems are framed, just as in sounds there are four notes out of which all the harmonies are composed. But of what sort of lives they are severally the imitations I am unable to say.

Then, I said, we must take Damon into our counsels; and he will tell us what rhythms are expressive of meanness, or insolence, or fury, or other unworthiness, and what are to be reserved for the expression of opposite feelings. . . .

But it does not require much analysis to see that grace or the absence of grace accompanies good or bad rhythm.

None at all.

And also that good and bad rhythm naturally assimilate to a good and bad style; and that harmony and discord in like manner follow style; for our principle is that rhythm and harmony are regulated by the words, and not the words by them.

Just so, he said, they should follow the words.

And will not the words and the character of the style depend on the temper of the soul?

Yes.

And everything else on the style?

Yes.

Then beauty of style and harmony and grace and good rhythm depend on simplicity,—I mean the true simplicity of a rightly and nobly ordered mind and character, not that other simplicity which is only a euphemism for folly?

Very true, he replied.

And if your youth are to do their work in life, must they not make these graces and harmonies their perpetual aim?

They must.

And surely the art of the painter and every other creative and [401] constructive art are full of them,—weaving, embroidery, architecture, and every kind of manufacture; also nature, animal and vegetable,—in all of them there is grace or the absence of grace. And ugliness and discord and inharmonious motion are nearly allied to ill words and ill nature, as grace and harmony are the twin sisters of goodness and self-restraint and bear their likeness.

That is quite true, he said.

But shall our superintendence go no further, and are the poets only to be required by us to express the image of the good in their works, on pain, if they do anything else, of expulsion from our State? Or is the same control to be extended to other artists, and are they also to be prohibited from exhibiting the opposite forms of vice and intemperance and meanness and deformity in sculpture and building and the other creative arts; and is he who cannot conform to this rule of ours to be prevented from practising his art in our State, lest the taste of our citizens be corrupted by him? We would not have our guardians grow up amid images of moral deformity, as in some noxious pasture, and there browse and feed upon many a baneful herb and flower day by day, little by little, until they silently gather a festering mass of corruption in their own soul. Let us rather search for artists who are gifted to discern the true nature of the beautiful and graceful; then will our youth dwell in a land of health, amid fair sights and sounds, and receive the good in everything; and beauty, the effluence of fair works, shall flow into the eye and ear, like a health-giving breeze from a purer region, and insensibly draw the soul from earliest years into likeness and sympathy with the beauty of reason.

There can be no nobler training than that, he replied.

And therefore, I said, Glaucon, musical training is a more potent instrument than any other, because rhythm and harmony find their way into the inward places of the soul, on which they mightily fasten, imparting grace, and making the soul of him who is rightly educated graceful, or of him who is ill-educated ungraceful; and also because he who has received this true education of the inner being will most shrewdly perceive omissions or faults in art and nature, and with a true [402] taste, while he praises and rejoices over and receives into his soul the good, and becomes noble and good, he will justly blame and hate the bad, now in the days of his youth, even before he is able to know the reason why; and when reason comes he will recognize and salute the friend with whom his education has made him long familiar.

Yes, he said, I quite agree with you in thinking that it is for such reasons that they should be trained in music.

Just as in learning to read, I said, we were satisfied when we knew the letters of the alphabet, few as they are, in all their recurring combinations; not slighting them as unimportant whether they occupy a space large or small, but everywhere eager to make them out, because we knew we should not be perfect in the art of reading until we could do so:

True—

And as we recognize the reflection of letters in water, or in a mirror, only when we know the letters themselves, the same art and study giving us the knowledge of both:

Exactly—

Even so, as I maintain, neither we nor the guardians, whom we say that we have to educate, can ever become musical until we and they know the essential forms of temperance, courage, liberality, magnanimity, and their kindred, as well as the contrary forms, in all their combinations, and can recognize them and their images wherever they are found, not slighting them either in small things or great, but believing them all to be within the sphere of one art and study.

Most assuredly.

And when nobility of soul is observed in harmonious union with beauty of form, and both are cast from the same mould, that will be the fairest of sights to him who has an eye to see it?

Republic: Book X [595–608b]

[595] Of the many excellences which I perceive in the order of our State, there is none which upon reflection pleases me better than the rule about poetry.

To what do you refer?

To our refusal to admit the imitative kind of poetry, for it certainly ought not to be received; as I see far more clearly now that the parts of the soul have been distinguished.

What do you mean?

Speaking in confidence, for you will not denounce me to the tragedians and the rest of the imitative tribe, all poetical imitations are ruinous to the understanding of the hearers, unless as an antidote they possess the knowledge of the true nature of the originals.

Explain the purport of your remark.

Well, I will tell you, although I have always from my earliest youth had an awe and love of Homer which even now makes the words falter on my lips, for he seems to be the great captain and teacher of the whole of that noble tragic company; but a man is not to be reverenced more than the truth, and therefore I will speak out.

Very good, he said.

Listen to me, then, or rather, answer me.

Put your question.

Can you give me a general definition of imitation? for I really do not myself understand what it professes to be.

A likely thing, then, that I should know.

[596] There would be nothing strange in that, for the duller eye may often see a thing sooner than the keener.

Very true, he said; but in your presence, even if I had any faint notion, I could not muster courage to utter it. Will you inquire yourself?

Well then, shall we begin the inquiry at this point, following our usual method: Whenever a number of individuals have a common name, we assume that there is one corresponding idea or form:[1]—do you understand me?

I do.

Let us take, for our present purpose, any instance of such a group; there are beds and tables in the world—many of each, are there not?

Yes.

But there are only two ideas or forms of such furniture—one the idea of a bed, the other of a table.

True.

And the maker of either of them makes a bed or he makes a table for our use, in accordance with the idea—that is our way of speaking in this and similar instances—but no artificer makes the idea itself: how could he?

Impossible.

And there is another artificer—I should like to know what you would say of him.

Who is he?

---

[1] [Or (probably better): "we have been accustomed to assume that there is one single idea corresponding to each group of particulars; and to these we give the same name (as we give the idea)." See J. A. Smith, C.R. xxxi (1917).]

One who is the maker of all the works of all other workmen.

What an extraordinary man!

Wait a little, and there will be more reason for your saying so. For this is the craftsman who is able to make not only furniture of every kind, but all that grows out of the earth, and all living creatures, himself included; and besides these he can make earth and sky and the gods, and all the things which are in heaven or in the realm of Hades under the earth.

He must be a wizard and no mistake.

Oh! you are incredulous, are you? Do you mean that there is no such maker or creator, or that in one sense there might be a maker of all these things but in another not? Do you see that there is a way in which you could make them all yourself?

And what way is this? he asked.

An easy way enough; or rather, there are many ways in which the feat might be quickly and easily accomplished, none quicker than that of turning a mirror round and round—you would soon enough make the sun and the heavens, and the earth and yourself, and other animals and plants, and furniture and all the other things of which we were just now speaking, in the mirror.

Yes, he said; but they would be appearances only.

Very good, I said, you are coming to the point now. And the painter too is, as I conceive, just such another—a creator of appearances, is he not?

Of course.

But then I suppose you will say that what he creates is untrue. And yet there is a sense in which the painter also creates a bed? Is there not?

Yes, he said, but here again, an appearance only.

[597] And what of the maker of the bed? were you not saying that he too makes, not the idea which according to our view is the real object denoted by the word bed, but only a particular bed?

Yes, I did.

Then if he does not make a real object he cannot make what *is*, but only some semblance of existence; and if any one were to say that the work of the maker of the bed, or of any other workman, has real existence, he could hardly be supposed to be speaking the truth.

Not, at least, he replied, in the view of those who make a business of these discussions.

No wonder, then, that his work too is an indistinct expression of truth.

No wonder.

Suppose now that by the light of the examples just offered we inquire who this imitator is?

If you please.

Well then, here we find three beds: one existing in nature, which is made by God, as I think that we may say—for no one else can be the maker?

No one, I think.

There is another which is the work of the carpenter?

Yes.

And the work of the painter is a third?

Yes.

Beds, then, are of three kinds, and there are three artists who superintend them: God, the maker of the bed, and the painter?

Yes, there are three of them.

God, whether from choice or from necessity, made one bed in nature and one only; two or more such beds neither ever have been nor ever will be made by God.

Why is that?

Because even if He had made but two, a third would still appear behind them of which they again both possessed the form, and that would be the real bed and not the two others.

Very true, he said.

God knew this, I suppose, and He desired to be the real maker of a real bed, not a kind of maker of a kind of bed, and therefore He created a bed which is essentially and by nature only one.

So it seems.

Shall we, then, speak of Him as the natural author or maker of the bed?

Yes, he replied; inasmuch as by the natural process of creation He is the author of this and of all other things.

And what shall we say of the carpenter—is not he also the maker of a bed?

Yes.

But would you call the painter an artificer and maker?

Certainly not.

Yet if he is not the maker, what is he in relation to the bed?

I think, he said, that we may fairly designate him as the imitator of that which the others make.

Good, I said; then you call him whose product is third in the descent from nature, an imitator?

Certainly, he said.

And so if the tragic poet is an imitator, he too is thrice removed from the king and from the truth; and so are all other imitators.

That appears to be so.

Then about the imitator we are agreed. And what about the painter?—Do you think he tries to imitate in each case that [598] which originally exists in nature, or only the creations of artificers?

The latter.

As they are or as they appear? you have still to determine this.

What do you mean?

I mean to ask whether a bed really becomes different when it is seen from different points of view, obliquely or directly or from any other point of view? Or does it simply appear different, without being really so? And the same of all things.

Yes, he said, the difference is only apparent.

Now let me ask you another question: Which is the art of painting designed to be —an imitation of things as they are, or as they appear—of appearance or of reality?

Of appearance, he said.

Then the imitator is a long way off the

truth, and can reproduce all things because he lightly touches on a small part of them, and that part an image. For example: A painter will paint a cobbler, carpenter, or any other artisan, though he knows nothing of their arts; and, if he is a good painter, he may deceive children or simple persons when he shows them his picture of a carpenter from a distance, and they will fancy that they are looking at a real carpenter.

Certainly.

And surely, my friend, this is how we should regard all such claims: whenever any one informs us that he has found a man who knows all the arts, and all things else that anybody knows, and every single thing with a higher degree of accuracy than any other man—whoever tells us this, I think that we can only retort that he is a simple creature who seems to have been deceived by some wizard or imitator whom he met, and whom he thought all-knowing, because he himself was unable to analyse the nature of knowledge and ignorance and imitation.

Most true.

And next, I said, we have to consider tragedy and its leader, Homer; for we hear some persons saying that these poets know all the arts; and all things human; where virtue and vice are concerned, and indeed all divine things too; because the good poet cannot compose well unless he knows his subject, and he who has not this knowledge can never be a poet. We ought to consider whether here also there may not be a similar illusion. Perhaps they may have come across imitators and been deceived by them; they may not have remembered when they [599] saw their works that these were thrice removed from the truth, and could easily be made without any knowledge of the truth, because they are appearances only and not realities? Or, after all, they may be in the right, and good poets do really know the things about which they seem to the many to speak so well?

The question, he said, should by all means be considered.

Now do you suppose that if a person were able to make the original as well as the image, he would seriously devote himself to the image-making branch? Would he allow imitation to be the ruling principle of his life, as if he had nothing higher in him?

I should say not.

But the real artist, who had real knowledge of those things which he chose also to imitate, would be interested in realities and not in imitations; and would desire to leave as memorials of himself works many and fair; and, instead of being the author of encomiums, he would prefer to be the theme of them.

Yes, he said, that would be to him a source of much greater honour and profit.

Now let us refrain, I said, from calling Homer or any other poet to account regarding those arts to which his poems incidentally refer: we will not ask them, in case any poet has been a doctor and not a mere imitator of medical parlance, to show what patients have been restored to health by a poet, ancient or modern, as they were by Asclepius; or what disciples in medicine a poet has left behind him, like the Asclepiads. Nor shall we press the same question upon them about the other arts. But we have a right to know respecting warfare, strategy, the administration of States and the education of man, which are the chiefest and noblest subjects of his poems, and we may fairly ask him about them. "Friend Homer," then we say to him, "if you are only in the second remove from truth in what you say of virtue, and not in the third —not an image maker, that is, by our definition, an imitator—and if you are able to discern what pursuits make men better or worse in private or public life, tell us what State was ever better governed by your help? The good order of Lacedaemon is due to Lycurgus, and many other cities great and small have been similarly benefited by others; but who says that you have been a good legislator to them and have done them any good? Italy and Sicily boast of Charondas, and there is Solon who is renowned among us; but what city has anything to say about you?" Is there any city which he might name?

I think not, said Glaucon; not even the Homerids themselves pretend that he was a legislator.

[600] Well, but is there any war on record which was carried on successfully owing to his leadership or counsel?

There is not.

Or is there anything comparable to those clever improvements in the arts, or in other operations, which are said to have been due to men of practical genius such as Thales the Milesian or Anacharsis the Scythian?

There is absolutely nothing of the kind.

But, if Homer never did any public service, was he privately a guide or teacher of any? Had he in his lifetime friends who loved to associate with him, and who handed down to posterity an Homeric way of life, such as was established by Pythagoras who was especially beloved for this reason and whose followers are to this day conspicuous among others by what they term the Pythagorean way of life?

Nothing of the kind is recorded of him. For surely, Socrates, Creophylus, the companion of Homer, that child of flesh, whose name always makes us laugh, might be more justly ridiculed for his want of breeding, if what is said is true, that Homer was greatly neglected by him in his own day when he was alive?

Yes, I replied, that is the tradition. But can you imagine, Glaucon, that if Homer had really been able to educate and improve mankind—if he had been capable of knowledge and not been a mere imitator—can you imagine, I say, that he would not have attracted many followers, and been honoured and loved by them? Protagoras of Abdera, and Prodicus of Ceos, and a host of others, have only to whisper to their contemporaries: "You will never be able to

manage either your own house or your own State until you appoint us to be your ministers of education"—and this ingenious device of theirs has such an effect in making men love them that their companions all but carry them about on their shoulders. And is it conceivable that the contemporaries of Homer, or again of Hesiod, would have allowed either of them to go about as rhapsodists, if they had really been able to help mankind forward in virtue? Would they not have been as unwilling to part with them as with gold, and have compelled them to stay at home with them? Or, if the master would not stay, then the disciples would have followed him about everywhere, until they had got education enough?

Yes, Socrates, that, I think, is quite true.

Then must we not infer that all these poetical individuals, beginning with Homer, are only imitators, who copy images of virtue and the other themes of their poetry, but have no contact with the truth? The poet is like a painter who, as we have already observed, will make a likeness of a cobbler though [601] he understands nothing of cobbling; and his picture is good enough for those who know no more than he does, and judge only by colours and figures.

Quite so.

In like manner the poet with his words and phrases[2] may be said to lay on the colours of the several arts, himself understanding their nature only enough to imitate them; and other people, who are as ignorant as he is, and judge only from his words, imagine that if he speaks of cobbling, or of military tactics, or of anything else, in metre and harmony and rhythm, he speaks very well—such is the sweet influence which melody and rhythm by nature have. For I am sure that you know what a poor appearance the works of poets make when stripped of the colours which art puts upon them,

[2] Or, "with his nouns and verbs."

and recited in simple prose. You have seen some examples?

Yes, he said.

They are like faces which were never really beautiful, but only blooming, seen when the bloom of youth has passed away from them?

Exactly.

Come now, and observe this point: The imitator or maker of the image knows nothing, we have said, of true existence; he knows appearances only. Am I not right?

Yes.

Then let us have a clear understanding, and not be satisfied with half an explanation.

Proceed.

Of the painter we say that he will paint reins, and he will paint a bit?

Yes.

And the worker in leather and brass will make them?

Certainly.

But does the painter know the right form of the bit and reins? Nay, hardly even the workers in brass and leather who make them; only the horseman who knows how to use them—he knows their right form.

Most true.

And may we not say the same of all things?

What?

That there are three arts which are concerned with all things: one which uses, another which makes, a third which imitates them?

Yes.

And the excellence and beauty and rightness of every structure, animate or inanimate, and of every action of man, is relative solely to the use for which nature or the artist has intended them.

True.

Then beyond doubt it is the user who has the greatest experience of them, and he must report to the maker the good or bad qualities which develop themselves in use;

for example, the flute-player will tell the flute-maker which of his flutes is satisfactory to the performer;[3] he will tell him how he ought to make them, and the other will attend to his instructions?

Of course.

So the one pronounces with knowledge about the goodness and badness of flutes, while the other, confiding in him, will make them accordingly?

True.

The instrument is the same, but about the excellence or badness of it the maker will possess a correct belief, since he [602] associates with one who knows, and is compelled to hear what he has to say; whereas the user will have knowledge?

True.

But will the imitator have either? Will he know from use whether or not that which he paints is correct or beautiful? or will he have right opinion from being compelled to associate with another who knows and gives him instructions about what he should paint?

Neither.

Then an imitator will no more have true opinion than he will have knowledge about the goodness or badness of his models?

I suppose not.

The imitative poet will be in a brilliant state of intelligence about the theme of his poetry?

Nay, very much the reverse.

And still he will go on imitating without knowing what makes a thing good or bad, and may be expected therefore to imitate only that which appears to be good to the ignorant multitude?

Just so.

Thus far then we are pretty well agreed that the imitator has no knowledge worth mentioning of what he imitates. Imitation

---

[3] [Or, to avoid the repetition of ὑπηρετεῖν in a different sense: "will make a report to the flute-maker, *who assists him in his playing*, about the flutes."]

is only a kind of play or sport, and the tragic poets, whether they write in iambic or in heroic verse, are imitators in the highest degree?

Very true.

And now tell me, I conjure you,—this imitation is concerned with an object which is thrice removed from the truth?

Certainly.

And what kind of faculty in man is that to which imitation makes its special appeal?

What do you mean?

I will explain: The same body does not appear equal to our sight when seen near and when seen at a distance?

True.

And the same objects appear straight when looked at out of the water, and crooked when in the water; and the concave becomes convex, owing to the illusion about colours to which the sight is liable. Thus every sort of confusion is revealed within us; and this is that weakness of the human mind on which the art of painting in light and shadow, the art of conjuring, and many other ingenious devices impose, having an effect upon us like magic.

True.

And the arts of measuring and numbering and weighing come to the rescue of the human understanding—there is the beauty of them—with the result that the apparent greater or less, or more or heavier, no longer have the mastery over us, but give way before the power of calculation and measuring and weighing?

Most true.

And this, surely, must be the work of the calculating and rational principle in the soul?

To be sure.

And often when this principle measures and certifies that some things are equal, or that some are greater or less than others, it is, at the same time, contradicted by the appearance which the objects present?

True.

But did we not say that such a contradiction is impossible—the same faculty cannot have contrary opinions at the same time about the same thing?

We did; and rightly.

[603] Then that part of the soul which has an opinion contrary to measure can hardly be the same with that which has an opinion in accordance with measure?

True.

And the part of the soul which trusts to measure and calculation is likely to be the better one?

Certainly.

And therefore that which is opposed to this is probably an inferior principle in our nature?

No doubt.

This was the conclusion at which I was seeking to arrive when I said that painting or drawing, and imitation in general, are engaged upon productions which are far removed from truth, and are also the companions and friends and associates of a principle within us which is equally removed from reason, and that they have no true or healthy aim.

Exactly.

The imitative art is an inferior who from intercourse with an inferior has inferior offspring.

Very true.

And is this confined to the sight only, or does it extend to the hearing also, relating in fact to what we term poetry?

Probably the same would be true of poetry.

Do not rely, I said, on a probability derived from the analogy of painting; but let us once more go directly to that faculty of the mind with which imitative poetry has converse, and see whether it is good or bad.

By all means.

We may state the question thus:—Imitation imitates the actions of men, whether voluntary or involuntary, on which, as they imagine, a good or bad result has ensued, and they rejoice or sorrow accordingly. Is there anything more?

No, there is nothing else.

But in all this variety of circumstances is the man at unity with himself—or rather, as in the instance of sight there was confusion and opposition in his opinions about the same things, so here also is there not strife and inconsistency in his life? Though I need hardly raise the question again, for I remember that all this has been already admitted; and the soul has been acknowledged by us to be full of these and ten thousand similar oppositions occurring at the same moment?

And we were right, he said.

Yes, I said, thus far we were right; but there was an omission which must now be supplied.

What was the omission?

Were we not saying that a good man, who has the misfortune to lose his son or anything else which is most dear to him, will bear the loss with more equanimity than another?

Yes, indeed.

But will he have no sorrow, or shall we say that although he cannot help sorrowing, he will moderate his sorrow?

The latter, he said, is the truer statement.

Tell me: will he be more likely to struggle and hold out [604] against his sorrow when he is seen by his equals, or when he is alone in a deserted place?

The fact of being seen will make a great difference, he said.

When he is by himself he will not mind saying many things which he would be ashamed of any one hearing, and also doing many things which he would not care to be seen doing?

True.

And doubtless it is the law and reason in him which bids him resist; while it is the affliction itself which is urging him to indulge his sorrow?

True.

But when a man is drawn in two opposite directions, to and from the same object, this, as we affirm, necessarily implies two distinct principles in him?

Certainly.

One of them is ready to follow the guidance of the law?

How do you mean?

The law would say that to be patient under calamity is best, and that we should not give way to impatience, as the good and evil in such things are not clear, and nothing is gained by impatience; also, because no human thing is of serious importance, and grief stands in the way of that which at the moment is most required.

What is most required? he asked.

That we should take counsel about what has happened, and when the dice have been thrown, according to their fall, order our affairs in the way which reason deems best; not, like children who have had a fall, keeping hold of the part struck and wasting time in setting up a howl, but always accustoming the soul forthwith to apply a remedy, raising up that which is sickly and fallen, banishing the cry of sorrow by the healing art.

Yes, he said, that is the true way of meeting the attacks of fortune.

Well then, I said, the higher principle is ready to follow this suggestion of reason?

Clearly.

But the other principle, which inclines us to recollection of our troubles and to lamentation, and can never have enough of them, we may call irrational, useless, and cowardly?

Indeed, we may.

Now does not the principle which is thus inclined to complaint, furnish a great variety of materials for imitation? Whereas the wise and calm temperament, being always nearly equable, is not easy to imitate or to appreciate when imitated, especially at a public festival when a promiscuous crowd is assembled in a theatre. For the feeling represented is one to which they are strangers.

Certainly.

[605] Then the imitative poet who aims at being popular is not by nature made, nor is his art intended, to please or to affect the rational principle in the soul; but he will appear rather to the lachrymose and fitful temper, which is easily imitated?

Clearly.

And now we may fairly take him and place him by the side of the painter, for he is like him in two ways: first, inasmuch as his creations have an inferior degree of truth—in this, I say, he is like him; and he is also like him in being the associate of an inferior part of the soul; and this is enough to show that we shall be right in refusing to admit him into a State which is to be well ordered, because he awakens and nourishes this part of the soul, and by strengthening it impairs the reason. As in a city when the evil are permitted to wield power and the finer men are put out of the way, so in the soul of each man, as we shall maintain, the imitative poet implants an evil constitution, for he indulges the irrational nature which has no discernment of greater and less, but thinks the same thing at one time great and at another small—he is an imitator of images and is very far removed from the truth.

Exactly.

But we have not yet brought forward the heaviest count in our accusation:—the power which poetry has of harming even the good (and there are very few who are not harmed), is surely an awful thing?

Yes, certainly, if the effect is what you say.

Hear and judge: The best of us, as I conceive, when we listen to a passage of Homer or one of the tragedians, in which he represents some hero who is drawling out his sorrows in a long oration, or singing, and smiting his breast—the best of us, you know, delight in giving way to sympathy, and are in raptures at the excellence of the poet who stirs our feelings most.

Yes, of course I know.

But when any sorrow of our own happens to us, then you may observe that we pride ourselves on the opposite quality—we would fain be quiet and patient; this is considered the manly part, and the other which delighted us in the recitation is now deemed to be the part of a woman.

Very true, he said.

Now can we be right in praising and admiring another who is doing that which any one of us would abominate and be ashamed of in his own person?

No, he said, that is certainly not reasonable.

[606] Nay, I said, quite reasonable from one point of view.

What point of view?

If you consider, I said, that when in misfortune we feel a natural hunger and desire to relieve our sorrow by weeping and lamentation, and that this very feeling which is starved and suppressed in our own calamities is satisfied and delighted by the poets; —the better nature in each of us, not having been sufficiently trained by reason or habit, allows the sympathetic element to break loose because the sorrow is another's; and the spectator fancies that there can be no disgrace to himself in praising and pitying any one who while professing to be a brave man, gives way to untimely lamentation; he thinks that the pleasure is a gain, and is far from wishing to lose it by rejection of the whole poem. Few persons ever reflect, as I should imagine, that the contagion must pass from others to themselves. For the pity which has been nourished and strengthened in the misfortunes of others is with difficulty repressed in our own.

How very true!

And does not the same hold also of the ridiculous? There are jests which you would be ashamed to make yourself, and yet on the comic stage, or indeed in private, when you hear them, you are greatly amused by them, and are not at all disgusted at their unseemliness;—the case of pity is repeated;—there is a principle in human nature which is disposed to raise a laugh, and this, which you once restrained by reason because you were afraid of being thought a buffoon, is now let out again; and having stimulated the risible faculty at the theatre, you are betrayed unconsciously to yourself into playing the comic poet at home.

Quite true, he said.

And the same may be said of lust and anger and all the other affections, of desire and pain and pleasure, which are held to be inseparable from every action—in all of them poetry has a like effect; it feeds and waters the passions instead of drying them up; she lets them rule, although they ought to be controlled if mankind are ever to increase in happiness and virtue.

I cannot deny it.

Therefore, Glaucon, I said, whenever you meet with any of the eulogists of Homer declaring that he has been the educator of Hellas, and that he is profitable for education and for the ordering of human things, and that you should take him up again and again and get to know him and regulate your whole life according to him, we may love and honour those who say these things —they are excellent people, as far as their lights [607] extend; and we are ready to acknowledge that Homer is the greatest of poets and first of tragedy writers; but we must remain firm in our conviction that hymns to the gods and praises of famous men are the only poetry which ought to be admitted into our State. For if you go beyond this and allow the honeyed Muse to enter, either in epic or lyric verse, not law and the reason of mankind, which by common consent have ever been deemed best,[4]

but pleasure and pain will be the rulers in our State.

That is most true, he said.

And now since we have reverted to the subject of poetry, let this our defence serve to show the reasonableness of our former judgement in sending away out of our State an art having the tendencies which we have described; for reason constrained us. But that she may not impute to us any harshness or want of politeness, let us tell her that there is an ancient quarrel between philosophy and poetry; of which there are many proofs, such as the saying of "the yelping hound howling at her lord," or of one "mighty in the vain talk of fools," and "the mob of sages circumventing Zeus," and the "subtle thinkers who are beggars after all";[5] and there are innumerable other signs of ancient enmity between them. Notwithstanding this, let us assure the poetry which aims at pleasure, and the art of imitation, that if she will only prove her title to exist in a well-ordered State we shall be delighted to receive her—we are very conscious of her charms; but it would not be right on that account to betray the truth. I dare say, Glaucon, that you are as much charmed by her as I am, especially when she appears in Homer?

Yes, indeed, I am greatly charmed.

Shall I propose, then, that she be allowed to return from exile, but upon this condition only—that she make a defence of herself in some lyrical or other metre?

Certainly.

And we may further grant to those of her defenders who are lovers of poetry and yet not poets the permission to speak in prose on her behalf: let them show not only that she is pleasant but also useful to States and to human life, and we will listen in a kindly spirit; for we shall surely be the gainers if this can be proved, that there is a use in poetry as well as a delight?

[4] [Or: "law, and the principle which the community in every case has pronounced to be the best."]

[5] [Reading and sense uncertain. The origin of all these quotations is unknown.]

Certainly, he said, we shall be the gainers.

If her defence fails, then, my dear friend, like other persons who are enamoured of something, but put a restraint upon themselves when they think their desires are opposed to their interests, so too must we after the manner of lovers give her up, though not without a struggle. We too are inspired by that love of such poetry which the education of noble States has implanted in us, [608] and therefore we shall be glad if she appears at her best and truest; but so long as she is unable to make good her defence, this argument of ours shall be a charm to us, which we will repeat to ourselves while we listen to her strains; that we may not fall away into the childish love of her which captivates the many. At all events we are well aware[6] that poetry,[7] such as we have described, is not to be regarded seriously as attaining to the truth; and he who listens to her, fearing for the safety of the city which is within him, should be on his guard against her seductions and make our words his law.

Yes, he said, I quite agree with you.

Yes, I said, my dear Glaucon, for great is the issue at stake, greater than appears, whether a man is to be good or bad. And what will any one be profited if under the influence of honour or money or power, aye, or under the excitement of poetry, he neglect justice and virtue?

Symposium [201C–212a]

Indeed, you made a very good speech, Agathon, replied Socrates; but there is yet one small question which I would fain ask: —Is not the good also the beautiful?

---

[6] Or, if we accept Madvig's ingenious but unnecessary emendation ἀσόμεθα, "At all events we will sing, that," etc.

[7] [i.e. *imitative* poetry. The word imitation, in the recent argument, had not the same sense as in Book III; but it has always been implied that there might be poetry which is not imitative.]

Yes.

Then in lacking the beautiful, love lacks also the good?

I cannot refute you, Socrates, said Agathon:—Be it as you say.

Say rather, beloved Agathon, that you cannot refute the truth; for Socrates is easily refuted.

And now, taking my leave of you, I will rehearse a tale of love which I heard from Diotima of Mantinea, a woman wise in this and many other kinds of knowledge, who in the days of old, when the Athenians offered sacrifice before the coming of the plague, delayed the disease ten years. She was my instructress in the art of love, and I shall try to repeat to you what she said to me, beginning with the propositions on which Agathon and I are agreed; I will do the best I can do without any help. As you, Agathon, suggested, it is proper to speak first of the being and nature of Love, and then of his work. (I think it will be easiest for me if in recounting my conversation with the wise woman I follow its actual course of question and answer.) First I said to her in nearly the same words which he used to me, that Love was a mighty god, and likewise fair; and she proved to me, as I proved to him, that by my own showing Love was neither fair nor good. "What do you mean, Diotima," I said, "is Love then evil and foul?" "Hush," she cried; "must that be foul which is not fair?" "Certainly," I said. "And is that which is [202] not wise, ignorant? do you not see that there is a mean between wisdom and ignorance?" "And what may that be?" I said. "Right opinion," she replied; "which, as you know, being incapable of giving a reason, is not knowledge (for how can knowledge be devoid of reason?) nor again ignorance (for neither can ignorance attain the truth), but is clearly something which is a mean between ignorance and wisdom." "Quite true," I replied. "Do not then insist," she said, "that what is not fair is of necessity foul, or what is not good evil; or infer that because Love is not fair and good he is therefore foul and evil; for he is in a mean between them." "Well," I said, "Love is surely admitted by all to be a great god." "By those who know or by those who do not know?" "By all." "And how, Socrates," she said with a smile, "can Love be acknowledged to be a great god by those who say that he is not a god at all?" "And who are they?" I said. "You and I are two of them," she replied. "How can that be?" I said. "It is quite intelligible," she replied; "for you yourself would acknowledge that the gods are happy and fair—of course you would—would you dare to say that any god was not?" "Certainly not," I replied. "And you mean by the happy, those who are the possessors of things good and things fair?" "Yes." "And you admitted that Love, because he was in want, desires those good and fair things of which he is in want?" "Yes, I did." "But how can he be a god who has no portion in what is good and fair?" "Impossible." "Then you see that you also deny the divinity of Love."

"What then is Love?" I asked; "Is he mortal?" "No." "What then?" "As in the former instance, he is neither mortal nor immortal, but in a mean between the two." "What is he, Diotima?" "He is a great spirit [δαίμων], and like all spirits he is intermediate between the divine and the mortal." "And what," I said, "is his power?" "He interprets between gods and men, conveying and taking across to the gods the prayers and sacrifices of men, and to men the commands of the gods and the benefits they return; he is the mediator who spans the chasm which divides them, and therefore by him the universe is bound together, and through him the arts of the prophet and the priest, [203] their sacrifices and mysteries and charms, and all prophecy and incantation, find their way. For God mingles not with man; but through Love all the intercourse and converse of gods with men, whether they be awake or asleep, is carried on. The wisdom which understands

this is spiritual; all other wisdom, such as that of arts and handicrafts, is mean and vulgar. Now these spirits or intermediate powers are many and diverse, and one of them is Love." "And who," I said, "was his father, and who his mother?" "The tale," she said, "will take time; nevertheless I will tell you. On the day when Aphrodite was born there was a feast of all the gods, among them the god Poros or Plenty, who is the son of Metis or Sagacity. When the feast was over, Penia or Poverty, as the manner is on such occasions, came about the doors to beg. Now Plenty, who was the worse for nectar (there was no wine in those days), went into the garden of Zeus and fell into a heavy sleep; and Poverty considering that for her there was no plenty, plotted to have a child by him, and accordingly she lay down at his side and conceived Love, who partly because he is naturally a lover of the beautiful, and because Aphrodite is herself beautiful, and also because he was begotten during her birthday feast, is her follower and attendant. And as his parentage is, so also are his fortunes. In the first place he is always poor, and anything but tender and fair, as the many imagine him; and he is rough and squalid, and has no shoes, nor a house to dwell in; on the bare earth exposed he lies under the open heaven, in the streets, or at the doors of houses, taking his rest; and like his mother he is always in distress. Like his father too, whom he also partly resembles, he is always plotting against the fair and good; he is bold, enterprising, strong, a mighty hunter, always weaving some intrigue or other, keen in the pursuit of wisdom, fertile in resources; a philosopher at all times, terrible as an enchanter, sorcerer, sophist. He is by nature neither mortal nor immortal, but alive and flourishing at one moment when he is in plenty, and dead at another moment in the same day, and again alive by reason of his father's nature. But that which is always flowing in is always flowing out, and so he is never in want and never in wealth; and, further, he is in a mean between ignorance and knowledge. The truth of the matter is this: No god is a philosopher [204] or seeker after wisdom, for he is wise already; nor does any man who is wise seek after wisdom. Neither do the ignorant seek after wisdom; for herein is the evil of ignorance, that he who is neither a man of honour nor wise is nevertheless satisfied with himself: there is no desire when there is no feeling of want." "But who then, Diotima," I said, "are the lovers of wisdom, if they are neither the wise nor the foolish?" "A child may answer that question," she replied; "they are those who are in a mean between the two; Love is one of them. For wisdom is a most beautiful thing, and Love is of the beautiful; and therefore Love is also a philosopher or lover of wisdom, and being a lover of wisdom is in a mean between the wise and the ignorant. And of this, too, his birth is the cause; for his father is wealthy and wise, and his mother poor and foolish. Such, my dear Socrates, is the nature of the spirit Love. The error in your conception of him was very natural; from what you say yourself, I infer that it arose because you thought that Love is that which is loved, not that which loves; and for that reason, I think, Love appeared to you supremely beautiful. For the beloved is the truly beautiful, and delicate, and perfect, and blessed; but the active principle of love is of another nature, and is such as I have described."

I said: "O thou stranger woman, thou sayest well; but, assuming Love to be such as you say, what is the use of him to men?" "That, Socrates," she replied, "I will attempt to unfold: of his nature and birth I have already spoken; and you acknowledge that love is of the beautiful. But someone will say: What does it consist in, Socrates and Diotima?—or rather let me put the question more clearly, and ask: When a man loves the beautiful, what does his love desire?" I answered her "That the beautiful

may be his." "Still," she said, "the answer suggests a further question: What is given by the possession of beauty?" "To what you have asked," I replied, "I have no answer ready." "Then," she said, "let me put the word 'good' in the place of the beautiful, and repeat the question once more: If he who loves loves the good, what is it then that he loves?" "The possession of the good." "And what does he gain who possesses the good?" "Happiness," I replied; "there is less difficulty in answering [205] that question." "Yes," she said, "the happy are made happy by the acquisition of good things. Nor is there any need to ask why a man desires happiness; the answer is already final." "You are right," I said. "And is this wish and this desire common to all? and do all men always desire their own good, or only some men?—what say you?" "All men," I replied; "the desire is common to all." "Why, then," she rejoined, "are not all men, Socrates, said to love, but only some of them? whereas you say that all men are always loving the same things." "I myself wonder," I said, "why this is." "There is nothing to wonder at," she replied; "the reason is that one part of love is separated off and receives the name of the whole, but the other parts have other names." "Give an illustration," I said. She answered me as follows: "There is creative activity which, as you know, is complex and manifold. All that causes the passage of non-being into being is a 'poesy' or creation, and the processes of all art are creative; and the masters of arts are all poets or creators." "Very true." "Still," she said, "you know that they are not called poets, but have other names; only that one portion of creative activity which is separated off from the rest, and is concerned with music and metre, is called by the name of the whole and is termed poetry, and they who possess poetry in this sense of the word are called poets." "Very true," I said. "And the same holds of love. For you may say generally that all desire of good and happiness is only the great and subtle power of love; but they who are drawn towards him by any other path, whether the path of money-making or gymnastics or philosophy, are not called lovers—the name of the whole is appropriated to those whose desire takes one form only—they alone are said to love, or to be lovers." "I dare say," I replied, "that you are right." "Yes," she added, "and you hear people say that lovers are seeking for their other half; but I say that they are seeking neither for the half of themselves, nor for the whole, unless the half or the whole be also a good; men will cut off their own hands and feet and cast them away, if they think them evil. They do not, I imagine, each cling to what is his own, unless perchance there be someone who calls what belongs to him the good, and what [206] belongs to another the evil; for there is nothing which men love but the good. Is there anything?" "Certainly, I should say, that there is nothing." "Then," she said, "the simple truth is, that men love the good." "Yes," I said. "To which must be added that they love the possession of the good?" "Yes, that must be added." "And not only the possession, but the everlasting possession of the good?" "That must be added too." "Then love," she said, "may be described generally as the love of the everlasting possession of the good?" "That is most true."

"Then if this be always the nature of love, can you tell me further," she went on, "what is the manner of the pursuit? what are they doing who show all this eagerness and heat which is called love? and what is the object which they have in view? Answer me." "Nay, Diotima," I replied, "if I knew, I should not be wondering at your wisdom, neither should I come to learn from you about this very matter." "Well," she said, "I will teach you:—The object which they have in view is birth in beauty, whether of body or soul." "I do not understand you," I said; "the oracle requires an explanation." "I will make my meaning clearer," she replied. "I mean to say, that all men are bringing to the birth in their bodies and in their souls. There is a certain age at which human nature is desirous of procreation—procreation which must be in beauty and not in deformity. The union of man and woman is a procreation; it is a divine thing, for conception and generation are an immortal principle in the mortal creature, and in the inharmonious they can never be. But the deformed is inharmonious with all divinity, and the beautiful harmonious. Beauty, then, is the destiny or goddess of parturition who presides at birth, and therefore, when approaching beauty, the procreating power is propitious, and expansive, and benign, and bears and produces fruit: at the sight of ugliness she frowns and contracts and has a sense of pain, and turns away, and shrivels up, and not without a pang refrains from procreation. And this is the reason why, when the hour of procreation comes, and the teeming nature is full, there is such a flutter and ecstasy about beauty whose approach is the alleviation of the bitter pain of travail. For love, Socrates, is not, as you imagine, the love of the beautiful only." "What then?" "The love of generation and of birth in beauty." "Yes," I said. "Yes, indeed," she replied. "But why of generation? Because to the mortal creature, generation is a sort of eternity and immortality, and if, as has been already admitted, love is of the [207] everlasting possession of the good, all men will necessarily desire immortality together with good: whence it must follow that love is of immortality."

All this she taught me at various times when she spoke of love. And I remember her once saying to me, "What is the cause, Socrates, of love, and the attendant desire? See you not how all animals, birds as well as beasts, in their desire of procreation, are in agony when they take the infection of love, which begins with the desire of union and then passes to the care of offspring, on whose behalf the weakest are ready to battle against the strongest even to the uttermost, and to die for them, and will let themselves be tormented with hunger, or make any other sacrifice, in order to maintain their young. Man may be supposed to act thus from reason; but why should animals have these passionate feelings? Can you tell me why?" Again I replied that I did not know. She said to me: "And do you expect ever to become a master in the art of love, if you do not know this?" "But I have told you already, Diotima, that my ignorance is the reason why I come to you, for I am conscious that I want a teacher; tell me then the cause of this and of the other mysteries of love." "Marvel not," she said, "if you believe that love is of the immortal, as we have several times acknowledged; for here again, and on the same principle too, the mortal nature is seeking as far as is possible to be everlasting and immortal: and this is only to be attained by generation, because generation always leaves behind a new and different existence in the place of the old. Nay, even in the life of the same individual there is succession and not absolute uniformity: a man is called the same, and yet in the interval between youth and age, during which every animal is said to have life and identity, he is undergoing a perpetual process of loss and reparation—hair, flesh, bones, blood, and the whole body are always changing. Which is true not only of the body, but also of the soul, whose habits, tempers, opinions, desires, pleasures, pains, fears, never remain the same in any one of us, but are always coming and going. What is still more surprising, it is equally true of science; not only do some of the sciences come to life in our minds, and others die away, so that we are [208] never the same in regard to them either: but the same fate happens to each of them individually. For what is implied in the word 'recollection,' but the departure of knowledge, which is ever being forgotten, and is renewed and preserved by recollection, and appears to be the same although in reality new, according to that law by which all mortal things are preserved, not absolutely the same, but by substitution, the old worn-out mortality leaving another new and similar existence behind—unlike the divine, which is wholly and eternally the same? And in this way, Socrates, the mortal body, or mortal anything, partakes of immortality; but the immortal in another way. Marvel not then at the love which all men have of their offspring; for that universal love and interest is for the sake of immortality."

I was astonished at her words, and said: "Is this really true, O most wise Diotima?" And she answered with all the authority of an accomplished sophist: "Of that, Socrates, you may be assured;—think only of the ambition of men, and you will wonder at the senselessness of their ways, unless you consider how they are stirred by the passionate love of fame. They are ready to run all risks, even greater than they would have run for their children, and to pour out money and undergo any sort of toil, and even to die, 'if so they leave an everlasting name.' Do you imagine that Alcestis would have died to save Admetus, or Achilles to avenge Patroclus, or your own Codrus in order to preserve the kingdom for his sons, if they had not imagined that the memory of their virtues, which still survives among us, would be immortal? Nay," she said, "I am persuaded that all men do all things, and the better they are the more they do them, in hope of the glorious fame of immortal virtue; for they desire the immortal.

"Those who are pregnant in the body only, betake themselves to women and beget children—this is the character of their love; their offspring, as they hope, will preserve their memory and give them the blessedness and immortality which [209] they desire for all future time. But souls which are pregnant—for there certainly are men who are more creative in their souls than in their bodies, creative of that which is proper for the soul to conceive and bring forth: and if you ask me what are these conceptions, I answer, wisdom, and virtue in general—among such souls are all creative poets and all artists who are deserving of the name inventor. But the greatest and fairest sort of wisdom by far is that which is concerned with the ordering of states and families, and which is called temperance and justice. And he who in youth has the seed of these implanted in his soul, when he grows up and comes to maturity desires to beget and generate. He wanders about seeking beauty that he may get offspring —for from deformity he will beget nothing —and naturally embraces the beautiful rather than the deformed body; above all, when he finds a fair and noble and well-nurtured soul, he embraces the two in one person, and to such a one he is full of speech about virtue and the nature and pursuits of a good man, and he tries to educate him. At the touch and in the society of the beautiful which is ever present to his memory, even when absent, he brings forth that which he had conceived long before, and in company with him tends that which he brings forth; and they are married by a far nearer tie and have a closer friendship than those who beget mortal children, for the children who are their common offspring are fairer and more immortal. Who, when he thinks of Homer and Hesiod and other great poets, would not rather have their children than ordinary human ones? Who would not emulate them in the creation of children such as theirs, which have preserved their memory and given them everlasting glory? Or who would not have such children as Lycurgus left behind him to be the saviours, not only of Lacedaemon, but of Hellas, as one may say? There is Solon, too, who is the revered father of Athenian laws; and many others there are in many other places, both among Hellenes and barbarians, who have given to the world many noble works, and have been the parents of virtue of every kind; and many temples have been raised in their honour for the sake of children such as theirs; which were never raised in honour of anyone, for the sake of his mortal children.

"These are the lesser mysteries of love, into which even you, Socrates, may enter; to the greater and more hidden ones which [210] are the crown of these, and to which, if you pursue them in a right spirit, they will lead, I know not whether you will be able to attain. But I will do my utmost to inform you, and do you follow if you can. For he who would proceed aright in this matter should begin in youth to seek the company of corporeal beauty; and first, if he be guided by his instructor aright, to love one beautiful body only—out of that he should create fair thoughts; and soon he will of himself perceive that the beauty of one body is akin to the beauty of another; and then if beauty of form in general is his pursuit, how foolish would he be not to recognize that the beauty in every body is one and the same! And when he perceives this he will abate his violent love of the one, which he will despise and deem a small thing, and will become a steadfast lover of all beautiful bodies. In the next stage he will consider that the beauty of the soul is more precious than the beauty of the outward form; so that if a virtuous soul have but a little comeliness, he will be content to love and tend him, and will search out and bring to the birth thoughts which may improve the young, until he is compelled next to contemplate and see the beauty in institutions and laws, and to understand that the beauty of them all is of one family, and that personal beauty is a trifle; and after institutions his guide will lead him on to the sciences, in order that, beholding the wide region already occupied by beauty, he may cease to be like a servant in love with one beauty only, that of a particular youth or man or institution, himself a slave mean and narrow-minded; but drawing towards and contemplating the vast sea of beauty, he will create many fair and noble thoughts and discourses in boundless love of wisdom, until on that shore he

grows and waxes strong, and at last the
vision is revealed to him of a single science,
which is the science of beauty everywhere.
To this I will proceed; please to give me
your very best attention:

"He who has been instructed thus far in
the things of love, and who has learned to
see the beautiful in due order and succession, when he comes toward the end will
suddenly perceive a nature of wondrous
beauty (and this, Socrates, is the [211] final
cause of all our former toils)—a nature
which in the first place is everlasting, knowing not birth or death, growth or decay; secondly, not fair in one point of view and foul
in another, or at one time or in one relation
or at one place fair, at another time or in
another relation or at another place foul,
as if fair to some and foul to others, or in
the likeness of a face or hands or any other
part of the bodily frame, or in any form of
speech or knowledge, or existing in any individual being, as for example, in a living
creature, whether in heaven, or in earth, or
anywhere else; but beauty absolute, separate, simple, and everlasting, which is imparted to the ever growing and perishing
beauties of all other beautiful things, without itself suffering diminution, or increase,
or any change. He who, ascending from
these earthly things under the influence of
true love, begins to perceive that beauty, is
not far from the end. And the true order of
going, or being led by another, to the things
of love, is to begin from the beauties of
earth and mount upwards for the sake of
that other beauty, using these as steps only,
and from one going on to two, and from two
to all fair bodily forms, and from fair bodily
forms to fair practices, and from fair practices to fair sciences, until from fair sciences
he arrives at the science of which I have
spoken, the science which has no other object than absolute beauty, and at last knows
that which is beautiful by itself alone. This,
my dear Socrates," said the stranger of Mantinea, "is that life above all others which
man should live, in the contemplation of

beauty absolute; a beauty which if you once
beheld, you would see not to be after the
measure of gold, and garments, and fair
boys and youths, whose presence now en-
trances you; and you and many a one would
be content to live seeing them only and conversing with them without meat or drink,
if that were possible—you only want to look
at them and to be with them. But what if a
man had eyes to see the true beauty—the
divine beauty, I mean, pure and clear and
unalloyed, not infected with the pollutions
of the flesh and all the colours and vanities
of mortal life—thither looking, and holding
converse with the true beauty simple and
divine? Remember how in that communion
only, beholding beauty with [212] that by
which it can be beheld, he will be enabled
to bring forth, not images of beauty, but
realities (for he has hold not of an image
but of a reality), and bringing forth and
nourishing true virtue will properly become
the friend of God and be immortal, if mortal man may. Would that be an ignoble
life?"

Phaedrus [243–245a]

Soc. Know then, fair youth, that the former discourse was the [244] word of Phae-
drus, the son of Pythocles, of the deme
Myrrhina. And this which I am about to
utter is the recantation of Stesichorus the
son of Euphemus, who comes from the
town of Himera, and is to the following
effect: "False was that word of mine" that
the beloved ought to accept the non-lover
when he might have the lover, because the
one is sane, and the other mad. It might be
so if madness were simply an evil; but there
is also a madness which is a divine gift, and
the source of the chiefest blessings granted
to men. For prophecy is a madness, and the
prophetess at Delphi and the priestesses at
Dodona when out of their senses have conferred great benefits on Hellas, both in public and private life, but when in their senses

few or none. And I might also tell you how the Sibyl and other inspired persons have given to many an one many an intimation of the future which has saved them from falling. But it would be tedious to speak of what every one knows.

There will be more reason in appealing to the ancient inventors of names, who would never have connected prophecy [μαντική], which foretells the future and is the noblest of arts, with madness [μανική], or called them both by the same name, if they had deemed madness to be a disgrace or dishonour;—they must have thought that there was an inspired madness which was a noble thing; for the two words, μαντική and μανική, are really the same, and the letter τ is only a modern and tasteless insertion. And this is confirmed by the name which was given by them to the rational investigation of futurity, whether made by the help of birds or other signs—this, for as much as it is an art which supplies from the reasoning faculty mind [νοῦς] and information [ἱστορία] to human thought [οἴησις], they originally termed οἰονοιστική, but the word has been lately altered and made sonorous by the modern introduction of the letter Omega [οἰονοιστική and οἰωνιστική], and in proportion as prophecy [μαντική] is more perfect and august than augury, both in name and fact, in the same proportion, as the ancients testify, is madness superior to a sane mind [σωφροσύνη], for the one is only of human, but the other of divine, origin. Again, where plagues and mightiest woes have bred in certain families, owing to some ancient blood-guiltiness, there madness, inspiring and taking possession of those whom destiny has appointed, has found deliverance, having recourse to prayers and religious rites. And learning thence the use of purifications and mysteries, it has sheltered from evil, future as well as present, the man who has some part in this gift, and has afforded a release from his present calamity to one who is truly possessed, and duly out of his [245] mind. The third kind is the madness

of those who are possessed by the Muses; which taking hold of a delicate and virgin soul, and there inspiring frenzy, awakens lyrical and all other numbers; with these adorning the myriad actions of ancient heroes for the instruction of posterity. But he who, having no touch of the Muses' madness in his soul, comes to the door and thinks that he will get into the temple by the help of art—he, I say, and his poetry are not admitted; the sane man disappears and is nowhere when he enters into rivalry with the madman.

Philebus [50e–51d]

Soc. Then after the mixed pleasures the unmixed should have their turn; this is the natural and necessary order.

[51] *Pro.* Excellent. ~~Pro~~ *Protarcus*

Soc. These, in turn, then, I will now endeavour to indicate; for with the maintainers of the opinion that all pleasures are a cessation of pain, I do not agree, but, as I was saying, I use them as witnesses, that there are pleasures which seem only and are not, and there are others again which have great power and appear in many forms, yet are intermingled with pains, and are partly alleviations of agony and distress, both of body and mind.

Pro. Then what pleasures, Socrates, should we be right in conceiving to be true?

Soc. True pleasures are those which are given by beauty of colour and form, and most of those which arise from smells; those of sound, again, and in general those of which the want is painless and unconscious, and of which the fruition is palpable to sense and pleasant and unalloyed with pain.

Pro. Once more, Socrates, I must ask what you mean.

Soc. My meaning is certainly not obvious, and I will endeavour to be plainer. I do not mean by beauty of form such beauty as that of animals or pictures, which the many would suppose to be my meaning; but, says the argument, understand me to mean straight lines and circles, and the plane or solid figures which are formed out of them by turning-lathes and rulers and measurers of angles; for these I affirm to be not only relatively beautiful, like other things, but they are eternally and absolutely beautiful, and they have peculiar pleasures, quite unlike the pleasures of scratching. And there are colours which are of the same character, and have similar pleasures; now do you understand my meaning?

Pro. I am trying to understand, Socrates, and I hope that you will try to make your meaning clearer.

Soc. When sounds are smooth and clear, and have a single pure tone, then I mean to say that they are not relatively but absolutely beautiful, and have natural pleasures of the same character.

Laws: Book II [652–660a]

Ath. Let me once more recall our doctrine of right education; [653] which, if I am not mistaken, depends on the due regulation of convivial intercourse.

Cle. You talk rather grandly. *Cleanias*

Ath. Pleasure and pain I maintain to be the first perceptions of children, and I say that they are the forms under which virtue and vice are originally present to them. As to wisdom and true and fixed opinions, happy is the man who acquires them, even when declining in years; and we may say that he who possesses them, and the blessings which are contained in them, is a perfect man. Now I mean by education that training which is given by suitable habits to the first instincts of virtue in children;— when pleasure, and friendship, and pain, and hatred are rightly implanted in souls not yet capable of understanding the nature of them, and who find them, after they have attained reason, to be in harmony with her. This harmony of the soul, taken as a

whole, is virtue; but the particular training in respect of pleasure and pain, which leads you always to hate what you ought to hate, and love what you ought to love, from the beginning of life to the end, may be separated off; and, in my view, will be rightly called education.

Cle. I think, stranger, that you are quite right in all that you have said and are saying about education.

Ath. I am glad to hear that you agree with me; for, indeed, the discipline of pleasure and pain which, when rightly ordered, is a principle of education, has been often relaxed and corrupted in human life. And the Gods, pitying the toils which our race is born to undergo, have appointed holy festivals, wherein men alternate rest with labour; and have given them the Muses and Apollo, the leader of the Muses, and Dionysus, to be companions in their revels, that these may be saved from degeneration, and men partake in spiritual nourishment in company with the Gods. I should like to know whether a common saying is in our opinion true to nature or not. For men say that the young of all creatures cannot be quiet in their bodies or in their voices; they are always wanting to move and cry out; some leaping and skipping, and overflowing with sportiveness and delight at something, others uttering all sorts of cries. But, whereas the animals have no perception of order or disorder in their movements, that is, of rhythm or harmony, as they are called, to us the Gods, who, as we say, have been appointed to be our companions in the dance, have given the pleasurable [654] sense of harmony and rhythm; and so they stir us into life, and we follow them, joining hands together in dances and songs; and these they call choruses, which is a term naturally expressive of cheerfulness. Shall we begin, then, with the acknowledgement that education is first given through Apollo and the Muses? What do you say?

Cle. I assent.

Ath. And the uneducated is he who has

(Plato - Athenian Stranger)

not been trained in the chorus, and the educated is he who has been well trained?

Cle. Certainly.

Ath. And the chorus is made up of two parts, dance and song?

Cle. True.

Ath. Then he who is well educated will be able to sing and dance well?

Cle. I suppose that he will.

Ath. Let us see; what are we saying?

Cle. What?

Ath. He sings well and dances well; now must we add that he sings what is good and dances what is good?

Cle. Let us make the addition.

Ath. We will suppose that he knows the good to be good, and the bad to be bad, and makes use of them accordingly: which now is the better trained in dancing and music —he who is able to move his body and use his voice in what he understands to be the right manner, but has no delight in good or hatred of evil; or he who is scarcely correct in gesture and voice and in understanding, but is right in his sense of pleasure and pain, and welcomes what is good, and is offended at what is evil?

Cle. There is a great difference, stranger, in the two kinds of education.

Ath. If we three know what is good in song and dance, then we truly know also who is educated and who is uneducated; but if not, then we certainly shall not know wherein lies the safeguard of education, and whether there is any or not.

Cle. True.

Ath. Let us follow the scent like hounds, and go in pursuit of beauty of figure, and melody, and song, and dance; if these escape us, there will be no use in talking about true education, whether Hellenic or barbarian.

Cle. Yes.

Ath. Now what is meant by beauty of figure, or beautiful [655] melody? When a manly soul is in trouble, and when a cowardly soul is in similar case, are they likely to use the same figures and gestures, or to give utterance to the same sounds?

Cle. How can they, when the very colours of their faces differ?

Ath. Good, my friend; I may observe, however, in passing, that in music there certainly are figures and there are melodies: and music is concerned with harmony and rhythm, so that you may speak of a melody or figure having good rhythm or good harmony—the term is correct enough; but to speak metaphorically of a melody or figure having a "good colour," as the masters of choruses do, is not allowable, although you can speak of the melodies or figures of the brave and the coward, praising the one and censuring the other. And not to be tedious, let us say that the figures and melodies which are expressive of virtue of soul or body, or of images of virtue, are without exception good, and those which are expressive of vice are the reverse of good.

Cle. Your suggestion is excellent; and let us answer that these things are so.

Ath. Once more, are all of us equally delighted with every sort of dance?

Cle. Far otherwise.

Ath. What, then leads us astray? Are beautiful things not the same to us all, or are they the same in themselves, but not in our opinion of them? For no one will admit that forms of vice in the dance are more beautiful than forms of virtue, or that he himself delights in the forms of vice, and others in a muse of another character. And yet most persons say, that the excellence of music is to give pleasure to our souls. But this is intolerable and blasphemous; there is, however, a much more plausible account of the delusion.

Cle. What?

Ath. The adaptation of art to the characters of men. Choric movements are imitations of manners and the performers range over all the various actions and chances of life with characterization and mimicry; and those to whom the words, or songs, or dances are suited, either by nature or habit or both, cannot help feeling pleasure in

what is critera for critic

them and applauding them, and calling them beautiful. But those whose natures, or ways, or habits are unsuited to them, cannot delight in them or applaud them, and they call them base. There are others, again, whose natures are right and their habits wrong, or whose habits are right and their natures wrong, and they praise one thing, but are pleased at another. For they say that all these imitations are pleasant, but not good. And in the presence of those whom they think wise, [656] they are ashamed of dancing and singing in the baser manner, in a way which would indicate deliberate approval; and yet, they have a secret pleasure in them.

Cle. Very true.

Ath. And is any harm done to the lover of vicious dances or songs, or any good done to the approver of the opposite sort of pleasure?

Cle. I think that there is.

Ath. "I think" is not the word, but I would say, rather, "I am certain." For must they not have the same effect as when a man associates with bad characters, whom he likes and approves rather than dislikes, and only censures playfully because he has but a suspicion of their badness? In that case, he who takes pleasure in them will surely become like those in whom he takes pleasure, even though he be ashamed to praise them. This result is quite certain; and what greater good or evil can a human being undergo?

Cle. I know of none.

Ath. Then in a city which has good laws, or in future ages is to have them, bearing in mind the instruction and amusement which are given by music, can we suppose that the poets are to be allowed to teach in the dance anything which they themselves like, in the way of rhythm, or melody, or words, to the young children of any well-conditioned parents? Is the poet to train his choruses as he pleases, without reference to virtue or vice?

Cle. That is surely quite unreasonable, and is not to be thought of.

Ath. And yet he may do this in almost any state with the exception of Egypt.

Cle. And what are the laws about music and dancing in Egypt?

Ath. You will wonder when I tell you: Long ago they appear to have recognized the very principle of which we are now speaking—that their young citizens must be habituated to forms and strains of virtue. These they fixed, and exhibited the patterns of them in their temples; and no painter, no other representative artist is allowed to innovate upon them, or to leave the traditional forms and invent new ones. To this day, no alteration is allowed either in these arts, or in music at all. And you find that their works of art are painted or moulded in the same forms which they had ten thousand years ago;—this is literally true and no exaggeration,—their ancient paintings and sculptures [657] are not a whit better or worse than the work of to-day, but are made with just the same skill.

Cle. How extraordinary!

Ath. I should rather say, How statesmanlike, how worthy of a legislator! I know that other things in Egypt are not so well. But what I am telling you about music is true and deserving of consideration, because showing that a lawgiver may institute melodies which have a natural truth and correctness without any fear of failure. To do this, however, must be the work of God, or of a divine person; in Egypt they have a tradition that their ancient chants which have been preserved for so many ages are the composition of the Goddess Isis. And therefore, as I was saying, if a person can only find in any way the natural melodies, he may confidently embody them in a fixed and legal form. For the love of novelty which arises out of pleasure in the new and weariness of the old, has not strength enough to corrupt the consecrated song and dance, under the plea that they have become antiquated. At any rate, they are far from being corrupted in Egypt.

Cle. Your arguments seem to prove your point.

Ath. May we not confidently say that the true use of music and of choral festivities is as follows: We rejoice when we think that we prosper, and again we think that we prosper when we rejoice?

Cle. Exactly.

Ath. And when rejoicing in our good fortune, we are unable to be still?

Cle. True.

Ath. Our young men break forth into dancing and singing, and we who are their elders deem that we are fulfilling our part in life when we look on at them. Having lost our agility, we delight in their sports and merry-making, because we love to think of our former selves; and gladly institute contests for those who are able to awaken in us the memory of our youth.

Cle. Very true.

Ath. Is it altogether unmeaning to say, as the common people do about festivals, that he should be adjudged the wisest of men, and the winner of the palm, who gives us the greatest amount of pleasure and mirth? For on such occasions, and when mirth is the order of the day, ought not he to be honoured most, and, as I was saying, bear the palm, who gives most mirth to the greatest number? Now is this a true way of speaking or of [658] acting?

Cle. Possibly.

Ath. But, my dear friend, let us distinguish between different cases, and not be hasty in forming a judgement: One way of considering the question will be to imagine a festival at which there are entertainments of all sorts, including gymnastic, musical, and equestrian contests: the citizens are assembled; prizes are offered, and proclamation is made that anyone who likes may enter the lists, and that he is to bear the palm who gives the most pleasure to the spectators—there is to be no regulation about

the manner how; but he who is most successful in giving pleasure is to be crowned victor, and deemed to be the pleasantest of the candidates. What is likely to be the result of such a proclamation?

Cle. In what respect?

Ath. There would be various exhibitions: one man, like Homer, will exhibit a rhapsody, another a performance on the lute; one will have a tragedy, and another a comedy. Nor would there be anything astonishing in someone imagining that he could gain the prize by exhibiting a puppet-show. Suppose these competitors to meet, and not these only, but innumerable others as well —can you tell me who ought to be the victor?

Cle. I do not see how anyone can answer you, or pretend to know, unless he has heard with his own ears the several competitors; the question is absurd.

Ath. Well, then, if neither of you can answer, shall I answer this question which you deem so absurd?

Cle. By all means.

Ath. If very small children are to determine the question, they will decide for the puppet-show.

Cle. Of course.

Ath. The older children will be advocates of comedy; educated women, and young men, and people in general, will favour tragedy.

Cle. Very likely.

Ath. And I believe that we old men would have the greatest pleasure in hearing a rhapsodist recite well the Iliad and Odyssey, or one of the Hesiodic poems, and would award an overwhelming victory to him. But, who would really be the victor? —that is the question.

Cle. Yes.

Ath. Clearly you and I will have to declare that those whom we old men adjudge victors ought to win; for our ways are far and away better than any which at present exist anywhere in the world.

Cle. Certainly.

Ath. Thus far I too should agree with the many, that the excellence of music is to be measured by pleasure. But the pleasure must not be that of chance persons; the fairest music is that which delights the best and best educated, and especially [659] that which delights the one man who is pre-eminent in virtue and education. And therefore the judges must be men of character, for they will require wisdom and have still greater need of courage; the true judge must not draw his inspiration from the theatre, nor ought he to be unnerved by the clamour of the many and his own incapacity; nor again, knowing the truth, ought he through cowardice and unmanliness carelessly to deliver a lying judgement, with the very same lips which have just appealed to the Gods before he judged. He is sitting not as the disciple of the theatre, but, in his proper place, as their instructor, and he ought to be the enemy of all pandering to the pleasure of the spectators.[1] The ancient and common custom of Hellas was the reverse of that which now prevails in Italy and Sicily, where the judgement is left to the body of spectators, who determine the victor by show of hands. But this custom has been the destruction of the poets themselves; for they are now in the habit of composing with a view to please the bad taste of their judges, and the result is that the spectators instruct themselves;—and also it has been the ruin of the theatre; they

---

[1] [Or, taking τοῖς with θεαταῖς, "the enemy of all spectators who respond with pleasure in a mistaken and unsuitable way."]

ought to be having characters put before them better than their own, and so receiving a higher pleasure, but now by their own act the opposite result follows. What inference is to be drawn from all this? Shall I tell you?

Cle. What?

Ath. The inference at which we arrive for the third or fourth time is, that education is the constraining and directing of youth towards that right reason, which the law affirms, and which the experience of the eldest and best has agreed to be truly right. In order, then, that the soul of the child may not be habituated to feel joy and sorrow in a manner at variance with the law, and those who obey the law, but may rather follow the law and rejoice and sorrow at the same things as the aged—in order, I say, to produce this effect, chants appear to have been invented, which really enchant, and are designed to implant that harmony of which we speak. And, because the mind of the child is incapable of enduring serious training, they are called plays and songs, and are performed in play; just as when men are sick and ailing in their bodies, their attendants [660] give them wholesome diet in pleasant meats and drinks, but unwholesome diet in disagreeable things, in order that they may learn, as they ought, to like the one, and to dislike the other. And similarly the true legislator will persuade, and, if he cannot persuade, will compel the poet to express, as he ought, by fair and noble words, in his rhythms, the figures, and in his melodies, the music of temperate and brave and in every way good men.

⤜⤜⤜⤜⤛⤛⤛⤛

On Poetic Art

I.

It is on poetic art itself that we propose to talk, and also on the forms it takes—what effectiveness each has; and how plots should be put together if the composition is to be good—also, then, of what parts a composition is in terms of quantity and quality; and on any other matters as well which belong to this particular investigation, beginning in the natural order first with the things which are first.

2. Epic, as I here define it, and the composing of tragedy—comedy, too, of course—and the art of dithyrambic composition, and most of the other arts which use the flute and lyre, all are found to be forms of imitation generically. 3. But they differ from one another in three respects: that is, in imitating either in other media, or other objects, or otherwise—not in the same way.

4. For, as some men, either by art or by practice, imitate many sorts of things making likenesses both in colors and in shapes—while others imitate with the voice—so it is in the arts named: as a group, they make their imitation in rhythm and language and tone. But these they may use either separately or in combination; for example, tone and rhythm, when the arts of the flute and the lyre use only them, and perhaps there are other arts which may be found similar in what they can do, such as that of the panpipes. 5. And by the very rhythm, without tone, some of the dancers imitate these men, in fact, by rhythms in gesture equally

imitate kinds of character and emotion and action.

6. "Epic" uses spoken words alone—prose or verse without music—and in the case of verse [1447b] it either mixes the various meters with one another or uses some one kind; it happens to have been without a name until now. 7. We were quite unable, that is, to give a common name to the mimes of Sophron and Xenarchus and the Socratic dialogues; and also if a man made his imitation in trimeters or elegiacs or any of the other meters like them—except that people, of course, connecting poetic composition with meter, call some men elegiac-poets and some hexameter-poets, speaking of them as poets not for their imitation but for their meter in common. 8. And, in fact, if they bring out something in verse on medicine or natural science, people are accustomed to call them poets. But Homer and Empedocles have nothing in common except the meter; so it is right to call the one poet, the other natural scientist rather than poet. 9. Equally, if a man makes his imitation combining every one of the meters, as Chaeremon did in composing the *Centaur*, a mixed rhapsody combining all the possible meters, he too should be spoken of as a poet.

10. These arts, then, are to be differentiated in this way. But there are some which use all the media named—I speak now of rhythm and music and verse; for example, the composing both of dithyrambs and nomes, and both tragedy and comedy; but these differ in that dithyrambs and nomes use all at the same time, tragedy and comedy according to the part.

11. These, then, I say, are the ways of differentiating the arts as respects the media in which they make their imitation.

"Aristotle: On Poetic Art," translated by Seymour Pitcher, *Journal of General Education,* VII (1952), pp. 56-76. Reprinted by permission of the University of Chicago Press.

II.

[1448a] Since the imitators imitate men acting, these must be relatively noble or base—the various kinds of character almost always are subsumed under just these two headings, for in wickedness and virtue all men differ in character—and so those imitated are nobler than we are, or baser, or such as we are. So it is with the painters, for Polygnotus made likenesses of nobler men, Pauson of baser, Dionysius of men like us. 2. And it is clear that each of the forms of imitation mentioned will have these differences and be unlike in imitating objects unlike in this way. 3. And, in fact, these differences can occur in dancing and in flute-playing and lyre-playing. And in the case of prose writings and verse without music: thus, Homer imitates nobler men; Cleophon, men like us; Hegemon of Thasos, who was first to make parodies, and Nichochares, who wrote the *Deliad,* baser men. 4. So it is, too, in respect to the dithyrambs and the nomes: a man might imitate as . . . Timotheus and Philoxenus the Cyclopses. In this difference, also, tragedy stands apart from comedy, for comedy prefers to imitate baser men; tragedy, men nobler than those nowadays.

III.

There is still a third way of differentiating these arts: how one imitates each of these objects. For it is possible to imitate in the same media the same objects, now narrating and now becoming someone else, as Homer does; or as one's self and not changing; or with all the imitators acting and shaping the action.

2. As we said at the beginning, the imitation occurs with these three indicated differences: media, objects, and manner. So in one respect Sophocles will be the same kind of imitator as Homer, for both imitate noble men; in another, as Aristophanes, for both imitate men acting and doing. And some say that dramas are so called because they imitate men doing. 3. That is why, too, the Dorians claim both tragedy and comedy—comedy, that is, the Dorians of Megara (those in Greece alleging that it came into being during their democracy and those in Sicily because Epicharmus the poet was from there, and much earlier than Chionides and Magnes), and tragedy some in the Peloponnesus claim—they make the words evidence, for they say they call outlying towns κῶμαι, the Athenians δῆμοι; so comedians are not named from κωμάζειν (*to revel*) but from their strolling *from town to town* (κατά κώμας) when out of favor in the city; [1448b] and for *to do* they say δρᾶν, the Athenians πράττειν.

4. On the differences in imitation, then, both how many and what they are, let these remarks suffice.

IV.

It seems that all in all some two causes have produced the poetic art, and those natural. 2. Imitating, that is, is native to men from childhood, and they differ from the other animals in being the most imitative and in getting their first lessons by imitation. And there is the fact that all men enjoy imitations. 3. Evidence of this is what happens in experience; and as for things, to be sure, which we dislike to see themselves, their likenesses, even those made particularly exact, we enjoy seeing—for example, forms both of the meanest beasts and of corpses. 4. And the reason for that, indeed, is that not only philosophers find it most pleasant to acquire understanding but others, too, though slightly they share it. 5. They enjoy seeing likenesses, that is, because in looking at them they come to understand and they reason out what everything is—for example, that "This man is so and so." But whenever one does not happen to have the object previously, the likeness will not give the pleasure as an imitation; rather, through the way it is carried out or the color or through another such cause.

6. Imitating being natural to us, and tone and rhythm—that meters are parts of rhythms is obvious—at the start men particularly inclined toward them from birth, little by little advancing, produced poetic composition from their improvisations. 7. But a split occurred in poetic composition according to their individual characters, for the more dignified imitated noble actions and those of men of that kind, while the more ordinary imitated those of base men, at first composing invectives, as others hymns and encomia. 8. We cannot, to be sure, mention such a poem by any of the poets before Homer, though it is probable that there were many who wrote them. But beginning with Homer we can—for example, his own *Margites* and poems like it. It was in these, too, that the appropriate invective meter came in, and it is now called iambic because in that meter they *iambized* [lampooned] one another. And of the early poets some became composers of heroic verses, some of iambics. 9. And as, indeed, Homer was particularly a poet for noble subjects—he is unique, in fact, not only in that he made imitations well but also in that he made them dramatic—so he first indicated the lines of comedy, dramatizing not invective but the ridiculous. The *Margites*, in fact, is analogous to our comedies, as the *Iliad* [1449a] and the *Odyssey* are to our tragedies.

10. When tragedy and comedy appeared, those moving toward one form of poetic composition or the other in accordance with their individual natures became, some of them, composers of comedy instead of invectives and, others, composers of tragedy instead of epics, these forms being more important and more in honor than those. 11. To consider whether tragedy is at long last adequate to its qualitative factors or not, and to judge that by itself and with regard to audiences, is, to be sure, another subject.

12. At the outset, to be sure, tragedy was improvised, and comedy as well; and the former came from men who began with the dithyramb, the latter from men who began with the phallic songs, which even now in many of our cities remain in common use. Little by little tragedy grew, the poets going ahead with as much of it as had become evident. And, having evolved through many changes, tragedy halted when it had achieved its proper nature.

13. The number of the "answerers" was first raised by Aeschylus from one to two, and he also reduced the choral passages and made the dialogue the leading part. 14. Three actors and scene painting were introduced by Sophocles. Further, as for size and importance: from slight stories and ridiculous language, because it evolved from the satyr-play, tragedy at length became dignified. The meter became iambic trimeter instead of trochaic tetrameter; at first, indeed, they used the tetrameter because the composition was satyric and more suited for dancing. But when dialogue developed, nature of itself found the suitable meter, for of the meters the iambic is most like speech. Evidence of it is that we use mostly iambics in our conversation with one another, hexameters rarely and when we depart from the conversational tone. 15. There is, further, the increase in episodes and the other matters; how they all are said to have been ordered we may take as discussed, for it would probably be a great task to go through them one by one.

V.

Comedy is, as we said, imitation of men who are relatively base; but not, of course, in every sort of evil. Ridiculousness is, rather, a kind of ignominy or ugliness, for it is to some degree a failure to hit the mark and a deformity, though it causes no pain and is not harmful; for example, at once the comic mask comes to mind—an ignominious thing, ugly and distorted, but not causing pain.

2. Now the changes in tragedy and through whom they came about have not

been overlooked, but comedy, through not [1449b] being taken seriously at the start, escaped notice; and, in fact, it was at a rather late date that the archon provided a chorus of comic actors, whereas they had been volunteers. Only when comedy already had definite forms are those called its poets recorded. 3. But who provided masks or prologues or increase in the number of actors, and all such matters, has been unknown. As for making plots, Epicharmus and Phormis; that came, then, originally from Sicily. Of the poets at Athens, however, it was Crates who, dismissing the idea of invective, first began to give stories and plots general meaning.

4. Now epic goes along with tragedy as far as being imitation, in meter, with story, of noble men, but in that it has the single meter and is narrative they differ. Then, as for length, tragedy is trying as best it can to keep under one circuit of the sun, or little to exceed it; epic, however, is unlimited in time and in this differs. But at first the practice was the same both in tragedies and in epics.

5. As for their parts, some are the same, some peculiar to tragedy; so whoever knows about tragedy—noble and base—knows also about epics. That is, the parts which epic has are present in tragedy, but those which are present in tragedy are not all in epic.

VI.

On the imitative art in hexameters and on comedy we shall speak later, but it is on tragedy we now propose to talk, gathering from the things already said the resulting definition of its essence.

2. Tragedy is, then, imitation of a course of action which is noble and complete, having size and importance; in speech made pleasing, each of the kinds separately in the various parts; with persons in action, and not by narrative; through pity and fear ordering the catharsis of the emotions like them.

3. I call speech *pleasing* when it has

rhythm and tone and music; *kinds separately* means that some parts are ordered by meters only, and again others by music.

4. Since men acting make the imitation, first, of necessity, the world of the spectacle would be some part of tragedy; then music and language, for in these they make the imitation. In this instance I mean by *language* the sum of the verses, while *music* is something which has its meaning entirely evident.

5. Tragedy, then, is imitation of a course of action and is performed by persons acting who necessarily are of a certain quality both by their character and by their process of thought (indeed, it is through these that we say that their [1450a] actions, also, are of a certain sort); there naturally are two causes of their actions—thought and character—and through these they both succeed and fail, one and all. 6. It is of action that plot is imitation. In this instance, that is, I define *plot* as the sum of the things done; and qualities of *character* as that by which we say those acting are of one sort or another; and *thought,* in whatever terms, in speaking, they demonstrate something or utter a generality.

7. Necessarily, then, of every tragedy the parts are six; by them the tragedy is of one sort or another. They are: plot, qualities of character, language, thought, spectacle, and music. Therefore, the media in which they imitate are two parts; the manner in which they imitate is one; the objects which they imitate are three. And besides these none. 8. These not a few of the poets have used, so to speak, as the qualitative factors; and every drama, in fact, uses spectacular effects—and character and plot and language and music and thought—thus.

9. But most important of these factors is the putting-together of the things done, for tragedy is an imitating not of people but of action and of life. Besides, happiness and unhappiness depend upon action, and the end is action of a certain kind, not quality. 10. It is by their qualities of character that

men are of one sort or another, but by their actions that they are happy or the opposite. They certainly do not act in order that they may imitate qualities of character; rather, they take on qualities of character with and through their actions. So the things done and the plot are tragedy's end, and the end is most important of all things whatsoever.

11. Again, without a course of action a tragedy could not exist; without qualities of character one might. The tragedies of most of the recent poets are, in fact, without character; and altogether there are many such poets. So, too, among the painters Zeuxis has suffered comparison with Polygnotus, for Polygnotus is a noble painter of character, whereas the painting of Zeuxis has no character whatever.

12. Further, if a man puts one after another speeches expressive of character and well constructed in language and thought, he will not accomplish what was the tragedy's task; but much rather the tragedy will do so which uses these more sparingly and has plot and structure in the things done. 13. Besides, the most effective means by which tragedy stirs the soul are parts of the plot: both reversals and recognitions. 14. And there is also evidence in that those beginning to compose are sooner successful in the language and the qualities of character than in putting together the things done; as was indeed the case with the early poets, nearly every one of them.

15. First principle, then, and, as it were, soul is the plot of the tragedy; second are the qualities of character. It is almost the same, too [1450b], in the art of painting: if a man daubed with the finest colors at random, he would not as much please as by drawing a likeness on white. It, too, is imitation of action and through that chiefly of those who act.

16. Third is the thought. That means the ability to say the possible and appropriate things, which in the speeches is work for the political and the rhetorical arts; the

early poets, in fact, made people talk like politicians—those nowadays, like rhetoricians.

17. Character is whatever reveals the moral choice, of whatever sort it may be. Hence, they have no character in the speeches in which it is not clear what the speaker chooses or avoids. There is thought, on the other hand, in the speeches in which they show that something is or is not the case, or make evident something of general significance.

18. Fourth is language. And I say, as has been said before, that language is revelation of meaning through application of words; and it has the same effectiveness both in verse and in prose.

19. Of the remaining parts music is chief of the pleasurable elements. But the spectacle, although, to be sure, it stirs the soul, is least a matter of the poetic art and least characteristic of it. The effectiveness of tragedy exists, in fact, without either audience or actors. Also, the art of the scene designer exercises more control over the working-out of the spectacular elements than does that of the poets.

VII.

These having been defined, let us next talk about what sort of structure the things done should have, since that is both first and most important in tragedy. 2. By our definition it is evident that tragedy is imitation of a complete and whole course of action which also has some size and importance. For there can be something which is whole and yet has no size. 3. But a whole is something which has a beginning and a middle and an end. A beginning is something which is not itself of necessity after anything else, but after it something else naturally is or comes to be. An end, on the other hand, is something which itself is naturally after something else, either of necessity or as a general rule, but after it there is nothing else. A middle both is itself after something else and after it there is something else. Plots well put together should, then, neither begin from wherever chances nor end wherever chances; rather, they should use the principles stated.

4. Again, what is beautiful, both living animal and each and every object that consists of parts, not only must have these parts ordered, but size must be present, and not just the size which chances; for beauty depends on size and order. That is why neither a very small animal would be beautiful—for sight does not focus when it occurs approximately in the imperceptible moment —nor a very large one—for then sight does not occur [1451a] at one time, but, instead, for the spectators the unity and the wholeness escape from sight. Suppose, for example, there were a creature ten thousand miles long! 5. So, just as in bodies and in living animals there ought to be size, and that easily seen as a unity, so, too, in plots there ought to be length, and that well suited to the memory. 6. A normative length considering audiences and perception is not the art's concern; indeed, if a hundred tragedies had to be presented, they might be timed by water-clocks, as they say, has been done sometimes elsewhere. But for the norm determined by the very nature of the object: always, the greater it is, provided it be clear as a whole, the more beautiful it is for its size; and, to speak defining generically, a proper norm for the size is such that a change takes place, with the events occurring one after another by probability or necessity, to good fortune from bad, or from good to bad.

VIII.

But a plot is not a unit, as some suppose, if it is about one man, for many and limitless things happen to one man, from some of which nothing unified results; similarly, too, the actions of one man are many from which no one course of action results. 2. That is why all the poets seem to miss the mark who have composed a *Heracleid* and a *Theseid* and poems of that kind, for

they suppose that, since Heracles was one man, the plot is consequently a unit. 3. But Homer, as he is different in all other respects, seems also to see this clearly, whether by art or by nature, for composing the *Odyssey* he did not treat every single thing which happened to Odysseus; his being wounded on Parnassus, for example, and his pretending to be mad at the muster— one of which having occurred, it was not at all necessary or probable the other should. Rather, he constructed the *Odyssey* around one course of action such as we mean, and likewise the *Iliad*.

4. Since also in the other imitative arts one imitation is of one thing, so too, then, the plot, since it is an imitating of a course of action, must be imitation of one course of action and that a whole, and the parts of the things done must join in such a way that if any part be shifted or removed the whole is injured and disordered. Anything which, present or not, makes no evident difference is no part of the whole.

IX.

It is also clear from the things said that to relate things which have happened is not a poet's task, but such as might happen, and things possible in terms of probability or necessity. 2. Indeed, the [1451b] compiler of facts and the poet do not differ in using verse or prose, for it would be possible to put the accounts of Herodotus into verse, and no less would they be compilations of a kind with meter than without. Rather, the difference is that the one relates things which have happened; the other, such as might happen. 3. That is why poetic composition in comparison with compilation of facts is both more philosophical and nobler; for poetic composition presents, rather, things in their general import, whereas factual compilation presents particulars. 4. It is of general import what sort of things it happens a man of a certain kind says or does by probability or necessity; at that poetic composition aims in assigning names.

It is a particular fact what Alcibiades did, or what he suffered.

5. Now in the case of comedy this has already become clear; for after they have thus put the plot together with probable events, they add the names they choose, and they do not, like the writers of invectives, write about the particular man. 6. But in the case of tragedy they hold to actual names; the reason is that what is possible is convincing. Things which have not happened we are not ready to believe are possible, but, as for things which have happened, it is clear they are possible; they would not have happened if they had been impossible.

7. Not but that also in certain tragedies there are one or two of the familiar names while the others are made up. And in some there is not even one, as in the *Anthus* of Agathon; in it, in fact, both the things done and the names have equally been made up, and it pleases no less. 8. So by no means need one try to hold to the stories handed down, with which our tragedies deal. And, in fact, it is ridiculous to try to do so, since even the familiar stories are familiar to few but yet please all.

9. Now it is clear from these things that the poet must be rather a maker of plots than of verses, inasmuch as he is a poet by his imitating and imitates courses of action. If, then, it happens that he writes about things which have occurred, no less is he a poet; and that is because nothing prevents some things which have occurred from being such as might probably occur and be possible—on that basis he is their poet.

10. Of simple plots and courses of action, the episodic are worst. I call *episodic* a plot in which it is neither probable nor necessary that the episodes follow one another. Such are made by the bad poets because they are bad, by the good because of the actors, for when they compose rhetorical debates and stretch the plot beyond its strength, they are [1452a] often forced to interrupt the sequence.

11. The imitation is not only of a complete course of action but also of fearful and pitiful events. These occur most effectively—and all the more—when they come about contrary to expectation, through one another. They will thus create surprise more than if without cause and by chance, for those chance things seem most surprising which appear to have occurred as by design. Thus, for example, the statue of Mitys in Argos killed the man who caused Mitys' death, falling upon him looking at it; such things, indeed, seem to occur not at random. So plots of this kind are necessarily finer.

x.

Some plots are simple, some complicated; and that is because courses of action, of which plots are imitations, are basically and obviously such. 2. I call a course of action *simple* in which, it being, as defined, continuous and one, the change occurs without reversal or recognition. A *complicated* course of action is one out of which the change develops with recognition or reversal, or with both. 3. These must arise from the very structure of the plot, so as to take place from the preceding events, either from necessity or by probability. It makes a great difference, indeed, whether events occur because of others or after them.

xi.

Reversal is the sudden change to the opposite of the things being done, as has been said, and that, as we are now saying, according to probability or necessity; for example, in the *Oedipus* the man who came to bring Oedipus joy and to relieve him from his fear as to his mother, in revealing who he was did the opposite. And in the *Lynceus*, Lynceus is led off to die, while Danaus follows to slay him; it comes about from the things already done that Danaus dies, but Lynceus is saved.

2. Recognition, as the word itself shows, is sudden change from ignorance to knowl-

edge, whether for love or for hate, on the part of those determined for good fortune or bad. The finest recognition occurs when reversals take place at the same time, as the one in the *Oedipus* has it. 3. There are also, to be sure, other kinds of recognition, for it can occur, as has been said, in relation to inanimate and chance objects; and it is possible to recognize whether someone did or did not do something. 4. But the recognition most a part of the plot and most a part of the action is that spoken of, for such a recognition—and reversal—will have either pity [1452b] or fear. Of such courses of action tragedy, by definition, is imitation; further, both bad fortune and good will occur in them. 5. Furthermore, some recognitions are of one person by the other alone, when it is clear to the first who the other is; sometimes each must recognize the other. Iphigenia, for example, was recognized by Orestes from the sending of the letters, but another recognition, of him by Iphigenia, was necessary.

6. Two parts of the plot, then, are these: reversal and recognition. A third is suffering. Of these, reversal and recognition have been discussed. *Suffering* is action destructive or painful; for example, deaths in plain sight, agonies, woundings, and all such.

XII.

The parts of a tragedy which are to be used as qualitative factors we have previously mentioned. In terms of quantity and the divisions into which a tragedy is separated, there are these: prologue, episode, exode, choric song (one section of which is parode and the other stasimon). These are common to tragedies one and all; peculiar to some are songs from the stage and laments. 2. A prologue is all that part of a tragedy before the parode of the chorus; and an episode is all that part of a tragedy between entire choric songs; an exode is all that part of a tragedy after which there is no song of the chorus. Of the choral part, a parode is the first speech of the entire

chorus; a stasimon is a song of the chorus without anapest or trochee; a lament is a dirge shared by the chorus and the actors.

3. As for the parts of a tragedy, those which are to be used as qualitative factors we have previously mentioned. In terms of quantity and the divisions into which a tragedy is separated they are these.

XIII.

What things poets should aim at and what they should shun in putting their plots together, and from what the effect of tragedy will derive, are next to be discussed after what has now been said.

2. Since, then, the structure of the finest tragedy should not be simple but complicated, and since the tragedy should be imitative of fearful and pitiful events (that is characteristic of this kind of imitation), first it is clear that the good and just men need not be shown changing from good fortune to bad (that is neither fearful nor pitiful, but repulsive); nor the wicked men changing from bad fortune to good (that is most unsuited to tragedy of all, since it has none of the qualities it should have—that is, it is not friendly to mankind, [1453a] it is not pitiful, and it is not fearful). And, in the second place, it is clear that the thorough scoundrel need not fall from good fortune into bad (such a structure would have the element of friendliness of mankind, but neither pity nor fear, because the one is for the man who does not deserve his misfortune, the other for the man who is like us—pity for the man who does not deserve his misfortune, fear for the man who is like us— so that what happens will be neither pitiful nor fearful). 3. The man, then, who is in the midst of them is left. Such a man is not one who is unlike us in virtue and sense of justice, nor does he change to bad fortune through evil and wickedness, but through some error; he is of those who are in great repute and good fortune, like Oedipus and Thyestes and the outstanding men from such families.

4. The good plot, then, must be single, rather than double as some say, and must change not to good fortune from bad but the opposite, from good to bad; not through wickedness but through a great error, either of such a man as was mentioned or of a better rather than a worse. 5. And what happens is evidence, for at first the poets told of the stories that occurred to them, but now the finest tragedies are composed about a few families; for example, about Alcmaeon, Oedipus, Orestes, Meleager, Thyestes, Telephus, and all the others whose lot it was either to suffer frightful things or to do them.

6. The finest tragedy in terms of the art is, then, of this structure. And hence those who complain against Euripides that he does this in his tragedies, many of which end in misfortune, make the same mistake —for this, as has been said, is right. There is the strongest evidence, for on the stage and in performance such tragedies appear particularly tragic, if they are correctly presented; and Euripides, if, indeed, he does not handle the other matters well, yet appears most tragic, at any rate, of the poets.

7. Second is the structure called first by some, that both having the double structure, as the *Odyssey* has, and ending in an opposite way for the better men and the worse. It is thought to be first because of the weakness of the audiences, for the poets follow along doing the bidding of the spectators. 8. But the pleasure is not the particular one which comes from tragedy; rather, it is characteristic of comedy, for there men who may be the direst enemies in the plot, like Orestes and Aegisthus, become friends at the end and go out, and nobody is killed by anybody.

XIV.

[1453b] Now fear and pity can derive from the spectacle, but also from the very structure of the things done; and that is preferable and the characteristic of a better poet. The plot must, in fact, so fit together that, even without seeing, anyone who hears the events which occur will both shudder and feel pity from what happens; these emotions one would experience in hearing the plot of the *Oedipus*. 2. To provide this through the spectacle is less a matter of the poetic art and requires a full-scale production. Those who create through the spectacle not fear but horror only have nothing in common with tragedy; that is to say, one should seek not every pleasure from tragedy but the one characteristic of it. 3. And since it is the pleasure deriving from pity and fear through imitation that the poet should provide, clearly that is to be put in the things done.

Let us, then, consider what sort of occurrences are found to be terrible and what sort piteous. 4. Actions of this kind are necessarily those of dear ones against each other, or of enemies, or of men who are neither. If, then, enemy against enemy, there is nothing pitiful, whether a man acts or only starts to—except in so far as the act of suffering itself arouses pity. Nor if the men are indifferent. But when acts of suffering occur in close relationships—for example, brother kills brother, or son father, or mother son, or son mother, or starts to do it, or some other deed of the kind—those are to be sought.

5. Now it is not possible to break up the plots handed down; I mean, for example, Clytemnestra being killed by Orestes and Eriphyle by Alcmaeon; but the poet should find out for himself how to use well even stories handed down.

Let us say more clearly what we mean by *well*. 6. It is possible for the action to occur as the early poets used to compose, with the persons knowing and comprehending what they did; in this manner also, Euripides made Medea kill her boys. And it is possible for them to do the terrible deed, but to do it in ignorance, then later to recognize the close relationship, as Sophocles' Oedipus does. In that case, to be sure, the deed is outside the drama, but it may be within the tragedy itself—for example, the deeds of Astydamas' Alcmaeon or of Telegonus in the *Odysseus Wounded*. 7. Further, there is a third possibility besides these: a man about to do some one of the irreparable things through ignorance recognizes before doing it. And besides these there is no other way, for necessarily they do the deed or not, knowing or not knowing.

The worst of these is for a man to be about to do the deed, knowing, and then not to do it; it has what is repulsive, and also it is not tragic, since it is without suffering. Hence, no one [1454a] writes that way, or but rarely; for example, in *Antigone* Haemon starts to kill Creon.

8. To do the deed is second, but it is better to do it without knowing and having done it to recognize what one has done. The repulsive is not present, and also the recognition is overwhelming.

9. Best is the last: I have in mind how in the *Cresphontes* Merope starts to kill her son; but she does not kill him, she recognizes him. And in the *Iphigenia* the sister recognizes the brother; and in the *Helle* the son, about to give up his mother, recognizes her.

10. That is why, as was said just now, our tragedies are not about many families; for, in looking about, the poets found not by art but by chance how to provide in their plots what we have spoken of; they are forced, then, to go to those families in which sufferings have occurred.

11. And now enough has been said about the structure of the things done and of what sort plots should be.

xv.

As for the qualities of character, there are four things to aim at. One thing and foremost is that they be good. Now a man will have character if, as was said, his speech or his action makes clear some choice; and good character if good choice. It is possible in each sex and kind, for surely a good woman is possible, and a good slave; and yet, all the same, of these, the former is inferior and the latter generally base.

2. Second is that they be appropriate; it is possible for a man to be courageous in character, but it is not appropriate for a woman to be as courageous—or as clever.

3. Third is likeness; that is different from making the character good and appropriate as said. – *line*

4. Fourth is consistency; even if the one offering the imitation were an inconsistent person and stamped with such a character, nevertheless he should be consistently inconsistent.

5. We might cite as an example of wickedness of character, quite unnecessary, Menelaus in the *Orestes*; of unfitting and inappropriate character, the lament of Odysseus in the *Scylla* and the speech of Melanippe; of inconsistency, Iphigenia at Aulis, for the suppliant girl is not at all like the later woman.

6. And in the qualities of character, as in the structure of the things done, one must always seek either the necessary or the probable, so that for a man of a certain kind to say or do things of a certain kind will be either necessary or probable; and so that for this to come after that will be either necessary or probable.

7. Now it is clear that the resolutions of plots must also come about from the [1454b] character itself and not as in the *Medea* from a machine, and in the *Iliad* in the matter of the sailing away. Rather, a machine is to be used for the things outside the drama: such as have occurred before it, or such as a human being cannot know, or such as occur later, which need foretelling and reporting. We admit that the gods see all things. But there should be nothing irrational in any of the things done; if that is impossible, it should be outside the tragedy, like that in the *Oedipus* of Sophocles.

8. Since a tragedy is imitation of men nobler than we are, the poet should imitate the good portrait painters, for, though they reproduce the individual form, in making

them like they paint them more beautiful. Thus, too, the poet, imitating both quick-tempered and slothful—and men who have the other qualities of that kind in their characters—though they are such, should make them good and just; as Homer has made Achilles good, though an example of obstinacy.

9. These things the poet should watch closely and, in addition, sensory effects beyond those necessarily accompanying poetic art; in them, indeed, it is possible to go wrong often. About them enough has been said in the published works.

XVI.

What recognition is has been said earlier. As for kinds of recognition, first is that which is most artificial and which poets use most, through lack of resourcefulness: that through signs. 2. Of these, some are birthmarks, like "the spear which the Earth-born bear" or the stars that Carcinus uses in the *Thyestes*. Others are acquired, and of these some are on the body, like scars, and some things worn, like necklaces and the things produced from the chest in the *Tyro*. 3. But these, too, may be used better or worse; for example, Odysseus was recognized through his scar in one way by the nurse and in another way by the swineherds. Those, that is, for proof are more artificial, and all like them. But those with a reversal, like the one in the *Bathing of Odysseus*, are better.

4. Second are those made up by the poet —hence, artificial. For example, Orestes in the *Iphigenia* makes it known that he is Orestes; she, to be sure, is revealed through the letter, but he says himself what the poet bids—not the story. So this is close to the error mentioned; he might also have carried some tokens. And in the *Tereus* of Sophocles there is the voice of the shuttle.

5. The third is through memory—by perceiving [1455a] on seeing something—like that in the *Cyprians* of Dicaeogenes, for when Teucer sees the picture, he bursts into tears; and like that in the *Reply to Alcinous,* for when Odysseus hears the lyre-player and remembers, he weeps. That is how they were recognized.

6. Fourth is that from inference (syllogism). For example, in the *Libation-bearers* Electra reasons that someone like her has come; there is no one like her but Orestes; he, therefore, has come. And that of Polyidus the sophist, for the *Iphigenia*, for it is probable that Orestes should reason that it is because his sister was sacrificed that it is also his lot to be sacrificed. And in the *Tydeus* of Theodectes, Tydeus says that he came to find his son, and himself perishes. And that in the *Phineidae*, for the women seeing the place inferred their fate: namely, that they were fated to die in this place since they had been exposed there.

7. And there is even a kind based on false reasoning (paralogism) of the audience, as in the *Odysseus the Bearer of False Tidings*. For it is made up by the poet that no one else but Odysseus can stretch the bow; and an assumption occurs if, to be sure, a man has said he will stretch the bow who would not have seen it. But to make that assumption supposing that he will thereby expose himself is false reasoning.

8. Of all, the best recognition is that resulting directly from the things done, the surprise coming about through likely events, as in the *Oedipus* of Sophocles and in the *Iphigenia*. It is likely, in fact, that Iphigenia should wish to send a letter. Such recognitions alone are free from artificial things—signs and necklaces. Second are those from inference.

XVII.

The poet should put his plots together and work them out with language setting the action as much as possible before his eyes; thus seeing it most vividly, as if present at the very events, he will find what is fitting, and contradictions will be least likely to escape him. Evidence of this is what was charged against Carcinus, for Amphiaraus was coming up from a temple

—which escaped the spectator, who did not see it. And on the stage the play failed, the audience misconstruing it.

2. And as far as possible the poet should work out his plots even with gestures, for, granted the similarity of human nature, persons in states of emotion are particularly convincing; and the enraged man will rage and the angered man storm most realistically. Hence, the poetic art requires a man of fine nature or inspired; of these the former are quite plastic, the latter ecstatic.

3. Plots—including those made up—the poet should also, [1455b] as he composes, set forth in general terms; then afterward he should work in episodes and expand. He would consider the general scheme, I say, as he might that of the *Iphigenia*: a certain girl was sacrificed and made to disappear mysteriously from the sight of those sacrificing her; she was set down in another country where it was the custom to sacrifice strangers to the goddess; she took over this priestly office; at a later time the brother of the priestess happened to come there—the fact that the god for some purpose ordered him to go there is outside the general scheme, and what he came for is outside the plot—he came and was captured; on the point of being sacrificed he made himself known, either as Euripides has it or as Polyidus contrived—saying, as he probably would, that not only his sister, then, but he too must be sacrificed; and thence his deliverance.

4. Next the poet, already having added names for support, should work in episodes. And the episodes are to be suitable—as, for Orestes, the mad fit through which he was captured and his deliverance through the purification.

5. Now in dramas the episodes are short, but epic is lengthened by them. The plot of the *Odyssey*, indeed, is not long: a man is away from home many years, closely watched by Poseidon, alone; further, matters at home are such that his goods are being wasted by suitors of his wife and

his son is being plotted against; he arrives, storm-tossed; making himself known to some, he sets upon his enemies; he is saved and destroys them. This, then, is the essence; the rest, episodes.

XVIII.

In every tragedy there is both complication and resolution. The things outside and some of those within usually make up the complication; the rest is resolution. I call *complication* everything from the beginning up to that part which comes just before there is a change to good fortune or to bad; *resolution,* everything from the beginning of the change to the end. Thus, in the *Lynceus* of Theodectes the complication includes the things done earlier, and the seizure of the little child, and afterward the revelation of these matters; the resolution is the part from the charge of murder to the end.

2. There are four forms of tragedy—as many, that is, as the parts have also been said to be: there is the complicated tragedy, the whole of which is reversal and recognition; another is expressive of suffering, like those about Ajax [1456a] and Ixion; another is expressive of character, like the *Phthiotides* and the *Peleus*; the fourth . . . like the *Phorcides* and the *Prometheus* and all those set in Hades.

3. One should, indeed, try very hard to combine these forms, one and all; or else the most important and as many as possible, particularly because men nowadays chide the poets; since there have been poets good at every part, they think the individual should surpass the peculiar virtue of each.

In nothing so much as in plot is it just to speak of a tragedy as different or the same; tragedies are the same if their complication and resolution are the same. Many who make good complications resolve them badly; but the poet should always master both.

4. The poet must remember what has often been said, and not make a tragedy an

epic-like system (*epic-like* I call that made up of many stories); suppose, for example, one should treat the whole story of the *Iliad*. There, on account of the length, the various parts are given their fitting importance, but in dramas it turns out quite contrary to expectation. 5. The evidence is that those who have treated the destruction of Ilium as a whole, and not by the part, like Euripides, or the story of Thebes, and not like Aeschylus, fail or come off badly in competition. Agathon, indeed, failed in this alone.

6. Both in their reversals and in their simple plots they come remarkably close to what they aim at: namely, what is tragic and friendly to mankind. That is the case when the clever, but wicked, man is outwitted, like Sisyphus, and the courageous, but unjust man is worsted. That is the case, and it is probable, as Agathon says; it is probable, that is, that many things will happen quite against probability.

7. The chorus, too, one should take to be one of the actors, and a part of the whole, and to share in the acting—not as in Euripides, but as in Sophocles. In most of the poets the parts sung belong no more to the plot than to another tragedy. For that reason they now sing inserted pieces, Agathon having first begun such a practice. And yet how does singing inserted pieces differ from fitting a speech (or a whole episode) from one play into another?

XIX.

Now we have already spoken about the other parts, but it remains to speak about language and thought.

The things to be said about thought may be left to our remarks about rhetoric, for the subject belongs rather to that investigation. Under thought, indeed, is what is to be brought about by speech. 2. It includes both proof and refutation; the stirring-up of emotions like [1456b] pity or fear or anger, and all such; and, further, importance and insignificance. 3. It is clear, also, that in the things done the poet should proceed from the same principles when he needs to produce pity or fear or importance or probability—except that there is this much difference, that these must appear without instruction, while in speech they must be furnished by the speaker and must occur along with his speech. What, indeed, would be the speaker's task if the idea were evident anyway, and not through his speech?

4. Among matters pertaining to language, one is a kind of study of the structural forms of language; these are for the actor to know and the man who has the related master-art; for example, what a command is, and what a prayer, and a statement, and a threat, and a question, and an answer, and anything else of the sort. 5. On the ground of knowledge or ignorance of these things no fault can be found with the poetic art which is at all worthy of serious attention. For why should anyone suppose Homer missed the mark in what Protagoras finds fault with: that intending to pray he gives a command, saying, "Sing, Goddess, the wrath——"? Bidding anyone, he says, to do something or not to do it is a command. So let this study be dismissed as belonging to another art and not to the poetic.

XX.

Of language as a whole these are the parts: letter, syllable, ligament, joint, name, verb, inflection, phrase.

2. A letter, then, is an indivisible sound —not every such sound, but one from which an intelligible sound is capable of being made. There are also, that is, indivisible sounds uttered by animals, but I call none of them a letter. 3. The kinds of letter are vowel, semivowel, and mute. A vowel has an audible sound without addition. A semivowel has an audible sound after addition; for example, *s* and *r*. A mute has no sound by itself, but by addition of one of the letters which have a sound of some sort it becomes audible; for example, *g* and *d*. 4. These differ in both the shapes and the re-

gions of the mouth which produce them; in aspiration and lack of it, in length and brevity, and, further, in acute, grave, and medial accentuation. About the details of these matters we must see the metrical treatises.

5. A syllable is a nonsignificant sound made up of a mute and a letter having a sound; *gr* without *a* is a syllable, as it is with *a*—that is, *gra*. But to study the differences of the syllables is also the business of metrics.

6. A ligament is a nonsignificant sound which neither [1457a] hinders nor helps the creation of a single significant sound out of several sounds; it is not appropriate to place it at the beginning of a phrasal unit by itself—for example, μέν, δή, τοι, δέ. Or it is a nonsignificant sound which is capable of making a single significant phrase out of two or more significant phrases—for example, ἀμφί, περί, and the rest.

7. A joint is a nonsignificant sound which marks the beginning of a phrase, or the end, or the separation of phrases, its natural place being either at the ends or in the middle.

8. A name is a composite, significant sound without tense, of which no part is by itself significant; in the case of compounds, that is, we do not use them as if one part also had significance by itself—for example, in Theodore, the *-dore* is not significant.

9. A verb is a composite, significant sound with tense, of which no part is significant by itself, as is also the case with the names. That is, *man* or *white* does not signify *when;* whereas *walks* also signifies the present time, *has walked* what has passed.

10. Inflection occurs in name or verb, one form signifying *of* or *to,* and the like; another signifying one or many, as *men* or *man;* another signifying mode, as by question or command—*Did he walk?* and *Walk!* show inflection in a verb by these formative principles.

11. A phrase is a composite, significant

sound of which some parts by themselves signify something. Not every phrase, indeed, is composed of verbs and names, such as *the definition of man;* rather, it is accepted as being a phrase without verbs. A phrase will always, however, have a part which is significant by itself, like *Cleon* in *Cleon walks.* 12. A phrase is a unit in two ways; either, that is, by signifying one thing or by conjunction of several phrases; for example, the *Iliad* is one by conjunction, *the definition of man* by signifying one thing.

XXI.

There are two forms of names: the simple (I call *simple* a word which is not made up of significant parts, like *earth*) and the double. Of the latter, one form is made up of a significant and a nonsignificant part (but not in the word significant and nonsignificant), and one form is made up of significant parts; there might even be a triple and quadruple name, and a multiple, like many of the words of the Massilians—for example, [1457b] Ἑρμοκαϊκόξανθος.

2. Every word is either a standard expression or dialectal or a metaphor or an ornament or artificial or lengthened or abbreviated or changed.

3. I call a word *standard* which we Athenians use, and dialectal one which other Greeks. So it is clear that the same word can be both dialectal and standard, but not to the same people; for example, σίγυνον [spear] is a standard word to Cyprians, but to us dialectal.

4. *Metaphor* means applying the name of something else, either from genus to species, or from species to genus, or from species to species, or by analogy. 5. I call *from genus to species* an example like "Here stands my ship." That is, *being at anchor* is a kind of *standing. From species to genus*—"Truly Odysseus has wrought ten thousand noble deeds" [*Iliad* ii. 272]. For *ten thousand* means *many,* and in this case Homer used it in place of *many. From species to species*—examples like "drawing off

life with bronze" and "cutting with indestructible bronze." There *draw* means cut and *cut* means *draw*; both are a kind of taking away. 6. I call it *by analogy* when the second term is so related to the first as the fourth to the third, for one will say for the second the fourth, or for the fourth the second, and sometimes they add for what is supplanted something it is related to. For example, the cup is so related to Dionysus as the shield to Ares; one will then say that the cup is "Dionysus' shield" and that the shield is "Ares' cup." Or what old age is to life, evening is to day; one will then say that evening is the "old age of day," as Empedocles puts it, and old age the "evening of life," or "sunset of life." 7. For some terms there is no existing word analogous, but nonetheless a comparison will also be made. For example, to scatter seed is to sow, but for scattering fire in the case of the sun there is no word; still, in relation to the sun this is like sowing in relation to seed; hence, "sowing god-created light" has been said. 8. And it is possible to use this style of metaphor in yet another way; applying a word appropriate to something else, to deny some one of its peculiar attributes. For example, one might speak of the shield as a cup not "of Ares" but "wineless."

9. An *artificial* word is one which, not being generally used by people, the poet himself establishes; some words seem to be of this kind, like ἐρνύγες for *horns* and ἀρητήρ for *priest*.

10. A word is *lengthened* [1458a] if it uses a longer vowel than the usual one or an added syllable, like πόληος for πόλεως and Πηληϊάδεω for Πηλείδον. A word is *abbreviated* when some part of it is taken away, like κρῖ for κριθή, δω for δῶμα, and ὄψ for ὄψις in μία γίγνεται ἀμφοτέρων ὄψ. 11. A word is *changed* when the poet leaves part of the ordinary form and makes up the rest, like δεξιτερόν for δεξίον, in δεξίτερον κατὰ μαζόν.

12. In the case of the names themselves some are masculine, some feminine, some intermediate. Masculines are those which end in Ν, Ρ, and Σ, and the letters which are composed with Σ (these are two, Ψ and Ξ); feminines are those which end in vowels—both those always long (like Η and Ω) and those sometimes lengthened (like Α). So it happens there are an equal number of endings for masculines and for feminines, since Ψ and Ξ are identical with Σ. No name ends in a mute, nor in a short vowel (Ε and Ο). Three, only, end in Ι and five in Υ. The intermediates end in long vowels, and in Ν (and Ρ) and Σ.

XXII.

Excellence in language is to be clear without being ordinary. Clearest, indeed, is that made up of standard words, but it is ordinary; examples are the poetry of Cleophon and Sthenelus. Language which uses distinctive words is, however, dignified, and it quite changes vulgar speech. I call *distinctive* a dialectal word, a metaphor, lengthening, and everything contrary to standard usage. 2. But if one composes wholly in such language, either a riddle or babble will result—if the language is made up of metaphors, a riddle; if of dialectal words, babble. The idea of a riddle is this: for the speaker to unite things which ordinarily cannot be united. It is, to be sure, impossible to make a riddle by putting together the other kinds of words; but with metaphor it can be done—for example, "I saw a man who had glued bronze upon a man with fire," and the like. Passages made up of dialectal words are babble.

3. Standard and distinctive words, should, then, in one way or another be mixed, for the latter will make for what is neither vulgar nor ordinary—such as the dialectal word, the metaphor, the ornament, and the other kinds mentioned—and what is standard will make for clarity.

4. No very small share [1458b] is contributed to clarity of language which is not ordinary by lengthenings, abbreviations, and alterations of words; through its being

different from what is standard—the language will avoid commonplaceness, but through its partially conforming to custom there will be clarity.

5. So men do not rightly find fault when they inveigh against such a style of discourse and ridicule the poet; for example, the early Euclid, claiming it easy to compose poetry if you let a poet lengthen words as he wishes, satirized that practice in his very reading of:

Ἐπιχάρην εἶδον Μαραθῶνάδε βαδίζοντα

and

οὐκ ἄν γ' ἐράμενος τὸν ἐκείνου ἐλλέβορον.[1]

6. To be at all obvious in using this style is ridiculous, to be sure, for meter is common to all the various kinds of words. In fact, using metaphors and dialectal words and the other forms improperly and expressly for ridiculous effects, one will achieve just that.

7. How great a difference the appropriate word makes is to be observed in hexameters when words are put in contrary to the meter. One might discover that we are speaking the truth in the case of the dialectal word, and metaphors, and all the other kinds, by substituting standard words. Thus, when Aeschylus and Euripides make the same iambic line, the latter changing one word only, a dialectic word for a standard and ordinary one, Euripides' line seems fine, Aeschylus' cheap. Aeschylus, that is, wrote in the *Philoctetes*

the cancer which *eats* the flesh of my foot.

Euripides wrote *feasts on* for *eats*. Or,

being now few and worthless and shabby
    [*Odyssey* ix. 515],

if one should say, substituting standard words

    being now small and weak and ugly.

---

[1] The meaning of these lines is unimportant. The point is that a short syllable may be lengthened by accentual stress; and this then can become an instrument of parody.—Ed.

Or,

putting down shabby chair and cheap table
    [*Odyssey* xx. 259]

changed into

putting down bad chair and small table.

Or,

the shores thundered [*Iliad* xvii. 265]

into

the shores screeched.

8. Again Ariphrades used to make fun of the tragedians because they used phrases and words in their writing which no one would utter in conversation, such as δωμάτων ἄπο [from the house away], instead of ἀπὸ δωμάτων [away from the house], and σέθεν, and ἐγὼ δέ νιν, and [1459a] Ἀχιττέως πέρι instead of περὶ Ἀχιττέως, and other like them. But all such, by not being among the standard expressions, make for what is not vulgar in language. Ariphrades did not realize that.

9. It is important to use properly each of the forms mentioned—and compounds and dialectal words. But much the most important is to be metaphorical, for this alone one cannot get from anyone else, and it is a sign of a fine nature, since to make metaphors well is to perceive likeness.

10. Of the various forms of words, compounds are especially suited to dithyrambs, dialectal words to heroic verse, metaphors to iambic. In heroic verse, all the forms mentioned are usable, but in iambic, since it imitates speech as closely as possible, such words are suited as one would also use in an oration—these are the standard word and metaphor and ornament.

11. And now we have said enough about tragedy and imitation in action.

XXIII.

As for the imitative art which is narrative and in meter, it is clear that the poet should put together his plots, as in tragedies, to be dramatic, and about one action which is whole and complete, having a beginning and middle parts and an end, so that, like a living animal which is one whole, it will create the pleasure characteristic of it; and it is clear that the structures should not be like historical accounts, in which it is necessary to reveal not one course of action but one period of time—whatever events happened in it, involving one man or more, each of which is only as it chanced related to the others. 2. For as the sea-battle at Salamis and the fight with the Carthaginians in Sicily took place at the same time, without at all tending toward the same result, so also in consecutive periods of time one event sometimes occurs after another without any one result occurring from them. Yet perhaps most of the poets do this.

3. Hence, as we have already said, in this respect, too, Homer would seem to be inspired beyond all the others, that he did not try to treat the war as a whole, although it had a beginning and an end, for the plot would have been too big and not easily seen as a unit; or if he cut it down in length, it would have been too complicated in its variety. But, as it is, selecting one part, he used many of the events as episodes, such as the *Catalogue of the Ships* and other episodes by which he diversifies his composition. The other poets write about one man and [1459b] about one period of time and one course of action in many parts —as do the authors of the *Cypria* and the *Little Iliad*. 4. So, then, whereas from the *Iliad* and the *Odyssey* only one tragedy each is made, or at most two, from the *Cypria* many have been made and from the *Little Iliad* more than eight—for example, *The Award of the Arms, Philoctetes, Neoptolemus, Eurypylus, The Begging, The Laconian Women, The Destruction of Ilium, The Departure of the Fleet, Sinon,* and *The Trojan Women.*

XXIV.

Further, epic must have the same forms as tragedy; as being, that is, either simple or complicated, or expressive of character, or of suffering. And the parts, except music and spectacle, must be the same, for there must be reversals and recognitions and acts of suffering, and the thoughts and the language must be good. 2. These, one and all, Homer used, both first and properly; and I say this because each of his poems is well constructed—the *Iliad,* simple and pathetic; the *Odyssey,* complicated, for there are recognitions throughout, and expressive of character. And, in addition, in language and in thought they excel all.

3. But epic differs both in the length of its structure and in its meter. As for normative length, indeed, that stated is sufficient; that is, the beginning and the end must be capable of being seen as a unit. That will probably be the case if the structures are less than those of the early poets and approximate the total length of the tragedies set for a single hearing. 4. And for extending its size epic has a considerable advantage characteristic of it, because in tragedy it is not possible to imitate several parts as being enacted at the same time, but only the part on the stage and presented by the actors. In epic, however, through its being narrative, it is possible to treat several parts as occurring at the same time, and by them, if they are germane, the weight of the poem will be increased. This advantage, then, it has for magnificence, and the fact that it diverts the hearer by using episodes of many kinds. Sameness, quickly satiating, makes tragedies fail.

5. As for meter, the heroic from experience has proved suitable, for if one should compose narrative imitation in any other meter, or in many meters, it would appear inept. The heroic is, in fact, the most stately and most impressive of the meters; hence, it very readily admits both dialectal words and metaphors. Narrative imitation, in fact, goes far beyond the others. The iambic and the trochaic, on the other hand, are [1460a] full of movement; the former suits action, the latter dancing. 6. Further,

it would be still more out of place if one should mix meters as Chaeremon did. That is why no one has composed a poem of lengthy structure in any other meter than the heroic, but, as we said, nature herself teaches us to choose what is appropriate to her.

7. Homer deserves to be praised for many reasons, but particularly because he alone of the poets is not ignorant of what he himself should do; as himself the poet should say as few things as possible, since he is not by them an imitator. The other poets, indeed, themselves compete throughout, and imitate few subjects and rarely; but Homer, after a brief introduction, straightway brings in a man or a woman or a person with some other character, and none characterless, rather each having character.

8. Now it is necessary in tragedies to create surprise, but the irrational, through which surprise particularly comes about, is better received in epic because one is not looking at the doer. While the business of the pursuit of Hector would prove laughable if it were on the stage—the men standing still and not pursuing, and Achilles shaking his head—in hexameters it escapes attention. Surprise is pleasant; the evidence is that all men report an event adding to it, to give pleasure.

9. It is Homer especially who has taught the other poets to tell lies as they ought. The method is false reasoning. For people suppose, whenever one thing exists or comes about because another does, that if the second does, the first does also. This is false. On account of it, even if the first is false, but the second necessarily exists or comes about if it is true, we postulate the first, for, since we know the second to be true, our mind falsely reasons that the first also is. An example of this is that from the *Bathing of Odysseus.*

10. And one should prefer impossibilities, rendered probable, to things possible but unconvincing. Plots should not be constructed from irrational parts; indeed, most

certainly they should have nothing irrational. If they do, it should be outside the story told, like Oedipus' not knowing how Laius died—not, however, in the drama, like the men giving an account of the Pythian games in the *Electra,* or in the *Mysians* the man coming from Tegea to Mysia without speaking. To say that the plot would have been destroyed is ridiculous, for in the first place such plots should not be constructed. But if the poet makes one and it appears fairly reasonable, it is to be accepted, even though absurd. Since the irrational matters in the Odyssey—those about Odysseus' disembarkment [1406b]—would also clearly not be tolerable if a bad poet composed them; as it is, with his other virtues, the poet conceals what is absurd, making it pleasurable.

11. And the poet must work hard at the language in the parts without action and expressive neither of character nor of thought; conversely, language which is too brilliant conceals both qualities of character and thoughts.

XXV.

About problems and their solutions—of how many and also of what kinds they are —will become clear if we look at the matter thus: since the poet is an imitator, just as if he were a painter or some other maker of likenesses, he necessarily and always imitates one of three possibilities—namely, what was or is; what men say and is believed to be; what ought to be. 2. These are narrated in language in which dialectal word and metaphor and the many modifications of language occur, for we grant these to the poets.

3. Besides, there is not the same exactness in the political and the poetic arts, or in any other art and the poetic. In the poetic art itself there is twofold possibility of error; one pertinent to the art, the other incidental. 4. That is, if the poet chooses to imitate impossibilities, the error pertains to the art itself. But if the poet is right in his

choice, although he has described the horse as throwing both right legs forward; or if he has made a mistake in respect to a particular art—for example, in respect to medicine or some other art; or if he has imitated miscellaneous impossibilities—the error does not pertain to the poetic art. So we must reply to the accusations in the problems looking at them from these facts.

5. First, then, the accusations against the art itself: the poet has presented impossibilities, he has erred. But, we may reply, he is right if he achieves the end of the art—the end, of course, has been stated—if thus he makes this or another part more striking. An example is the pursuit of Hector.

If, to be sure, the end might more or less have been realized and according to the art governing these matters, he is wrong to have erred; for, if possible, one should not err at all. Still, we may ask whether the error is one of those which pertains to the art or to another incidental matter. It is less serious of a man does not know that a doe does not have horns than if he depicts her unimitatively.

6. In addition, if it is charged that things are not true, we may reply that they nonetheless ought to be. Thus, Sophocles said for himself that he presented men as they ought to be, Euripides men as they are. By this answer the problem is to be solved.

7. But if neither is the case we may reply that men say things are thus—for example, the stories about gods. Perhaps, indeed, it is not better to tell them and they are not true; rather, things have chanced [1461a] as it seemed to Xenophanes. Still we may reply that men say so.

In other cases, perhaps it is not better, but so it was. For example, what Homer says about the weapons: "Their spears were upright on the spike" [*Iliad* x. 152]. They were so accustomed then, as are Illyrians even now.

8. As to whether something was said or done well or ill by someone, that is to be considered by looking not only at the thing done or said itself, seeing whether it is noble or base, but also at the one who does or says it, to whom, or when, or how, or for what reason—whether, for example, that a greater good may occur or that a greater evil may be avoided.

9. One must solve some problems by considering the language. Thus, for a dialectal word: οὐρῆας μὲν πρῶτον [*Iliad* i. 50]. For Homer is not speaking of *mules* but of *guards*. As for Dolon ὅς ῥ᾽ ἦ τοι εἶδος μὲν ἔην κακός [he was indeed of evil form] [*Iliad* x. 316], it is not his body that is shapeless, but his face that is ugly; for the Cretans use εὐειδές to mean *fair of face*. And ζωρότερον δὲ κέραιε [mix it livelier] [*Iliad* ix. 203] does not mean *unmixed wine*, as for some drunkards, but *more rapidly*.

10. Some are explicated metaphorically, as "All gods and men slept through the night" [*Iliad* ii. 1]; whereas he says, "When he looked toward the Trojan plain, a noise of flutes and pipes. . . ." [*Iliad* x. 11-13]. *All* has been said instead of *many* by metaphor, for all is a form of many. And "She alone has no part. . . ." [*Iliad* xviii. 489] is metaphorical, for the best known is the only one.

11. Some are solved by accentuation and breathing. Thus Hippias of Thasos explained δίδομεν δέ οἱ εὖχος ἀρέσθαι [*Iliad* ii. 15] and τὸ μὲν οὗ καταπύθεται ὄμβρῳ [*Iliad* xxiii. 328].

12. Some are solved by punctuation, as in Empedocles' "Suddenly mortal things were created, which formerly had learned to be immortal; things unmixed before were mixed."

13. Some are solved by indicating ambiguity, as in "The greater part of the night had passed" [*Iliad* x. 252], for in that case "the greater part" is ambiguous.

14. Some are solved by appeal to the custom of language. A mixed drink men call wine, and braziers they call workers in iron. On this basis, "a greave of new-wrought tin" [*Iliad* xxi. 592] was written. On this basis, Ganymede was said to "pour

wine for Zeus" [*Iliad* xx. 234], although the gods do not drink wine. This practice might also be explained, perhaps as metaphorical.

15. And when a word seems to indicate a contradiction, we should consider in how many ways it may have meaning in what is said. In the case of "There was held the spear of bronze" [*Iliad* xx. 272], we should consider in how many ways it is possible to be fixed in that place—so or so.

16. We should take up the matter as far as possible doing the opposite of what [1461b] Glaucon remarks—that some men from the beginning take up problems irrationally and, having voted against the poet, draw conclusions and censure him for having said what they think he said—if it is opposed to their own opinion. The matter of Icarius has been treated in this way, for they suppose him to be a Lacedemonian, and it is consequently absurd that Telemachus did not meet him when he came to Lacedemon. But perhaps it is as the Cephallenians say; for they claim that Odysseus married among them and that Penelope's father was Icadius, not Icarius. Through an error the problem is plausible.

17. All in all, we must refer the impossible to poetic composition, or to what is better, or to opinion. As for poetic composition, we may say that something convincing, though impossible, is rather to be chosen than something unconvincing and possible. And perhaps it is impossible that men should be such as Zeuxis painted them. But, we may say, it is better, and that is because the representation should be superior. The irrational may be justified on the basis of what men say, and also because sometimes a thing is not, in fact, irrational, since it is probable for things to happen even against probability.

18. Statements which contradict each other we should examine like proofs in speeches, whether the same thing is meant, and in relation to the same thing, and in the same thing, and in the same way—so as to examine the speaker himself, in terms of what he himself says or what a sensible man assumes.

19. There is proper objection both to irrationality and to depravity when, there being no necessity at all, the poet uses the irrational, as does Euripides in the case of Aegeus, or wickedness, like that of Menelaus in the *Orestes*.

20. So they bring charges of five kinds, alleging things to be either impossible or irrational or disgusting or contradictory or against the exactness appropriate to the art. The solutions are to be examined under the headings mentioned: they are twelve.

XXVI.

Someone may raise the question whether the epic imitation is better than the tragic. It is argued that if the less vulgar imitation is better and always is that directed toward better audiences, very clearly the one imitating everything whatsoever is vulgar. And it is said that the actors, supposing the audience will not perceive unless the actor himself adds something, stir up a great commotion, like the cheap flute-players who whirl about if they have to imitate the discus and drag the leader of the chorus if they are playing the *Scylla*. 2. Such, people claim, is tragedy—as, indeed, the earlier actors judged those who came after them. Mynniscus called Callipides a monkey, thinking him very extravagant, and such was the opinion also about [1462a] Pindarus. As these later actors are to the earlier ones, the whole art is to epic. Epic, they say, is for audiences of good and just men, who do not need gestures at all, while tragedy is for cheap people. And the art which is vulgar will clearly be inferior.

3. In the first place, it may be replied, the criticism is not of the poetic art but of the art of acting, since it also is possible to overdo gesticulations both in reciting, as Sosistratus did, and in singing, as Mnasith-

eus the Opuntian did. Then, too, not every sort of movement is to be disapproved, unless dancing is; rather, that of cheap persons. It was, in fact, charged against both Callipides and now others, that they imitated licentious women. Further, tragedy produces its effect even without movement, just as epic does; for through reading it is clear what sort of thing it is. Now if in the other respects it is superior, this need not be essential to it.

4. Then, it is superior because it has everything that epic has, for it can even use its meter; and also because it has, as no small part, music and spectacular elements, through which its delights most vividly unite. Further, it has vividness both in reading and on the stage. 5. Again, it is superior in that the purpose of the imitation [1462b] is achieved in less space, for the more intense effect is more delightful than one weakened by length of time. Suppose a man should put the *Oedipus* of Sophocles into as many hexameters as the *Iliad!* Again, the imitation of hexameter poets is less a unit—and the evidence is that from any imitation of the sort several tragedies are constructed—so that if they unify a plot, either it appears curtailed when it is briefly set forth, or, conforming to the length usual to the meter, waterish. 6. And I have in mind what happens if the epic is composed of several actions—like the *Iliad* and the *Odyssey,* which have many such parts that in themselves have size. These poems, nevertheless, are constructed in the best way possible, and as far as possible each is imitation of one course of action.

7. Now if in all these respects tragedy differs and also in the effectiveness of the art—for epic and tragedy are not to create a chance pleasure but the one mentioned—it is clear that tragedy will be superior, achieving the end better than epic.

8. So much, then, concerning tragedy and epic: themselves, their forms, and their parts; in how many ways and in what they differ; what the causes of success and failure are; and concerning accusations and solutions.

About invectives and comedy. . . .

Politics: Book VIII [5–7]

[5] Concerning music there are some questions which we have already raised; these we may now resume and carry further; and our remarks will serve as a prelude to this or any other discussion of the subject. It is not easy to determine the nature of music, or why any one should have a knowledge of it. Shall we say, for the sake of amusement and relaxation, like sleep or drinking, which are not good in themselves, but are pleasant, and at the same time "make care to cease," as Euripides says? And for this end men also appoint music, and make use of all three alike,—sleep, drinking, music,—to which some add dancing. Or shall we argue that music conduces to virtue, on the ground that it can form our minds and habituate us to true pleasures as our bodies are made by gymnastic to be of a certain character? Or shall we say that it contributes to the enjoyment of leisure and mental cultivation, which is a third alternative? Now obviously youths are not to be instructed with a view to their amusement, for learning is no amusement, but is accompanied with pain. Neither is intellectual enjoyment suitable to boys of that age, for it is the end, and that which is imperfect cannot attain the perfect or end. But perhaps it may be said that boys learn music for the sake of the amusement which they will have when they are grown up. If so, why should they learn themselves, and not, like the Persian and Median kings, enjoy the pleasure and instruction which is

From Aristotle's *Politics,* translated by B. Jowett, revised by W. D. Ross (Oxford: Oxford University Press, 1921). Reprinted by permission of the Clarendon Press, Oxford.

derived from hearing others? . . . And even granting that music may form the character, the objection still holds: why should we learn ourselves? Why cannot we attain true pleasure and form a correct judgement from hearing others, like the Lacedaemonians?—for they, without learning music, nevertheless can correctly judge, as they say, of good and bad melodies. Or again, if music should be used to promote cheerfulness and refined intellectual enjoyment, the objection still remains—why should we learn ourselves instead of enjoying the performances of others? . . .

The first question is whether music is or is not to be a part of education. Of the three things mentioned in our discussion, which does it produce?—education or amusement or intellectual enjoyment, for it may be reckoned under all three, and seems to share in the nature of all of them. Amusement is for the sake of relaxation, and relaxation is of necessity sweet, for it is the remedy of pain caused by toil; and intellectual enjoyment is universally acknowledged to contain an element not only of the noble, but of the pleasant, for happiness is made up of both. All men agree that music is one of the pleasantest things, whether with or without song; as Musaeus says,

"Song is to mortals of all things the sweetest."

Hence and with good reason it is introduced into social gatherings and entertainments, because it makes the hearts of men glad; so that on this ground alone we may assume that the young ought to be trained in it. For innocent pleasures are not only in harmony with the perfect end of life, but they also provide relaxation. And whereas men rarely attain the end, but often rest by the way and amuse themselves, not only with a view to a further end, but also for the pleasure's sake, it may be well at times to let them find a refreshment in music. It sometimes happens that men make amusement the end, for the end probably contains

some element of pleasure, though not any ordinary or lower pleasure; but they mistake the lower for the higher, and seeking for the one find the other, since every pleasure has a likeness to the end of action. For the end is not eligible for the sake of any future good, nor do the pleasures which we have described exist for the sake of any future good but of the past, that is to say, they are the alleviation of past toils and pains. And we may infer this to be the reason why men seek happiness from these pleasures. But music is pursued, not only as an alleviation of past toil, but also as providing recreation. And who can say whether, having this use, it may not also have a nobler one? In addition to this common pleasure, felt and shared in by all (for the pleasure given by music is natural, and therefore adapted to all ages and characters), may it not have also some influence over the character and the soul? It must have such an influence if characters are affected by it. And that they are so affected is proved in many ways, and not least by the power which the songs of Olympus exercise; for beyond question they inspire enthusiasm, and enthusiasm is an emotion of the ethical part of the soul. Besides, when men hear imitations, even apart from the rhythms and tunes themselves, their feelings move in sympathy. Since then music is a pleasure, and virtue consists in rejoicing and loving and hating aright, there is clearly nothing which we are so much concerned to acquire and to cultivate as the power of forming right judgements, and of taking delight in good dispositions and noble actions. Rhythm and melody supply imitations of anger and gentleness, and also of courage and temperance, and of all the qualities contrary to these, and of the other qualities of character, which hardly fall short of the actual affections, as we know from our own experience, for in listening to such strains our souls undergo a change. The habit of feeling pleasure or pain at mere representations is not far removed from the same feeling about realities;

for example, if any one delights in the sight of a statue for its beauty only, it necessarily follows that the sight of the original will be pleasant to him. The objects of no other sense, such as taste or touch, have any resemblance to moral qualities; in visible objects there is only a little, for there are figures which are of a moral character, but only to a slight extent, and all do not participate in the feeling about them. Again, figures and colours are not imitations, but signs, of moral habits, indications which the body gives of states of feeling. . . . On the other hand, even in mere melodies there is an imitation of character, for the musical modes differ essentially from one another, and those who hear them are differently affected by each. Some of them make men sad and grave, like the so-called Mixolydian, others enfeeble the mind, like the relaxed modes, another, again, produces a moderate and settled temper, which appears to be the peculiar effect of the Dorian; the Phrygian inspires enthusiasm. The whole subject has been well treated by philosophical writers on this branch of education, and they confirm their arguments by facts. The same principles apply to rhythms; some have a character of rest, others of motion, and of these latter again, some have a more vulgar, others a nobler movement. Enough has been said to show that music has a power of forming the character, and should therefore be introduced into the education of the young. The study is suited to the stage of youth, for young persons will not, if they can help, endure anything which is not sweetened by pleasure, and music has a natural sweetness. There seems to be in us a sort of affinity to musical modes and rhythms, which makes some philosophers say that the soul is a tuning, others, that it possesses tuning.

[6] And now we have to determine the question which has been already raised, whether children should be themselves taught to sing and play or not. Clearly there is a considerable difference made in the character by the actual practice of the art. It is difficult, if not impossible, for those who do not perform to be good judges of the performance of others. Besides, children should have something to do, and the rattle of Archytas, which people give to their children in order to amuse them and prevent them from breaking anything in the house, was a capital invention, for a young thing cannot be quiet. The rattle is a toy suited to the infant mind, and education is a rattle or toy for children of a larger growth. We conclude then that they should be taught music in such a way as to become not only critics but performers.

The question what is or is not suitable for different ages may be easily answered; nor is there any difficulty in meeting the objection of those who say that the study of music is vulgar. We reply (1) in the first place, that they who are to be judges must also be performers, and that they should begin to practise early, although when they are older they may be spared the execution; they must have learned to appreciate what is good and to delight in it, thanks to the knowledge which they acquired in their youth. As to (2) the vulgarizing effect which music is supposed to exercise, this is a question which we shall have no difficulty in determining, when we have considered to what extent freemen who are being trained to political virtue should pursue the art, what melodies and what rhythms they should be allowed to use, and what instruments should be employed in teaching them to play; for even the instrument makes a difference. The answer to the objection turns upon these distinctions; for it is quite possible that certain methods of teaching and learning music do really have a degrading effect. It is evident then that the learning of music ought not to impede the business of riper years, or to degrade the body or render it unfit for civil or military training, whether for bodily exercises at the time or for later studies.

The right measure will be attained if students of music stop short of the arts which are practised in professional contests, and do not seek to acquire those fantastic marvels of execution which are now the fashion in such contests, and from these have passed into education. Let the young practise even such music as we have prescribed, only until they are able to feel delight in noble melodies and rhythms, and not merely in that common part of music in which every slave or child and even some animals find pleasure.

From these principles we may also infer what instruments should be used. The flute, or any other instrument which requires great skill, as for example the harp, ought not to be admitted into education, but only such as will make intelligent students of music or of the other parts of education. Besides, the flute is not an instrument which is expressive of moral character; it is too exciting. The proper time for using it is when the performance aims not at instruction, but at the relief of the passions. And there is a further objection; the impediment which the flute presents to the use of the voice detracts from its educational value. The ancients therefore were right in forbidding the flute to youths and freemen, although they had once allowed it. . . . Later experience enabled men to judge what was or was not really conducive to virtue, and they rejected both the flute and several other old-fashioned instruments, . . . — which are intended only to give pleasure to the hearer, and require extraordinary skill of hand. There is a meaning also in the myth of the ancients, which tells how Athene invented the flute and then threw it away. It was not a bad idea of theirs, that the Goddess disliked the instrument because it made the face ugly; but with still more reason may we say that she rejected it because the acquirement of flute-playing contributes nothing to the mind, since to Athene we ascribe both knowledge and art.

Thus then we reject the professional instruments and also the professional mode of education in music (and by professional we mean that which is adopted in contests), for in this the performer practises the art, not for the sake of his own improvement, but in order to give pleasure, and that of a vulgar sort, to his hearers. For this reason the execution of such music is not the part of a freeman but of a paid performer, and the result is that the performers are vulgarized, for the end at which they aim is bad. The vulgarity of the spectator tends to lower the character of the music and therefore of the performers; they look to him— he makes them what they are, and fashions even their bodies by the movements which he expects them to exhibit.

We have also to consider rhythms and modes, and [7] their use in education. Shall we use them all or make a distinction? and shall the same distinction be made for those who practise music with a view to education, or shall it be some other? Now we see that music is produced by melody and rhythm, and we ought to know what influence these have respectively on education, and whether we should prefer excellence in melody or excellence in rhythm. But as the subject has been very well treated . . . we shall only speak of it now after the manner of the legislator, stating the general principles.

We accept the division of melodies proposed by certain philosophers into ethical melodies, melodies of action, and passionate or inspiring melodies, each having, as they say, a mode corresponding to it. But we maintain further that music should be studied, not for the sake of one, but of many benefits, that is to say, with a view to (1) education, (2) purgation (the word "purgation" we use at present without explanation, but when hereafter we speak of poetry, we will treat the subject with more precision); music may also serve (3) for intellectual enjoyment, for relaxation and for recreation after exertion. It is clear, therefore, that all the modes must be employed by us, but not all of them in the same manner. In education the most ethical modes are to be preferred, but in listening to the performances of others we may admit the modes of action and passion also. For feelings such as pity and fear, or, again, enthusiasm, exist very strongly in some souls, and have more or less influence over all. Some persons fall into a religious frenzy, whom we see as a result of the sacred melodies—when they have used the melodies that excite the soul to mystic frenzy—restored as though they had found healing and purgation. Those who are influenced by pity or fear, and every emotional nature, must have a like experience, and others in so far as each is susceptible to such emotions, and all are in a manner purged and their souls lightened and delighted. The purgative melodies likewise give an innocent pleasure to mankind. Such are the modes and the melodies in which those who perform music at the theatre should be invited to compete. But since the spectators are of two kinds—the one free and educated, and the other a vulgar crowd composed of mechanics, labourers, and the like—there ought to be contests and exhibitions instituted for the relaxation of the second class also. And the music will correspond to their minds; for as their minds are perverted from the natural state, so there are perverted modes and highly strung and unnaturally coloured melodies. A man receives pleasure from what is natural to him, and therefore professional musicians may be allowed to practise this lower sort of music before an audience of a lower type. But, for the purposes of education, . . . those modes and melodies should be employed which are ethical, such as the Dorian, . . . though we may include any

others which are approved by philosophers who have had a musical education. The Socrates of the *Republic* is wrong in retaining only the Phrygian mode along with the Dorian, and the more so because he rejects the flute; for the Phrygian is to the modes what the flute is to musical instruments—both of them are exciting and emotional. Poetry proves this, for Bacchic frenzy and all similar emotions are most suitably expressed by the flute, and are better set to the Phrygian than to any other mode. . . . All men agree that the Dorian music is the gravest and manliest. And whereas we say that the extremes should be avoided and the mean followed, and whereas the Dorian is a mean between the other modes, it is evident that our youth should be taught the Dorian music.

Two principles have to be kept in view, what is possible, what is becoming: at these every man ought to aim. But even these are relative to age; the old, who have lost their powers, cannot very well sing the high-strung modes, and nature herself seems to suggest that their songs should be of the more relaxed kind. Wherefore the musicians likewise blame Socrates, and with justice, for rejecting the relaxed modes in education under the idea that they are intoxicating, not in the ordinary sense of intoxication (for wine rather tends to excite men), but because they have no strength in them. And so, with a view also to the time of life when men begin to grow old, they ought to practise the gentler modes and melodies as well as the others, and, further, any mode, such as the Lydian above all others appears to be, which is suited to children of tender age, and possesses the elements both of order and of education. Thus it is clear that education should be based upon three principles—the mean, the possible, the becoming, these three.

LONGINUS

≻≻≻≻≺≺≺≺≺

From *On the Sublime*
[first century A.D.]

I. . . . As I am addressing a person so accomplished in literature, I need only state, without enlarging further on the matter, that the Sublime, wherever it occurs, consists in a certain loftiness and excellence of language, and that it is by this, and this only, that the greatest poets and prose-writers have gained eminence. . . . A lofty passage does not convince the reason of the reader, but takes him out of himself. That which is admirable ever confounds our judgment, and eclipses that which is merely reasonable or agreeable. To believe or not is usually in our own power; but the Sublime, acting with an imperious and irresistible force, sways every reader whether he will or no. Skill in invention, lucid arrangement and disposition of facts, are appreciated not by one passage, or by two, but gradually manifest themselves in the general structure of a work; but a sublime thought, if happily timed, illumines an entire subject with the vividness of a lightning-flash, and exhibits the whole power of the orator in a moment of time. . . .

II. The first question which presents itself for solution is whether there is any art which can teach sublimity or loftiness in writing. For some hold generally that there is mere delusion in attempting to reduce such subjects to technical rules. "The Sublime," they tell us, "is born in a man, and not to be acquired by instruction; genius is the only master who can teach it. The vig-

For centuries the treatise *On the Sublime* was attributed to the Greek rhetorician, Cassius Longinus (third century A.D.). It is now widely held to have been written by an unknown author in the first century. The translation is by H. L. Havell (London: 1890).

orous products of nature are weakened and in every respect debased, when robbed of their flesh and blood by frigid technicalities." But I maintain that the truth can be shown to stand otherwise in this matter. Let us look at the case in this way; Nature in her loftier and more passionate moods, while detesting all appearance of restraint, is not wont to show herself utterly wayward and reckless; and though in all cases the vital informing principle is derived from her, yet to determine the right degree and the right moment, and to contribute the precision of practice and experience, is the particular province of scientific method. The great passions, when left to their own blind and rash impulses without the control of reason, are in the same danger as a ship let drive at random without ballast. Often they need the spur, but sometimes also the curb. The remark of Demosthenes with regard to human life in general—that the greatest of all blessings is to be fortunate, but next to that and equal in importance is to be well advised—for good fortune is utterly ruined by the absence of good counsel —may be applied to literature, if we substitute genius for fortune, and art for counsel. Then, again (and this is the most important point of all), a writer can only learn from art when he is to abandon himself to the direction of his genius.

. . .

VII. It is proper to observe that in human life nothing is truly great which is despised by all elevated minds. . . . Now let us apply this principle to the Sublime in poetry or in prose; let us ask in all cases, is it merely a specious sublimity? is this gorgeous exterior a mere false and clumsy pageant, which if laid open will be found to conceal nothing but emptiness? for if so, a noble mind will scorn instead of admiring it. It is natural to us to feel our soul uplifted by the true Sublime, and in a sort of generous exultation to be filled with joy and pride, as though we ourselves had originated the ideas which we read. If then any work, on being repeatedly submitted to the judgment of an acute and cultivated critic, fails to dispose his mind to lofty ideas; if the thoughts which it suggests do not extend beyond what is actually expressed; and if, the longer you read it, the less you think of it—there can be here no true sublimity, when the effect is not sustained beyond the mere act of perusal. But when a passage is pregnant in suggestion, when it is hard, nay impossible, to distract the attention from it, and when it takes a strong and lasting hold on the memory, then we may be sure that we have lighted on the true Sublime. In general we may regard those words as truly noble and sublime which always please and please all readers. For when the same book always produces the same impression on all who read it, whatever be the difference in their pursuits, their manner of life, their aspirations, their ages, or their language, such a harmony of opposites gives irresistible authority to their favorable verdict.

VIII. I shall now enumerate the five principal sources from which almost all sublimity is derived, assuming, of course, the preliminary gift on which all these depend, namely, command of language. The first and the most important is (1) grandeur of thought. The second is (2) a vigorous and spirited treatment of the passions. These two conditions of sublimity depend mainly on natural endowments, whereas those which follow derive assistance from Art. The third is (3) a certain artifice in the employment of figures, which are of two kinds, figures of thought and figures of speech. The fourth is (4) dignified expression, which is subdivided into (a) the proper choice of words, and (b) the use of metaphors and other ornaments of diction. The fifth cause of sublimity, which em-braces all those preceding, is (5) majesty and elevation of structure.

. . .

IX. Of all these five conditions of the Sublime the most important is the first, that is, a certain lofty cast of mind. Therefore, although this is rather natural than acquired, nevertheless it will be well for us in this instance to train up our souls to sublimity, and make them as it were ever big with noble thoughts. How, it may be asked, is this to be done? I have hinted elsewhere in my writings that sublimity is, so to say, the image of greatness of soul. Hence a thought in its naked simplicity, even though unuttered, is sometimes admirable by the sheer greatness of soul implied. Thus, the silence of Ajax in the underworld is great, and grander than anything he could have said. It is absolutely essential, then, first of all to settle the question whence this grandeur of conception arises; and the answer is that true eloquence can be found only in those whose spirit is generous and aspiring. For those whose whole lives are wasted in paltry and illiberal thoughts and habits cannot possibly produce any work worthy of the lasting reverence of mankind. It is only natural that their words should be full of sublimity whose thoughts are full of majesty. Hence sublime thoughts belong properly to the loftiest minds.

. . .

XXXIII. But supposing now that we assume the existence of a really unblemished and irreproachable writer. Is it not worth while to raise the whole question whether in poetry and prose we should prefer sublimity accompanied by some faults, or a style which never rising above moderate excellence never stumbles and never requires correction? and again, whether the first place in literature is justly to be assigned to the more numerous, or the loftier excellences? For these are questions proper to an inquiry on the Sublime, and urgently demanding settlement.

I know, then, that the largest intellects

are far from being the most exact. A mind always intent on correctness is apt to be dissipated in trifles; but in great affluence of thought, as in vast material wealth, there must needs be an occasional neglect of detail. And is it not inevitably so? Is it not by risking nothing, by never aiming high, that a writer of low or middling powers keeps generally clear of faults and secure of blame? whereas the loftier walks of literature are by their very loftiness perilous? I am well aware, again, that there is a law by which in all human productions the weak points catch the eye first, by which their faults remain indelibly stamped on the memory, while their beauties quickly fade away. Yet, though I have myself noted not a few faulty passages in Homer and in other authors of the highest rank, and though I am far from being partial to their failings, nevertheless I would call them not so much wilfull blunders as oversights which were allowed to pass unregarded through that contempt of little things, that "brave disorder" which is natural to an exalted genius; and I still think that the greater excellences, though not everywhere equally sustained, ought always to be voted to the first place in literature, if for no other reason, for the mere grandeur of soul they evince.

. . .

XXXV. . . . What truth, then, was it that was present to those mighty spirits of the past, who, making whatever is greatest in writing their aim, thought it beneath them to be exact in every detail? Among many others especially this, that it was not in nature's plan for us her chosen children to be creatures base and ignoble—no, she brought us into life, and into the whole universe, as into some great field of contest, that we should be at once spectators and ambitious rivals of her mighty deeds, and from the first implanted in our souls an invincible yearning for all that is great, all that is diviner than ourselves. Therefore even the whole world is not wide enough for the soaring range of human thought, but man's mind often overleaps the very bounds of space. When we survey the whole circle of life, and see it abounding everywhere in what is elegant, grand, and beautiful, we learn at once what is the true end of man's being. And this is why nature prompts us to admire, not the clearness and usefulness of a little stream, but the Nile, the Danube, the Rhine, and far beyond all the Ocean; not to turn our wandering eyes from the heavenly fires, though often darkened, to the little flame kindled by human hands, however pure and steady its light; not to think that tiny lamp more wondrous than the caverns of Aetna, from whose raging depths are hurled up stones and whole masses of rock, and torrents sometimes come pouring from earth's center of pure and living fire.

To sum the whole: Whatever is useful or needful lies easily within man's reach; but he keeps his homage for what is astounding.

PLOTINUS [A.D. 204–269]

>>>>>-<<<<<

From *The Enneads*

1ST ENNEAD, 6TH TRACTATE: *Beauty*

Beauty addresses itself chiefly to sight; but there is a beauty for the hearing too, as in certain combinations of words and in all kinds of music, for melodies and cadences are beautiful; and minds that lift themselves above the realm of sense to a higher order are aware of beauty in the conduct of life, in actions, in character, in the pursuits of the intellect; and there is the beauty of the virtues. What loftier beauty there may be, yet, our argument will bring to light.

What, then, is it that gives comeliness to material forms and draws the ear to the sweetness perceived in sounds, and what is the secret of the beauty there is in all that derives from Soul?

Is there some One Principle from which all take their grace, or is there a beauty peculiar to the embodied and another for the bodiless? Finally, one or many, what would such a Principle be?

Consider that some things, material shapes for instance, are gracious not by anything inherent but by something communicated, while others are lovely of themselves, as, for example, Virtue.

The same bodies appear sometimes beautiful, sometimes not; so that there is a good deal between being body and being beautiful.

What, then, is this something that shows itself in certain material forms? This is the natural beginning of our enquiry.

What is it that attracts the eyes of those

Plotinus, *The Enneads*, translated by Stephen MacKenna (London: The Medici Society, 1926).

to whom a beautiful object is presented, and calls them, lures them, towards it, and fills them with joy at the sight? If we possess ourselves of this, we have at once a standpoint for the wider survey.

Almost everyone declares that the symmetry of parts towards each other and towards a whole, with, besides, a certain charm of colour, constitutes the beauty recognised by the eye, that in visible things, as indeed in all else, universally, the beautiful thing is essentially symmetrical, patterned.

But think what this means.

Only a compound can be beautiful, never anything devoid of parts; and only a whole; the several parts will have beauty, not in themselves, but only as working together to give a comely total. Yet beauty in an aggregate demands beauty in details: it cannot be constructed out of ugliness; its law must run throughout.

All the loveliness of colour and even the light of the sun, being devoid of parts and so not beautiful by symmetry, must be ruled out of the realm of beauty. And how comes gold to be a beautiful thing? And lightning by night, and the stars, why are these so fair?

In sounds also the simple must be proscribed, though often in a whole noble composition each several tone is delicious in itself.

Again since the one face, constant in symmetry, appears sometimes fair and sometimes not, can we doubt that beauty is something more than symmetry, that symmetry itself owes its beauty to a remoter principle?

Turn to what is attractive in methods of life or in the expression of thought; are we to call in symmetry here? What symmetry is to be found in noble conduct, or excellent laws, in any form of mental pursuit?

What symmetry can there be in points of abstract thought?

The symmetry of being accordant with each other? But there may be accordance or entire identity where there is nothing but ugliness: the proposition that honesty is merely a generous artlessness chimes in the most perfect harmony with the proposition that morality means weakness of will; the accordance is complete.

Then again, all the virtues are a beauty of the soul, a beauty authentic beyond any of these others; but how does symmetry enter here? The soul, it is true, is not a simple unity, but still its virtue cannot have the symmetry of size or of number: what standard of measurement could preside over the compromise or the coalescence of the soul's faculties or purposes?

Finally, how by this theory would there be beauty in the Intellectual-Principle, essentially the solitary?

2. Let us, then, go back to the source, and indicate at once the Principle that bestows beauty on material things.

Undoubtedly this Principle exists; it is something that is perceived at the first glance, something which the soul names as from an ancient knowledge and, recognising, welcomes it, enters into unison with it. But let the soul fall in with the Ugly and at once it shrinks within itself, denies the thing, turns away from it, not accordant, resenting it.

Our interpretation is that the soul—by the very truth of its nature, by its affiliation to the noblest Existents in the hierarchy of Being—when it sees anything of that kin, or any trace of that kinship, thrills with an immediate delight, takes its own to itself, and thus stirs anew to the sense of its nature and of all its affinity.

But, is there any such likeness between the loveliness of this world and the splendours in the Supreme? Such a likeness in the particulars would make the two orders alike: but what is there in common between beauty here and beauty There?

We hold that all the loveliness of this world comes by communion in Ideal-Form.

All shapelessness whose kind admits of pattern and form, as long as it remains outside of Reason and Idea, is ugly by that very isolation from the Divine-Thought. And this is the Absolute Ugly: an ugly thing is something that has not been entirely mastered by pattern, that is by Reason, the Matter not yielding at all points and in all respects to Ideal-Form.

But where the Ideal-Form has entered, it has grouped and co-ordinated what from a diversity of parts was to become a unity: it has rallied confusion into co-operation: it has made the sum one harmonious coherence: for the Idea is a unity and what it moulds must come to unity as far as multiplicity may.

And on what has thus been compacted to unity, Beauty enthrones itself, giving itself to the parts as to the sum: when it lights on some natural unity, a thing of like parts, then it gives itself to that whole. Thus, for an illustration, there is the beauty, conferred by craftsmanship, of all a house with all its parts, and the beauty which some natural quality may give to a single stone.

This, then, is how the material thing becomes beautiful—by communicating in the thought that flows from the Divine.

3. And the soul includes a faculty peculiarly addressed to Beauty—one incomparably sure in the appreciation of its own, never in doubt whenever any lovely thing presents itself for judgment.

Or perhaps the soul itself acts immediately, affirming the Beautiful where it finds something accordant with the Ideal-Form within itself, using this Idea as a canon of accuracy in its decision.

But what accordance is there between the material and that which antedates all Matter?

On what principle does the architect, when he finds the house standing before him correspondent with his inner ideal of a house, pronounce it beautiful? Is it not that the house before him, the stones apart, is the inner idea stamped upon the mass of exterior matter, the indivisible exhibited in diversity?

So with the perceptive faculty: discerning in certain objects the Ideal-Form which has bound and controlled shapeless matter, opposed in nature to Idea, seeing further stamped upon the common shapes some shape excellent above the common, it gathers into unity what still remains fragmentary, catches it up and carries it within, no longer a thing of parts, and presents it to the Ideal-Principle as something concordant and congenial, a natural friend: the joy here is like that of a good man who discerns in a youth the early signs of a virtue consonant with the achieved perfection within his own soul.

The beauty of colour is also the outcome of a unification: it derives from shape, from the conquest of the darkness inherent in Matter by the pouring-in of light, the unembodied, which is a Rational-Principle and an Ideal-Form.

Hence it is that Fire itself is splendid beyond all material bodies, holding the rank of Ideal-Principle to the other elements, making ever upwards, the subtlest and sprightliest of all bodies, as very near to the unembodied; itself alone admitting no other, all the others penetrated by it: for they take warmth but this is never cold; it has colour primally; they receive the Form of colour from it: hence the splendour of its light, the splendour that belongs to the Idea. And all that has resisted and is but uncertainly held by its light remains outside of beauty, as not having absorbed the plenitude of the Form of colour.

And harmonies unheard in sound create the harmonies we hear and wake the soul to the consciousness of beauty, showing it the one essence in another kind: for the measures of our sensible music are not arbitrary but are determined by the Principle whose labour is to dominate Matter and bring pattern into being.

Thus far of the beauties of the realm of sense, images and shadow-pictures, fugitives that have entered into Matter—to adorn, and to ravish, where they are seen.

4. But there are earlier and loftier beauties than these. In the sense-bound life we are no longer granted to know them, but the soul, taking no help from the organs, sees and proclaims them. To the vision of these we must mount, leaving sense to its own low place.

As it is not for those to speak of the graceful forms of the material world who have never seen them or known their grace—men born blind, let us suppose—in the same way those must be silent upon the beauty of noble conduct and of learning and all that order who have never cared for such things, nor may those tell of the splendour of virtue who have never known the face of Justice and of Moral-Wisdom beautiful beyond the beauty of Evening and of Dawn.

Such vision is for those only who see with the Soul's sight—and at the vision, they will rejoice, and awe will fall upon them and a trouble deeper than all the rest could ever stir, for now they are moving in the realm of Truth.   *Truth*

This is the spirit that Beauty must ever induce, wonderment and a delicious trouble, longing and love and a trembling that is all delight. For the unseen all this may be felt as for the seen; and this the Souls feel for it, every soul in some degree, but those the more deeply that are the more truly apt to this higher love—just as all take delight in the beauty of the body but all are not stung as sharply, and those only that feel the keener wound are known as Lovers.

5. These Lovers, then, lovers of the beauty outside of sense, must be made to declare themselves.

as in plato's symposium — higher love

What do you feel in presence of the grace you discern in actions, in manners, in sound morality, in all the works and fruits of virtue, in the beauty of souls? When you see that you yourselves are beautiful within, what do you feel? What is this Dionysiac exultation that thrills through your being, this training upwards of all your Soul, this longing to break away from the body and live sunken within the veritable self?

These are no other than the emotions of Souls under the spell of love.

But what is it that awakens all this passion? No shape, no colour, no grandeur of mass: all is for a Soul, something whose beauty rests upon no colour, for the moral wisdom the Soul enshrines and all the other hueless splendour of the virtues. It is that you find in yourself, or admire in another, loftiness of spirit; righteousness of life; disciplined purity; courage of the majestic face; gravity; modesty that goes fearless and tranquil and passionless; and, shining down upon all, the light of godlike Intellection.

All these noble qualities are to be reverenced and loved, no doubt, but what entitles them to be called beautiful? They exist: they manifest themselves to us: anyone that sees them must admit that they have reality of Being; and is not Real-Being, really beautiful?

But we have not yet shown by what property in them they have wrought the Soul to loveliness: what is this grace, this splendour as of Light, resting upon all the virtues?

Let us take the contrary, the ugliness of the Soul, and set that against its beauty: to understand, at once, what this ugliness is and how it comes to appear in the Soul will certainly open our way before us.

Let us then suppose an ugly Soul, dissolute, unrighteous: teeming with all the lusts; torn by internal discord; beset by the fears of its cowardice and the envies of its pettiness; thinking, in the little thought it has, only of the perishable and the base; perverse in all its impulses; the friend of unclean pleasures; living the life of aban-

donment to bodily sensation and delighting in its deformity.

What must we think but that all this shame is something that has gathered about the Soul, some foreign bane outraging it, soiling it, so that, encumbered with all manner of turpitude, it has no longer a clean activity or a clean sensation, but commands only a life smouldering dully under the crust of evil; that, sunk in manifold death, it no longer sees what a Soul should see, may no longer rest in its own being, dragged ever as it is toward the outer, the lower, the dark?

An unclean thing, I dare to say; flickering hither and thither at the call of objects of sense, deeply infected with the taint of body, occupied always in Matter, and absorbing Matter into itself; in its commerce with the Ignoble it has trafficked away for an alien nature its own essential Idea.

If a man has been immersed in filth or daubed with mud his native comeliness disappears and all that is seen is the foul stuff besmearing him: his ugly condition is due to alien matter that has encrusted him, and if he is to win back his grace it must be his business to scour and purify himself and make himself what he was.

So, we may justly say, a Soul becomes ugly—by something foisted upon it, by sinking itself into the alien, by a fall, a descent into body, into Matter. The dishonour of the Soul is in its ceasing to be clean and apart. Gold is degraded when it is mixed with earthy particles; if these be worked out, the gold is left and is beautiful, isolated from all that is foreign, gold with gold alone. And so the Soul; let it be but cleared of the desires that come by its too intimate converse with the body, emancipated from all the passions, purged of all that embodiment has thrust upon it, withdrawn, a solitary, to itself again—in that moment the ugliness that came only from the alien is stripped away.

6. For, as the ancient teaching was, moral-

discipline and courage and every virtue, not even excepting Wisdom itself, all is purification.

Hence the Mysteries with good reason adumbrate the immersion of the unpurified in filth, even in the Nether-World, since the unclean loves filth for its very filthiness, and swine foul of body find their joy in foulness.

What else is Sophrosyny, rightly so-called, but to take no part in the pleasures of the body, to break away from them as unclean and unworthy of the clean? So, too, Courage is but being fearless of the death which is but the parting of the Soul from the body, an event which no one can dread whose delight is to be his unmingled self. And Magnanimity is but disregard for the lure of things here. And Wisdom is but the Act of the Intellectual-Principle withdrawn from the lower places and leading the Soul to the Above.

The Soul thus cleansed is all Idea and Reason, wholly free of body, intellective, entirely of that divine order from which the wellspring of Beauty rises and all the race of Beauty.

Hence the Soul heightened to the Intellectual-Principle is beautiful to all its power. For Intellection and all that proceeds from Intellection are the Soul's beauty, a graciousness native to it and not foreign, for only with these is it truly Soul. And it is just to say that in the Soul's becoming a good and beautiful thing is its becoming like to God, for from the Divine comes all the Beauty and all the Good in beings.

We may even say that Beauty *is* the Authentic-Existent and Ugliness is the Principle contrary to Existence: and the Ugly is also the primal evil; therefore its contrary is at once good and beautiful, or is Good and Beauty: and hence the one method will discover to us the Beauty-Good and the Ugliness-Evil.

And Beauty, this Beauty which is also The Good, must be posed as The First: directly deriving from this First is the Intellectual-Principle which is pre-eminently the manifestation of Beauty; through the Intellectual-Principle Soul is beautiful. The beauty in things of a lower order—actions and pursuits for instance—comes by operation of the shaping Soul which is also the author of the beauty found in the world of sense. For the Soul, a divine thing, a fragment as it were of the Primal Beauty, makes beautiful to the fulness of their capacity all things whatsoever that it grasps and moulds.

7. Therefore we must ascend again towards the Good, the desired of every Soul. Anyone that has seen This, knows what I intend when I say that it is beautiful. Even the desire of it is to be desired as a Good. To attain it is for those that will take the upward path, who will set all their forces towards it, who will divest themselves of all that we have put on in our descent:—so, to those that approach the Holy Celebrations of the Mysteries, there are appointed purifications and the laying aside of the garments worn before, and the entry in nakedness—until, passing, on the upward way, all that is other than the God, each in the solitude of himself shall behold that solitary-dwelling Existence, the Apart, the Unmingled, the Pure, that from Which all things depend, for Which all look and live and act and know, the Source of Life and of Intellection and of Being.

And one that shall know this vision—with what passion of love shall he not be seized, with what pang of desire, what longing to be molten into one with This, what wondering delight! If he that has never seen this Being must hunger for It as for all his welfare, he that has known must love and reverence It as the very Beauty; he will be flooded with awe and gladness, stricken by a salutary terror; he loves with a veritable love, with sharp desire; all other loves than this he must despise, and disdain all that once seemed fair.

This, indeed, is the mood even of those who, having witnessed the manifestation of

Gods or Supernals, can never again feel the old delight in the comeliness of material forms: what then are we to think of one that contemplates Absolute Beauty in Its essential integrity, no accumulation of flesh and matter, no dweller on earth or in the heavens—so perfect Its purity—far above all such things in that they are non-essential, composite, not primal but descending from This?

Beholding this Being—the Choragos of all Existence, the Self-Intent that ever gives forth and never takes—resting, rapt, in the vision and possession of so lofty a loveliness, growing to Its likeness, what Beauty can the soul yet lack? For This, the Beauty supreme, the absolute, and the primal, fashions Its lovers to Beauty and makes them also worthy of love.

And for This, the sternest and the uttermost combat is set before the Souls; all our labour is for This, lest we be left without part in this noblest vision, which to attain is to be blessed in the blissful sight, which to fail of is to fail utterly.

For not he that has failed of the joy that is in colour or in visible forms, not he that has failed of power or of honours or of kingdom has failed, but only he that has failed of only This, for Whose winning he should renounce kingdoms and command over earth and ocean and sky, if only, spurning the world of sense from beneath his feet, and straining to This, he may see.

how lies the path?

8. But what must we do? How lies the path? How come to vision of the inaccessible Beauty, dwelling as if in consecrated precincts, apart from the common ways where all may see, even the profane?

He that has the strength, let him arise and withdraw into himself, foregoing all that is known by the eyes, turning away for ever from the material beauty that once made his joy. When he perceives those shapes of grace that show in body, let him not pursue: he must know them for copies, vestiges, shadows, and hasten away towards

That they tell of. For if anyone follow what is like a beautiful shape playing over water —is there not a myth telling in symbol of such a dupe, how he sank into the depths of the current and was swept away to nothingness? So too, one that is held by material beauty and will not break free shall be precipitated, not in body but in Soul, down to the dark depths loathed of the Intellective-Being, where, blind even in the Lower-World, he shall have commerce only with shadows, there as here.

"Let us flee then to the beloved Fatherland": this is the soundest counsel. But what is this flight? How are we to gain the open sea? For Odysseus is surely a parable to us when he commands the flight from the sorceries of Circe or Calypso—not content to linger for all the pleasure offered to his eyes and all the delight of sense filling his days.

The Fatherland to us is There whence we have come, and There is The Father.

What then is our course, what the manner of our flight? This is not a journey for the feet; the feet bring us only from land to land; nor need you think of coach or ship to carry you away; all this order of things you must set aside and refuse to see: you must close the eyes and call instead upon another vision which is to be waked within you, a vision, the birth-right of all, which few turn to use.

9. And this inner vision, what is its operation?

Newly awakened it is all too feeble to bear the ultimate splendour. Therefore the Soul must be trained—to the habit of remarking, first, all noble pursuits, then the works of beauty produced not by the labour of the arts but by the virtue of men known for their goodness: lastly, you must search the souls of those that have shaped these beautiful forms.

But how are you to see into a virtuous soul and know its loveliness?

Withdraw into yourself and look. And if

you do not find yourself beautiful yet, act as does the creator of a statue that is to be made beautiful: he cuts away here, he smooths there, he makes this line lighter, this other purer, until a lovely face has grown upon his work. So do you also: cut away all that is excessive, straighten all that is crooked, bring light to all that is overcast, labour to make all one glow of beauty and never cease chiselling your statue, until there shall shine out on you from it the godlike splendour of virtue, until you shall see the perfect goodness surely established in the stainless shrine.

When you know that you have become this perfect work, when you are self-gathered in the purity of your being, nothing now remaining that can shatter that inner unity, nothing from without clinging to the authentic man, when you find yourself wholly true to your essential nature, wholly that only veritable Light which is not measured by space, not narrowed to any circumscribed form nor again diffused as a thing void of term, but ever unmeasurable as something greater than all measure and more than all quantity—when you perceive that you have grown to this, you are now become very vision: now call up all your confidence, strike forward yet a step—you need a guide no longer—strain, and see.

This is the only eye that sees the mighty Beauty. If the eye that adventures the vision be dimmed by vice, impure, or weak, and unable in its cowardly blenching to see the uttermost brightness, then it sees nothing even though another point to what lies plain to sight before it. To any vision must be brought an eye adapted to what is to be seen, and having some likeness to it. Never did eye see the sun unless it had first become sunlike, and never can the soul have vision of the First Beauty unless itself be beautiful.

Therefore, first let each become godlike and each beautiful who cares to see God and Beauty. So, mounting, the Soul will come first to the Intellectual-Principle and survey all the beautiful Ideas in the Supreme and will avow that this is Beauty, that the Ideas are Beauty. For by their efficacy comes all Beauty else, by the offspring and essence of the Intellectual-Being. What is beyond the Intellectual-Principle we affirm to be the nature of Good radiating Beauty before it. So that, treating the Intellectual-Kosmos as one, the first is the Beautiful: if we make distinction there, the Realm of Ideas constitutes the Beauty of the Intellectual Sphere; and The Good, which lies beyond, is the Fountain at once and Principle of Beauty: the Primal Good and the Primal Beauty have the one dwelling-place and, thus, always, Beauty's seat is There.

— a flight from the alone to the alone.

5TH ENNEAD, 8TH TRACTATE: *On the Intellectual Beauty*

1. It is a principle with us that one who has attained to the vision of the Intellectual Beauty and grasped the beauty of the Authentic Intellect will be able also to come to understanding the Father and Transcendent of that Divine Being. It concerns us, then, to try to see and say, for ourselves and as far as such matters may be told, how the Beauty of the divine Intellect and of the Intellectual Cosmos may be revealed to contemplation.

Let us go to the realm of magnitudes:— Suppose two blocks of stone lying side by side: one is unpatterned, quite untouched by art; the other has been minutely wrought by the craftsman's hands into some statue of god or man, a Grace or a Muse, or if a human being, not a portrait but a creation in which the sculptor's art has concentrated all loveliness.

Now it must be seen that the stone thus brought under the artist's hand to the beauty of form is beautiful not as stone—for so the crude block would be as pleasant— but in virtue of the form or idea introduced by the art. This form is not in the material; it is in the designer before ever it enters the stone; and the artificer holds it not by his equipment of eyes and hands but by his participation in his art. The beauty, therefore, exists in a far higher state in the art; for it does not come over integrally into the work; that original beauty is not transferred; what comes over is a derivative and a minor: and even that shows itself upon the statue not integrally and with entire realisation of intention but only so far as it has subdued the resistance of the material.

Art, then, creating in the image of its own nature and content, and working by the Idea or Reason-Principle of the beautiful object it is to produce, must itself be beautiful in a far higher and purer degree since it is the seat and source of that beauty, indwelling in the art, which must naturally be more complete than any comeliness of the external. In the degree in which the beauty is diffused by entering into matter, it is so much the weaker than that concentrated in unity; everything that reaches outwards is the less for it, strength less strong, heat less hot, every power less potent, and so beauty less beautiful.

Then again every prime cause must be, within itself, more powerful than its effect can be: the musical does not derive from an unmusical source but from music; and so the art exhibited in the material work derives from an art yet higher.

Still the arts are not to be slighted on the ground that they create by imitation of natural objects; for, to begin with, these natural objects are themselves imitations; then, we must recognise that they give no bare reproduction of the thing seen but go back to the Ideas from which Nature itself derives, and, furthermore, that much of their work is all their own; they are holders of beauty and add where nature is lacking. Thus Pheidias wrought the Zeus upon no model among things of sense but by apprehending what form Zeus must take if he chose to become manifest to sight.

2. But let us leave the arts and consider those works produced by Nature and admitted to be naturally beautiful which the creations of art are charged with imitating, all reasoning life and unreasoning things alike, but especially the consummate among them, where the moulder and maker has subdued the material and given the form he desired. Now what is the beauty here? It has nothing to do with the blood or the menstrual process: either there is also a colour and form apart from all this or there is nothing unless sheer ugliness or (at best) a bare recipient, as it were the mere Matter of beauty.

Whence shone forth the beauty of Helen, battle-sought; or of all those women like in loveliness to Aphrodite; or of Aphrodite herself; or of any human being that has been perfect in beauty; or of any of those gods manifest to sight, or unseen but carrying what would be beauty if we saw?

In all these is it not the Idea, something of that realm but communicated to the producer just as in works of art, we held, it is communicated from the arts to their creations? Now we can surely not believe that, while the made thing and the Idea thus impressed upon Matter are beautiful, yet the Idea not so alloyed but resting still with the creator—the Idea primal, immaterial, firmly a unity—is not Beauty.

If material extension were in itself the ground of beauty, then the creating principle, being without extension could not be beautiful: but beauty cannot be made to depend upon magnitude since, whether in a large object or a small, the one Idea equally moves and forms the mind by its inherent power. A further indication is that as long as the object remains outside us we know nothing of it; it affects us by entry; but only as an Idea can it enter through the eyes which are not of scope to take an extended mass: we are, no doubt, simultaneously possessed of the magnitude which, however, we take in not as mass but by an elaboration upon the presented form.

Then again the principle producing the

beauty must be, itself, ugly, neutral or beautiful: ugly, it could not produce the opposite; neutral, why should its product be the one rather than the other? The Nature, then, which creates things so lovely must be itself of a far earlier beauty; we, undisciplined in discernment of the inward, knowing nothing of it, run after the outer, never understanding that it is the inner which stirs us; we are in the case of one who sees his own reflection but not realising whence it comes goes in pursuit of it.

But that the thing we are pursuing is something different and that the beauty is not in the concrete object is manifest from the beauty there is in matters of study, in conduct and custom; briefly in soul or mind. And it is precisely here that the greater beauty lies, perceived whenever you look to the wisdom in a man and delight in it, not wasting attention on the face, which may be hideous, but passing all appearance by and catching only at the inner comeliness, the truly personal; if you are still unmoved and cannot acknowledge beauty under such conditions, then looking to your own inner being you will find no beauty to delight you and it will be futile in that state to seek the greater vision, for you will be questing it through the ugly and impure.

This is why such matters are not spoken of to everyone; you, if you are conscious of beauty within, remember.

3. Thus there is in the Nature-Principle itself an Ideal archetype of the beauty that is found in material forms and, of that archetype again, the still more beautiful archetype in Soul, source of that in Nature. In the proficient soul this is brighter and of more advanced loveliness: adorning the soul and bringing to it a light from that greater light which is beauty primally, its immediate presence sets the soul reflecting upon that quality of this prior, the archetype which has no such entries, and is present nowhere but remains in itself alone, and thus is not even to be called a Reason-Principle but is the creative source of the very first Reason-Principle which is the Beauty to which Soul serves as Matter.

This prior, then, is the Intellectual-Principle, the veritable, abiding and not fluctuant since not taking intellectual quality from outside itself. By what image thus, can we represent it? We have nowhere to go but to what is less. Only from itself can we take an image of it; that is, there can be no representation of it, except in the sense that we represent gold by some portion of gold—purified, either actually or mentally, if it be impure—insisting at the same time that this is not the total thing gold, but merely the particular gold of a particular parcel. In the same way we learn in this matter from the purified Intellect in ourselves or, if you like, from the Gods and the glory of the Intellect in them.

For assuredly all the gods are august and beautiful in a beauty beyond our speech. And what makes them so? Intellect; and especially Intellect operating within them (the divine sun and stars) to visibility. It is not through the loveliness of their corporeal forms: even those that have body are not gods by that beauty; it is in virtue of Intellect that they too, are gods, and as gods beautiful. They do not veer between wisdom and folly: in the immunity of intellect unmoving and pure, they are wise always, all-knowing, taking cognisance not of the human but of their own being and of all that lies within the contemplation of Intellect. Those of them whose dwelling is in the heavens, are ever in this meditation—what task prevents them?—and from afar they look, too, into that further heaven by a lifting of the head. The Gods belonging to that higher Heaven itself, they whose station is upon it and in it, see and know in virtue of their omnipresence to it. For all There is heaven; earth is heaven, and sea heaven; and animal and plant and man; all is the heavenly content of that heaven: and the Gods in it, despising neither men nor anything else that is there where all is of the heavenly order, traverse all that country and all space in peace.

4. To "live at ease" is There; and to these divine beings verity is mother and nurse, existence and sustenance; all that is not of process but of authentic being they see, and themselves in all: for all is transparent, nothing dark, nothing resistant; every being is lucid to every other, in breadth and depth; light runs through light. And each of them contains all within itself, and at the same time sees all in every other, so that everywhere there is all, and all is all and each all, and infinite the glory. Each of them is great; the small is great; the sun, There, is all the stars; and every star, again, is all the stars and sun. While some one manner of being is dominant in each, all are mirrored in every other.

Movement There is pure (as self-caused) for the moving principle is not a separate thing to complicate it as it speeds.

So, too, Repose is not troubled, for there is no admixture of the unstable; and the Beauty is all beauty since it is not merely resident (as an attribute or addition) in some beautiful object. Each There walks upon no alien soil; its place is its essential self; and, as each moves, so to speak, towards what is Above, it is attended by the very ground from which it starts: there is no distinguishing between the Being and the Place; all is Intellect, the Principle and the ground on which it stands, alike. Thus we might think that our visible sky (the ground or place of the stars), lit, as it is, produces the light which reaches us from it, though of course this is really produced by the stars (as it were, by the Principles of light alone, not also by the ground as the analogy would require).

In our realm all is part rising from part and nothing can be more than partial; but There each being is an eternal product of a whole and is at once a whole and an individual manifesting as part but, to the keen

vision There, known for the whole it is.

The myth of Lynceus seeing into the very deeps of the earth tells us of those eyes in the divine. No weariness overtakes this vision which yet brings no such satiety as would call for its ending; for there never was a void to be filled so that, with the fulness and the attainment of purpose, the sense of sufficiency be induced: nor is there any such incongruity within the divine that one Being there could be repulsive to another: and of course all There are unchangeable. This absence of satisfaction means only a satisfaction leading to no distaste for that which produces it; to see is to look the more, since for them to continue in the contemplation of an infinite self and of infinite objects is but to acquiesce in bidding of their nature.

Life, pure, is never a burden; how then could there be weariness There where the living is most noble? That very life is wisdom, not a wisdom built up by reasoning but complete from the beginning, suffering no lack which could set in enquiring, a wisdom primal, unborrowed, not something added to the Being, but its very essence. No wisdom, thus, is greater; this is the authentic knowing, assessor to the divine Intellect as projected into manifestation simultaneously with it; thus, in the symbolic saying, Justice is assessor to Zeus.

[Perfect wisdom] for all the Principles of this order, dwelling There, are as it were visible images projected from themselves, so that all becomes an object of contemplation to contemplators immeasurably blessed. The greatness and power of the wisdom There we may know from this, that it embraces all the real Beings, and has made all and all follow it, and yet that it is itself those beings, which sprang into being with it, so that all is one and the essence There is wisdom. If we have failed to understand, it is that we have thought of knowledge as a mass of theorems and an accumulation of propositions, though that is false even for our sciences of the sense-realm. But in case this should be questioned, we may leave our own sciences for the present, and deal with the knowing in the Supreme at which Plato glances where he speaks of "that knowledge which is not a stranger in something strange to it"—though in what sense, he leaves us to examine and declare, if we boast ourselves worthy of the discussion. This is probably our best starting point.

5. All that comes to be, work of nature or of craft, some wisdom has made: everywhere a wisdom presides at a making.

No doubt the wisdom of the artist may be the guide of the work; it is sufficient explanation of the wisdom exhibited in the arts; but the artist himself goes back, after all, to that wisdom in Nature which is embodied in himself; and this is not a wisdom built up of theorems but one totality, not a wisdom consisting of manifold detail co-ordinated into a unity but rather a unity working out into detail.

Now, if we could think of this as the primal wisdom, we need look no further, since, at that, we have discovered a principle which is neither a derivative nor a "stranger in something strange to it." But if we are told that, while this Reason-Principle is in Nature, yet Nature itself is its source, we ask how Nature came to possess it; and, if Nature derived it from some other source, we ask what that other source may be; if, on the contrary, the principle is self-sprung, we need look no further: but if (as we assume) we are referred to the Intellectual-Principle we must make clear whether the Intellectual-Principle engendered the wisdom: if we learn that it did, we ask whence: if from itself, then inevitably, it is itself Wisdom.

The true Wisdom, then (found to be identical with the Intellectual-Principle) is Real Being; and Real Being is Wisdom; it is wisdom that gives value to Real Being; and Being is Real in virtue of its origin in wisdom. It follows that all forms of existence not possessing wisdom are, indeed, Beings in right of the wisdom which went to their forming, but, as not in themselves possessing it, are not Real Beings.

We cannot therefore think that the divine Beings of that sphere, or the other supremely blessed There, need look to our apparatus of science: all of that realm (the very Beings themselves), all is noble image, such images as we may conceive to lie within the soul of the wise—but There not as inscription but as authentic existence. The ancients had this in mind when they declared the Ideas to be Beings, Essentials.

6. Similarly, as it seems to me, the wise of Egypt—whether in precise knowledge or by a prompting of nature—indicated the truth where, in their effort towards philosophical statement, they left aside the writing forms that take in the detail of words and sentences—those characters that represent sounds and convey the propositions of reasoning—and drew pictures instead, engraving in the temple-inscriptions a separate image for every separate item: thus they exhibited the mode in which the Supreme goes forth.

For each manifestation of knowledge and wisdom is a distinct image, an object in itself, an immediate unity, not an aggregate of discursive reasoning and detailed willing. Later from this wisdom in unity there appears, in another form of being, an image, already less compact, which announces the original in an outward stage and seeks the causes by which things are such that the wonder rises how a generated world can be so excellent.

For, one who knows must declare his wonder that this Wisdom, while not itself containing the causes by which Being exists and takes such excellence, yet imparts them to the entities produced in Being's realm. This excellence, whose necessity is scarcely or not at all manifest to search, exists, if we could but find it out, before all searching and reasoning.

What I say may be considered in one chief thing, and thence applied to all the particular entities:—

7. Consider the universe: we are agreed that its existence and its nature come to it from beyond itself; are we, now, to imagine that its maker first thought it out in detail —the earth, and its necessary situation in the middle; water and, again, its position as lying upon the earth; all the other elements and objects up to the sky in due place and order; living beings with their appropriate forms as we know them, their inner organs and their outer limbs—and that having thus appointed every item beforehand, he then set about the execution?

Such designing was not even possible; how could the plan for a universe come to one that had never looked outward? Nor could he work on material gathered from elsewhere as our craftsmen do, using hands and tools; feet and hands are of the later order.

One way, only, remains: all things must exist in something else; of that prior—since there is no obstacle, all being continuous within the realm of reality—there has suddenly appeared a sign, an image, whether given forth directly or through the ministry of soul or of some phase of soul, matters nothing for the moment: thus the entire aggregate of existence springs from the divine world, in greater beauty There because There unmingled but mingled here.

From the beginning to end all is gripped by the Forms of the Intellectual-Realm: Matter itself is held by the Ideas of the elements and to these Ideas are added other Ideas and others again, so that it is hard to work down to crude Matter beneath all that sheathing of Idea. Indeed since Matter itself is, in its degree, an Idea—the lowest— all this universe is Idea and there is nothing that is not Idea as the archetype was. And all is made silently, since nothing had part in the making but Being and Idea—a further reason why creation went without toil. The Exemplar was the Idea of an All and so an All must come into being.

Thus nothing stood in the way of the Idea, and even now it dominates, despite all the clash of things: the creation is not hindered on its way even now; it stands firm in virtue of being All. To me, moreover, it seems that if we ourselves were archetypes, Ideas, veritable Being, and the Idea with which we construct here were our veritable Essence, then our creative power too would toillessly effect its purpose: as man now stands, he does not produce in his work a true image of himself: become man, he has ceased to be the All; ceasing to be man—we read—"he soars aloft and administers the Cosmos entire"; restored to the All he is maker of the All.

But—to our immediate purpose—it is possible to give a reason why the earth is set in the midst and why it is round and why the ecliptic runs precisely as it does, but, looking to the creative principle, we cannot say that because this was the way therefore things were so planned: we can say only that because the All is what it is, therefore there is a total of good; the causing principle, we might put it, reached the conclusion before all formal reasoning and not from any premises, not by sequence or plan but before either, since all of that order is later, all reason, demonstration, persuasion.

Since there is a Source, all the created must spring from it and in accordance with it; and we are rightly told not to go seeking the causes impelling a Source to produce, especially when this is the perfectly sufficient Source and identical with the Term: a Source which is Source and Term must be the All-Unity, complete in itself.

8. This then is Beauty primally: it is entire and omnipresent as an entirety; and therefore in none of its parts or members lacking in beauty; beautiful thus beyond denial. Certainly it cannot be anything (be,

for example, Beauty) without being wholly that thing; it can be nothing which it is to possess partially or in which it utterly fails (and therefore it must entirely be Beauty entire).

If this principle were not beautiful, what other could be? Its prior does not deign to be beautiful; that which is the first to manifest itself—Form an object of vision to the intellect—cannot but be lovely to see. It is to indicate this that Plato, drawing on something well within our observation, represents the Creator as approving the work he has achieved: the intention is to make us feel the lovable beauty of the autotype and of the Divine Idea; for to admire a representation is to admire the original upon which it was made.

It is not surprising if we fail to recognise what is passing within us: lovers, and those in general that admire beauty here, do not stay to reflect that it is to be traced, as of course it must be, to the Beauty There. That the admiration of the Demiurge is to be referred to the Ideal Exemplar is deliberately made evident by the rest of the passage: "He admired; and determined to bring the work into still closer likeness with the Exemplar": he makes us feel that magnificent beauty of the Exemplar by telling us that the Beauty sprung from this world is, itself, a copy from That.

And indeed if the divine did not exist, the transcendently beautiful, in a beauty beyond all thought, what could be lovelier than the things we see? Certainly no reproach can rightly be brought against this world save only that it is not That.

9. Let us, then, make a mental picture of our universe: each member shall remain what it is, distinctly apart; yet all is to form, as far as possible, a complete unity so that whatever comes into view shall show as if it were the surface of the orb over all, bringing immediately with it the vision, on the one plane, of the sun and of all the stars with earth and sea and all living things as

if exhibited upon a transparent globe.

Bring this vision actually before your sight, so that there shall be in your mind the gleaming representation of a sphere, a picture holding all the things of the universe moving or in repose or (as in reality) some at rest, some in motion. Keep this sphere before you, and from it imagine another, a sphere stripped of magnitude and of spatial differences; cast out your inborn sense of Matter, taking care not merely to attenuate it: call on God, maker of the sphere whose image you now hold, and pray Him to enter. And may He come bringing His own Universe with all the Gods that dwell in it—He who is the one God and all the gods, where each is all, blending into a unity, distinct in powers but all one God in virtue of that one divine power of many facets.

More truly, this is the one God who is all the gods; for, in the coming to be of all those, this, the one, has suffered no diminishing. He and all have one existence, while each again is distinct. It is distinction by state without interval: there is no outward form to set one here and another there and to prevent any from being an entire identity; yet there is no sharing of parts from one to another. Nor is each of those divine wholes a power in fragment, a power totalling to the sum of the measurable segments: the divine is one all-power, reaching out to infinity, powerful to infinity: and so great is God that his very members are infinities. What place can be named to which He does not reach?

Great, too, is this firmament of ours and all the powers constellated within it, but it would be greater still, unspeakably, but that there is inbound in it something of the petty power of body; no doubt the powers of fire and other bodily substances might themselves be thought very great, but in fact, it is through their failure in the true power that we see them burning, destroying, wearing things away, and slaving towards the production of life; they destroy because they are themselves in process of destruction, and they produce because they belong to the realm of the produced.

The power in that other world has merely Being and Beauty of Being. Beauty without Being could not be, nor Being voided of Beauty: abandoned of Beauty, Being loses something of its essence. Being is desirable because it is identical with Beauty; and Beauty is loved because it is Being. How then can we debate which is the cause of the other, where the nature is one? The very figment of Being needs some imposed image of Beauty to make it passable, and even to ensure its existence; it exists to the degree in which it has taken some share in the beauty of Idea; and the more deeply it has drawn on this, the less imperfect it is, precisely because the nature which is essentially the beautiful has entered into it the more intimately.

10. This is why Zeus, although the oldest of the gods and their sovereign, advances first (in the Phaidros myth) towards that vision, followed by gods and demigods and such souls as are of strength to see. That Being appears before them from some unseen place and rising loftily over them pours its light upon all things, so that all gleams in its radiance; it upholds some beings, and they see; the lower are dazzled and turn away, unfit to gaze upon that sun, the trouble falling the more heavily on those most remote.

Of those looking upon that Being and its content, and able to see, all take something but not all the same vision always: intently gazing, one sees the fount and principle of Justice, another is filled with the sight of Moral Wisdom, the original of that quality as found, sometimes at least, among men, copied by them in their degree from the divine virtue which, covering all the expanse, so to speak, of the Intellectual Realm is seen, last attainment of all, by

those who have known already many splendid visions.

The gods see, each singly and all as one. So, too, the souls; they see all There in right of being sprung, themselves, of that universe and therefore including all from beginning to end and having their existence There if only by that phase which belongs inherently to the Divine, though often too they are There entire, those of them that have not incurred separation.

This vision Zeus takes and it is for such of us, also, as share his love and appropriate our part in the Beauty There, the final object of all seeing, the entire beauty upon all things; for all There sheds radiance, and floods those that have found their way thither so that they too become beautiful; thus it will often happen that men climbing heights where the soil has taken a yellow glow will themselves appear so, borrowing colour from the place on which they move. The colour flowering on that other height we speak of is Beauty; or rather all There is light and beauty, through and through, for the beauty is no mere bloom upon the surface.

To those that do not see entire, the immediate impression is alone taken into account; but those drunken with this wine, filled with the nectar, all their soul penetrated by this beauty, cannot remain mere gazers: no longer is there a spectator outside gazing on an outside spectacle; the clear-eyed hold the vision within themselves, though for the most part, they have no idea that it is within but look towards it as to something beyond them and see it as an object of vision caught by a direction of the will.

All that one sees as a spectacle is still external; one must bring the vision within and see no longer in that mode of separation but as we know ourselves; thus a man filled with a god—possessed by Apollo or by one of the Muses—need no longer look outside for his vision of the divine being; it is but finding the strength to see divinity within.

11. Similarly any one, unable to see himself, but possessed by that God, has but to bring that divine-within before his consciousness and at once he sees an image of himself, himself lifted to a better beauty: now let him ignore that image, lovely though it is, and sink into a perfect self-identity, no such separation remaining; at once he forms a multiple unity with the God silently present; in the degree of his power and will, the two become one; should he turn back to the former duality, still he is pure and remains very near to the God; he has but to look again and the same presence is there.

This conversion brings gain: at the first stage, that of separation, a man is aware of self; but retreating inwards, he becomes possessor of all; he puts sense away behind him in dread of the separated life and becomes one in the Divine; if he plans to see in separation, he sets himself outside.

The novice must hold himself constantly under some image of the Divine Being and seek in the light of a clear conception; knowing thus, in a deep conviction, whither he is going—into what a sublimity he penetrates—he must give himself forthwith to the inner and, radiant with the Divine Intellections (with which he is now one), be no longer the seer, but, as that place has made him, the seen.

Still, we will be told, one cannot be in beauty and yet fail to see it. The very contrary: to see the divine as something external is to be outside of it; to become it is to be more truly in beauty: since sight deals with the external, there can here be no vision unless in the sense of identification with the object.

And this identification amounts to a self-knowing, a self-consciousness, guarded by the fear of losing the self in the desire of a too wide awareness.

It must be remembered that sensations of the ugly and evil impress us more violently than those of what is agreeable and yet leave less knowledge as the residue of the shock: sickness makes the rougher mark, but health, tranquilly present, explains itself better; it takes the first place, it is the natural thing, it belongs to our being; illness is alien, unnatural and thus makes itself felt by its very incongruity, while the other conditions are native and we take no notice. Such being our nature, we are most completely identified with the object of our knowledge.

This is why in that other sphere, when we are deepest in that knowledge by intellection, we are aware of none; we are expecting some impression on sense, which has nothing to report since it has seen nothing and never could in that order see anything. The unbelieving element is sense; it is the other, the Intellectual-Principle, that sees; and if this too is doubted, it could not even credit its own existence, for it can never stand away and with bodily eyes apprehend itself as a visible object.

12. We have told how this vision is to be procured, whether by the mode of separation or in identity; now, seen in either way, what does it give to report?

The vision has been of God in travail of a beautiful offspring, God engendering a universe within himself in a painless labour and—rejoiced in what he has brought into being, proud of his children—keeping all closely by Him, for the pleasure He has in his radiance and in theirs.

Of this offspring—all beautiful, but most beautiful those that have remained within —only one has become manifest without; from him (Zeus, sovereign over the visible universe) the youngest born, we may gather, as from some image, the greatness of the Father and of the Brothers that remain within the Father's house.

Still the manifested God cannot think

that he has come forth in vain from the father; for through him another universe has arisen, beautiful as the image of beauty, and it could not be lawful that Beauty and Being should fail of a beautiful image.

This second Cosmos at every point copies the archetype: it has life and being in copy, and has beauty as springing from that diviner world. In its character of images it holds, too, that divine perpetuity without which it would only at times be truly representative and sometimes fail like a construction of art; for every image whose existence lies in the nature of things must stand during the entire existence of the archetype.

Hence it is false to put an end to the visible sphere as long as the Intellectual endures, or to found it upon a decision taken by its maker at some given moment.

That teaching shirks the penetration of such a making as is here involved: it fails to see that as long as the Supreme is radiant there can be no failing of its sequel but, that existing, all exists. And—since the necessity of conveying our meaning compels such terms—the Supreme has existed for ever and for ever will exist.

13. The God fettered (as in the Kronos Myth) to an unchanging identity leaves the ordering of this universe to his son (to Zeus), for it could not be in his character to neglect his rule within the divine sphere, and, as though sated with the Authentic-Beauty, seek a lordship too recent and too poor for his might. Ignoring this lower world, Kronos (Intellectual-Principle)

claims for his own father (Ouranos, the Absolute, or One) with all the upward tending between them: and he counts all that tends to the inferior, beginning from his son (Zeus the All-Soul), as ranking beneath him. Thus he holds a mid position determined on the one side by the differentiation implied in the severance from the very highest and, on the other, by that which keeps him apart from the link between himself and the lower: he stands between a greater father and an inferior son. But since that father is too lofty to be thought of under the name of Beauty, the second God remains the primally beautiful.

Soul also has beauty, but is less beautiful than Intellect as being its image and therefore, though beautiful in nature, taking increase of beauty by looking to that original. Since then the All-Soul—to use the more familiar term—since Aphrodite herself is so beautiful, what name can we give to that other? If Soul is so lovely in its own right, of what quality must that prior be? And since its being is derived, what must that power be from which the Soul takes the double beauty, the borrowed and the inherent?

We ourselves possess beauty when we are true to our own being; our ugliness is in going over to another order; our self-knowledge, that is to say, is our beauty; in self-ignorance we are ugly.

Thus beauty is of the Divine and comes Thence only.

Do these considerations suffice to a clear understanding of the Intellectual Sphere or must we make yet another attempt by another road?

＞＞＞＞＞＜＜＜＜＜

From *The Soliloquies*

After all our inquiry I see that nothing remains that we may justly term false except that which feigns itself to be what it is not, or pretends to be when it does not exist. The former kind is either fallacious or mendacious. Fallacious, strictly speaking, is that which has a certain desire to deceive and this cannot be understood apart from the soul. But deceit is practised partly by reason and partly by nature; by reason in rational beings like men, by nature in beasts like foxes. What I call lying is done by liars. The difference between the fallacious and the mendacious is that the former all wish to deceive while the latter do not all wish to do so. Mimes and comedies and many poems are full of lies, but the aim is to delight rather than to deceive. Nearly all who make jokes lie. But the fallacious person, strictly speaking, is he whose design is to deceive. Those who feign without intent to deceive are mendacious, or at least no one hesitates to call them liars. Have you any objection to urge against this?

17. A.—Please go on. Perhaps you have begun to teach me the truth about falsity. But I am waiting to hear what you have to say about the other kind that pretends it is and is not. R.—What do you expect? I have given you many examples already. Don't you think that your image in a mirror wants to be you but is false because it is not? A.— Yes, I do. R.—And every picture, statue, or similar work of art tries to be that on which it is modelled. A.—I must agree. R.—You will agree that the things which deceive

Quotations from Augustine are all from *Early Writings: Augustine,* edited by J. H. S. Burleigh, Vol. VI, LCC (Philadelphia: The Westminster Press, and London: S.C.M. Press, Ltd., 1953). Reprinted by permission.

dreamers and madmen are in the same class? A.—Yes, these above all. More than anything else these pretend to be what men see when they are awake and sane. And they are false just because they pretend to be what they cannot be. R.—Why need I say more about the apparent movement of towers, or the oar plunged in water, or the shadows of bodies? It is clear, I think, that they all come under this rule. A.—Most clear. R.—I say nothing of the other senses. For no one who considers the matter will fail to discover that in the realm of the senses that is called false which pretends to be something and is not.

x, 18. A.—You are right. But I wonder why you think poems and jests and other fallacious things are to be kept separate from this class. R.—It is one thing to will to be false and another not to be able to be true. We can classify comedies, tragedies, mimes and the like with the works of painters and sculptors. The picture of a man, though it tries to be like him, cannot be a true man any more than a character in the books of the comedians. These things are false not from any will or desire of their own, but from the necessity of following the will of their authors. On the stage, Roscius wants to be a false Hecuba, but by nature he is a true man. By so wanting, he is also a true tragedian, so far as he fulfils the part. But he would be a false Priam if he gave himself out as Priam and was not. But here emerges a strange fact which nobody doubts. A.—What is that? R.—In all such matters truth and falsehood are inevitably intertwined; indeed, if there is to be truth in one respect there must be falsehood in another. How could Roscius be truly a tragic actor if he refused to be a false Hector, Andromache, Hercules or the like?

How could a picture of a horse be truly a picture if the horse were not false? How could there be a man's face in a glass, true as such, though not truly a man? So if a certain kind of falsity is necessary in order that there should be truth, why do we dread falsity and seek truth as a great boon? *A.*—I don't know, unless it is because there is in these examples nothing worthy of our imitation. After all, unlike actors, reflections in mirrors, or Myron's brass cow, we ought not to be both true and false: true in our proper garb but false as dressed up to represent something else. We ought to seek the absolute truth, not that double-faced thing that is partly true and partly false. *R.*—You are asking something great, nay divine. If we find that, we shall agree that we have found Truth itself, from which everything that is called true derives its quality. *A.*—I agree most heartily.

xi, 19. *R.*—Well now, do you think the art of dialectic is true or false? *A.*—Clearly true, and so is the art of literary studies [*grammatica*]. *R.*—Are both equally true? *A.*—I don't see that there can be degrees of truth. *R.*—Yet there may be a truth that has no falsehood in it. You have just said that you objected to things that cannot be true without an element of falsehood in them. You know that literary studies include fables and obvious falsehoods. *A.*—Yes. But the study of literature is not responsible for the falsehood. It demonstrates their nature. A fable is a falsehood composed for use and pleasure; while literary study is the art which guards and controls composition. By its very profession it must handle all the products of human speech, whether transmitted orally or in writing. It does not originate these falsehoods, but gives us scientific knowledge about them. *R.*—Quite right. But I am not concerned at the moment as to whether your definition is correct. I want to know whether this is properly the function of literary studies or of dialectic. *A.*—I do not deny that the power

and skill to define and distinguish, as I did just now, belong to dialectic.

20. *R.*—Literary study is true inasmuch as it is a school discipline. Discipline derives its name from *discere* [to learn]. No one who has learnt and who retains what he has learnt can be said not to know, and no one can know what is false. Therefore, every school discipline is true. *A.*—I see no rashness in accepting that reasoning. I do, however, wonder whether any one will think that the fables are true, for we learn and memorize them. *R.*—Surely our teacher did not want us to believe what he taught us as well as to know it? *A.*—Oh no. What he insisted on was that we should know it. *R.*—He never insisted that we should believe the tale of Daedalus flying? *A.*—Never. But if we did not hold the tale in memory he made our hands unable to hold anything! *R.*—You do agree that there is such a fable and that such is reported of Daedalus? *A.*—Certainly that is true. *R.*—Then you learned a truth when you learned that fable. If on the contrary it were true that Daedalus *had* wings, and boys accepted and repeated it as merely a fictitious fable, their conception of the tale would be false for the very reason that the story they were repeating was true. Here is an example of what astonished us a moment ago. There could not truly be a fable about the flight of Daedalus unless it were false that Daedalus had actually flown in the air. *A.*—Now I understand. But where are we to go from that point? *R.*—We have shown that the reasoning was not false by which we proved that a school discipline can be such only if it teach what is true. *A.*—What has that got to do with our problem? *R.*—Tell me, please, why literature is a school discipline, for that will be the answer to the question why it is true. *A.*—I do not know the answer. *R.*—Don't you think it could not be a discipline if there were no definitions in it, no distinctions and distributions into classes and parts? *A.*—Now I know what

you mean. I cannot imagine a discipline in which there are no definitions, divisions and reasonings, where the nature of each thing is not set forth, where each part does not receive its due attention without confusion, where anything relevant is omitted and anything irrelevant is admitted. All this is the function of a so-called discipline. R.—And because it performs all these functions it is said to be true. A.—I see that follows.

21. R.—Now to what discipline belongs a reasoned account of definitions, divisions and distinctions of parts? A.—As was said before, all that is contained in the rules of dialectic. R.—Therefore, literature as a true discipline is created by the same art as you have just defended against the charge of falsehood.

From *On Free Will*

xvi, 41. *Aug.*—What do we do when we are eager to be wise? Don't we with all possible keenness give our whole soul, so to speak, to what is mentally discerned, and keep it steadfastly fixed on that, so that it may not rejoice in any private possession of its own which will implicate it in transient things, but, having put off all affections for things temporal and spatial, it may apprehend what remains ever one and the same? For as the soul is the whole life of the body, so is God the happy life of the soul. While we do as I have just described, so long as we continue, we are in the way [*in via*]. If it is given us to rejoice in these true and certain blessings as they glimmer for us even now on our still darkly shadowed way, perhaps this is what Scripture means when it describes how wisdom deals with the lovers who come to her. For it is written: "In their paths she appeareth unto them graciously, and in every purpose she meeteth them" (Wisdom 6:16). Wherever you turn she speaks to you through certain traces of her operations. When you are falling away to external things she recalls you to return within by the very forms of external things. Whatever delights you in corporeal objects and entices you by appeal to the bodily senses, you may see is governed by number, and when you ask how that is so, you will return to your mind within, and know that you could neither approve nor disapprove things of sense unless you had within you, as it were, laws of beauty by which you judge all beautiful things which you perceive in the world.

42. Behold the heaven, the earth, the sea; all that is bright in them or above them; all that creep or fly or swim; all have forms because all have number. Take away number and they will be nothing. From whom have they their being if not from him who has made number? For they exist only in so far as they have number. The artificers of all corporeal forms work by number and regulate their operations thereby. In working they move their hands and tools until that which is fashioned in the outer world, being referred to the inward light of number, receives such perfection as is possible, and, being reported on by the senses, pleases the internal judge who beholds the supernal ideal numbers. Do you ask who moves the limbs of the artificer? It will be number, for they, too, move by number. Suppose there is no actual work in hand and no intention to make anything, but the motions of the limbs are done for pleasure, that will be dancing. Ask what delights you in dancing and number will reply: "Lo, here am I." Examine the beauty of bodily form, and you will find that everything is in its place by number. Examine the beauty of bodily motion and you will find everything in its due time by number. Examine the art which produces all these things and you never anywhere find in it either space or time, but it is alive with number. It has neither place in space nor length of days. And yet those who want to become artificers, while they accustom themselves to

learning their art, move their bodies in space and time, and their minds at least in time. They become more skilled, I mean, with the passing of time. But rise above even the mind of the artificer to behold the eternal realm of number. Then wisdom will shine upon you from its inward seat, from the secret place of truth. If truth repels you still because you look for it somewhat languidly, direct your mental vision to that path in which "she shows herself graciously." Remember that you have postponed a vision that you will seek again when you have become stronger and sounder.

From *The True Religion*

xxx, 54. If rational life judges by itself alone, then there is nothing more excellent. But clearly it is mutable, since it can be skilled at one moment and unskilled at another. The more skilled it is the better it judges, and its skill is in proportion to its participation in some art, discipline or wisdom. Now we must ask what is the nature of an art. By an art in this context I would have you understand not something that is observed by experience but something that is found out by reason. There is nothing very remarkable in knowing that sand and lime bind stones more securely together than mud, or that he who would build elegantly, must put a feature that is to be unique in the middle of the building, and, if there are several features, they must be made to correspond, like with like. That is sense-knowledge, but it is not far from reason and truth. We must indeed inquire what is the cause of our being dissatisfied if two windows are placed not one above the other but side by side, and one of them is greater or less than the other, for they ought to have been equal; while, if they are placed one directly above the other, even though they are unlike, the inequality does not offend us in the same way. Why don't we notice very much how much the one is greater or less than the other? If there are three windows, sense itself seems to demand either that they should not be unequal, or that between the largest and the smallest there should be an intermediate one as much larger than the smallest as it is smaller than the largest. In this way we take counsel with nature, as it were, to see what she approves. And here we must observe how that which displeases us only a little when we simply look at it, is rejected when we compare it with what is better. Thus we discover that art in the popular sense is nothing but the memory of things we have experienced and which have given us pleasure, with the addition of some skilled bodily activity. If you lack the skill you can still judge of the works produced even though you cannot produce them. And the power of judging is much better.

55. In all the arts it is symmetry that gives pleasure, preserving unity and making the whole beautiful. Symmetry demands unity and equality, the similarity of like parts, or the graded arrangements of parts which are dissimilar. But who can find absolute equality or similarity in bodily objects? Who would venture to say, after due consideration, that any body is truly and simply one? All are changed by passing from form to form or from place to place, and consist of parts each occupying its own place and extended in space. True equality and similitude, true and primal unity, are not perceived by the eye of flesh or by any bodily sense, but are known by the mind. How is equality of any kind demanded in bodies, and how are we convinced that any equality that may be seen there is far different from perfect equality, unless the mind sees that which is perfect? If indeed that which is not made [*facta*] can be called perfect [*perfecta*].

56. All things which are beautiful to the senses, whether they are produced by nature or are worked out by the arts, have a spatial or temporal beauty, as for example the body and its movements. But the equality and

unity which are known only by the mind, and according to which the mind judges of corporeal beauty by the intermediary of the senses, are not extended in space or unstable in time. It would be wrong to say that a wheel can be judged to be round by this standard, while a little jar cannot, or a jar can but a penny cannot. So in the case of times and motions of corporeal things, it would be ridiculous to say that years can be judged by any standard to be of equal length but months cannot, or that months can and days cannot. Whether a proper movement occupies a larger space of time or is measured by hours or brief minutes, all are judged by one and the same standard of changeless equality. If greater and smaller movements and spatial figures are all judged according to the same standard of equality or similitude or fitness, the standard is greater than all of them in potency. But it is neither greater nor less in a spatial or a temporal sense. If it were greater we should not use the whole of it to judge things that are less. If it were smaller we could not use it to judge things that are larger. As it is, we use the absolute standard of squareness to judge the squareness of a market-place, a stone, a table or a gem. And we use the absolute standard of equality to judge the movements of the feet of a running ant and those of an elephant on the march. Who then can doubt that it is neither greater nor less in a spatial or temporal sense, but in potency surpasses all else? This standard of all the arts is absolutely unchangeable, but the human mind, which is given the power to see the standard, can suffer the mutability of error. Clearly, then, the standard which is called truth is higher than our minds. . . .

xxxii, 59. But many stop with what delights men and are unwilling to rise to higher things, so that they may judge why visible things give pleasure. If I ask a workman why, after constructing one arch, he builds another like it over against it, he will reply, I dare say, that in a building like parts must correspond to like. If I go further and ask why he thinks so, he will say that it is fitting, or beautiful, or that it gives pleasure to those who behold it. But he will venture no further. He will bow and direct his eyes downward and not understand the cause for all this. But if I have to do with a man with inward eyes who can see the invisible, I shall not cease to press the query why these things give pleasure, so that he may dare to be the judge of human pleasure. He transcends it and escapes from its control in judging pleasure and not according to pleasure. First I shall ask him whether things are beautiful because they give pleasure, or give pleasure because they are beautiful. Then I shall ask him why they are beautiful, and if he is perplexed, I shall add the question whether it is because its parts correspond and are so joined together as to form one harmonious whole.

60. When he sees that that is so, I shall ask whether they completely achieve the unity they aim at, or fall far short of it, and in a measure misrepresent it. No one who is put on his guard can fail to see that there is no form or material thing which does not have some trace of unity, or that no material thing however beautiful can possibly achieve the unity it aims at, since it must necessarily have its parts separated by intervals of space. If this is so, I shall ask him to tell me where he sees that unity, and what is its source; and if he cannot see it, how does he know what it is that material things imitate but cannot completely achieve. If he says of material things: You would not exist unless some kind of unity held you together, but on the other hand if you were unity itself you would not be material things? the correct reply would be: Whence have you acquired the knowledge of unity according to which you judge material things. Unless you had seen it you would not be able to judge that they come short of it. You would not be right to say that you see it with your bodily eyes, although things do show traces of it, but

they come nowhere near it. With the bodily eyes you see nothing but corporeal things. Therefore it is with the mind that we see true unity. But where? If it were here where our body is, it would not be visible to a man who in eastern parts judges in the same way about corporeal things. It is not, then, circumscribed by space. It is present wherever anyone judges in this way. It is nowhere present spatially, but its potency is nowhere absent.

xxxiii, 61. If corporeal things travesty unity, we must not trust things that deceive, lest we fall into the vanities of them that are vain. Since they deceive by appearing to show to the eye of flesh the unity which is seen by the mind alone, we must rather ask whether they deceive by resembling unity or in failing to achieve unity. If they achieved it they would be completely identical with what they imitate. In that case there would be no difference at all. If that were so there would be no deception. They would be exactly what unity is. In any case, if you consider the matter closely they do not actively deceive. He is a deceiver who wants to appear what he is not. He who, without willing it, is thought to be other than he is, is not a deceiver but simply causes mistakes. This is how a deceiver is distinguished from one who causes mistakes. Every deceiver has the will to deceive, whether he is believed or not. But mistakes can be caused by one who has no intention to deceive. Therefore a corporeal form, which can have no will of its own, does not deceive. Nor does it cause mistakes if it is not thought to be what it is not.

Part Two

>>>>><<<<<

THE DEVELOPMENT OF MODERN AESTHETICS

Boileau to Kant

NICHOLAS BOILEAU [1636–1711]

>>>>><<<<<

From *The Art of Poetry* [1674]

CANTO I

Rash author, 'tis a vain presumptuous crime,
To undertake the sacred art of rhyme;
If at thy birth the stars that ruled thy sense
Shone not with a poetic influence,
In thy strait genius thou wilt still be bound,
Find Phoebus deaf, and Pegasus unsound.

You, then, that burn with the desire to try
The dangerous course of charming poetry,
Forbear in fruitless verse to lose your time,
Or take for genius the desire of rhyme;
Fear the allurements of a specious bait,
And well consider your own force and
    weight.
Nature abounds in wits of every kind,
And for each author can a talent find.
One may in verse describe an amorous
    flame,
Another sharpen a short epigram;
Waller a hero's mighty acts extol,
Spenser sing Rosalind in pastoral:
But authors, that themselves too much es-
    teem,
Lose their own genius, and mistake their
    theme;
Thus in times past Dubartas vainly writ,
Alloying sacred truth with trifling wit;
Impertinently, and without delight,
Described the Israelites triumphant flight;
And, following Moses o'er the sandy plain,
Perished with Pharaoh in the Arabian main.
Whate'er you write of pleasant or sub-
    lime,
Always let sense accompany your rhyme.
Falsely they seem each other to oppose;

From *L'Art Poétique* by Nicholas Boileau-
Despréaux, translated by William Soame and
John Dryden. The translation was first published
in 1683.

Rhyme must be made with reason's laws to
    close;
And when to conquer her you bend your
    force,
The mind will triumph in the noble course.
To reason's yoke she quickly will incline,
Which, far from hurting, renders her di-
    vine;
But if neglected, will as easily stray,
And master reason, which she should obey.
Love reason then; and let whate'er you
    write
Borrow from her its beauty, force, and light.
Most writers mounted on a resty muse,
Extravagant and senseless objects chuse;
They think they err, if in their verse they
    fall
On any thought that's plain or natural.
Fly this excess; and let Italians be
Vain authors of false glittering poetry.
All ought to aim at sense; but most in vain
Strive the hard pass and slippery path to
    gain;
You drown, if to the right or left you stray;
Reason to go has often but one way.
Sometimes an author, fond of his own
    thought,
Pursues its object till it's over wrought:
If he describes a house, he shows the face,
And after walks you round from place to
    place;
Here is a vista, there the doors unfold,
Balconies here are ballustred with gold;
Then counts the rounds and ovals in the
    halls,
"The festoons, freezes, and the astragals":
Tired with his tedious pomp, away I run,
And skip o'er twenty pages, to be gone.
Of such descriptions the vain folly see,
And shun their barren superfluity.
All that is needless carefully avoid;
The mind once satisfied is quickly cloyed:

He cannot write, who knows not to give o'er;
To mend one fault, he makes a hundred more:
A verse was weak, you turn it much too strong,
And grow obscure for fear you should be long.
Some are not gaudy, but are flat and dry;
Not to be low, another soars too high.
Would you of every one deserve the praise?
In writing vary your discourse and phrase;
A frozen style, that neither ebbs nor flows,
Instead of pleasing, makes us gape and doze.
Those tedious authors are esteemed by none
Who tire us, humming the same heavy tone.
Happy who in his verse can gently steer,
From grave to light; from pleasant to severe:
His works will be admired wherever found,
And oft with buyers will be compassed round.
In all you write, be neither low nor vile;
The meanest theme may have a proper style.
    The dull burlesque appeared with impudence,
And pleased by novelty in spite of sense.
All, except trivial points, grew out of date;
Parnassus spoke the cant of Billingsgate;
Boundless and mad, disordered rhyme was seen;
Disguised Apollo changed to Harlequin.
This plague, which first in country towns began,
Cities and kingdoms quickly over-ran;
The dullest scribblers some admirers found,
And the "Mock Tempest" was a while renowned.
But this low stuff the town at last despised,
And scorned the folly that they once had prized;
Distinguished dull from natural and plain,
And left the villages to Flecknoe's reign.
Let not so mean a style your muse debase,
But learn from Butler the buffooning grace;
And let burlesque in ballads be employed,
Yet noisy bombast carefully avoid;
Nor think to raise, though on Pharsalia's plain,
"Millions of mourning mountains of the slain."
Nor with Dubartas, "bridle up the floods,
And periwig with wool the baldpate woods."
Choose a just style; Be grave without constraint,
Great without pride, and lovely without paint:
Write what your reader may be pleased to hear,
And for the measure have a careful ear.
On easy numbers fix your happy choice;
Of jarring sounds avoid the odious noise:
The fullest verse, and the most laboured sense,
Displease us, if the ear once take offence.
Our ancient verse, as homely as the times,
Was rude, unmeasured, only tagged with rhymes;
Number and cadence, that have since been shown,
To those unpolished writers were unknown.
Fairfax was he, who, in that darker age,
By his just rules restrained poetic rage;
Spenser did next in pastorals excel,
And taught the noble art of writing well;
To stricter rules the stanza did restrain,
And found for poetry a richer vein.
Then D'Avenant came, who, with a new-found art,
Changed all, spoiled all, and had his way apart;
His haughty muse all others did despise,
And thought in triumph to bear off the prize,
'Till the sharp-sighted critics of the times,
In their Mock-Gondibert, exposed his rhymes;
The laurels he pretended did refuse,
And dashed the hopes of his aspiring muse.
This headstrong writer falling from on high,
Made following authors take less liberty.

Waller came last, but was the first whose art
Just weight and measure did to verse impart;
That of a well-placed word could teach the force,
And showed for poetry a nobler course;
His happy genius did our tongue refine,
And easy words with pleasing numbers join;
His verses to good method did apply,
And changed hard discord to soft harmony.
All owned his laws; which, long approved and tried,
To present authors now may be a guide;
Tread boldly in his steps, secure from fear,
And be, like him, in your expressions clear.
If in your verse you drag, and sense delay,
My patience tires, my fancy goes astray;
And from your vain discourse I turn my mind,
Nor search an author troublesome to find.
There is a kind of writer pleased with sound,
Whose fustian head with clouds is compassed round—
No reason can disperse them with its light;
Learn then to think ere you pretend to write.
As your idea's clear, or else obscure,
The expression follows perfect or impure;
What we conceive with ease we can express;
Words to the notions flow with readiness.
    Observe the language well in all you write,
And swerve not from it in your loftiest flight.
The smoothest verse, and the exactest sense,
Displease us, if ill English give offence;
A barbarous phrase no reader can approve;
Nor bombast, noise, or affectation love.
In short, without pure language, what you write
Can never yield us profit or delight.
Take time for thinking; never work in haste;

And value not yourself for writing fast.
A rapid poem, with such fury writ,
Shows want of judgment, not abounding wit.
More pleased we are to see a river lead
His gentle streams along a flowery mead,
Than from high banks to hear loud torrents roar,
With foamy waters on a muddy shore.
Gently make haste, of labour not afraid;
A hundred times consider what you've said:
Polish, repolish, every colour lay,
And sometimes add, but oftener take away.
'Tis not enough, when swarming faults are writ,
That here and there are scattered sparks of wit:
Each object must be fixed in the due place,
And differing parts have corresponding grace;
Till, by a curious art disposed, we find
One perfect whole, of all the pieces joined.
Keep to your subject close in all you say;
Nor for a sounding sentence ever stray.
The public censure for your writings fear,
And to yourself be critic most severe.
Fantastic wits their darling follies love;
But find you faithful friends that will reprove,
That on your works may look with careful eyes,
And of your faults be zealous enemies:
Lay by an author's pride and vanity,
And from a friend a flatterer descry,
Who seems to like, but means not what he says;
Embrace true counsel, but suspect false praise.
A sycophant will every thing admire;
Each verse, each sentence sets his soul on fire;
All is divine! there's not a word amiss!
He shakes with joy, and weeps with tenderness;
He overpowers you with his mighty praise.
Truth never moves in those impetuous ways;

A faithful friend is careful of your fame,
And freely will your heedless errors blame;
He cannot pardon a neglected line,
But verse to rule and order will confine;
Reprove of words the too-affected sound;—
Here the sense flags, and your expression's
    round,
Your fancy tires, and your discourse grows
    vain,
Your terms improper; make it just and
    plain.—
Thus 'tis a faithful friend will freedom use;
But authors, partial to their darling muse,
Think to protect it they have just pretence,
And at your friendly counsel take offence.—
"Said you of this, that the expression's flat?
Your servant, sir, you must excuse me
    that,"
He answers you.—"This word has here no
    grace,
Pray leave it out";—"that, sir's the properest
    place."—
"This turn I like not";—"'tis approved by
    all."
Thus, resolute not from one fault to fall,
If there's a syllable of which you doubt,
'Tis a sure reason not to blot it out.
Yet still he says you may his faults confute,
And over him your power is absolute.
But of his feigned humility take heed;
'Tis a bait laid to make you hear him read.
And, when he leaves you, happy in his
    muse,
Restless he runs some other to abuse.
And often finds; for in our scribbling times
No fool can want a sot to praise his rhymes.
The flattest work has ever in the court
Met with some zealous ass for its support;
And in all times a forward scribbling fop
Has found some greater fool to cry him up.

. . . .

CANTO III

Tragedy

There's not a monster bred beneath the sky,
But well-disposed by art, may please the eye:
A curious workman by his skill divine,

From an ill object makes a good design.
Thus to delight us, Tragedy, in tears
For Oedipus, provokes our hopes and fears;
For parricide Orestes asks relief,
And, to encrease our pleasure, causes grief,
You then that in this noble art would rise,
Come, and in lofty verse dispute the prize.
Would you upon the stage acquire renown,
And for your judges summon all the town?
Would you your works for ever should re-
    main,
And after ages past be sought again?
If all you write, observe with care and art
To move the passions, and incline the
    heart.
If in a laboured act, the pleasing rage
Cannot our hopes and fears by turns en-
    gage,
Nor in our mind a feeling pity raise,
In vain with learned scenes you fill your
    plays:
Your cold discourse can never move the
    mind
Of a stern critic, naturally unkind,
Who, justly tired with your pedantic flight,
Or falls asleep, or censures all you write.
The secret is, attention first to gain;
To move our minds, and then to entertain;
That from the very opening of the scenes,
The first may show us what the author
    means.
I'm tired to see an actor on the stage,
That knows not whether he's to laugh or
    rage;
Who, an intrigue unravelling in vain,
Instead of pleasing keeps my mind in pain.
I'd rather much the nauseous dunce should
    say
Downright, "my name is Hector in the
    play";
Than with a mass of miracles, ill-joined,
Confound my ears, and not instruct my
    mind.
The subject's never soon enough exprest;
Your place of action must be fixed, and
    rest.
A Spanish poet may with good event,
In one day's space whole ages represent;

There oft the hero of a wandering stage
Begins a child, and ends the play of age:
But we, that are by reason's rules confined,
Will, that with art the poem be designed;
That unity of action, time, and place,
Keep the stage full, and all our labours
    grace.
Write not what cannot be with ease con-
    ceived;
Some truths may be too strong to be be-
    lieved.
A foolish wonder cannot entertain;
My mind's not moved if your discourse be
    vain.
You may relate what would offend the eye:
Seeing, indeed, would better satisfy;
But there are objects that a curious art
Hides from the eyes, yet offers to the heart.
The mind is most agreeably surprised,
When a well-woven subject, long dis-
    guised,
You on a sudden artfully unfold,
And give the whole another face and
    mould.

       .   .   .   .

Of romance heroes shun the low design;
Yet to great hearts some human frailties
    join:
Achilles must with Homer's heat engage;
For an affront I'm pleased to see him rage.
Those little failings in your hero's heart
Show that of man and nature he has part.
To leave known rules you cannot be al-
    lowed;
Make Agamemnon covetous and proud,
Aeneas in religious rites austere.
Keep to each man his proper character.
Of countries and of times the humours
    know;
From different climates different customs
    grow;
And strive to shun their fault, who vainly
    dress
An antique hero like some modern ass;
Who make old Romans like our English
    move,
Show Cato sparkish, or make Brutus love.

In a romance those errors are excused:
There 'tis enough that, reading, we're
    amused:
Rules too severe would there be useless
    found;
But the strict scene must have a juster
    bound;
Exact decorum we must always find.
If then you form some hero in your mind,
Be sure your image with itself agree;
For what he first appears, he still must be,
Affected wits will naturally incline
To paint their figures by their own design;
Your bully poets, bully heroes write;
Chapman in Bussy D'Ambois took delight,
And thought perfection was to huff and
    fight.
Wise nature by variety does please;
Clothe differing passions in a differing
    dress.
Bold anger, in rough haughty words ap-
    pears;
Sorrow is humble, and dissolves in tears.
Make not your Hecuba with fury rage,
And show a ranting grief upon the stage;
Or tell in vain how the rough Tanais bore
His sevenfold waters to the Euxine shore:
These swoln expressions, this affected
    noise,
Shows like some pedant that declaims to
    boys.
In sorrow you must softer methods keep;
And, to excite our tears, yourself must
    weep.
Those noisy words with which ill plays
    abound,
Come not from hearts that are in sadness
    drowned.
    The theatre for a young poet's rhymes
Is a bold venture in our knowing times:
An author cannot easily purchase fame;
Critics are always apt to hiss, and blame:
You may be judged by every ass in town,
The privilege is bought for half-a-crown.
To please, you must a hundred changes try;
Sometimes be humble, then must soar on
    high;
In noble thoughts must everywhere abound,

Be easy, pleasant, solid, and profound;
To these you must surprising touches join,
And show us a new wonder in each line;
That all, in a just method well-designed,
May leave a strong impression in the mind.
These are the arts that tragedy maintain:

. . . .

Would you in this great art acquire renown?
Authors, observe the rules I here lay down.
In prudent lessons every where abound;
With pleasant join the useful and the sound:
A sober reader a vain tale will slight;
He seeks as well instruction as delight.
Let all your thoughts to virtue be confined,
Still offering nobler figures to our mind:
I like not those loose writers, who employ
Their guilty muse, good manners to destroy;
Who with false colours still deceive our eyes,
And show us vice dressed in a fair disguise.
Yet do I not their sullen muse approve,
Who from all modest writings banish love;
That stript the play-house of its chief intrigue,
And make a murderer of Roderigue:
The lightest love, if decently exprest,
Will raise no vitious motions in our breast.
Dido in vain may weep, and ask relief;
I blame her folly, whilst I share her grief.
A virtuous author, in his charming art,
To please the sense needs not corrupt the heart:
His heat will never cause a guilty fire:
To follow virtue then be your desire.
In vain your art and vigour are exprest;
The obscene expression shows the infected breast.
But, above all, base jealousies avoid,
In which detracting poets are employed.
A noble wit dares liberally commend,
And scorns to grudge at his deserving friend.
Base rivals, who true wit and merit hate,
Caballing still against it with the great,

Maliciously aspire to gain renown,
By standing up, and pulling others down.
Never debase yourself by treacherous ways,
Nor by such abject methods seek for praise:
Let not your only business be to write;
Be virtuous, just, and in your friends delight.
'Tis not enough your poems be admired;
But strive your conversation be desired:
Write for immortal fame; nor ever choose
Gold for the object of a generous muse.
I know a noble wit may, without crime,
Receive a lawful tribute for his time:
Yet I abhor those writers, who despise
Then honour, and alone their profits prize;
Who their Apollo basely will degrade,
And of a noble science make a trade.
Before kind reason did her light display,
And government taught mortals to obey,
Men, like wild beasts, did nature's laws pursue,
They fed on herbs, and drink from rivers drew;
Their brutal force, on lust and rapine bent,
Committed murder without punishment:
Reason at last, by her all-conquering arts,
Reduced these savages, and tuned their hearts;
Mankind from bogs, and woods, and caverns calls,
And towns and cities fortifies with walls:
Thus fear of justice made proud rapine cease,
And sheltered innocence by laws and peace.
  These benefits from poets we received;
From whence are raised those fictions since believed,
That Orpheus, by his soft harmonious strains,
Tamed the fierce tygers of the Thracian plains;
Amphion's notes, by their melodious powers,
Drew rocks and woods, and raised the Theban towers:

These miracles from numbers did arise;
Since which, in verse heaven taught his
　mysteries,
And by a priest, possessed with rage
　divine,
Apollo spoke from his prophetic shrine.
Soon after, Homer the old heroes praised,
And noble minds by great examples raised;
Then Hesiod did his Grecian swains in-
　cline

To till the fields, and prune the bounteous
　vine.
Thus useful rules were, by the poet's aid,
In easy numbers to rude men conveyed,
And pleasingly their precepts did impart;
First charmed the ear, and then engaged
　the heart;
The muses thus their reputation raised,
And with just gratitude in Greece were
　praised.

ANTHONY ASHLEY COOPER [1671–1713]

THIRD EARL OF SHAFTESBURY

→→→→→←←←←←

From *Characteristics of Men, Manners, Opinions, Times* [1711]

And thus, after all, the most natural beauty in the world is honesty and moral truth. For all beauty is truth. True features make the beauty of a face; and true proportions, the beauty of architecture; as true measures, that of harmony and music. In Poetry, which is all fable, truth still is the perfection. And whoever is scholar enough to read the ancient philosopher, or his modern copyists, upon the nature of a dramatic and epic poem will easily understand this account of truth.

A painter, if he has any genius, understands the truth and unity of design and knows he is even then unnatural when he follows nature too close and strictly copies life. For his art allows him not to bring all nature into his piece, but a part only. However, his piece, if it be beautiful, and carries truth, must be a whole, by itself, complete, independent, and withal as great and comprehensive as he can make it. So that

From *Characteristics of Men, Manners, Opinions, Times* by Anthony, Earl of Shaftesbury, edited by J. M. Robertson (New York: 1900), Vol I, pp. 94-6, 296; Vol. II, pp. 126-31.

particulars, on this occasion, must yield to the general design, and all things be subservient to that which is principal, in order to form a certain easiness of sight, a simple, clear, and united view, which would be broken and disturbed by the expression of anything peculiar or distinct.

Now the variety of Nature is such as to distinguish everything she forms, by a peculiar original character, which, if strictly observed, will make the subject appear unlike to anything extant in the world besides. But this effect the good poet and painter seek industriously to prevent. They hate minuteness and are afraid of singularity, which would make their images or characters appear capricious and fantastical. The mere face painter, indeed, has little in common with the poet but, like the mere historian, copies what he sees and minutely traces every feature and odd mark. It is otherwise with the men of invention and design. It is from the many objects of nature, and not from a particular one, that those geniuses form the idea of their work. Thus the best artists are said to have been indefatigable in studying the best statues, as esteeming them a better rule than the perfectest human bodies could afford. And thus some considerable wits have recommended the best poems as preferable to the best of histories, and better teaching the truth of characters and nature of mankind.

. . .

There is no one who, by the least progress in science or learning, has come to know barely the principles of mathematics, but has found, that in the exercise of his mind on the discoveries he there makes, though merely of speculative truths, he receives a pleasure and delight superior to that of sense. When we have thoroughly searched into the nature of this contemplative delight, we shall find it of a kind which relates not in the least to any private interest of the creature, nor has for its object any self-good or advantage of the private system. The admiration, joy, or love turns wholly upon what is exterior and foreign to ourselves. And though the reflected joy or pleasure which arises from the notice of this pleasure once perceived, may be interpreted a self-passion or interested regard, yet the original satisfaction can be no other than what results from the love of truth, proportion, order and symmetry in the things without. If this be the case, the passion ought in reality to be ranked with natural affection. For having no object within the compass of the private system, it must either be esteemed superfluous and unnatural (as having no tendency towards the advantage of good of anything in Nature) or it must be judged to be what it truly is, "A natural joy in the contemplation of those numbers, that harmony, proportion, and concord which supports the universal nature, and is essential in the constitution and form of every particular species or order of beings."

. . .

For if we may trust to what our reasoning has taught us, whatever in Nature is beautiful or charming is only the faint shadow of that first beauty. So that every real love depending on the mind, and being only the contemplation of beauty either as it really is in itself or as it appears imperfectly in the objects which strike the sense, how can the rational mind rest here, or be satisfied with the absurd enjoyment which reaches the sense alone?

From this time forward then, said I, I shall no more have reason to fear those beauties which strike a sort of melancholy, like the places we have named, or like these solemn groves. No more shall I avoid the moving accents of soft music, or fly from the enchanting features of the fairest human face.

If you are already, replied he, such a proficient in this new love that you are sure never to admire the representative beauty except for the sake of the original, nor aim at other enjoyment than of the rational kind, you may then be confident. I am so, and presume accordingly to answer for myself. However, I should not be ill satisfied if you explained yourself a little better as to this mistake of mine you seem to fear. Would it be any help to tell you, "That the absurdity lay in seeking the enjoyment elsewhere than in the subject loved"? The matter, I must confess, is still mysterious. Imagine then, good Philocles, if being taken with the beauty of the ocean, which you see yonder at a distance, it should come into your head to seek how to command it, and, like some mighty admiral, ride master of the sea, would not the fancy be a little absurd?

Absurd enough, in conscience. The next thing I should do, 'tis likely, upon this frenzy, would be to hire some bark and go in nuptial ceremony, Venetian-like, to wed the gulf, which I might call perhaps as properly my own.

Let who will call it theirs, replied Theocles, you will own the enjoyment of this kind to be very different from that which should naturally follow from the contemplation of the ocean's beauty. The bridegroom-Doge, who in his stately Bucentaur floats on the bosom of his Thetis, has less possession than the poor shepherd, who from a hanging rock or point of some high promontory, stretched at his ease, forgets his feeding flocks, while he admires her beauty. But to come nearer home, and make the question still more familiar. Suppose (my Philocles) that, viewing such a tract of country as this delicious vale we see beneath us, you should, for the enjoyment of the prospect, require the property or possession of the land.

The covetous fancy, replied I, would be as absurd altogether as that other ambitious one.

O Philocles! said he, may I bring this yet a little nearer, and will you follow me once more? Suppose that, being charmed as you seem to be with the beauty of those trees under whose shade we rest, you should long for nothing so much as to taste some delicious fruit of theirs; and having obtained of Nature some certain relish by which these acorns or berries of the wood became as palatable as the figs or peaches of the garden, you should afterwards, as oft as you revisited these groves, seek hence the enjoyment of them by satiating yourself in these new delights.

The fancy of this kind, replied I, would be sordidly luxurious, and as absurd, in my opinion, as either of the former.

Can you not then, on this occasion, said he, call to mind some other forms of a fair kind among us, where the admiration of beauty is apt to lead to as irregular a consequence?

I feared, said I, indeed, where this would end, and was apprehensive you would force me at least to think of certain powerful forms in human kind which draw after them a set of eager desires, wishes, and hopes; no way suitable, I must confess, to your rational and refined contemplation of beauty. The proportions of this living architecture, as wonderful as they are, inspire nothing of a studious or contemplative kind. The more they are viewed, the further they are from satisfying by mere view. Let that which satisfies be ever so disproportionable an effect, or ever so foreign to its cause, censure it as you please, you must allow, however, that it is natural. So that you, Theocles, for aught I see, are become the accuser of Nature by condemning a natural enjoyment.

Far be it from us both, said he, to condemn a joy which is from Nature. But when we spoke of the enjoyment of these woods and prospects, we understood by it a far different kind from that of the inferior creatures, who, rifling in these places, find here their choicest food. Yet we too live by tasteful food, and feel those other joys of sense in common with them. But 'twas not here (my Philocles) that we had agreed to place our good, nor consequently our enjoyment. We who were rational, and had minds, methought, should place it rather in those minds which were indeed abused, and cheated of their real good, when drawn to seek absurdly the enjoyment of it in the objects of sense, and not in those objects they might properly call their own, in which kind, as I remember, we comprehended all which was truly fair, generous, or good.

So that beauty, said I, and good with you, Theocles, I perceive, are still one and the same.

'Tis so, said he. And thus are we returned again to the subject of our yesterday's morning conversation. Whether I have made good my promise to you in showing the true good, I know not. But so, doubtless, I should have done with good success had I been able in my poetic ecstasies, or by any other efforts, to have led you into some deep view of Nature and the sovereign genius. We then had proved the force of divine beauty, and formed in ourselves an object capable and worthy of real enjoyment.

O Theocles! said I, well do I remember now the terms in which you engaged me that morning when you bespoke my love of this mysterious beauty. You have indeed made good your part of the condition, and may now claim me for a proselyte. If there be any seeming extravagance in the case I must comfort myself the best I can, and consider that all sound love and admiration is enthusiasm: "The transports of poets, the sublime of orators, the rapture of musicians, the high strains of the virtuosi—all mere enthusiasm! Even learning itself, the love of arts and curiosities, the spirit of travellers and adventurers, gallantry, war, heroism—all, all enthusiasm!" 'Tis enough; I am content to be this new enthusiast in a way unknown to me before.

And I, replied Theocles, am content you should call this love of ours enthusiasm, allowing it the privilege of its fellow-passions. For is there a fair and plausible enthusiasm, a reasonable ecstasy and transport allowed to other subjects, such as architecture, painting, music; and shall it be exploded here? Are there senses by which all those other graces and perfections are perceived, and none by which this higher perfection and grace is comprehended? Is it so preposterous to bring that enthusiasm hither, and transfer it from those secondary and scanty objects to this original and comprehensive one? Observe how the case stands in all those other subjects of art or science. What difficulty to be in any degree knowing! How long ere a true taste is gained! How many things shocking, how many offensive at first, which afterwards are known and acknowledged the highest beauties! For 'tis not instantly we acquire the sense by which these beauties are discoverable. Labour and pains are required, and time to cultivate a natural genius ever so apt or forward. But who is there once thinks of cultivating this soil, or of improving any sense or faculty which Nature may have given of this kind? And is it a wonder we should be dull then, as we are, confounded and at a loss in these affairs, blind as to this higher scene, these nobler representations? Which way should we come to understand better? which way be knowing in these beauties? Is study, science, or learning necessary to understand all beauties else? And for the sovereign beauty, is there no skill or science required? In painting there are shades and masterly strokes which the vulgar understand not, but find fault with; in architecture there is the rustic; in music the chromatic kind, and skilful mixture of dissonancies: and is there nothing which answers to this in the whole?

I must confess, said I, I have hitherto been one of those vulgar who could never relish the shades, the rustic, or the dissonancies you talk of. I have never dreamt of such masterpieces in Nature. 'Twas my way to censure freely on the first view. But I perceive I am now obliged to go far in the pursuit of beauty, which lies very absconded and deep; and if so, I am well assured that my enjoyments hitherto have been very shallow. I have dwelt, it seems, all this while upon the surface, and enjoyed only a kind of slight superficial beauties, having never gone in search of beauty itself, but of what I fancied such. Like the rest of the unthinking world, I took for granted that what I liked was beautiful, and what I rejoiced in was my good. I never scrupled loving what I fancied, and aiming only at the enjoyment of what I loved; I never troubled myself with examining what the subjects were, nor ever hesitated about their choice.

Begin then, said he, and choose. See what the subjects are, and which you would prefer, which honour with your admiration, love, and esteem. For by these again you will be honoured in your turn. Such, Philocles, as is the worth of these companions, such will your worth be found. As there is emptiness or fulness here, so will there be in your enjoyment. See therefore where fulness is, and where emptiness. See in what subject resides the chief excellence, where beauty reigns, where 'tis entire, perfect, absolute; where broken, imperfect, short. View these terrestrial beauties and whatever has the appearance of excellence and is able to attract. See that which either really is, or stands as in the room of fair, beautiful, and good. "A mass of metal, a tract of land, a number of slaves, a pile of stones, a human body of certain lineaments and proportions." Is this the highest of the kind? Is beauty founded then in body only, and not in action, life, or operation? . . .

Hold! hold! said I, good Theocles, you take this in too high a key above my reach. If you would have me accompany you, pray lower this strain a little, and talk in a more familiar way.

Thus then, said he (smiling), whatever passion you may have for other beauties, I know, good Philocles, you are no such admirer of wealth in any kind as to allow much beauty to it, especially in a rude heap or mass. But in medals, coins, embossed work, statues, and well-fabricated pieces, of whatever sort, you can discover beauty and admire the kind. True, said I, but not for the metal's sake. 'Tis not then the metal or matter which is beautiful with you? No. But the art? Certainly. The art then is the beauty? Right. And the art is that which beautifies? The same. So that the beautifying, not the beautified, is the really beautiful? It seems so. For that which is beautified, is beautiful only by the accession of something beautifying, and by the recess or withdrawing of the same, it ceases to be beautiful? Be it. In respect of bodies therefore, beauty comes and goes? So we see. Nor is the body itself any cause either of its coming or staying? None. So that there is no principle of beauty in body? None at all. For body can no way be the cause of beauty to itself? No way. Nor govern nor regulate itself? Nor yet this. Nor mean nor intend itself? Nor this neither. Must not that, therefore, which means and intends for it, regulates and orders it, be the principle of beauty to it? Of necessity. And what must that be? Mind, I suppose, for what can it be else?

JOSEPH ADDISON [1672–1719]

→→→→→←←←←←

From *The Spectator*, #409–418
[1712]

I shall next Saturday enter upon an essay on "the pleasures of the imagination" which, though it shall consider that subject at large, will perhaps suggest to the reader what it is that gives a beauty to many passages of the finest writers, both in prose and verse. As an undertaking of this nature is entirely new, I question not but it will be received with candor. . . .

From *The Works of Joseph Addison* (London: 1811), Vol. IV, pp. 335-66.

Our sight is the most perfect and most delightful of all our senses. It fills the mind with the largest variety of ideas, converses with its objects at the greatest distance, and continues the longest in action without being tired or satiated with its proper enjoyments. The sense of feeling can indeed give us a notion of extension, shape, and all other ideas that enter at the eye, except colors; but at the same time it is very much straitened and confined in its operations to the number, bulk, and distance of its particular objects. Our sight seems designed to supply all these defects, and may be considered as a more delicate and diffusive kind of touch, that spreads itself over an infinite multitude of bodies, comprehends the largest figures, and brings into our reach some of the most remote parts of the universe.

It is this sense which furnishes the imagination with its ideas; so that by the pleasures of the imagination or fancy (which I shall use promiscuously) I here mean such as arise from visible objects, either when we have them actually in our view or when we call up their ideas into our minds by paintings, statues, descriptions, or any the like occasion. We cannot indeed have a single image in the fancy that did not make its first entrance through the sight; but we have the power of retaining, altering, and compounding those images which we have once received into all the varieties of picture and vision that are most agreeable to the imagination; for by this faculty a man in a dungeon is capable of entertaining himself with scenes and landscapes more beautiful than any that can be found in the whole compass of nature.

There are few words in the English language which are employed in a more loose and uncircumscribed sense than those of the fancy and the imagination. I therefore thought it necessary to fix and determine the notion of these two words as I intend to make use of them in the thread of my following speculations, that the reader may conceive rightly what is the subject which I proceed upon. I must therefore desire him to remember that by the pleasures of the imagination I mean only such pleasures as arise originally from sight, and that I divide these pleasures into two kinds: my design being first of all to discourse of those primary pleasures of the imagination which entirely proceed from such objects as are before our eyes; and, in the next place, to speak of those secondary pleasures of the imagination which flow from the ideas of visible objects when the objects are not actually before the eye, but are called up into our memories, or formed into agree-able visions of things that are either absent or fictitious.

The pleasures of the imagination, taken in their full extent, are not so gross as those of sense, nor so refined as those of the understanding. The last are, indeed, *more preferable*, because they are founded on some new knowledge or improvement in the mind of man; yet it must be confest, that those of the imagination are as great and as transporting as the other. A beautiful prospect delights the soul, as much as a demonstration; and a description in Homer has charmed more readers than a chapter in Aristotle. Besides, the pleasures of the imagination have this advantage above those of the understanding, that they are more obvious, and more easy to be acquired. It is but opening the eye and the scene enters. The colors paint themselves on the fancy, with very little attention of thought or application of mind in the beholder. We are struck, we know not how, with the symmetry of anything we see, and immediately assent to the beauty of an object, without inquiring into the particular causes and occasions of it. . . .

. . . A man should endeavor to make the sphere of his innocent pleasures as wide as possible, that he may retire into them with safety, and find in them such a satisfaction as a wise man would not blush to take. Of this nature are those of the imagination, which do not require such a bent of thought as is necessary to our more serious employments, nor, at the same time suffer the mind to sink into that intelligence and remissness, which are apt to accompany our more sensual delights, but, like a gentle exercise to the faculties, awaken them from sloth and idleness, without putting them upon any labor or difficulty. . . .

I shall first consider those pleasures of the imagination, which arise from the actual view and survey of outward objects: And these, I think, all proceed from the sight of what is great, uncommon, or beautiful. There may, indeed, be something so terrible or offensive that the horror or loathsomeness of an object may overbear the pleasure which results from its greatness, novelty, or beauty; but still there will be such a mixture of delight in the very disgust it gives us as any of these three qualifications are most conspicuous and prevailing.

By greatness I do not only mean the bulk of any single object, but the largeness of a whole view, considered as one entire piece. Such are the prospects of an open champaign country, a vast uncultivated desert, of huge heaps of mountains, high rocks and precipices, or a wide expanse of waters, where we are not struck with the novelty or beauty of the sight, but with that rude kind of magnificence which appears in many of these stupendous works of nature. Our imagination loves to be filled with an object, or to grasp at anything that is too big for its capacity. We are flung into a pleasing astonishment at such unbounded views, and feel a delightful stillness and amazement in the soul at the apprehension of them. The mind of man naturally hates everything that looks like a restraint upon it, and is apt to fancy itself under a sort of confinement when the sight is pent up in a narrow compass and shortened on every side by the neighborhood of walls or mountains. On the contrary, a spacious horizon is an image of liberty, where the eye has room to range abroad, to expatiate at large on the immensity of its views, and to lose itself amidst the variety of objects that offer themselves to its observation. Such wide and undetermined prospects are as pleasing to the fancy as the speculations of eternity or infinitude are to the understanding. But if there be a beauty or uncommonness joined with this grandeur, as in a troubled ocean, a heaven adorned with stars and meteors, or a spacious landscape cut out into rivers, woods, rocks, and meadows, the pleasure still grows upon us, as it arises from more than a single principle.

Everything that is new or uncommon raises a pleasure in the imagination because it fills the soul with an agreeable surprise, gratifies its curiosity, and gives it an idea of which it was not before possessed. . . .

As the fancy delights in everything that is great, strange, or beautiful, and is still more pleased the more it finds of these perfections in the same object, so it is capable of receiving a new satisfaction by the assistance of another sense. Thus any continued sound, as the music of birds or a fall of water, awakens every moment the mind of the beholder, and makes him more attentive to the several beauties of the place that lie before him. Thus if there arises a fragrancy of smells or perfumes, they heighten the pleasures of the imagination, and make even the colors and verdure of the landscape appear more agreeable; for the ideas of both senses recommend each other and are pleasanter together than when they enter the mind separately: as the different colors of a picture, when they are well disposed, set off one another and receive an additional beauty from the advantage of their situation. . . .

Though in yesterday's paper we considered how everything that is great, new, or beautiful is apt to affect the imagination with pleasure, we must own that it is impossible for us to assign the necessary cause of this pleasure, because we know neither the nature of an idea, nor the substance of a human soul, which might help us to discover the conformity or disagreeableness of the one to the other; and therefore, for want of such a light, all that we can do in speculations of this kind is to reflect on those operations of the soul that are most agreeable, and to range under their proper heads what is pleasing or displeasing to the mind, without being able to trace out the several necessary and efficient causes from whence the pleasure or displeasure arises.

Final causes lie more bare and open to our observation, as there are often a great variety that belong to the same effect; and these, though they are not altogether so satisfactory, are generally more useful than the other, as they give us greater occasion of admiring the goodness and wisdom of the First Contriver. . . .

If we consider the works of nature and art as they are qualified to entertain the imagination, we shall find the last very defective in comparison of the former; for though they may sometimes appear as beautiful or strange, they can have nothing in them of that vastness and immensity which afford so great an entertainment to the mind of the beholder. The one may be as polite and delicate as the other but can never show herself so august and magnificent in the design. There is something more bold and masterly in the rough, careless strokes of nature than in the nice touches and embellishments of art. The beauties of the most stately garden or palace lie in a narrow compass; the imagination immediately runs them over and requires something else to gratify her; but in the wide fields of nature the sight wanders up and down without confinement and is fed with an infinite variety of images without any certain stint or number. For this reason we always find the poet in love with a country life, where nature appears in the greatest perfection and furnishes out all those scenes that are most apt to delight the imagination. . . .

I at first divided the pleasures of the imagination into such as arise from objects that are actually before our eyes or that once entered in at our eyes and are afterwards called up into the mind, either barely by its own operations or on occasion of something without us, as statues or descriptions. We have already considered the first division and shall, therefore, enter on the other, which, for distinction's sake, I have called the secondary pleasures of the imagination. When I say the ideas we receive from statues, descriptions, or such like occasions are the same that were once actually in our view, it must not be understood

that we had once seen the very place, action, or person which are carved or described. It is sufficient that we have seen places, persons, or actions, in general, which bear a resemblance, or at least some remote analogy, with what we find represented—since it is in the power of the imagination, when it is once stocked with particular ideas, to enlarge, compound, and vary them at her own pleasure.

Among the different kinds of representation, statuary is the most natural, and shows us something likest the object that is represented. To make use of a common instance, let one who is born blind take an image in his hands and trace out with his fingers the different furrows and impressions of the chisel, and he will easily conceive how the shape of a man or beast may be represented by it; but should he draw his hand over a picture, where all is smooth and uniform, he would never be able to imagine how the several prominences and depressions of a human body could be shown on a plain piece of canvas, that has in it no unevenness or irregularity. Description runs yet further from the things it represents than painting; for a picture bears a real resemblance to its original which letters and syllables are wholly void of. Colors speak all languages, but words are understood only by such a people or nation. For this reason, though men's necessities quickly put them on finding out speech, writing is probably of a later invention than painting; particularly we are told that in America, when the Spaniards first arrived there, expresses were sent to the Emperor of Mexico in paint, and the news of his country delineated by the strokes of a pencil, which was a more natural way than that of writing, though at the same time much more imperfect, because it is impossible to draw the little connections of speech or to give the picture of a conjunction or an adverb. It would be yet more strange to represent visible objects by sounds that have no ideas annexed to them, and to make something like description in music. Yet it is certain there may be confused, imperfect notions of this nature raised in the imagination by an artificial composition of notes; and we find that great masters in the art are able sometimes to set their hearers in the heat and hurry of a battle, to overcast their minds with melancholy scenes and apprehensions of deaths and funerals, or to lull them into pleasing dreams of groves and Elysiums.

In all these instances this secondary pleasure of the imagination proceeds from that action of the mind which compares the ideas arising from the original objects with the ideas we receive from the statue, picture, description, or sound that represents them. It is impossible for us to give the necessary reason why this operation of the mind is attended with so much pleasure, as I have before observed on the same occasion, but we find a great variety of entertainments derived from this single principle; for it is this that not only gives us a relish of statuary, painting, and description, but makes us delight in all the actions and arts of mimicry. It is this that makes the several kinds of wit pleasant, which consists, as I have formerly shown, in the affinity of ideas—and, we may add, it is this also that raises the little satisfaction we sometimes find in the different sorts of false wit, whether it consists in the affinity of letters, as in anagram, acrostic; or of syllables, as in doggerel rhymes, echoes; or of words, as in puns, quibbles; or of a whole sentence or poem to wings and altars. The final cause, probably, of annexing pleasure to this operation of the mind was to quicken and encourage us in our searches after truth, since the distinguishing one thing from another and the right discerning betwixt our ideas depends wholly upon our comparing them together and observing the congruity or disagreement that appears among the several works of nature.

But I shall here confine myself to those pleasures of the imagination which proceed from ideas raised by words, because most of the observations that agree with descriptions are equally applicable to painting and statuary.

Words, when well chosen, have so great a force in them that a description often gives us more lively ideas than the sight of things themselves. The reader finds a scene drawn in stronger colors and painted more to the life in his imagination by the help of words than by an actual survey of the scene which they describe. In this case the poet seems to get the better of nature; he takes, indeed, the landscape after her but gives it more vigorous touches, heightens its beauty, and so enlivens the whole piece that the images which flow from the objects themselves appear weak and faint in comparison of those that come from the expressions. The reason probably may be because in the survey of any object we have only so much of it painted on the imagination as comes in at the eye; but in its description the poet gives us as free a view of it as he pleases and discovers to us several parts that either we did not attend to or that lay out of our sight when we first beheld it. As we look on any object, our idea of it is perhaps made up of two or three simple ideas; but when the poet represents it, he may either give us a more complex idea of it or only raise in us such ideas as are most apt to affect the imagination. . . .

The pleasures of these secondary views of the imagination are of a wider and more universal nature than those it has when joined with sight, for not only what is great, strange, or beautiful but anything that is disagreeable when looked upon pleases us in an apt description. Here, therefore, we must inquire after a new principle of pleasure, which is nothing else but the action of the mind which compares the ideas that arise from words with the ideas that arise from the objects themselves; and why this operation of the mind is attended with so much pleasure we have before considered. For this reason, therefore, the description of a dunghill is pleasing to the imagination if the image be represented to our minds by suitable expressions, though perhaps this may be more properly called the pleasure of the understanding than of the fancy, because we are not so much delighted with the image that is contained in the description as with the aptness of the description to excite the image.

But if the description of what is little, common, or deformed be acceptable to the imagination, the description of what is great, surprising, or beautiful is much more so, because here we are not only delighted with comparing the representation with the original but are highly pleased with the original itself. Most readers, I believe, are more charmed with Milton's description of Paradise than of Hell; they are both perhaps equally perfect in their kind, but in the one the brimstone and sulphur are not so refreshing to the imagination as the beds of flowers and the wilderness of sweets in the other.

There is yet another circumstance which recommends a description more than all the rest, and that is if it represents to us such objects as are apt to raise a secret ferment in the mind of the reader and to work with violence upon his passions. For in this case we are at once warmed and enlightened; so that the pleasure becomes more universal and is several ways qualified to entertain us. Thus, in painting it is pleasant to look on the picture of any face where the resemblance is hit, but the pleasure increases if it be the picture of a face that is beautiful, and is still greater if the beauty be softened with an air of melancholy or sorrow. The two leading passions which the more serious parts of poetry endeavor to stir up in us are terror and pity. And here, by the way, one would wonder how it comes to pass that such passions as are very unpleasant at all other times are very agreeable when excited by proper descriptions. It is not strange that we should take delight in such passages as are apt to produce hope, joy, admiration, love, or the like emotions in us, because they never rise in the mind without an inward pleasure which attends them. But how comes it to pass that we should take delight in being terrified or dejected by a description, when we find so much uneasiness in the fear or grief which we receive from any other occasion?

If we consider, therefore, the nature of this pleasure, we shall find that it does not arise so properly from the description of what is terrible as from the reflection we make on ourselves at the time of reading it. When we look on such hideous objects, we are not a little pleased to think we are in no danger of them. We consider them at the same time as dreadful and harmless; so that the more frightful appearance they make, the greater is the pleasure we receive from the sense of our own safety. In short, we look upon the terrors of a description with the same curiosity and satisfaction that we survey a dead monster.

FRANCIS HUTCHESON [1694–1746]

>>>>><<<<<

From *An Inquiry into the Original of Our Ideas of Beauty and Virtue* [1725]

THE PREFACE

There is no part of Philosophy of more importance, than a just Knowledge of Human Nature, and its various Powers and Dispositions. Our late Inquirys have been very much employ'd about our Understanding, and the several Methods of obtaining Truth. We generally acknowledge, that the Importance of any Truth is nothing else than its Moment, or Efficacy to make Men happy, or to give them the greatest and most lasting Pleasure; and Wisdom denotes only a Capacity of pursuing this End by the best Means. It must surely then be of the greatest importance, to have distinct Conceptions of this End it self, as well as of the Means, necessary to obtain it; that we may find out which are the greatest and most lasting Pleasures, and not employ our Reason, after all our laborious Improvements of it, in trifling Pursuits, It is to be fear'd indeed, that most of our Studys, without this Inquiry, will be of very little use to us; for they seem to have scarce any other tendency than to lead us into speculative Knowledge it self. Nor are we distinctly told how it is that Knowledge, or Truth, is pleasant to us.

This Consideration put the Author of the following Papers upon inquiring into the various Pleasures which Human Nature is capable of receiving. We shall generally find in our modern philosophick Writings, nothing farther on this Head, than some bare Division of them into Sen-

Reprinted from the 3rd edition (London: 1729).

sible, and Rational, and some trite Common-place Arguments to prove the latter more valuable than the former. Our sensible Pleasures are slightly passed over, and explain'd only by some Instances in Tastes, Smells, Sounds, or such like, which Men of any tolerable Reflection generally look upon as very trifling Satisfactions. Our rational Pleasures have had much the same kind of treatment. We are seldom taught any other Notion of rational Pleasure than that which we have upon reflecting on our Possession, or Claim to those Objects, which may be Occasions of Pleasure. Such Objects we call advantageous; but Advantage, or Interest, cannot be distinctly conceiv'd, till we know what those Pleasures are which advantageous Objects are apt to excite; and what Senses or Powers of Perception we have with respect to such Objects. We may perhaps find such an Inquiry of more importance in Morals, to prove what we call the Reality of Virtue, or that it is the surest Happiness of the Agent, than one would at first imagine.

In reflecting upon our external Senses, we plainly see, that our Perceptions of Pleasure, or Pain, do not depend directly on our Will. Objects do not please us, according as we incline they should. The presence of some Objects necessarily pleases us, and the presence of others as necessarily displeases us. Nor can we by our Will, any otherwise procure Pleasure, or avoid Pain, than by procuring the former kind of Objects, and avoiding the latter. By the very Frame of our Nature the one is made the occasion of Delight, and the other of Dissatisfaction.

The same Observation will hold in all many other sorts of Objects, which please, our other Pleasures and Pains. For there are or displease us as necessarily, as material Objects do when they operate upon our Organs of Sense. There is scarcely any Object which our Minds are employ'd about, which is not thus constituted the necessary occasion of some Pleasure or Pain. Thus we find our selves pleas'd with a regular Form, a piece of Architecture or Painting, a Composition of Notes, a Theorem, an Action, an Affection, a Character. And we are conscious that this Pleasure necessarily arises from the Contemplation of the Idea, which is then present to our Minds, with all its Circumstances, altho some of these Ideas have nothing of what we commonly call sensible Perception in them; and in those which have, the Pleasure arises from some Uniformity, Order, Arrangement, Imitation; and not from the simple Ideas of Colour, or Sound, or mode of Extension separately consider'd.

These Determinations to be pleas'd with any Forms, or Ideas which occur to our Observation, the Author chooses to call SENSES; distinguishing them from the Powers which commonly go by that Name, by calling our Power of perceiving the Beauty of Regularity, Order, Harmony, an INTERNAL SENSE; and that Determination to approve Affections, Actions, or Characters of rational Agents, which we call virtuous, he marks by the name of a MORAL SENSE.

His principal Design is to shew, "That Human Nature was not left quite indifferent in the affair of Virtue, to form to it self Observations concerning the Advantage, or Disadvantage of Actions, and accordingly to regulate its Conduct." The weakness of our Reason, and the avocations arising from the Infirmities and Necessities of our Nature, are so great, that very few Men could ever have form'd those long Deductions of Reason, which shew some Actions to be in the whole advantageous to the Agent, and their Contrarys pernicious. The AUTHOR of Nature has much better furnish'd us for a virtuous Conduct, than our Moralists seem to imagine, by almost as quick and powerful Instructions, as we have for the preservation of our Bodys. He has given us strong Affections to be the Springs of each virtuous Action; and made Virtue a lovely form, that we might easily distinguish it from its contrary, and be made happy by the pursuit of it.

This moral Sense of Beauty in Actions and Affections, may appear strange at first View. Some of our Moralists themselves are offended at it in my LORD SHAFTESBURY; so much are they accustom'd to deduce every Approbation, or Aversion, from rational Views of Interest, (except it be merely in the Simple Ideas of the external Senses) and have such a Horror at innate Ideas, which they imagine this borders upon. But this moral Sense has no relation to innate Ideas, as will appear in the second Treatise. Our Gentlemen of good Taste can tell us of a great many Senses, Tastes, and Relishes for Beauty, Harmony, Imitation in Painting and Poetry; and may not we find too in Mankind a Relish for a Beauty in Characters, in Manners? I doubt we have made Philosophy, as well as Religion, by our foolish management of it, so austere and ungainly a Form, that a Gentleman cannot easily bring himself to like it; and those who are strangers to it, can scarcely bear to hear our Description of it. So much it is changed from what was once the delight of the finest Gentlemen among the Antients, and their Recreation after the Hurry of publick Affairs!

In the first Treatise, the Author perhaps in some Instances has gone too far, in supposing a greater Agreement of Mankind in their Sense of Beauty, than Experience will confirm; but all he is sollicitous about is to shew "That there is some Sense of Beauty natural to Men; that we find as great an Agreement of Men in their Relishes of Forms, as in their external Senses, which all agree to be natural; and that Pleasure or Pain, Delight or Aversion, are naturally join'd to their Perceptions." If the Reader be convinc'd of such Determination of the

Mind to be pleas'd with Forms, Proportions, Resemblances, Theorems; it will be no difficult matter to apprehend another superior Sense, natural also to Men, determining them to be pleas'd with Actions, Characters, Affections. This is the moral Sense, which makes the Subject of the second Treatise.

The proper Occasions of Perception by the external Senses, occur to us as soon as we come into the World; whence perhaps we easily look upon these Senses to be natural; but the Objects of the superior Senses of Beauty and Virtue generally do not. It is probably some little time before Children reflect, or at least let us know that they reflect upon Proportion and Similitude; upon Affections, Characters, Tempers; or come to know the external Actions which are Evidences of them. Hence we imagine that their Sense of Beauty, and their moral Sentiments of Actions, must be entirely owing to Instruction, and Education; whereas it is as easy to conceive, how a Character, a Temper, as soon as they are observ'd, may be constituted by NATURE the necessary occasion of Pleasure, or an Object of Approbation, as a Taste or a Sound; tho these Objects present themselves to our Observation sooner than the other.

SECT. I

Concerning some Powers of Perception, distinct from what is generally understood by Sensation

To make the following Observations understood, it may be necessary to premise some Definitions, and Observations, either universally acknowledg'd, or sufficiently prov'd by many Writers both antient and modern, concerning our Perceptions called Sensations, and the Actions of the Mind consequent upon them.

Art. I. Those Ideas which are rais'd in the Mind upon the presence of external Objects, and their acting upon our Bodys, are call'd Sensations. We find that the Mind in such Cases is passive, and has not

Power directly to prevent the Perception or Idea, or to vary it at its Reception, as long as we continue our Bodys in a state fit to be acted upon by the external Object.

II. When two Perceptions are intirely different from each other, or agree in nothing but the general Idea of Sensation, we call the Powers of receiving those different Perceptions, different Senses. Thus Seeing and Hearing denote the different Powers of receiving the Ideas of Colours and Sounds. And altho Colours have great Differences among themselves, as also have Sounds, yet there is a greater Agreement among the most opposite Colours, than between any Colour and a Sound: Hence we call all Colours Perceptions of the same Sense. All the several Senses seem to have their distinct Organs, except Feeling, which is in some degree diffus'd over the whole Body.

III. The Mind has a Power of compounding Ideas, which were receiv'd separately; of comparing Objects by means of the Ideas, and of observing their Relations and Proportions; of enlarging and diminishing its Ideas at pleasure, or in any certain Ratio, or Degree; and of considering separately each of the simple Ideas, which might perhaps have been impress'd jointly in the Sensation. This last Operation we commonly call Abstraction.

IV. The Ideas of Substances are compounded of the various simple Ideas jointly impress'd, when they presented themselves to our Senses. We define Substances only by enumerating these sensible Ideas: And such Definitions may raise an Idea clear enough of the Substance in the Mind of one who never immediately perceiv'd the Substance; provided he has separately receiv'd by his Senses all the simple Ideas which are in the Composition of the complex one of the Substance defin'd: But if there be any simple Ideas which he has not receiv'd, or if he wants any of the Senses necessary for the Perception of them, no Definition can raise any simple

Idea which has not been before perceived by the Senses.

v. Hence it follows, "That when Instruction, Education, or Prejudice of any kind, raise any Desire or Aversion toward an Object, this Desire or Aversion must be founded upon an Opinion of some Perfection, or of some Deficiency in those Qualitys, for Perception of which we have the proper Senses." Thus if Beauty be desir'd by one who has not the Sense of Sight, the Desire must be rais'd by some apprehended Regularity of Figure, Sweetness of Voice, Smoothness, or Softness, or some other Quality perceivable by the other Senses without relation to the Ideas of Colour.

vi. Many of our sensitive Perceptions are pleasant, and many painful, immediately, and that without any knowledge of the Cause of this Pleasure or Pain, or how the Objects excite it, or are the Occasions of it; or without seeing to what farther Advantage or Detriment the Use of such Objects might tend: Nor would the most accurate Knowledge of these things vary either the Pleasure or Pain of the Perception, however it might give a rational Pleasure distinct from the sensible; or might raise a distinct Joy, from a prospect of farther Advantage in the Object, or Aversion, from an apprehension of Evil.

vii. The simple Ideas rais'd in different Persons by the same Object, are probably some way different, when they disagree in their Approbation or Dislike; and in the same Person, when his Fancy at one time differs from what it was at another. This will appear from reflecting on those Objects, to which we have now an Aversion tho they were formerly agreeable: And we shall generally find that there is some accidental Conjunction of a disagreeable Idea, which always recurs with the Object. . . .

viii. The only Pleasure of Sense, which many Philosophers seem to consider, is that which accompanys the simple Ideas of Sensation: But there are far greater Pleasures in those complex Ideas of Objects, which obtain the Names of Beautiful, Regular, Harmonious. Thus every one acknowledges he is more delighted with a fine Face, a just Picture, than with the View of any one Colour, were it as strong and lively as possible; and more pleas'd with a Prospect of the Sun arising among settled Clouds, and colouring their Edges with a starry Hemisphere, a fine Landskip, a regular Building, than with a clear blue Sky, a smooth Sea, or a large open Plain, not diversify'd by Woods, Hills, Waters, Buildings: And yet even these latter Appearances are not quite simple. So in Musick, the Pleasure of fine Composition is incomparably greater than that of any one Note, how sweet, full, or swelling soever.

ix. Let it be observ'd, that in the following Papers, the Word Beauty is taken for the Idea rais'd in us, and a Sense of Beauty for our Power of receiving this Idea. Harmony also denotes our pleasant Ideas arising from Composition of Sounds, and a good Ear (as it is generally taken) a Power of perceiving this Pleasure. In the following Section, an Attempt is made to discover "what is the immediate Occasion of these pleasant Ideas, or what real Quality in the Objects ordinarily excites them."

x. It is of no consequence whether we call these Ideas of Beauty and Harmony, Perceptions of the External Senses of Seeing and Hearing, or not. I should rather choose to call our Power of perceiving these Ideas, an INTERNAL SENSE, were it only for the Convenience of distinguishing them from other Sensations of Seeing and Hearing, which Men may have without Perception of Beauty and Harmony. It is plain from Experience, that many Men have in the common meaning, the Senses of Seeing and Hearing perfect enough; they perceive all the simple Ideas separately, and have their Pleasures; they distinguish them from each other, such as one Colour from another, either quite different, or the stronger or fainter of the same Colour, when they are plac'd beside each other, altho they may often confound their Names when they occur a-part from each other; as some do the Names of Green and Blue: they can tell in separate Notes, the higher, lower, sharper or flatter, when separately sounded; in Figures they discern the Length, Breadth, Wideness of each Line, Surface, Angle; and may be as capable of hearing and seeing at great distances as any Men whatsoever: And yet perhaps they shall find no Pleasure in Musical Compositions, In painting, Architecture, natural Land-skip; or but a very weak one in comparison of what others enjoy from the same Objects. This greater Capacity of receiving such pleasant Ideas we commonly call a fine Genius or Taste: in Musick we seem universally to acknowledge something like a distinct Sense from the External one of Hearing, and call it a good Ear; and the like distinction we should probably acknowledge in other Objects, had we also got distinct Names to denote these Powers of Perception by.

xi. There will appear another Reason perhaps hereafter, for calling this Power of perceiving the Ideas of Beauty, an Internal Sense, from this, that in some other Affairs, where our External Senses are not much concern'd, we discern a sort of Beauty, very like, in many respects, to that observ'd in sensible Objects, and accompany'd with like Pleasure: Such is that Beauty perceiv'd in Theorems, or universal Truths, in general Causes, and in some extensive Principles of Action.

xii. Let every one here consider, how different we must suppose the Perception to be, with which a Poet is transported upon the Prospect of any of those Objects of natural Beauty, which ravish us even in his Description; from that cold lifeless Conception which we imagine in a dull Critick, or one of the Virtuosi, without what we call a fine Taste. This latter Class of Men may have greater Perfection in that Knowledge which is deriv'd from external Sensation; they can tell all the specifick Differences of Trees, Herbs, Minerals, Metals; they know the Form of every Leaf, Stalk, Root, Flower, and Seed of all the Species, about which the Poet is often very ignorant: And yet the Poet shall have a much more delightful Perception of the Whole; and not only the Poet but any Man of a fine Taste. Our External Senses may by measuring teach us all the Proportions of Architecture to the Tenth of an Inch, and the Situation of every Muscle in the human Body; and a good Memory may retain these: and yet there is still something farther necessary, not only to make a Man a compleat Master in Architecture, Painting or Statuary, but even a tolerable Judge in these Works; or capable of receiving the highest Pleasure in contemplating them. Since then there are such different Powers of Perception, where what are commonly called the External Senses are the same; since the most accurate Knowledge of what the External Senses discover often does not give the Pleasure of Beauty or Harmony, which yet one of a good Taste will enjoy at once without much Knowledge; we may justly use another Name for these higher, and more delightful Perceptions of Beauty and Harmony, and call the Power of receiving such Impressions, an Internal Sense. The Difference of the Perceptions seems sufficient to vindicate the Use of a different Name, especially when we are told in what meaning the Word is applied.

xiii. This superior Power of Perception is justly called a Sense, because of its Affinity to the other Senses in this, that the Pleasure does not arise from any Knowledge of Principles, Proportions, Causes, or of the Usefulness of the Object; but strikes us at first with the Idea of Beauty: nor does the most accurate Knowledge increase this Pleasure of Beauty, however it may superadd a distinct rational Pleasure from prospects of Advantage, or from the Increase of Knowledge.

xiv. And farther, the Ideas of Beauty

and Harmony, like other sensible Ideas, are necessarily pleasant to us, as well as immediately so; neither can any Resolution of our own, nor any Prospect of Advantage or Disadvantage, vary the Beauty or Deformity of an Object: For as in the external Sensations, no View of Interest will make an Object grateful, nor View of Detriment, distinct from immediate Pain in the Perception, make it disagreeable to the Sense; so propose the whole World as a Reward, or threaten the greatest Evil, to make us approve a deform'd Object, or disapprove a beautiful one; Dissimulation may be procur'd by Rewards or Threatenings, or we may in external Conduct abstain from any pursuit of the Beautiful, and pursue the Deform'd; but our Sentiments of the Former and our Perceptions, would continue invariably the same.

xv. Hence it plainly appears, "that some Objects are immediately the Occasions of this Pleasure of Beauty, and that we have Senses fitted for perceiving it; and that it is distinct from that Joy which arises upon prospect of Advantage." Nay, do not we often see Convenience and Use neglected to obtain Beauty, without any other prospect of Advantage in the Beautiful Form, than the suggesting the pleasant Ideas of Beauty? Now this shews us, that however we may pursue beautiful Objects from Self-love, with a view to obtain the Pleasures of Beauty, as in Architecture, Gardening, and many other Affairs; yet there must be a Sense of Beauty, antecedent to Prospects even of this Advantage, without which Sense, these Objects would not be thus Advantageous, nor excite in us this Pleasure which constitutes them advantageous. Our Sense of Beauty from Objects, by which they are constituted good to us, is very distinct from our Desire of them when they are thus constituted: Our Desire of Beauty may be counter-balanc'd by Rewards or Threatnings, but never our Sense of it; even as Fear of Death may make us desire a bitter Potion, or neglect those Meats which the Sense of Taste would recommend as pleasant; and yet no prospect of Advantage, or Fear of Evil, can make that Potion agreeable to the Sense, or Meat disagreeable to it, which was not so antecedently to this Prospect. The same holds true of the Sense of Beauty and Harmony; that the Pursuit of such Objects if frequently neglected, from prospects of Advantage, Aversion to Labour, or any other Motive or Interest, does not prove that we have no Sense of Beauty, but only that our Desire of it may be counter-balanc'd by a stronger Desire. . . .

xvii. Beauty is either Original or Comparative; or, if any like the Terms better, Absolute, or Relative: Only let it be observ'd, that by Absolute or Original Beauty, is not understood any Quality suppos'd to be in the Object, which should itself be beautiful, without relation to any Mind which perceives it: For Beauty, like other Names of sensible Ideas, properly denotes the Perception of some Mind; so Cold, Hot, Sweet, Bitter, denote the Sensations in our Minds, to which perhaps there is no resemblance in the Objects, which excite these Ideas in us, however we generally imagine otherwise. The Ideas of Beauty and Harmony being excited upon our Perception of some primary Quality, and having relation to Figure and Time, may indeed have a nearer resemblance to Objects, than these Sensations, which seem not so much any Pictures of Objects, as Modifications of the perceiving Mind; and yet were there no Mind with a Sense of Beauty to contemplate Objects, I see not how they could be call'd beautiful. We therefore by Absolute Beauty understand only that Beauty, which we perceive in Objects without comparison to any thing external, of which the Object is suppos'd an Imitation, or Picture; such as that Beauty perceiv'd from the Works of Nature, artificial Forms, Figures, Theorems. Comparative or Relative Beauty is that which we perceive in Objects, commonly considered as Imitations or Resemblances of something else. These two Kinds of Beauty employ the three following Sections.

SECT. II

Of Original or Absolute Beauty

I. Since it is certain that we have Ideas of Beauty and Harmony, let us examine what Quality in Objects excites these Ideas, or is the occasion of them. And let it be here observ'd, that our Inquiry is only about the Qualitys which are beautiful to Men; or about the Foundation of their Sense of Beauty: for, as was above hinted, Beauty has always relation to the Sense of some Mind; and when we afterwards shew how generally the Objects which occur to us, are beautiful, we mean that such Objects are agreeable to the Sense of Men: for there are many Objects which seem no way beautiful to Men, and yet other Animals seem delighted with them; they may have Senses otherwise constituted than those of Men, and may have the Ideas of Beauty excited by Objects of a quite different Form. We see Animals fitted for every Place; and what to Men appears rude and shapeless, or loathsom, may be to them a Paradise.

II. That we may more distinctly discover the general Foundation or Occasion of the Ideas of Beauty among Men, it will be necessary to consider it first in its simpler Kinds, such as occurs to us in regular Figures; and we may perhaps find that the same Foundation extends to all the more complex Species of it. _Most Important_

III. The Figures which excite in us the Ideas of Beauty, seem to be those in which there is Uniformity amidst Variety. There are many Conceptions of Objects which are agreeable upon other accounts, such as Grandeur, Novelty, Sanctity, and some others, which shall be mention'd hereafter. But what we call Beautiful in objects, to speak in the Mathematical Style, seems to be in a compound Ratio of Uniformity and Variety: so that where the Uniformity of Bodys is equal, the Beauty is as the Variety;

and where the Variety is equal, the Beauty is as the Uniformity. This will be plain from Examples. . . . _(cavil on notes)_

V. The same Foundation we have for our Sense of Beauty in the Works of NATURE. In every Part of the World which we call Beautiful, there is a surprizing Uniformity amidst an almost infinite Variety. Many Parts of the Universe seem not at all design'd for the use of Man; nay, it is but a very small Spot with which we have any acquaintance. The Figures and Motions of the great Bodys are not obvious to our Senses, but found out by Reasoning and Reflection, upon many long Observations: and yet as far as we can by Sense discover or by Reasoning enlarge our Knowledge, and extend our Imagination, we generally find their Structure, Order, and Motion, agreeable to our Sense of Beauty. Every particular Object in Nature does not indeed appear beautiful to us; but there is a great Profusion of Beauty over most of the Objects which occur either to our Senses, or Reasonings upon Observation: For not to mention the apparent Situation of the heavenly Bodys in the Circumference of a great Sphere, which is wholly occasion'd by the Imperfection of our Sight in discerning Distances; the Forms of all the great Bodys in the Universe are nearly Spherical; the Orbits of their Revolutions generally Elliptick, and without great Eccentricity, in those which continually occur to our Observation: now these are Figures of great Uniformity, and therefore pleasing to us.

. . .

XIV. But in all these Instances of Beauty let it be observ'd, That the Pleasure is communicated to those who never reflected on this general Foundation; and that all here alleg'd is this, "That the pleasant Sensation arises only from Objects, in which there is Uniformity amidst Variety": We may have the Sensation without knowing what is the Occasion of it; as a Man's Taste may suggest Ideas of Sweets, Acids, Bitters, tho he be ignorant of the Forms of the small Bodys, or their Motions, which excite these Perceptions in him.

Of the Beauty of Theorems

I. The Beauty of Theorems, or universal Truths demonstrated, deserves a distinct Consideration, being of a Nature pretty different from the former kinds of Beauty; and yet there is none in which we shall see such an amazing Variety with Uniformity: and hence arises a very great Pleasure distinct from Prospects of any farther Advantage.

II. For in one Theorem we may find included, with the most exact Agreement, an infinite Multitude of particular Truths; nay, often an Infinity of Infinites: so that altho the Necessity of forming abstract Ideas and universal Theorems, arises perhaps from the Limitation of our Minds, which cannot admit an infinite Multitude of singular Ideas or Judgments at once, yet this Power gives us an Evidence of the Largeness of the human Capacity above our Imagination. Thus for instance, the 47th Proposition of the first Book of EUCLID's *Elements* contains an infinite Multitude of Truths, concerning the infinite possible Sizes of right-angled Triangles, as you make the Area greater or less; and in each of these Sizes you may find an infinite Multitude of dissimilar Triangles, as you vary the Proportion of the Base to the Perpendicular; all which Infinitys of Infinites agree in the general Theorem. In Algebraick, and the Fluxional Calculations, we shall still find a greater Variety of particular Truths included in general Theorems; not only in general Equations applicable to all Kinds of Quantity, but in more particular Investigations of Areas and Tangents: In which one Manner of Operation shall discover Theorems applicable to infinite Orders or Species of Curves, to the infinite Sizes of each Species, and to the infinite Points of the infinite Individuals of each Size.

III. That we may the better discern this Agreement, or Unity of an Infinity of Objects, in the general Theorem, to be the Foundation of the Beauty or Pleasure attending their Discovery, let us compare our Satisfaction in such Discoverys, with the uneasy state of Mind in which we are, when we can only measure Lines, or Surfaces, by a Scale, or are making Experiments which we can reduce to no general Canon, but only heaping up a Multitude of particular incoherent Observations. Now each of these Trials discovers a new Truth, but with no Pleasure or Beauty, notwithstanding the Variety, till we can discover some sort of Unity, or reduce them to some general Canon.

IV. Again, let us take a Metaphysical Axiom, such as this, Every Whole is greater than its Part; and we shall find no Beauty in the Contemplation. For tho this Proposition contains many Infinitys of particular Truths; yet the Unity is inconsiderable, since they all agree only in a vague, undetermin'd Conception of Whole and Part, and in an indefinite Excess of the former above the latter, which is sometimes great and sometimes small. So, should we hear that the Cylinder is greater than the inscrib'd Sphere, and this again greater than the Cone of the same Altitude and Diameter of the Base, we shall find no pleasure in this Knowledge of a general Relation of greater and less, without any precise Difference or Proportion. But when we see the universal exact Agreement of all possible Sizes of such Systems of Solids, that they preserve to each other the constant Ration of 3,2,1; how beautiful is the Theorem, and how we are ravish'd with its first Discovery.

We may likewise observe, that easy or obvious Propositions, even where the Unity is sufficiently distinct, and determinate, do not please us so much as those, which being less obvious, give us some Surprize in the Discovery: Thus we find little Pleasure in discovering that a Line bisecting the vertical Angle of an Isosceles Triangle, bisects the Base, or the Reverse; or, that Equilateral Triangles are Equiangular. These Truths we almost know Intuitively, without Demonstration: They are like common Goods, or those which Men have long possessed, which do not give such sensible Joys as much smaller new Additions may give us. But let none hence imagine, that the sole Pleasure of Theorems is from Surprize; for the same Novelty of a single Experiment does not please us much: nor ought we to conclude from the greater Pleasure accompanying a new, or unexpected Advantage, that Surprize, or Novelty is the only Pleasure of Life, or the only ground of Delight in Truth. Another kind of Surprize in certain Theorems increases our pleasure above that we have in Theorems of greater Extent; when we discover a general Truth, which upon some confused Notion we had reputed false: as that Assymptotes always approaching should never meet the Curve. This is like the Joy of unexpected Advantage where we dreaded Evil. But still the Unity of many Particulars in the general Theorem is necessary to give Pleasure in any Theorem. . . .

It is easy to see how Men are charm'd with the Beauty of such Knowledge, besides its Usefulness; and how this sets them upon deducing the Propertys of each Figure from one Genesis, and demonstrating the mechanick Forces from one Theorem of the Composition of Motion; even after they have sufficient Knowledge and Certainty in all these Truths from distinct independent Demonstrations. And this Pleasure we enjoy even when we have no Prospect of obtaining any other Advantage from such Manner of Deduction, than the immediate Pleasure of contemplating the Beauty: nor could Love of Fame excite us to such regular Methods of Deduction, were we not conscious that Mankind are pleas'd with them immediately, by this internal Sense of their Beauty.

It is no less easy to see into what absurd Attempts Men have been led by this Sense of Beauty, and an Affection of obtaining it

in the other Sciences as well as the Mathematicks. 'Twas this probably which set DESCARTES on that hopeful Project of deducing all human Knowledge from one Proposition, viz. *Cogito, ergo sum;* while others with as little Sense contended, that *Impossibile est idem simul esse and non esse,* had much fairer Pretensions to the Style and Title of *Principium humanae Cognitionis absolute primum.* Mr. LEIBNITZ had an equal Affection for his favourite Principle of a sufficient Reason for every thing in Nature, and brags to Dr. CLARKE of the Wonders he had wrought in the intellectual World by its Assistance; but his learned Antagonist seems to think he had not sufficient Reason for his Boasting. If we look into particular Sciences, we may see in the Systems learned Men have given us of them, the Inconveniences of this Love of Uniformity. . . .

SECT. IV

Of Relative or Comparative Beauty

I. If the preceding Thoughts concerning the Foundation of absolute Beauty be just, we may easily understand wherein relative Beauty consists. All Beauty is relative to the Sense of some Mind perceiving it; but what we call relative is that which is apprehended in any Object, commonly consider'd as an Imitation of some Original: And this Beauty is founded on a Conformity, or a kind of Unity between the Original and the Copy. The Original may be either some Object in Nature, or some establish'd Idea; for if there be any known Idea as a Standard, and Rules to fix this Image or Idea by, we may make a beautiful Imitation. Thus a Statuary, Painter, or Poet, may please us with an HERCULES, if his Piece retains that Grandeur, and those marks of Strength, and Courage, which we imagine in that Hero.

And farther, to obtain comparative Beauty alone, it is not necessary that there be any Beauty in the Original; the Imitation of absolute Beauty may indeed in the whole make a more lovely Piece, and yet an exact Imitation shall still be beautiful, tho the Original were intirely void of it: Thus the Deformitys of old Age in a Picture, the rudest Rocks or Mountains in a Landskip, if well represented, shall have abundant Beauty, tho perhaps not so great as if the Original were absolutely beautiful, and as well represented: Nay, perhaps the Novelty may make us prefer the representation of Irregularity.

II. The same Observation holds true in the Descriptions of the Poets either of natural Objects or Persons; and this relative Beauty is what they should principally endeavour to obtain, as the peculiar Beauty of their Works. By the *Moratoe Fabulae*, we are not to understand virtuous Manners in a moral Sense, but a just Representation of Manners or Characters as they are in Nature; and that the Actions and Sentiments be suited to the Characters of the Persons to whom they are ascrib'd in Epick and Dramatick Poetry. Perhaps very good Reasons may be suggested from the Nature of our Passions, to prove that a Poet should not draw his Characters perfectly Virtuous; these Characters indeed abstractly consider'd might give more Pleasure, and have more Beauty than the imperfect ones which occur in Life with a mixture of Good and Evil: But it may suffice at present to suggest against this Choice, that we have more lively Ideas of imperfect Men with all their Passions, than of morally perfect Heroes, such as really never occur to our Observation; and of which consequently we cannot judge exactly as to their Agreement with the Copy. And farther, thro' Consciousness of our own State, we are more nearly touch'd and affected by the imperfect Characters; since in them we see represented, in the Persons of others, the Contrasts of Inclinations, and the Struggles between the Passions of Self-Love and those of Honour and Virtue, which we often feel in our own Breasts. This is the

Perfection of Beauty for which HOMER is justly admir'd, as well as for the Variety of his Characters.

III. Many other Beautys of Poetry may be reduc'd under this Class of relative Beauty: The Probability is absolutely necessary to make us imagine Resemblance; it is by Resemblance that the Similitudes, Metaphors and Allegorys are made either the Subject or the Thing compar'd to it have Beauty or not; the Beauty indeed is greater, when both have some original Beauty or Dignity as well as Resemblance: and this is the foundation of the Rule of studying Decency in Metaphors and Similys as well as Likeness. The Measures and Cadence are instances of Harmony, and come under the head of absolute Beauty.

IV. We may here observe a strange Proneness in our Minds to make perpetual Comparisons of all things which occur to our Observation, even of those which are very different from each other. There are certain Resemblances in the Motions of all Animals upon like Passions, which easily found a Comparison; but this does not serve to entertain our Fancy: Inanimate Objects have often such Positions as resemble those of the human Body in various Circumstances; these Airs or Gestures of the Body are Indications of certain Dispositions in the Mind, so that our very Passions and Affections as well as other Circumstances obtain a Resemblance to natural inanimate Objects. Thus a Tempest at Sea is often an Emblem of Wrath; a Plant or Tree drooping under the Rain, of a Person in Sorrow; a Poppy bending its Stalk, or a Flower withering when cut by the Plow, resembles the Death of a blooming Hero; an aged Oak in the Mountains shall represent an old Empire, a Flame seizing a Wood shall represent other things, even the most remote, especially the Passions and Circumstances of human Nature in which we are more nearly concern'd; and to confirm this and furnish Instances of it, one need only look into HOMER or VIRGIL.

A fruitful Fancy would find in a Grove, or a Wood, an Emblem for every Character in a Commonwealth, and every turn of Temper, or Station in Life.

v. Concerning that kind of comparative Beauty which has a necessary relation to some establish'd Idea, we may observe, that some Works of Art acquire a distinct Beauty by their Correspondence to some universally suppos'd Intention in the Artificers, or the Persons who employ'd him: And to obtain this Beauty, sometimes they do not form their Works so as to attain the highest Perfection of original Beauty separately consider'd; because a Composition of this relative Beauty, along with some degree of the original Kind, may give more Pleasure, than a more perfect original Beauty separately. Thus we see, that strict Regularity in laying out of Gardens in Parterres, Vistas, parallel Walks, is often neglected, to obtain an Imitation of Nature even in some of its Wildnesses. And we are more pleas'd with this Imitation, especially when the Scene is large and spacious, than with the more confin'd Exactness of regular Works. So likewise in the Monuments erected in honour of deceased Heroes, altho a Cylinder, or Prism, or regular Solid, may have more original Beauty than a very acute Pyramid or Obelisk, yet the latter pleases more, by answering better the suppos'd Intentions of Stability, and being conspicuous. For the same reason Cubes, or square Prisms, are generally chosen for the Pedestals of Statues, and not any of the more beautiful Solids, which do not seem so secure from rolling. This may be the reason too, why Columns or Pillars look best when made a little taper from the middle, or a third from the bottom, that they may not seem top-heavy and in danger of falling.

vi. The like reason may influence Artists, in many other Instances, to depart from the Rules of original Beauty, as above laid down. And yet this is no Argument against our Sense of Beauty being founded, as was above explain'd, on Uniformity amidst Variety, but only an Evidence that our Sense of Beauty of the Original Kind may be vary'd and overbalanc'd by another kind of Beauty.

SECT. VI

Of the Universality of the Sense of Beauty among Men

I. We before insinuated, "That all Beauty has a relation to some perceiving Power"; and consequently since we know not how great a Variety of Senses there may be among Animals, there is no Form in Nature concerning which we can pronounce, "That it has no Beauty"; for it may still please some perceiving Power. But our Inquiry is confin'd to Men; and before we examine the Universality of this Sense of Beauty, or their agreement in approving Uniformity, it may be proper to consider, "whether, as the other Senses which give us Pleasure do also give us Pain, so this Sense of Beauty does make some Objects disagreeable to us, and the occasion of Pain."

That many Objects give no pleasure to our Sense is obvious; many are certainly void of Beauty: But then there is no Form which seems necessarily disagreeable of itself, when we dread no other Evil from it, and compare it with nothing better of the Kind. Many Objects are naturally displeasing, and distasteful to our external Senses, as well as others pleasing and agreeable; as Smells, Tastes, and some separate Sounds: but as to our Sense of Beauty, no Composition of Objects which give not unpleasant simple Ideas, seems positively unpleasant or painful of itself, had we never observ'd any thing better of the kind. Deformity is only the absence of Beauty, or deficiency in the Beauty expected in any Species: Thus bad Musick pleases Rusticks who never heard any better, and the finest Ear is not offended with tuning of Instruments if it be not too tedious, where no Harmony is expected; and yet much small Dissonancy shall offend amidst the Performance, where Harmony is expected. A rude Heap of Stones is no way offensive to one who shall be displeas'd with Irregularity in Architecture, where Beauty was expected. And had there been a Species of that Form which we now call ugly or deform'd, and had we never seen or expected greater Beauty, we should have receiv'd no disgust from it, altho the Pleasure would not have been so great in this Form as in those we now admire. Our Sense of Beauty seems design'd to give us positive Pleasure, but not positive Pain or Disgust, any farther than what arises from disappointment.

II. There are indeed many Faces which at first View are apt to raise Dislike; but this is generally not from any Deformity which of it self is positively displeasing, but either from want of expected Beauty, or much more from their carrying some natural indications of morally bad Dispositions, which we all acquire a Faculty of discerning in Countenances, Airs, and Gestures. That this is not occasion'd by any Form positively disgusting, will appear from this, That if upon long acquaintance we are sure of finding sweetness of Temper, Humanity and Cheerfulness, altho the bodily Form continues, it shall give us no Disgust or Displeasure; whereas if any thing were naturally disagreeable, or the occasion of Pain, or positive Distaste, it would always continue so, even altho the Aversion we might have toward it were counterbalanc'd by other Considerations. There are Horrors rais'd by some Objects, which are only the Effect of Fear for our selves, or Compassion towards others, when either Reason, or some foolish Association of Ideas, makes us apprehend Danger, and not the Effect of any thing in the Form it self: for we find that most of those Objects which excite Horror at first, when Experience or Reason has remov'd the Fear, may become the occasions of Pleasure; as ravenous Beasts, a tempestuous Sea, a craggy Precipice, a dark shady Valley.

III. We shall see hereafter, "That Associations of Ideas make Objects pleasant, and delightful, which are not naturally apt to give any such Pleasures; and the same way, the casual Conjunctions of Ideas may give a Disgust, where there is nothing disagreeable in the Form it self." And this is the occasion of many fantastick Aversions to Figures of some Animals, and to some other Forms: Thus Swine, Serpents of all Kinds, and some Insects really beautiful enough, are beheld with Aversion by many People, who have got some accidental Ideas associated to them. And for Distastes of this Kind, no other Account can be given.

IV. But as the universal Agreement of Mankind in their Sense of Beauty from Uniformity amidst Variety, we must consult Experience: and as we allow all Men Reason, since all Men are capable of understanding simple Arguments, tho few are capable of complex Demonstrations; so in this Case it must be sufficient to prove this sense of Beauty universal, "if all Men are better pleas'd with Uniformity in the simpler Instances than the contrary, even when there is no Advantage observ'd attending it; and likewise if all Men, according as their Capacity enlarges, so as to receive and compare more complex Ideas, have a greater Delight in Uniformity, and are pleas'd with its more complex Kinds, both Original and Relative."

Now let us consider if ever any Person was void of this Sense in the simpler Instances. Few Trials have been made in the simplest Instances of Harmony, because as soon as we find an Ear incapable of relishing complex Compositions, such as our Tunes are, no farther Pains are employ'd about such. But in Figures, did ever any Man make choice of a Trapezium, or any irregular Curve, for the Ichnography or Plan of his House, without Necessity, or some great Motive of Convenience? or to make the opposite Walls not parallel, or unequal in Height? Were ever Trapeziums, irregular Polygons or Curves chosen for the Forms of Doors or Windows, tho these

Figures might have answer'd the Uses as well, and would have often sav'd a great part of the Time, Labour and Expence to Workmen, which is now employ'd in suiting the Stones and Timber to the regular Forms? Among all the fantastick Modes of Dress, none was ever quite void of Uniformity, if it were only in the resemblance of the two Sides of the same Robe, and in some general Aptitude to the human Form. The Pictish Painting had always relative Beauty, by resemblance to other Objects, and often those Objects were originally beautiful. . . . But never were any so extravagant as to affect such Figures as are made by the casual spilling of liquid Colours. Who was ever pleas'd with an inequality of Heights in Windows of the same Range, or dissimilar Shapes of them? with unequal Legs or Arms, Eyes or Cheeks in a Mistress? It must however be acknowledg'd, "That Interest may often counterbalance our Sense of Beauty, in this Affair as well as in others, and superior good qualitys may make us overlook such Imperfections."

v. Nay farther, it may perhaps appear, "That Regularity and Uniformity are so copiously diffus'd thro' the Universe, and we are so readily determin'd to pursue this as the Foundation of Beauty in Works of Art, that there is scarcely any thing ever fancy'd as Beautiful, where there is not really something of this Uniformity and Regularity." We are indeed often mistaken in imagining that there is the greatest possible Beauty, where it is but very imperfect; but still it is some degree of Beauty, which pleases, altho there may be higher Degrees which we do not observe; and our Sense acts with full Regularity when we are pleas'd, altho we are kept by a false Prejudice from pursuing Objects which would please us more.

A goth, for instance, is mistaken, when from Education he imagines the Architecture of his Country to be the most perfect: and a Conjunction of some hostile Ideas, may make him have an Aversion to Roman Buildings, and study to demolish them, as some of our Reformers did the Popish Buildings, not being able to separate the Ideas of the superstitious Worship from the Forms of the Buildings where it was practised: and yet it is still real Beauty which pleases the GOTH, founded upon Uniformity amidst Variety. For the Gothick Pillars are uniform to each other, not only in their Sections, which are Lozengeform'd; but also in their Heights and Ornaments: Their Arches are not one uniform Curve, but yet they are Segments of similar Curves, and generally equal in the same Ranges. The very Indian Buildings have some kind of Uniformity, and many of the EASTERN NATIONS, tho they differ much from us, yet have great Regularity in their Manner, as well as the ROMANS in theirs. Our Indian Screens, which wonderfully supply our Imaginations with Ideas of Deformity, in which Nature is very churlish and sparing, do want indeed all the Beauty arising from Proportion of Parts, and Conformity to Nature; and yet they cannot disvest themselves of all Beauty and Uniformity in the separate Parts: And this diversifying the human Body into various Contortions, may give some wild Pleasure from Variety, since some Uniformity to the human Shape is still retain'd.

vi. There is one sort of Beauty which might perhaps have been better mention'd before, but will not be impertinent here, because the Taste or Relish of it is universal in all Nations, and with the Young as well as the Old, and that is the Beauty of History. Every one knows how dull a Study is to read over a Collection of Gazettes, which shall perhaps relate all the same Events with the Historian: The superior Pleasure then of History must arise, like that of Poetry, from the Manners; when we see a Character well drawn, wherein we find the secret Causes of a great Diversity of seemingly inconsistent Actions; or an Interest of State laid open, or an artful View nicely unfolded, the Execution of which influences very different and opposite Actions as the Circumstances may alter. Now this reduces the whole to an Unity of Design at least: And this may be observ'd in the very Fables which entertain Children, otherwise we cannot make them relish them.

VII. What has been said will probably be assented to, if we always remember in our Inquirys into the Universality of the Sense of Beauty, That there may be real Beauty, "where there is not the greatest; and that there are an Infinity of different Forms which may all have some Unity, and yet differ from each other." So that Men may have different Fancys of Beauty, and yet Uniformity be the universal Foundation of our Approbation of any Form whatsoever as Beautiful. And we shall find that it is so in the Architecture, Gardening, Dress, Equipage, and Furniture of Houses, even among the most uncultivated Nations; where Uniformity still pleases, without any other Advantage than the Pleasure of the Contemplation of it.

VIII. It will deserve our Consideration on this Subject, how, in like Cases, we form very different Judgments concerning the internal and external Senses. Nothing is more ordinary among those, who after Mr. LOCKE have rejected innate Ideas, than to alledge, "That all our Relish for Beauty, and Order, is either from prospect of Advantage, Custom, or Education," for no other Reason but the Variety of Fancys in the World: and from this they conclude, "That our Fancys do not arise from any natural Power of Perception, or Sense." And yet all allow our external Senses to be Natural, and that the Pleasures or Pains of their Sensations, however they may be increas'd, or diminish'd, by Custom, or Education, and counterbalanc'd by Interest, yet are really antecedent to Custom, Habit, Education, or Prospect of Interest. Now it is certain, "That there is at least as great a variety of Fancys about their Objects, as the

Objects of Beauty": Nay it is much more difficult, and perhaps impossible, to bring the Fancys or Relishes of the external Senses to any general Foundation at all, or to find any Rule for the agreeable or disagreeable: and yet we all allow "that these are natural Powers of Perception."

IX. The Reason of this different Judgment can be no other than this, That we have got distinct Names for the external Senses, and none, or very few, for the Internal; and by this are led, as in many other Cases, to look upon the former as some way more fix'd and real and natural, than the latter. The Sense of Harmony has got its Name, viz. a good Ear; and we are generally brought to acknowledge this a natural Power of Perception, or a Sense some way distinct from Hearing: now it is certain, "That there is as necessary a Perception of Beauty upon the presence of regular Objects, as of Harmony upon hearing certain Sounds."

X. But let it be observ'd here once for all, "That an internal Sense no more presupposes an innate Idea, or principle of Knowledge, than the external." Both are natural Powers of Perception, or Determinations of the Mind to receive necessarily certain Ideas from the presence of Objects. The internal Sense is, a passive Power of receiving Ideas of Beauty from all Objects in which there is Uniformity amidst Variety. Nor does there seem any thing more difficult in this matter, than that the Mind should always be determin'd to receive the Idea of Sweet, when Particles of such a Form enter the Pores of the Tongue; or to have as little Connection with its Idea, as the other: And the same Power could with equal ease constitute the former the occasion of Ideas as the latter.

XI. The Association of Ideas above hinted at, is one great Cause of the apparent Diversity of Fancys in the Sense of Beauty, as well as in the external Senses; and often makes Men have an aversion to Objects of Beauty, and a liking to others void of it, but under different Conceptions than those of Beauty or Deformity. And here it may not be improper to give some Instances of some of these Associations. The Beauty of Trees, their cool Shades, and their Aptness to conceal from Observation, have made Groves and Woods, the usual Retreat to those who love Solitude, especially to the Religious, the Pensive, the Melancholy, and the Amorous. And do not we find that we have so join'd the Ideas of these Dispositions of Mind with those external Objects, that they always recur to us along with them? The Cunning of the Heathen Priests might make such obscure Places the Scene of the fictitious Appearances of their Deitys; and hence we join Ideas of something Divine to them. We know the like Effect in the Ideas of our Churches, from the perpetual use of them only in religious Exercises. The faint Light in Gothick Buildings has had the same Association of a very foreign Idea, which our Poet shews in his Epithet, A Dim religious Light.

In like manner it is known, That often all the Circumstances of Actions, or Places, or Dresses of Persons, or Voice, or Song, which have occur'd at any time together, when we were strongly affected by any Passion, will be so connected that any one of these will make all the rest recur. And this is often the occasion both of great Pleasure and Pain, Delight and Aversion to many Objects, which of themselves might have been perfectly indifferent to us: but these Approbations, or Distastes, are remote from the Ideas of Beauty, being plainly different Ideas.

XII. There is also another Charm in Musick to various Persons, which is distinct from the Harmony, and is occasion'd by its raising agreeable Passions. The human Voice is obviously vary'd by all the stronger Passions; now when our Ear discerns any resemblance between the Air of a Tune, whether sung or play'd upon an Instrument, either in its Time, or Modulation, or any other Circumstance, to the sound of the human Voice in any Passion, we shall be touch'd by it in a very sensible manner, and have Melancholy, Joy, Gravity, Thoughtfulness, excited in us by a sort of Sympathy or Contagion. The same Connexion is observable between the very Air of a Tune, and the Words expressing any Passion which we have heard it fitted to, so that they shall both recur to us together, tho but one of them affects our Senses.

Now in such a diversity of pleasing or displeasing Ideas which may be join'd with Forms of Bodys, or Tunes, when Men are of such different Dispositions, and prone to such a variety of Passions, it is no wonder "that they should often disagree in their Fancys of Objects, even altho their Sense of Beauty and Harmony were perfectly uniform"; because many other Ideas may either please or displease, according to Persons' Tempers, and past Circumstances. We know how agreeable a very wild Country may be to any Person who has spent the chearful Days of his Youth in it, and how disagreeable very beautiful places may be, if they were the Scenes of his Misery. And this may help us in many Cases to account for the Diversitys of Fancy, without denying the Uniformity of our internal Sense of Beauty.

XIII. Grandeur and Novelty are two Ideas different from Beauty, which often recommend Objects to us. The Reason of this is foreign to the present Subject. See Spectator N 412.

SECT. VII

Of the Power of Custom, Education, and Example, as to our Internal Senses

1. Custom, Education, and Example are so often alledg'd in this Affair, as the occasion of our Relish for beautiful Objects, and for our Approbation of, or Delight in a certain Conduct in Life in a moral Species, that it is necessary to examine these three particularly, to make it appear "that

there is a natural Power of Perception, or Sense of Beauty in Objects, antecedent to all Custom, Education, or Example."

II. Custom, as distinct from the other two, operates in this manner. As to Actions, it only gives a disposition to the Mind or Body more easily to perform those Actions which have been frequently repeated, but never leads us to apprehend them under any other View than what we were capable of apprehending them under at first; nor gives us any new Power of Perception about them. We are naturally capable of Sentiments of Fear, and Dread of any powerful Presence; and so Custom may connect the Ideas of religious Horror to certain Buildings: but Custom could never have made a Being naturally incapable of Fear, receive such Ideas. So had we no other Power of perceiving, or forming Ideas of Actions, but as they were advantageous or disadvantageous, Custom could only have made us more ready at perceiving the Advantage or Disadvantage of Actions. But this is not to our present purpose.

As to our Approbation of, or Delight in external Objects. When the Blood or Spirits, of which Anatomists talk, are rous'd, quicken'd, or fermented as they call it, in any agreeable manner by Medicine or Nutriment; or any Glands frequently stimulated to Secretion; it is certain that to preserve the Body easy, we shall delight in Objects of Taste which of themselves are not immediately pleasant to it, if they promote that agreeable State which the Body had been accustom'd to. Farther, Custom will so alter the State of the Body, that what at first rais'd uneasy Sensations will cease to do so, or perhaps raise another agreeable Idea of the same Sense; but Custom can never give us any Idea of a Sense different from those we had antecedent to it: It will never make the Blind approve Objects as coloured, or those who have no Taste approve Meats as delicious, however they might approve them as Strengthening or Exhilarating. Were our Glands and the

Parts about them void of Feeling, did we perceive no Pleasure from certain brisker Motions in the Blood, Custom could never make stimulating or intoxicating Fluids or Medicines agreeable, when they were not so to the Taste: So by like Reasoning, had we no natural Sense of Beauty from Uniformity, Custom could never have made us imagine any Beauty in Objects; if we had had no Ear, Custom could never have given us the Pleasures of Harmony. When we have these natural Senses antecedently, Custom may make us capable of extending our Views farther, and of receiving more complex Ideas of Beauty in Bodys, or Harmony in Sounds, by increasing our Attention and quickness of Perception. But however Custom may increase our Power of receiving or comparing complex Ideas, yet it seems rather to weaken than strengthen the Ideas of Beauty, or the Impressions of Pleasure from regular Objects; else how is it possible that any Person could go into the open Air on a sunny Day, or clear Evening, without the most extravagant Raptures, such as MILTON represents our ancestor upon his first Creation? For such any Person would certainly fall into, upon the first Representation of such a Scene.

Custom in like manner may make it easier for any Person to discern the Use of a complex Machine, and approve it as advantageous; but he would never have imagin'd it Beautiful, had he no natural Sense of Beauty. Custom may make us quicker in apprehending the Truth of complex Theorems, but we all find the Pleasure or Beauty of Theorems as strong at first as ever. Custom makes us more capable of retaining and comparing complex Ideas, so as to discern more complicated Uniformity, which escapes the Observation of Novices in any Art; but all this presupposes a natural Sense of Beauty in Uniformity: for had there been nothing in Forms, which was constituted the necessary occasion of Pleasure to our Senses, no Repetition of indifferent Ideas as to Pleasure or Pain, Beauty or Deformity, could ever have made them grow pleasing or displeasing.

III. The Effect of Education is this, that thereby we receive many speculative Opinions, which are sometimes true and sometimes false; and are often led to believe that Objects may be naturally apt to give Pleasure or Pain to our external Senses, which in reality have no such Qualitys. And farther, by Education there are some strong Associations of Ideas without any Reason, by mere Accident sometimes, as well as by Design, which it is very hard for us ever after to break asunder. Thus Aversions are rais'd to Darkness, and to many kinds of Meat, and to certain innocent Actions: Approbations without Ground are aris'd in like manner. But in all these Instances, Education never makes us apprehend any Qualitys in Objects, which we have not naturally Senses capable of perceiving. We know what Sickness of the Stomach is, and may without Ground believe that very healthful Meats will raise this; we by our Sight and Smell receive disagreeable Ideas of the Food of Swine, and their Styes, and perhaps cannot prevent the recurring of these Ideas at Table: but never were Men naturally Blind prejudic'd against Objects as of a disagreeable Colour, or in favour of others as of a beautiful Colour; they perhaps hear Men dispraise one Colour, and may imagine this Colour to be some quite different sensible Quality of the other Senses, but that is all. And the same way, a Man naturally void of Taste could by no Education receive the Ideas of Taste, or be prejudic'd in favour of Meats as delicious: So, had we no natural Sense of Beauty and Harmony, we could never be prejudic'd in favour of Objects or Sounds as Beautiful or Harmonious. Education may make an unattentive GOTH imagine that his Countrymen have attain'd the Perfection of Architecture; and an Aversion to their Enemys the ROMANS, may have join'd some disagreeable Ideas to their very Buildings, and excited them to their Demolition; but he

had never form'd these Prejudices, had he been void of a Sense of Beauty. Did ever blind Men debate whether Purple or Scarlet were the finer Colour? or could any Education prejudice them in favour of either as Colours?

Thus Education and Custom may influence our internal Senses, where they are antecedently, by enlarging the Capacity of our Minds to retain and compare the Parts of complex Compositions: And then if the finest Objects are presented to us, we grow conscious of a Pleasure far superior to what common Performances excite. But all this presupposes our Sense of Beauty to be natural. Instruction in Anatomy, Observation of Nature, and of those Airs of the Countenance and Attitudes of Body, which accompany any Sentiment, Action, or Passion, may enable us to know where there is a just Imitation: but why should an exact Imitation please upon Observation, if we had not naturally a Sense of Beauty in it, more than the observing the Situation of fifty or a hundred Pebbles thrown at random? and should we observe them ever so often, we should never dream of their growing Beautiful. . . .

SECT. VIII

Of the Importance of the internal Senses in Life, and the final Causes of them

I. The busy part of Mankind may look upon these things as airy Dreams of an inflam'd Imagination, which a wise Man should despise, who rationally pursues more solid Possessions independent on Fancy: but a little Reflection will convince us, "That the Gratifications of our internal Senses are as natural, real, and satisfying Enjoyments as any sensible Pleasure whatsoever; and that they are the chief Ends for which we commonly pursue Wealth and Power." For how is Wealth or Power advantageous? How do they make us happy, or prove good to us? No otherwise than as they supply

Gratifications to our Senses or Facultys of perceiving Pleasure. Now, are these Senses or Facultys only the External ones? No: Every body sees, that a small portion of Wealth or Power will supply more Pleasures of the external Senses than we can enjoy; we know that Scarcity often heightens these Perceptions more than Abundance, which cloys that Appetite which is necessary to all Pleasure in Enjoyment . . . In short, the only use of a great Fortune above a very small one (except in good Offices and moral Pleasures) must be to supply us with the Pleasures of Beauty, Order, and Harmony.

It is true indeed, that the noblest Pleasures of the internal Senses, in the Contemplation of the Works of Nature, are expos'd to every one without Expence; the Poor and the Low, may have as free use of these Objects, in this way, as the Wealthy or Powerful. And even in Objects which may be appropriated, the Property is of little Consequence to the Enjoyment of their Beauty, which is often enjoy'd by others beside the Proprietor. But then there are other Objects of these internal Senses, which require Wealth, or Power to procure the use of them as frequently as we desire; as appears in Architecture, Musick, Gardening, Painting, Dress, Equipage, Furniture; of which we cannot have the full Enjoyment without Property. And there are some confus'd Imaginations, which often lead us to pursue Property, even in Objects where it is not necessary to the true Enjoyment of them. These are the ultimate Motives of our pursuing the greater Degrees of Wealth, where there are no generous Intentions of virtuous Actions.

This is confirm'd by the constant Practice of the very Enemys to these Senses. As soon as they think they are got above the World, or extricated from the Hurrys of Avarice and Ambition; banish'd Nature will return upon them, and set them upon Pursuits of Beauty and Order in their Houses, Gardens, Dress, Table, Equipage.

They are never easy without some degree of this; and were their Hearts open to our View, we should see Regularity, Decency, Beauty, as what their Wishes terminate upon, either to themselves or their Posterity; and what their Imagination is always presenting to them as the possible Effects of their Labours. Nor without this, could they ever justify their Pursuits to themselves.

 II. As to the final Causes of this internal Sense, we need not inquire, "Whether, to an almighty, and all-knowing Being, there be any real Excellence in regular Forms, in acting by general Laws, in knowing by Theorems?" We seem scarce capable of answering such Questions any way; nor need we inquire, "Whether other Animals may not discern Uniformity and Regularity in Objects which escape our Observation, and may not perhaps have their Senses constituted so as to perceive Beauty from the same Foundation which we do, in Objects which our Senses are not fit to examine or compare?" We shall confine our selves to a Subject where we have some certain Foundation to go upon, and only inquire, "if we can find any Reasons worthy of the great AUTHOR of Nature, for making such a Connection between regular Objects, and the Pleasure which accompanys our Perceptions of them; or, what Reasons might possibly influence him to create the World, as it at present is, as far as we can observe, every where full of Regularity and Uniformity?"

Let it be here observ'd, that as far as we know concerning any of the great Bodys of the Universe, we see Forms and Motions really Beautiful to our Senses; and if we were plac'd in any Planet, the apparent Courses would still be Regular and Uniform, and consequently Beautiful to us. Now this gives us no small Ground to imagine, that if the Senses of their Inhabitants are in the same manner adapted to their Habitations, and the Objects occurring to their View, as ours as here, their Senses must be upon the same general Foundation with ours.

But to return to the Questions: What occurs to resolve them, may be contain'd in the following Propositions.

1. The Manner of Knowledge by universal Theorems, and of Operation by universal Causes, as far as we can attain it, must be most convenient for Beings of limited Understanding and Power; since this prevents Distraction in their Understandings thro' the Multiplicity of Propositions, and Toil and Weariness to their Powers of Action: and consequently their Reason, without any Sense of Beauty, must approve of such Methods when they reflect upon their apparent Advantage.

2. Those Objects of Contemplation in which there is Uniformity amidst Variety, are more distinctly and easily comprehended and retain'd, than irregular Objects; because the accurate Observation of one or two Parts often leads to the Knowledge of the Whole: Thus we can from a Pillar or two, with an intermediate Arch, and Cornice, form a distinct Idea of a whole regular Building, if we know of what Species it is, and have its Length and Breadth: From a Side and solid Angle, we have the whole regular Solid; the measuring one Side, gives the whole Square; one Radius, the whole Circle; two Diameters, an Oval; one Ordinate and Abscissa, the Parabola; thus also other Figures, if they have any Regularity, are in every point determin'd from a few Data: Whereas it must be a long Attention to a vast Multiplicity of Parts, which can ascertain or fix the Idea of any irregular Form, or give any distinct Idea of it, or make us capable of retaining it; as appears in the Forms of rude Rocks, and Pebbles, and confus'd Heaps, even when the Multitude or sensible Parts is not so great as in the regular Forms: for such irregular Objects distract the Mind with Variety, since for every sensible Part we must have a quite different Idea.

3. From these two Propositions it follows,

"That Beings of limited Understanding and Power, if they act rationally for their own Interest, must choose to operate by the simplest Means, to invent general Theorems, and to study regular Objects, if they be as useful as irregular ones; that they may avoid the endless Toil of producing each Effect by a separate Operation, of searching out each different Truth by a different Inquiry, and of imprinting the endless Variety of dissimilar Ideas in irregular Objects."

4. But then, beside this Consideration of Interest, there does not appear to be any necessary Connection, antecedent to the Constitution of the AUTHOR of Nature, between regular Forms, Actions, Theorems, and that sudden sensible Pleasure excited in us upon observation of them, even when we do not reflect upon the Advantage mention'd in the former Proposition. And possibly, the DEITY could have form'd us so as to have receiv'd no immediate Pleasure from such Objects, or connected Pleasure to those of a quite contrary Nature. We have a tolerable Presumption of this in the Beautys of various Animals; they give some small Pleasure indeed to every one who views them, but then every one seems far more delighted with the peculiar Beautys of its own Species, than with those of a different one, which seldom raise any desire. This makes it probable, that the Pleasure is not the necessary Result of the Form it self, otherwise it would equally affect all Apprehensions in what Species soever; but depends upon a voluntary Constitution, adapted to preserve the Regularity of the Universe, and is probably not the Effect of Necessity but Choice in the SUPREME AGENT, who constituted our Senses.

5. Now from the whole we may conclude, "That supposing the DEITY so kind as to connect sensible Pleasure with certain Actions or Contemplations, beside the rational Advantage perceivable in them; there is a great moral Necessity, from his Goodness, that the internal Sense of Men should be constituted as it is at present, so as to

make Uniformity amidst Variety the Occasion of Pleasure." For were it not so, but on the contrary, if irregular Objects, particular Truths and Operations pleased us, beside the endless Toil this would involve us in, there must arise a perpetual Dissatisfaction in all rational Agents with themselves; since Reason and Interest would lead us to simple general Causes, while a contrary Sense of Beauty would make us disapprove them: Universal Theorems would appear to our Understanding the best Means of increasing our Knowledge of what might be useful; while a contrary Sense would set us on the search after particular Truths: Thought and Reflection would recommend Objects with Uniformity amidst Variety, and yet this perverse Instinct would involve us in Labyrinths of Confusion and Dissimilitude. And hence we see "how suitable it is to the sagacious Bounty which we suppose in the DEITY, to constitute our internal Senses in the manner in which they are; by which Pleasure is join'd to the Contemplation of those Objects which a finite Mind can best imprint and retain the Ideas of with the least Distraction; to those Actions which are most efficacious, and fruitful in useful Effects; and to those Theorems which most enlarge our Minds."

III. As to the other Question, "What Reason might influence the DEITY, whom no Diversity of Operation could distract or weary, to choose to operate by simplest Means and general Laws, and to diffuse Uniformity, Proportion and Similitude thro' all the Parts of Nature which we can observe?" Perhaps there may be some real Excellence in this Manner of Operation, and in these Forms, which we know not: but this we may probably say, that since the divine Goodness, for the Reasons above mention'd, has constituted our Sense of Beauty as it is at present, the Same Goodness might have determined the Great ARCHITECT to adorn this stupendous Theatre in a manner agreeable to the Spectators, and that part which is expos'd to the Observation of Men, so as to be pleasant to them; especially if we suppose that he design'd to discover himself to them as Wise and Good, as well as Powerful: for thus he has given them greater Evidences, thro' the whole Earth, of his Art, Wisdom, Design, and Bounty, than they can possibly have for the Reason, Counsel, and Good-will of their fellow-Creatures, with whom they converse, with full Persuasion of these qualities in them, about their common Affairs.

EDMUND BURKE [1728–97]

++++>+<<<<+

From *A Philosophical Inquiry into the Origin of Our Ideas of the Sublime and Beautiful* [1756]

PART ONE

Sect. I. Novelty

The first and the simplest emotion which we discover in the human mind, is Curios-

From *The Works of the Right Honourable Edmund Burke*, Vol. I (London: 1906).

ity. By curiosity, I mean whatever desire we have for, or whatever pleasure we take in, novelty. We see children perpetually running from place to place, to hunt out something new: they catch with great eagerness, and with very little choice, at whatever comes before them; their attention is engaged by everything, because everything has, in that stage of life, the charm of novelty to recommend it. But as those things, which engage us merely by their novelty, cannot attach us for any length of time, curiosity is the most superficial of all the affections; it changes its object perpetually, it has an appetite which is very sharp, but very easily satisfied; and it has always an appearance of giddiness, restlessness, and anxiety. Curiosity, from its nature, is a very active principle; it quickly runs over the greatest part of its objects, and soon exhausts the variety which is commonly to be met with in nature; the same things make frequent returns, and they return with less and less of any agreeable effect. In short, the occurrences of life, by the time we come to know it a little, would be incapable of affecting the mind with any other sensations than those of loathing and weariness, if many things were not adapted to affect the mind by means of other powers besides novelty in them, and of other passions besides curiosity in ourselves. These powers and passions shall be considered in their place. But whatever these powers are, or upon what principle soever they affect the mind, it is absolutely necessary that they should not be exerted in those things which a daily and vulgar use have brought into a stale unaffecting familiarity. Some degree of novelty must be one of the materials in every instrument which works upon the mind; and curiosity blends itself more or less with all our passions.

Sect. II. Pain and Pleasure

It seems then necessary towards moving the passions of people advanced in life to any considerable degree, that the objects designed for that purpose, besides their being in some measure new, should be capable of exciting pain or pleasure from other causes. Pain and pleasure are simple ideas, incapable of definition. People are not liable to be mistaken in their feelings, but they are very frequently wrong in the names they give them, and in their reasonings about them. Many are of the opinion, that pain arises necessarily from the removal of some pleasure; as they think pleasure does from the ceasing or diminution of some pain. For my part, I am rather inclined to imagine, that pain and pleasure, in their most simple and natural manner of affecting, are each of a positive nature, and by no means necessarily dependent on each other for their existence. The human mind is often, and I think it is for the most part, in a state neither of pain nor pleasure, which I call a state of indifference. When I am carried from this state into a state of actual pleasure, it does not appear necessary that I should pass through the medium of any sort of pain. If in such a state of indifference, or ease, or tranquillity, or call it what you please, you were to be suddenly entertained with a concert of music; or suppose some object of a fine shape, and bright, lively colours, to be presented before you; or imagine your smell is gratified with the fragrance of a rose; or if without any previous thirst you were to drink of some pleasant kind of wine, or to taste of some sweetmeat without being hungry; in all the several senses, of hearing, smelling and tasting, you undoubtedly find a pleasure; yet if I inquire into the state of your mind previous to these gratifications, you will hardly tell me that they found you in any kind of pain; or, having satisfied these several senses with their several pleasures, will you say that any pain has succeeded, though the pleasure is absolutely over? Suppose on the other hand, a man in the same state of indifference, to receive a violent blow, or to drink of some bitter potion, or to have his ears wounded with some harsh and grating sound; here is no removal of pleasure; and yet here is felt in every sense which is affected, a pain very distinguishable. It may be said, perhaps, that the pain in these cases had its rise from the removal of the pleasure which the man enjoyed before, though that pleasure was of so low a degree as to be perceived only by the removal. But this seems to me a subtilty, that is not discoverable in nature. For if, previous to the pain, I do not feel any actual pleasure, I have no reason to judge that any such thing exists; since pleasure is only pleasure as it is felt. The same may be said of pain, and with equal reason. I can never persuade myself that pleasure and pain are mere relations, which can only exist as they are contrasted; but I think I can discern clearly that they are positive pains and pleasures, which do not at all depend upon each other. Nothing is more certain to my own feelings than this. There is nothing which I can distinguish in my mind with more clearness than the three states, of indifference, of pleasure, and of pain. Every one of these I can perceive without any sort of idea of its relation to anything else. Caius is afflicted with a fit of the colic; this man is actually in pain; stretch Caius upon the rack, he will feel a much greater pain: but does this pain of the rack arise from the removal of any pleasure? or is the fit of the colic a pleasure or a pain, just as we are pleased to consider it?

Sect. III. The Difference between the Removal of Pain, and Positive Pleasure

We shall carry this proposition yet a step farther. We shall venture to propose, that pain and pleasure are not only not necessarily dependent for their existence on their mutual diminution or removal, but that, in reality, the diminution or ceasing of pleasure does not operate like positive pain; and that the removal or diminution of pain, in its effect, has very little resemblance to positive pleasure. The former of these propositions will, I believe, be much more readily allowed than the latter; because it is very evident that pleasure, when it has run its career, sets us down very nearly where it found us. Pleasure of every kind quickly satisfies; and when it is over, we relapse into indifference, or rather we fall into a soft tranquillity, which is tinged with the agreeable colour of the former sensation. I own it is not at first view so apparent, that the removal of a great pain does not resemble positive pleasure; but let us recollect in

what state we have found our minds upon escaping some imminent danger, or on being released from the severity of some cruel pain. We have on such occasions found, if I am not much mistaken, the temper of our minds in a tenor very remote from that which attends the presence of positive pleasure; we have found them in a state of much sobriety, impressed with a sense of awe, in a sort of tranquillity shadowed with horror. The fashion of the countenance and the gesture of the body on such occasions is so correspondent to this state of mind, that any person, a stranger to the cause of the appearance, would rather judge us under some consternation, than in the enjoyment of anything like positive pleasure. . . .

Sect. IV. Of Delight and Pleasure as opposed to each Other

But shall we therefore say, that the removal of pain or its diminution is always simply painful? or affirm that the cessation or the lessening of pleasure is always attended itself with a pleasure? By no means. What I advance is no more than this; first, that there are pleasures and pains of a positive and independent nature; and, secondly, that the feeling which results from the ceasing or diminution of pain does not bear a sufficient resemblance to positive pleasure, to have it considered as of the same nature, or to entitle it to be known by the same name; and, thirdly, that upon the same principle the removal or qualification of pleasure has no resemblance to positive pain. It is certain that the former feeling (the removal or moderation of pain) has something in it far from distressing or disagreeable in its nature. This feeling, in many cases so agreeable, but in all so different from positive pleasure, has no name which I know; but that hinders not its being a very real one, and very different from all others. It is most certain that every species of satisfaction or pleasure, how different soever in its manner of affecting, is of a positive nature in the mind of him who feels it. The affection is undoubtedly positive; but the cause may be, as in this case it certainly is, a sort of *Privation*. And it is very reasonable that we should distinguish by some term two things so distinct in nature, as a pleasure that is such simply, and without any relation, from that pleasure which cannot exist without a relation, and that too a relation to pain. Very extraordinary it would be, if these affections, so distinguishable in their causes, so different in their effects, should be confounded with each other, because vulgar use has ranged them under the same general title. Whenever I have occasion to speak of this species of relative pleasure, I call it *Delight*; and I shall take the best care I can to use that world in no other sense. I am satisfied the word is not commonly used in this appropriated signification; but I thought it better to take up a word already known, and to limit its signification, than to introduce a new one, which would not perhaps incorporate so well with the language. I should never have presumed the least alteration in our words, if the nature of the language, framed for the purposes of business rather than those of philosophy, and the nature of my subject, that leads me out of the common track of discourse, did not in a manner necessitate me to it. I shall make use of this liberty with all possible caution. As I make use of the word *Delight* to express the sensation which accompanies the removal of pain or danger; so when I speak of positive pleasure, I shall for the most part call it simply *Pleasure*.

Sect. V. Joy and Grief

It must be observed that the cessation of pleasure affects the mind three ways. If it simply ceases, after having continued a proper time, the effect is *indifference*; if it be abruptly broken off, there ensues an uneasy sense called *disappointment*; if the object be so totally lost that there is no chance of enjoying it again, a passion arises in the mind, which is called *grief*. Now there is none of these, not even grief, which is the most violent, that I think has any resemblance to positive pain. The person who grieves, suffers his passion to grow upon him; he indulges it, he loves it: but this never happens in the case of actual pain, which no man ever willingly endured for any considerable time. That grief should be willingly endured, though far from a simply pleasing sensation, is not so difficult to be understood. It is the nature of grief to keep its object perpetually in its eye, to present it in its most pleasurable views, to repeat all the circumstances that attend it, even to the last minuteness; to go back to every particular enjoyment, to dwell upon each, and to find a thousand new perfections in all, that were not sufficiently understood before; in grief, the *pleasure* is still uppermost; and the affliction we suffer has no resemblance to absolute pain, which is always odious, and which we endeavor to shake off as soon as possible. . . . On the other hand, when we recover our health, when we escape an imminent danger, is it with joy that we are affected? The sense on these occasions is far from that smooth and voluptuous satisfaction which the assured prospect of pleasure bestows. The delight which arises from the modification of pain confesses the stock from whence it sprung, in its solid, strong, and severe nature.

Sect. VI. Of the Passions which Belong to Self-preservation

Most of the ideas which are capable of making a powerful impression on the mind, whether simply of Pain or Pleasure, or of the modifications of those, may be reduced very nearly to these two heads, *self-preservation* and *society*; to the ends of one or the other of which all our passions are calculated to answer. The passions which concern self-preservation, turn mostly on *pain* or *danger*. The ideas of *pain, sickness,* and *death*, fill the mind with strong emotions of horror; but *life* and *health*, though they put us in a capacity of being affected with pleasure, make no such impression by the simple enjoyment. The passions therefore which are conversant about the preservation of the individual turn chiefly on *pain* and *danger,* and they are the most powerful of all the passions.

Sect. VII. Of the Sublime

Whatever is fitted in any sort to excite the ideas of pain and danger, that is to say, whatever is in any sort terrible, or is conversant about terrible objects, or operates in a manner analogous to terror, is a source of the *sublime;* that is, it is productive of the strongest emotion which the mind is capable of feeling. I say the strongest emotion, because I am satisfied the ideas of pain are much more powerful than those which enter on the part of pleasure. Without all doubt, the torments which we may be made to suffer are much greater in their effect on the body and mind, than any pleasures which the most learned voluptuary could suggest, or than the liveliest imagination, and the most sound and exquisitely sensible body, could enjoy. Nay, I am in great doubt whether any man could be found, who would earn a life of the most perfect satisfaction, at the price of ending it in the torments, which justice inflicted in a few hours on the late unfortunate regicide in France. But as pain is stronger in its operation than pleasure, so death is in general a much more affecting idea than pain; because there are very few pains, however exquisite, which are not preferred to death: nay, what generally makes pain itself, if I may say so, more painful, is, that it is considered as an emissary of this king of terrors. When danger or pain press too nearly, they are incapable of giving any delight, and are simply terrible; but at certain distances, and with certain modifications, they may be, and they are, delightful, as we every day experience. The cause of this I shall endeavour to investigate hereafter.

Sect. VIII. Of the Passions which Belong to Society

The other head under which I class our passions, is that of *society,* which may be divided into two sorts. I. The society of the *sexes,* which answers the purposes of propagation; and next, that more *general society,* which we have with men and with other animals, and which we may in some sort be said to have even with the inanimate world. The passions belonging to the preservation of the individual turn wholly on pain and danger: those which belong to *generation* have their origin in gratifications and *pleasures;* the pleasure most directly belonging to this purpose is of a lively character, rapturous and violent, and confessedly the highest pleasure of sense; yet the absence of this so great an enjoyment scarce amounts to an uneasiness; and, except at particular times, I do not think it affects at all. When men describe in what manner they are affected by pain and danger, they do not dwell on the pleasure of health and the comfort of security, and then lament the *loss* of these satisfactions: the whole turns upon the actual pains and horrors which they endure. But if you listen to the complaints of a forsaken lover, you observe that he insists largely on the pleasures which he enjoyed, or hoped to enjoy, and on the perfection of the object of his desires; it is the *loss* which is always uppermost in his mind. The violent effects produced by love, which has sometimes been even wrought up to madness, is no objection to the rule which we seek to establish. When men have suffered their imaginations to be long affected with any idea, it so wholly engrosses them as to shut out by degrees almost every other, and to break down every partition of the mind which would confine it. Any idea is sufficient for the purpose, as is evident from the infinite variety of causes, which give rise to madness: but this at most can only prove, that the passion of love is capable of producing very extraordinary effects, not that its extraordinary emotions have any connexion with positive pain.

Sect. IX. *The Final Cause of the Difference between the Passions belonging to Self-preservation, and Those which Regard the Society of the Sexes*

The final cause of the difference in character between the passions which regard self-preservation, and those which are directed to the multiplication of the species, will illustrate the foregoing remarks yet further; and it is, I imagine, worthy of observation even upon its own account. As the performance of our duties of every kind depends upon life, and the performing them with vigour and efficacy depends upon health, we are very strongly affected with whatever threatens the destruction of either: but as we are not made to acquiesce in life and health, the simple enjoyment of them is not attended with any real pleasure, lest, satisfied with that, we should give ourselves over to indolence and inaction. On the other hand, the generation of mankind is a great purpose, and it is requisite that men should be animated to the pursuit of it by some great incentive. It is therefore attended with a very high pleasure; but as it is by no means designed to be our constant business, it is not fit that the absence of this pleasure should be attended with any considerable pain. The difference between men and brutes, in this point, seems to be remarkable. Men are at all times pretty equally disposed to the pleasures of love, because they are to be guided by reason in the time and manner of indulging them. Had any great pain arisen from the want of this satisfaction, reason, I am afraid, would find great difficulties in the performance of its office. But brutes, who obey laws, in the execution of which their own reason has but little share, have their stated seasons; at such times it is not improbable that the sensation from the want is very troublesome, because the end must be then answered, or be missed in many, perhaps

for ever; as the inclination returns only with its season.

Sect. X. *Of Beauty*

The passion which belongs to generation, merely as such, is lust only. This is evident in brutes, whose passions are more unmixed, and which pursue their purposes more directly than ours. The only distinction they observe with regard to their mates, is that of sex. It is true, that they stick severally to their own species in preference to all others. But this preference, I imagine, does not arise from any sense of beauty which they find in their species, as Mr. Addison supposes, but from a law of some other kind, to which they are subject; and this we may fairly conclude, from their apparent want of choice amongst those objects to which the barriers of their species have confined them. But man, who is a creature adapted to a greater variety and intricacy of relation, connects with the general passion the idea of some *social* qualities, which direct and heighten the appetite which he has in common with all other animals; and as he is not designed like them to live at large, it is fit that he should have something to create a preference, and fix his choice; and this in general should be some sensible quality; as no other can so quickly, so powerfully, or so surely produce its effect. The object therefore of this mixed passion, which we call love, is the *beauty* of the *sex*. Men are carried to the sex in general, as it is the sex, and by the common law of nature; but they are attached to particulars by personal *beauty*. I call beauty a social quality; for where women and men, and not only they, but when other animals give us a sense of joy and pleasure in beholding them (and there are many that do so), they inspire us with sentiments of tenderness and affection towards their persons; we like to have them near us, and we enter willingly into a kind of relation with them, unless we should have strong reasons to the contrary. But to what end, in many cases;

this was designed, I am unable to discover; for I see no greater reason for a connexion between man and several animals who are attired in so engaging a manner, than between him and some others who entirely want this attraction, or possess it in a far weaker degree. But it is probable, that Providence did not make even this distinction, but with a view to some great end; though we cannot perceive distinctly what it is, as his wisdom is not our wisdom, nor our ways his ways.

Sect. XVIII. The Recapitulation

To draw the whole of what has been said into a few distinct points. The passions which belong to self-preservation, turn on pain and danger; they are simply painful when their causes immediately affect us; they are delightful when we have an idea of pain and danger, without being actually in such circumstances; this delight I have not called pleasure, because it turns on pain, and because it is different enough from any idea of positive pleasure. Whatever excites this delight, I call *sublime*. The passions belonging to self-preservation are the strongest of all the passions.

The second head to which the passions are referred with relation to their final cause, is society. There are two sorts of societies. The first is, the society of sex. The passion belonging to this is called love, and it contains a mixture of lust; its object is the beauty of women. The other is the great society with man and all other animals. The passion subservient to this is called likewise love, but it has no mixture of lust, and its object is beauty; which is a name I shall apply to all such qualities in things as induce in us a sense of affection and tenderness, or some other passion the most nearly resembling these. The passion of love has its rise in positive pleasure; it is, like all things which grow out of pleasure, capable of being mixed with a mode of uneasiness, that is, when an idea of its object is excited in the mind with an idea at the same time of having irretrievably lost it. This mixed sense of pleasure I have not called *pain,* because it turns upon actual pleasure, and because it is both in its cause and in most of its effects of a nature altogether different.

Next to the general passion we have for society, to a choice in which we are directed by the pleasure we have in the object, the particular passion under this head called sympathy has the greatest extent. The nature of this passion is to put us in the place of another in whatever circumstance he is in, and to affect us in a like manner; so that this passion may, as the occasion requires, turn either on pain or pleasure; but with the modifications mentioned in some cases in section II. As to imitation and preference nothing more need be said.

PART TWO

Sect. I. Of the Passion Caused by the Sublime

The passion caused by the great and sublime in *nature,* when those causes operate most powerfully, is Astonishment; and astonishment is that state of the soul, in which all its motions are suspended, with some degree of horror. In this case the mind is so entirely filled with its object, that it cannot entertain any other, nor by consequence reason on that object with employs it. Hence arises the great power of the sublime, that far from being produced by them, it anticipates our reasonings, and hurries us on by an irresistible force. Astonishment, as I have said, is the effect of the sublime in its highest degree; the inferior effects are admiration, reverence and respect.

Sect. II. Terror

No passion so effectually robs the mind of all its powers of acting and reasoning as fear. For fear being an apprehension of pain or death, it operates in a manner that resembles actual pain. Whatever therefore is terrible, with regard to sight, is sublime too, whether this cause of terror, be endured with greatness of dimensions or not; for it is impossible to look on any thing as trifling, or contemptible, that may be dangerous. There are many animals, who though far from being large, are yet capable of raising ideas of the sublime, because they are considered as objects of terror. As serpents and poisonous animals of almost all kinds. And to things of great dimensions, if we annex an adventitious idea of terror, they become without comparison greater. A level plain of a vast extent on land, is certainly no mean idea; the prospect of such a plain may be as extensive as a prospect of the ocean; but can it ever fill the mind with any thing so great as the ocean itself? This is owing to several causes, but it is owing to none more than this, that the ocean is an object of no small terror. Indeed terror is in all cases whatsoever, either more openly or latently the ruling principle of the sublime. . . .

PART THREE

Sect. I. Of Beauty

It is my design to consider beauty as distinguished from the sublime; and in the course of the enquiry, to examine how far it is consistent with it. But previous to this, we must take a short review of the opinions already entertained of this quality; which I think are hardly to be reduced to any fixed principles; because men are used to talk of beauty in a figurative manner, that is to say, in a manner extremely uncertain, and indeterminate. By beauty I mean, that quality or those qualities in bodies by which they cause love, or some passion similar to it. I confine this definition to the merely sensible qualities of things, for the sake of preserving the utmost simplicity in a subject which must always distract us, whenever we take in those various causes of sympathy which attach us to any persons

or things from secondary considerations, and not from the direct force which they have merely on being viewed. I likewise distinguish love, by which I mean that satisfaction which arises to the mind upon contemplating any thing beautiful, of whatsoever nature it may be, from desire or lust; which is an energy of the mind, that hurries us on to the possession of certain objects, that do not affect us as they are beautiful, but by means altogether different. We shall have a strong desire for a woman of no remarkable beauty; whilst the greatest beauty in men, or in other animals, though it causes love, yet excites nothing at all of desire. Which shews that beauty, and the passion caused by beauty, which I call love, is different from desire, though desire may sometimes operate along with it; but it is to this latter that we must attribute those violent and tempestuous passions, and the consequent emotions of the body which attend what is called love in some of its ordinary acceptations, and not to the effects of beauty merely as it is such.

Sect. XII. The real cause of Beauty

Having endeavoured to shew what beauty is not, it remains that we should examine, at least with equal attention, in what it really consists. Beauty is a thing much too affecting not to depend upon some positive qualities. And, since it is no creature of our reason, since it strikes us without any reference to use, and even where no use at all can be discerned, since the order and method of nature is generally very different from our measures and proportions, we must conclude that beauty is, for the greater part, some quality in bodies, acting mechanically upon the human mind by the intervention of the senses. We ought therefore to consider attentively in what manner those sensible qualities are disposed, in such things as by experience we find beautiful, or which excite in us the passion of love, or some correspondent affection.

Sect. XXVII. The Sublime and Beautiful compared

On closing this general view of beauty, it naturally occurs, that we should compare it with the sublime; and in this comparison there appears a remarkable contrast. For sublime objects are vast in their dimensions, beautiful ones comparatively small; beauty should be smooth, and polished; the great, rugged and negligent; beauty should shun the right line, yet deviate from it insensibly; the great in many cases love the right line, and when it deviates, it often makes a strong deviation; beauty should not be obscure; the great ought to be dark and gloomy; beauty should be light and delicate; the great ought to be solid, and even massive. They are indeed ideas of a very different nature, one being founded on pain, the other on pleasure; and however they may vary afterwards from the direct nature of their causes, yet these causes keep up an eternal distinction between them, a distinction never to be forgotten by any whose business it is to affect the passions. In the infinite variety of natural combinations we must expect to find the qualities of things the most remote imaginable from each other united in the same object. We must expect also to find combinations of the same kind in the works of art. But when we consider the power of an object upon our passions, we must know that when any thing is intended to affect the mind by the force of some predominant property, the affection produced is like to be the more uniform and perfect, if all the other properties or qualities of the object be of the same nature, and tending to the same design as the principal; . . .

PART FOUR

Sect. I. Of the Efficient Cause of the Sublime and Beautiful

When I say I intend to inquire into the efficient cause of Sublimity and Beauty, I would not be understood to say, that I can come to the ultimate cause. I do not pretend that I shall ever be able to explain, why certain affections of the body produce such a distinct emotion of mind, and no other; or why the body is at all affected by the mind, or the mind by the body. A little thought will show this to be impossible. But I conceive, if we can discover what affections of the mind produce certain emotions of the body, and what distinct feelings and qualities of body shall produce certain determinate passions in the mind, and no others, I fancy a great deal will be done; something not unuseful towards a distinct knowledge of our passions, so far at least as we have them at present under our consideration. This is all, I believe, we can do. If we could advance a step farther, difficulties would still remain, as we should be still equally distant from the first cause. When Newton first discovered the property of attraction, and settled its laws, he found it served very well to explain several of the most remarkable phaenomena in nature; but yet, with reference to the general system of things, he could consider attraction but as an effect, whose cause at that time he did not attempt to trace. But when he afterwards began to account for it by a subtle elastic æther, this great man (if in so great a man it be not impious to discover anything like a blemish) seemed to have quitted his usual cautious manner of philosophizing; since, perhaps, allowing all that has been advanced on this subject to be sufficiently proved, I think it leaves us with as many difficulties as it found us. The great chain of causes, which links one to another, even to the throne of God himself, can never be unravelled by any industry of ours. When we go but one step beyond the immediate sensible qualities of things, we go out of our depth. All we do after is but a faint struggle, that shows we are in an element which does not belong to us. So that when I speak of cause, and efficient cause, I only mean certain affections of the mind, that cause certain changes in the body; or certain powers and properties in bodies, that work a change in the mind. As if I were to explain the motion of a body falling to the ground, I would say it was caused by gravity; and I would endeavour to show after what manner this power operated, without attempting to show why it operated in this manner: or if I were to explain the effects of bodies striking one another by the common laws of percussion, I should not endeavour to explain how motion itself is communicated.

Sect. II. Association

It is no small bar in the way of our inquiry into the cause of our passions, that the occasions of many of them are given, and that their governing motions are communicated at a time when we have not capacity to reflect on them; at a time of which all sort of memory is worn out of our minds. For besides such things as affect us in various manners, according to their natural powers, there are associations made at that early season, which we find it very hard afterwards to distinguish from natural effects. Not to mention the unaccountable antipathies which we find in many persons, we all find it impossible to remember when a steep became more terrible than a plain; or fire or water more terrible than a clod of earth; though all these are very probably either conclusions from experience, or arising from the premonitions of others; and some of them impressed, in all likelihood, pretty late. But as it must be allowed that many things affect us after a certain manner, not any natural powers they have for that purpose, but by association; so it would be absurd, on the other hand, to say that all things affect us by association only; since some things must have been originally and naturally agreeable or disagreeable, from which the others derive their associated powers; and it would be, I fancy, to little purpose to look for the cause of our passions in association, until we fail of it in the natural properties of things.

Sect. III. Cause of Pain and Fear

I have before observed, that whatever is qualified to cause terror is a foundation capable of the sublime; to which I add, that not only these, but many things from which we cannot probably apprehend any danger, have a similar effect, because they operate in a similar manner. I observed too, that whatever produces pleasure, positive and original pleasure, is fit to have beauty ingrafted on it. Therefore, to clear up the nature of these qualities, it may be necessary to explain the nature of pain and pleasure on which they depend. A man who suffers under violent bodily pain (I suppose the most violent, because the effect may be the more obvious), I say a man in great pain has his teeth set, his eyebrows are violently contracted, his forehead is wrinkled, his eyes are dragged inwards, and rolled with great vehemence, his hair stands on end, the voice is forced out in short shrieks and groans, and the whole fabric totters. Fear, or terror, which is an apprehension of pain or death, exhibits exactly the same effects, approaching in violence to those just mentioned, in proportion to the nearness of the cause, and the weakness of the subject. This is not only so in the human species; but I have more than once observed in dogs, under an apprehension of punishment, that they have writhed their bodies, and yelped, and howled, as if they had actually felt the blows. From hence I conclude, that pain and fear act upon the same parts of the body, and in the same manner, though somewhat differing in degree; that pain and fear consist in an unnatural tension of the nerves; that this is sometimes accompanied with an unnatural strength, which sometimes suddenly changes into an extraordinary weakness; that these effects often come on alternately, and are sometimes mixed with each other. This is the nature of all convulsive agitations, especially in weaker subjects, which are the most liable to the severest impressions of pain and fear.

The only difference between pain and terror is, that things which cause pain operate on the mind by the intervention of the body; whereas things that cause terror generally affect the bodily organs by the operation of the mind suggesting the danger; but both agreeing, either primarily or secondarily, in producing a tension, contraction, or violent emotion of the nerves,[1] they agree likewise in everything else. For it appears very clearly to me, from this, as well as from many other examples, that when the body is disposed, by any means whatsoever, to such emotions as it would acquire by the means of a certain passion; it will of itself excite something very like that passion in the mind.

Sect. IV. Continued

To this purpose Mr. Spon, in his *Récherches d' Antiquité*, gives us a curious story of the celebrated physiognomist Campanella. This man, it seems, had not only made very accurate observations on human faces, but was very expert in mimicking such as were any way remarkable. When he had a mind to penetrate into the inclinations of those he had to deal with, he composed his face, his gesture, and his whole body, as nearly as he could into the exact similitude of the person he intended to examine; and then carefully observed what turn of mind he seemed to acquire by this change. So that, says my author, he was able to enter into the dispositions and thoughts of people as effectually as if he had been changed into the very men. I have often observed, that on mimicking the looks and gestures of angry, or placid, or frighted, or daring men, I have involuntarily found my mind turned to that passion, whose appearance I endeavoured to imitate; nay, I am convinced

---

[1] I do not here enter into the question debated among physiologists, whether pain be the effect of a contraction, or a tension of the nerves. Either will serve my purpose; for by tension, I mean no more than a violent pulling of the fibres, which compose any muscle or membrane, in whatever way this is done.

it is hard to avoid it, though one strove to separate the passion from its correspondent gestures. Our minds and bodies are so closely and intimately connected, that one is incapable of pain or pleasure without the other. Campanella, of whom we have been speaking, could so abstract his attention from any sufferings of his body, that he was able to endure the rack itself without much pain; and in lesser pains everybody must have observed, that, when we can employ our attention on anything else, the pain has been for a time suspended: on the other hand, if by any means the body is indisposed to perform such gestures, or to be stimulated into such emotions, as any passion usually produces in it, that passion itself never can arise, though its cause should be never so strongly in action; though it should be merely mental, and immediately affecting none of the senses. As an opiate or spirituous liquors, shall suspend the operation of grief, or fear, or anger, in spite of all our efforts to the contrary; and this by inducing in the body a disposition contrary to that which it receives from these passions.

Sect. V. How the Sublime is Produced

Having considered terror as producing an unnatural tension and certain violent emotions of the nerves; it easily follows, from what we have just said, that whatever is fitted to produce such a tension must be productive of a passion similar to terror, and consequently must be a source of the sublime, though it should have no idea of danger connected with it. So that little remains towards showing the cause of the sublime, but to show that the instances we have given of it in the second part relate to such things as are fitted by nature to produce this sort of tension, either by the primary operation of the mind or the body. With regard to such things as effect by the associated idea of danger, there can be no doubt but that they produce terror, and act by some modification of that passion; and that terror, when sufficiently violent, raises the emotions of the body just mentioned, can as little be doubted. But if the sublime is built on terror, or some passion like it, which has pain for its object, it is previously proper to inquire how any species of delight can be derived from a cause so apparently contrary to it. I say *delight*, because, as I have often remarked, it is very evidently different in its cause, and in its own nature, from actual and positive pleasure.

Sect. VI. How Pain can be a cause of Delight

Providence has so ordered it, that a state of rest and inaction, however it may flatter our indolence, should be productive of many inconveniences; that it should generate such disorders, as may force us to have recourse to some labour, as a thing absolutely requisite to make us pass our lives with tolerable satisfaction; for the nature of rest is to suffer all the parts of our bodies to fall into a relaxation, that not only disables the members from performing their functions, but takes away the vigorous tone of fibre which is requisite for carrying on the natural and necessary secretions. At the same time, that in this languid inactive state, the nerves are more liable to the most horrid convulsions, than when they are sufficiently braced and strengthened. Melancholy, dejection, despair, and often self-murder, is the consequence of the gloomy view we take of things in this relaxed state of body. The best remedy for all these evils is exercise or *labour*; and labour is a surmounting of *difficulties*, an exertion of the contracting power of the muscles; and as such resembles pain, which consists in tension or contraction, in everything but degree. Labour is not only requisite to preserve the coarser organs in a state fit for their functions; but it is equally necessary to those finer and more delicate organs, on which, and by which, the imagination, and perhaps the other mental powers, act. Since it is probable, that not only the inferior parts of the soul, as the passions are called, but the understanding itself, makes use of some fine corporeal instruments in its operation; though what they are, and where they are, may be somewhat hard to settle; but that it does make use of such, appears from hence; that a long exercise of the mental powers induces a remarkable lassitude of the whole body; and, on the other hand, that great bodily labour, or pain, weakens, and sometimes actually destroys, the mental faculties. Now, as a due exercise is essential to the coarse muscular parts of the constitution, and that without this rousing they would become languid and diseased, the very same rule holds with regard to those finer parts we have mentioned; to have them in proper order, they must be shaken and worked to a proper degree.

Sect. VII. Exercise Necessary for the Finer Organs

As common labour, which is a mode of pain, is the exercise of the grosser, a mode of terror is the exercise of the finer parts of the system; and if a certain mode of pain be of such a nature as to act upon the eye or the ear, as they are the most delicate organs, the affection approaches more nearly to that which has a mental cause. In all these cases, if the pain and terror are so modified as not to be actually noxious; if the pain is not carried to violence, and the terror is not conversant about the present destruction of the person, as these emotions clear the parts, whether fine or gross, of a dangerous and troublesome encumbrance, they are capable of producing delight; not pleasure, but a sort of delightful horror, a sort of tranquillity tinged with terror; which, as it belongs to self-preservation, is one of the strongest of all the passions. Its object is the sublime. Its highest degree I call *astonishment*; the subordinate degrees are awe, reverence, and respect, which, by the very etymology of the words show from what source they are derived, and how they stand distinguished from positive pleasure.

PART FIVE

Sect. I. Of Words

Natural objects affect us, by the laws of that connexion which Providence has established between certain motions and configurations of bodies, and certain consequent feelings in our mind. Painting affects us in the same manner, but with the superadded pleasure of imitation. Architecture affects by the laws of nature, and the law of reason: from which latter result the rules of proportion, which make a work to be praised or censured, in the whole or in some part, when the end for which it was designed is or is not properly answered. But as to words; they seem to me to affect us in a manner very different from that in which we are affected by natural objects, or by painting or architecture; yet words have as considerable a share in exciting ideas of beauty and of the sublime as many of those, and sometimes a much greater than any of them: therefore an inquiry into the manner by which they excite such emotions is far from being unnecessary in a discourse of this kind.

Sect. II. The Common Effects of Poetry, not by Raising Ideas of things

The common notion of the power of poetry and eloquence, as well as that of words in ordinary conversation, is that they affect the mind by raising in it ideas of those things for which custom has appointed them to stand. To examine the truth of this notion, it may be requisite to observe, that words may be divided into three sorts. The first are such as represent many simple ideas *united by nature* to form some one determinate composition, as man, horse, tree, castle, &c. These I call *aggregate words*. The second are they that stand for one simple idea of such compositions, and no more; as red, blue, round, square, and the like. These I call *simple abstract* words. The third are those which are formed by an union, an *arbitrary* union, of both the

others, and of the various relations between them in greater or less degrees of complexity; as virtue, honour, persuasion, magistrate, and the like. These I call *compound abstract* words. Words, I am sensible, are capable of being classed into more curious distinctions; but these seem to be natural, and enough for our purpose; and they are disposed in that order in which they are commonly taught, and in which the mind gets the ideas they are substituted for. I shall begin with the third sort of words; compound abstracts, such as virtue, honour, persuasion, docility. Of these I am convinced, that whatever power they may have on the passions, they do not derive it from any representation raised in the mind of the things for which they stand. As compositions, they are not real essences, and hardly cause, I think, any real ideas. Nobody, I believe, immediately on hearing the sounds, virtue, liberty, or honour, conceives any precise notions of the particular modes of action and thinking together with the mixt and simple ideas and the several relations of them for which these words are substituted; neither has he any general idea, compounded of them; for if he had, then some of those particular ones, though indistinct perhaps, and confused, might come soon to be perceived. But this, I take it, is hardly ever the case. For, put yourself upon analyzing one of these words, and you must reduce it from one set of general words to another, and then into the simple abstracts and aggregates, in a much longer series than may be at first imagined, before any real idea emerges to light, before you come to discover anything like the first principles of such compositions; and when you have made such a discovery of the original ideas, the effect of the composition is utterly lost. A train of thinking of this sort is much too long to be pursued in the ordinary ways of conversation; nor is it at all necessary that it should. Such words are in reality but mere sounds; but they are sounds which being used on particular occasions, wherein we receive some good, or suffer some evil, or see others affected with good or evil; or which we hear applied to other interesting things or events; and being applied in such a variety of cases, that we know readily by habit to what things they belong, they produce in the mind, whenever they are afterwards mentioned, effects similar to those of their occasions. The sounds being often used without reference to any particular occasion, and carrying still their first impressions, they at last utterly lose their connexion with the particular occasion that gave rise to them; yet the sound, without any annexed notion, continues to operate as before.

Sect. III. General Words before Ideas

Mr. Locke has somewhere observed, with his usual sagacity, that most general words, those belonging to virtue and vice, good and evil, especially, are taught before the particular modes of action to which they belong are presented to the mind; and with them, the love of the one, and the abhorrence of the other; for the minds of children are so ductile, that a nurse, or any person about a child, by seeming pleased or displeased with anything, or even any word, may give the disposition of the child a similar turn. When, afterwards, the several occurrences in life come to be applied to these words, and that which is pleasant often appears under the name of evil; and what is disagreeable to nature is called good and virtuous; a strange confusion of ideas and affections arises in the minds of many; and an appearance of no small contradiction between their notions and their actions. There are many who love virtue and who detest vice, and this not from hypocrisy or affectation, who notwithstanding very frequently act ill and wickedly in particulars without the least remorse; because these particular occasions never come into view, when the passions on the side of virtue were so warmly affected by certain words heated originally by the breath of others; and for this reason, it is hard to repeat certain sets of words, though owned by themselves unoperative, without being in some degree affected; especially if a warm and affecting tone of voice accompanies them, as suppose,

"Wise, valiant, generous, good, and great."

These words, by having no application, ought to be unoperative; but when words commonly sacred to great occasions are used, we are affected by them even without the occasions. When words which have been generally so applied are put together without any rational view, or in such a manner that they do not rightly agree with each other, the style is called bombast. And it requires in several cases much good sense and experience to be guarded against the force of such language; for when propriety is neglected, a greater number of these affecting words may be taken into the service and a greater variety may be indulged in combining them.

Sect. IV. The Effect of Words

If words have all their possible extent of power, three effects arise in the mind of the hearer. The first is, the *sound;* the second, the *picture,* or representation of the thing signified by the sound; the third is, the *affection* of the soul produced by one or by both of the foregoing. *Compounded abstract* words of which we have been speaking (honour, justice, liberty, and the like), produce the first and the last of these effects, but not the second. *Simple abstracts* are used to signify some one simple idea, without much adverting to others which may chance to attend it, as blue, green, hot, cold, and the like; these are capable of affecting all three of the purposes of words; as the *aggregate* words, man, castle, horse, &c., are in a yet higher degree. But I am of opinion, that the most general effect, even of these words, does not arise from their forming pictures of the several things they would represent in the imagination; because, on a very diligent examination of my own mind, and getting others to consider theirs, I do not find that once in twenty times any such picture is formed, and when it is, there is most commonly a particular effort of the imagination for that purpose. But the aggregate words operate, as I said of the compound-abstracts, not by presenting any image to the mind, but by having from use the same effect on being mentioned, that their original has when it is seen. Suppose we were to read a passage to this effect: "The river Danube rises in a moist and mountainous soil in the heart of Germany, where winding to and fro, it waters several principalities, until, turning into Austria, and leaving the walls of Vienna, it passes into Hungary; there with a vast flood, augmented by the Saave and the Drave, it quits Christendom, and rolling through the barbarous countries which border on Tartary, it enters by many mouths in the Black Sea." In this description many things are mentioned, as mountains, rivers, cities, the sea, &c. But let anybody examine himself, and see whether he has had impressed on his imagination any pictures of a river, mountain, watery soil, Germany, &c. Indeed it is impossible, in the rapidity and quick succession of words in conversation to have ideas both of the sound of the word, and of the thing represented: besides, some words, expressing real essences, are so mixed with others of a general and nominal import, that it is impracticable to jump from sense to thought, from particulars to generals, from things to words, in such a manner as to answer the purposes of life; nor is it necessary that we should.

Sect. VI. Poetry not strictly an Imitative Art

Hence we may observe that poetry, taken in its most general sense, cannot with strict propriety be called an art of imitation. It is indeed an imitation so far as it describes the manners and passions of men which their words can express; where *animi motus*

effert interprete lingua. There it is strictly imitation; and all merely *dramatic* poetry is of this sort. But *descriptive* poetry operates chiefly by *substitution*; by the means of sounds, which by custom have the effect of realities. Nothing is an imitation further than as it resembles some other thing; and words undoubtedly have no sort of resemblance to the ideas for which they stand.

Sect. VII. How Words influence the Passions

Now, as words affect, not by any original power, but by representation, it might be supposed, that their influence over the passions should be but light; yet it is quite otherwise; for we find by experience that eloquence and poetry are as capable, nay indeed much more capable of making deep and lively impressions than any other arts, and even than nature itself in very many cases. And this arises chiefly from these three causes. First, that we take an extraordinary part in the passions of others, and that we are easily affected and brought into sympathy by any tokens which are shewn of them; and there are no tokens which can express all the circumstances of most passions so fully as words; so that if a person speaks upon any subject, he can not only convey the subject to you, but likewise the manner in which he is himself affected by it. Certain it is, that the influence of most things on our passions is not so much from the things themselves, as from our opinions concerning them; and these again depend very much on the opinions of other men, conveyable for the most part by words only. Secondly; there are many things of a very affecting nature, which can seldom occur in the reality, but the words which represent them often do; and thus they have an opportunity of making a deep impression and taking root in the mind, whilst the idea of the reality was transient; and to some perhaps never really occurred in any shape, to whom it is notwithstanding very affecting, as war, death, famine, &c. Besides, many ideas have never been at all presented to the senses of any men but by words, as God, angels, devils, heaven and hell, all of which have however a great influence over the passions. Thirdly; by words we have it in our power to make such *combinations* as we cannot possibly do otherwise. By this power of combining we are able, by the addition of well-chosen circumstances, to give a new life and force to the simple object. In painting we may represent any fine figure we please; but we never can give it those enlivening touches which it may receive from words. To represent an angel in a picture, you can only draw a beautiful young man winged; but what painting can furnish out any thing so grand as the addition of one word, "the angel of the *Lord?*" It is true, I have here no clear idea, but these words affect the mind more than the sensible image did, which is all I contend for. . . . but still it will be difficult to conceive how words can move the passions which belong to real objects, without representing these objects clearly. This is difficult to us, because we do not sufficiently distinguish, in our observations upon language, between a clear expression, and a strong expression. These are frequently confounded with each other, though they are in reality extremely different. The former regards the understanding; the latter belongs to the passions. The one describes a thing as it is; the other describes it as it is felt. Now, as there is a moving tone of voice, an impassioned countenance, an agitated gesture, which affect independently of the things about which they are exerted, so there are words, and certain dispositions of words, which being peculiarly devoted to passionate subjects, and always used by those who are under the influence of any passion; they touch and move us more than those which far more clearly and distinctly express the subject matter. We yield to sympathy, what we refuse to description.

The truth is, all verbal description, merely as naked description, though never so exact, conveys so poor and insufficient an idea of the thing described, that it could scarcely have the smallest effect, if the speaker did not call in to his aid those modes of speech that mark a strong and lively feeling in himself. Then, by the contagion of our passions, we catch a fire already kindled in another, which probably might never have been struck out by the object described. Words, by strongly conveying the passions, by those means which we have already mentioned, fully compensate for their weakness in other respects. It may be observed that very polished languages, and such as are praised for their superior clearness and perspicuity, are generally deficient in strength. The French language has that perfection, and that defect. Whereas the oriental tongues, and in general the languages of most unpolished people, have a great force and energy of expression; and this is but natural. Uncultivated people are but ordinary observers of things, and not critical in distinguishing them; but, for that reason, they admire more, and are more affected with what they see, and therefore express themselves in a warmer and more passionate manner. If the affection be well conveyed, it will work its effect without any clear idea; often without any idea at all of the thing which has originally given rise to it.

It might be expected from the fertility of the subject, that I should consider poetry as it regards the sublime and beautiful more at large; but it must be observed that in this light it has been often and well handled already. It was not my design to enter into the criticism of the sublime and beautiful in any art, but to attempt to lay down such principles as may tend to ascertain, to distinguish, and to form a sort of standard for them; which purposes I thought might be best effected by an enquiry into the properties of such things in nature as raise love and astonishment in us; and by shewing in what manner they operated to produce these passions. Words were only so far to be considered, as to shew upon what principle they were capable of being the representatives of these natural things, and by what powers they were able to affect us often as strongly as the things they represent, and sometimes much more strongly.

DAVID HUME [1711–76]

≻≻≻≻≺≺≺≺

Of the Standard of Taste [1757]

The great variety of Taste, as well as of opinion, which prevails in the world, is too obvious not to have fallen under every one's observation. Men of the most confined knowledge are able to remark a difference of taste in the narrow circle of their acquaintance, even where the persons have been educated under the same government, and have early imbibed the same prejudices. But those, who can enlarge their view to contemplate distant nations and remote ages, are still more surprised at the great inconsistence and contrariety. We are apt to call *barbarous* whatever departs widely from our own taste and apprehension: But soon find the epithet of reproach retorted on us. And the highest arrogance and self-conceit is at last startled, on observing an equal assurance on all sides, and scruples, amidst such a contest of sentiment to pronounce positively in its own favour.

As this variety of taste is obvious to the most careless enquirer; so will it be found, on examination, to be still greater in reality than in appearance. The sentiments of men often differ with regard to beauty and deformity of all kinds, even while their general discourse is the same. There are certain terms in every language, which import blame, and others praise; and all men, who use the same tongue, must agree in their

From *Essays Moral, Political, and Literary* by David Hume, edited by T. H. Greene and T. H. Grose (London: 1875).

application of them. Every voice is united in applauding elegance, propriety, simplicity, spirit in writing; and in blaming fustian, affectation, coldness, and a false brilliancy: But when critics come to particulars, this seeming unanimity vanishes; and it is found, that they had affixed a very different meaning to their expressions. In all matters of opinion and science, the case is opposite: The difference among men is there oftener found to lie in generals than in particulars; and to be less in reality than in appearance. An explanation of the terms commonly ends the controversy; and the disputants are surprized to find, that they had been quarrelling, while at bottom they agreed in their judgment.

Those who found morality on sentiment, more than on reason, are inclined to comprehend ethics under the former observation, and to maintain, that, in all questions, which regard conduct and manners, the difference among men is really greater than at first sight it appears. It is indeed obvious, that writers of all nations and all ages concur in applauding justice, humanity, magnanimity, prudence, veracity; and in blaming the opposite qualities. Even poets and other authors, whose compositions are chiefly calculated to please the imagination, are yet found, from Homer down to Fenelon, to inculcate the same moral precepts, and to bestow their applause and blame on the same virtues and vices. This great unanimity is usually ascribed to the influence of plain reason; which, in all these cases, maintains similar sentiments in all men, and prevents those controversies, to which the abstract sciences are so much exposed. So far as the unanimity is real, this account may be admitted as satisfactory: But we must also allow that some part of the seeming harmony in morals may be accounted for from the very nature of language. The word *virtue,* with its equivalent in every tongue, implies praise; as that of *vice* does blame: And no one, without the most obvious and grossest impropriety, could affix reproach to a term, which in general acceptation is understood in a good sense; or bestow applause, where the idiom requires disapprobation. Homer's general precepts, where he delivers any such, will never be controverted; but it is obvious, that, when he draws particular pictures of manners, and represents heroism in Achilles and prudence in Ulysses, he intermixes a much greater degree of ferocity in the former, and of cunning and fraud in the latter, than Fenelon would admit of. The sage Ulysses in the Greek poet seems to delight in lies and fictions, and often employs them without any necessity or even advantage: But his more scrupulous son, in the French epic writer, exposes himself to the most imminent perils, rather than depart from the most exact line of truth and veracity.

The admirers and followers of the *Alcoran* insist on the excellent moral precepts interspersed throughout that wild and absurd performance. But it is to be supposed, that the Arabic words, which correspond to the English, equity, justice, temperance, meekness, charity, were such as, from constant use of that tongue, must always be taken in a good sense; and it would have argued the greatest ignorance, not of morals, but of language, to have mentioned them with any epithets, besides those of applause and approbation. But would we know, whether the pretended prophet had really attained a just sentiment of morals? Let us attend to his narration; and we shall soon find, that he bestows praise on such instances of treachery, inhumanity, cruelty, revenge, bigotry, as are utterly incompatible with civilized society. No steady rule of right seems there to be attained to; and every action is blamed or praised, so far only as it is beneficial or hurtful to the true believers.

The merit of delivering true general precepts in ethics is indeed very small. Whoever recommends any moral virtues, really does no more than is implied in the terms themselves. That people, who invented the word *charity,* and used it in a good sense, inculcated more clearly and much more efficaciously, the precept, *be charitable,* than any pretended legislator or prophet, who should insert such a *maxim* in his writings. Of all expressions, those, which, together with their other meaning, imply a degree either of blame or approbation, are the least liable to be perverted or mistaken.

It is natural for us to seek a *Standard of Taste;* a rule, by which the various sentiments of men may be reconciled; at least, a decision afforded, confirming one sentiment, and condemning another.

There is a species of philosophy, which cuts off all hopes of success in such an attempt, and represents the impossibility of ever attaining any standard of taste. The difference, it is said, is very wide between judgment and sentiment. All sentiment is right; because sentiment has a reference to nothing beyond itself, and is always real, wherever a man is conscious of it. But all determinations of the understanding are not right; because they have a reference to something beyond themselves, to wit, real matter of fact; and are not always conformable to that standard. Among a thousand different opinions which different men may entertain of the same subject, there is one, and but one, that is just and true; and the only difficulty is to fix and ascertain it. On the contrary, a thousand different sentiments, excited by the same object, are all right: Because no sentiment represents what is really in the object. It only marks a certain conformity or relation between the object and the organs or faculties of the mind; and if that conformity did not really exist, the sentiment could never possibly have being. Beauty is no quality in things themselves: It exists merely in the mind which contemplates them; and each mind perceives a different beauty. One person may even perceive deformity, where another is sensible of beauty; and every individual ought to acquiesce in his own sentiment, without pretending to regulate those of others. To seek the real beauty, or real deformity, is as fruitless an enquiry, as to pretend to ascertain the real sweet or real bitter. According to the disposition of the organs, the same object may be both sweet and bitter; and the proverb has justly determined it to be fruitless to dispute concerning tastes. It is very natural, and even quite necessary, to extend this axiom to mental, as well as bodily taste; and thus common sense, which is so often at variance with philosophy, especially with the sceptical kind, is found, in one instance at least, to agree in pronouncing the same decision.

But though this axiom, by passing into a proverb, seems to have attained the sanction of common sense; there is certainly a species of common sense which opposes it, at least serves to modify and restrain it. Whoever would assert an equality of genius and elegance between Ogilby and Milton, or Bunyan and Addison, would be thought to defend no less an extravagance, than if he had maintained a mole-hill to be as high as Teneriffe, or a pond as extensive as the ocean. Though there may be found persons, who give the preference to the former authors, no one pays attention to such a taste; and we pronounce without scruple the sentiment of these pretended critics to be absurd and ridiculous. The principle of the natural equality of tastes is then totally forgot, and while we admit it on some occasions, where the objects seem near an equality, it appears an extravagant paradox, or rather a palpable absurdity,

where objects so disproportioned are compared together.

It is evident that none of the rules of composition are fixed by reasoning a priori, or can be esteemed abstract conclusions of the understanding, from comparing those habitudes and relations of ideas, which are eternal and immutable. Their foundation is the same with that of all the practical sciences, experience; nor are they any thing but general observations, concerning what has been universally found to please in all countries and in all ages. Many of the beauties of poetry and even of eloquence are founded on falsehood and fiction, on hyperboles, metaphors, and an abuse or perversion of terms from their natural meaning. To check the sallies of the imagination, and to reduce every expression to geometrical truth and exactness, would be the most contrary to the laws of criticism; because it would produce a work, which, by universal experience, has been found the most insipid and disagreeable. But though poetry can never submit to exact truth, it must be confined by rules of art, discovered to the author either by genius or observation. If some negligent or irregular writers have pleased, they have not pleased by their transgressions of rule or order, but in spite of these transgressions: They have possessed other beauties, which were conformable to just criticism; and the force of these beauties has been able to overpower censure, and give the mind a satisfaction superior to the disgust arising from the blemishes. Ariosto pleases; but not by his monstrous and improbable fictions, by his bizarre mixture of the serious and comic styles, by the want of coherence in his stories, or by the continual interruptions of his narration. He charms by the force and clearness of his expression, by the readiness and variety of his inventions, and by his natural pictures of the passions, especially those of the gay and amorous kind: And however his faults may diminish our satisfaction, they are not able entirely to destroy it. Did our pleasure really arise from those parts of his poem, which we denominate faults, this would be no objection to criticism in general: It would only be an objection to those particular rules of criticism, which would establish such circumstances to be faults, and would represent them as universally blameable. If they are found to please, they cannot be faults; let the pleasure, which they produce, be ever so unexpected and unaccountable.

But though all the general rules of art are founded only on experience and on the observation of the common sentiments of human nature, we must not imagine, that, on every occasion, the feelings of men will be conformable to these rules. Those finer emotions of the mind are of a very tender and delicate nature, and require the concurrence of many favourable circumstances to make them play with facility and exactness, according to their general and established principles. The least exterior hindrance to such small springs, or the least internal disorder, disturbs their motion, and confounds the operation of the whole machine. When we would make an experiment of this nature, and would try the force of any beauty or deformity, we must choose with care a proper time and place, and bring the fancy to a suitable situation and disposition. A perfect serenity of mind, a recollection of thought, a due attention to the object; if any of these circumstances be wanting, our experiment will be fallacious, and we shall be unable to judge of the catholic and universal beauty. The relation, which nature has placed between the form and the sentiment, will at least be more obscure; and it will require greater accuracy to trace and discern it. We shall be able to ascertain its influence not so much from the operation of each particular beauty, as from the durable admiration, which attends those works, that have survived all the caprices of mode and fashion, all the mistakes of ignorance and envy.

The same Homer, who pleased at Athens and Rome two thousand years ago, is still admired at Paris and at London. All the changes of climate, government, religion, and language, have not been able to obscure his glory. Authority or prejudice may give a temporary vogue to a bad poet or orator; but his reputation will never be durable or general. When his compositions are examined by posterity or by foreigners, the enchantment is dissipated, and his faults appear in their true colours. On the contrary, a real genius, the longer his works endure, and the more wide they are spread, the more sincere is the admiration which he meets with. Envy and jealousy have too much place in a narrow circle; and even familiar acquaintance with his person may diminish the applause due to his performances: But when these obstructions are removed, the beauties, which are naturally fitted to excite agreeable sentiments, immediately display their energy; and while the world endures, they maintain their authority over the minds of men.

It appears then, that, amidst all the variety and caprice of taste, there are certain general principles of approbation or blame, whose influence a careful eye may trace in all operations of the mind. Some particular forms or qualities, from the original structure of the internal fabric, are calculated to please, and others displease; and if they fail of their effect in any particular instance, it is from some apparent defect or imperfection in the organ. A man in a fever would not insist on his palate as able to decide concerning flavours; nor would one, affected with the jaundice, pretend to give a verdict with regard to colours. In each creature, there is a sound and defective state; and the former alone can be supposed to afford us a true standard of taste and sentiment. If, in the sound state of the organ, there be an entire or a considerable uniformity of sentiment among men, we may thence derive an idea of the perfect beauty; in like manner as the appearance of objects in day-light, to the eye of a man in health, is denominated their true and real colour, even while colour is allowed to be merely a phantasm of the senses.

Many and frequent are the defects in the internal organs which prevent or weaken the influence of those general principles, on which depends our sentiment of beauty or deformity. Though some objects, by the structure of the mind, be naturally calculated to give pleasure, it is not to be expected, that in every individual the pleasure will be equally felt. Particular incidents and situations occur, which either throw a false light on the objects, or hinder the true from conveying to the imagination the proper sentiment and perception.

One obvious cause, why many feel not the proper sentiment of beauty, is the want of that *delicacy* of imagination, which is requisite to convey a sensibility of those finer emotions. This delicacy every one pretends to: Every one talks of it; and would reduce every kind of taste or sentiment to its standard. But as our intention in this essay is to mingle some light of the understanding with the feeling of sentiment, it will be proper to give a more accurate definition of delicacy, than has hitherto been attempted. And not to draw our philosophy from too profound a source, we shall have recourse to a noted story in *Don Quixote*.

It is with good reason, says Sancho to the squire with the great nose, that I pretend to have a judgment in wine: This is a quality hereditary in our family. Two of my kinsmen were once called to give their opinion of a hogshead, which was supposed to be excellent, being old and of a good vintage. One of them tastes it; considers it; and after mature reflection pronounces the wine to be good, were it not for a small taste of leather, which he perceived in it. The other, after using the same precautions, gives also his verdict in favour of the wine; but with the reserve of a taste of iron, which he could easily distinguish. You cannot imagine how much they were both ridiculed for their judgment. But who laughed in the end? On emptying the hogshead, there was found at the bottom, an old key with a leathern thong tied to it.

The great resemblance between mental and bodily taste will easily teach us to apply this story. Though it be certain that beauty and deformity, more than sweet and bitter, are not qualities in objects, but belong entirely to the sentiment, internal or external; it must be allowed, that there are certain qualities in objects, which are fitted by nature to produce those particular feelings. Now as these qualities may be found in a small degree, or may be mixed and confounded with each other, it often happens, that the taste is not affected with such minute qualities, or is not able to distinguish all the particular flavours, amidst the disorder, in which they are presented. Where the organs are so fine, as to allow nothing to escape them; and at the same time so exact as to perceive every ingredient in the composition: This we call delicacy of taste, where we employ these terms in the literal or metaphorical sense. Here then the general rules of beauty are of use; being drawn from established models, and from the observation of what pleases or displeases, when presented singly and in a high degree: And if the same qualities, in a continued composition and in a smaller degree, affect not the organs with a sensible delight or uneasiness, we exclude the person from all pretensions to this delicacy. To produce these general rules or avowed patterns of composition is like finding the key with the leathern thong; which justified the verdict of Sancho's kinsmen, and confounded those pretended judges who had condemned them. Though the hogshead had never been emptied, the taste of the one was still equally delicate, and that of the other equally dull and languid: But it would have been more difficult to have proved the superiority of the former, to the conviction of every by-stander. In like manner, though the beauties of writing had never been methodized, or reduced to general principles; though no excellent models had ever been acknowledged; the different degrees of taste would still have subsisted, and the judgment of one man been preferable to that of another; but it would not have been so easy to silence the bad critic, who might always insist upon his particular sentiment, and refuse to submit to his antagonist. But when we show him an avowed principle of art; when we illustrate this principle by examples, whose operation, from his own particular taste, he acknowledges to be conformable to the principle; when we prove, that the same principle may be applied to the present case, where he did not perceive or feel its influence: He must conclude, upon the whole, that the fault lies in himself, and that he wants the delicacy, which is requisite to make him sensible of every beauty and every blemish, in any composition or discourse.

It is acknowledged to be the perfection of every sense or faculty, to perceive with exactness its most minute objects, and allow nothing to escape its notice and observation. The smaller the objects are, which become sensible to the eye, the finer is that organ, and the more elaborate its make and composition. A good palate is not tried by strong flavours; but by a mixture of small ingredients, where we are still sensible of each part, notwithstanding its minuteness and its confusion with the rest. In like manner, a quick and acute perception of beauty and deformity must be the perfection of our mental taste; nor can a man be satisfied with himself while he suspects, that any excellence or blemish in a discourse has passed him unobserved. In this case, the perfection of the man, and the perception of the sense or feeling, are found to be united. A very delicate palate, on many occasions, may be a great inconvenience both to a man himself and to his friends: But a delicate taste of wit or beauty must always be a desirable quality; because it is the source of all the finest and most innocent enjoyments, of which human nature is susceptible. In this decision the sentiments of all mankind are agreed. Wherever you can ascertain a delicacy of taste, it is sure to meet with approbation; and the best way of ascertaining it is to appeal to those models and principles, which have been established by the uniform consent and experience of nations and ages.

But though there be naturally a wide difference in point of delicacy between one person and another, nothing tends further to encrease and improve this talent, than practice in a particular art, and the frequent survey or contemplation of a particular species of beauty. When objects of any kind are first presented to the eye or imagination, the sentiment, which attends them, is obscure and confused; and the mind is, in a great measure, incapable of pronouncing concerning their merits or defects. The taste cannot perceive the several excellences of the performance; much less distinguish the particular character of each excellency, and ascertain its quality and degree. If it pronounce the whole in general to be beautiful or deformed, it is the utmost that can be expected; and even this judgment, a person, so unpractised, will be apt to deliver with great hesitation and reserve. But allow him to acquire experience in those objects, his feeling becomes more exact and nice: He not only perceives the beauties and defects of each part, but marks the distinguishing species of each quality, and assigns it suitable praise or blame. A clear and distinct sentiment attends him through the whole survey of the objects; and he discerns that very degree and kind of approbation or displeasure, which each part is naturally fitted to produce. The mist dissipates, which seemed formerly to hang over the object: The organ acquires greater perfection in its operations; and can pronounce, without danger of mistake, concerning the merits of every performance. In a word, the same address and dexterity, which practice gives to the execution of any work, is also acquired by the same means, in the judging of it.

So advantageous is practice to the discernment of beauty, that, before we can give judgment on any work of importance, it will even be requisite, that that very individual performance be more than once perused by us, and be surveyed in different lights with attention and deliberation. There is a flutter or hurry of thought which attends the first perusal of any piece, and which confounds the genuine sentiment of beauty. The relation of the parts is not discerned: The true characters of style are little distinguished: The several perfections and defects seem wrapped up in a species of confusion, and present themselves indistinctly to the imagination. Not to mention, that there is a species of beauty, which, as it is florid and superficial, pleases at first; but being found incompatible with a just expression either of reason or passion, soon palls upon the taste, and is then rejected with disdain, at least rated at a much lower value.

It is impossible to continue in the practice of contemplating any order of beauty, without being frequently obliged to form *comparisons* between the several species and degrees of excellence, and estimating their proportion to each other. A man, who has had no opportunity of comparing the different kinds of beauty, is indeed totally unqualified to pronounce an opinion with regard to any object presented to him. By comparison alone we fix the epithets of praise or blame, and learn how to assign the due degree of each. The coarsest daubing contains a certain lustre of colours and exactness of imitation, which are so far beauties, and would affect the mind of a peasant or Indian with the highest admiration. The most vulgar ballads are not entirely destitute of harmony or nature; and none but a person familiarized to superior beauties, would pronounce their numbers harsh, or narration uninteresting. A great inferiority of beauty gives pain to a person conversant in the highest excellence of the kind, and is for that reason pronounced a deformity: As

the most finished object, with which we are acquainted, is naturally supposed to have reached the pinnacle of perfection, and to be entitled to the highest applause. One accustomed to see, and examine, and weigh the several performances, admired in different ages and nations, can only rate the merits of a work exhibited to his view, and assign its proper rank among the productions of genius.

But to enable a critic the more fully to execute this undertaking, he must preserve his mind free from all *prejudice*, and allow nothing to enter into his consideration, but the very object which is submitted to his examination. We may observe, that every work of art, in order to produce its due effect on the mind, must be surveyed in a certain point of view, and cannot be fully relished by persons, whose situation, real or imaginary, is not conformable to that which is required by the performance. An orator addresses himself to a particular audience, and must have a regard to their particular genius, interests, opinions, passions, and prejudices; otherwise he hopes in vain to govern their resolution, and inflame their affections. Should they even have entertained some prepossessions against him, however unreasonable, he must not overlook this disadvantage; but, before he enters upon the subject, must endeavour to conciliate their affection, and acquire their good graces. A critic of a different age or nation, who should peruse this discourse, must have all these circumstances in his eye, and must place himself in the same situation as the audience, in order to form a true judgment of the oration. In like manner, when any work is addressed to the public, though I should have a friendship or enmity with the author, I must depart from this situation; and considering myself as a man in general, forget, if possible, my individual being and my peculiar circumstances. A person influenced by prejudice, complies not with this condition, but obstinately maintains his natural position, without placing himself in that point of view, which the performance supposes. If the work be addressed to persons of a different age or nation, he makes no allowance for their peculiar views and prejudices; but, full of the manners of his own age and country, rashly condemns what seemed admirable in the eyes of those for whom alone the discourse was calculated. If the work be executed for the public, he never sufficiently enlarges his comprehension, or forgets his interest as a friend or enemy, as a rival or commentator. By this means, his sentiments are perverted; nor have the same beauties and blemishes the same influence upon him, as if he had imposed a proper violence on his imagination, and had forgotten himself for a moment. So far his taste evidently departs from the true standard; and of consequence loses all credit and authority.

It is well known, that in all questions, submitted to the understanding, prejudice is destructive of sound judgment, and perverts all operations of the intellectual faculties: It is no less contrary to good taste; nor has it less influence to corrupt our sentiment of beauty. It belongs to *good sense* to check its influence in both cases; and in this respect, as well as in many others, reason, if not an essential part of taste, is at least requisite to the operations of this latter faculty. In all the nobler productions of genius, there is a mutual relation and correspondence of parts; nor can either the beauties or blemishes be perceived by him, whose thought is not capacious enough to comprehend all those parts, and compare them with each other, in order to perceive the consistence and uniformity of the whole. Every work of art has also a certain end or purpose, for which it is calculated; and is to be deemed more or less perfect, as it is more or less fitted to attain this end. The object of eloquence is to persuade, of history to instruct, of poetry to please by means of the passions and the imagination. These ends we must carry constantly in our view, when we peruse any performance; and we must be able to judge how far the means employed are adapted to their respective purposes. Besides every kind of composition, even the most poetical, is nothing but a chain of propositions and reasonings; not always, indeed, the justest and most exact, but still plausible and specious, however disguised by the colouring of the imagination. The persons introduced in tragedy and epic poetry, must be represented as reasoning, and thinking, and concluding, and acting, suitably to their character and circumstances; and without judgment, as well as taste and invention, a poet can never hope to succeed in so delicate an undertaking. Not to mention, that the same excellence of faculties which contributes to the improvement of reason, the same clearness of conception, the same exactness of distinction, the same vivacity of apprehension, are essential to the operations of true taste, and are its infallible concomitants. It seldom, or never happens, that a man of sense, who has experience in any art, cannot judge of its beauty; and it is no less rare to meet with a man who has a just taste without a sound understanding.

Thus, though the principles of taste be universal, and, nearly, if not entirely the same in all men; yet few are qualified to give judgment of any work of art, or establish their own sentiment as the standard of beauty. The organs of internal sensation are seldom so perfect as to allow the general principles their full play, and produce a feeling correspondent to those principles. They either labour under some defect, or are vitiated by some disorder; and by that means, excite a sentiment, which may be pronounced erroneous. When the critic has no delicacy, he judges without any distinction, and is only affected by the grosser and more palpable qualities of the object: The finer touches pass unnoticed and disregarded. Where he is not aided by practice, his verdict is attended with confusion and hesitation. Where no comparison has been employed, the most frivolous beauties, such as rather merit the name of defects, are the objects of his admiration. Where he lies under the influence of prejudice, all his natural sentiments are perverted. Where good sense is wanting, he is not qualified to discern the beauties of design and reasoning, which are the highest and most excellent. Under some or other of these imperfections, the generality of men labour; and hence a true judge in the finer arts is observed, even during the most polished ages, to be so rare a character: Strong sense, united to delicate sentiment, improved by practice, perfected by comparison, and cleared of all prejudice, can alone entitle critics to this valuable character; and the joint verdict of such, wherever they are to be found, is the true standard of taste and beauty.

But where are such critics to be found? By what marks are they to be known? How distinguish them from pretenders? These questions are embarrassing; and seem to throw us back into the same uncertainty, from which, during the course of this essay, we have endeavoured to extricate ourselves.

But if we consider the matter aright, these are questions of fact, not of sentiment. Whether any particular person be endowed with good sense and a delicate imagination, free from prejudice, may often be the subject of dispute, and be liable to great discussion and enquiry; But that such a character is valuable and estimable will be agreed in by all mankind. Where these doubts occur, men can do no more than in other disputable questions, which are submitted to the understanding: They must produce the best arguments, that their invention suggests to them; they must acknowledge a true and decisive standard to exist somewhere, to wit, real existence and matter of fact; and they must have indulgence to such as differ from them in their appeals to this standard. It is sufficient for our present purpose, if we have proved, that the taste of all individuals is not upon an equal footing, and that some men in general, however difficult to be particularly pitched upon, will be acknowledged by universal sentiment to have a preference above others.

But in reality the difficulty of finding, even in particulars, the standard of taste, is not so great as it is represented. Though in speculation, we may readily avow a certain criterion in science and deny it in sentiment, the matter is found in practice to be much more hard to ascertain in the former case than in the latter. Theories of abstract philosophy, systems of profound theology, have prevailed during one age: In a successive period, these have been universally exploded: Their absurdity has been detected: Other theories and systems have supplied their place, which again gave place to their successors: And nothing has been experienced more liable to the revolutions of chance and fashion than these pretended decisions of science. The case is not the same with beauties of eloquence and poetry. Just expressions of passion and nature are sure, after a little time, to gain public applause, which they maintain for ever. Aristotle, and Plato, and Epicurus, and Descartes, may successively yield to each other: But Terence and Virgil maintain an universal, undisputed empire over the minds of men. The abstract philosophy of Cicero has lost its credit: The vehemence of his oratory is still the object of our admiration.

Though men of delicate taste be rare, they are easily to be distinguished in society, by the soundness of their understanding and the superiority of their faculties above the rest of mankind. The ascendant, which they acquire, gives a prevalence to that lively approbation, with which they receive any productions of genius, and renders it generally predominant. Many men, when left to themselves, have but a faint and dubious perception of beauty, who yet are capable of relishing any fine stroke, which is pointed out to them. Every con-

vert to the admiration of the real poet or
orator is the cause of some new conversion.
And though prejudices may prevail for a
time, they never unite in celebrating any
rival to the true genius, but yield at last to
the force of nature and just sentiment.
Thus, though a civilized nation may easily
be mistaken in the choice of their admired
philosopher, they never have been found
long to err, in their affection for a favorite
epic or tragic author.

But notwithstanding all our endeavours
to fix a standard of taste, and reconcile the
discordant apprehensions of men, there still
remain two sources of variation, which are
not sufficient indeed to confound all the
boundaries of beauty and deformity, but
will often serve to produce a difference in
the degrees of our approbation or blame.
The one is the different humours of particular men; the other, the particular manners and opinions of our age and country.
The general principles of taste are uniform
in human nature: Where men vary in their
judgments, some defect or perversion in the
faculties may commonly be remarked; proceeding either from prejudice, from want of
practice, or want of delicacy; and there is
just reason for approving one taste, and
condemning another. But where there is
such a diversity in the internal frame or
external situation as is entirely blameless on
both sides, and leaves no room to give one
the preference above the other; in that case
a certain degree of diversity in judgment is
unavoidable, and we seek in vain for a
standard, by which we can reconcile the
contrary sentiments.

A young man, whose passions are warm,
will be more sensibly touched with amorous
and tender images, than a man more advanced in years, who takes pleasure in wise,
philosophical reflections concerning the
conduct of life and moderation of the passions. At twenty, Ovid may be the favourite
author; Horace at forty; and perhaps Taci-
tus at fifty. Vainly would we, in such cases,
endeavour to enter into the sentiments of

others, and divest ourselves of those propensities, which are natural to us. We
choose our favourite author as we do our
friend, from a conformity of humour and
disposition. Mirth or passion, sentiment or
reflection; whichever of these most predominates in our temper, it gives us a peculiar
sympathy with the writer who resembles us.

One person is more pleased with the sublime; another with the tender; a third with
raillery. One has a strong sensibility to
blemishes, and is extremely studious of correctness: Another has a more lively feeling
of beauties, and pardons twenty absurdities
and defects for one elevated or pathetic
stroke. The ear of this man is entirely
turned towards conciseness and energy;
that man is delighted with a copious, rich,
and harmonious expression. Simplicity is
affected by one; ornament by another. Comedy, tragedy, satire, odes, have each its
partisans, who prefer that particular species
of writing to all others. It is plainly an error
in a critic, to confine his approbation to one
species or style of writing, and condemn all
the rest. But it is almost impossible not to
feel a predilection for that which suits our
particular turn and disposition. Such pref-
erences are innocent and unavoidable, and
can never reasonably be the object of dispute, because there is no standard, by
which they can be decided.

For a like reason, we are more pleased,
in the course of our reading, with pictures
and characters, that resemble objects which
are found in our own age or country, than
with those which describe a different set of
customs. It is not without some effort, that
we reconcile ourselves to the simplicity of
ancient manners, and behold princesses
carrying water from the spring, and kings
and heroes dressing their own victuals. We
may allow in general, that the representation of such manners is no fault in the author, nor deformity in the piece; but we are
not so sensibly touched with them. For this
reason, comedy is not easily transferred
from one age or nation to another. A

Frenchman or Englishman is not pleased with the *Andria* of Terence, or *Clitia* of Machiavel; where the fine lady, upon whom all the play turns, never once appears to the spectators, but is always kept behind the scenes, suitably to the reserved humour of the ancient Greeks and modern Italians. A man of learning and reflection can make allowance for these peculiarities of manners; but a common audience can never divest themselves so far of their usual ideas and sentiments, as to relish pictures which in no wise resemble them.

But here there occurs a reflection, which may, perhaps, be useful in examining the celebrated controversy concerning ancient and modern learning; where we often find the one side excusing any seeming absurdity in the ancients from the manners of the age, and the other refusing to admit this excuse, or at least, admitting it only as an apology for the author, not for the performance. In my opinion, the proper boundaries in this subject have seldom been fixed between the contending parties. Where any innocent peculiarities of manner are represented, such as those above mentioned, they ought certainly to be admitted; and a man, who is shocked with them, gives an evident proof of false delicacy and refinement. The poet's *monument more durable than brass,* must fall to the ground like common brick or clay, were men to make no allowance for the continual revolutions of manners and customs, and would admit of nothing but what was suitable to the prevailing fashion. Must we throw aside the pictures of our ancestors, because of their ruffs and fardingales? But where the ideas of morality and decency alter from one age to another, and where vicious manners are described, without being marked with the proper characters of blame and disapprobation; this must be allowed to disfigure the poem, and to be a real deformity. I cannot, nor is it proper I should, enter into such sentiments; and however I may excuse the poet, on account of the manners of his age,

I never can relish the composition. The want of humanity and of decency, so conspicuous in the characters drawn by several of the ancient poets, even sometimes by Homer and the Greek tragedians, diminishes considerably the merit of their noble performances, and gives modern authors an advantage over them. We are not interested in the fortunes and sentiments of such rough heroes: We are displeased to find the limits of vice and virtue so much confounded: And whatever indulgence we may give to the writer on account of his prejudice, we cannot prevail on ourselves to enter into his sentiments, or bear an affection to characters, which we plainly discover to be blameable.

The case is not the same with moral principles, as with speculative opinions of any kind. These are in continual flux and revolution. The son embraces a different system from the father. Nay, there scarcely is any man, who can boast of great constance and uniformity in this particular. Whatever speculative errors may be found in the polite writings of any age or country, they detract but little from the value of those compositions. There needs but a certain turn of thought or imagination to make us enter into all the opinions, which then prevailed, and relish the sentiments or conclusions derived from them. But a very violent effort is requisite to change our judgment of manners, and excite sentiments of approbation or blame, love or hatred, different from those to which the mind from long custom has been familiarized. And where a man is confident of the rectitude of that moral standard, by which he judges, he is justly jealous of it, and will not pervert the sentiments of his heart for a moment, in complaisance to any writer whatsoever.

Of all speculative errors, those, which regard religion, are the most excusable in compositions of genius; nor is it ever permitted to judge of the civility or wisdom of any people, or even of single persons, by the grossness or refinement of their theological principles. The same good sense, that directs men in the ordinary occurrences of life, is not hearkened to in religious matters, which are supposed to be placed altogether above the cognizance of human reason. On this account, all the absurdities of the pagan system of theology must be overlooked by every critic, who would pretend to form a just notion of ancient poetry; and our posterity, in their turn, must have the same indulgence to their forefathers. No religious principles can ever be imputed as a fault to any poet, while they remain merely principles, and take no such strong possession of his heart, as to lay him under the imputation of *bigotry* or *superstition*. Where that happens, they confound the sentiments of morality, and alter the natural boundaries of vice and virtue. They are therefore eternal blemishes, according to the principle above mentioned; nor are the prejudices and false opinions of the age sufficient to justify them.

It is essential to the Roman Catholic religion to inspire a violent hatred of every other worship, and to represent all pagans, mahometans, and heretics as the objects of divine wrath and vengeance. Such sentiments, though they are in reality very blameable, are considered as virtues by the zealots of that communion, and are represented in their tragedies and epic poems as a kind of divine heroism. This bigotry has disfigured two very fine tragedies of the French theatre, *Polieucte* and *Athalia;* where an intemperate zeal for particular modes of worship is set off with all the pomp imaginable, and forms the predominant character of the heroes. "What is this," says the sublime Joad to Josabet, finding her in discourse with Nathan, the priest of Baal, "does the daughter of David speak to this traitor? Are you not afraid, lest the earth should open and pour forth flames to devour you both? Or lest these holy walls should fall and crush you together? What is his purpose? Why comes that enemy of God hither to poison the air, which we breathe, with his horrid presence?" Such sentiments are received with great applause in the theatre of Paris; but at London the spectators would be full as much pleased to hear Achilles tell Agamemnon, that he was a dog in his forehead, and a deer in his heart, or Jupiter threaten Juno with a sound drubbing, if she will not be quiet.

Religious principles are also a blemish in any polite composition, when they rise up to superstition, and intrude themselves into every sentiment, however remote from any connection with religion. It is no excuse for the poet, that the customs of his country had burthened life with so many religious ceremonies and observances, that no part of it was exempt from that yoke. It must for ever be ridiculous in Petrarch to compare his mistress Laura, to Jesus Christ. Nor is it less ridiculous in that agreeable libertine, Boccace, very seriously to give thanks to God Almighty and the ladies, for their assistance in defending him against his enemies.

Role of Art in Society
Religious Art ?

ALEXANDER GERARD [1728–95]

>>>><<<<

From *An Essay on Taste* [1759]

A fine taste is neither wholly the gift of *nature,* nor wholly the effect of *art.* It derives its origin from certain powers natural to the mind; but these powers cannot attain their full perfection, unless they be assisted by proper culture. Taste consists chiefly in the improvement of those principles which are commonly called *the powers of imagination,* and are considered by modern philosophers as *internal* or *reflex senses,* supplying us with fine and more delicate perceptions than any which can properly be referred to our external organs. These are reducible to the following principles; the senses of novelty, of sublimity, of beauty, of imitation, of harmony, of ridicule, and of virtue. With the explication of these, we must, therefore, begin our inquiry into the nature of taste. . . .

PART I. SECTION II

Of the sense or taste of Grandeur and Sublimity

Grandeur or sublimity gives us a still higher and nobler pleasure (than novelty), by means of a sense appropriated to the perception of it; while meanness renders any object to which it adheres, disagreeable and distasteful. Objects are sublime, which possess *quantity,* or amplitude, and *simplicity,* in conjunction. . . .

We always contemplate objects and ideas with a disposition similar to their nature. When a large object is presented, the mind expands itself to the extent of that object, and is filled with one grand sensation, which totally possessing it, composes it

From *An Essay on Taste* by Alexander Gerard, 3rd edition (Edinburgh: 1780).

into a solemn sedateness, and strikes it with deep silent wonder and admiration: it finds such a difficulty in spreading itself to the dimensions of its object, as enlivens and invigorates its frame: and having overcome the opposition which this occasions, it sometimes imagines itself present in every part of the scene which it contemplates; and from the sense of this immensity, feels a noble pride, and entertains a lofty conception of its own capacity. . . .

It must also be remarked, that whatever excites in the mind a sensation or emotion similar to what is excited by vast objects, is on this account denominated sublime; it being natural to reduce to the same species, to express by the same name, and even frequently to confound together, those objects which we contemplate with the same or a like disposition. Hence the raging of the sea in a storm, and the loud roaring thunder, which inspire an awful sedateness, are termed sublime. Objects exciting terror are, for this reason, in general sublime; for terror always implies astonishment, occupies the whole soul, and suspends all its motions.

In like manner, we admire as sublime superior excellence of many kinds; such iminence in strength, or power, or genius, as is uncommon, and overcomes difficulties which are unsurmountable by lower degrees of ability; such vigor of mind as indicates the absence of low and groveling passions, and enables a person to despise honours, riches, power, pain, death; setting him above those enjoyments on which men generally put a high value, and those sufferings which they think intolerable. Such degrees of excellence, by an original principle of the mind, excite wonder and astonishment, the same emotion which is produced by amplitude. A great degree of *quality* has here the same effect upon the mind, as vastness of *quantity*, and it produces this effect in the same manner, by stretching and elevating the mind in the conception of it. . . .

But in order to comprehend the whole extent of the sublime, it is proper to take notice, that objects which do not themselves possess that quality, may nevertheless acquire it by *association* with such as do. It is the nature of association, to unite different ideas so closely, that they become in a manner one. In that situation, the qualities of one part are naturally attributed to the whole, or to the other part. At least, association renders the transition of the mind from one idea to another so quick and easy, that we contemplate both with the same disposition; and are therefore similarly affected by both. Whenever, then, any object uniformly and constantly introduces into the mind the idea of another that is grand, it will, by its connection with the latter, be itself rendered grand. Hence words and phrases are denominated lofty and majestic. Sublimity of style arises, not so much from the sound of the words, though that doubtless may have some influence, as from the nature of the ideas which we are accustomed to annex to them, and the character of the persons among whom they are in most common use. This too is the origin of the grandeur which we ascribe to objects high and elevated in place; . . .

But the fine arts present the most numerous examples of grandeur produced by association. In all of them, the sublime is attained chiefly by the artist's exciting *ideas* of sublime objects; and in such as are mimical, this quality is chiefly owing to our being led by the exactness of the imitation to form ideas and conceive images of sublime originals. Thought is a less intense energy than sense; yet *ideas,* especially when lively, never fail to be contemplated with some degree of the same emotion which attends their original *sensations;* and often yield almost equal pleasure to the reflex senses, when impressed upon the mind by a skilful imitation. . . .

SECTION III

Of the sense or taste of Beauty

Beautiful objects are of different kinds, and produce pleasure by means of different principles of human nature.

The first species of beauty is that of figure; and belongs to objects possessed of *uniformity, variety,* and proportion. Each of these qualities pleases in some degree; but all of them united give exquisite satisfaction.

Facility in the conception of an object, if it be moderate, gives us pleasure: the mind thinks well of itself, when it is able to form its conception without pain or labour. This constitutes the value of perspicuity of thought and language; which is agreeable in opposition to obscurity, as this occasions an uneasy search into the meaning of the parts, or the tendency of the whole, which requires greater labour than we are willing to bestow. Hence too it is that *uniformity* and *simplicity* become agreeable. Objects endued with these qualities enter easily into the mind: they do not distract our attention, or hurry us too fast from one scene to another: each part is distinctly and strongly conceived: the view of a part suggests the whole, and, impelling the mind to imagine the rest, produces a grateful exertion of its energy. . . .

There is perhaps no term used in a looser sense than *beauty,* which is applied to almost everything that pleases us. Though this usage is doubtless too indefinite, we may, without a faulty deviation from precision, apply this epithet to every pleasure which is conveyed by the eye, and which has not got a proper and peculiar name; to the pleasure we receive, either when an object of sight suggests pleasant ideas of other senses, or when the ideas suggested are agreeable ones formed from the sensations of sight, or when both these circumstances concur. In all these cases, beauty is, at least in part, resolveable into association. . . .

How far Taste depends on the Imagination

It has been observed above, that those internal senses, from which taste is formed, are commonly referred to the *imagination,* which is considered as holding a middle rank between the bodily senses, and the rational and moral faculties. . . .

. . . If we will but recollect and compare those qualities of human nature from which taste has been explained, we shall be convinced, that all its phenomena proceed, either from the general laws of *sensation,* or from certain operations of the *imagination.* Taste, therefore, though itself a species of sensation, is, in respect of its principles, justly reduced to imagination.

That taste is properly a kind of sensation, can scarcely be called in question, by any one who has clear and distinct ideas. It supplies us with simple perceptions, entirely different from all that we receive by external, sense, or by reflection. These make us acquainted with the forms and inherent qualities of things external, and with the nature of our own powers and operations: but taste exhibits a set of perceptions, which, though consequent on these, are really different; which result from, but are not included in, the primary and direct perception of objects. They are however equally uncompounded in their feeling, as incapable of being conceived prior to experience, as immediately, necessarily, and regularly exhibited in certain circumstances, as any other sensations whatsoever.[1] Taste

[1] Indeed, as our external senses are *ultimate* and *original* principles, it may perhaps be taken for granted, that this circumstance is essential to the idea of a sense, and that no power of the mind can be properly expressed by this name, which is derived and compounded, and capable of being resolved into simpler principles. According to this hypothesis, the powers of taste would not be

is subjected to the same general laws which regulate our other senses. . . . We shall mention but one law of sensation, which has been so often hinted at already, and which, by its immediate effects and its remoter consequences, has so great influence on the sentiments of taste, that it will be proper in a few words to illustrate it. The law of sensation which we have in view, is this: When an object is presented to any of our senses, the mind conforms itself to its nature and appearance, feels an emotion, and is put in a frame suitable and analo-

---

senses. To enquire whether they are, or are not, may perhaps be deemed a dispute about words, as the determination will depend upon the definition of a sense. It is however of some real moment, that the powers of the mind be reduced into classes, according to their real differences and analogies; and, therefore, that no definition be received which would disturb the regular distribution of them. And that the powers of taste may, with the greatest propriety, be reckoned senses, though they be derived faculties, will, it is hoped, appear from the following observations. We are directed by the phaenomena of our faculties in reducing them to classes. The obvious phaenomena of a *sense* are these. It is a power which supplies us with such *simple* perceptions, as cannot be conveyed by any other channel to those who are destitute of that sense. It is a power which receives its perception *immediately,* as soon as its object is exhibited, previous to any reasoning concerning the qualities of the object, or the causes of the perception. It is a power which exerts itself independent of *volition;* so that, while we remain in proper circumstances, we cannot, by any act of the will, prevent our receiving certain sensations, nor alter them at pleasure; nor can we, by any means, procure these sensations, as long as we are not in the proper situation for receiving them by their peculiar organ. These are the circumstances which characterize a sense. . . . These characters evidently belong to all the external senses, and to reflection or consciousness, by which we perceive what passes in our minds. They likewise belong to the powers of taste: harmony, for example, is a simple perception, which no man who has not a musical ear can receive, and which every one who has an ear immediately and necessarily receives on hearing a good tune. The powers of taste are therefore to be reckoned senses. Whether they are ultimate powers, is a subsequent question. Those who are unacquainted with philosophy reckon all our powers ultimate qualities of the mind: but nature delights in simplicity, and produces numerous effects, by a few causes of extensive influence; and it gous; of which we have a perception by consciousness or reflection. Thus, difficulty produces a consciousness of a grateful exertion of energy; facility, of an even and composed motion of soul; excellence, perfection, or sublimity, begets an enlargement of mind, and conscious pride; deficience or imperfection, a depression of soul and painful humility. This adapting of the mind to its present object, is the *immediate* cause of many of the pleasures and the pains of taste which have been pointed out: and by its consequences, it augments or diminishes many others.

---

is the business of philosophy to investigate these causes, and to explain the phaenomena from them. On inquiry, it appears, that the internal senses are not ultimate principles, because all their phaenomena can be accounted for, by simpler qualities of the mind. Thus the pleasure we receive from beautiful forms is resolveable into the pleasure of facility, that of moderate exertion, and that which results from the discovery of art and wisdom in the cause. But, notwithstanding this investigation of the causes of our reflex sensations, we may continue to term them *senses*, since it does not contradict any of the phaenomena, on account of which this name was originally bestowed upon them. Beautiful forms have uniformity, variety, and proportion; but the pleasure they give us, is an immediate sensation, prior to our analyzing them, or discovering by reason that they have these qualities. We find, on examination, that uniformity and proportion are agreeable, as they enable us to conceive the object with facility; and variety, as it hinders this facility from degenerating into langour; and that all of them are agreeable, as being indications of art and skill; and thence we conclude, that the pleasant sentiment of beauty is the result of those simple principles which dispose us to relish moderate facility, and moderate difficulty, and to approve intelligence and design; but the sentiment of beauty arises, without our reflecting on this mixture. This sentiment is compound in its *principles*, but perfectly simple in its *feeling*. . . . Just so, each principle of taste is with reason accounted a particular sense, because its perceptions, however produced, are peculiar to it, and specifically different from all others. Each conveys perceptions, which, in respect of their feeling, are original, though the powers, by which they are conveyed, are derived. It is scarce necessary to observe, that our ascribing the sentiments of taste to mental processes is totally different from asserting that they are deductions of reason. We do not prove that certain objects are grand by arguments, but we perceive them to be grand in consequence of the natural constitution of our mind, which disposes us, without reflection, to be pleased with largeness and simplicity. Reasoning may, however, be employed in exhibiting an object to the mind; and yet the perception that it has, when the object is once exhibited, may properly belong to a sense. Thus reasoning may be necessary to ascertain the circumstances, and determine the motive, of an action; but it is the moral sense that perceives it to be either virtuous or vicious, after reason has discovered its motive and its circumstances.

GOTTHOLD EPHRAIM LESSING [1729–81]

➤➤➤➤✦◀◀◀◀

From *Laokoon* [1766]

PREFACE

The first person who compared painting and poetry with one another was a man of refined feeling, who become aware of a similar effect produced upon himself by both arts. He felt that both represent what

From Lessing, *Selected Prose Works*, translated by E. C. Beasley & Helen Zimmern, edited by Edward Bell (London: G. Bell & Sons, Ltd., 1890). Some minor revisions have been made in the translation.

is absent as if it were present, and appearance as if it were reality; that both deceive, and that the deception of both is pleasing.

A second observer sought to penetrate below the surface of this pleasure, and discovered that in both it flowed from the same source. Beauty, the idea of which we first deduce from bodily objects, possesses universal laws, applicable to more things than one; to actions and to thoughts as well as to forms.

A third reflected upon the value and distribution of these universal laws, and noticed that some are more predominant in painting, others in poetry; that thus, in the latter case, poetry will help to explain and illustrate painting; in the former, painting will do the same for poetry.

The first was the amateur, the second the philosopher, the third the critic.

The two first could not easily make a wrong use of either their feelings or conclusions. On the other hand, the value of the critic's observations mainly depends upon the correctness of their application to the individual case; and since for one clear-sighted critic there have always been fifty ingenious ones, it would have been a wonder if this application had always been applied with all that caution which is required to hold the balance equally between the two arts. . . .

The dazzling antithesis of the Greek Voltaire, "Painting is dumb poetry, and poetry speaking painting," could never have been found in any didactic work; it was an idea, among others, of Simonides, and the truth it contains is so evident that we feel compelled to overlook the indistinctness and error which accompany it.

And yet the ancients did not overlook them. They confined the expression of Simonides to the effect of either art, but at the same time forgot not to teach that notwithstanding the complete similarity of this effect, the two were different, both in the objects which they imitated and in the mode of their imitation.

But, just as though no such difference existed, many recent critics have drawn from this harmony of poetry and painting the most ill-digested conclusions. At one time they compress poetry into the narrower limits of painting; at another they allow painting to occupy the whole wide sphere of poetry. Everything, say they, that the one is entitled to should be conceded to the other; everything that pleases or displeases in one is necessarily pleasing or displeasing in the other. . . .

Indeed, this false criticism has misled in

some degree the professors of art. It has produced the love of description in poetry, and of allegory in painting: while the critics strove to reduce poetry to a speaking painting, without properly knowing what it could and ought to paint; and painting to a dumb poem, without having considered in what degree it could express general ideas, without alienating itself from its destiny, and degenerating into an arbitrary method of writing.

To counteract this false taste and these groundless judgments is the principle aim of the following essay.

. . .

CHAPTER II-III

Be it fable or history that Love inspired the first effort in the plastic arts, it is certain that it never wearied of guiding the hands of the great masters of old. Painting . . . may be defined generally as the art of imitating figures on a flat surface; but the wise Greek allotted it far narrower limits, and confined it to the imitation of beautiful figures only; his artist painted nothing but the beautiful. Even the commonly beautiful, the beauty of a lower order, was only his accidental subject, his exercise, his relaxation. It was the perfection of the object itself that was to make his work delightful; he was too great to ask beholders to be satisfied with the mere cold pleasure that comes from a striking resemblance, or the consideration of his skill. In his art nothing was dearer or seemed nobler to him than its proper end.

"Who would paint you when nobody will look at you?" asks an old epigrammatist of an exceedingly deformed man. Many modern artists would say, "However misshapen you are, I will paint you; and although no one could look at you with pleasure, they will look with pleasure at my picture; not because it is your likeness, but because it will be an evidence of my skill in knowing how to present such a horror so faithfully." . . .

. . . all I want to establish is that among the ancients beauty was the highest law of the plastic arts. And this, once proved, it is a necessary consequence that everything else over which their range could be extended, if incompatible with beauty, gave way entirely to it; and if compatible was at least subordinate. Let us consider expression. There are passions and degrees of passion, which are expressed by the ugliest possible contortions of the face and throw the whole body into such a forced position that all the beautiful contours of its natural state are lost. From all such emotions the ancient masters either abstained entirely, or reduced them to a degree in which they are capable of a certain measure of beauty.

Rage and despair degraded none of their productions: I dare maintain that they have never painted a Fury. Wrath was softened down to seriousness. In poetry it was the wrathful Jupiter who hurled the lightning; in art it was only the serious. . . .

But, as has already been mentioned, art has in modern times been given a far wider sphere. Its imitations, it is said, extend over the whole of visible nature, of which the beautiful is but a small part: truth and expression is its first law; and as nature herself is ever ready to sacrifice beauty to higher aims, so likewise the artist must render it subordinate to his general design, and not pursue it farther than truth and expression permit. Enough that truth and expression change what is most ugly in nature into a beauty of art.

But are there not other considerations, independent of this idea, which would compel the artist to put certain limits to expression, and prevent him from ever drawing it at its highest intensity?

I believe the fact that it is to a single moment that the material limits of art confine all its imitations, will lead us to such considerations.

If the artist, out of ever-varying nature, can only make use of a single moment, and the painter especially can only use this moment from one point of view, whilst their works are intended to stand the test not only of a passing glance, but of long and repeated contemplation, it is clear that this moment, and the point from which this moment is viewed, cannot be chosen with too great a regard for its effect. But that only is a happy choice which allows the imagination free rein. The longer we gaze, the more must our imagination add; and the more our imagination adds, the more we must believe we see. In the whole course of an emotion no moment possesses this advantage so little as its climax. There is nothing beyond this; and the presentation of extremes to the eye clips the wings of fancy, prevents her form soaring beyond the impression of the senses, and compels her to occupy herself with weak images; further than these she ventures not, but shrinks from the visible fulness of expression as her limit. Thus, if Laokoon sighs, the imagination can hear him shriek; but if he shrieks, it can neither rise a step higher above nor descend a step below this representation, without seeing him in a condition which, as it will be more endurable, becomes less interesting. It either hears him merely moaning, or sees him already dead.

Furthermore, this single moment receives through art an unchangeable duration; therefore it must not express anything, of which we can think only as transitory. All appearances, to whose very being it is essential that they suddenly break forth and as suddenly vanish, that they can be what they are but for a moment—all such appearances, be they pleasing or be they horrible, receive through the prolongation which art gives them, such as unnatural character, that at every repeated glance the impression they make grows weaker and weaker and at last fills us with dislike or disgust of the whole object. La Mettrie, who had himself painted as a second Democritus, laughs only the first time we look at him. Look at him oftener and he changes from a philosopher into a fool. His laugh becomes a grin.

So it is with shrieks; the violent pain which compels their utterance either soon subsides, or destroys its suffering subject altogether. If therefore, even the most resolute man shrieks, he does not do so unremittingly; and it is only the seeming continuance of his cries in art which turns them into effeminate impotence or childish petulance. This, at least, the artist of the Laokoon must needs have avoided, even if beauty were not injured by a shriek, and even had his art allowed of his expressing suffering without beauty.

. . .

CHAPTER XVI

However, I will endeavor to trace the matter from its first principles.

I reason thus: if it is true that painting and poetry in their imitations make use of entirely different means or symbols—the first, form and color in space; the second, articulated sounds in time—if these symbols indisputably require a suitable relation to the thing symbolized, then it is clear that symbols arranged in juxtaposition can only express subjects of which the wholes or parts exist in juxtaposition; while consecutive symbols can only express subjects of which the wholes or parts are themselves consecutive.

Subjects whose wholes or parts exist in juxtaposition are called bodies. Consequently, bodies with their visible properties are the true subjects of painting.

Subjects whose wholes or parts are consecutive are called actions. Consequently, actions are the true subjects of poetry.

Still, bodies do not exist in space only, but also in time. They endure, and in each moment of their duration may assume a different appearance, or stand in a different combination. Each of these momentary appearances and combinations is the effect of a preceding one, and may be the cause of a subsequent one, and is therefore, as it were, the center of an action. Consequently, painting too can imitate actions, but only indicatively, by means of bodies.

On the other hand, actions cannot exist in themselves, they must depend on certain beings. So far as these beings are bodies, or are regarded as such, poetry depicts bodies, but only indicatively, by means of actions.

In its coexisting compositions painting can only make use of a single instant of the action, and must therefore chose the one which is most pregnant, and from which what precedes and what follows can be most easily gathered.

In like manner, poetry, in its progressive imitations, is confined to the use of a single property of bodies, and must therefore choose that which calls up the most sensible image of the body in the aspect in which she makes use of it. From this flows the rule of the unity of descriptive epithets and moderation in the description of bodily objects.

CHAPTER XVII

But, it will be answered, symbols of poetry are not merely progressive, but they are also arbitrary; and as arbitrary symbols, they are certainly capable of representing bodies as they exist in space. . . .

It is true that, since the symbols of speech are arbitrary, it is quite possible that by it the parts of a body may be made to follow upon one another just as easily as they stand side by side in nature. But this is a peculiarity of language and its signs generally, and not in so far forth as they are most adapted to the aim of poetry. The poet does not merely wish to be intelligible; the prose writer is contented with simply rendering his descriptions clear and distinct, but not the poet. He must awaken in us conceptions so lively, that, from the rapidity with which they arise, the same impression should be made upon our senses which the sight of the material objects that these conceptions represent would produce. In this moment of illusion we should cease to be conscious of the instruments—his words

—by which this effect is obtained. This was the source of the explanation of poetical painting which we have given. But a poet should always produce a picture; and we will now inquire how far bodies, according to their parts in juxtaposition, are adapted for this.

How do we attain to a distinct conception of an object in space? First we look at its parts singly; then at their combination; and lastly, at the whole. The different operations are performed by our senses with such astonishing rapidity that they appear to us to be but one; and this rapidity is indispensable, if we are to form an idea of the whole, which is nothing more than the resultant of the ideas of the parts and of their combination. Supposing, therefore, that the poet could lead us, in the most beautiful order, from one part of the object to another; supposing that he knew how to make the combination of these parts ever so clear to us; still, how much time would he spend in the process? What the eye takes in at a glance he enumerates slowly and by degrees; and it often happens that we have already forgotten the first traits before we come to the last; yet from these traits we are to form our idea of the whole. To the eye the parts once seen are continually present; it can run over them time after time, while the ear, on the contrary, entirely loses those parts it has heard, if they are not retained in the memory. And even if they are retained, what trouble and effort it costs us to renew their whole impression in the same order, and with the same liveliness; to pass them at one time under review with but moderate rapidity, in order to attain any possible idea of the whole! . . .

Once more, therefore, I do not deny to language generally the power of depicting a corporeal whole according to its parts. It can do so, because its symbols, although consecutive, are still arbitrary; but I do deny it to language, as the means of poetry, because such verbal descriptions are entirely deficient in that illusion which is the principal end of poetry. And this illusion, I repeat, cannot fail to be wanting to them, because the coexistence of the body comes into collision with the consecutiveness of language, and though dissolving the former into the latter renders the division of the whole into its parts easier to us, the ultimate recomposition of these parts into their whole is rendered extremely difficult, and often impossible.

. . .

CHAPTER XVIII

And yet could even Homer be said to have fallen into this cold description of material objects? I venture to hope that there are but few passages which can be cited in support of this; and I feel assured that these will prove to be of such a kind as to confirm the rule from which they appear to be exceptions.

I maintain that succession of time is the department of the poet, as space is that of the painter.

To introduce two necessarily distant points of time in one and the same painting . . . as Titian has the whole history of the prodigal son . . . is an encroachment by the painter upon the sphere of the poet which good taste could never justify.

To enumerate one by one to the reader, in order to afford him an idea of the whole, several parts or things which, if they are to produce a whole, I must necessarily in nature take in at one glance, is an encroachment by the poet upon the sphere of the painter, whereby he squanders much imagination to no purpose. . . .

JOSHUA REYNOLDS [1723–92]

>>>>><<<<<

From *Discourses* [1769–90]

DISCOURSE XIII

*Delivered to the Students of the Royal
Academy, on the Distribution of the
Prizes, December 11, 1786.*

Gentlemen, To discover beauties, or to
point out faults, in the works of celebrated
masters, and to compare the conduct of one
artist with another, is certainly no mean or
inconsiderable part of criticism; but this is
still no more than to know the art through
the artist. This test of investigation must
have two capital defects; it must be narrow,
and it must be uncertain. To enlarge the
boundaries of the art of painting, as well as
to fix its principles, it will be necessary, that
that art and *those* principles should be considered in their correspondence with the
principles of the other arts which, like this,
address themselves primarily and principally to the imagination. When those connected and kindred principles are brought
together to be compared, another comparison will grow out of this; that is, the comparison of them all with those of human
nature, from whence arts derive the materials upon which they are to produce their
effects.

When this comparison of art with art,
and of all arts with the nature of man, is
once made with success, our guiding lines
are as well ascertained and established, as
they can be in matters of this description.

This, as it is the highest style of criticism,
is at the same time the soundest; for it refers
to the eternal and immutable nature of
things.

You are not to imagine that I mean to

From *The Literary Works of Sir Joshua Reynolds* (London: 1852).

open to you at large, or to recommend to
your research, the whole of this vast field
of science. It is certainly much above my
faculties to reach it; and though it may not
be above yours to comprehend it fully, if it
were fully and properly brought before you,
yet perhaps the most perfect criticism requires habits of speculation and abstraction,
not very consistent with the employment
which ought to occupy and the habits of
mind which ought to prevail in a practical
artist. I only point out to you these things,
that when you do criticise (as all who work
on a plan will criticise more or less), your
criticism may be built on the foundation of
true principles; and that though you may
not always travel a great way, the way that
you do travel may be the right road.

I observe, as a fundamental ground, common to all the arts with which we have any
concern in this discourse, that they address
themselves only to two faculties of the
mind, its imagination and its sensibility.

All theories which attempt to direct or
to control the art, upon any principles
falsely called rational, which we form to
ourselves upon a supposition of what ought
in reason to be the end or means of art, independent of the known first effect produced by objects on the imagination, must
be false and delusive. For though it may
appear bold to say it, the imagination is
here the residence of truth. If the imagination be affected, the conclusion is fairly
drawn; if it be not affected, the reasoning
is erroneous, because the end is not obtained; the effect itself being the test, and
the only test, of the truth and efficacy of the
means.

There is in the commerce of life, as in
art, a sagacity which is far from being contradictory to right reason, and is superior to

any occasional exercise of that faculty; which supersedes it; and does not wait for the slow progress of deduction, but goes at once, by what appears a kind of intuition, to the conclusion. A man endowed with this faculty feels and acknowledges the truth, though it is not always in his power, perhaps, to give a reason for it; because he cannot recollect and bring before him all the materials that gave birth to his opinion; for very many and very intricate considerations may unite to form the principle, even of small and minute parts, involved in, or dependent on, a great system of things: though these in process of time are forgotten, the right impression still remains fixed in his mind.

This impression is the result of the accumulated experience of our whole life, and has been collected, we do not always know how, or when. But this mass of collective observation, however acquired, ought to prevail over that reason, which, however powerfully exerted on any particular occasion, will probably comprehend but a partial view of the subject; and our conduct in life as well as in the arts is, or ought to be, generally governed by this habitual reason: it is our happiness that we are enabled to draw on such funds. If we were obliged to enter into a theoretical deliberation on every occasion, before we act, life would be at a stand, and art would be impracticable.

It appears to me, therefore, that our first thoughts, that is, the effect which anything produces on our minds, on its first appearance, is never to be forgotten; and it demands for that reason, because it is the first, to be laid up with care. If this be not done, the artist may happen to impose on himself by partial reasoning; by a cold consideration of those animated thoughts which proceed, not perhaps from caprice or rashness (as he may afterwards conceit), but from the fulness of his mind, enriched with the copious stores of all the various inventions which he had ever seen, or had ever passed in his mind. These ideas are infused into his de-sign, without any conscious effort; but if he be not on his guard, he may reconsider and correct them, till the whole matter is reduced to a commonplace invention.

This is sometimes the effect of what I mean to caution you against; that is to say, an unfounded distrust of the imagination and feeling, in favour of narrow, partial, confined, argumentative theories; and of principles that seem to apply to the design in hand; without considering those general impressions on the fancy in which real principles of *sound reason,* and of much more weight and importance, are involved, and, as it were, lie hid, under the appearance of a sort of vulgar sentiment.

Reason, without doubt, must ultimately determine everything; at this minute it is required to inform us when that very reason is to give way to feeling.

Though I have often spoken of that mean conception of our art which confines it to mere imitation, I must add, that it may be narrowed to such a mere matter of experiment, as to exclude from it the application of science, which alone gives dignity and compass to any art. But to find proper foundations for science is neither to narrow nor to vulgarise it; and this is sufficiently exemplified in the success of experimental philosophy. It is the false system of reasoning, grounded on a partial view of things, against which I would most earnestly guard you. And I do it the rather, because those narrow theories, so coincident with the poorest and most miserable practice, and which are adopted to give it countenance, have not had their origin in the poorest minds, but in the mistakes, or possibly in the mistaken interpretations, of great and commanding authorities. We are not therefore in this case misled by feeling, but by false speculation.

When such a man as Plato speaks of painting as only an imitative art, and that our pleasure proceeds from observing and acknowledging the truth of the imitation, I think he misleads us by a partial theory.

It is in this poor, partial, and so far false view of the art, that Cardinal Bembo has chosen to distinguish even Raffaelle himself, whom our enthusiasm honours with the name of Divine. The same sentiment is adopted by Pope in his epitaph on Sir Godfrey Kneller; and he turns the panegyric solely on imitation, as it is a sort of deception.

I shall not think my time misemployed, if by any means I may contribute to confirm your opinion of what ought to be the object of your pursuit; because, though the best critics must always have exploded this strange idea, yet I know that there is a disposition towards a perpetual recurrence to it, on account of its simplicity and superficial plausibility. For this reason I shall beg leave to lay before you a few thoughts on this subject; to throw out some hints that may lead your minds to an opinion (which I take to be the truth), that painting is not only to be considered as an imitation, operating by deception, but that it is, and ought to be, in many points of view, and strictly speaking, no imitation at all of external nature. Perhaps it ought to be as far removed from the vulgar idea of imitation, as the refined civilised state in which we live, is removed from a gross state of nature; and those who have not cultivated their imaginations, which the majority of mankind certainly have not, may be said, in regard to arts, to continue in this state of nature. Such men will always prefer imitation to that excellence which is addressed to another faculty that they do not possess; but these are not the persons to whom a painter is to look, any more than a judge of morals and manners ought to refer controverted points upon those subjects to the opinions of people taken from the banks of the Ohio, or from New Holland.

It is the lowest style only of arts, whether of painting, poetry, or music, that may be said, in the vulgar sense, to be naturally pleasing. The higher efforts of those arts, we know by experience, do not affect minds wholly uncultivated. This refined taste is the consequence of education and habit; we are born only with a capacity of entertaining this refinement, as we are born with a disposition to receive and obey all the rules and regulations of society; and so far it may be said to be natural to us, and no further.

What has been said, may show the artist how necessary it is, when he looks about him for the advice and criticism of his friends, to make some distinction of the character, taste, experience, and observation in this art of those from whom it is received. An ignorant uneducated man may, like Apelles's critic, be a competent judge of the truth of the representation of a sandal; or to go somewhat higher, like Molière's old woman, may decide upon what is nature, in regard to comic humour; but a critic in the higher style of art ought to possess the same refined taste, which directed the artist in his work.

To illustrate this principle by a comparison with other arts, I shall now produce some instances to show, that they, as well as our own art, renounce the narrow idea of nature, and the narrow theories derived from that mistaken principle, and apply to that reason only which informs us not what imitation is—a natural representation of a given object—but what it is natural for the imagination to be delighted with. And perhaps there is no better way of acquiring this knowledge, than by this kind of analogy: each art will corroborate and mutually reflect the truth on the other. Such a kind of juxtaposition may likewise have this use, that whilst the artist is amusing himself in the contemplation of other arts, he may habitually transfer the principles of those arts to that which he professes; which ought to be always present to his mind, and to which everything is to be referred.

So far is art from being derived from, or having any immediate intercourse with, particular nature as its model, that there are many arts that set out with a professed deviation from it.

This is certainly not so exactly true in regard to painting and sculpture. Our elements are laid in gross common nature—an exact imitation of what is before us: but when we advance to the higher state, we consider this power of imitation, though first in the order of acquisition, as by no means the highest in the scale of perfection.

Poetry addresses itself to the same faculties and the same dispositions as painting, though by different means. The object of both is to accommodate itself to all the natural propensities and inclinations of the mind. The very existence of poetry depends on the licence it assumes of deviating from actual nature, in order to gratify natural propensities by other means, which are found by experience full as capable of affording such gratification. It sets out with a language in the highest degree artificial, a construction of measured words, such as never is, nor ever was used by man. Let this measure be what it may, whether hexameter or any other metre used in Latin or Greek—or rhyme, or blank verse varied with pauses and accents, in modern languages—they are all equally removed from nature, and equally a violation of common speech. When this artificial mode has been established as the vehicle of sentiment, there is another principle in the human mind, to which the work must be referred, which still renders it more artificial, carries it still further from common nature, and deviates only to render it more perfect. That principle is the sense of congruity, coherence, and consistency, which is a real existing principle in man; and it must be gratified. Therefore having once adopted a style and a measure not found in common discourse, it is required that the sentiments also should be in the same proportion elevated above common nature, from the necessity of there being an agreement of the parts among themselves, that one uniform whole may be produced.

To correspond therefore with this general system of deviation from nature, the manner in which poetry is offered to the ear, the tone in which it is recited, should be as far removed from the tone of conversation, as the words of which that poetry is composed. This naturally suggests the idea of modulating the voice by art, which I suppose may be considered as accomplished to the highest degree of excellence in the recitative of the Italian Opera; as we may conjecture it was in the chorus that attended the ancient drama. And though the most violent passions, the highest distress, even death itself, are expressed in singing or recitative, I would not admit as sound criticism the condemnation of such exhibitions on account of their being unnatural.

If it is natural for our senses, and our imaginations, to be delighted with singing, with instrumental music, with poetry, and with graceful action, taken separately (none of them being in the vulgar sense natural, even in that separate state); it is conformable to experience, and therefore agreeable to reason as connected with and referred to experience, that we should also be delighted with this union of music, poetry, and graceful action, joined to every circumstance of pomp and magnificence calculated to strike the senses of the spectator. Shall reason stand in the way, and tell us that we ought not to like what we know we do like, and prevent us from feeling the full effect of this complicated exertion of art? This is what I would understand by poets and painters being allowed to dare everything; for what can be more daring, than accomplishing the purpose and end of art, by a complication of means, none of which have their archetypes in actual nature?

So far therefore is servile imitation from being necessary, that whatever is familiar, or in any way reminds us of what we see and hear every day, perhaps does not belong to the higher provinces of art, either in poetry or painting. The mind is to be transported, as Shakespeare expresses it, *beyond the ignorant present* to ages past. Another and a higher order of beings is supposed; and to those beings everything which is introduced into the work must correspond. Of this conduct, under these circumstances, the Roman and Florentine schools afford sufficient examples. Their style by this means is raised and elevated above all others; and by the same means the compass of art itself is enlarged.

We often see grave and great subjects attempted by artists of another school; who, though excellent in the lower class of art, proceeding on the principles which regulate that class, and not recollecting, or not knowing, that they were to address themselves to another faculty of the mind, have become perfectly ridiculous.

The picture which I have at present in my thoughts is a sacrifice of Iphigenia, painted by Jan Steen, a painter of whom I have formerly had occasion to speak with the highest approbation; and even in this picture, the subject of which is by no means adapted to his genius, there is nature and expression; but it is such expression, and the countenances are so familiar, and consequently so vulgar, and the whole accompanied with such finery of silks and velvets, that one would be almost tempted to doubt, whether the artist did not purposely intend to burlesque his subject.

Instances of the same kind we frequently see in poetry. Parts of Hobbes's translation of Homer are remembered and repeated merely for the familiarity and meanness of their phraseology, so ill corresponding with the ideas which ought to have been expressed, and, as I conceive, with the style of the original.

We may proceed in the same manner through the comparatively inferior branches of art. There are in works of that class, the same distinction of a higher and a lower style; and they take their rank and degree in proportion as the artist departs more, or less, from common nature, and makes it an object of his attention to strike the imagina-

tion of the spectator by ways belonging specially to art—unobserved and untaught out of the school of its practice.

If our judgments are to be directed by narrow, vulgar, untaught, or rather ill-taught reason, we must prefer a portrait by Denner or any other high finisher, to those of Titian or Vandyck; and a landscape of Vanderheyden to those of Titian or Rubens; for they are certainly more exact representations of nature.

If we suppose a view of nature represented with all the truth of the *camera obscura,* and the same scene represented by a great artist, how little and mean will the one appear in comparison of the other, where no superiority is supposed from the choice of the subject. The scene shall be the same, the difference only will be in the manner in which it is presented to the eye. With what additional superiority then will the same artist appear when he has the power of selecting his materials, as well as elevating his style? Like Nicolas Poussin, he transports us to the environs of ancient Rome, with all the objects which a literary education makes so precious and interesting to man: or, like Sebastian Bourdon, he leads us to the dark antiquity of the Pyramids of Egypt; or, like Claude Lorrain, he conducts us to the tranquillity of arcadian scenes and fairyland.

Like the history-painter, a painter of landscapes in this style and with this conduct sends the imagination back into antiquity; and, like the poet, he makes the elements sympathise with his subject; whether the mountains have sudden and bold projections, or are gently sloped; whether the branches of his trees shoot out abruptly in right angles from their trunks, or follow each other with only a gentle inclination. All these circumstances contribute to the general character of the work, whether it be of the elegant, or of the more sublime kind. If we add to this the powerful materials of lightness and darkness, over which the artist has complete dominion, to vary and dispose them as he pleases; to diminish, or increase them, as will best suit his purpose, and correspond to the general idea of his work; a landscape thus conducted, under the influence of a poetical mind, will have the same superiority over the more ordinary and common views, as Milton's *Allegro* and *Penseroso* have over a cold prosaic narration or description; and such a picture would make a more forcible impression on the mind than the real scenes, were they presented before us.

If we look abroad to other arts, we may observe the same distinction, the same division into two classes; each of them acting under the influence of two different principles, in which the one follows nature, the other varies it, and sometimes departs from it.

The theatre, which is said *to hold the mirror up to nature,* comprehends both those sides. The lower kind of comedy or farce, like the inferior style of painting, the more naturally it is represented, the better; but the higher appears to me to aim no more at imitation, so far as it belongs to anything like deception, or to expect that the spectators should think that the events there represented are really passing before them, than Raffaelle in his cartoons, or Poussin in his sacraments, expected it to be believed, even for a moment, that what they exhibited were real figures.

For want of this distinction, the world is filled with false criticism. Raffaelle is praised for naturalness and deception, which he certainly has not accomplished, and as certainly never intended; and our late great actor, Garrick, has been as ignorantly praised by his friend Fielding; who doubtless imagined he had hit upon an ingenious device, by introducing in one of his novels (otherwise a work of the highest merit) an ignorant man, mistaking Garrick's representation of a scene in Hamlet for reality. A very little reflection will convince us, that there is not one circumstance in the whole scene that is of the nature of deception. The merit and excellence of Shakespeare, and of Garrick, when they were engaged in such scenes, is of a different and much higher kind. But what adds to the falsity of this intended compliment is that the best stage-representation appears even more unnatural to a person of such a character, who is supposed never to have seen a play before, than it does to those who have had a habit of allowing for those necessary deviations from nature which the art requires.

In theatric representation, great allowances must always be made for the place in which the exhibition is represented; for the surrounding company, the lighted candles, the scenes visibly shifted in your sight, and the language of blank verse, so different from common English; which merely as English must appear surprising in the mouths of Hamlet, and all the court and natives of Denmark. These allowances are made; but their being made puts an end to all manner of deception: and further, we know that the more low, illiterate, and vulgar any person is, the less he will be disposed to make these allowances, and of course to be deceived by any imitation; the things in which the trespass against nature and common probability is made in favour of the theatre being quite within the sphere of such uninformed men.

Though I have no intention of entering into all the circumstances of unnaturalness in theatrical representations, I must observe, that even the expression of violent passion is not always the most excellent in proportion as it is the most natural; so great terror and such disagreeable sensations may be communicated to the audience, that the balance may be destroyed by which pleasure is preserved, and holds its predominance in the mind: violent distortion of action, harsh screamings of the voice, however great the occasion, or however natural on such occasion, are therefore not admissible in the theatric art. Many of these allowed deviations from nature arise from the necessity which there is, that everything should be raised and enlarged beyond its natural state; that the full effect may come home to the spectator, which otherwise would be lost in the comparatively extensive space of the theatre. Hence the deliberate and stately step, the studied grace of action, which seems to enlarge the dimensions of the actor, and alone to fill the stage. All this unnaturalness, though right and proper in its place, would appear affected and ridiculous in a private room; *quid enim deformius, quam scenam in vitam transferre?*[1]

And here I must observe, and I believe it may be considered as a general rule, that no art can be engrafted with success on another art. For though they all profess the same origin, and to proceed from the same stock, yet each has its own peculiar modes both of imitating nature, and of deviating from it, each for the accomplishment of its own particular purpose. These deviations, more especially, will not bear transplantation to another soil.

If a painter should endeavour to copy the theatrical pomp and parade of dress and attitude, instead of that simplicity, which is not a greater beauty in life than it is in painting, we should condemn such pictures, as painted in the meanest style.

So also gardening, as far as gardening is an art, or entitled to that appellation, is a deviation from nature; for if the true taste consists, as many hold, in banishing every appearance of art, or any traces of the footsteps of a man, it would then be no longer a garden. Even though we define it, "Nature to advantage dress'd," and in some sense is such, and much more beautiful and commodious for the recreation of man; it is, however, when so dressed, no longer a subject for the pencil of a landscape-painter, as all landscape-painters know, who love to have recourse to nature herself, and to dress her according to the principles

of their own art; which are far different from those of gardening, even when conducted according to the most approved principles; and such as a landscape-painter himself would adopt in the disposition of his own grounds, for his own private satisfaction.

I have brought together as many instances as appear necessary to make out the several points which I wished to suggest to your consideration in this discourse, that your own thoughts may lead you further in the use that may be made of the analogy of the arts, and of the restraint which a full understanding of the diversity of many of their principles ought to impose on the employment of that analogy.

The great end of all those arts is, to make an impression on the imagination and the feeling. The imitation of nature frequently does this. Sometimes it fails, and something else succeeds. I think therefore the true test of all the arts is not solely whether the production is a true copy of nature, but whether it answers the end of art, which is to produce a pleasing effect upon the mind.

It remains only to speak a few words of architecture, which does not come under the denomination of an imitative art. It applies itself, like music (and I believe we may add poetry), directly to the imagination, without the intervention of any kind of imitation.

There is in architecture, as in painting, an inferior branch of art, in which the imagination appears to have no concern. It does not, however, acquire the name of a polite and liberal art, from its usefulness, or administering to our wants or necessities, but from some higher principle: we are sure that in the hands of a man of genius it is capable of inspiring sentiment, and of filling the mind with great and sublime ideas.

It may be worth the attention of artists to consider what materials are in their hands, that may contribute to this end; and

[1] For what [would be] more unbecoming than to carry a scene from drama over into actual life?

whether this art has it not in its power to address itself to the imagination with effect, by more ways than are generally employed by architects.

To pass over the effect produced by that general symmetry and proportion, by which the eye is delighted, as the ear is with music, architecture certainly possesses many principles in common with poetry and painting. Among those which may be reckoned as the first is that of affecting the imagination by means of association of ideas. Thus, for instance, as we have naturally a veneration for antiquity, whatever building brings to our remembrance ancient customs and manners, such as the castles of the barons of ancient chivalry, is sure to give this delight. Hence it is that *towers and battlements* are so often selected by the painter and the poet, to make a part of the composition of their ideal landscape; and it is from hence in a great degree, that in the buildings of Vanbrugh, who was a poet as well as an architect, there is a greater display of imagination than we shall find perhaps in any other, and this is the ground of the effect we feel in many of his works, notwithstanding the faults with which many of them are justly charged. For this purpose, Vanbrugh appears to have had recourse to some of the principles of the Gothic architecture; which, though not so ancient as the Grecian, is more so to our imagination, with which the artist is more concerned than with absolute truth.

The barbaric splendour of those Asiatic buildings, which are now publishing by a member of this Academy, may possibly, in the same manner, furnish an architect, not with models to copy, but with hints of composition and general effect, which would not otherwise have occurred.

It is, I know, a delicate and hazardous thing (and as such I have already pointed it out), to carry the principles of one art to another, or even to reconcile in one object the various modes of the same art, when they proceed on different principles. The sound rules of the Grecian architecture are not to be lightly sacrificed. A deviation from them, or even an addition to them, is like a deviation or addition to, or from, the rules of other arts,—fit only for a great master, who is thoroughly conversant in the nature of man, as well as all combinations in his own art.

It may not be amiss for the architect to take advantage *sometimes* of that to which I am sure the painter ought always to have his eyes open, I mean the use of accidents; to follow when they lead, and to improve them, rather than always to trust to a regular plan. It often happens that additions have been made to houses, at various times, for use or pleasure. As such buildings depart from regularity, they now and then acquire something of scenery by this accident, which I should think might not unsuccessfully be adopted by an architect, in an original plan, if it does not too much interfere with convenience. Variety and intricacy is a beauty and excellence in every other of the arts which address the imagination; and why not in architecture?

The forms and turnings of the streets of London, and other old towns, are produced by accident, without any original plan or design; but they are not always the less pleasant to the walker or spectator, on that account. On the contrary, if the city had been built on the regular plan of Sir Christopher Wren, the effect might have been, as we know it is in some new parts of the town, rather unpleasing; the uniformity might have produced weariness, and a slight degree of disgust.

I can pretend to no skill in the detail of architecture. I judge now of the art, merely as a painter. When I speak of Vanbrugh, I mean to speak of him in the language of our art. To speak then of Vanbrugh in the language of a painter, he had originality of invention, he understood light and shadow, and had great skill in composition. To support his principal object he produced his second and third groups of masses; he perfectly understood in his art what is the most difficult in ours, the conduct of the background, by which the design and invention is set off to the greatest advantage. What the background is in painting, in architecture is the real ground on which the building is erected; and no architect took greater care than he that his work should not appear crude and hard: that is, it did not abruptly start out of the ground without expectation or preparation.

This is a tribute which a painter owes to an architect who composed like a painter; and was defrauded of the due reward of his merit by the wits of his time, who did not understand the principles of composition in poetry better than he; and who knew little or nothing of what he understood perfectly, the general ruling principles of architecture and painting. His fate was that of the great Perrault; both were the objects of the petulant sarcasms of factious men of letters; and both have left some of the fairest ornaments which to this day decorate their several countries; the façade of the Louvre, Blenheim, and Castle Howard.

Upon the whole, it seems to me, that the object and intention of all the arts is to supply the natural imperfection of things, and often to gratify the mind by realising and embodying what never existed but in the imagination.

It is allowed on all hands, that facts and events, however they may bind the historian, have no dominion over the poet or the painter. With us, history is made to bend and conform to this great idea of art. And why? Because these arts, in their highest province, are not addressed to the gross senses, but to the desires of the mind, to that spark of divinity which we have within, impatient of being circumscribed and pent up by the world which is about us. Just so much as our art has of this, just so much of dignity, I had almost said of divinity, it exhibits; and those of our artists who possessed this mark of distinction in the highest degree acquired from thence the glorious appellation of Divine.

ARCHIBALD ALISON [1757–1839]

>>>><<<<

From *Essays on the Nature and Principles of Taste* [1790, 1811]

INTRODUCTION

Taste, is, in general, considered as that Faculty of the Human mind, by which we perceive and enjoy whatever is Beautiful or Sublime in the works of Nature or Art.

The perception of these qualities is attended with an Emotion of Pleasure, very distinguishable from every other pleasure of our Nature, and which is accordingly

Reprinted from the 6th edition (Edinburgh: 1825).

distinguished by the name of the Emotion of Taste. The distinction of the objects of Taste into the Sublime and the Beautiful, has produced a similar division of this Emotion, into the Emotion of Sublimity, and the Emotion of Beauty. . . .

The Qualities [that produce these Emotions], however, though so important to human happiness, are not the objects of immediate observation; and in the attempt to investigate them, various circumstances unite to perplex our research. They are often obscured under the number of qualities with which they are accidentally combined: They result often from peculiar combinations of the qualities of objects, or the relation of certain parts of objects to each other: They are still oftener, perhaps, dependent upon the state of our own minds, and vary in their effects with the dispositions in which they happen to be observed. In all cases, while we feel the Emotions they excite, we are ignorant of the causes by which they are produced; and when we seek to discover them, we have no other method of discovery, than that varied and patient Experiment, by which, amid these complicated circumstances, we may gradually ascertain the peculiar qualities which, by the Constitution of our Nature, are permanently connected with the Emotions we feel.

In the employment of this mode of Investigation, there are two great objects of attention and inquiry, which seem to include all that is necessary, or perhaps possible, for us to discover on the subject of Taste.

These objects are,

I. To investigate the Nature of those Qualities that produce the Emotions of Taste: And,

II. To investigate the Nature of that Faculty, by which these Emotions are received. . . .

With the Emotions of Taste, in almost every instance, many other accidental Emotions of Pleasure are united: the various simple pleasures that arise from other qualities of the object; the pleasure of agreeable Sensation, in the case of Material objects; and in all, that pleasure which, by the Constitution of our Nature, is annexed to the Exercise of our Faculties. Unless, therefore, we have previously acquired a distinct and accurate conception of that *peculiar* effect which is produced on our Minds, when the Emotions of Taste are felt, and can precisely distinguish it from the effects that are produced by these accidental Qualities, we must necessarily include in the Causes of such Emotions, those Qualities also, which are the causes of the accidental pleas-

ures with which this Emotion is accompanied. The variety of Systems that Philosophers have adopted upon this subject, and the various Emotions into which they have resolved the Emotion of Taste . . . afford a strong illustration of the necessity of previously ascertaining the Nature of this Effect before we attempt to investigate its Cause. With regard, therefore, to both these Inquiries, the first and most important step is accurately to examine the Nature of this Emotion itself, and its distinction from every other Emotion of Pleasure; and our capacity of discovering either the Nature of the Qualities that produce the Emotions of Taste, or the Nature of the Faculty by which they are received, will be exactly proportioned to our accuracy in ascertaining the Nature of the Emotion itself.

When we look back to the history of these investigations, and to the Theories . . . formed upon the subject, there is one fact which must necessarily strike us, *viz.* That all these Theories have uniformly taken for granted the *Simplicity* of this Emotion; that they have considered it as an Emotion too plain, and too commonly felt, to admit of any analysis; that they have as uniformly, therefore, referred it to some *one* Principle or Law of the Human Mind; and that they have therefore concluded, that the Discovery of that *one* Principle was the essential key by which all the Pleasures of Taste were to be resolved. . . .

. . . It seemed to me that the Simplicity of the Emotion of Taste, was a Principle much too hastily adopted; and that the consequences which followed from it were very little reconcileable with the most common experience of Human Feeling; and from the examination of this preliminary Question, I was led gradually to conclusions which seemed . . . of an importance not unworthy of being presented to the public. In doing this, I am conscious that I have entered upon a new and untrodden path; . . .

The Inquiries which follow, naturally divide themselves into the following parts; and are to be prosecuted in the following order.

1. I shall begin with an Analysis of the Effect which is produced upon the Mind, when the Emotions of Beauty or Sublimity are felt. I shall endeavor to show, that this effect is very different from the determination of a Sense; that it is not in fact a Simple, but a Complex Emotion; that it involves, in all cases, 1st, the production of some Simple Emotion, or the exercise of some moral affectation, and, 2dly, the consequent Excitement of a peculiar Exercise of the Imagination; that these concomitant effects are distinguishable, and very often distinguished in our experience; and that the *peculiar* pleasure of the Beautiful or the Sublime is only felt when these two effects are conjoined, and the Complex Emotion produced.

The prosecution of this Subject will lead to another Inquiry . . . , *viz.* into the origin of the Beauty and Sublimity of the Qualities of Matter. I shall endeavor to show, that all the Phenomena are reducible to the same general Principle, and that the Qualities of Matter are not beautiful or sublime in themselves, but as they are, by various means, the Signs or Expressions of Qualities capable of producing Emotion.

II. From this Examination of the Effect I shall proceed, in the Second Part, to investigate the Causes which are productive of it; in other words, the Sources of the Beautiful and the Sublime in Nature and Art.

In the course of this investigation, I shall endeavor to show, 1st, That there is no single emotion into which these varied effects can be resolved; that on the contrary, every simple emotion, and therefore every object which is capable of producing any simple emotion, *may* be the foundation of the complex emotion of Beauty or Sublimity. But, in the second place, that this complex emotion of Beauty or Sublimity is never produced, unless, beside the excite-

ment of some simple emotion, the imagination also is excited, and the exercise of the two faculties combined in the general effect. The prosecution of the subject, will lead me to the *principal object of the inquiry,* to show what is that Law of Mind, according to which, in actual life, this exercise or employment of imagination is excited; and what are the means by which . . . the artist is able to awaken this important exercise of imagination, and to exalt objects of simple and common pleasure into objects of Beauty or Sublimity.

On the Nature of the Emotions of Sublimity and Beauty

CHAP. I. SEC. I. The Emotions of Sublimity and Beauty are uniformly ascribed, both in popular and in philosophical language, to the Imagination. The Fine Arts are considered as the arts which are addressed to the imagination; and the pleasures they afford are described, by way of distinction, as the Pleasures of the Imagination. . . .

Although, however, this connexion is so generally acknowledged, it is not perhaps as generally understood in what it consists, or what is the nature of that effect which is produced upon the imagination by objects of sublimity and beauty. I shall endeavor, therefore, . . . to state what seems to me the nature of this Effect, or, in what that exercise of imagination consists, which is so generally supposed to take place, when these emotions are felt.

When any object, either of sublimity or beauty, is presented to the mind, I believe every man is conscious of a train of thought being immediately awakened in his imagination, analogous to the character or expression of the original object. The simple perception of the object, we frequently find, is insufficient to excite these emotions, unless it is accompanied with this operation of mind—unless, according to common expression, our imagination is seized, and our fancy busied in the pursuit of all those trains of thought which are allied to this character or expression.

Thus, when we feel either the beauty or sublimity of natural scenery . . . we are conscious of a variety of images in our minds, very different from those which the objects themselves can present to the eye. Trains of pleasing or of solemn thought arise spontaneously within our minds; our hearts swell with emotions, of which the objects before us seem to afford no adequate cause; and we are never so much satiated with delight, as when in recalling our attention we are unable to trace either the progress or the connexion of those thoughts, which have passed with so much rapidity through our imagination. . . .

SEC. II. That unless this exercise of imagination is excited, the emotions of Beauty or Sublimity are unfelt, seems capable of illustration from many instances of a very familiar kind.

If the mind is in such a state as to prevent this freedom of imagination, the emotion, whether of sublimity or beauty, is unperceived. In so far as the beauties of art or nature affect the external senses, their effect is the same upon every man who is in possession of these senses. But to a man in pain or in grief, whose mind, by these means, is attentive only to one object or consideration, the same scene, or the same form, will produce no feeling of admiration, which, at other times, when his imagination was at liberty, would have produced it in its fullest perfection. Whatever is great or beautiful in the scenery of external nature, is almost constantly before us; and not a day passes, without presenting us with appearances, fitted both to charm and to elevate our minds; yet it is in general with a heedless eye that we regard them, and only in particular moments that we are sensible of their power. . . . In these, and similar cases of difference in our feelings, from the same objects, it will always be found, that the difference arises from the state of our imaginations; from our dispositions to follow out the train of thought which some objects naturally produce, or our incapacity to do it, from some other idea, which has at that time taken possession of our minds, and renders us unable to attend to anything else. That state of mind . . . is most favorable to the emotions of taste, in which the imagination is free and unembarrassed, or, in which the attention is so little occupied by any private or particular object of thought, as to leave us open to all the impressions which the objects that are before us can produce. It is upon the vacant and the unemployed, accordingly, that the objects of taste make the strongest impression. It is in such hours alone, that we turn to the compositions of music, or of poetry for amusement. The seasons of care, of grief, or of business, have other occupations, and destroy, for the time at least, our sensibility to the beautiful or the sublime, in the same proportion that they produce a state of mind unfavorable to the indulgence of imagination.

The same thing is observable in criticism. When we sit down to appreciate the value of a poem, or of a painting, and attend minutely to the language or composition of the one, or to the coloring or design of the other, we feel no longer the delight which they at first produce. Our imagination in this employment is restrained, and instead of yielding to its suggestions, we studiously endeavor to resist them, by fixing our attention upon minute and partial circumstances of the composition. How much this operation of mind tends to diminish our sense of its beauty, every one will feel, who attends to his own thoughts on such an occasion. . . .

SEC. III. There are many other instances equally familiar, which are sufficient to show, that whatever increases this exercise or employment of Imagination, increases also the Emotion of beauty or sublimity.

This is very obviously the effect of all

Associations. There is no man who has not some interesting associations with particular scenes, or airs, or books, and who does not feel their beauty or sublimity enhanced by such connexions. The view of the house where one was born, of the school where one was educated, and where the gay years of infancy were passed, is indifferent to no man. They recall so many images of past happiness, and past affections—they are connected with so many strong or interesting emotions, and lead altogether to so long a train of feelings and recollections, that there is hardly any scene which one ever beholds with so much rapture. . . . There are scenes, undoubtedly, more beautiful than Runnymede; yet, to those who recollect the great event which passed there, there is no scene, perhaps, which so strongly seizes upon the imagination; and although the emotions this recollection produces, are of a very different kind from those which the mere natural scenery can excite, yet they unite themselves so well with these inferior emotions, and spread so venerable a charm over the whole, that one can hardly persuade one's self, that the scene itself is not entitled to this admiration. . . .

The Sublime is increased, in the same manner, by whatever tends to increase this exercise of imagination. The field of any celebrated battle becomes sublime from such associations. No man, acquainted with English history, could behold the field of Agincourt, without some emotion of this kind. The additional conceptions which this association produces, and which fill the mind of the spectator on the prospect of that memorable field, diffuse themselves in some measure over the scene, and give it a sublimity which does not naturally belong to it.

. . .

CHAP. II. SEC. I. The illustrations in the preceding chapter seem to show, that whenever the emotions of Sublimity or Beauty are felt, that exercise of Imagination is produced, which consists in the indulgence of a train of thought; that when this exercise is prevented, these emotions are unfelt or unperceived; and that whatever tends to increase this exercise of mind, tends in the same proportion to increase these emotions. If these illustrations are just, it seems reasonable to conclude, that the effect produced upon the mind, by objects of Sublimity or Beauty, consists in the production of this exercise of Imagination.

Although, however, this conclusion seems to be both just and consonant to experience, yet it is in itself too general, to be considered as a sufficient account of the nature of that operation of mind which takes place in the case of such Emotions. There are many other trains of ideas of which we are conscious, which are unattended by any kind of pleasure. There are other operations of mind, in which such trains of thought are necessarily produced, without exciting any similar emotion. . . .

If therefore some train of thought, or some exercise of Imagination is necessary for the production of the emotions of Taste, it is obvious that this is not every train of thought of which we are capable. To ascertain, therefore, with any precision, either the nature or the causes of these emotions, it is previously necessary to investigate the nature of those trains of thought that are produced by objects of sublimity and beauty, and their difference from those ordinary trains which are unaccompanied with such pleasure.

As far as I am able to judge, this difference consists in two things. 1st, In the Nature of the ideas or conceptions which compose such trains: and 2dly, In the Nature or Law of their succession.

In our ordinary trains of thought, every man must be conscious that the ideas which compose them, are very frequently of a kind which excite no emotions either of pleasure or pain. There is an infinite variety of our ideas, as well as of our sensations, that may be termed indifferent, which are perceived without any sentiment either of pain or pleasure, and which pass as it were before the mind without making any further impression than simply exciting the consciousness of their existence. . . .

The trains of thought which are suggested by external objects are very frequently of a similar kind. The greater part of such objects are simply indifferent, or at least are regarded as indifferent in our common hours either of occupation or amusement: the conceptions which they produce, by the laws of association, partake of the nature or character of the object which originally excited them; and the whole train passes through our mind without leaving any further emotion, than perhaps that general emotion of pleasure which accompanies the exercise of our faculties. . . .

In the case of those trains of thought, on the contrary, which are suggested by objects either of Sublimity or Beauty, I apprehend it will be found, that they are in all cases composed of ideas capable of exciting some affection or emotion; and that not only the whole succession is accompanied with that peculiar emotion which we call the emotion of Beauty or Sublimity, but that every individual idea of such a succession is in itself productive of some simple Emotion or other. Thus the ideas suggested by the scenery of Spring, are ideas productive of emotions of Cheerfulness, of Gladness and of Tenderness. . . . The ideas . . . awakened by the view of the ocean in a storm, are ideas of Power, of Majesty and of Terror. In every case where the emotions of Taste are felt, I conceive it will be found, that the train of thought which is excited, is distinguished by some character of emotion, and that it is by this means distinguished from our common or ordinary successions of thought. To prevent a very tedious and unnecessary circumlocution, such ideas may . . . be termed ideas of Emotion: and I shall . . . use the expression in this sense. . . .

In our ordinary trains of thought, there seldom appears any general principle of connexion among the ideas which compose them. Each idea, indeed, is related, by an established law of our nature, to that which immediately preceded and that which immediately follows it; but in the whole series there is no predominant relation or bond of connexion. This want of general connexion is so strong, that even that most general of all relations, the relation either of pleasure or pain, is frequently violated. Images both of the one kind and the other succeed each other in the course of the train; and when we put an end to it we are often at a loss to say whether the whole series was pleasant or painful. . . .

In those trains, on the contrary, which are suggested by objects of Sublimity or Beauty, however slight the connexion between individual thoughts may be, I believe it will be found, that there is always some general principle of connexion which pervades the whole, and gives them some certain and definite character. They are either gay, or pathetic, or melancholy, or solemn, or awful, or elevating, &c. according to the nature of the emotion which is first excited. Thus the prospect of a serene evening in summer, produces first an emotion of peacefulness and tranquillity, and then suggests a variety of images corresponding to this primary impression. The sight of a torrent, or of a storm, in the same manner, impresses us first with sentiments of awe, or solemnity, or terror, and then awakens in our minds a series of conceptions allied to this peculiar emotion. Whatever may be the character of the original emotion, the images which succeed seem all to have a relation to this character; and if we trace them back, we shall discover not only a connexion between the individual thoughts of the train, but also a general relation among the whole, and a conformity to that peculiar emotion which first excited them.

The train of thought, therefore, which takes place in the mind, upon the prospect of objects of sublimity and beauty, may be considered as consisting in a regular or consistent train of ideas of emotion, and as distinguished from our ordinary trains of thought: 1st, In respect of the Nature of the ideas of which it is composed, by their being ideas productive of Emotion; and 2dly, In respect of their succession, by their being distinguished by some general principle of connexion, which subsists through the whole extent of the train. . . .

SEC. II. . . . Wherever the Emotions of Sublimity or Beauty are felt, I believe it will be found, that some affection is uniformly excited by the presence of the object, before the more complex Emotion of Beauty is felt; and that if no such affection is excited, no Emotion of Beauty or Sublimity is produced. The truth of this observation may be illustrated both from common language and common experience.

1. If any man were to assert, that some object, though positively indifferent or uninteresting, was yet beautiful or sublime, everyone would consider it as asserting an absurdity. If, on the other hand, he were to assert, that the object had neither beauty nor sublimity to him, because there was no quality in it which could give him any emotion, . . . we should not only clearly understand his meaning, but very readily allow his reason; and if the object were such as appeared to us in the light either of Sublimity or Beauty, and we wished to make him sensible of it, the way that we should naturally take, would be to point out to him some affecting or interesting quality which we imagined he had overlooked, and which we felt was the foundation of our own emotion.

There is undoubtedly a very great difference between the Emotion of Taste, and any Simple Emotion, as of Cheerfulness, Tenderness . . . Terror, &c. as such emotions are frequently felt without any sentiment of Beauty or Sublimity; but there is no case, I believe, where the Emotions of Taste are felt, without the previous production of some such Simple Emotion . . . so strong is our conviction of the dependence

of the Emotion of Taste upon some such previous simple emotion, that whenever we endeavor to explain the Beauty or Sublimity of any object, we uniformly proceed by pointing out the interesting or affecting quality in it, which is fitted to produce this previous emotion. It is not only impossible for us to imagine an object of Taste, that is not an object of Emotion; but it is impossible to describe any such object, without resting the description upon that quality, or those qualities in it, which are productive of Simple Emotion. . . .

Besides the influence of permanent habits of thought, or of the diversities of original disposition upon our sentiments of Beauty, every man must have had occasion to observe, that the perception of Beauty depends also on the temporary sensibility of his mind; and that even objects of the most experienced Beauty, fail in exciting their usual delight, when they occur to him in moments when he is under the dominion of different emotions from those with which he usually regards them. In our seasons of gaiety, we behold with indifference the same objects which delight our imaginations when we are under the impressions of tenderness or melancholy. . . . The husbandman who goes out to observe the state of his grounds, the man of business who walks forth to ruminate about his affairs, or the philosopher, to reason or reflect, whatever their natural sensibilities may be, are at such times insensible to every beauty that the scenery of nature may exhibit; nor do they begin to feel them, until they withdraw their attention from the particular objects of their thought, and abandon themselves to the emotions which such scenes may happen to inspire. . . .

It is further observable, that our sense of the Beauty or Sublimity of every object depends upon that quality, or those qualities of it which we consider; and that objects of the most acknowledged beauty cease to affect us with such emotions, when we make any of their indifferent or uninteresting qualities the object of our consideration. . . .

It is difficult, for instance, to enumerate the various qualities which may produce the emotion of Beauty, in the statues of the Venus de Medicis, or the Apollo Belvidere; yet it is undoubtedly possible for any man to see these masterpieces of statuary, and yet feel no emotion of Beauty. The delicacy, the modesty, the timidity of the one—the grace, the dignity, the majesty of the other—and, in both, the inimitable art with which these characters are expressed, are, in general, the qualities which first impress themselves upon the imagination of the spectator; yet the man of the best taste may afterwards see them, without thinking of any such expressions. He may observe their dimensions, he may study their proportions, he may attend to the particular state of their preservation, the history of their discovery, or even the nature of the marble of which they are made. All these are as truly qualities of these statues, as their majesty or grace, and may certainly, at particular times, happen to engage the attention of the man of the most refined taste. That, in such cases, no Emotion of Beauty would be felt, and that, before it could be felt, it would be necessary for the spectator to withdraw his mind from the consideration of such unaffecting qualities, is too obvious to require any illustration. . . .

. . . It is in consequence of this that the exercise of Criticism never fails to destroy, for the time, our sensibility to the beauty of every composition, and that habits of this kind so generally end in destroying the sensibility of Taste. They accustom us to consider every composition in relation only to rules; they turn our attention from those qualities upon which their effect is founded as objects of Taste, to the consideration of the principles by which this effect is attained; and instead of that deep and enthusiastic delight which the perception of Beauty or Sublimity bestows, they afford us at last no higher enjoyment, than what

arises from the observation of the servile dexterity of Art.

The effect of Familiarity, which has so often been observed, in diminishing our sensibility to the objects of Taste, may serve also as an illustration of the same principle. This effect indeed is generally resolved into the influence of habit, which in this, as in every other case, is supposed to diminish the strength of our emotions; yet, that it is not solely to be ascribed to habit, seems evident from the following consideration, that such indifference is never permanent, and that there are times when the most familiar objects awaken us to the fullest sense of their beauty. The necessity which we are under of considering all such objects when familiar, in very different aspects from those in which they appear to us as objects of Beauty, and of attending only to their unaffecting qualities, may perhaps better account both for this gradual decay of our sensibility and for its temporary return.

When a man of any taste, for instance, first settles in a romantic country, he is willing to flatter himself that he can never be satiated with its beauties, and that in their contemplation he shall continue to receive the same exquisite delight. The aspect in which he now sees them, is solely that in which they are calculated to produce Emotion. The streams are known to him only by their solemnity, the rocks by their awfulness or terror. In a very short time, however, he is forced to consider them in very different lights. They are useful to him for some purposes, either of occupation or amusement. They serve as distinctions of different properties, or of different divisions of the country. They become boundaries or land-marks, by which his knowledge of the neighborhood is ascertained. It is with these qualities that he hears them usually spoken of by all who surround him. It is in this light that he must often speak and think of them himself. It is with these qualities, accordingly, that he comes at last insensibly to consider them, in the common hours of his life. Even a circumstance so trifling as the assignation of particular names, contributes in a great degree to produce this effect; because the use of such names, in marking the particular situation or place of such objects, naturally leads him to consider the objects themselves in no other light than that of their place or situation. It is with very different feelings that he must now regard the objects that were once so full of beauty. They now occur to his mind, only as topographical distinctions, and are beheld with the indifference such qualities naturally produce. Their majesty, their solemnity, their terror, &c. are gradually obscured, under the mass of unaffecting qualities with which he is obliged to consider them: and, excepting at those times when either their appearances or their expressions are new, or when some other incident has awakened that tone or temper of thought with which their expressions agree, and when, of consequence, he is disposed to consider them in the light of this expression alone, he must be content at last to pass his life without any perception of their beauty. . . .

SEC. III. If it is true, that those trains of thought which attend the Emotions of Taste, are uniformly distinguished by some general principle of connexion, it ought to be found, that no Composition of Objects or qualities in fact produces such emotions, in which this unity of character or of emotion is not preserved. This proposition also may be illustrated from the most superficial review of the Principles of Composition, in the different arts of Taste. . . .

The art of Landscape-painting is yet superior in its effect, from the capacity which the artist enjoys, of giving both greater extent and greater unity to his composition. . . . In a landscape the painter has the choice of the circumstances he is to represent, and can give whatever force or extent he pleases to the expression he wishes to convey. . . . He may select from a thousand scenes, the circumstances which are to characterize a single composition, and may unite into one expression, the scattered features with which Nature has feebly marked a thousand situations. . . .

While it is by the Invention of such circumstances that we estimate the genius of the artist, it is by their Composition that his Taste is uniformly determined. The mere assemblage of picturesque incidents, the most unimproved Taste will condemn. Some general principle is universally demanded, some decided expression, to which the meaning of the several parts may be referred; and which, by affording us, as it were, the key of the scene, may lead us to feel, from the whole of the composition, that full and undisturbed emotion which we are prepared to indulge. It is this purity and simplicity of composition, accordingly, which has uniformly distinguished the great masters of the art from the mere copiers of Nature. . . .

It is not, however, on our first acquaintance with this art, that we either discover its capacity, or feel its effects; and perhaps the progress of Taste, in this respect, may afford a further illustration of the great and fundamental Principle of Composition. What we first understand of painting is, that it is a simple art of imitation; and what we expect to find in it, is the representation of the common scenes of Nature that surround us. It is with some degree of surprise, accordingly, that we at first observe the different scenery with which the Painter presents us, and with an emotion rather of wonder, than of delight, that we gaze at a style of landscape, which has so little resemblance to the ordinary views to which we are accustomed. In the copy of a real scene, we can discover and admire the skill of the artist; but in the representation of desert or of desolate prospects, in appearances of Solitude or Tempest, we perceive no traces of imitation, and wonder only at the perversity of Taste, which could have led to the choice of so disagreeable subjects.

As soon however as . . . we begin to

connect expression with such views of Nature, we begin also to understand and to feel the beauties of landscape painting. It is with a different view that we now consider it. It is not for imitation we look, but for character. It is not the art, but the genius of the Painter, which now gives value to his composition: and the language he employs is found not only to speak to the eye, but to affect the imagination and the heart. It is not now a simple copy which we see, nor is our Emotion limited to the cold pleasure which arises from the perception of accurate Imitation. It is a creation of Fancy with which the artist presents us, in which only the greater expressions of Nature are retained, and where more interesting emotions are awakened, than those which we experience from the usual tameness of common scenery. In the same proportion in which we thus discover the expression of landscape, we begin to collect the principles of its composition. The crowd of incidents which used to dazzle our earlier Taste, as expressive both of the skill and of the invention of the artist, begin to appear to us as inconsistence or confusion. When our hearts are affected, we seek only for objects congenial to our emotion: and the Simplicity, which we used to call the Poverty of landscape, begins now to be welcome to us, as permitting us to indulge, without interruption, those interesting trains of thought which the character of the scene is fitted to inspire. As our knowledge of the expressions of Nature increases, our sensibility to the beauty and to the defects of composition becomes more keen, until at last our admiration attaches itself only to those greater productions of the art, in which one pure and unmingled character is preserved, and in which no feature is admitted, which may prevent it from falling upon the heart with one full and harmonious effect.

In this manner, the object of Painting is no sooner discovered, than the unity of expression is felt to be the great secret of its power: The superiority which it at last assumes over the scenery of Nature, is found to arise, in one important respect, from the greater purity and simplicity which its composition can attain; and perhaps this simple rule comprehends all that Criticism can prescribe for the regulation of this delightful art. . . .

CONCLUSION: The illustrations in the first Chapter of this Essay are intended to show, that whenever the Emotions of Beauty or Sublimity are felt, that exercise of Imagination is produced which consists in the prosecution of a train of thought.

The illustrations in the second Chapter are intended to point out the distinction between such trains, and our ordinary trains of thought, and to show that this difference consists, 1st, In the ideas which compose them being in all cases Ideas of Emotion; and 2dly, In their possessing an uniform principle of connexion through the whole train. The effect, therefore, which is produced upon the mind by objects of Taste may be considered as consisting in the production of a regular or consistent train of Ideas of Emotion.

The account . . . given of this effect may perhaps serve to point out an important distinction between the Emotions of Taste, and all our different Emotions of Simple Pleasure. In the case of these last emotions, no additional train of thought is necessary. The pleasurable feeling follows immediately the presence of the object or quality, and has no dependence upon anything for its perfection, but the sound state of the sense by which it is received. . . .

In the case of the Emotions of Taste it seems evident that this exercise of mind is necessary, and that unless this train of thought is produced, these emotions are unfelt. Whatever may be the nature of that simple emotion which any object is fitted to excite, . . . if it produce not a train of kindred thought in our minds, we are conscious only of that simple Emotion. Whenever, on the contrary, this train of thought, or this exercise of imagination is produced, we are conscious of an emotion of a higher and more pleasing kind; and which, though it is impossible to describe in language, we may yet distinguish by the name of the Emotion of Taste. . . .

As in every operation of Taste there are thus two different faculties employed, *viz.* some affection or emotion raised, and the imagination excited to a train of thought corresponding to this emotion, the peculiar pleasure which attends, and which constitutes the Emotions of Taste, may naturally be considered as composed of the pleasures which separately attend the exercise of these faculties, or, in other words, as produced by the union of pleasing emotion, with the pleasure which, by the constitution of our nature, is annexed to the exercise of imagination. That both these pleasures are felt in every operation of Taste, seems to me very agreeable to common experience and observation. . . .

If it is allowed, then, that there is a pleasure annexed, by the constitution of our nature, to the Exercise of Imagination; and if the illustrations in the first chapter are just, which are intended to show, that when this exercise of mind is not produced, the Emotions of Taste are unfelt, and that when it is increased these Emotions are increased with it, we seem to possess sufficient evidence to conclude, that this Pleasure exists, and forms a part of that peculiar pleasure which we receive from objects of Sublimity and Beauty.

The pleasure, therefore, which accompanies the Emotions of Taste, may be considered not as a simple, but as a complex pleasure; and as arising not from any separate and peculiar Sense, but from the union of the pleasure of *Simple Emotion,* with that which is annexed, by the constitution of the human mind, to the exercise of *Imagination.*

The distinction which thus appears to subsist between the Emotions of Simple Pleasure, and that complex pleasure which accompanies the Emotions of Taste, seems to require a similar distinction in philosophical language. I believe, indeed, that the distinction is actually to be found in the common language of conversation; and I apprehend that the term *Delight* is very generally used to express the peculiar pleasure which attends the Emotions of Taste, in contradistinction to the general term Pleasure, which is appropriated to Simple Emotion. We are *pleased,* we say, with the gratification of any appetite or affection, . . . But, we say, we are *delighted* with the prospect of a fine landscape, the sight of a fine statue, . . . with the perusal of a celebrated poem. . . . I acknowledge, indeed, that this distinction is not very accurately adhered to in common language, because, in most cases, either of the terms equally expresses our meaning; but I apprehend that the observation of it is sufficiently general, to show some consciousness in mankind of a difference between these pleasures, and to justify such a distinction in philosophical language as may express it.

If it were permitted me, therefore, I should wish to appropriate the term Delight, to signify the peculiar pleasure which attends the Emotions of Taste, or which is felt, *when the Imagination is employed in the prosecution* of a regular train of *Ideas of Emotion.*

ESSAY II

Of the Sublimity and Beauty of the Material World

CHAP. I. If the illustrations in the preceding essay are just, if that exercise of mind which takes place when the Emotions of Beauty or Sublimity are felt consists in the prosecution of a regular train of Ideas of Emotion, and if no other objects are in fact productive of the Emotions of Taste, but such as are fitted to produce some simple Emotion, there arises a question of some difficulty, and of very considerable importance, *viz.* What is the source of the *Sublimity and Beauty of the Material World?*

It cannot be doubted, that many objects of the Material World are productive of the Emotions of Sublimity and Beauty: some of the fine arts are altogether employed about material objects; and far the greater part of the instances of Beauty or Sublimity which occur in every man's experience, are found in matter, or in some of its qualities.

On the other hand, I think it must be allowed, that Matter in itself is unfitted to produce any kind of emotion. The various qualities of matter are known to us only by means of our external senses; but all that such powers of our nature convey, is Sensation and Perception; and whoever will take the trouble of attending to the effect which such qualities, when simple and unassociated, produce upon his mind, will be satisfied, that in no case do they produce Emotion, or the exercise of any of his affections. The common language of mankind upon this subject, perfectly coincides with this observation. Such qualities, when simple, are always spoken of as producing sensation, but in no case as producing emotion; and although perhaps the general word Feeling (as applied both to our external and internal senses) may sometimes be used ambiguously, yet if we attend to it, we shall find, that, with regard to material qualities, it is uniformly used to express Sensation, and that, if we substitute Emotion for it, every man will perceive the mistake. The smell of a rose, the color of scarlet, the taste of a pineapple, when spoken of merely as qualities, and abstracted from the objects in which they are found, are said to produce agreeable Sensations, but not agreeable Emotions. . . . If we could conceive ourselves possessed only of those powers which we have by means of our external senses, I apprehend there can be no doubt, that, in such a case, the qualities of matter would produce only sensation and perception: that such sensations might be either pleasing or painful, but that in no case could they be attended with any emotion.

But although the qualities of matter are in themselves incapable of producing emotion, or the exercise of any affection, yet it is obvious that they may produce this effect, from their association with other qualities; and as being either the signs or expression of such qualities as are fitted by the constitution of our nature to produce Emotion. Thus, in the human body, particular forms or colors are the signs of particular passions or affections. In works of art, particular forms are the signs of Dexterity, of Taste, of Convenience, of Utility. In the works of nature, particular sounds and colors &c. are the signs of Peace, or Danger, or Plenty, or Desolation, &c. In such cases, the constant connexion we discover between the sign and the thing signified, between the material quality and the quality productive of Emotion, renders at last the one expressive to us of the other, and very often disposes us to attribute to the sign, that effect which is produced only by the quality signified. . . .

Whatever may be the truth of these observations, it cannot at least be doubted, that the Qualities of Matter are often associated with others, and that they affect us in such cases, like all other signs, by leading our imaginations to the qualities they signify. It seems to be equally obvious, that in all cases where Matter, or any of its qualities, produces the Emotion of Sublimity or Beauty, this effect must arise either from these material Qualities themselves; from their being fitted by the constitution of our nature to produce such Emotions; or from some other qualities with which they are associated, and of which they operate as the Signs or Expressions.

It should seem, therefore, that a very simple, and a very obvious principle is sufficient to guide our investigation into the source of the sublimity and beauty of the qualities of Matter. If these qualities are in themselves fitted to produce the Emotions of Sublimity or Beauty (or, in other words, are in themselves beautiful or sublime), I think it is obvious that they must produce these Emotions, independently of any association. If, on the contrary, it is found that these qualities only produce such Emotions when they are associated with interesting or affecting qualities, and that when such associations are destroyed, they no longer produce the same emotions, I think it must also be allowed that their Beauty or Sublimity is to be ascribed, not to the material, but to the associated qualities.

That this is in reality the case, I shall endeavor to show, by a great variety of illustrations.

. . .

CHAP. VI, SEC. VI. *Conclusion of this Essay.* The illustrations that have been offered in the course of this *Essay* upon the origin of the *Sublimity* and *Beauty* of some of the principal qualities of *Matter,* seem to afford sufficient evidence for the following conclusions.

I. That each of these qualities is, either from nature, from experience, or from accident, the sign of some quality capable of producing Emotion, or the exercise of some moral affection. And,

II. That when these associations are dissolved, or in other words when the material qualities cease to be significant of the associated qualities, they also cease to produce the emotions, either of Sublimity or Beauty.

If these conclusions are admitted, it appears necessarily to follow, that the Beauty and Sublimity of such objects is to be ascribed not to the material qualities themselves, but to the qualities they signify; and of consequence, that the qualities of matter are not to be considered as sublime or beautiful in themselves, but as being the *Signs* or *Expressions* of such qualities as, by the constitution of our nature, are fitted to produce pleasing or interesting emotions.

The opinion I have now stated coincides, in a great degree, with a *Doctrine* that appears very early to have distinguished the *Platonic* school; . . . The doctrine to which I allude is, that matter is not beautiful in itself, but derives its Beauty from the expression of *Mind.*

As this doctrine . . . has somewhat the air of a paradox, I shall beg leave, in a few words, to explain in what sense I understand and adopt it, by enumerating what appear to me the principal classes of this expression, or the principal means by which the qualities of matter become significant to us of those qualities of mind which are destined to affect us with pleasing or interesting emotions.

The qualities of *Mind* which are capable of producing emotion are, either its *Active,* or its *Passive* qualities; either its powers and capacities, as beneficence, wisdom, fortitude, invention, fancy, &c.; or its feelings and affections, as love, joy, hope, gratitude, purity, fidelity, innocence, &c. In the observation or belief of these qualities of mind, we are formed, by the original and moral constitution of our nature, to experience various and powerful emotions.

As it is only, however, through the medium of matter, that, in the present condition of our being, the qualities of mind are known to us, the qualities of matter become necessarily expressive to us of all the qualities of mind they signify. They may be the signs, therefore, or expressions of these mental qualities, in the following ways.

I. As the immediate signs of the *Powers* or capacities of mind. It is thus, that all the works of human Art or Design, are directly significant to us of the wisdom, the invention, the taste, or the benevolence of the artist; and the works of Nature, of the power, the wisdom, and the beneficence of the Divine Artist.

II. As the signs of all those *Affections,* or dispositions of mind, which we love, or with which we are formed to sympathise. It is thus that the notes and motions of animals are expressive to us of their happiness and joy; that the tones of the human voice are significant of the various emotions by which it is animated; and that all the affections which we either love or admire in the

Human Mind, are directly signified to us by the various appearances of the countenance and form.

These may be called the direct expressions of Mind; and the material qualities which signify such powers or affections, produce in us immediately the peculiar emotions which, by the laws of our nature, the mental qualities are fitted to produce. But besides these, there are other means by which the qualities of matter may be significant to us of the qualities of mind, indirectly, or by means of less universal and less permanent relations.

1. From Experience; when peculiar forms or appearances of matter are considered as the means or instruments by which those feelings or affections of mind are produced with which we sympathize, or in which we are interested. It is thus that the productions of art are in so many various ways significant to us of the conveniences, the pleasures, or the happiness they bestow upon human life, and, as the signs of happiness, affect us with the emotion this happiness itself is destined to produce. It is thus also, that the scenes of Nature acquire such an accession of Beauty, when we consider them as fitted, with such exquisite wisdom, for the habitation of so many classes of sentient being; and when they become thus expressive to us of all the varied happiness they produce, and contain, and conceal.

2. From Analogy or Resemblance; from that resemblance which has everywhere been felt between the qualities of matter and of mind, and by which the former becomes so powerfully expressive to us of the latter. It is thus that the colors, the sounds, the forms, and above all, the motions of inanimate objects, are so universally felt as resembling peculiar qualities or affections of mind, and, when thus felt, are so productive of the analogous emotion; that the personification of matter is so strongly marked in every period of the history of human thought; and that the poet, while he gives life and animation to every thing around him, is not displaying his own invention, but only obeying one of the most powerful laws which regulate the imagination of man.

3. From Association (in the proper sense of the term); when by means of education, of fortune, or of accident, material objects are connected with pleasing and interesting qualities of mind; and from this connexion become forever afterwards expressive of them. It is thus that colors, forms, &c. derive their temporary beauty from fashion; that the objects which have been devoted to religion, to patriotism, or to honour, affect us with all the emotions of the qualities of which they become significant; that the Beauty of natural scenery is so often exalted by the record of the events it has witnessed; and that in every country, the scenes which have the deepest effect upon the admiration of the people, are those which have become sacred by the memory of ancient virtue, or ancient glory.

4. From individual Association; when certain qualities or appearances of matter, are connected with our own private affections or remembrances; and when they give to these material qualities or appearances a character of interest which is solely the result of our own memory and affections.

Of the reality of these expressions I believe no person can doubt; and whoever will attend to the power and extent of their influence, will, I think, soon be persuaded that they are sufficient to account for all the Beauty or sublimity we discover in the qualities of matter.

The conclusion, therefore, in which I wish to rest is, *that the Beauty and Sublimity which is felt in the various appearances of matter, are finally to be ascribed to their Expression of Mind; or to their being, either directly or indirectly, the signs of those qualities of Mind which are fitted, by the constitution of our Nature, to affect us with pleasing or interesting Emotion.*

IMMANUEL KANT [1724–1804]

>>>>><<<<<

From *The Critique of Aesthetic Judgement* [1790]

INTRODUCTION

VII. *The Aesthetic Representation of the Finality of Nature*

That which is purely subjective in the representation of an Object, i.e. what constitutes its reference to the Subject, not to the object, is its aesthetic quality. On the other hand, that which in such a representation serves, or is available, for the determination of the object (for the purpose of knowledge), is its logical validity. In the cognition of an object of sense both sides are present conjointly. In the sense-representation of external things the Quality of space in which we intuit them is the merely subjective side of my representation of them . . . and it is on account of that reference that the object in being intuited in space is also thought merely as a phenomenon. But despite its purely subjective Quality, space is still a constituent of the knowledge of things as phenomena. *Sensation* (here external) also agrees in expressing a merely subjective side of our representations of external things, but one which is properly their matter (through which we are given something with real existence), just as space is the mere *a priori* form of the possibility of their intuition; and so sensation is, none the less, also employed in the cognition of external Objects.

But that subjective side of a representation *which is incapable of becoming an element of cognition*, is the *pleasure* or *displeasure*

From Immanuel Kant, *The Critique of Judgement*, translated by J. C. Meredith (Oxford: Oxford University Press, 1952). Reprinted by permission of the Clarendon Press, Oxford.

connected with it; for through it I cognize nothing in the object of the representation, although it may easily be the result of the operation of some cognition or other. Now the finality[1] of a thing, so far as represented in our perception of it, is in no way a quality of the object itself (for a quality of this kind is not one that can be perceived), although it may be inferred from a cognition of things. In the finality, therefore, which is prior to the cognition of an Object, and which, even apart from any desire to make use of the representation of it for the purpose of a cognition, is yet immediately connected with it, we have the subjective quality belonging to it that is incapable of becoming a constituent of knowledge. Hence we only apply the term "final" to the object on account of its representation being immediately coupled with the feeling of pleasure: and this representation itself is an aesthetic representation of the finality. The

[1] Translators of Kant have disagreed vigorously about the proper rendering of the German word translated here as "finality." In Bernard's translation of *The Critique of Judgment* the terms "final" and "finality" do not appear; they are replaced by "purpose" and "purposiveness." Kant's explanation of the meaning intended is given in Book I, Section 10 of the *Critique* (*infra*, p. 205). Meredith's note defending his use of "finality" reads: "*Zweckmässigkeit* has been variously rendered by different writers as: 'purposiveness,' 'purposefulness,' 'adaptation to ends.' 'Adaptation to ends,' at all events, sounds better than 'purposiveness' but it is equally misleading. Kant gives *forma finalis* as its equivalent, and it is difficult to see why the rendering 'finality' should be so consistently avoided, unless it be that the word as most commonly used refers to termination in time. But why should philosophy only recognize the one meaning of the word that is practically useless in philosophy? Throughout the present translation the word 'finality' is used in its strict technical sense, and, to avoid ambiguity, the word 'final' is never used to mean 'ultimate,' but always as in the expression 'final cause.' " (ed.)

only question is whether such a representation of finality exists at all.

If pleasure is connected with the mere apprehension (*apprehensio*) of the form of an object of intuition, apart from any reference it may have to a concept for the purpose of a definite cognition, this does not make the representation referable to the Object, but solely to the Subject. In such a case the pleasure can express nothing but the conformity of the Object to the cognitive faculties brought into play in the reflective judgement, and so far as they are in play, and hence merely a subjective formal finality of the Object. For that apprehension of forms in the imagination can never take place without the reflective judgement, even when it has no intention of so doing, comparing them at least with its faculty of referring intuitions to concepts. If, now, in this comparison, imagination (as the faculty of intuitions a priori) is undesignedly brought into accord with understanding (as the faculty of concepts) by means of a given representation, and a feeling of pleasure is thereby aroused, then the object must be regarded as final for the reflective judgement. A judgement of this kind is an aesthetic judgement upon the finality of the Object, which does not depend upon any present concept of the object, and does not provide one. When the form of an object (as opposed to the matter of its presentation, as sensation) is, in the mere act of reflecting upon it, without regard to any concept to be obtained from it, estimated as the ground of a pleasure in the representation of such an Object, then this pleasure is also judged to be combined necessarily with the representation of it, and so not merely for the Subject apprehending this form, but for all in general who pass judgement. The object is then called beautiful; and the faculty of judging by means of such a pleasure (and so also with universal validity) is called taste. For since the ground of the pleasure is made to reside merely in the

form of the object for reflection generally, consequently not in any sensation of the object, and without any reference, either, to any concept that might have something or other in view, it is with the conformity to law in the empirical employment or judgement generally (unity of imagination and understanding) in the Subject, and with this alone, that the representation of the Object in reflection, the conditions of which are universally valid a priori, accords. And, as this accordance of the object with the faculties of the Subject is contingent, it gives rise to a representation of a finality on the part of the object in respect of the cognitive faculties of the Subject.

Here, now, is a pleasure which . . . no concepts could ever enable us to regard as necessarily connected with the representation of an object. It must always be only through reflective perception that it is cognized as conjoined with this representation. As with all empirical judgements, it is, consequently, unable to announce objective necessity or lay claim to a priori validity. But then, the judgement of taste in fact only lays claim, like every other empirical judgement, to be valid for everyone, and despite its inner contingency this is always possible. The only point that is strange . . . about it, is that it is not an empirical concept, but a feeling of pleasure (and so not a concept at all) that is yet exacted from everyone by the judgement of taste, just as if it were a predicate united to the cognition of the Object, and that is meant to be conjoined with its representation.

A singular empirical judgement rightly looks to everyone finding the fact as stated, since the judgement has been formed according to the universal conditions of the determinant judgement under the laws of a possible experience generally. In the same way one who feels pleasure in simple reflection on the form of an object, without having any concept in mind, rightly lays claim to the agreement of everyone, although this judgement is empirical and a singular judgement. For the ground of this pleasure is found in the universal, though subjective, condition of reflective judgements, namely, the final harmony of an object . . . with the mutual relation of the faculties of cognition (imagination and understanding) which are requisite for every empirical cognition. The pleasure in judgements of taste is, therefore, dependent doubtless upon an empirical representation, and cannot be united *a priori* to any concept (one cannot determine *a priori* what object will be in accordance with taste or not—one must find out the object that is so); but then it is only made the determining ground of this judgement by virtue of our consciousness of its resting simply upon reflection and the universal, though only subjective, conditions of the harmony of that reflection with the knowledge of objects generally, for which the form of the Object is final.

This is why judgements of taste are subjected to a Critique in respect of their possibility. For their possibility presupposes an *a priori* principle, although that principle is neither a cognitive principle for understanding nor a practical principle for the will, and is thus in no way determinant *a priori*.

Susceptibility to pleasure arising from reflection on the forms of things (whether of nature or of art) betokens, however, not only a finality on the part of Objects in their relation to the reflective judgement in the Subject, in accordance with the concept of nature, but also, conversely, a finality on the part of the Subject, answering to the concept of freedom, in respect of the form, or even formlessness, of objects. The result is that the aesthetic judgement refers not merely, as a judgement of taste, to the beautiful, but also, as springing from a higher intellectual feeling, to the *sublime*. Hence the above-mentioned Critique of Aesthetic Judgement must be divided on these lines into two main parts. . . .

ANALYTIC OF THE BEAUTIFUL
FIRST MOMENT

Of the Judgement of Taste: Moment of Quality

1. *The judgement of taste is aesthetic.* If we wish to discern whether anything is beautiful or not, we do not refer the representation of it to the Object by means of understanding with a view to cognition, but by means of the imagination (acting perhaps in conjunction with understanding) we refer the representation to the Subject and its feeling of pleasure or displeasure. The judgement of taste, therefore, is not a cognitive judgement, and so not logical, but is aesthetic—which means that it is one whose determining ground *cannot be other than subjective.* Every reference of representations is capable of being objective, even that of sensations (in which case it signifies the real in an empirical representation). The one exception to this is the feeling of pleasure or displeasure. This denotes nothing in the object, but is a feeling which the Subject has of itself and of the manner in which it is affected by the representation.

To apprehend a regular and appropriate building with one's cognitive faculties, be the mode of representation clear or confused, is quite a different thing from being conscious of this representation with an accompanying sensation of delight. Here the representation is referred wholly to the Subject, and what is more to its feeling of life —under the name of the feeling of pleasure or displeasure—and this forms the basis of a quite separate faculty of discriminating and estimating, that contributes nothing to knowledge. All it does is to compare the given representation in the Subject with the entire faculty of representations of which the mind is conscious in the feeling of its state. Given representations in a judgement may be empirical, and so aesthetic; but the judgement which is pronounced by their means is logical, provided it refers them to the Object. Conversely, be the given representations even rational, but referred in a judgement solely to the Subject (to its feeling), they are always to that extent aesthetic.

2. *The delight which determines the judgement of taste is independent of all interest.* The delight which we connect with the representation of the real existence of an object is called interest. Such a delight, therefore, always involves a reference to the faculty of desire, either as its determining ground, or else as necessarily implicated with its determining ground. Now, where the question is whether something is beautiful, we do not want to know, whether we, or any one else, are, or even could be, concerned in the real existence of the thing, but rather what estimate we form of it on mere contemplation (intuition or reflection). . . . All one wants to know is whether the mere representation of the object is to my liking, no matter how indifferent I may be to the real existence of the object of this representation. It is quite plain that in order to say that the object *is beautiful*, and to show that I have taste, everything turns on the meaning which I can give to this representation, and not on any factor which makes me dependent on the real existence of the object. Every one must allow that a judgement on the beautiful which is tinged with the slightest interest, is very partial and not a pure judgement of taste. One must not be in the least prepossessed in favour of the real existence of the thing, but must preserve complete indifference in this respect, in order to play the part of judge in matters of taste.

This proposition, which is of the utmost importance, cannot be better explained than by contrasting the pure disinterested delight which appears in the judgement of taste with that allied to an interest. . . .

3. *Delight* IN THE AGREEABLE *is coupled with interest. That is* AGREEABLE *which the senses find pleasing in sensation.* This at once affords a convenient opportunity for

(*gratifying*)

condemning and directing particular attention to a prevalent confusion of the double meaning of which the word "sensation" is capable. All delight (as is said or thought) is itself sensation (of a pleasure). Consequently everything that pleases, and for the very reason that it pleases, is agreeable—and according to its different degrees, or its relations to other agreeable sensations, is attractive, charming, delicious, enjoyable, etc. But if this is conceded, then impressions of sense, which determine inclination, or principles of reason, which determine the will, or mere contemplated forms of intuition, which determine judgement, are all on a par in everything relevant to their effect upon the feeling of pleasure, for this would be agreeableness in the sensation of one's state; and since, in the last resort, all the elaborate work of our faculties must issue in and unite in the practical as its goal, we could credit our faculties with no other appreciation of things and the worth of things, than that consisting in the gratification which they promise. . . .

When a modification of the feeling of pleasure or displeasure is termed sensation, this expression is given quite a different meaning to that which it bears when I call the representation of a thing (through sense as a receptivity pertaining to the faculty of knowledge) sensation. For in the latter case the representation is referred to the Object, but in the former it is referred solely to the Subject and is not available for any cognition, not even for that by which the Subject *cognizes* itself.

Now in the above definition the word sensation is used to denote an objective representation of sense; and, to avoid continually running the risk of misinterpretation, we shall call that which must always remain purely subjective, and is absolutely incapable of forming a representation of an object, by the familiar name of feeling. The green colour of the meadows belongs to *objective* sensation, as the perception of an object of sense; but its agreeableness to *sub-*

jective sensation, by which no object is represented: i.e. to feeling, through which the object is regarded as an Object of delight (which involves no cognition of the object).

Now, that a judgement on an object by which its agreeableness is affirmed, expresses an interest in it, is evident from the fact that through sensation it provokes a desire for similar objects, consequently the delight presupposes, not the simple judgement about it, but the bearing its real existence has upon my state so far as affected by such an Object. Hence we do not merely say of the agreeable that it *pleases,* but that it gratifies. I do not accord it a simple approval, but inclination is aroused by it, and where agreeableness is of the liveliest type a judgement on the character of the Object is so entirely out of place, that those who are always intent on enjoyment . . . would fain dispense with all judgement.

4. *Delight* IN THE GOOD *is coupled with interest.* That is *good* which by means of reason commends itself by its mere concept. We call that *good for something* (useful) which only pleases as a means; but that which pleases on its own account we call *good in itself.* In both cases the concept of an end is implied, and consequently the relation of reason to (at least possible) willing, and thus a delight in the *existence* of an Object or action, i.e. some interest or other.

To deem something good, I must always know what sort of a thing the object is intended to be, i.e. I must have a concept of it. That is not necessary to enable me to see beauty in a thing. Flowers, free patterns, lines aimlessly intertwining . . . have no signification, depend upon no definite concept, and yet please. Delight in the beautiful must depend upon the reflection on an object precursory to some (not definitely determined) concept. It is thus also differentiated from the agreeable, which rests entirely upon sensation.

In many cases, no doubt, the agreeable and the good seem convertible terms. Thus it is commonly said that all (especially lasting) gratification is of itself good; which is almost equivalent to saying that to be permanently agreeable and to be good are identical. But it is readily apparent that this is merely a vicious confusion of words, for the concepts appropriate to these expressions are far from interchangeable. The agreeable, which, as such, represents the object solely in relation to sense, must in the first instance be brought under principles of reason through the concept of an end, to be, as an object of will, called good. But that the reference to delight is wholly different where what gratifies is at the same time called *good,* is evident from the fact that with the good the question always is whether it is mediately or immediately good, i.e. useful or good in itself; whereas with the agreeable this point can never arise, since the word always means what pleases immediately—and it is just the same with what I call beautiful. . . .

5. *Comparison of the three specifically different kinds of delight.* Both the Agreeable and the Good involve a reference to the faculty of desire, and are thus attended, the former with a delight pathologically conditioned (by stimuli), the latter with a pure practical delight. Such delight is determined not merely by the representation of the object, but also by the represented bond of connexion between the Subject and the real existence of the object. It is not merely the object, but also its real existence, that pleases. On the other hand the judgement of taste is simply *contemplative,* i.e. it is a judgement which is indifferent as to the existence of an object, and only decides how its character stands with the feeling of pleasure and displeasure. But not even is this contemplation itself directed to concepts; for the judgement of taste is not a cognitive judgement (neither a theoretical one nor a practical), and hence, also, is not *grounded* on concepts, nor yet *intentionally directed* to them.

The agreeable, the beautiful, and the good thus denote three different relations of representations to the feeling of pleasure and displeasure, as a feeling in respect of which we distinguish different objects or modes of representation. Also, the corresponding expressions which indicate our satisfaction in them are different. The agreeable is what GRATIFIES a man; the beautiful what simply PLEASES him; the good what is ESTEEMED (approved), i.e. that on which he sets an objective worth. Agreeableness is a significant factor even with irrational animals; beauty has purport and significance only for human beings, . . . whereas the good is good for every rational being in general;—a proposition which can only receive its complete justification and explanation in the sequel. Of all these three kinds of delight, that of taste in the beautiful may be said to be the one and only disinterested and free delight; for, with it, no interest, whether of sense or reason, extorts approval. And so we may say that delight, in the three cases mentioned, is related to inclination, to favour, or to respect. For FAVOUR is the only free liking. An object of inclination, and one which a law of reason imposes upon our desire, leaves us no freedom to turn anything into an object of pleasure. All interest presupposes a want, or calls one forth; and, being a ground determining approval, deprives the judgement on the object of its freedom. . . .

DEFINITION OF THE BEAUTIFUL DERIVED FROM THE FIRST MOMENT

Taste is the faculty of estimating an object or a mode of representation by means of a delight or aversion apart from any interest. The object of such a delight is called beautiful.

SECOND MOMENT

Of the Judgement of Taste: Moment of Quantity

6. The beautiful is that which, apart from concepts, is represented as the Object of a UNIVERSAL delight. This definition of the beautiful is deducible from the foregoing definition of it as an object of delight apart from any interest. For where any one is conscious that his delight in an object is with him independent of interest, it is inevitable that he should look on the object as one containing a ground of delight for all men. For, since the delight is not based on any inclination of the Subject (or on any other deliberate interest), but the Subject feels himself completely free in respect of the liking which he accords to the object, he can find as reason for his delight no personal conditions to which his own subjective self might alone be party. Hence he must regard it as resting on what he may also presuppose in every other person; and therefore he must believe that he has reason for demanding a similar delight from every one. Accordingly he will speak of the beautiful as if beauty were a quality of the object and the judgement logical (forming a cognition of the Object by concepts of it); although it is only aesthetic, and contains merely a reference of the representation of the object to the Subject;—because it still bears this resemblance to the logical judgement, that it may be presupposed to be valid for all men. But this universality cannot spring from concepts. For from concepts there is no transition to the feeling of pleasure or displeasure (save in the case of pure practical laws, which, however, carry an interest with them; and such an interest does not attach to the pure judgement of taste). The result is that the judgement of taste, with its attendant consciousness of detachment from all interest, must involve a claim to validity for all men, and must do so apart from universality attached to Objects, i.e. there must be coupled with it a claim to subjective universality.

7. Comparison of the beautiful with the agreeable and the good by means of the above characteristic. As regards the agreeable every one concedes that his judgement, which he bases on a private feeling, and in

which he declares that an object pleases him, is restricted merely to himself personally. Thus he does not take it amiss if, when he says that Canary-wine is agreeable, another corrects the expression and reminds him that he ought to say: It is agreeable *to me*. This applies not only to the taste of the tongue, the palate, and the throat, but to what may with any one be agreeable to eye or ear . . . With the agreeable, therefore, the axiom holds good: *Every one has his own taste* (that of sense).

The beautiful stands on quite a different footing. It would, on the contrary, be ridiculous if any one who plumed himself on his taste were to think of justifying himself by saying: This object (the building we see, the dress that person has on, the concert we hear, the poem submitted to our criticism) is beautiful *for me*. For if it merely pleases *him,* he must not call it *beautiful.* Many things may for him possess charm and agreeableness—no one cares about that; but when he puts a thing on a pedestal and calls it beautiful, he demands the same delight from others. He judges not merely for himself, but for all men, and then speaks of beauty as if it were a property of things. Thus he says the *thing* is beautiful; and it is not as if he counted on others agreeing in his judgement of liking owing to his having found them in such agreement on a number of occasions, but he *demands* this agreement of them. He blames them if they judge differently, and denies them taste, which he still requires of them as something they ought to have; and to this extent it is not open to men to say: Every one has his own taste. This would be equivalent to saying that there is no such thing at all as taste, i.e. no aesthetic judgement capable of making a rightful claim upon the assent of all men.

. . . In respect of the good it is true that judgements also rightly assert a claim to validity for every one; but the good is only represented as an Object of universal delight *by means of a concept,* which is the case neither with the agreeable nor the beautiful.

8. *In a judgement of taste the universality of delight is only represented as subjective.* First, one must get firmly into one's mind that by the judgement of taste (upon the beautiful) the delight in an object is imputed to *every one,* yet without being founded on a concept (for then it would be the good), and that this claim to universality is such an essential factor of a judgement by which we describe anything as *beautiful,* that were it not for its being present to the mind it would never enter into any one's head to use this expression, but everything that pleased without a concept would be ranked as agreeable. For in respect of the agreeable every one is allowed to have his own opinion, and no one insists upon others agreeing with his judgement of taste, which is what is invariably done in the judgement of taste about beauty. The first of these I may call the taste of sense, the second, the taste of reflection: the first laying down judgements merely private, the second, on the other hand, judgements ostensibly of general validity (public), but both alike being aesthetic (not practical) judgements about an object merely in respect of the bearings of its representation on the feeling of pleasure or displeasure. Now it does seem strange that while with the taste of sense it is not alone experience that shows that its judgement (of pleasure or displeasure in something) is not universally valid, but every one willingly refrains from imputing this agreement to others . . . the taste of reflection, which, as experience teaches, has often enough to put up with a rude dismissal of its claims to universal validity of its judgement (upon the beautiful), can (as it actually does) find it possible for all that, to formulate judgements capable of demanding this agreement in its universality. Such agreement it does in fact require from every one for each of its judgements of taste—the persons who pass these judgements not quarrelling over

the possibility of such a claim, but only failing in particular cases to come to terms as to the correct application of this faculty.

First of all we have here to note that a universality which does not rest upon concepts of the Object . . . is in no way logical, but aesthetic, i.e. does not involve any objective quantity of the judgement, but only one that is subjective. For this universality I use the expression *general validity*, which denotes the validity of the reference of a representation, not to the cognitive faculties, but to the feeling of pleasure or displeasure for every Subject. . . .

Now a judgement that has *objective universal validity* has always got the subjective also, i.e. if the judgement is valid for everything which is contained under a given concept, it is valid also for all who represent an object by means of this concept. But from a *subjective universal validity*, i.e. the aesthetic, that does not rest on any concept, no conclusion can be drawn to the logical; because judgements of that kind have no bearing upon the Object. But for this very reason the aesthetic universality attributed to a judgement must also be of a special kind, seeing that it does not join the predicate of beauty to the concept of the *Object* taken in its entire logical sphere, and yet does extend this predicate over the whole sphere of *judging Subjects*.

In their logical quantity all judgements of taste are *singular* judgements. . . . Yet by taking the singular representation of the Object of the judgement of taste, and by comparison converting it into a concept according to the conditions determining that judgement, we can arrive at a logically universal judgement. For instance, by a judgement of taste I describe the rose at which I am looking as beautiful. The judgement, on the other hand, resulting from the comparison of a number of singular representations: Roses in general are beautiful, is no longer pronounced as a purely aesthetic judgement, but as a logical judgement founded on one that is aesthetic. . . .

In forming an estimate of Objects merely from concepts, all representation of beauty goes by the board. There can, therefore, be no rule according to which any one is to be compelled to recognize anything as beautiful. Whether a dress, a house, or a flower is beautiful is a matter upon which one declines to allow one's judgement to be swayed by any reasons or principles. We want to get a look at the Object with our own eyes, just as if our delight depended on sensation. And yet, if upon so doing, we call the object beautiful, we believe ourselves to be speaking with a universal voice, and lay claim to the concurrence of every one, whereas no private sensation would be decisive except for the observer alone and *his* liking.

Here, now, we may perceive that nothing is postulated in the judgement of taste but such a *universal voice* in respect of delight that is not mediated by concepts; consequently, only the *possibility* of an aesthetic judgement capable of being at the same time deemed valid for every one. The judgement of taste itself does not *postulate* the agreement of every one (for it is only competent for a logically universal judgement to do this, in that it is able to bring forward reasons); it only *imputes* this agreement to every one, as an instance of the rule in respect of which it looks for confirmation, not from concepts, but from the concurrence of others. The universal voice is, therefore, only an idea—resting upon grounds the investigation of which is here postponed. It may be a matter of uncertainty whether a person who thinks he is laying down a judgement of taste is, in fact, judging in conformity with that idea; but that this idea is what is contemplated in his judgement, and that, consequently, it is meant to be a judgement of taste, is proclaimed by his use of the expression "beauty." For himself he can be certain on the point from his mere consciousness of the separation of everything belonging to the agreeable and the good from the delight remaining to him; and this is all for which he promises himself the agreement of every one. . . .

9. *Investigation of the question of the relative priority in a judgement of taste of the feeling of pleasure and the estimating of the object.*

The solution of this problem is the key to the Critique of taste. . . .

Were the pleasure in a given object to be the antecedent, and were the universal communicability of this pleasure to be all that the judgement of taste is meant to allow to the representation of the object, such a sequence would be self-contradictory. For a pleasure of that kind would be nothing but the feeling of mere agreeableness to the senses, and so, from its very nature, would possess no more than private validity, seeing that it would be immediately dependent on the representation through which the object *is given.*

Hence it is the universal capacity for being communicated incident to the mental state in the given representation which, as the subjective condition of the judgement of taste, must be fundamental, with the pleasure in the object as its consequent. Nothing, however, is capable of being universally communicated but cognition and representation so far as appurtenant to cognition. For it is only as thus appurtenant that the representation is objective, and it is this alone that gives it a universal point of reference with which the power of representation of every one is obliged to harmonize. If, then, the determining ground of the judgement as to this universal communicability of the representation is to be merely subjective, that is to say, is to be conceived independently of any concept of the object, it can be nothing else than the mental state that presents itself in the mutual relation of the powers of representation so far as they refer a given representation *to cognition in general.*

The cognitive powers brought into play by this representation are here engaged in a free play, since no definite concept restricts them to a particular rule of cognition. Hence the mental state in this representation must be one of a feeling of the free play of the powers of representation in a given representation for a cognition in general. Now a representation, whereby an object is given, involves, in order that it may become a source of cognition at all, *imagination* for bringing together the manifold of intuition, and *understanding* for the unity of the concept uniting the representations. This state of *free play* of the cognitive faculties attending a representation by which an object is given must admit of universal communication: because cognition, as a definition of the Object with which given representations (in any Subject whatever) are to accord, is the one and only representation which is valid for every one.

As the subjective universal communicability of the mode of representation in a judgement of taste is to subsist apart from the presupposition of any definite concept, it can be nothing else than the mental state present in the free play of imagination and understanding (so far as these are in mutual accord, as is requisite for *cognition in general*): for we are conscious that this subjective relation suitable for a cognition in general must be just as valid for every one, and consequently as universally communicable, as is any determinate cognition, which always rests upon that relation as its subjective condition.

Now this purely subjective (aesthetic) estimating of the object, or of the representation through which it is given, is antecedent to the pleasure in it, and is the basis of this pleasure in the harmony of the cognitive faculties. Again, the above-described universality of the subjective conditions of estimating objects forms the sole foundation of this universal subjective validity of the delight which we connect with the representation of the object that we call beautiful.

That an ability to communicate one's mental state, even though it be only in respect of our cognitive faculties, is attended with a pleasure, is a fact which might easily be demonstrated from the natural propensity of mankind to social life, i.e. empirically and psychologically. But what we have here in view calls for something more than this. In a judgement of taste the pleasure felt by us is exacted from every one else as necessary, just as if, when we call something beautiful, beauty was to be regarded as a quality of the object forming part of its inherent determination according to concepts; although beauty is for itself, apart from any reference to the feeling of the Subject, nothing. . . .

At present we are exercised with the . . . question of the way in which we become conscious, in a judgement of taste, of a reciprocal subjective common accord of the powers of cognition. Is it aesthetically by sensation and our mere internal sense? Or is it intellectually by consciousness of our intentional activity in bringing these powers into play?

Now if the given representation occasioning the judgement of taste were a concept which united understanding and imagination in the estimate of the object so as to give a cognition of the Object, the consciousness of this relation would be intellectual. . . . But, then, in that case the judgement would not be laid down with respect to pleasure and displeasure, and so would not be a judgement of taste. But, now, the judgement of taste determines the Object, independently of concepts, in respect of delight and of the predicate of beauty. There is, therefore, no other way for the subjective unity of the relation in question to make itself known than by sensation. The quickening of both faculties (imagination and understanding) to an indefinite, but yet, thanks to the given representation, harmonious activity, such as belongs to cognition generally, is the sensation whose universal communicability is

postulated by the judgement of taste. An objective relation can, of course, only be thought, yet in so far as, in respect of its conditions, it is subjective, it may be felt in its effect upon the mind, and, in the case of a relation (like that of the powers of representation to a faculty of cognition generally) which does not rest on any concept, no other consciousness of it is possible beyond that through sensation of its effect upon the mind—an effect consisting in the more facile play of both mental powers (imagination and understanding) as quickened by their mutual accord. A representation which is singular and independent of comparison with other representations, and, being such, yet accords with the conditions of the universality that is the general concern of understanding, is one that brings the cognitive faculties into that proportionate accord which we require for all cognition and which we therefore deem valid for every one who is so constituted as to judge by means of understanding and sense conjointly (i.e. for every man).

DEFINITION OF THE BEAUTIFUL DRAWN FROM THE SECOND MOMENT

The *beautiful* is that which, apart from a concept, pleases universally.

THIRD MOMENT

Of Judgements of Taste: Moment of the Relation of the Ends (purpose) Brought under Review in Such Judgements

10. *Finality in general.* Let us define the meaning of "an end" in transcendental terms (i.e. without presupposing anything empirical, such as the feeling of pleasure). An end is the object of a concept so far as this concept is regarded as the cause of the object (the real ground of its possibility); and the causality of a *concept* in respect of its *Object* is finality (*forma finalis*). Where, then, not the cognition of an object merely,

but the object itself (its form or real existence) as an effect, is thought to be possible
only through a concept of it, there we imagine an end. The representation of the effect is here the determining ground of its
cause and takes the lead of it. The consciousness of the causality of a representation in respect of the state of the Subject as
one tending *to preserve a continuance* of
that state, may here be said to denote in a
general way what is called pleasure; whereas
displeasure is that representation which
contains the ground for converting the
state of the representations into their opposite (for hindering or removing them).

The faculty of desire, so far as determinable only through concepts, i.e. so as to act
in conformity with the representation of
an end, would be the will. But an Object,
or state of mind, or even an action may, although its possibility does not necessarily
presuppose the representation of an end, be
called final simply on account of its possibility being only explicable and intelligible
for us by virtue of an assumption on our
part of a fundamental causality according
to ends, i.e. a will that would have so or-
dained it according to a certain represented
rule. Finality, therefore, may exist apart
from an end, in so far as we do not locate
the causes of this form in a will, but yet
are able to render the explanation of its
possibility intelligible to ourselves only by
deriving it from a will. Now we are not always obliged to look with the eye of reason
into what we observe (i.e. to consider it in
its possibility). So we may at least observe
a finality of form, and trace it in objects—
though by reflection only—without resting
it on an end. . . .

11. *The sole foundation of the judgement of taste is the FORM OF FINALITY
of an object (or mode of representing
it).* Whenever an end is regarded as a
source of delight it always imports an interest as determining ground of the judgement on the object of pleasure. Hence the
judgement of taste cannot rest on any sub-

jective end as its ground. But neither can
any representation of an objective end, i.e.
of the possibility of the object itself on
principles of final connexion, determine the
judgement of taste, and, consequently,
neither can any concept of the good. For
the judgement of taste is an aesthetic and
not a cognitive judgement, and so does not
deal with any *concept* of the nature or of
the internal or external possibility, by this
or that cause, of the object, but simply with
the relative bearing of the representative
powers so far as determined by a representation.

Now this relation, present when an object is characterized as beautiful, is coupled
with the feeling of pleasure. This pleasure
is by the judgement of taste pronounced
valid for every one; hence an agreeableness
attending the representation is just as incapable of containing the determining ground
of the judgement as the representation of
the perfection of the object or the concept
of the good. We are thus left with the subjective finality in the representation of an
object, exclusive of any end (objective or
subjective)—consequently the bare form of
finality in the representation whereby an
object is *given* to us, so far as we are conscious of it—as that which is alone capable
of constituting the delight which, apart
from any concept, we estimate as universally communicable, and so of forming the
determining ground of the judgement of
taste. . . .

13. *The pure judgement of taste is independent of charm and emotion.* Every
interest vitiates the judgement of taste and
robs it of its impartiality. This is especially
so where instead of, like the interest of reason, making finality take the lead of the
feeling of pleasure, it grounds it upon this
feeling—which is what always happens in
aesthetic judgements upon anything so far
as it gratifies or pains. Hence judgements
so influenced can either lay no claim at all
to a universally valid delight, or else must
abate their claim in proportion as sensations

of the kind in question enter into the determining grounds of taste. Taste that requires an added element of *charm* and *emotion* for its delight, not to speak of adopting this as the measure of its approval, has not yet emerged from barbarism. . . .

A judgement of taste which is uninfluenced by charm or emotion (though these may be associated with the delight in the beautiful), and whose determining ground, therefore, is simply finality of form, is *a pure judgement of taste*.

14. *Exemplification.* Aesthetic, just like theoretical (logical) judgements, are divisible into empirical and pure. The first are those by which agreeableness or disagreeableness, the second those by which beauty, is predicated of an object or its mode of representation. The former are judgements of sense (material aesthetic judgements), the latter (as formal) alone judgements of taste proper.

A judgement of taste, therefore, is only pure so far as its determining ground is tainted with no merely empirical delight. But such a taint is always present where charm or emotion have a share in the judgement by which something is to be described as beautiful.

Here now there is a recrudescence of a number of specious pleas that go the length of putting forward the case that charm is not merely a necessary ingredient of beauty, but is even of itself sufficient to merit the name of beautiful. A mere colour . . . or a mere tone is described by most people as in itself beautiful, notwithstanding the fact that both seem to depend merely on the matter of the representations—in other words, simply on sensation, which only entitles them to be called agreeable. But it will at the same time be observed that sensations of colour as well as of tone are only entitled to be immediately regarded as beautiful where, in either case, they are *pure*. This is a determination which at once goes to their form, and it is the only one which these representations possess that admits

with certainty of being universally communicated. For it is not to be assumed that even the quality of the sensations agrees in all Subjects, and we can hardly take it for granted that the agreeableness of a colour, or of the tone of a musical instrument, which we judge to be preferable to that of another, is given a like preference in the estimate of every one. . . .

But as for the beauty ascribed to the object on account of its form, and the supposition that it is capable of being enhanced by charm, this is a common error and one very prejudicial to genuine, uncorrupted, sincere taste. Nevertheless charms may be added to beauty to lend to the mind, beyond a bare delight, an adventitious interest in the representation of the object, and thus to advocate taste and its cultivation. This applies especially where taste is as yet crude and untrained. But they are positively subversive of the judgement of taste, if allowed to obtrude themselves as grounds of estimating beauty. . . .

In painting, sculpture, and in fact in all the formative arts, in architecture and horticulture, so far as fine arts, the *design* is what is essential. Here it is not what gratifies in sensation but merely what pleases by its form, that is the fundamental prerequisite for taste. The colours which give brilliancy to the sketch are part of the charm. They may no doubt, in their own way, enliven the object for sensation, but make it really worth looking at and beautiful they cannot. Indeed, more often than not the requirements of the beautiful form restrict them to a very narrow compass, and, even where charm is admitted, it is only this form that gives them a place of honour.

All form of objects of sense (both of external and also, mediately, of internal sense) is either *figure* or *play*. In the latter case it is either play of figures (in space: mimic and dance), or mere play of sensations (in time). The *charm* of colours, or of the agreeable tones of instruments, may be added: but the *design* in the former and the *composition* in the latter constitute the proper object of the pure judgement of taste. To say that the purity alike of colours and of tones, or their variety and contrast, seem to contribute to beauty, is by no means to imply that, because in themselves agreeable, they therefore yield an addition to the delight in the form and one on a par with it. The real meaning rather is that they make this form more clearly, definitely, and completely intuitable, and besides stimulate the representation by their charm, as they excite and sustain the attention directed to the object itself. . . .

Emotion—a sensation where an agreeable feeling is produced merely by means of a momentary check followed by a more powerful outpouring of the vital force—is quite foreign to beauty. Sublimity (with which the feeling of emotion is connected) requires, however, a different standard of estimation from that relied upon by taste. A pure judgement of taste has, then, for its determining ground neither charm nor emotion, in a word, no sensation as matter of the aesthetic judgement.

15. *The judgement of taste is entirely independent of the concept of perfection.* Objective finality can only be cognized by means of a reference of the manifold to a definite end, and hence only through a concept. This alone makes it clear that the beautiful, which is estimated on the ground of a mere formal finality, i.e. a finality apart from an end, is wholly independent of the representation of the good. For the latter presupposes an objective finality, i.e. the reference of the object to a definite end.

Objective finality is either external, i.e. the *utility,* or internal, i.e. the *perfection,* of the object. That the delight in an object on account of which we call it beautiful is incapable of resting on the representation of its utility, is abundantly evident from the two preceding articles; for in that case, it would not be an immediate delight in the object, which latter is the essential condition of the judgement upon beauty. But in an objective, internal finality, i.e. perfection, we have what is more akin to the predicate of beauty, and so this has been held even by philosophers of reputation to be convertible with beauty, though subject to the qualification: *where it is thought in a confused way.* In a Critique of taste it is of the utmost importance to decide whether beauty is really reducible to the concept of perfection.

For estimating objective finality we always require the concept of an end, and, where such finality has to be, not an external one (utility), but an internal one, the concept of an internal end containing the ground of the internal possibility of the object. Now an end is in general that, the *concept* of which may be regarded as the ground of the possibility of the object itself. So in order to represent an objective finality in a thing we must first have a concept of *what sort of a thing it is to be.* The agreement of the manifold in a thing with this concept (which supplies the rule of its synthesis) is the *qualitative perfection* of the thing. *Quantitative* perfection is entirely distinct from this. It consists in the completeness of anything after its kind, and is a mere concept of quantity (of totality). . . . What is formal in the representation of a thing, i.e. the agreement of its manifold with a unity (i.e. irrespective of what it is to be) does not, of itself, afford us any cognition whatsoever of objective finality. For since abstraction is made from this unity as *end* (what the thing is to be) nothing is left but the subjective finality of the representations in the mind of the Subject intuiting. This gives a certain finality of the representative state of the Subject, in which the Subject feels itself quite at home in its effort to grasp a given form in the imagination, but no perfection of any Object, the latter not being here thought through any concept. . . . To suppose a formal *objective* finality that is yet devoid of an end, i.e. the mere form of a *perfection* (apart from any matter or *concept* of that to which the agreement relates, even though there was the mere general idea of a conformity to law) is a veritable contradiction.

Now the judgement of taste is an aesthetic judgement, i.e. one resting on subjective grounds. No concept can be its determining ground, and hence not one of a definite end. Beauty, therefore, as a formal subjective finality, involves no thought whatsoever of a perfection of the object, as a would-be formal finality which yet, for all that, is objective: and the distinction between the concepts of the beautiful and the good, which represents both as differing only in their logical form, the first being merely a confused, the second a clearly defined, concept of perfection, while otherwise alike in content and origin, all goes for nothing: for then there would be no *specific* difference between them, but the judgement of taste would be just as much a cognitive judgement as one by which something is described as good. . . . But I have already stated that an aesthetic judgement is quite unique, and affords absolutely no (not even a confused), knowledge of the Object. It is only through a logical judgement that we get knowledge. The aesthetic judgement, on the other hand, refers the representation, by which an Object is given, solely to the Subject, and brings to our notice no quality of the object, but only the final form in the determination of the powers of representation engaged upon it. The judgement is called aesthetic for the very reason that its determining ground cannot be a concept, but is rather the feeling (of the internal sense) of the concert in the play of the mental powers as a thing only capable of being felt. If, on the other hand, confused concepts, and the objective judgement based on them, are going to be called aesthetic, we shall find ourselves with an understanding judging by sense, or a sense representing its objects by concepts—a mere choice of contradictions. The faculty of concepts, be they confused or be they

clear, is understanding; and although understanding has (as in all judgements) its role in the judgement of taste, as an aesthetic judgement, its role there is not that of a faculty for cognizing an object, but of a faculty for determining that judgement and its representation (without a concept) according to its relation to the Subject and its internal feeling, and for doing so in so far as that judgement is possible according to a universal rule.

16. *A judgement of taste by which an object is described as beautiful under the condition of a definite concept is not pure.* There are two kinds of beauty: free beauty (*pulchritudo vaga*), or beauty which is merely dependent (*pulchritudo adhaerens*). The first presupposes no concept of what the object should be; the second does presuppose such a concept and, with it, an answering perfection of the object. Those of the first kind are said to be (self-subsisting) beauties of this thing or that thing; the other kind of beauty, being attached to a concept (conditioned beauty), is ascribed to Objects which come under the concept of a particular end.

Flowers are free beauties of nature. Hardly any one but a botanist knows the true nature of a flower, and even he, while recognizing in the flower the reproductive organ of the plant, pays no attention to this natural end when using his taste to judge of its beauty. Hence no perfection of any kind—no internal finality, as something to which the arrangement of the manifold is related—underlies this judgement. Many birds . . . and a number of crustacea, are self-subsisting beauties which are not appurtenant to any object defined with respect to its end, but please freely and on their own account. So designs *à la grecque*, foliage for framework or on wall-papers, etc., have no intrinsic meaning; they represent nothing—no Object under a definite concept—and are free beauties. We may also rank in the same class what in music are called fantasias (without a theme), and, indeed, all music that is not set to words.

In the estimate of a free beauty (according to mere form) we have the pure judgement of taste. No concept is here presupposed of any end for which the manifold should serve the given Object, and which the latter, therefore, should represent—an incumbrance which would only restrict the freedom of the imagination that, as it were, is at play in the contemplation of the outward form.

But the beauty of man . . . the beauty of a horse, or of a building . . . presupposes a concept of the end that defines what the thing has to be, and consequently a concept of its perfection; and is therefore merely appendant beauty. Now, just as it is a clog on the purity of the judgement of taste to have the agreeable (of sensation) joined with beauty to which properly only the form is relevant, so to combine the good with beauty (the good, namely, of the manifold to the thing itself according to its end), mars its purity. . . .

Now the delight in the manifold of a thing, in reference to the internal end that determines its possibility, is a delight based on a concept, whereas delight in the beautiful is such as does not presuppose any concept, but is immediately coupled with the representation through which the object is given (not through which it is thought). If, now, the judgement of taste in respect of the latter delight is made dependent upon the end involved in the former delight as a judgement of reason, and is thus placed under a restriction, then it is no longer a free and pure judgement of taste.

Taste, it is true, stands to gain by this combination of intellectual delight with the aesthetic. For it becomes fixed, and, while not universal, it enables rules to be prescribed for it in respect of certain definite final Objects. But these rules are then not rules of taste, but merely rules for establishing a union of taste with reason, i.e. of the beautiful with the good—rules by which the former becomes available as an inten-

tional instrument in respect of the latter, for the purpose of bringing that temper of the mind which is self-sustaining and of subjective universal validity to the support and maintenance of that mode of thought which, while possessing objective universal validity, can only be preserved by a resolute effort. But, strictly speaking, perfection neither gains by beauty, nor beauty by perfection. The truth is rather this, when we compare the representation through which an object is given to us with the Object (in respect of what it is meant to be) by means of a concept, we cannot help reviewing it also in respect of the sensation in the Subject. Hence there results a gain to the *entire faculty* of our representative power when harmony prevails between both states of mind. . . .

17. *The Ideal of beauty*. There can be no objective rule of taste by which what is beautiful may be defined by means of concepts. For every judgement from that source is aesthetic, i.e. its determining ground is the feeling of the Subject, and not any concept of an Object. . . . But in the universal communicability of the sensation (of delight or aversion) . . . in the accord, so far as possible, of all ages and nations as to this feeling in the representation of certain objects, we have the empirical criterion, weak indeed and scarce sufficient to raise a presumption, of the derivation of a taste, thus confirmed by examples, from grounds deep-seated and shared alike by all men, underlying their agreement in estimating the forms under which objects are given to them.

For this reason some products of taste are looked on as *exemplary*—not meaning thereby that by imitating others taste may be acquired. For taste must be an original faculty; whereas one who imitates a model, while showing skill commensurate with his success, only displays taste as himself a critic of this model. Hence it follows that the highest model, the archetype of taste, is a mere idea, which each person must beget in his own consciousness, and according to which he must form his estimate of everything that is an Object of taste, or that is an example of critical taste, and even of universal taste itself. Properly speaking, an *idea* signifies a concept of reason, and an *ideal* the representation of an individual existence as adequate to an idea. Hence this archetype of taste . . . may more appropriately be called the ideal of the beautiful. While not having this ideal in our possession, we still strive to beget it within us. But it is bound to be merely an <u>ideal of the imagination</u>, seeing that it rests, not upon concepts, but upon the presentation—the faculty of presentation being the imagination.—Now, how do we arrive at such an ideal of beauty? Is it *a priori* or empirically? Further, what species of the beautiful admits of an ideal?

First of all, we do well to observe that the beauty for which an ideal has to be sought cannot be a beauty that is *free and at large,* but must be one fixed by a concept of objective finality. Hence it cannot belong to the Object of an altogether pure judgement of taste, but must attach to one that is partly intellectual. In other words, where an ideal is to have place among the grounds upon which any estimate is formed, then beneath grounds of that kind there must lie some idea of reason according to determinate concepts, by which the end underlying the internal possibility of the object is determined *a priori*. An ideal of beautiful flowers . . . or of a beautiful view, is unthinkable. But, it may also be impossible to represent an ideal of a beauty dependent on definite ends, e.g. a beautiful residence, a beautiful tree, a beautiful garden, etc., presumably because their ends are not sufficiently defined and fixed by their concept, with the result that their finality is nearly as free as with beauty that is quite *at large.* Only what has in itself the end of its real existence—only *man* that is able himself to determine his ends by reason, or, where he has to derive them from external percep-

tion, can still compare them with essential and universal ends, and then further pronounce aesthetically upon their accord with such ends, only he, among all objects in the world, admits, therefore, of an ideal of *beauty,* just as humanity in his person, as intelligence, alone admits of the ideal of *perfection.*

Two factors are here involved. *First,* there is the aesthetic *normal idea,* which is an individual intuition (of the imagination). This represents the norm by which we judge of a man as a member of a particular animal species. *Secondly,* there is the *rational idea.* This deals with the ends of humanity so far as capable of sensuous representation, and converts them into a principle for estimating his outward form, through which these ends are revealed in their phenomenal effect. The normal idea must draw from experience the constituents which it requires for the form of an animal of a particular kind. But the greatest finality in the construction of this form—that which would serve as a universal norm for forming an estimate of each individual of the species in question—the image that, as it were, forms an intentional basis underlying the technic of nature, to which no separate individual, but only the race as a whole, is adequate, has its seat merely in the idea of the judging Subject. Yet it is, with all its proportions, an aesthetic idea, and, as such, capable of being fully presented *in concreto* in a model image. Now, how is this effected? In order to render the process to some extent intelligible . . . let us attempt a psychological explanation.

It is of note that the imagination . . . is able on occasion . . . not alone to recall the signs for concepts, but also to reproduce the image and shape of an object out of a countless number of others of a different, or even of the very same, kind. And, further, if the mind is engaged upon comparisons, we may well suppose that it can in actual fact, though the process is unconscious, superimpose as it were one image upon another, and from the coincidence of a number of the same kind arrive at a mean contour which serves as a common standard for all. Say, for instance, a person has seen a thousand full-grown men. Now if he wishes to judge normal size determined upon a comparative estimate, then imagination . . . allows a great number of these images . . . to fall one upon the other, and . . . to extend to the case the analogy of optical presentation, in the space where they come most together, and within the contour where the place is illuminated by the greatest concentration of colour, one gets a perception of the *average size*, which alike in height and breadth is equally removed from the extreme limits of the greatest and smallest statures; and this is the stature of a beautiful man. . . . But the power of imagination does all this by means of a dynamical effect upon the organ of internal sense, arising from the frequent apprehension of such forms. If, again, for our average man we seek on similar lines for the average head, and for this the average nose, and so on, then we get the figure that underlies the normal idea of a beautiful man in the country where the comparison is instituted. . . . This *normal idea* is not derived from proportions taken from experience *as definite rules:* rather is it according to this idea that rules for forming estimates first become possible. It is an intermediate between all singular intuitions of individuals, with their manifold variations—a floating image for the whole genus, which nature has set as an archetype underlying those of her products that belong to the same species. . . . But the normal idea is far from giving the complete *archetype* of *beauty* in the genus. It only gives the form that constitutes the indispensable condition of all beauty, and, consequently, only *correctness* in the presentation of the genus. It is, as the famous *Doryphorus* of *Polycletus* was called, the *rule*. . . . It cannot, for that very reason, contain anything specifi-

cally characteristic; for otherwise it would not be the *normal idea* for the genus. Further, it is not by beauty that its presentation pleases, but merely because it does not contradict any of the conditions under which alone a thing belonging to this genus can be beautiful. The presentation is merely academically correct.

But the *ideal* of the beautiful is still something different from its *normal idea*. For reasons already stated it is only to be sought in the *human figure*. Here the ideal consists in the expression of the *moral*, apart from which the object would not please at once universally and positively (not merely negatively in a presentation academically correct). The visible expression of moral ideas that govern men inwardly can, of course, only be drawn from experience; but their combination with all that our reason connects with the morally good in the idea of the highest finality—benevolence, purity, strength, or equanimity, etc.—may be made, as it were, visible in bodily manifestation (as effect of what is internal), and this embodiment involves a union of pure ideas of reason and great imaginative power, in one who would even form an estimate of it, not to speak of being the author of its presentation. The correctness of such an ideal of beauty is evidenced by its not permitting any sensuous charm to mingle with the delight in its Object, in which it still allows us to take a great interest. This fact in turn shows that an estimate formed according to such a standard can never be purely aesthetic, and that one formed according to an ideal of beauty cannot be a simple judgement of taste.

DEFINITION OF THE BEAUTIFUL DERIVED FROM THIS THIRD MOMENT

Beauty is the form of *finality* in an object, so far as perceived in it *apart from the representation of an end*. *(purpose)*

purposiveness without purpose

FOURTH MOMENT

Of the Judgement of Taste: Moment of the Modality of the Delight in the Object

18. *Nature of the modality in a judgement of taste.* I may assert in the case of every representation that the synthesis of a pleasure with the representation (as a cognition) is at least *possible*. Of what I call *agreeable* I assert that it *actually* causes pleasure in me. But what we have in mind in the case of the *beautiful* is a *necessary* reference on its part to delight. However, this necessity is of a special kind. It is not a theoretical objective necessity—such as would let us cognize a priori that every one *will feel* this delight in the object that is called beautiful by me. Nor yet is it a practical necessity, in which case, thanks to concepts of a pure rational will in which free agents are supplied with a rule, this delight is the necessary consequence of an objective law, and simply means that one ought absolutely . . . to act in a certain way. Rather, being such a necessity as is thought in an aesthetic judgement, it can only be termed *exemplary*. In other words it is a necessity of the assent of *all* to a judgement regarded as exemplifying a universal rule incapable of formulation. Since an aesthetic judgement is not an objective or cognitive judgement, this necessity is not derivable from definite concepts, and so is not apodictic. Much less is it inferable from universality of experience. . . . For, apart from the fact that experience would hardly furnish evidences sufficiently numerous for this purpose, empirical judgements do not afford any foundation for a concept of the necessity of these judgements.

19. *The subjective necessity attributed to a judgement of taste is conditioned.* The judgement of taste exacts agreement from every one; and a person who describes something as beautiful insists that every one *ought* to give the object in question his approval and follow suit in describing it as beautiful. The *ought* in aesthetic judgements, therefore, despite an accordance with all the requisite data for passing judgement, is still only pronounced conditionally. We are suitors for agreement from every one else, because we are fortified with a ground common to all. Further, we would be able to count on this agreement, provided we were always assured of the correct subsumption of the case under that ground as the rule of approval.

20. *The condition of the necessity advanced by a judgement of taste is the idea of a common sense.* Were judgements of taste (like cognitive judgements) in possession of a definite objective principle, then one who in his judgement followed such a principle would claim unconditioned necessity for it. Again, were they devoid of any principle, as are those of the mere taste of sense, then no thought of any necessity on their part would enter one's head. Therefore they must have a subjective principle, and one which determines what pleases or displeases, by means of feeling only and not through concepts, but yet with universal validity. Such a principle, however, could only be regarded as a *common sense*. This differs essentially from common understanding, which is also sometimes called common sense (*sensus communis*): for the judgement of the latter is not one by feeling, but always one by concepts, though usually only in the shape of obscurely represented principles.

The judgement of taste, therefore, depends on our presupposing the existence of a common sense. (But this is not to be taken to mean some external sense, but the effect arising from the free play of our powers of cognition.) Only under the presupposition, I repeat, of such a common sense, are we able to lay down a judgement of taste.

21. *Have we reason for presupposing a common sense?* Cognitions and judgements

must, together with their attendant conviction, admit of being universally communicated; for otherwise a correspondence with the Object would not be due to them. They would be a conglomerate constituting a mere subjective play of the powers of representation, just as scepticism would have it. But if cognitions are to admit of communication, then our mental state, i.e. the way the cognitive powers are attuned for cognition generally, and, in fact, the relative proportion suitable for a representation (by which an object is given to us) from which cognition is to result, must also admit of being universally communicated, as, without this, which is the subjective condition of the act of knowing, knowledge, as an effect, would not arise. And this is always what actually happens where a given object, through the intervention of sense, sets the imagination at work in arranging the manifold, and the imagination, in turn, the understanding in giving to this arrangement the unity of concepts. But this disposition of the cognitive powers has a relative proportion differing with the diversity of the Objects that are given. However, there must be one in which this internal ratio suitable for quickening (one faculty by the other) is best adapted for both mental powers in respect of cognition . . . generally; and this disposition can only be determined through feeling (and not by concepts). Since, now, this disposition itself must admit of being universally communicated, and hence also the feeling of it (in the case of a given representation), while again, the universal communicability of a feeling presupposes a common sense: it follows that our assumption of it is well founded. And here, too, we do not have to take our stand on psychological observations, but we assume a common sense as the necessary condition of the universal communicability of our knowledge, which is presupposed in every logic and every principle of knowledge that is not one of scepticism.

22. *The necessity of the universal assent that is thought in a judgement of taste, is a subjective necessity which, under the presupposition of a common sense, is represented as objective.* In all judgements by which we describe anything as beautiful we tolerate no one else being of a different opinion, and in taking up this position we do not rest our judgement upon concepts, but only on our feeling. Accordingly we introduce this fundamental feeling not as a private feeling, but as a public sense. Now, for this purpose, experience cannot be made the ground of this common sense, for the latter is invoked to justify judgements containing an "ought." The assertion is not that every one *will* fall in with our judgement, but rather that every one *ought* to agree with it. Here I put forward my judgement of taste as an example of the judgement of common sense, and attribute to it on that account *exemplary* validity. Hence common sense is a mere ideal norm. With this as presupposition, a judgement that accords with it, as well as the delight in an Object expressed in that judgement, is rightly converted into a rule for every one. For the principle, while it is only subjective, being yet assumed as subjectively universal (a necessary idea for every one), could, in what concerns the consensus of different judging Subjects, demand universal assent like an objective principle, provided we were assured of our subsumption under it being correct.

This indeterminate norm of a common sense is, as a matter of fact, presupposed by us; as is shown by our presuming to lay down judgements of taste. But does such a common sense in fact exist as a constitutive principle of the possibility of experience, or is it formed for us as a regulative principle by a still higher principle of reason, that for higher ends first seeks to beget in us a common sense? Is taste, in other words, a natural and original faculty, or is it only the idea of one that is artificial and to be acquired by us, so that a judgement of taste, with its demand for universal assent, is but a requirement of reason for generating such a con*sensus,* and does the "ought," i.e. the objective necessity of the coincidence of the feeling of all with the particular feeling of each, only betoken the possibility of arriving at some sort of unanimity in these matters, and the judgement of taste only adduce an example of the application of this principle? These are questions which as yet we are neither willing nor in a position to investigate. . . .

DEFINITION OF THE BEAUTIFUL

DRAWN FROM THE

FOURTH MOMENT

The beautiful is that which, apart from a concept, is cognized as object of a *necessary* delight.

GENERAL REMARK ON THE

FIRST SECTION OF

THE ANALYTIC

The result to be extracted from the foregoing analysis is in effect this: that everything runs up into the concept of taste as a critical faculty by which an object is estimated in reference to the *free conformity to law* of the imagination. If, now, imagination must in the judgement of taste be regarded in its freedom, then, to begin with, it is not taken as reproductive, as in its subjection to the laws of association, but as productive and exerting an activity of its own (as originator of arbitrary forms of possible intuitions). And although in the apprehension of a given object of sense it is tied down to a definite form of this Object and, to that extent, does not enjoy free play (as it does in poetry), still it is easy to conceive that the object may supply readymade to the imagination just such a form of the arrangement of the manifold, as the imagination, if it were left to itself, would freely project in harmony with the general *conformity to law of the understanding.* But that the *imagination* should be both *free* and *of itself conformable to law,* i.e. carry autonomy with it, is a contradiction.

The understanding alone gives the law. Where, however, the imagination is compelled to follow a course laid down by a definite law, then what the form of the product is to be is determined by concepts; but, in that case, as already shown, the delight is not delight in the beautiful, but in the good (in perfection, though it be no more than formal perfection), and the judgement is not one due to taste. Hence it is only a conformity to law without a law, and a subjective harmonizing of the imagination and the understanding without an objective one . . . that can consist with the free conformity to law of the understanding (which has also been called finality apart from an end) and with the specific character of a judgement of taste. . . .

ANALYTIC OF THE SUBLIME

23. *Transition from the faculty of estimating the beautiful to that of estimating the sublime.* The beautiful and the sublime agree on the point of pleasing on their own account. Further they agree in not presupposing either a judgement of sense or one logically determinant, but one of reflection. Hence it follows that the delight does not depend upon a sensation, as with the agreeable, nor upon a definite concept, as does the delight in the good, although it has, for all that, an indeterminate reference to concepts. Consequently the delight is connected with the mere presentation or faculty of presentation, and is thus taken to express the accord, in a given intuition, of the faculty of presentation, or the imagination, with the *faculty of concepts* that belongs to understanding or reason, in the sense of the former assisting the latter. Hence both kinds of judgements are *singular,* and yet such as profess to be universally valid in respect of every Subject, despite the fact that their claims are directed merely to the feeling of pleasure and not to any knowledge of the object.

There are, however, also important and striking differences between the two. The beautiful in nature is a question of the form of the object, and this consists in limitation, whereas the sublime is to be found in an object even devoid of form, so far as it immediately involves, or else by its presence provokes, a representation of *limitlessness*, yet with a superadded thought of its totality. Accordingly the beautiful seems to be regarded as a presentation of an indeterminate concept of understanding, the sublime as a presentation of an indeterminate concept of reason. Hence the delight is in the former case coupled with the representation of *Quality*, but in this case with that of *Quantity*. Moreover, the former delight is very different from the latter in kind. For the beautiful is directly attended with a feeling of the furtherance of life, and is thus compatible with charms and a playful imagination. On the other hand, the feeling of the sublime is a pleasure that only arises indirectly, being brought about by the feeling of a momentary check to the vital forces followed at once by a discharge all the more powerful, and so it is an emotion that seems to be no sport, but dead earnest in the affairs of the imagination. Hence charms are repugnant to it; and, since the mind is not simply attracted by the object, but is also alternately repelled thereby, the delight in the sublime does not so much involve positive pleasure as admiration or respect, i.e. merits the name of a negative pleasure.

But the most important and vital distinction between the sublime and the beautiful is certainly this: that if, as is allowable, we here confine our attention in the first instance to the sublime in Objects of nature (that of art being always restricted by the conditions of an agreement with nature), we observe that whereas natural beauty (such as is self-subsisting) conveys a finality in its form making the object appear, as it were, pre-adapted to our power of judgement, so that it thus forms of itself an object of our delight, that which . . . simply in our apprehension of it, excites the feeling of the sublime, may appear, indeed, in point of form to contravene the ends of our power of judgement, to be ill-adapted to our faculty of presentation, and to be, as it were, an outrage on the imagination, and yet it is judged all the more sublime on that account.

From this it may be seen at once that we express ourselves on the whole inaccurately if we term any *Object of nature* sublime, although we may with perfect propriety call many such objects beautiful. For how can that which is apprehended as inherently contra-final be noted with an expression of approval? All that we can say is that the object lends itself to the presentation of a sublimity discoverable in the mind. For the sublime, in the strict sense of the word, cannot be contained in any sensuous form, but rather concerns ideas of reason, which, although no adequate presentation of them is possible, may be excited and called into the mind by that very inadequacy itself which does admit of sensuous presentation. Thus the broad ocean agitated by storms cannot be called sublime. Its aspect is horrible, and one must have stored one's mind in advance with a rich stock of ideas, if such an intuition is to raise it to the pitch of a feeling which is itself sublime—sublime because the mind has been incited to abandon sensibility, and employ itself upon ideas involving higher finality.

Self-subsisting natural beauty reveals to us a technic of nature which shows it in the light of a system ordered in accordance with laws the principle of which is not to be found within the range of our entire faculty of understanding. This principle is that of a finality relative to the employment of judgement in respect of phenomena which have thus to be assigned, not merely to nature regarded as aimless mechanism, but also to nature regarded after the analogy of art. Hence it gives a veritable extension, not, of course, to our knowledge of Objects of nature, but to our conception of nature itself—nature as mere mechanism being enlarged to the conception of nature as art—an extension inviting profound inquiries as to the possibility of such a form. But in what we are wont to call sublime in nature there is such an absence of anything leading to particular objective principles and corresponding forms of nature, that it is rather in its chaos, or in its wildest and most irregular disorder and desolation, provided it gives signs of magnitude and power, that nature chiefly excites the ideas of the sublime. Hence we see that the concept of the sublime in nature is far less important and rich in consequences than that of its beauty. It gives on the whole no indication of anything final in nature itself, but only in the possible *employment* of our intuitions of it in inducing a feeling in our own selves of a finality quite independent of nature. For the beautiful in nature we must seek a ground external to ourselves, but for the sublime one merely in ourselves and the attitude of mind that introduces sublimity into the representation of nature.

A. *The Mathematically Sublime*

25. *Definition of the term "sublime."* *Sublime* is the name given to what is *absolutely great.* But to be great and to be a magnitude are entirely different concepts (*magnitudo* and *quantitas*). In the same way to *assert without qualification* (*simpliciter*) that something is great, is quite a different thing from saying that it is *absolutely great* (*absolute, non comparative magnum*). The latter is *what is beyond all comparison great.* . . . Given a multiplicity of the homogeneous together constituting one thing, and we may at once cognize from the thing itself that it is a *magnitude* (*quantum*). No comparison with other things is required. But to determine *how great* it is always requires something else, which itself has magnitude, for its measure. Now, since in the estimate of magnitude we have to take into account not merely the multiplicity (number of units) but also the magnitude of the unit (the measure), and since the magnitude of this unit in turn

always requires something else as its measure and the standard of its comparison, . . . we see that the computation of the magnitude of phenomena is, in all cases, utterly incapable of affording us any absolute concept of a magnitude, and can, instead, only afford one that is always based on comparison.

If, now, I assert without qualification that anything is great, it would seem that I have nothing in the way of a comparison present to my mind, or at least nothing involving an objective measure, for no attempt is thus made to determine how great the object is. But, despite the standard of comparison being merely subjective, the claim of the judgement is none the less one to universal agreement; the judgements: "That man is beautiful" and "He is tall" do not purport to speak only for the judging Subject, but, like theoretical judgements, they demand the assent of every one.

Now in a judgement that without qualification describes anything as great, it is not merely meant that the object has a magnitude, but greatness is ascribed to it preeminently among many other objects of a like kind, yet without the extent of this preeminence being determined. Hence a standard is certainly laid at the basis of the judgement, which standard is presupposed to be one that can be taken as the same for every one, but which is available only for an aesthetic estimate of the greatness, and not for one that is logical (mathematically determined), for the standard is a merely subjective one underlying the reflective judgement upon the greatness. Furthermore, this standard may be empirical, as, let us say, the average size of the men known to us, . . . Or it may be a standard given *a priori,* which by reason of the imperfections of the judging Subject is restricted to subjective conditions of presentation *in concreto:* as, in the practical sphere, the greatness of a particular virtue, or of public liberty and justice in a country; or, in the theoretical sphere, the greatness of the accuracy or inaccuracy of an experiment or measurement, &c.

Here now, it is of note that, although we have no interest whatever in the Object, i.e. its real existence may be a matter of no concern to us, still its mere greatness, regarded even as devoid of form, is able to convey a universally communicable delight and so involve the consciousness of a subjective finality in the employment of our cognitive faculties, . . .

If (subject as above) we say of an object, without qualification, that it is great, this is not a mathematically determinant, but a mere reflective judgement upon its representation, which is subjectively final for a particular employment of our cognitive faculties in the estimation of magnitude, and we then always couple with the representation a kind of respect, just as we do a kind of contempt with what we call absolutely small. . . .

If, however, we call anything not alone great, but, without qualification, absolutely, and in every respect (beyond all comparison) great, that is to say, sublime, we soon perceive that for this it is not permissible to seek an appropriate standard outside itself, but merely in itself. It is a greatness comparable to itself alone. Hence it comes that the sublime is not to be looked for in the things of nature, but only in our own ideas. . . .

The above definition may also be expressed in this way: _that is sublime in comparison with which all else is small._ Here we readily see that nothing can be given in nature, no matter how great we may judge it to be, which regarded in some other relation, may not be degraded to the level of the infinitely little, and nothing so small which in comparison with some still smaller standard may not for our imagination be enlarged to the greatness of a world. Telescopes have put within our reach an abundance of material to go upon in making the first observation, and microscopes the same

in making the second. Nothing, therefore, which can be an object of the senses is to be termed sublime when treated on this footing. But precisely because there is a striving in our imagination towards progress _ad infinitum,_ while reason demands absolute totality, as a real idea, that same inability on the part of our faculty for the estimation of the magnitude of things of the world of sense to attain to this idea, is the awakening of a feeling of a supersensible faculty within us; and it is the use to which judgement naturally put particular objects on behalf of this latter feeling, and not the object of sense, that is absolutely great, and every other contrasted employment small. Consequently it is the disposition of soul evoked by a particular representation engaging the attention of the reflective judgement, and not the Object, that is to be called sublime.

The foregoing formulae defining the sublime may, therefore, be supplemented by yet another: _The sublime is that, the mere capacity of thinking which evidences a faculty of mind transcending every standard of sense._

26. _The estimation of the magnitude of natural things requisite for the idea of the sublime._ The estimation of magnitude by means of concepts of number . . . is mathematical, but that in mere intuition (by the eye) is aesthetic. Now we can only get definite concepts of _how great_ anything is by having recourse to numbers . . . , the unit being the measure; and to this extent all logical estimation of magnitude is mathematical. But, as the magnitude of the measure has to be assumed as a known quantity, if, to form an estimate of this, we must again have recourse to numbers involving another standard for their unit, and consequently must again proceed mathematically, we can never arrive at a first or fundamental measure, and so cannot get any definite concept of a given magnitude. The estimation of the magnitude of the

fundamental measure must, therefore, consist merely in the immediate grasp which we can get of it in intuition, and the use to which our imagination can put this in presenting the numerical concepts: i.e. all estimation of the magnitude of objects of nature is in the last resort aesthetic (i.e. subjectively and not objectively determined).

Now for the mathematical estimation of magnitude there is, of course, no greatest possible (for the power of numbers extends to infinity), but for the aesthetic estimation there certainly is, and of it I say that where it is considered an absolute measure beyond which no greater is possible subjectively (i.e. for the judging Subject), it then conveys the idea of the sublime, and calls forth that emotion which no mathematical estimation of magnitudes by numbers can evoke . . . : Because the latter presents only the relative magnitude due to comparison with others of a like kind, whereas the former presents magnitude absolutely, so far as the mind can grasp it in an intuition.

To take in a quantum intuitively in the imagination so as to be able to use it as a measure, or unit for estimating magnitude by numbers, involves two operations of this faculty: *apprehension* (*apprehensio*) and *comprehension* (*comprehensio aesthetica*). Apprehension presents no difficulty: for this process can be carried on *ad infinitum;* but with the advance of apprehension, comprehension becomes more difficult at every step and soon attains its maximum, and this is the aesthetically greatest fundamental measure for the estimation of magnitude. For if the apprehension has reached a point beyond which the representations of sensuous intuition in the case of the parts first apprehended begin to disappear from the imagination as this advances to the apprehension of yet others, as much, then, is lost at one end as is gained at the other, and for comprehension we get a maximum which the imagination cannot exceed. . . .

Since whatever is to be a source of pleasure, apart from interest, to the merely reflective judgement must involve in its representation subjective, and, as such, universally valid finality—though here, however, no finality of the *form* of the object underlies our estimate of it (as it does in the case of the beautiful)—the question arises, What is this subjective finality, and what enables it to be prescribed as a norm so as to yield a ground for universally valid delight in the mere estimation of magnitude, and that, too, in a case where it is pushed to the point at which our faculty of imagination breaks down in presenting the concept of a magnitude, and proves unequal to its task?

In the successive aggregation of units requisite for the representation of magnitudes the imagination of itself advances *ad infinitum* without let or hindrance—understanding, however, conducting it by means of concepts of number for which the former must supply the schema. This procedure belongs to the logical estimation of magnitude, and as such, is doubtless something objectively final according to the concept of an end (as all measurement is), but it is not anything which for the aesthetic judgement is final or pleasing. Further, in this intentional finality there is nothing compelling us to tax the utmost powers of the imagination, and drive it as far as ever it can reach in its presentations, so as to enlarge the size of the measure, and thus make the single intuition holding the many in one (the *comprehension*) as great as possible. . . . In this mathematical estimation of magnitude understanding is as well served and as satisfied whether imagination selects for the unit a magnitude which one can take in at a glance, e.g. a foot, . . . , or else a German mile, or even the earth's diameter, the apprehension of which is indeed possible, but not its comprehension in an intuition of the imagination (i.e. it is not possible by means of a *comprehensio aesthetica,* though quite so by means of a *comprehensio logica* in a numerical concept). In each case the logical estimation of magnitude advances *ad infinitum* with nothing to stop it.

The mind, however, hearkens now to the voice of reason, which for all given magnitudes—even for those which can never be completely apprehended, though (in sensuous representation) estimated as completely given—requires totality, and consequently comprehension in *one* intuition, and which calls for a *presentation* answering to all the above members of a progressively increasing numerical series, and does not exempt even the infinite (space and time past) from this requirement, but rather renders it inevitable for us to regard this infinite (in the judgement of common reason) as *completely given* (i.e. given in its totality).

But the infinite is absolutely . . . great. In comparison with this all else (in the way of magnitudes of the same order) is small. But the point of capital importance is that the mere ability even to think it as *a whole* indicates a faculty of mind transcending every standard of sense. For the latter would entail a comprehension yielding as unit a standard bearing to the infinite a definite ratio expressible in numbers, which is impossible. Still the *mere ability even to think* the given infinite without contradiction, is something that requires the presence in the human mind of a faculty and its idea of a noumenon, which latter, while not itself admitting of any intuition, is yet introduced as substrate underlying the intuition of the world as mere phenomenon, that the infinite of the world of sense, in the pure intellectual estimation of magnitude, is *completely* comprehended *under* a concept, although in the mathematical estimation *by means of numerical concepts* it can never be completely thought. Even a faculty enabling the infinite of supersensible intuition to be regarded as given (in its intelligible substrate), tran-

scends every standard of sensibility, and is great beyond all comparison even with the faculty of mathematical estimation: . . .

Nature, therefore, is sublime in such of its phenomena as in their intuition convey the idea of their infinity. But this can only occur through the inadequacy of even the greatest effort of our imagination in the estimation of the magnitude of an object. But, now, in the case of the mathematical estimation of magnitude imagination is quite competent to supply a measure equal to the requirements of any object. For the numerical concepts of the understanding can by progressive synthesis make any measure adequate to any given magnitude. Hence it must be the *aesthetic* estimation of magnitude in which we get at once a feeling of the effort towards a comprehension that exceeds the faculty of imagination for mentally grasping the progressive apprehension in a whole of intuition, and, with it, a perception of the inadequacy of this faculty . . . for taking in and using for the estimation of magnitude a fundamental measure that understanding could turn to account without the least trouble. Now the proper unchangeable fundamental measure of nature is its absolute whole, which, with it, regarded as a phenomenon, means infinity comprehended. But, since this fundamental measure is a self-contradictory concept (owing to the impossibility of the absolute totality of an endless progression), it follows that where the size of a natural Object is such that the imagination spends its whole faculty of comprehension upon it in vain, it must carry our concept of nature to a supersensible substrate (underlying both nature and our faculty of thought) which is great beyond every standard of sense. Thus, instead of the object, it is rather the cast of the mind in appreciating it that we have to estimate as *sublime*.

Therefore, just as the aesthetic judgement in its estimate of the beautiful refers the imagination in its free play to the *understanding*, to bring out its agreement with the *concepts* of the latter in general (apart from their determination): so in its estimate of a thing as sublime it refers that faculty to *reason* to bring out its subjective accord with *ideas* of reason (indeterminately indicated), i.e. to induce a temper of mind conformable to that which the influence of definite (practical) ideas would produce upon feeling, and in common accord with it.

This makes it evident that true sublimity must be sought only in the mind of the judging Subject, and not in the Object of nature that occasions this attitude by the estimate formed of it. Who would apply the term "sublime" even to shapeless mountain masses towering one above the other in wild disorder, with their pyramids of ice, or to the dark tempestuous ocean, or such like things? But in the contemplation of them, without any regard to their form, the mind abandons itself to the imagination and to a reason placed, though quite apart from any definite end, in conjunction therewith, and merely broadening its view, and it feels itself elevated in its own estimate of itself on finding all the might of imagination still unequal to its ideas. . . .

27. Quality of the delight in our estimate of the sublime. The feeling of our incapacity to attain to an idea *that is a law for us*, is RESPECT. Now the idea of the comprehension of any phenomenon whatever, that may be given us, in a whole of intuition, is an idea imposed upon us by a law of reason, which recognizes no definite, universally valid and unchangeable measure except the absolute whole. But our imagination, even when taxing itself to the uttermost on the score of this required comprehension of a given object in a whole of intuition (and so with a view to the presentation of the idea of reason), betrays its limits and its inadequacy, but still, at the same time, its proper vocation of making itself adequate to the same as a law. Therefore the feeling of the sublime in nature is respect for our own vocation, which we

attribute to an Object of nature by a certain subreption (substitution of a respect for the Object in place of one for the idea of humanity in our own self—the Subject); and this feeling renders, as it were, intuitable the supremacy of our cognitive faculties on the rational side over the greatest faculty of sensibility.

The feeling of the sublime, is, therefore, at once a feeling of displeasure, arising from the inadequacy of imagination in the aesthetic estimation of magnitude to attain to its estimation by reason, and a simultaneously awakened pleasure, arising from this very judgement of the inadequacy of the greatest faculty of sense being in accord with ideas of reason, so far as the effort to attain to these is for us a law. It is, in other words, for us a law (of reason), which goes to make us what we are, that we should esteem as small in comparison with ideas of reason everything which for us is great in nature as an object of sense; and that which makes us alive to the feeling of this supersensible side of our being harmonizes with that law. Now the greatest effort of the imagination in the presentation of the unit for the estimation of magnitude involves in itself a reference to something *absolutely great,* consequently a reference also to the law of reason that this alone is to be adopted as the supreme measure of what is great. Therefore the inner perception of the inadequacy of every standard of sense to serve for the rational estimation of magnitude is a coming into accord with reason's laws, and a displeasure that makes us alive to the feeling of the supersensible side of our being, according to which it is final, and consequently a pleasure, to find every standard of sensibility falling short of the ideas of reason.

The mind feels itself *set in motion* in the representation of the sublime in nature; whereas in the aesthetic judgement upon what is beautiful therein it is in *restful* contemplation. This movement, especially in its inception, may be compared with a vi-

bration, i.e. with a rapidly alternating repulsion and attraction produced by one and the same Object. The point of excess for the imagination (towards which it is driven in the apprehension of the intuition) is like an abyss in which it fears to lose itself; yet again for the rational idea of the supersensible it is not excessive, but conformable to law, and directed to drawing out such an effort on the part of the imagination: and so in turn as much a source of attraction as it was repellent to mere sensibility. But the judgement itself all the while steadfastly preserves its aesthetic character, because it represents, without being grounded on any definite concept of the Object, merely the subjective play of the mental powers (imagination and reason) as harmonious by virtue of their very contrast. For just as in the estimate of the beautiful imagination and *understanding* by their concert generate subjective finality of the mental faculties, so imagination and *reason* do so here by their conflict—that is to say they induce a feeling of our possessing a pure and self-sufficient reason, or a faculty for the estimation of magnitude, whose preeminence can only be made intuitively evident by the inadequacy of that faculty which in the presentation of magnitudes (of objects of sense) is itself unbounded.
. . .

B. The Dynamically Sublime in Nature

28. *Nature as Might. Might* is a power which is superior to great hindrances. It is termed *dominion* if it is also superior to the resistance of that which itself possesses might. Nature considered in an aesthetic judgement as might that has no dominion over us, is *dynamically sublime*.

If we are to estimate nature as dynamically sublime, it must be represented as a source of fear (though the converse, that every object that is a source of fear is, in our aesthetic judgement, sublime, does not hold). For in forming an aesthetic estimate (no concept being present) the superiority

to hindrances can only be estimated according to the greatness of the resistance. Now that which we strive to resist is an evil, and, if we do not find our powers commensurate to the task, an object of fear. Hence the aesthetic judgement can only deem nature a might, and so dynamically sublime, in so far as it is looked upon as an object of fear.

But we may look upon an object as *fearful*, and yet not be afraid *of* it, if, that is, our estimate takes the form of our simply *picturing to ourselves* the case of our wishing to offer some resistance to it, and recognizing that all such resistance would be quite futile. So the righteous man fears God without being afraid of Him, . . .

Bold, overhanging, and, as it were, threatening rocks, thunderclouds piled up the vault of heaven, borne along with flashes and peals, volcanoes in all their violence of destruction, hurricanes leaving desolation in their track, the boundless ocean rising with rebellious force, the high waterfall of some mighty river, and the like, make our power of resistance of trifling moment in comparison with their might. But, provided our own position is secure, their aspect is all the more attractive for its fearfulness; and we readily call these objects sublime, because they raise the forces of the soul above the height of vulgar common place, and discover within us a power of resistance of quite another kind, which gives us courage to be able to measure ourselves against the seeming omnipotence of nature.

In the immeasurableness of nature and the incompetence of our faculty for adopting a standard proportionate to the aesthetic estimation of the magnitude of its *realm*, we found our own limitation. But with this we also found in our rational faculty another non-sensuous standard, one which has that infinity itself under it as unit, and in comparison with which everything in nature is small, and so found in our minds a preeminence over nature even in its immeasurability. Now in just the same way the irresistibility of the might of nature forces upon us the recognition of our physical helplessness as beings of nature, but at the same time reveals a faculty of estimating ourselves as independent of nature, and discovers a pre-eminence above nature that is the foundation of a self-preservation of quite another kind from that which may be assailed and brought into danger by external nature. This saves humanity in our own person from humiliation, even though as mortal men we have to submit to external violence. In this way external nature is not estimated in our aesthetic judgement as sublime so far as exciting fear, but rather because it challenges our power (one not of nature) to regard as small those things of which we are wont to be solicitous (worldly goods, health, and life), and hence to regard its might . . . as exercising over us and our personality no such rude dominion that we should bow down before it, once the question becomes one of our highest principles and of our asserting or forsaking them. Therefore nature is here called sublime merely because it raises the imagination to a presentation of those cases in which the mind can make itself sensible of the appropriate sublimity of the sphere of its own being, even above nature. . . .

29. *Modality of the judgement on the sublime in nature.* Beautiful nature contains countless things as to which we at once take every one as in their judgement concurring with our own, and as to which we may further expect this concurrence without facts finding us far astray. But in respect of our judgement upon the sublime in nature we cannot so easily vouch for ready acceptance by others. For a far higher degree of culture, not merely of the aesthetic judgement, but also of the faculties of cognition which lie at its basis, seems to be requisite to enable us to lay down a judgement upon this high distinction of natural objects.

The proper mental mood for a feeling of the sublime postulates the mind's susceptibility for ideas, since it is precisely in the failure of nature to attain to these—and consequently only under presupposition of this susceptibility and of the straining of the imagination to use nature as a schema for ideas—that there is something forbidding to sensibility, but which, for all that, has an attraction for us, arising from the fact of its being a dominion which reason exercises over sensibility with a view to extending it to the requirements of its own realm (the practical) and letting it look out beyond itself into the infinite, which for it is an abyss. In fact, without the development of moral ideas, that which, thanks to preparatory culture, we call sublime, merely strikes the untutored man as terrifying. . . .

But the fact that culture is requisite for the judgement upon the sublime in nature (more than for that upon the beautiful) does not involve its being an original product of culture and something introduced in a more or less conventional way into society. Rather is it in human nature that its foundations are laid, and, in fact, in that which, at once with common understanding, we may expect every one to possess and may require of him, namely, a native capacity for the feeling for (practical) ideas, i.e. for moral feeling.

This, now, is the foundation of the necessity of that agreement between other men's judgements upon the sublime and our own, which we make our own imply. For just as we taunt a man who is quite inappreciative when forming an estimate of an object of nature in which we see beauty, with want *of taste,* so we say of a man who remains unaffected in the presence of what we consider sublime, that he has no *feeling.* But we demand both taste and feeling of every man, and, granted some degree of culture, we give him credit for both. Still, we do so with this difference: that, in the case of the former, since judgement there refers the imagination merely to the understanding, as the faculty of concepts, we make the requirement as a matter of course, whereas in the case of the latter, since here the judgement refers the imagination to reason, as a faculty of ideas, we do so only under a subjective presupposition (which, however, we believe we are warranted in making), namely, that of the moral feeling in man. And, on this assumption, we attribute necessity to the latter aesthetic judgement also.

In this modality of aesthetic judgements, namely their assumed necessity, lies what is for the Critique of Judgement a moment of capital importance. For this is exactly what makes an *a priori* principle apparent in their case, and lifts them out of the sphere of empirical psychology, in which otherwise they would remain buried amid the feelings of gratification and pain (only with the senseless epithet of *finer* feeling), so as to place them, and, thanks to them, to place the faculty of judgement itself, in the class of judgements of which the basis of an *a priori* principle is the distinguishing feature, and, thus distinguished, to introduce them into transcendental philosophy. . . .

30. *Taste as a kind of* sensus communis. The name of sense is often given to judgement where what attracts attention is not so much its reflective act as merely its result. So we speak of a sense of truth, of a sense of propriety, or of justice, &c. And yet, of course, we know, or at least ought well enough to know, that a sense cannot be the true abode of these concepts, not to speak of its being competent, even in the slightest degree, to pronounce universal rules. On the contrary, we recognize that a representation of this kind, be it of truth, propriety, beauty, or justice, could never enter our thoughts were we not able to raise ourselves above the level of the senses to that of higher faculties of cognition. *Common human understanding* which, as mere sound (not yet cultivated) understanding, is looked upon as the least we can expect from any one claiming the name of man, has therefore the doubtful honour of having

the name of common sense (*sensus communis*) bestowed upon it; and bestowed, too, in an acceptation of the word *common* . . . which makes it amount to what is *vulgar*—what is everywhere to be met with—a quality which by no means confers credit or distinction upon its possessor.

However, by the name *sensus communis* is to be understood the idea of a *public* sense, i.e. a critical faculty which in its reflective act takes account (*a priori*) of the mode of representation of everyone else, in order, *as it were*, to weigh its judgement with the collective reason of mankind, and thereby avoid the illusion arising from subjective and personal conditions which could readily be taken for objective, an illusion that would exert a prejudicial influence upon its judgement. This is accomplished by weighing the judgement, not so much with actual, as rather with the merely possible, judgements of others, and by putting ourselves in the position of everyone else, as the result of a mere abstraction from the limitations which contingently affect our own estimate. This, in turn, is effected by so far as possible letting go the element of matter, i.e. sensation, in our general state of representative activity, and confining attention to the formal peculiarities of our representation or general state of representative activity. Now it may seem that this operation of reflection is too artificial to be attributed to the faculty which we call *common* sense. But this is an appearance due only to its expression in abstract formulae. In itself nothing is more natural than to abstract from charm and emotion where one is looking for a judgement intended to serve as a universal rule. . . .

. . . I say that taste can with more justice be called a *sensus communis* than can sound understanding; and that the aesthetic, rather than the intellectual, judgement can bear the name of a public sense, i.e. taking it that we are prepared to use the word "sense" of an effect that mere reflection has upon the mind; for then by sense we mean the feeling of pleasure. We might even define taste as the faculty of estimating what makes our feeling in a given representation *universally communicable* without the mediation of a concept.

The aptitude of men for communicating their thoughts requires, also, a relation between the imagination and the understanding, in order to connect intuitions with concepts, and concepts, in turn, with intuitions, which both unite in cognition. But there the agreement of both mental powers is *according to law,* and under the constraint of definite concepts. Only when the imagination in its freedom stirs the understanding, and the understanding apart from concepts puts the imagination into regular play, does the representation communicate itself not as thought, but as an internal feeling of a final state of the mind.

Taste is, therefore, the faculty of forming an *a priori* estimate of the communicability of the feelings that, without the mediation of a concept, are connected with a given representation.

Supposing, now, that we could assume that the mere universal communicability of our feeling must of itself carry with it an interest for us (an assumption, however, which we are not entitled to draw as a conclusion from the character of a merely reflective judgement), we should then be in a position to explain how the feeling in the judgement of taste comes to be exacted from every one as a sort of duty.

41. *The empirical interest in the beautiful.* Abundant proof has been given above to show that the judgement of taste by which something is declared beautiful must have no interest *as its determining ground.* But it does not follow from this that after it has once been posited as a pure aesthetic judgement, an interest cannot then enter into combination with it. This combination, however, can never be anything but indirect. Taste must, that is to say, first of all be represented in conjunction with something else, if the delight attending the mere reflection upon an object is to admit of having further conjoined with it *a pleasure in the real existence* of the object (as that wherein all interest consists). . . . Now this "something else" may be something empirical, such as an inclination proper to the nature of human beings, or it may be something intellectual, as a property of the will whereby it admits of rational determination *a priori.* Both of these involve a delight in the existence of the Object, and so can lay the foundation for an interest in what has already pleased of itself and without regard to any interest whatsoever.

The empirical interest in the beautiful exists only in *society.* And if we admit that the impulse to society is natural to mankind, and that the suitability for and the propensity towards it, i.e. *sociability,* is a property essential to the requirements of man as a creature intended for society, and one, therefore, that belongs to *humanity,* it is inevitable that we should also look upon taste in the light of a faculty for estimating whatever enables us to communicate even our *feeling* to every one else, and hence as a means of promoting that upon which the natural inclination of every one is set.

With no one to take into account but himself a man abandoned on a desert island would not adorn either himself or his hut, nor would he look for flowers, and still less plant them, with the object of providing himself with personal adornments. Only in society does it occur to him to be not merely a man, but a man refined after the manner of his kind (the beginning of civilization) —for that is the estimate formed of one who has the bent and turn for communicating his pleasure to others, and who is not quite satisfied with an Object unless his feeling of delight in it can be shared in communion with others. Further, a regard to universal communicability is a thing which everyone expects and requires from every one else, just as if it were part of an original compact dictated by humanity itself. And thus, no doubt, at first only charms, e.g. colours for painting oneself. . . , or flowers, sea-shells, beautifully coloured feathers, then, in the course of time, also beautiful forms . . . which convey no gratification, i.e. delight of enjoyment, become of moment in society and attract a considerable interest. Eventually, when civilization has reached its height it makes this work of communication almost the main business of refined inclination, and the entire value of sensations is placed in the degree to which they permit of universal communication. At this stage, then, even where the pleasure which each one has in an object is but insignificant and possesses of itself no conspicuous interest, still the idea of its universal communicability almost indefinitely augments its value.

This interest, indirectly attached to the beautiful by the inclination towards society, and consequently, empirical, is however, of no importance for us here. For that to which we have alone to look is what can have a bearing *a priori,* even though indirect, upon the judgement of taste. For, if even in this form an associated interest should betray itself, taste would then reveal a transition on the part of our critical faculty from the enjoyment of sense to the moral feeling. This would not merely mean that we should be supplied with a more effectual guide for the final employment of taste, but taste would further be presented as a link in the chain of the human faculties *a priori* upon which all legislation must depend. This much may certainly be said of the empirical interest in objects of taste, and in taste itself, that as taste thus pays homage to inclination, however refined, such interest will nevertheless readily fuse also with all inclinations and passions, which in society attain to their greatest variety and highest degree, and the interest in the beautiful, if this is made its ground, can but afford a very ambiguous transition from the agreeable to the good. We have reason, however, to inquire whether this

transition may not still in some way be furthered by means of taste when taken in its purity.

42. *The intellectual interest in the beautiful.* It has been with the best intentions that those who love to see in the ultimate end of humanity, namely the morally good, the goal of all activities to which men are impelled by the inner bent of their nature, have regarded it as a mark of a good moral character to take an interest in the beautiful generally. But they have . . . been contradicted by others who appeal to the fact of experience, that *virtuosi* in matters of taste, being not alone often, but one might say as a general rule, vain, capricious, and addicted to injurious passions, could perhaps more rarely than others lay claim to any pre-eminent attachment to moral principles. And so it would seem, not only that the feeling for the beautiful is specifically different from the moral feeling (which as a matter of fact is the case), but also that the interest which we may combine with it, will hardly consort with the moral, and certainly not on grounds of inner affinity.

Now I willingly admit that the interest in the *beautiful of art* . . . gives no evidence at all of a habit of mind attached to the morally good, or even inclined that way. But, on the other hand, I do maintain that to take an *immediate interest* in the beauty of *nature* (not merely to have taste in estimating it) is always a mark of a good soul; and that, where this interest is habitual, it is at least indicative of a temper of mind favourable to the moral feeling that it should readily associate itself with the *contemplation of nature*. It must, however, be borne in mind that I mean to refer strictly to the beautiful *forms* of nature, and to put to one side the *charms* which she is wont so lavishly to combine with them; because, though the interest in these is no doubt immediate, it is nevertheless empirical.

One who alone (and without any intention of communicating his observations to other) regards the beautiful form of a wild flower, a bird, an insect, or the like, out of admiration and love of them, and being loath to let them escape him in nature, even at the risk of some misadventure to himself —so far from there being any prospect of advantage to him—such a one takes an immediate, and in fact intellectual, interest in the beauty of nature. This means that he is not alone pleased with nature's product in respect of its form, but is also pleased at its existence, and is so without any charm of sense having a share in the matter, or without his associating with it any end whatsoever.

In this connexion, however, it is of note that were we to play a trick on our lover of the beautiful, and plant in the ground artificial flowers . . . , and perch artfully carved birds on the branches of trees, and he were to find out how he had been taken in, the immediate interest which these things previously had for him would at once vanish. . . . The fact is that our intuition and reflection must have as their concomitant the thought that the beauty in question is nature's handiwork; and this is the sole basis of the immediate interest that is taken in it. Failing this we are either left with a bare judgement of taste void of all interest whatever, or else only with one that is combined with an interest that is mediate, involving, namely, a reference to society; which latter affords no reliable indication of morally good habits of thought.

The superiority which natural beauty has over that of art, even where it is excelled by the latter in point of form, in yet being alone able to awaken an immediate interest, accords with the refined and well-grounded habits of thought of all men who have cultivated their moral feeling. If a man with taste enough to judge of works of fine art with the greatest correctness and refinement readily quits the room in which he meets with those beauties that minister to vanity or, at least, social joys, and be-

takes himself to the beautiful in nature, so that he may there find as it were a feast for his soul in a train of thought which he can never completely evolve, we will then regard this his choice even with veneration, and give him credit for a beautiful soul, to which no connoisseur or art collector can lay claim on the score of the interest which his objects have for him.—Here, now, are two kinds of Objects which in the judgement of mere taste could scarcely contend with one another for a superiority. What then, is the distinction that makes us hold them in such different esteem?

We have a faculty of judgement which is merely aesthetic—a faculty of judging of forms without the aid of concepts, and of finding, in the mere estimate of them, a delight that we at the same time make into a rule for everyone, without this judgement being founded on an interest, or yet producing one.—On the other hand we have also a faculty of intellectual judgement for the mere forms of practical maxims (so far as they are of themselves qualified for universal legislation)—a faculty of determining an *a priori* delight, which we make into a law for every one, without our judgement being founded on any interest, *though here it produces one*. The pleasure or displeasure in the former judgement is called that of taste; the latter is called that of the moral feeling.

But, now, reason is further interested in ideas (for which in our moral feeling it brings about an immediate interest) having also objective reality. That is to say, it is of interest to reason that nature should at least show a trace or give a hint that it contains in itself some ground or other for assuming a uniform accordance of its products with our wholly disinterested delight (a delight which we cognize *a priori* as a law for every one without being able to ground it upon proofs). That being so, reason must take an interest in every manifestation on the part of nature of some such accordance. Hence the mind cannot reflect on the beauty of *nature* without at the same time finding its interest engaged. But this interest is akin to the moral. One, then, who takes such an interest in the beautiful in nature can only do so in so far as he has previously set his interest deep in the foundations of the morally good. On these grounds we have reason for presuming the presence of at least the germ of a good moral disposition in the case of a man to whom the beauty of nature is a matter of immediate interest.

It will be said that this interpretation of aesthetic judgements on the basis of kinship with our moral feeling has far too studied an appearance to be accepted as the true construction of the cypher in which nature speaks to us figuratively in its beautiful forms. But, first of all, this immediate interest in the beauty of nature is not in fact common. It is peculiar to those whose habits of thought are already trained to the good or else are eminently susceptible of such training; and under these circumstances the analogy in which the pure judgement of taste that, without relying upon any interest, gives us a feeling of delight, and at the same time represents it *a priori* as proper to mankind in general, stands to the moral judgement that does just the same from concepts, is one which, without any clear, subtle, and deliberate reflection, conduces to a like immediate interest being taken in the objects of the former judgement as in those of the latter —with this one difference, that the interest in the first case is free, while in the latter it is one founded on objective laws. In addition to this there is our admiration of nature which in her beautiful products displays herself as art, not as mere matter of chance, but, as it were, designedly, according to a law-directed arrangement, and as finality apart from any end. As we never meet with such an end outside ourselves, we naturally look for it in ourselves, and, in fact, in that which constitutes the ultimate end of our existence—the moral side of our being. . . .

The fact that the delight in beautiful art does not, in the pure judgement of taste, involve an immediate interest, as does that in beautiful nature, may be readily explained. For the former is either such an imitation of the latter as goes the length of deceiving us, in which case it acts upon us in the character of a natural beauty, which we take it to be; or else it is an intentional art obviously directed to our delight. In the latter case, however, the delight in the product would, it is true, be brought about immediately by taste, but there would be nothing but a mediate interest in the cause that lay beneath—an interest, namely, in an art only capable of interesting by its end, and never in itself. It will, perhaps, be said that this is also the case where an Object of nature only interests by its beauty so far as a moral idea is brought into partnership therewith. But it is not the object that is of immediate interest, but rather the inherent character of the beauty qualifying it for such a partnership—a character, therefore, that belongs to the very essence of beauty.

The charms in natural beauty, which are to be found blended, as it were, so frequently with beauty of form, belong either to the modifications of light (in colouring) or of sound (in tones). For these are the only sensations which permit not merely of a feeling of the senses, but also of reflection upon the form of these modifications of sense, and so embody as it were a language in which nature speaks to us and which has the semblance of a higher meaning. . . .

43. *Art in general.* (1) *Art* is distinguished from *nature* as making (*facere*) from acting or operating in general (*agere*), and the product or the result of the former is distinguished from that of the latter as work (*opus*) from operation (*effectus*).

By right it is only production through freedom, i.e. through an act of will that places reason at the basis of its action, that should be termed art. For, although we are pleased to call what bees produce (their regularly constructed cells) a work of art, we only do so on the strength of an analogy with art; that is to say, as soon as we call to mind that no rational deliberation forms the basis of their labour, we say at once that it is a product of their nature (of instinct), and it is only to their Creator that we ascribe it as art.

If, as sometimes happens, in a search through a bog, we light on a piece of hewn wood, we do not say it is a product of nature but of art. Its producing cause had an end in view to which the object owes its form. Apart from such cases, we recognize an art in everything formed in such a way that its actuality must have been preceded by a representation of the thing in its cause (as even in the case of the bees), although the effect could not have been *thought* by the cause. But where anything is called absolutely a work of art, to distinguish it from a natural product, then some work of man is always understood.

(2) *Art*, as human skill, is distinguished also from *science* (as *ability* from *knowledge*), as a practical from a theoretical faculty, as technic from theory (as the art of surveying from geometry). For this reason, also, what one *can* do the moment one only *knows* what is to be done, hence without anything more than sufficient knowledge of the desired result, is not called art. To art that alone belongs for which the possession of the most complete knowledge does not involve one's having then and there the skill to do it. . . .

(3) *Art* is further distinguished from *handicraft*. The first is called *free,* the other may be called *industrial art.* We look on the former as something which could only prove final (be a success) as play, i.e. an occupation which is agreeable on its own account; but on the second as labour, i.e. a business, which on its own account is disagreeable (drudgery), and is only attractive by means of what it results in (e.g. the pay), and which is consequently capable of being a compulsory imposition. . . . It is

not amiss, however, to remind the reader of this: that in all free arts something of a compulsory character is still required, or, as it is called a *mechanism,* without which the *soul,* which in art must be *free,* and which alone gives life to the work, would be bodyless and evanescent (e.g. in the poetic art there must be correctness and wealth of language, likewise prosody and metre). For not a few leaders of a newer school believe that the best way to promote a free art is to sweep away all restraint, and convert it from labour into mere play.

44. *Fine Art.* There is no science of the beautiful, but only a Critique. Nor, again, is there an elegant [*schöne*] science, but only a fine [*schöne*] art. For a science of the beautiful would have to determine scientifically, i.e. by means of proofs, whether a thing was to be considered beautiful or not; and the judgement upon beauty, consequently, would, if belonging to science, fail to be a judgement of taste. As for a beautiful science—a science which, as such, is to be beautiful, is a nonentity. For if, treating it as a science, we were to ask for reasons and proofs, we would be put off with elegant phrases (*bons mots*).
  . . .

Where art, merely seeking to actualize a possible object to the *cognition* of which it is adequate, does whatever acts are required for that purpose, then it is *mechanical.* But should the feeling of pleasure be what it has immediately in view it is then termed *aesthetic* art. As such it may be either *agreeable* or *fine* art. The description "agreeable art" applies where the end of the art is that the pleasure should accompany the representations considered as mere *sensations,* the description "fine art" where it is to accompany them considered as *modes of cognition.*

Agreeable arts are those which have mere enjoyment for their object. Such are all the charms that can gratify a dinner party: entertaining narrative, the art of starting the whole table in unrestrained and sprightly conversation, or with jest and laughter inducing a certain air of gaiety. . . . In addition must be included play of every kind which is attended with no further interest than that of making the time pass by unheeded.

Fine art, on the other hand, is a mode of representation which is intrinsically final, and which, although devoid of an end, has the effect of advancing the culture of the mental powers in the interests of social communication.

The universal communicability of a pleasure involves in its very concept that the pleasure is not one of enjoyment arising out of mere sensation, but must be one of reflection. Hence aesthetic art, as art which is beautiful, is one having for its standard the reflective judgement and not organic sensation.

45. *Fine art is an art, so far as it has at the same time the appearance of being nature.* A product of fine art must be recognized to be art and not nature. Nevertheless the finality in its form must appear just as free from the constraint of arbitrary rules as if it were a product of mere nature. Upon this feeling of freedom in the play of our cognitive faculties—which play has at the same time to be final—rests that pleasure which alone is universally communicable without being based on concepts. Nature proved beautiful when it wore the appearance of art; and art can only be termed beautiful, where we are conscious of its being art, while yet it has the appearance of nature.

For whether we are dealing with beauty of nature or beauty of art, we may make the universal statement: *that is beautiful which pleases in the mere estimate of it* (not in a sensation or by means of a concept). Now art has always got a definite intention of producing something. Were this "something," however, to be mere sensation (something merely subjective), intended to be accompanied with pleasure, then such product would, in our estimation

of it, only please through the agency of the feeling of the senses. On the other hand, were the intention one directed to the production of a definite object, then, supposing this were attained by art, the object would only please by means of a concept. But in both cases the art would please, not in *the mere estimate of it,* i.e. not as fine art, but rather as mechanical art.

Hence the finality in the product of fine art, intentional though it be, must not have the appearance of being intentional; i.e. fine art must be clothed *with the aspect of nature,* although we recognize it to be art. But the way in which a product of art seems like nature, is by the presence of perfect *exactness* in the agreement with rules prescribing how alone the product can be what it is intended to be, but with an absence of *laboured effect* (without academic form betraying itself), i.e. without a trace appearing of the artist having always had the rule present to him and of its having fettered his mental powers.

46. *Fine art is the art of genius. Genius* is the talent (natural endowment) which gives the rule to art. Since talent, as an innate productive faculty of the artist, belongs itself to nature, we may put it this way: *Genius is the innate mental aptitude (ingenium) through which* nature gives the rule to art.

Whatever may be the merits of this definition, and whether it is merely arbitrary, or whether it is adequate or not to the concept usually associated with the word *genius,* . . . it may still be shown at the outset that, according to this acceptation of the word, fine arts must necessarily be regarded as arts of *genius.*

For every art presupposes rules which are laid down as the foundation which first enables a product, if it is to be called one of art, to be represented as possible. The concept of fine art, however, does not permit of the judgement upon the beauty of its product being derived from any rule that has a *concept* for its determining ground, and that depends, consequently, on a concept of the way in which the product is possible. Consequently fine art cannot of its own self excogitate the rule according to which it is to effectuate its product. But since, for all that, a product can never be called art unless there is a preceding rule, it follows that nature in the individual (and by virtue of the harmony of his faculties) must give the rule to art, i.e. fine art is only possible as a product of genius.

From this it may be seen that genius (1) is a *talent* for producing that for which no definite rule can be given: and not an aptitude in the way of cleverness for what can be learned according to some rule; and that consequently *originality* must be its primary property. (2) Since there may also be original nonsense, its products must at the same time be models, i.e. be *exemplary*; and, consequently, though not themselves derived from imitation, they must serve that purpose for others, i.e. as a standard or rule of estimating. (3) It cannot indicate scientifically how it brings about its product, but rather gives the rule as *nature*. Hence, where an author owes a product to his genius, he does not himself know how the *ideas* for it have entered into his head, nor has he it in his power to invent the like at pleasure, or methodically, and communicate the same to others in such precepts as would put them in a position to produce similar products. . . . (4) Nature prescribes the rule through genius not to science but to art, and this also only in so far as it is to be fine art.

47. *Elucidation and confirmation of the above explanation of genius.* Every one is agreed on the point of the complete opposition between genius and the *spirit of imitation.* Now since learning is nothing but imitation, the greatest ability, or aptness as a pupil (capacity), is still, as such, not equivalent to genius. Even though a man weaves his own thoughts or fancies, instead of merely taking in what others have thought, and even though he go so far as to bring fresh gains to art and science, this does not afford a valid reason for calling such a man of *brains,* and often great brains, a *genius,* in contradistinction to one who goes by the name of *shallow-pate,* because he can never do more than merely learn and follow a lead. For what is accomplished in this way is something that *could* have been learned. Hence it all lies in the natural path of investigation and reflection according to rules, and so is not specifically distinguishable from what may be acquired as the result of industry backed up by imitation. So all that *Newton* has set forth in his immortal work on the Principles of Natural Philosophy may well be learned, however great a mind it took to find it all out, but we cannot learn to write in a true poetic vein, no matter how complete all the precepts of the poetic art may be, or however excellent its models. The reason is that all the steps that Newton had to take from the first elements of geometry to his greatest and most profound discoveries were such as he could make intuitively evident and plain to follow, not only for himself but for every one else. On the other hand no Homer . . . can show how his ideas, . . . , enter and assemble themselves in his brain, for the good reason that he does not himself know, and so cannot teach others. In matters of science, therefore, the greatest inventor differs only in degree from the most laborious imitator and apprentice, whereas he differs specifically from one endowed by nature for fine art. . . .

Seeing, then, that the natural endowment of art (as fine art) must furnish the rule, what kind of rule must this be? It cannot be one set down in a formula and serving as a precept—for then the judgement upon the beautiful would be determinable according to concepts. Rather must the rule be gathered from the performance, i.e. from the product, which others may use to put their own talent to the test, so as to let it serve as a model, not for *imitation,* but for *following.* The possibility of this is difficult to explain. The artist's ideas arouse like ideas on the part of his pupil, presuming nature to have visited him with a like proportion of the mental powers. For this reason the models of fine art are the only means of handing down this art to posterity. . . .

Despite the marked difference that distinguishes mechanical art, as an art merely depending upon industry and learning, from fine art, as that of genius, there is still no fine art in which something mechanical, capable of being at once comprehended and followed in obedience to rules, and consequently something *academic* does not constitute the essential condition of the art. For the thought of something as end must be present, or else its product would not be ascribed to an art at all, but would be a mere product of chance. But the effectuation of an end necessitates determinate rules which we cannot venture to dispense with. Now, seeing that originality of talent is one . . . essential factor that goes to make up the character of genius, shallow minds fancy that the best evidence they can give of their being full-blown geniuses is by emancipating themselves from all academic constraint of rules, . . . Genius can do no more than furnish rich *material* for products of fine art; its elaboration and its *form* require a talent academically trained, so that it may be employed in such a way as to stand the test of judgement. But, for a person to hold forth and pass sentence like a genius in matters that fall to the province of the most patient rational investigation, is ridiculous in the extreme. . . .

48. *The relation of genius to taste.* For *estimating* beautiful objects, as such, what is required is *taste*; but for fine art, i.e. the *production* of such objects, one needs *genius.*

If we consider genius as the talent for fine art . . . , and if we would analyse it from this point of view into the faculties which must concur to constitute such a talent, it is imperative at the outset accu-

rately to determine the difference between beauty of nature, which it only requires taste to estimate, and beauty of art, which requires genius for its possibility (a possibility to which regard must also be paid in estimating such an object).

A beauty of nature is a *beautiful thing*; beauty of art is a *beautiful representation* of a thing.

To enable me to estimate a beauty of nature, as such, I do not need to be previously possessed of a concept of what sort of a thing the object is intended to be, i.e. I am not obliged to know its material finality (the end), but, rather, in forming an estimate of it apart from any knowledge of the end, the mere form pleases on its own account. If, however, the object is presented as a product of art, and is as such to be declared beautiful, then, seeing that art always presupposes an end in the cause (and its causality), a concept of what the thing is intended to be must first of all be laid at its basis. And, since the agreement of the manifold in a thing with an inner character belonging to it as its end constitutes the perfection of the thing, it follows that in estimating beauty of art the perfection of the thing must be also taken into account—a matter which in estimating a beauty of nature, as beautiful, is quite irrelevant.—It is true that in forming an estimate, especially of animate objects of nature, e.g. of a man or a horse, objective finality is also commonly taken into account with a view to judgement upon their beauty; but then the judgement also ceases to be purely aesthetic, i.e. a mere judgement of taste. Nature is no longer estimated as it appears like art, but rather in so far as it actually *is* art, though superhuman art; and the teleological judgement serves as basis and condition of the aesthetic, and one which the latter must regard. In such a case, where one says, for example, "that is a beautiful woman," what one in fact thinks is only this, that in her form nature excellently portrays the ends present in the female figure. For one has to extend one's view beyond the mere form to a concept, to enable the object to be thought in such manner by means of an aesthetic judgement logically conditioned.

Where fine art evidences its superiority is in the beautiful descriptions it gives of things that in nature would be ugly or displeasing. The Furies, diseases, devastations of war, and the like, can (as evils) be very beautifully described, nay even represented in pictures. One kind of ugliness alone is incapable of being represented conformably to nature without destroying all aesthetic delight, and consequently artistic beauty, namely, that which excites *disgust*. For, as in this strange sensation, which depends purely on the imagination, the object is represented as insisting, as it were, upon our enjoying it, while we still set our face against it, the artificial representation of the object is no longer distinguishable from the nature of the object itself in our sensation, and so it cannot possibly be regarded as beautiful. . . .

So much for the beautiful representation of an object, which is properly only the form of the presentation of a concept, and the means by which the latter is universally communicated. To give this form, however, to the product of fine art, taste merely is required. By this the artist, having practised and corrected his taste by a variety of examples from nature or art, controls his work and, after many, and often laborious, attempts to satisfy taste, finds the form which commends itself to him. Hence this form is not, as it were, a matter of inspiration, or of a free swing of the mental powers, but rather of a slow and even painful process of improvement, directed to making the form adequate to his thought without prejudice to the freedom in the play of those powers.

Taste is, however, merely a critical, not a productive faculty; and what conforms to it is not, merely on that account, a work of fine art. It may belong to useful and me-chanical art, or even to science, as a product following definite rules which are capable of being learned and which must be closely followed. But the pleasing form imparted to the works is only the vehicle of communication and a mode, as it were, of execution, in respect of which one remains to a certain extent free, notwithstanding being otherwise tied down to a definite end. So we demand that table appointments, or even a moral dissertation, . . . , must bear this form of fine art, yet without its appearing *studied*. But one would not call them on this account works of fine art. A poem, a musical composition, a picture-gallery, . . . , would, however, be placed under this head; and so in a would-be work of fine art we may frequently recognize genius without taste, and in another taste without genius.

49. *The faculties of the mind which constitute genius.* Of certain products which are expected, partly at least, to stand on the footing of fine art, we say they are *soul*less; and this, although we find nothing to censure in them as far as taste goes. A poem may be very pretty and elegant, but is soulless. A narrative has precision and method, but is soulless. A speech . . . may be good in substance and ornate withal, but may be soulless. Conversation frequently is not devoid of entertainment, but yet soulless. Even of a woman we may well say, she is pretty, affable, and refined, but soulless. Now what do we here mean by "soul"?

"Soul" [*Geist*] in an aesthetical sense, signifies the animating principle in the mind. But that whereby this principle animates the psychic substance [*Seele*]—the material which it employs for that purpose—is that which sets the mental powers into a swing that is final, i.e. into a play which is self-maintaining and which strengthens those powers for such activity.

Now my proposition is that this principle is nothing else than the faculty of presenting *aesthetic ideas*. But, by an aesthetic idea I mean that representation of the imagina·

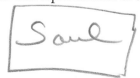
Soul

tion which induces much thought, yet without the possibility of any definite thought whatever, i.e. *concept*, being adequate to it, and which language, consequently, can never get quite on level terms with or render completely intelligible.—It is easily seen, that an aesthetic idea is the counterpart (pendant) of a *rational idea*, which, conversely, is a concept, to which no *intuition* (representation of the imagination) can be adequate.

The imagination (as a productive faculty of cognition) is a powerful agent for creating, as it were, a second nature out of the material supplied to it by actual nature. It affords us entertainment where experience proves too commonplace; and we even use it to remodel experience, always following, no doubt, laws that are based on analogy, but still also following principles which have a higher seat in reason (and which are every whit as natural to us as those followed by the understanding in laying hold of empirical nature). By this means we get a sense of our freedom from the law of association (which attaches to the empirical employment of the imagination), with the result that the material can be borrowed by us from nature in accordance with that law, but be worked up by us into something else —namely, what surpasses nature.

Such representations of the imagination may be termed *ideas*. This is partly because they at least strain after something lying out beyond the confines of experience, and so seek to approximate to a presentation of rational concepts (i.e. intellectual ideas), thus giving to these concepts the semblance of an objective reality. But, on the other hand, there is this most important reason, that no concept can be wholly adequate to them as internal intuitions. The poet essays the task of interpreting to sense the rational ideas of invisible beings, the kingdom of the blessed, hell, eternity, creation, &c. Or, again, as to things of which examples occur in experience, e.g. death, envy, and all vices, as also love, fame, and the like, trans-

gressing the limits of experience he attempts with the aid of an imagination which emulates the display of reason in its attainment of a maximum, to body them forth to sense with a completeness of which nature affords no parallel; and it is in fact precisely in the poetic art that the faculty of aesthetic ideas can show itself to full advantage. This faculty, however, regarded solely on its own account, is properly no more than a talent (of the imagination).

If now, we attach to a concept a representation of the imagination belonging to its presentation, but inducing solely on its own account such a wealth of thought as would never admit of comprehension in a definite concept, and, as a consequence, giving aesthetically an unbounded expansion to the concept itself, then the imagination here displays a creative activity, and it puts the faculty of intellectual ideas (reason) into motion—a motion, at the instance of a representation, towards an extension of thought, that, while germane, no doubt, to the concept of the object, exceeds what can be laid hold of in that representation or clearly expressed.

Those forms which do not constitute the presentation of a given concept itself, but which, as secondary representations of the imagination, express the derivatives connected with it, and its kinship with other concepts, are called (aesthetic) *attributes* of an object, the concept of which, as an idea of reason, cannot be adequately presented. In this way Jupiter's eagle, with the lightning in its claws, is an attribute of the mighty king of heaven, and the peacock of its stately queen. They do not, like *logical attributes*, represent what lies in our concepts of the sublimity and majesty of creation, but rather something else—something that gives the imagination an incentive to spread its flight over a whole host of kindred representations that provoke more thought than admits of expression in a concept determined by words. They furnish an *aesthetic idea*, which serves the above rational idea as a substitute for logical presentation, but with the proper function, however, of animating the mind by opening out for it a prospect into a field of kindred representations stretching beyond its ken. But it is not alone in the arts of painting or sculpture, where the name of attribute is customarily employed, that fine art acts in this way; poetry and rhetoric also derive the soul that animates their works wholly from the aesthetic attributes of the objects—attributes which go hand in hand with the logical, and give the imagination an impetus to bring more thought into play in the matter, though in an undeveloped manner, than allows of being brought within the embrace of a concept, or, therefore, of being definitely formulated in language. . . . —even an intellectual concept may serve . . . as attribute for a representation of sense, and so animate the latter with the idea of the supersensible; but only by the aesthetic factor subjectively attaching to the consciousness of the supersensible being employed for the purpose. So, for example, a certain poet says in his description of a beautiful morning: "The sun arose, as out of virtue rises peace." The consciousness of virtue, even where we put ourselves only in thought in the position of a virtuous man, diffuses in the mind a multitude of sublime and tranquillizing feelings, and gives a boundless outlook into a happy future, such as no expression within the compass of a definite concept completely attains.

In a word, the aesthetic idea is a representation of the imagination, annexed to a given concept, with which, in the free employment of imagination, such a multiplicity of partial representations are bound up, that no expression indicating a definite concept can be found for it—one which on that account allows a concept to be supplemented in thought by much that is indefinable in words, and the feeling of which quickens the cognitive faculties, and with language, as a mere thing of the letter, binds up the spirit (soul) also.

The mental powers whose union in a certain relation constitutes *genius* are imagination and understanding. Now, since the imagination, in its employment on behalf of cognition, is subjected to the constraint of the understanding and the restriction of having to be conformable to the concept belonging thereto, whereas aesthetically it is free to furnish of its own accord, over and above that agreement with the concept, a wealth of undeveloped material for the understanding, to which the latter paid no regard in its concept, but which it can make use of, not so much objectively for cognition, as subjectively for quickening the cognitive faculties, and hence also indirectly for cognitions, it may be seen that genius properly consists in the happy relation, which science cannot teach nor industry learn, enabling one to find out ideas for a given concept, and, besides, to hit upon the expression for them—the expression by means of which the subjective mental condition induced by the ideas as the concomitant of a concept may be communicated to others. This latter talent is properly that which is termed soul. For to get an expression for what is indefinable in the mental state accompanying a particular representation and to make it universally communicable . . . is a thing requiring a faculty for laying hold of the rapid and transient play of the imagination, and for unifying it in a concept (which for that very reason is original, and reveals a new rule which could not have been inferred from any preceding principles or examples) that admits of communication without any constraint of rules.

———————

If, after this analysis, we cast a glance back upon the above definition of what is called *genius*, we find: *First*, that it is a talent for art—not one for science, in which clearly known rules must take the lead and determine the procedure. *Secondly*, being a talent in the line of art, it presupposes a definite concept of the product—as its end. Hence it presupposes understanding, but in addition, a representation, indefinite though it be, of the material, i.e. of the intuition, required for the presentation of that concept, and so a relation of the imagination to the understanding. *Thirdly,* it displays itself, not so much in the working out of the projected end in the presentation of a definite *concept,* as rather in the portrayal, or expression of *aesthetic ideas* containing a wealth of material for effecting that intention. Consequently the imagination is represented by it in its freedom from all guidance of rules, but still as final for the presentation of the given concept. *Fourthly,* and lastly, the unsought and undesigned subjective finality in the free harmonizing of the imagination with the understanding's conformity to law presupposes a proportion and accord between these faculties such as cannot be brought about by any observance of rules, whether of science or mechanical imitation, but can only be produced by the nature of the individual.

Genius, according to these presuppositions, is the exemplary originality of the natural endowments of an individual in the *free* employment of his cognitive faculties. On this showing, the product of a genius . . . is an example, not for imitation (for that would mean the loss of the element of genius, and just the very soul of the work), but to be followed by another genius—one whom it arouses to a sense of his own originality in putting freedom from the constraint of rules so into force in his art, that for art itself a new rule is won—which is what shows a talent to be exemplary. Yet, since the genius is one of nature's elect—a type that must be regarded as but a rare phenomenon—for other clever minds his example gives rise to a school, that is to say a methodical instruction according to rules, collected, so far as the circumstances admit, from such products of genius and their peculiarities. And, to that extent, fine art is for such persons a matter of imitation, for which nature, through the medium of a genius, gave the rule.

But this imitation becomes *aping* when the pupil *copies* everything down to the deformities which the genius only of necessity suffered to remain, because they could hardly be removed without loss of force to the idea. This courage has merit only in the case of a genius. A certain *boldness* of expression, and, in general, many a deviation from the common rule becomes him well, but in no sense is it a thing worthy of imitation. On the contrary it remains all through intrinsically a blemish, which one is bound to try to remove, but for which the genius is, as it were, allowed to plead a privilege, on the ground that a scrupulous carefulness would spoil what is inimitable in the impetuous ardour of his soul. *Mannerism* is another kind of aping—an aping of *peculiarity* (originality) in general, for the sake of removing oneself as far as possible from imitators, while the talent requisite to enable one to be at the same time *exemplary* is absent.—There are, in fact, two modes (*modi*) in general of arranging one's thoughts for utterance. The one is called a *manner* (*modus aestheticus*), the other a *method* (*modus logicus*). The distinction between them is this: the former possesses no standard other than the *feeling* of unity in the presentation, whereas the latter here follows definite *principles.* As a consequence the former is alone admissible for fine art. It is only, however, where the manner of carrying the idea into execution in a product of art is *aimed at* singularity instead of being made appropriate to the idea, that *mannerism* is properly ascribed to such a product. The ostentatious (*précieux*), forced, and affected styles, intended to mark one out from the common herd (though soul is wanting), resemble the behaviour of a man who, as we say, hears himself talk, or who stands and moves about as if he were on a stage to be gaped at—action which invariably betrays a tyro.

50. *The combination of taste and genius in products of fine art.* To ask whether more stress should be laid in matters of fine art

upon the presence of genius or upon that of taste, is equivalent to asking whether more turns upon imagination or upon judgement. Now imagination rather entitles an art to be called an *inspired* [*geistreiche*] than a *fine* art. It is only in respect of judgement that the name of fine art is deserved. Hence it follows that judgement, being the indispensable condition (*conditio sine qua non*), is at least what one must look to as of capital importance in forming an estimate of art as fine art. So far as beauty is concerned, to be fertile and original in ideas is not such an imperative requirement as it is that the imagination in its freedom should be in accordance with the understanding's conformity to law. For in lawless freedom imagination, with all its wealth, produces nothing but nonsense; the power of judgement, on the other hand, is the faculty that makes it consonant with understanding.

Taste, like judgement in general, is the discipline (or corrective) of genius. It severely clips its wings, and makes it orderly or polished; but at the same time it gives it guidance, directing and controlling its flight, so that it may preserve its character of finality. It introduces a clearness and order into the plenitude of thought, and in so doing gives stability to the ideas, and qualifies them at once for permanent and universal approval, for being followed by others, and for a continually progressive culture. And so, where the interests of both these qualities clash in a product, and there has to be a sacrifice of something, then it should rather be on the side of genius; and judgement, which in matters of fine art bases its decision on its own proper principles, will more readily endure an abatement of the freedom and wealth of the imagination than that the understanding should be compromised.

The requisites for fine art are, therefore, *imagination, understanding, soul*, and *taste*.

51. *The division of the fine arts.* Beauty (whether it be of nature or of art) may in general be termed the *expression* of aesthetic ideas. But the proviso must be added that with beauty of art this idea must be excited through the medium of a concept of the Object, whereas with beauty of nature the bare reflection upon a given intuition, apart from any concept of what the object is intended to be, is sufficient for awakening and communicating the idea of which that Object is regarded as the *expression*.

Accordingly, if we wish to make a division of the fine arts, we can choose for that purpose, tentatively at least, no more convenient principle than the analogy which art bears to the mode of expression of which men avail themselves in speech, with a view to communicating themselves to one another as completely as possible, i.e. not merely in respect of their concepts but in respect of their sensations also. —Such expression consists in *word, gesture*, and *tone* (articulation, gesticulation, and modulation). It is the combination of these three modes of expression which alone constitutes a complete communication of the speaker. For thought, intuition, and sensation are in this conveyed to others simultaneously and in conjunction.

Hence there are only three kinds of fine art: the art of *speech, formative* art, and the art of the *play of sensations* (as external sense impressions). This division might also be arranged as a dichotomy, so that fine art would be divided into that of the expression of thoughts or intuitions, the latter being subdivided according to the distinction between the form and the matter (sensation). It would, however, in that case appear too abstract, and less in line with popular conceptions.

(1) The arts of SPEECH are *rhetoric* and *poetry*. *Rhetoric* is the art of transacting a serious business of the understanding as if it were a free play of the imagination; *poetry* that of conducting a free play of the imagination as if it were a serious business of the understanding.

Thus the *orator* announces a serious business, and for the purpose of entertaining his audience conducts it as if it were a mere *play* with ideas. The poet promises merely an entertaining *play* with ideas, and yet for the understanding there enures as much as if the promotion of its business had been his one intention. The combination and harmony of the two faculties of cognition, sensibility and understanding, which, though, doubtless, indispensable to one another, do not readily permit of being united without compulsion and reciprocal abatement, must have the appearance of being undesigned and a spontaneous occurrence —otherwise it is not *fine* art. For this reason what is studied and laboured must be here avoided. For fine art must be free art in a double sense: i.e. not alone in a sense opposed to contract work, as not being a work the magnitude of which may be estimated, exacted, or paid for according to a definite standard, but free also in the sense that, while the mind, no doubt, occupies itself, still it does so without ulterior regard to any other end, and yet with a feeling of satisfaction and stimulation (independent of reward).

. . .

(2) The FORMATIVE arts, or those for the expression of ideas in *sensuous intuition* (not by means of representations of mere imagination that are excited by words) are arts either of *sensuous truth* or of *sensuous semblance*. The first is called *plastic* art, the second *painting*. Both use figures in space for the expression of ideas: the former makes figures discernible to two senses, sight and touch (though, so far as the latter sense is concerned, without regard to beauty), the latter makes them so to the former sense alone. The aesthetic idea (archetype, original) is the fundamental basis of both in the imagination; but the figure which constitutes its expression (the ectype, the copy) is given either in its bodily extension (the way the object itself exists) or else in accordance with the picture which it forms of itself in the eye (according to its appearance when projected on a flat surface). Or, whatever the archetype is, either the reference to an actual end or only the semblance of one may be imposed upon reflection as its condition.

To *plastic* art, as the first kind of formative art, belong *sculpture* and *architecture*. The first is that which presents concepts of things corporeally, as they *might exist in nature* (though as fine art it directs its attention to aesthetic finality). The *second* is the art of presenting concepts of things which are possible *only through art,* and the determining ground of whose form is not nature but an arbitrary end—and of presenting them both with a view to this purpose and yet, at the same time, with aesthetic finality. In architecture the chief point is a certain *use* of the artistic object to which, as the condition, the aesthetic ideas are limited. In sculpture the mere *expression* of aesthetic ideas is the main intention. . . .

Painting, as the second kind of formative art, which presents the *sensuous semblance* in artful combination with ideas, I would divide into that of the beautiful *portrayal of nature,* and that of the beautiful *arrangement* of its *products.* The first is *painting proper,* the second *landscape gardening.* For the first gives only the semblance of bodily extension; whereas the second, giving this, no doubt, according to its truth, gives only the semblance of utility and employment for ends other than the play of the imagination in the contemplation of its forms. The latter consists in no more than decking out the ground with the same manifold variety . . . as that with which nature presents it to our view, only arranged differently and in obedience to certain ideas. The beautiful arrangement of corporeal things, however, is also a thing for the eye only, just like painting—the sense of touch can form no intuitable representation of such a form. In addition I would place under the head of painting, in the wide sense, the decoration of rooms by means of hangings, ornamental accessories, and all beautiful furniture the sole function of which is *to be looked at;* and in the same way the art of tasteful dressing. . . .

(3) The art of the BEAUTIFUL PLAY OF SENSATIONS (sensations that arise from external stimulation), which is a play of sensations that has nevertheless to permit of universal communication, can only be concerned with the proportion of the different degrees of tension in the sense to which the sensation belongs, i.e. with its tone. In this comprehensive sense of the word it may be divided into the artificial play of sensations of hearing and of sight, consequently into *music* and the *art of colour.* — It is of note that these two senses, over and above such susceptibility for impressions as is required to obtain concepts of external objects by means of these impressions, also admit a peculiar associated sensation of which we cannot well determine whether it is based on sense or reflection; and that this sensibility may at times be wanting, although the sense, in other respects, and in what concerns its employment for the cognition of objects, is by no means deficient but particularly keen. In other words, we cannot confidently assert whether a colour or a tone (sound) is merely an agreeable sensation, or whether they are in themselves a beautiful play of sensations, and in being estimated aesthetically, convey, as such, a delight in their form. . . .

52. *The combination of the fine arts in one and the same product.* Rhetoric may in a *drama* be combined with a pictorial presentation as well of its Subjects as of objects; as may poetry with music in a *song;* and this again with a pictorial (theatrical) presentation in an *opera;* and so may the play of sensations in a piece of music with the play of figures in a *dance,* and so on. Even the presentation of the sublime, so far as it belongs to fine art, may be brought into union with beauty in a *tragedy in verse,* a *didactic poem* or an *oratorio,* and in this combination fine art is even more artistic. Whether it is also more beautiful (having regard to the multiplicity of different kinds of delight which cross one another) may in some of these instances be doubted. Still in all fine art the essential element consists in the form which is final for observation and for estimating. Here the pleasure is at the same time culture, and disposes the soul to ideas, making it thus susceptible of such pleasure and entertainment in greater abundance. The matter of sensation (charm or emotion) is not essential. Here the aim is merely enjoyment, which leaves nothing behind it in the idea, and renders the soul dull, the object in the course of time distasteful, and the mind dissatisfied with itself and ill-humoured, owing to a consciousness that in the judgement of reason its disposition is perverse.

Where fine arts are not, either proximately or remotely, brought into combination with moral ideas, which alone are attended with self-sufficing delight, the above is the fate that ultimately awaits them. They then only serve for a diversion, of which one continually feels an increasing need in proportion as one has availed oneself of it as a means of dispelling the discontent of one's mind, with the result that one makes oneself ever more and more unprofitable and dissatisfied with oneself. With a view to the purpose first named the beauties of nature are in general the most beneficial, if one is early habituated to observe, estimate, and admire them.

53. *Comparative estimate of the aesthetic worth of the fine arts.* Poetry (which owes its origin almost entirely to genius and is least willing to be led by precepts or example) holds the first rank among all the arts. It expands the mind by giving freedom to the imagination and by offering, from among the boundless multiplicity of possible forms accordant with a given concept, to whose bounds it is restricted, that one which couples with the presentation of the concept a wealth of thought to which no verbal expression is completely adequate,

and by thus rising aesthetically to ideas. It invigorates the mind by letting it feel its faculty—free, spontaneous, and independent of determination by nature—of regarding and estimating nature as phenomenon in the light of aspects which nature of itself does not afford us in experience, either for sense or understanding, and of employing it accordingly in behalf of, and as a sort of scheme for, the supersensible. It plays with semblance, which it produces at will, but not as an instrument of deception; for its avowed pursuit is merely one of play, which, however, understanding may turn to good account and employ for its own purpose. — Rhetoric, so far as this is taken to mean the art of persuasion, i.e. the art of deluding by means of a fair semblance (as *ars oratoria*), and not merely excellence of speech (eloquence and style), is a dialectic which borrows from poetry only so much as is necessary to win over men's minds to the side of the speaker before they have weighed the matter, and to rob their verdict of its freedom. Hence it can be recommended neither for the bar nor the pulpit. . . . In poetry everything is straight and above board. It shows its hand: it desires to carry on a mere entertaining play with the imagination, and one consonant, in respect of form, with the laws of understanding; and it does not seek to steal upon and ensnare the understanding with a sensuous presentation.

After poetry, *if we take charm and mental stimulation into account,* I would give the next place to that art which comes nearer to it than to any other art of speech, and admits of very natural union with it, namely the art of *tone.* For though it speaks by means of mere sensations without concepts, and so does not, like poetry, leave behind it any food for reflection, still it moves the mind more diversely, and, although with transient, still with intenser effect. It is certainly, however, more a matter of enjoyment than of culture—the play of thought incidentally excited by it being merely the effect of a more or less mechanical association—and it possesses less worth in the eyes of reason than any other of the fine arts. Hence, like all enjoyment, it calls for constant change, and does not stand frequent repetition without inducing weariness. Its charm, which admits of such universal communication, appears to rest on the following facts. Every expression in language has an associated tone suited to its sense. This tone indicates, more or less, a mode in which the speaker is affected, and in turn evokes it in the hearer also, in whom conversely it then also excites the idea which in language is expressed with such a tone. Further, just as modulation is, as it were, a universal language of sensations intelligible to every man, so the art of tone wields the full force of this language wholly on its own account, namely, as a language of the affections, and in this way, according to the law of association, universally communicates the aesthetic ideas that are naturally combined therewith. But, further, inasmuch as those aesthetic ideas are not concepts or determinate thoughts, the form of the arrangement of these sensations (harmony and melody) taking the place of the form of a language, only serves the purpose of giving an expression to the aesthetic idea of an integral whole of an unutterable wealth of thought that fills the measure of a certain theme forming the dominant *affection* in the piece. This purpose is effectuated by means of a proportion in the accord of the sensations (an accord which may be brought mathematically under certain rules, since it rests, in the case of tones, upon the numerical relation of the vibrations of the air in the same time, so far as there is a combination of the tones simultaneously or in succession). Although this mathematical form is not represented by means of determinate concepts, to it alone belongs the delight which the mere reflection upon such a number of concomitant or consecutive sensations couples with this their play, as the universally valid condition of its beauty, and it is with reference to it alone that taste can lay claim to a right to anticipate the judgement of every man.

But mathematics, certainly, does not play the smallest part in the charm and movement of the mind produced by music. Rather is it only the indispensable condition (*conditio sine qua non*) of that proportion of the combining as well as changing impressions which makes it possible to grasp them all in one and prevent them from destroying one another, and to let them, rather, conspire towards the production of a continuous movement and quickening of the mind by affections that are in unison with it, and thus towards a serene self-enjoyment.

If, on the other hand, we estimate the worth of the fine arts by the culture they supply to the mind, and adopt for our standard the expansion of the faculties whose confluence, in judgement, is necessary for cognition, music, then, since it plays merely with sensations, has the lowest place among the fine arts—just as it has perhaps the highest among those valued at the same time for their agreeableness. Looked at in this light it is far excelled by the formative arts. For, in putting the imagination into a play which is at once free and adapted to the understanding, they all the while carry on a serious business, since they execute a product which serves the concepts of understanding as a vehicle, permanent and appealing to us on its own account for effectuating their union with sensibility, and thus for promoting, as it were, the urbanity of the higher powers of cognition. The two kinds of art pursue completely different courses. Music advances from sensations to indefinite ideas: formative art from definite ideas to sensations. The latter gives a *lasting* impression, the former one that is only *fleeting*. The former sensations imagination can recall and agreeably entertain itself with, while the latter either vanish entirely, or else if involuntarily repeated by the imagination, are more annoying to us than agreeable. . . .

Among the formative arts I would give the palm to *painting*; partly because it is the art of design and, as such, the groundwork of all the other formative arts; partly because it can penetrate much further into the region of ideas, and in conformity with them give a greater extension to the field of intuition than it is open to the others to do.

Part Three

⤙⤙⤙⤙⤙⤙⤙⤙⤙

POST-KANTIAN AESTHETICS

Schiller to Tolstoy

FRIEDRICH SCHILLER [1759–1805]

➤➤➤➤✕◄◄◄◄

From *Letters on the Aesthetic Education of Man* [1795]

Man is not better treated by nature originally than her other works are; so long as he is unable to act for himself as an independent intelligence she acts for him. But the very fact that constitutes him a man is that he does not remain stationary, where nature has placed him, but can pass with his reason, retracing the steps nature had made him anticipate; he can convert the work of necessity into one of free choice, and elevate physical necessity into a moral law.

When man is raised from his slumber in the senses he recognizes that he is a man; he surveys his surroundings and finds that he is in a state. He was introduced into this state by the power of circumstances, before he could freely choose his own position. But as a moral being he cannot possibly rest satisfied with a political condition forced upon him by necessity, and only calculated for that condition; and it would be unfortunate if this did satisfy him. In many cases man shakes off this blind law of necessity, by his free spontaneous action, of which among many others we have an instance, in his ennobling by beauty and suppressing by moral influence the powerful impulse implanted in him by nature in the passion of love. Thus, when arrived at maturity, he recovers his childhood by an artificial process, he forms a state of nature in his ideas, not given him by any experience, but established by the necessary laws

From Friedrich Schiller, *Aesthetical and Philosophical Essays,* edited by Nathan Haskell Dole (New York: 1902). Selections are from Letters #3, 4, 9, 11, 12, 13, 14, 15, 16, 18, 20, 21, 22, 23, 26. The anonymous and sometimes faulty translation has been revised where necessary by the editor of the present volume.

and conditions of his reason, and he attributes to this ideal condition an object, an aim, of which he was not cognisant in the actual reality of nature. He gives himself a choice of which he was not capable before, and sets to work just as if he were beginning anew, and were exchanging his original state of bondage for one of complete independence, doing this with complete insight and of his free decision. . . .

Now the term natural state can be applied to every political body which owes its establishment originally to forces and not to laws. Such a state contradicts the moral nature of man, because lawfulness can alone have authority over this. At the same time this natural condition is quite sufficient for the physical man, who only gives himself laws in order to get rid of brute force. Moreover, the physical man is a *reality,* and the moral man *problematical.* Therefore when the reason suppresses the natural condition, as she must if she wishes to substitute her own, she weighs the real physical man against the problematical moral man, she weighs the existence of society against a possible, though morally necessary, ideal of society. She takes from man something which he really possesses, and without which he possesses nothing, and refers him as a substitute to something that he ought to possess and might possess; and if reason had relied too exclusively on him she might, in order to secure him a state of humanity in which he is wanting and can want without injury to his life, have robbed him even of the means of animal existence which is the first necessary *condition* of his being a man. Before he had opportunity to hold firm to the law with his will, reason would have withdrawn from his feet the ladder of nature.

The great point is, therefore, to reconcile these two considerations, to prevent physical society from ceasing for a moment *in time,* while the moral society is being formed in the *idea;* in other words, to prevent its existence from being placed in jeopardy for the sake of the moral dignity of man. When the mechanic has to mend a watch he lets the wheels run out; but the living watchworks of the state have to be repaired while they act, and a wheel has to be exchanged for another during its revolutions. Accordingly props must be sought for to support society and keep it going while it is made independent of the natural state from which it is sought to emancipate it.

This prop is not found in the natural character of man, who, being selfish and violent, directs his energies rather to the destruction than to the preservation of society. Nor is it found in his moral character, which has yet to be formed, which can never be worked upon or calculated on by the lawgiver, because it is free and *never appears.* It would seem, therefore, that another measure must be adopted. It would seem that the physical character of the arbitrary must be separated from moral freedom; that it is incumbent to make the former harmonise with the laws and the latter dependent on impressions; it would be expedient to remove the former still farther from matter and to bring the latter somewhat more near to it; in short, to produce a third character related to both the others—the physical and the moral—paving the way to a transition from the sway of mere force to that of law, without preventing the proper development of the moral character, but serving rather as a pledge in the sensuous sphere of a morality in the unseen.

. . .

Now man can be opposed to himself in a twofold manner; either as a savage, when his feelings rule over his principles; or as a barbarian, when his principles destroy his feelings. The savage despises art, and acknowledges nature as his despotic ruler; the barbarian laughs at nature, and dishonours it, but he often proceeds in a more contemptible way than the savage to be the slave of his senses. The cultivated man makes of nature his friend, and honours its friendship, while only bridling its caprice.

Consequently, when reason brings her moral unity into physical society, she must not injure the manifold in nature. When nature strives to maintain her manifold character in the moral structure of society, this must not create any breach in moral unity; the victorious form is equally remote from uniformity and confusion. Therefore, *totality* of character must be found in the people which is capable and worthy to exchange the state of necessity for that of freedom.

. . .

All improvement in the political sphere must proceed from the ennobling of the character. But, subject to the influence of a social constitution still barbarous, how can character become ennobled? It would then be necessary to seek for this end an instrument that the state does not furnish, and to open sources that would have preserved themselves pure in the midst of political corruption.

I have now reached the point to which all previous considerations tended. This instrument is the art of the beautiful; these sources are open to us in its immortal models.

. . .

Thus, therefore, the *matter* of activity, or reality, that the supreme intelligence creates from its own being, must be *received* by man; and he does, in fact, receive it, through the medium of perception, as something which is outside him in space, and which changes in him in time. This matter which changes in him is always accompanied by the Ego, the personality, that never changes; and the rule prescribed for man by his rational nature is to remain immutably *himself* in the midst of change, to refer all perceptions to experience, that is, to the unity of knowledge, and to make of each of its manifestations in time the law of all time. The matter only exists in as far as it changes: *he,* his personality, only exists in as far as he does not change. Consequently, represented in his perfection, man would be the permanent unity, which remains always the same, among the waves of change. . . .

Considered in itself, and independently of all sensuous matter, his personality is nothing but the pure potentiality of a possible infinite manifestation; and so long as there is neither intuition nor feeling, it is nothing more than a form, an empty power. Considered in itself, and independently of all spontaneous activity of the mind, sensuousness can only make a material man; without it, he is pure form; but it cannot in any way establish a union between matter and him. So long as he only feels, wishes, and acts under the influence of desire, he is nothing more than the world, if by this word we point out only the formless contents of time. Without doubt, it is only his sensuousness that makes his strength pass into efficacious acts, but it is his personality alone that makes this activity his own. Thus, that he may not be merely world, he must give form to matter, and in order not to be a mere form, he must give reality to the potentiality that he bears in him. He gives matter to form by creating time, and by opposing the immutable to change, the diversity of the world to the external unity of the Ego. He gives a form to matter by again suppressing time, by maintaining permanence in change, and by placing the diversity of the world under the unity of the Ego.

Now from this source issue for man two opposite demands, the two fundamental laws of sensuous-rational nature. The first has for its object absolute *reality;* it must make a world of what is only form, manifest all that in it is only a force. The second law has for its object absolute *for-*

mality; it must destroy in him all that is only world, and carry out harmony in all changes. In other terms, he must manifest all that is internal, and give form to all that is external. . . .

This twofold labour or task, which consists in making the necessary pass into reality *in us* and in making reality *outside us* subject to the law of necessity, is urged upon us as a duty by two opposing forces, which are justly styled impulsions or instincts, because they impel us to realise their object. The first of these impulsions, which I shall call the *sensuous instinct,* issues from the physical existence of man, or from sensuous nature; and it is this instinct which tends to enclose him in the limits of time, and to make of him a material being; I do not say to give him matter, for to do that a certain free activity of the personality would be necessary, which, receiving matter, distinguishes it from the Ego, or what is permanent. By matter I only understand here the change or reality that fills time. Consequently the instinct requires that there should be change, and that time should contain something. This simply filled state of time is named sensation, and it is only in this state that physical existence manifests itself.

As all that is in time is *successive,* it follows by the mere fact that something is that all else is excluded. When one note on an instrument is touched, among all those that it virtually offers, this note alone is real. When man is actually modified, the infinite possibility of all his modifications is limited to this single mode of existence. Thus, then, the exclusive action of sensuous impulsion has for its necessary consequence the narrowest limitation. In this state man is only a unity of magnitude, a complete moment in time; or, to speak more correctly, *he* is not, for his personality is suppressed as long as sensation holds sway over him and carries time along with it.

This instinct extends its domains over the entire sphere of the finite in man, and as form is only revealed in matter, and the absolute by means of its limits, the total manifestation of human nature is connected on a close analysis with the sensuous instinct. . . .

The second impulse, which may be named the *formal instinct,* issues from the absolute existence of man, or from his rational nature, and tends to set free, and bring harmony into the diversity of its manifestations, and to maintain personality notwithstanding all the changes of state. As this personality, being an absolute and indivisible unity, can never be in contradiction with itself, as *we are ourselves,* for ever, this impulse, which tends to maintain personality, can never exact in one time anything but what it exacts and requires for ever. It therefore decides for always what it decides now, and orders now what it orders for ever. Hence it embraces the whole series of times, or what comes to the same thing, it suppresses time and change. It wishes the real to be necessary and eternal, and it wishes the eternal and the necessary to be real; in other terms, it tends to truth and justice.

If the sensuous instinct only produces *accidents,* the formal instinct gives laws, laws for every judgment when it is a question of knowledge, laws for every will when it is a question of action. Whether, therefore, we recognise an object or conceive an objective value to a state of the subject, whether we act in virtue of knowledge or make of the objective the determining principle of our state; in both cases we withdraw this state from the jurisdiction of time, and we attribute to it reality for all men and for all time, that is, universality and necessity. Feeling can only say: "That is true *for this subject* and *at this moment,*" and there may come another moment, another subject, which withdraws the affirmation from the actual feeling. But when once thought pronounces and says: *"That is,"* it decides for ever and ever, and the validity of its decision is guaranteed by the personality itself, which defies all change. Inclination can only say: "That is good *for your individuality* and *present necessity*"; but the changing current of affairs will sweep them away, and what you ardently desire to-day will form the object of your aversion to-morrow. But when the moral feeling says: "That ought to be," it decides for ever. If you confess the truth because it is the truth, and if you practise justice because it is justice, you have made of a particular case the law of all possible cases, and treated one moment of your life as eternity.

Accordingly, when the formal impulse holds sway and the pure object acts in us, the being attains its highest expansion, all barriers disappear, and from the unity of magnitude in which man was enclosed by a narrow sensuousness, he rises to the *unity of idea,* which embraces the entire sphere of phenomena. During this operation we are no longer in time, but time is in us with its infinite succession. We are no longer individuals but a species; the judgment of all spirits is expressed by our own, and the choice of all hearts is represented by our own act.

On a first survey, nothing appears more opposed than these two impulsions; one having for its object change, the other immutability, and yet it is these two notions that exhaust the notion of humanity, and a third *fundamental impulsion,* holding a medium between them, is quite inconceivable. How then shall we re-establish the unity of human nature, a unity that appears completely destroyed by this primitive and radical opposition?

. . .

We have been brought to the idea of such a correlation between the two impulsions that the action of the one establishes and limits at the same time the action of the other, and that each of them, taken in isolation, does arrive at its highest manifestation just because the other is active.

No doubt this correlation of the two impulsions is simply a problem advanced by reason, and which man will only be able to solve in the perfection of his being. It is in the strictest signification of the term: *the idea of his humanity;* accordingly, it is an infinite to which he can approach nearer and nearer in the course of time, but without ever reaching it. . . . It is only in conformity with this idea that he is a man in the full sense of the word; but he cannot be convinced of this so long as he gives himself up exclusively to one of these two impulsions, or only satisfies them one after the other. For as long as he only feels, his absolute personality and existence remain a mystery to him, and as long as he only thinks, his condition or existence in time escapes him. But if there were cases in which he could have *at once* this twofold experience in which he would have the consciousness of his freedom and the feeling of his existence together, in which he would simultaneously feel as matter and know himself as spirit, in such cases, and in such only, would he have a complete intuition of his humanity, and the object that would procure him this intuition would be a symbol of his accomplished destiny and consequently serve to express the infinite to him—since this destination can only be fulfilled in the fulness of time.

Presuming that cases of this kind could present themselves in experience, they would awake in him a new impulsion, which, precisely because the other two impulsions would coöperate in it, would be opposed to each of them taken in isolation, and might, with good grounds, be taken for a new impulsion. The sensuous impulsion requires that there should be change, that time should have contents; the formal impulsion requires that time should be suppressed, that there should be no change. Consequently, the impulsion in which both of the others act in concert—allow me to call it the *instinct of play,* till I explain the term—the instinct of play would have as its object to suppress time

in time, to conciliate the state of transition or *becoming* with the absolute being, change with identity.

The sensuous instinct wishes to be determined, to receive an object; the formal instinct wishes to determine itself, to produce an object. Therefore the instinct of play will endeavour to receive as it would itself have produced, and to produce as it aspires to receive.

The sensuous impulsion excludes from its subject all autonomy and freedom; the formal impulsion excludes all dependence and passivity. But the exclusion of freedom is physical necessity; the exclusion of passivity is moral necessity. Thus the two impulsions subdue the mind: the former to the laws of nature, the latter to the laws of reason. It results from this that the instinct of play, which unites the double action of the two other instincts, will content the mind at once morally and physically. Hence, as it suppresses all that is contingent, it will also suppress all coercion, and will set man free physically and morally. When we welcome with effusion some one who deserves our contempt, we feel painfully that *nature is constrained.* When we have a hostile feeling against a person who commands our esteem, we feel painfully the *constraint of reason.* But if this person inspires us with interest, and also wins our esteem, the constraint of feeling vanishes together with the constraint of reason, and we begin to love him, that is to say, to play, to take recreation, at once with our inclination and our esteem.

Moreover, as the sensuous impulsion controls us physically, and the formal impulsion morally, the former makes our formal constitution contingent, and the latter makes our material constitution contingent, that is to say, there is contingence in the agreement of our happiness with our perfection, and reciprocally. The instinct of play, in which both act in concert, will render both our formal and our material constitution contingent; accordingly, our perfection and our happiness in like manner. And on the other hand, exactly because it makes *both of them* contingent, and because the contingent disappears with necessity, it will suppress this contingence in both, and will thus give form to matter and reality to form. In proportion that it will lessen the dynamic influence of feeling and passion, it will place them in harmony with rational ideas, and by taking from the laws of reason their moral constraint, it will reconcile them with the interest of the senses.

The object of the sensuous instinct, expressed in a universal conception, is named Life in the widest acceptation; a conception that expresses all material existence and all that is immediately present in the senses. The object of the formal instinct, expressed in a universal conception, is called shape or form, as well in a literal as in a metaphoric sense; a conception that embraces all formal qualities of things and all relations of the same to the thinking powers. The object of the play instinct, represented in a general statement, may therefore bear the name *living form;* a term that serves to describe all aesthetic qualities of phenomena, and what people style, in the widest sense, *beauty.*

Beauty is neither extended to the whole field of all living things nor merely enclosed in this field. A marble block, though it is and remains lifeless, can nevertheless become a living form by the architect and sculptor; a man, though he lives and has a form, is far from being a living form on that account. For this to be the case, it is necessary that his form should be life, and that his life should be a form. As long as we only think of his form, it is lifeless, a mere abstraction; as long as we only feel his life, it is without form, a mere impression. It is only when his form lives in our feeling, and his life takes form in our understanding, he is the living form, and this will everywhere be the case where we judge him to be beautiful.

But the genesis of beauty is by no means explained because we know how to point out the component parts, which in their combination produce beauty. For to this end it would be necessary to comprehend that *combination itself,* which continues to defy our exploration, as does all mutual operation between the finite and the infinite. The reason, on transcendental grounds, makes the following demand: There shall be a communion between the formal impulse and the material impulse— that is, there shall be a play instinct— because it is only in the unity of reality with form, of the accidental with the necessary, of passivity with freedom, that the conception of humanity is completed. Reason is obliged to make this demand, because her nature impels her to completeness and to the removal of all bounds; while every exclusive activity of one or the other impulse leaves human nature incomplete and places a limit in it. Accordingly, as soon as reason issues the mandate, "A humanity shall exist," it proclaims at the same time the law, "There shall be a beauty." Experience can answer us if there is a beauty, and we shall know it as soon as she has taught us if a humanity can exist. But neither reason nor experience can tell us how beauty can be and how a humanity is possible.

We know that man is neither exclusively matter, nor exclusively spirit. Accordingly, beauty, as the consummation of humanity, can neither be exclusively mere life, . . . nor can beauty be mere form; it is rather the common object of both impulses, that guage completely justifies this name, as it is, of the play-instinct. The use of language is wont to qualify with the word play what is neither subjectively nor objectively accidental, and yet does not impose necessity either externally or internally. As the mind in the intuition of the beautiful finds itself in a happy medium between law and necessity, it is, because it divides itself between both, emancipated from the pressure of both. The formal impulse and the material impulse are equally earnest in their demands, because one relates in its cognition to things in their reality, and the other to their necessity; because in action the first is directed to the preservation of life, the second to the perservation of dignity, and therefore both to truth and perfection. But life becomes more indifferent when dignity blends with it, and duty no longer coerces when inclination attracts. In like manner the mind takes in the reality of things, material truth, more freely and tranquilly as soon as it encounters formal truth, the law of necessity; nor does the mind find itself strained by abstraction as soon as immediate intuition can accompany it. In one word, when the mind comes into communion with ideas, all reality loses its serious value because it becomes *small;* and as it comes in contact with feeling, necessity parts also with its serious value because it is *easy.*

But perhaps the objection has for some time occurred to you, is not the beautiful degraded by this, that it is made a mere play, and is it not reduced to the level of frivolous objects which have for ages passed under that name? Does it not contradict the conception of the reason and the dignity of beauty, which is nevertheless regarded as an instrument of culture, to confine it to the work of being a mere play, and does it not contradict the empirical conception of play, which can coexist with the exclusion of all taste, to confine it merely to beauty?

But what is meant by a *mere play,* when we know that in all conditions of humanity that very thing is play, and *only* that is play which makes man complete, and develops simultaneously his twofold nature? What you style *limitation,* according to your representation of the matter, according to my views, which I have justified by proofs, I name *enlargement.* Consequently I should have said exactly the reverse: man is serious *only* with the agree-

able, with the good, and with the perfect, but he *plays* with beauty. In saying this we must not indeed think of the games that are in vogue in real life, and which commonly refer only to his material state. But in real life we should also seek in vain for the beauty of which we are here speaking. The actually present beauty is worthy of the really, of the actually present play-impulse; but by the ideal of beauty, which is set up by the reason, an ideal of the play-instinct is also presented, which man ought to have before his eyes in all his games.

Therefore, no error will ever be incurred if we seek the ideal of beauty on the same road on which we satisfy our play-impulse. . . . Now the reason pronounces that the beautiful must not only be life and form, but a living form, that is, beauty, inasmuch as it dictates to man the twofold law of absolute formality and absolute reality. Reason also utters the decision that man shall *only play* with beauty, and he shall play *only with beauty.*

For, to speak out once for all, man only plays when in the full meaning of the word he is a man, and *he is only completely a man when he plays.* This proposition, which at this moment perhaps appears paradoxical, will receive a great and deep meaning if we have advanced far enough to apply it to the twofold seriousness of duty and of destiny. I promise you that the whole edifice of aesthetic art and the still more difficult art of life will be supported by this principle. But this proposition is only unexpected in science; long ago it lived and worked in art, and in the feeling of the Greeks, her most accomplished masters; only they removed to Olympus what ought to have been preserved on earth. Influenced by the truth of this principle they effaced from the brow of their gods the earnestness and labour which furrow the cheeks of mortals, and also the hollow lust that smoothes the empty face. They set free the ever serene from the chains of every purpose, of every duty, of every care, and they made *indolence* and *indifference* the envied condition of the godlike race; merely human appellations for the freest and highest mind. As well the material pressure of natural laws as the spiritual pressure of moral laws lost itself in its higher idea of necessity, which embraced at the same time both worlds, and out of the union of these two necessities issued true freedom. Inspired by this spirit the Greeks also effaced from the features of their ideal, together with *desire or inclination,* all traces of *volition,* or, better still, they made both unrecognisable, because they knew how to wed them both in the closest alliance. . . .

From the antagonism of the two impulsions, and from the association of two opposite principles, we have seen beauty to result, of which the highest ideal must therefore be sought in the most perfect union and equilibrium possible of the reality and of the form. But this equilibrium remains always an idea that reality can never completely reach. In reality there will always remain a preponderance of one of these elements over the other, and the highest point to which experience can reach will consist in an oscillation between two principles, when sometimes reality, and at others form will have the advantage. Ideal beauty is therefore eternally one and indivisible, because there can only be one single equilibrium; on the contrary, experienced beauty will be eternally double, because in the oscillation the equilibrium may be destroyed in two ways—this side and that.

I have called attention in the foregoing letters to a fact that can also be rigorously deduced from the considerations that have engaged our attention to the present point; this fact is that an exciting and also a moderating action may be expected from the beautiful. The *tempering* action is directed to keep within proper limits the sensuous and the formal impulsions; the *exciting,* to

maintain both of them in their full force. But these two modes of action of beauty ought to be completely identified in the idea. The beautiful ought to temper while uniformly exciting the two natures, and it ought also to incite while uniformly moderating them. This result flows at once from the idea of a correlation, in virtue of which the two terms mutually imply each other, and are the reciprocal condition one of the other, a correlation of which the purest product is beauty. But experience does not offer an example of so perfect a correlation. In the field of experience it will always happen more or less that excess on the one side will give rise to deficiency on the other, and deficiency will give birth to excess. It results from this that what in the beau-ideal is only distinct in the idea is different in reality in empirical beauty. The beau-ideal, though simple and indivisible, discloses, when viewed in two different aspects, on the one hand, a property of gentleness and grace, and on the other, an energetic property; in experience there is a gentle and graceful beauty, and there is an energetic beauty. It is so, and it will be always so, so long as the absolute is enclosed in the limits of time, and the ideas of reason have to be realised in humanity. For example, the intellectual man has the ideal of virtue, of truth, and of happiness; but the active man will only practise *virtues,* will only grasp *truths,* and enjoy *happy days.* The business of physical and moral education is to bring back this multiplicity to unity, to put morality in the place of manners, science in the place of knowledge; the business of aesthetic education is to make out of beauties the beautiful.

. . .

By beauty the sensuous man is led to form and to thought; by beauty the spiritual man is brought back to matter and restored to the world of sense.

From this statement it would appear to follow that between matter and form, between passivity and activity, there must be a *middle state,* and that beauty plants us in this state. It actually happens that the greater part of mankind really form this conception of beauty as soon as they begin to reflect on its operations, and all experience seems to point to this conclusion. But, on the other hand, nothing is more unwarrantable and contradictory than such a conception, because the aversion of matter and form, the passive and the active, feeling and thought, is *eternal,* and cannot be mediated in any way. How can we remove this contradiction? Beauty weds the two opposed conditions of feeling and thinking, and yet there is absolutely no medium between them. The former is immediately certain through experience, the other through the reason.

This is the point to which the whole question of beauty leads, and if we succeed in settling the point in a satisfactory way, we have at length found the clue that will conduct us through the whole labyrinth of aesthetics.

But this requires two very different operations, which must necessarily support each other in this inquiry. Beauty, it is said, weds two conditions with one another *which are opposite to each other,* and can never be one. We must start from this opposition; we must grasp and recognise them in their entire purity and strictness, so that both conditions are separated in the most definite manner; otherwise we mix, but we do not unite them. Secondly, it is usual to say, beauty *unites* those two opposed conditions, and therefore removes the opposition. But because both conditions remain eternally opposed to one another, they cannot be united in any other way than by being suppressed.

. . .

That freedom is an active and not a passive principle results from its very conception; but that liberty itself should be an effect of nature (taking this word in its widest sense), and not the work of man,

and therefore that it can be favoured or thwarted by natural means, is the necessary consequence of that which precedes. It begins only when man is complete, and when these two fundamental impulsions have been developed. It will then be wanting whilst he is incomplete, and while one of these impulsions is excluded, and it will be re-established by all that gives back to man his integrity.

Thus it is possible, both with regard to the entire species as to the individual, to remark the moment when man is yet incomplete, and when one of the two exclusions act solely in him. We know that man commences with life simply, to end with form; that he is an individual before he is a person, and that he starts from the limited or finite to approach the infinite. The sensuous impulsion comes into play therefore before the rational impulsion, because sensation precedes consciousness; and in this priority of sensuous impulsion we find the key of the history of the whole of human liberty.

There is a moment, in fact, when the instinct of life, not yet opposed to the instinct of form, acts as nature and as necessity; when the sensuous is a power because man has not begun; for in man there can be no other power than his will. But when man shall have attained to the power of thought, reason, on the contrary, will be an authority, and moral or logical necessity will take the place of physical necessity. Sensuous power must then be annihilated before the law which must govern it can be established. It is not enough that something shall begin which as yet was not; previously something must end which had begun. Man cannot pass immediately from sensuousness to thought. He must step backward, for it is only when one determination is suppressed that the contrary determination can take place. Consequently, in order to exchange passive against active liberty, a passive determination against an active, he must be momentarily free from all determination, and must traverse a state of pure determinability. He has then to return in some degree to that state of pure negative indetermination in which he was before his senses were affected by anything. But this state was absolutely empty of all contents, and now the question is to reconcile an equal determination and a determinability equally without limit, with the greatest possible fulness, because from this situation something positive must immediately follow. The determination which man received by sensation must be preserved, because he should not lose the reality; but at the same time, in so far as finite, it should be suppressed, because a determinability without limit is to take place. The problem consists then in annihilating the determination of the mode of existence, and yet at the same time in preserving it, which is only possible in one way: *in opposing to it another*. The two sides of a balance are in equilibrium when empty; they are also in equilibrium when their contents are of equal weight.

Thus, to pass from sensation to thought, the soul traverses a medium position, in which sensibility and reason are at the same time active, and thus they mutually destroy their determinate power, and, by their antagonism produce a negation. This middle situation in which the soul is neither physically nor morally constrained, and yet is in both ways active, merits essentially the name of a free situation; and if we call the state of sensuous determinaion *physical,* and the state of rational determination *logical* or *moral,* that state of real and active determination should be called the *aesthetic.*

I have remarked that there is a twofold condition of determinableness and a twofold condition of determination. And now I can clear up this proposition.

The mind is determinable only in as far as it is not determined; it is, however, determinable also, in as far as it is not exclusively determined; that is, if it is not limited in its determination. The former is only indeterminacy—it is without limits, because it is without reality; but the latter, the aesthetic determinableness, has no limits, because it unites all reality.

The mind is determined, inasmuch as it is limited at all; but it is also determined because it limits itself of its own absolute capacity. It is situated in the former position when it feels, in the second when it thinks. Accordingly the aesthetic constitution is in relation to determinableness what thought is in relation to determination. The former is a negative from internal and infinite completeness, the latter a limitation from internal infinite power. Feeling and thought come into contact in one single point, the mind is determined in both conditions, the man becomes something and exists —either as individual or person—by exclusion; in other cases these two faculties stand infinitely apart. Just in the same manner the aesthetic determinableness comes in contact with mere indeterminacy in a single point, by both excluding every distinct determined existence; in all other points they are as nothing and everything, and hence infinitely different. Therefore if the latter, in the absence of determination from deficiency, is represented as an *empty* infiniteness, the aesthetic freedom of determination, which forms the proper counterpart to the former, can be considered as a *completed infiniteness;* an idea which exactly agrees with the teachings of the previous investigations.

Man is therefore *nothing* in the aesthetic state, if attention is given to the single result, and not to the whole faculty, and if we regard only the absence of every special determination. We must therefore do justice to those who pronounce the beautiful, and the disposition in which it places the mind, as entirely indifferent and unprofitable, in relation to *knowledge* and *feeling.* They are perfectly right; for it is certain that beauty gives no separate, single result, either for the understanding or for the will; it does not realize a single intellectual or moral purpose; it discovers no truth, does not help us to fulfill a single duty, and, in *one* word, is equally unfit to found the character or to clear the head. Accordingly, the personal worth of a man, or his dignity, as far as this can only depend on himself, remains entirely undetermined by aesthetic culture, and nothing further is attained than that, on the *part* of *nature,* it is made possible for him to make of himself what he will; that the freedom to be what he ought to be is restored completely to him.

But by this something infinite is attained. For as soon as we remember that freedom is taken from man by the one-sided compulsion of nature in feeling, and by the exclusive legislation of the reason in thinking, we must consider the capacity restored to him by the aesthetical disposition, as the highest of all gifts, as the gift of humanity. I admit that he possesses this capacity for humanity, before every definite determination in which he may be placed. But, as a matter of fact, he loses it with every determined condition into which he may come; and if he is to pass over to an opposite condition, humanity must be in every case restored to him by the aesthetic life.

It is therefore not only a poetical license, but also philosophically correct, when beauty is named our second creator. Nor is this inconsistent with the fact that she only makes it possible for us to attain and realise humanity, leaving this to our free will. For in this she acts in common with our original creator, nature, which has imparted to us nothing further than this capacity for humanity, but leaves the use of it to our own determination of will.

Accordingly, if the aesthetic disposition of the mind must be looked upon in *one* respect as *nothing*—that is, when we confine our view to separate and determined operations—it must be looked upon in another respect as a state of the highest reality, in as far as we attend to the absence of all limits and the sum of powers which are commonly active in it. Accordingly we cannot pronounce them, again, to be wrong who describe the aesthetic state to be the most productive in relation to knowledge and morality. They are perfectly right, for a state of mind which comprises the whole of humanity in itself must of necessity include in itself also—necessarily and potentially—every separate expression of it. Again, a disposition of mind that removes all limitation from the totality of human nature must also remove it from every individual expression of it. Exactly because its "aesthetic disposition" does not exclusively shelter any separate function of humanity, it is favourable to all without distinction; nor does it favour any particular functions, precisely because it is the foundation of the possibility of all. All other exercises give to the mind some special aptitude, but for that very reason give it some definite limits; only the aesthetical leads him to the unlimited. Every other condition in which we can live refers us to a previous condition, and requires for its solution a following condition; only the aesthetic is a complete whole in itself, for it unites in itself all conditions of its source and of its duration. Here alone we feel ourselves swept out of time, and our humanity expresses itself with purity and *integrity* as if it had not yet received any impression or interruption from the operation of external powers.

That which flatters our senses in immediate sensation opens our weak and volatile spirit to every impression, but makes us in the same degree less apt for exertion. That which stretches our thinking power and invites us to abstract conceptions, strengthens our mind for every kind of resistance, but hardens it also in the same proportion, and deprives us of sensibility in the same ratio that it helps us to greater mental activity. For this very reason, one as well as the other brings us at length to exhaustion, because matter cannot long do without the shaping, constructive force, and the force cannot do without the constructible material. But on the other hand, if we have resigned ourselves to the enjoyment of genuine beauty, we are at such a moment master of our passive and active powers in the same degree, and we shall turn with ease from grave to gay, from rest to movement from submission to resistance, to abstract thinking or intuition.

This high indifference and freedom of mind, united with power and elasticity, is the disposition in which a true work of art ought to leave us, and there is no better test of true aesthetic excellence. If after an enjoyment of this kind we find ourselves specially impelled to a particular mode of feeling or action, and unfit for other modes, this serves as an infallible proof that we have not experienced *any pure aesthetic* effect, whether this is owing to the object, to our own mode of feeling— as generally happens—or to both together.

As in reality no purely aesthetical effect can be met with—for man can never leave his dependence on material forces—the excellence of a work of art can only consist in its greater approximation to its ideal of aesthetic purity, and however high we may raise the freedom of this effect we shall always leave it with a particular disposition and a particular bias. Any type of production or individual work in the world of art is noble and excellent in proportion to the universality of the disposition and the unlimited character of the bias thereby presented to our mind. This truth can be applied to works in various branches of art, and also to different works in the same branch. We leave a grand musical performance with our feelings excited, the reading of a noble poem with a quickened imagination, a beautiful statue or building with an awakened understanding; but a man would not choose an opportune moment who attempted to invite us to abstract thinking

after a high musical enjoyment, or to attend to a prosaic affair of common life after a high poetical enjoyment, or to kindle our imagination and astonish our feelings directly after inspecting a fine statue or edifice. The reason of this is that music, *by its matter,* even when most spiritual, presents a greater affinity with the senses than is permitted by aesthetic liberty; it is because even the most happy poetry, having *for its medium* the arbitrary and contingent play of the imagination, always shares in it more than the intimate necessity of the really beautiful allows; it is because the best sculpture touches on severe science *by what is determinate in its conception.* However, these particular affinities are lost in proportion as the works of these three kinds of art rise to a greater elevation, and it is a natural and necessary consequence of their perfection that, without confounding their objective limits, the different arts come to resemble each other more and more in the action *which they exercise on the mind.* At its highest degree of ennobling, music ought to become a form, and act on us with the calm power of an antique statue; in its most elevated perfection the plastic art ought to become music, and move us by the immediate action exercised on the mind by the senses; in its most complete development poetry ought both to stir us powerfully like music, and like plastic art to surround us with a peaceful light. In each art the perfect style consists exactly in knowing how to remove specific limits, without sacrificing at the same time the particular advantages of the art, and to give it by a wise use of what belongs to it specially a more universal character.

Nor is it only the limits inherent in the specific character of each kind of art that the artist ought to overcome in putting his hand to the work; he must also triumph over those which are inherent in the particular subject of which he treats. In a really beautiful work of art the substance ought to be inoperative, the form should do everything; for by the form the whole man is acted on; the substance acts on nothing but isolated forces. Thus, however vast and sublime it may be, the substance always exercises a restrictive action on the mind, and true aesthetic liberty can only be expected from the form. Consequently the true secret of the master consists in *destroying matter by the form;* and the triumph of art is great in proportion as it overcomes matter, and maintains its sway over those who enjoy its work by form. It is great particularly in destroying matter when most imposing, ambitious, and attractive, when therefore matter has most power to produce the effect proper to it, or, again, when it leads those who consider it more closely to enter directly into relation with it. The mind of the spectator and of the hearer must remain perfectly free and intact; it must issue pure and entire from the magic circle of the artist, as from the hands of the Creator. The most frivolous subject ought to be treated in such a way that we prepare the faculty to exchange it immediately for the most serious work. The arts which have passion for their object, as a tragedy for example, do not present a difficulty here; for, in the first place, these arts are not entirely free, because they are in the service of a particular end (the pathetic), and then no connoisseur will deny that even in this class a work is perfect in proportion as amidst the most violent storms of passion it respects the liberty of the soul. There is a fine art of passion, but an impassioned fine art is a contradiction in terms, for the infallible effect of the beautiful is emancipation from the passions. The idea of an instructive fine art (didactic art) or improving (moral) art is no less contradictory, for nothing agrees less with the idea of the beautiful than to give a determinate tendency to the mind.

However, from the fact that a work produces effects only by its substance, it must not always be inferred that there is a want of form in this work; this conclusion may quite as well testify to a want of form in the observer. If his mind is too taut or too relaxed, if it is only accustomed to receive things either by the senses or the intelligence, even in the most perfect combination, it will only stop to look at the parts, and it will only see matter in the most beautiful form. Only sensible of the coarse *elements,* he must first destroy the aesthetic organisation of a work to find enjoyment in it, and carefully disinter the details which genius has caused to vanish, with infinite art, in the harmony of the whole. The interest he takes in the work is either solely moral or exclusively physical; the only thing wanting to it is to be exactly what it ought to be—aesthetical. The readers of this class enjoy a serious and pathetic poem as they do a sermon; a simple and playful work, as an inebriating draught . . .

. . .

I take up the threat of my researches, which I broke off only to apply the principles I laid down to practical art and the appreciation of its works.

The transition from the passivity of sensuousness to the activity of thought and of will can be effected only by the intermediary state of aesthetic liberty; and though in itself this state decides nothing respecting our opinions and our sentiments, and therefore it leaves our intellectual and moral value entirely problematical, it is, however, the necessary condition without which we should never attain to an opinion or a sentiment. In a word, there is no other way to make a reasonable being out of a sensuous man than by making him first aesthetic.

. . .

What phenomenon accompanies the initiation of the savage into humanity? However far we look back into history, the phenomenon is identical among all people who have shaken off the slavery of the animal state: the love of appearance, the inclination for dress and for games.

Extreme stupidity and extreme intelligence have a certain affinity in only seeking the real and being completely insensible to mere appearance. The former is only drawn forth by the immediate presence of an object in the senses, and the second is reduced to a quiescent state only by referring conceptions to the facts of experience. In short, stupidity cannot rise above reality, nor the intelligence descend below truth. Thus, in as far as the want of reality and attachment to the real are only the consequence of a want and a defect, indifference to the real and an interest taken in appearances are a real enlargement of humanity and a decisive step toward culture. In the first place it is the proof of an exterior liberty, for as long as necessity commands and want solicits, the fancy is strictly chained down to the real: only when want is satisfied does it develop without hinderance. But it is also the proof of an internal liberty, because it reveals to us a force which, independent of an external substratum, sets itself in motion, and has sufficient energy to remove from itself the solicitations of nature. The reality of things is effected by things, the appearance of things is the work of man, and a soul that takes pleasure in appearance does not take pleasure in what it receives but in what it does.

It is self-evident that I am speaking of aesthetical appearance different from reality and truth, and not of logical appearance identical with them. Therefore if it is liked it is because it is an appearance, and not because it is held to be something better than it is: the first principle alone is a play, whilst the second is a deception. To give a value to the appearance of the first kind can never injure truth, because it is never to be feared that it will supplant it—the

only way in which truth can be injured. To despise this appearance is to despise in general all the fine arts of which it is the essence. Nevertheless, it happens sometimes that the understanding carries its zeal for reality as far as this intolerance, and strikes with a sentence of ostracism all the arts relating to beauty in appearance, because it is only an appearance. However, the intelligence only shows this vigorous spirit when it calls to mind the affinity pointed out further back. . . .

It is nature herself which raises man from reality to appearance by endowing him with two senses which only lead him to the knowledge of the real through appearance. In the eye and the ear the organs of the senses are already freed from the persecutions of nature, and the object with which we are immediately in contact through the animal senses is remoter from us. What we *see* by the eye differs from what we *perceive;* for the understanding to reach objects overleaps the light which separates us from them. In touch, we are passive to an object: in sight and hearing the object is a form we create. While still a savage, man only enjoys through touch merely aided by sight and sound. He either does not rise to perception through sight, or does not rest there. As soon as he begins to enjoy through sight, vision has an independent value, he is aesthetically free, and the instinct of play is developed.

The instinct of play likes appearance, and directly it is awakened it is followed by the formal imitative instinct which treats appearance as an independent thing. Directly man has come to distinguish the appearance from the reality, the form from the body, he can separate one from the other, in fact he has already done so. Thus the faculty of the art of imitation is given with the faculty of form in general. The inclination that draws us to it reposes on another tendency I have not to notice here. Exactly when the aesthetic instinct, or that of art, develops, depends entirely on the attraction that mere appearance has for men.

As every real existence proceeds from nature as an external power, whilst every appearance comes in the first place from man as a percipient subject, he only uses his absolute sight in separating semblance from essence, and arranging according to subjective law. With an unbridled liberty he can unite what nature has severed, provided he can imagine this union, and he can separate what nature has united, provided this separation can take place in his intelligence. Here nothing can be sacred to him but his own law: the only condition imposed upon him is to respect the border which separates his own sphere from the existence of things or from the realm of nature.

The human right of sovereignty is exercised by man in the art of appearance; and his success in extending the empire of the beautiful, and guarding the frontiers of truth, will be in proportion with the strictness with which he separates form from substance: for if he frees appearance from reality, he must also free reality from appearance.

But man possesses sovereign power only in the world of appearance, in the unsubstantial realm of imagination, only by abstaining from affirming existence of appearance in theory, and from giving it being in practice. It follows that the poet transgresses his proper limits when he attributes being to his ideal, and when he gives this ideal aim as a determined existence. For he can only reach this result by exceeding his right as a poet, that of encroaching by the ideal on the field of experience, and by pretending to determine real existence in virtue of a simple possibility, or else he renounces his right as a poet by letting experience encroach on the sphere of the ideal, and by restricting possibility to the conditions of reality.

It is only by being frank or disclaiming all reality, and by being independent or doing without reality, that the appearance is aesthetical. Directly it apes reality or needs reality for effect, it is nothing more than a vile instrument for material ends, and can prove nothing for the freedom of the mind. Moreover, the object in which we find beauty need not be unreal if our judgment disregards this reality; for if it regards this the judgment is no longer aesthetical. A beautiful woman, if living, would no doubt please us as much and rather more than an equally beautiful woman seen in painting; but what makes the former please men is not her being an independent appearance; she no longer pleases the pure aesthetic feeling. In the painting, life must only attract as an appearance, and reality as an idea. But it is certain that to feel in a living object only the pure appearance requires a greatly higher aesthetic culture than to do without life in the appearance.

When the frank and independent appearance is found in an individual man, or in a whole people, it may be inferred they have intellect, taste, and all prerogatives connected with them. In this case the ideal will be seen to govern real life, honour triumphing over fortune, thought over enjoyment, the dream of immortality over a transitory existence.

In this case public opinion will no longer be feared, and an olive crown will be more valued than a purple mantle. Impotence and perversity alone have recourse to false and paltry semblance, and individuals as well as nations who lend to reality the support of appearance, or to the aesthetic appearance the support of reality, show their moral unworthiness and their aesthetical impotence. Therefore, a short and conclusive answer can be given to this question—how far will appearance be permitted in the moral world? It will run thus: in so far as this appearance is aesthetical, that is, an appearance that does not try to replace reality, nor requires to be made up for by it. Aesthetical appearance can never endanger the truth of morals: wherever it seems to do so the appearance is not aesthetical. Only a stranger to the fashionable world can take polite assurances, which are only a form, for proofs of affection, and say he has been deceived; but only a clumsy fellow in good society calls in the aid of duplicity and flatters to become amiable. The former lacks the pure sense for independent appearance; therefore he can only give a value to appearance by truth. The second lacks reality, and wishes to replace it by appearance. Nothing is more common than to hear depreciators of the times utter these paltry complaints—that all solidity has disappeared from the world, and that reality is neglected for semblance. Though I feel by no means called upon to defend this age against these reproaches, I must say that the wide application of these criticisms shows that they attach blame to the age, not only on the score of the false, but also of the frank appearance. And even the exceptions they admit in favour of the beautiful have for their object less the independent appearance than the needy appearance. Not only do they attack the artificial colouring that hides truth and replaces reality, but also the beneficent appearance that fills a vacuum and clothes poverty; and they even attack the ideal appearance that ennobles a vulgar reality. Their strict sense of truth is rightly offended by the falsity of manners; unfortu-

nately, they class politeness in this category. It displeases them that the noisy and showy so often eclipse true merit, but they are no less shocked that appearance is also demanded from merit, and that a real substance does not dispense with an agreeable form. They regret the cordiality, the energy, and solidity of ancient times; they would restore with them ancient coarseness, heaviness, and the old Gothic profusion. By judgments of this kind they show an esteem for matter itself unworthy of humanity, which ought only to value matter inasmuch as it can receive a form and enlarge the empire of ideas. Accordingly, the taste of the age need not much fear these criticisms if it can clear itself before better judges. Our defect is not to grant a value to aesthetic appearance (we do not do this enough): a severe judge of the beautiful might rather reproach us with not having arrived at pure appearance, with not having separated clearly enough existence from the phenomenon, and thus established their limits. We shall deserve this reproach so long as we cannot enjoy the beautiful in living nature without desiring it; as long as we cannot admire the beautiful in the imitative arts without having an end in view; as long as we do not grant to imagination an absolute legislation of its own; and as long as we do not inspire it with care for its dignity by the esteem we show for its works.

WILLIAM WORDSWORTH [1770–1850]

>>>>><<<<<

Observations Prefixed to "Lyrical Ballads" [1800]

The first volume of these Poems has already been submitted to general perusal. It was published, as an experiment, which, I hoped, might be of some use to ascertain, how far, by fitting to metrical arrangement a selection of the real language of men in a state of vivid sensation, that sort of pleasure and that quantity of pleasure may be imparted, which a Poet may rationally endeavour to impart.

I had formed no very inaccurate estimate of the probable effect of those Poems: I flattered myself that they who should be pleased with them would read them with more than common pleasure: and, on the other hand, I was well aware, that by those who should dislike them, they would be read with more than common dislike. The result has differed from my expectation in this only, that a greater number have been pleased than I ventured to hope I should please.

Several of my Friends are anxious for the success of these Poems, from a belief, that, if the views with which they were composed were indeed realized, a class of Poetry would be produced, well adapted to interest mankind permanently, and not unimportant in the quality, and in the multiplicity of its moral relations: and on this account they have advised me to prefix a systematic defence of the theory upon which the Poems were written. But I was unwilling to undertake the task, knowing

From *Prose Works of William Wordsworth*, edited by William Knight (London, New York: Macmillan, 1896).

that on this occasion the Reader would look coldly upon my arguments, since I might be suspected of having been principally influenced by the selfish and foolish hope of *reasoning* him into an approbation of these particular Poems: and I was still more unwilling to undertake the task, because, adequately to display the opinions, and fully to enforce the arguments, would require a space wholly disproportionate to a preface. For, to treat the subject with the clearness and coherence of which it is susceptible, it would be necessary to give a full account of the present state of the public taste in this country, and to determine how far this taste is healthy or depraved; which, again, could not be determined, without pointing out in what manner language and the human mind act and re-act on each other, and without retracing the revolutions, not of literature alone, but likewise of society itself. I have therefore altogether declined to enter regularly upon this defence; yet I am sensible, that there would be something like impropriety in abruptly obtruding upon the Public, without a few words of introduction, Poems so materially different from those upon which general approbation is at present bestowed.

It is supposed, that by the act of writing in verse an Author makes a formal engagement that he will gratify certain known habits of association; that he not only thus apprises the Reader that certain classes of ideas and expressions will be found in his book, but that others will be carefully excluded. This exponent or symbol held forth by metrical language must in different eras of literature have excited very different expectations: for example, in the age of Catullus, Terence, and Lucretius, and that of Statius or Claudian; and in our own country, in the age of Shakespeare and Beaumont and Fletcher, and that of Donne and Cowley, or Dryden, or Pope. I will not take upon me to determine the exact import of the promise which, by the act of writing in verse, an Author in the present day makes to his reader: but it will undoubtedly appear to many persons that I have not fulfilled the terms of an engagement thus voluntarily contracted. They who have been accustomed to the gaudiness and inane phraseology of many modern writers, if they persist in reading this book to its conclusion, will, no doubt, frequently have to struggle with feelings of strangeness and awkwardness: they will look round for poetry, and will be induced to inquire by what species of courtesy these attempts can be permitted to assume that title. I hope therefore the reader will not censure me for attempting to state what I have proposed to myself to perform; and also (as far as the limits of a preface will permit) to explain some of the chief reasons which have determined me in the choice of my purpose: that at least he may be spared any unpleasant feeling of disappointment, and that I myself may be protected from one of the most dishonourable accusations which can be brought against an Author; namely, that of an indolence which prevents him from endeavouring to ascertain what is his duty, or, when his duty is ascertained, prevents him from performing it.

The principal object, then, proposed in these Poems was to choose incidents and situations from common life, and to relate or describe them, throughout, as far as was possible in a selection of language really used by men, and, at the same time, to throw over them a certain colouring of imagination, whereby ordinary things should be presented to the mind in an unusual aspect; and, further, and above all, to make these incidents and situations interesting by tracing in them, truly though not ostentatiously, the primary laws of our nature: chiefly, as far as regards the manner in which we associate ideas in a state of excitement. Humble and rustic life was generally chosen, because, in that condition, the essential passions of the heart find a better soil in which they can attain their maturity, are less under restraint, and speak a plainer and more emphatic language; because in that condition of life our elementary feelings coexist in a state of greater simplicity, and, consequently, may be more accurately contemplated, and more forcibly communicated; because the manners of rural life germinate from those elementary feelings, and, from the necessary character of rural occupations, are more easily comprehended, and are more durable; and, lastly, because in that condition the passions of men are incorporated with the beautiful and permanent forms of nature. The language, too, of these men has been adopted (purified indeed from what appear to be its real defects, from all lasting and rational causes of dislike or disgust) because such men hourly communicate with the best objects from which the best part of language is originally derived; and because, from their rank in society and the sameness and narrow circle of their intercourse, being less under the influence of social vanity, they convey their feelings and notions in simple and unelaborated expressions. Accordingly, such a language, arising out of repeated experience and regular feelings, is a more permanent, and a far more philosophical language, than that which is frequently substituted for it by Poets, who think that they are conferring honour upon themselves and their art, in proportion as they separate themselves from the sympathies of men, and indulge in arbitrary and capricious habits of expression, in order to furnish food for fickle tastes, and fickle appetites, of their own creation.

I cannot, however, be insensible to the

present outcry against the triviality and meanness, both of thought and language, which some of my contemporaries have occasionally introduced into their metrical compositions; and I acknowledge that this defect, where it exists, is more dishonourable to the Writer's own character than false refinement or arbitrary innovation, though I should contend at the same time, that it is far less pernicious in the sum of its consequences. From such verses the Poems in these volumes will be found distinguished at least by one mark of difference, that each of them has a worthy *purpose*. Not that I always began to write with a distinct purpose formerly conceived; but habits of meditation have, I trust, so prompted and regulated my feelings, that my descriptions of such objects as strongly excite those feelings, will be found to carry along with them a *purpose*. If this opinion be erroneous, I can have little right to the name of a Poet. For all good poetry is the spontaneous overflow of powerful feelings: and though this be true, Poems to which any value can be attached were never produced on any variety of subjects but by a man who, being possessed of more than usual organic sensibility, had also thought long and deeply. For our continued influxes of feelings are modified and directed by our thoughts, which are indeed the representatives of all our past feelings; and, as by contemplating the relation of these general representatives to each other, we discover what is really important to men, so, by the repetition and continuance of this act, our feelings will be connected with important subjects, till at length, if we be originally possessed of much sensibility, such habits of mind will be produced, that, by obeying blindly and mechanically the impulses of those habits, we shall describe objects, and utter sentiments, of such a nature, and in such connexion with each other, that the understanding of the Reader must necessarily be in some degree enlightened, and his affections strengthened and purified.

It has been said that each of these poems has a purpose. Another circumstance must be mentioned which distinguishes these Poems from the popular Poetry of the day; it is this, that the feeling therein developed gives importance to the action and situation, and not the action and situation to the feeling.

A sense of false modesty shall not prevent me from asserting, that the Reader's attention is pointed to this mark of distinction, far less for the sake of these particular Poems than from the general importance of the subject. The subject is indeed important! For the human mind is capable of being excited without the application of gross and violent stimulants; and he must have a very faint perception of its beauty and dignity who does not know this, and who does not further know, that one being is elevated above another, in proportion as he possesses this capability. It has therefore appeared to me, that to endeavour to produce or enlarge this capability is one of the best services in which, at any period, a Writer can be engaged; but this service, excellent at all times, is especially so at the present day. For a multitude of causes, unknown to former times, are now acting with a combined force to blunt the discriminating powers of the mind, and, unfitting it for all voluntary exertion, to reduce it to a state of almost savage torpor. The most effective of these causes are the great national events which are daily taking place, and the increasing accumulation of men in cities, where the uniformity of their occupations produces a craving for extraordinary incident, which the rapid communication of intelligence hourly gratifies. To this tendency of life and manners the literature and theatrical exhibitions of the country have conformed themselves. The invaluable works of our elder writers, I had almost said the works of Shakespeare and Milton, are driven into neglect by frantic novels, sickly and stupid German Tragedies, and deluges of idle and extravagant stories in verse.—When I think upon this degrading thirst after outrageous stimulation, I am almost ashamed to have spoken of the feeble endeavour made in these volumes to counteract it; and, reflecting upon the magnitude of the general evil, I should be oppressed with no dishonourable melancholy, had I not a deep impression of certain inherent and indestructible qualities of the human mind, and likewise of certain powers in the great and permanent objects that act upon it, which are equally inherent and indestructible; and were there not added to this impression a belief, that the time is approaching when the evil will be systematically opposed, by men of greater powers, and with far more distinguished success.

Having dwelt thus long on the subjects and aim of these Poems, I shall request the Reader's permission to apprise him of a few circumstances relating to their *style,* in order, among other reasons, that he may not censure me for not having performed what I never attempted. The Reader will find that personifications of abstract ideas rarely occur in these Volumes; and are utterly rejected, as an ordinary device to elevate the style, and raise it above prose. My purpose was to imitate, and, as far as possible, to adopt the very language of men; and assuredly such personifications do not make any natural or regular part of that language. They are, indeed, a figure of speech occasionally prompted by passion, and I have made use of them as such; but have endeavoured utterly to reject them as a mechanical device of style, or as a family language which Writers in metre seem to lay claim to by prescription. I have wished to keep the Reader in the company of flesh and blood, persuaded that by so doing I shall interest him. Others who pursue a different track will interest him likewise; I do not interfere with their claim, but wish to prefer a claim of my own. There will also be found in these volumes little of what is usually called poetic diction; as

much pains has been taken to avoid it as is ordinarily taken to produce it; this has been done for the reason already alleged, to bring my language near to the language of men; and further, because the pleasure which I have proposed to myself to impart, is of a kind very different from that which is supposed by many persons to be the proper object of poetry. Without being culpably particular, I do not know how to give my Reader a more exact notion of the style in which it was my wish and intention to write, than by informing him that I have at all times endeavoured to look steadily at my subject; consequently, there is I hope in these Poems little falsehood of description, and my ideas are expressed in language fitted to their respective importance. Something must have been gained by this practice, as it is friendly to one property of all good poetry, namely, good sense: but it has necessarily cut me off from a large portion of phrases and figures of speech which from father to son have long been regarded as the common inheritance of Poets. I have also thought it expedient to restrict myself still further, having abstained from the use of many expressions, in themselves proper and beautiful, but which have been foolishly repeated by bad Poets, till such feelings of disgust are connected with them as it is scarcely possible by any art of association to overpower.

If in a poem there should be found a series of lines, or even a single line, in which the language, though naturally arranged, and according to the strict laws of metre, does not differ from that of prose, there is a numerous class of critics, who, when they stumble upon these prosaisms, as they call them, imagine that they have made a notable discovery, and exult over the Poet as over a man ignorant of his own profession. Now these men would establish a canon of criticism which the Reader will conclude he must utterly reject, if he wishes to be pleased with these volumes.

And it would be a most easy task to prove to him, that not only the language of a large portion of every good poem, even of the most elevated character, must necessarily, except with reference to the metre, in no respect differ from that of good prose, but likewise that some of the most interesting parts of the best poems will be found to be strictly the language of prose when prose is well written. The truth of this assertion might be demonstrated by innumerable passages from almost all the poetical writings, even of Milton himself. To illustrate the subject in a general manner, I will here adduce a short composition of Gray, who was at the head of those who, by their reasonings, have attempted to widen the space of separation betwixt Prose and Metrical composition, and was more than any other man curiously elaborate in the structure of his own poetic diction.

In vain to me the smiling mornings shine,
And reddening Phoebus lifts his golden fire:
The birds in vain their amorous descant join,
Or cheerful fields resume their green attire.
These ears, alas! for other notes repine;
A different object do these eyes require;
My lonely anguish melts no heart but mine;
And in my breast the imperfect joys expire;
Yet morning smiles the busy race to cheer,
And new-born pleasure brings to happier men;
The fields to all their wonted tribute bear;
To warm their little loves the birds complain,
I fruitless mourn to him that cannot hear,
And weep the more because I weep in vain.

It will easily be perceived, that the only part of this Sonnet which is of any value is the lines printed in Italics; it is equally obvious, that, except in the rhyme, and in the use of the single word "fruitless" for fruitlessly, which is so far a defect, the language of these lines does in no respect differ from that of prose.

By the foregoing quotation it has been shown that language of Prose may yet be well adapted to Poetry; and it was previously asserted, that a large portion of the language of every good poem can in no respect differ from that of good Prose. We will go further. It may be safely affirmed, that there neither is, nor can be, any *essential* difference between the language of prose and metrical composition. We are fond of tracing the resemblance between Poetry and Painting, and, accordingly, we call them Sisters: but where shall we find bonds of connexion sufficiently strict to typify the affinity betwixt metrical and prose composition? They both speak by and to the same organs; the bodies in which both of them are clothed may be said to be of the same substance, their affections are kindred, and almost identical, not necessarily differing even in degrees; Poetry[1] sheds no tears "such as Angels weep," but natural and human tears; she can boast of no celestial ichor that distinguishes her vital juices from those of prose; the same human blood circulates through the veins of them both.

If it be affirmed that rhyme and metrical arrangement of themselves constitute a distinction which overturns what has just been said on the strict affinity of metrical language with that of prose, and paves the way for other artificial distinctions which the mind voluntarily admits, I answer that the language of such Poetry as is here recommended is, as far as is possible, a selection of the language really spoken by men; that this selection, wherever it is made with true taste and feeling, will of itself form a distinction far greater than would at first be imagined, and will entirely separate the composition from the

---

[1] I here use the word "Poetry" (though against my own judgement) as opposed to the word Prose, and synonymous with metrical composition. But much confusion has been introduced into criticism by this contradistinction of Poetry and Prose, instead of the more philosophical one of Poetry and Matter of Fact, or Science. The only strict antithesis to Prose is Metre; nor is this, in truth, a *strict* antithesis, because lines and passages of metre so naturally occur in writing prose, that it would be scarcely possible to avoid them, even were it desirable.

vulgarity and meanness of ordinary life; and, if metre be superadded thereto, I believe that a dissimilitude will be produced altogether sufficient for the gratification of a rational mind. What other distinction would we have? Whence is it to come? And where is it to exist? Not, surely, where the Poet speaks through the mouths of his characters: it cannot be necessary here, either for elevation of style, or any of its supposed ornaments: for, if the Poet's subject be judiciously chosen, it will naturally, and upon fit occasion, lead him to passions the language of which, if selected truly and judiciously, must necessarily be dignified and variegated, and alive with metaphors and figures. I forbear to speak of an incongruity which would shock the intelligent Reader, should the Poet interweave any foreign splendour of his own with that which the passion naturally suggests: it is sufficient to say that such addition is unnecessary. And, surely, it is more probable that those passages, which with propriety abound with metaphors and figures, will have their due effect, if, upon other occasions where the passions are of a milder character, the style also be subdued and temperate.

But, as the pleasure which I hope to give by the Poems now presented to the Reader must depend entirely on just notions upon this subject, and, as it is in itself of high importance to our taste and moral feelings, I cannot content myself with these detached remarks. And if, in what I am about to say, it shall appear to some that my labour is unnecessary, and that I am like a man fighting a battle without enemies, such persons may be reminded, that, whatever be the language outwardly holden by men, a practical faith in the opinions which I am wishing to establish is almost unknown. If my conclusions are admitted, and carried as far as they must be carried if admitted at all, our judgments concerning the works of the greatest Poets both ancient and modern

will be far different from what they are at present, both when we praise, and when we censure: and our moral feelings influencing and influenced by these judgments will, I believe, be corrected and purified.

Taking up the subject, then, upon general grounds, let me ask, what is meant by the word Poet? What is a Poet? To whom does he address himself? And what language is to be expected from him?—He is a man speaking to men: a man, it is true, endowed with more lively sensibility, more enthusiasm and tenderness, who has a greater knowledge of human nature, and a more comprehensive soul, than are supposed to be common among mankind; a man pleased with his own passions and volitions, and who rejoices more than other men in the spirit of life that is in him; delighting to contemplate similar volitions and passions as manifested in the goings-on of the Universe, and habitually impelled to create them where he does not find them. To these qualities he has added a disposition to be affected more than other men by absent things as if they were present; an ability of conjuring up in himself passions, which are indeed far from being the same as those produced by real events, yet (especially in those parts of the general sympathy which are pleasing and delightful) do more nearly resemble the passions produced by real events, than anything which, from the motions of their own minds merely, other men are accustomed to feel in themselves:—whence, and from practice, he had acquired a greater readiness and power in expressing what he thinks and feels, and especially those thoughts and feelings which, by his own choice, or from the structure of his own mind, arise in him without immediate external excitement.

But whatever portion of this faculty we may suppose even the greatest Poet to possess, there cannot be a doubt that the language which it will suggest to him, must often, in liveliness and truth, fall short of that which is uttered by men in real life, under the actual pressure of those passions, certain shadows of which the Poet thus produces, or feels to be produced, in himself.

However exalted a notion we would wish to cherish of the character of a Poet, it is obvious, that while he describes and imitates passions, his employment is in some degree mechanical, compared with the freedom and power of real and substantial action and suffering. So that it will be the wish of the Poet to bring his feelings near to those of the persons whose feelings he describes, nay, for short spaces of time, perhaps, to let himself slip into an entire delusion, and even confound and identify his own feelings with theirs; modifying only the language which is thus suggested to him by a consideration that he describes for a particular purpose, that of giving pleasure. Here, then, he will apply the principle of selection which has been already insisted upon. He will depend upon this for removing what would otherwise be painful or disgusting in the passion; he will feel that there is no necessity to trick out or to elevate nature: and, the more industriously he applies this principle, the deeper will be his faith that no words, which *his* fancy or imagination can suggest, will be to be compared with those which are the emanations of reality and truth.

But it may be said by those who do not object to the general spirit of these remarks, that, as it is impossible for the Poet to produce upon all occasions language as exquisitely fitted for the passion as that which the real passion itself suggests, it is proper that he should consider himself as in the situation of a translator, who does not scruple to substitute excellencies of another kind for those which are unattainable by him; and endeavours occasionally to surpass his original, in order to make some amends for the general inferiority to which he feels that he must submit. But

this would be to encourage idleness and unmanly despair. Further, it is the language of men who speak of what they do not understand; who talk of Poetry as of a matter of amusement and idle pleasure; who will converse with us as gravely about a *taste* for Poetry, as they express it, as if it were a thing as indifferent as a taste for rope-dancing, or Frontiniac or Sherry. Aristotle, I have been told, has said, that Poetry is the most philosophic of all writing: it is so: its object is truth, not individual and local, but general, and operative; not standing upon external testimony, but carried alive into the heart by passion; truth which is its own testimony, which gives competence and confidence to the tribunal to which it appeals, and receives them from the same tribunal. Poetry is the image of man and nature. The obstacles which stand in the way of the fidelity of the Biographer and Historian, and of their consequent utility, are incalculably greater than those which are to be encountered by the Poet who comprehends the dignity of his art. The Poet writes under one restriction only, namely, the necessity of giving immediate pleasure to a human Being possessed of that information which may be expected from him, not as a lawyer, a physician, a mariner, an astronomer, or a natural philosopher, but as a Man. Except this one restriction, there is no object standing between the Poet and the image of things; between this, and the Biographer and Historian, there are a thousand.

Nor let this necessity of producing immediate pleasure be considered as a degradation of the Poet's art. It is far otherwise. It is an acknowledgement of the beauty of the universe, an acknowledgement the more sincere, because not formal, but indirect; it is a task light and easy to him who looks at the world in the spirit of love: further, it is a homage paid to the native and naked dignity of man, to the grand elementary principle of pleasure, by which he knows, and feels, and lives, and moves. We have no sympathy but what is propagated by pleasure: I would not be misunderstood; but wherever we sympathize with pain, it will be found that the sympathy is produced and carried on by subtle combinations with pleasure. We have no knowledge, that is, no general principles drawn from the contemplation of particular facts, but what has been built up by pleasure, and exists in us by pleasure alone. The Man of science, the Chemist and Mathematician, whatever difficulties and disgusts they may have had to struggle with, know and feel this. However painful may be the objects with which the Anatomist's knowledge is connected, he feels that his knowledge is pleasure; and where he has no pleasure he has no knowledge. What then does the Poet? He considers man and the objects that surround him as acting and reacting upon each other, so as to produce an infinite complexity of pain and pleasure; he considers man in his own nature and in his ordinary life as contemplating this with a certain quantity of immediate knowledge, with certain convictions, intuitions, and deductions, which from habit acquire the quality of intuitions; he considers him as looking upon this complex scene of ideas and sensations, and finding everywhere objects that immediately excite in him sympathies which, from the necessities of his nature, are accompanied by an overbalance of enjoyment.

   To this knowledge which all men carry about with them, and to these sympathies in which, without any other discipline than that of our daily life, we are fitted to take delight, the Poet principally directs his attention. He considers man and nature as essentially adapted to each other, and the mind of man as naturally the mirror of the fairest and most interesting properties of nature. And thus the Poet, prompted by this feeling of pleasure, which accompanies him through the whole course of his studies, converses with general nature, with affections akin to those, which, through

labour and length of time, the Man of science has raised up in himself, by conversing with those particular parts of nature which are the objects of his studies. The knowledge both of the Poet and the Man of science is pleasure; but the knowledge of the one cleaves to us as a necessary part of our existence, our natural and unalienable inheritance; the other is a personal and individual acquisition, slow to come to us, and by no habitual and direct sympathy connecting us with our fellow-beings. The Man of science seeks truth as a remote and unknown benefactor; he cherishes and loves it in his solitude: the Poet singing a song in which all human beings join with him, rejoices in the presence of truth as our visible friend and hourly companion. Poetry is the breath and finer spirit of all knowledge; it is the impassioned expression which is in the countenance of all Science. Emphatically may it be said of the Poet, as Shakespeare hath said of man, "that he looks before and after." He is the rock of defence for human nature; an upholder and preserver, carrying everywhere with him relationship and love. In spite of difference of soil and climate, of language and manners, of laws and customs: in spite of things silently gone out of mind, and things violently destroyed; the Poet binds together by passion and knowledge the vast empire of human society, as it is spread over the whole earth, and over all time. The objects of the Poet's thoughts are everywhere; though the eyes and senses of man are, it is true, his favourite guides, yet he will follow wheresoever he can find an atmosphere of sensation in which to move his wings. Poetry is the first and last of all knowledge—it is as immortal as the heart of man. If the labours of Men of science should ever create any material revolution, direct or indirect, in our condition, and in the impressions which we habitually receive, the Poet will sleep then no more than at present; he will be ready to follow the steps of the Man of science, not only in those general indirect effects, but he will be at his side, carrying sensation into the midst of the objects of the science itself. The remotest discoveries of the Chemist, the Botanist, or Mineralogist, will be as proper objects of the Poet's art as any upon which it can be employed, if the time should ever come when these things shall be familiar to us, and the relations under which they are contemplated by the followers of these respective sciences shall be manifestly and palpably material to us as enjoying and suffering beings. If the time should ever come when what is now called science, thus familiarized to men, shall be ready to put on, as it were, a form of flesh and blood, the Poet will lend his divine spirit to aid the transfiguration, and will welcome the Being thus produced, as a dear and genuine inmate of the household of man.—It is not, then, to be supposed that any one, who holds that sublime notion of Poetry which I have attempted to convey, will break in upon the sanctity and truth of his pictures by transitory and accidental ornaments, and endeavour to excite admiration of himself by arts, the necessity of which must manifestly depend upon the assumed meanness of his subject.

What has been thus far said applies to Poetry in general; but especially to those parts of composition where the Poet speaks through the mouths of his characters; and upon this point it appears to authorize the conclusion that there are few persons of good sense, who would not allow that the dramatic parts of composition are defective, in proportion as they deviate from the real language of nature, and are coloured by a diction of the Poet's own, either peculiar to him as an individual Poet or belonging simply to Poets in general; to a body of men who, from the circumstance of their compositions being in metre, it is expected will employ a particular language.

It is not, then, in the dramatic parts of composition that we look for this distinction of language; but still it may be proper and necessary where the Poet speaks to us in his own person and character. To this I answer by referring the Reader to the description before given of a Poet. Among the qualities there enumerated as principally conducing to form a Poet, is implied nothing differing in kind from other men, but only in degree. The sum of what was said is, that the Poet is chiefly distinguished from other men by a greater promptness to think and feel without immediate external excitement, and a greater power in expressing such thoughts and feelings as are produced in him in that manner. But these passions and thoughts and feelings are the general passions and thoughts and feelings of men. And with what are they connected? Undoubtedly with our moral sentiments and animal sensations, and with the causes which excite these; with the operations of the elements, and the appearances of the visible universe; with storm and sunshine, with the revolutions of the seasons, with cold and heat, with loss of friends and kindred, with injuries and resentments, gratitude and hope, with fear and sorrow. These, and the like, are the sensations and objects which the Poet describes, as they are the sensations of other men, and the objects which interest them. The Poet thinks and feels in the spirit of human passions. How, then, can his language differ in any material degree from that of all other men who feel vividly and see clearly? It might be *proved* that it is impossible. But supposing that this were not the case, the Poet might then be allowed to use a peculiar language when expressing his feelings for his own gratification, or that of men like himself. But Poets do not write for Poets alone, but for men. Unless therefore we are advocates for that admiration which subsists upon ignorance, and that pleasure which arises from hearing what we do not understand, the Poet must descend from this supposed height; and, in order to excite rational sympathy he must express himself as other men express themselves. To this it may be added, that while he is only selecting from the real language of men, or, which amounts to the same thing, composing accurately in the spirit of such selection, he is treading upon safe ground, and we know what we are to expect from him. Our feelings are the same with respect to metre; for, as it may be proper to remind the Reader, the distinction of metre is regular and uniform, and not, like that which is produced by what is usually called POETIC DICTION, arbitrary, and subject to infinite caprices upon which no calculation whatever can be made. In the one case, the Reader is utterly at the mercy of the Poet, respecting what imagery or diction he may choose to connect with the passion; whereas, in the other, the metre obeys certain laws, to which the Poet and Reader both willingly submit because they are certain, and because no interference is made by them with the passion, but such as the concurring testimony of ages has shown to heighten and improve the pleasure which co-exists with it.

It will now be proper to answer an obvious question, namely, Why, professing these opinions, have I written in verse? To this, in addition to such answer as is included in what has been already said, I reply, in the first place, Because, however I may have restricted myself, there is still left open to me what confessedly constitutes the most valuable object of all writing, whether in prose or verse; the great and universal passions of men, the most general and interesting of their occupations, and the entire world of nature before me—to supply endless combinations of forms and imagery. Now, supposing for a moment that whatever is interesting in these objects may be as vividly described in prose, why should I be condemned for attempting to superadd to such description the charm which, by the consent of all nations, is acknowledged to exist in metri-

cal language? To this, by such as are yet unconvinced, it may be answered that a very small part of the pleasure given by Poetry depends upon the metre, and that it is injudicious to write in metre, unless it be accompanied with the other artificial distinctions of style with which metre is usually accompanied, and that, by such deviation, more will be lost from the shock which will thereby be given to the Reader's associations than will be counterbalanced by any pleasure which he can derive from the general power of numbers. In answer to those who still contend for the necessity of accompanying metre with certain appropriate colours of style in order to the accomplishment of its appropriate end, and who also, in my opinion, greatly underrate the power of metre in itself, it might, perhaps, as far as relates to these Volumes, have been almost sufficient to observe, that poems are extant, written upon more humble subjects, and in a still more naked and simple style, which have continued to give pleasure from generation to generation. Now, if nakedness and simplicity be a defect, the fact here mentioned affords a strong presumption that poems somewhat less naked and simple are capable of affording pleasure at the present day; and, what I wish *chiefly* to attempt, at present, was to justify myself for having written under the impression of this belief.

But various causes might be pointed out why, when the style is manly and the subject of some importance, words metrically arranged will long continue to impart such a pleasure to mankind as he who proves the extent of that pleasure will be desirous to impart. The end of Poetry is to produce excitement in co-existence with an overbalance of pleasure; but, by the supposition, excitement is an unusual and irregular state of the mind; ideas and feelings do not, in that state, succeed each other in accustomed order. If the words, however, by which this excitement is produced be in themselves powerful, or the

images and feelings have an undue proportion of pain connected with them, there
is some danger that the excitement may
be carried beyond its proper bounds. Now
the co-presence of something regular, something to which the mind has been accustomed in various moods and in a less excited state, cannot but have great efficacy
in tempering and restraining the passion
by an inter-texture of ordinary feeling,
and of feeling not strictly and necessarily
connected with the passion. This is unquestionably true; and hence, though the
opinion will at first appear paradoxical,
from the tendency of metre to divest language, in a certain degree, of its reality,
and thus to throw a sort of half-conscious-
ness of unsubstantial existence over the
whole composition, there can be little doubt
but that more pathetic situations and sentiments, that is, those which have a greater
proportion of pain connected with them,
may be endured in metrical composition,
especially in rhyme, than in prose. The
metre of the old ballads is very artless;
yet they contain many passages which
would illustrate this opinion; and, I hope,
if the following Poems be attentively perused, similar instances will be found in
them. This opinion may be further illustrated by appealing to the Reader's own
experience of the reluctance with which
he comes to the re-perusal of the distressful
parts of *Clarissa Harlowe,* or *The Game-
ster;* while Shakespeare's writings, in the most
pathetic scenes, never act upon us, as
pathetic, beyond the bounds of pleasure—
an effect which, in a much greater degree
than might at first be imagined, is to be
ascribed to small, but continual and regular impulses of pleasurable surprise from
the metrical arrangement.—On the other
hand (what it must be allowed will much
more frequently happen) if the Poet's
words should be incommensurate with the
passion, and inadequate to raise the Reader
to a height of desirable excitement, then
(unless the Poet's choice of his metre has

been grossly injudicious), in the feelings
of pleasure which the Reader has been accustomed to connect with metre in general,
and in the feeling, whether cheerful or
melancholy, which he has been accustomed
to connect with that particular movement
of metre, there will be found something
which will greatly contribute to impart passion to the words, and to effect the complex end which the Poet proposes to himself.

If I had undertaken a SYSTEMATIC defence of the theory here maintained, it
would have been my duty to develop the
various causes upon which the pleasure
received from metrical language depends.
Among the chief of these causes is to be
reckoned a principle which must be well
known to those who have made any of the
Arts the object of accurate reflection;
namely, the pleasure which the mind derives from the perception of similitude in
dissimilitude. This principle is the great
spring of the activity of our minds, and
their chief feeder. From this principle the
direction of the sexual appetite, and all the
passions connected with it, take their origin: it is the life of our ordinary conversation; and upon the accuracy with which
similitude in dissimilitude, and dissimilitude in similitude are perceived, depend
our taste and our moral feelings. It would
not be a useless employment to apply this
principle to the consideration of metre, and
to show this metre is hence enabled to
afford much pleasure, and to point out in
what manner that pleasure is produced.
But my limits will not permit me to enter
upon this subject, and I must content myself with a general summary.

I have said that poetry is the spontaneous
overflow of powerful feelings: it takes its
origin from emotion recollected in tranquillity: the emotion is contemplated till,
by a species of reaction, the tranquillity
gradually disappears, and an emotion, kindred to that which was before the subject
of contemplation, is gradually produced,

and does itself actually exist in the mind. In this mood successful composition generally begins, and in a mood similar to this it is carried on; but the emotion, of whatever kind, and in whatever degree, from various causes, is qualified by various pleasures, so that in describing any passions whatsoever, which are voluntarily described, the mind will, upon the whole, be in a state of enjoyment. If Nature be thus cautious to preserve in a state of enjoyment a being so employed, the Poet ought to profit by the lesson held forth to him, and ought especially to take care, that, whatever passions he communicates to his Reader, those passions, if his Reader's mind be sound and vigorous, should always be accompanied with an overbalance of pleasure. Now the music of harmonious metrical language, the sense of difficulty overcome, and the blind association of pleasure which has been previously received from works of rhyme or metre of the same or similar construction, an indistinct perception perpetually renewed of language closely resembling that of real life, and yet, in the circumstance of metre, differing from it so widely—all these imperceptibly make up a complex feeling of delight, which is of the most important use in tempering the painful feeling always found intermingled with powerful descriptions of the deeper passions. This effect is always produced in pathetic and impassioned poetry; while, in lighter compositions, the ease and gracefulness with which the Poet manages his numbers are themselves confessedly a principal source of the gratification of the Reader. All that it is *necessary* to say, however, upon this subject, may be effected by affirming, what few persons will deny, that, of two descriptions, either of passions, manners, or characters, each of them equally well executed, the one in prose and the other in verse, the verse will be read a hundred times where the prose is read once.

Having thus explained a few of my reasons for writing in verse, and why I have chosen subjects from common life, and endeavoured to bring my language near to the real language of men, if I have been two minute in pleading my own cause, I have at the same time been treating a subject of general interest; and for this reason a few words shall be added with reference solely to these particular poems, and to some defects which will probably be found in them. I am sensible that my associations must have sometimes been particular instead of general, and that, consequently, giving to things a false importance, I may have sometimes written upon unworthy subjects; but I am less apprehensive on this account, than that my language may frequently have suffered from those arbitrary connexions of feelings and ideas with particular words and phrases, from which no man can altogether protect himself. Hence I have no doubt, that, in some instances, feelings, even of the ludicrous, may be given to my Readers by expressions which appeared to me tender and pathetic. Such faulty expressions, were I convinced they were faulty at present, and that they must necessarily continue to be so, I would willingly take all reasonable pains to correct. But it is dangerous to make these alterations on the simple authority of a few individuals, or even of certain classes of men; for where the understanding of an Author is not convinced, or his feelings altered, this cannot be done without great injury to himself: for his own feelings are his stay and support; and, if he set them aside in one instance, he may be induced to repeat this act till his mind shall lose all confidence in itself, and become utterly debilitated. To this it may be added, that the critic ought never to forget that he is himself exposed to the same errors as the Poet, and, perhaps, in a much greater degree: for there can be no presumption in saying of most readers, that it is not probable they will be so well acquainted with the various stages of meaning through which words have passed, or with the fickleness or stability of the relations of particular ideas to each other; and, above all, since they are so much less interested in the subject, they may decide lightly and carelessly.

Long as the Reader has been detained, I hope he will permit me to caution him against a mode of false criticism which has been applied to Poetry, in which the language closely resembled that of life and nature. Such verses have been triumphed over in parodies, of which Dr. Johnson's stanza is a fair specimen:—

> I put my hat upon my head
> And walked into the Strand,
> And there I met another man
> Whose hat was in his hand.

Immediately under these lines let us place one of the most justly admired stanzas of the "Babes in the Wood."

> These pretty Babes with hand in hand
> Went wandering up and down;
> But never more they saw the Man
> Approaching from the Town.

In both these stanzas the words, and the order of the words, in no respect differ from the most unimpassioned conversation. There are words in both, for example, "the Strand," and "the Town," connected with none but the most familiar ideas; yet the one stanza we admit as admirable, and the other as a fair example of the superlatively contemptible. Whence arises this difference? Not from the metre, not from the language, not from the order of the words; but the *matter* expressed in Dr. Johnson's stanza is contemptible. The proper method of treating trivial and simple verses, to which Dr. Johnson's stanza would be a fair parallelism, is not to say, this is a bad kind of poetry, or, this is not poetry; but, this wants sense; it is neither interesting in itself nor can *lead* to anything interesting; the images neither origi-

nate in that sane state of feeling which arises out of thought, nor can excite thought or feeling in the Reader. This is the only sensible manner of dealing with such verses. Why trouble yourself about the species till you have previously decided upon the genus? Why take pains to prove than an ape is not a Newton, when it is self-evident that he is not a man?

One request I must make of my reader, which is, that in judging these Poems he would decide by his own feelings genuinely, and not by reflection upon what will probably be the judgment of others. How common is it to hear a person say, I myself do not object to this style of composition, or this or that expression, but, to such and such classes of people it will appear mean or ludicrous! This mode of criticism, so destructive of all sound unadulterated judgement, is almost universal: let the Reader then abide, independently, by his own feelings, and, if he finds himself affected, let him not suffer such conjectures to interfere with his pleasure.

If an Author, by any single composition, has impressed us with respect for his talents, it is useful to consider this as affording a presumption, that on other occasions where we have been displeased, he, nevertheless, may not have written ill or absurdly; and further, to give him so much credit for this one composition as may induce us to review what has displeased us, with more care than we should otherwise have bestowed upon it. This is not only an act of justice, but, in our decisions upon poetry especially, may conduce, in a high degree, to the improvement of our own taste; for an *accurate* taste in poetry, and in all the other arts, as Sir Joshua Reynolds has observed, is an *acquired* talent, which can only be produced by thought and a long continued intercourse with the best models of composition. This is mentioned, not with so ridiculous a purpose as to prevent the most inexperienced Reader from judging for himself (I have already said that I wish him to judge for himself), but merely to temper the rashness of decision, and to suggest, that, if Poetry be a subject on which much time has not been bestowed, the judgment may be erroneous; and that, in many cases, it necessarily will be so.

Nothing would, I know, have so effectually contributed to further the end which I have in view, as to have shown of what kind the pleasure is, and how that pleasure is produced, which is confessedly produced by metrical composition essentially different from that which I have here endeavoured to recommend: for the Reader will say that he has been pleased by such composition; and what more can be done for him? The power of any art is limited; and he will suspect, that, if it be proposed to furnish him with new friends, that can be only upon condition of his abandoning his old friends. Besides, as I have said, the Reader is himself conscious of the pleasure which he has received from such composition, composition to which he has peculiarly attached the endearing name of Poetry; and all men feel an habitual gratitude, and something of an honourable bigotry, for the objects which have long continued to please them: we not only wish to be pleased, but to be pleased in that particular way in which we have been accustomed to be pleased. There is in these feelings enough to resist a host of arguments; and I should be the less able to combat them successfully, as I am willing to allow, that, in order entirely to enjoy the Poetry which I am recommending, it would be necessary to give up much of what is ordinarily enjoyed. But, would my limits have permitted me to point out how this pleasure is produced, many obstacles might have been removed, and the Reader assisted in perceiving that the powers of language are not so limited as he may suppose; and that it is possible for poetry to give other enjoyments, of a purer, more lasting, and more exquisite nature. This part of the subject has not been altogether neglected, but it has not been so much my present aim to prove, that the interest excited by some other kinds of poetry is less vivid, and less worthy of the nobler powers of the mind, as to offer reasons for presuming, that if my purpose were fulfilled, a species of poetry would be produced, which is genuine poetry; in its nature well adapted to interest mankind permanently, and likewise important in the multiplicity and quality of its moral relations.

From what has been said, and from a perusal of the Poems, the Reader will be able clearly to perceive the object which I had in view: he will determine how far it has been attained; and, what is a much more important question, whether it be worth attaining: and upon the decision of these two questions will rest my claim to the approbation of the Public.

FRIEDRICH WILHELM JOSEPH VON SCHELLING [1775-1854]

>>>>>><<<<<

On the Relation of the Plastic Arts to Nature [1807]

Plastic art, according to the most ancient expression, is silent Poetry. The inventor of this definition no doubt meant thereby that the former, like the latter, is to express spiritual thoughts—conceptions whose source is the soul; not only by speech, but, like silent Nature, by shape, by form, by corporeal, independent works.

Plastic Art, therefore, evidently stands as a uniting link between the soul and Nature, and can be apprehended only in the living centre of both. Indeed, since Plastic Art has its relation to the soul in common with every other art, and particularly with Poetry, that by which it is connected with Nature, and, like Nature, a productive force, remains as its sole peculiarity; so that to this alone can a theory relate which shall be satisfactory to the understanding, and helpful and profitable to Art itself.

We hope, therefore, in considering Plastic Art in relation to its true prototype and original source, Nature, to be able to contribute something new to its theory—to give some additional exactness or clearness to the conceptions of it; but, above all, to set forth the coherence of the whole structure of Art in the light of a higher necessity.

But has not Science always recognized this relation? Has not indeed every theory of modern times taken its departure from this very position, that Art should be the imitator of Nature? Such has indeed been

From *The German Classics,* Vol. V, edited by K. Francke (New York: The German Publication Society, 1913). The translation is by J. Elliot Cabot.

the case. But what should this broad general proposition profit the artist, when the notion of Nature is of such various interpretation, and when there are almost as many differing views of it as there are various modes of life? Thus, to one, Nature is nothing more than the lifeless aggregate of an indeterminable crowd of objects, or the space in which, as in a vessel, he imagines things placed; to another, only the soil from which he draws his nourishment and support; to the inspired seeker alone, the holy, ever-creative original energy of the world, which generates and busily evolves all things out of itself.

The proposition would indeed have a high significance, if it taught Art to emulate this creative force; but the sense in which it was meant can scarcely be doubtful to one acquainted with the universal condition of Science at the time when it was first brought forward. Singular enough that the very persons who denied all life to Nature should set it up for imitation in Art! To them might be applied the words of a profound writer: "Your lying philosophy has put Nature out of the way; and why do you call upon us to imitate her? Is it that you may renew the pleasure by perpetrating the same violence on the disciples of Nature?"

Nature was to them not merely a dumb, but an altogether lifeless image, in whose inmost being even no living word dwelt; a hollow scaffolding of forms, of which as hollow an image was to be transferred to the canvas, or hewn out of stone.

This was the proper doctrine of those more ancient and savage nations, who, as they saw in Nature nothing divine, fetched idols out of her; whilst, to the susceptive

Greeks, who everywhere felt the presence of a vitally efficient principle, genuine gods arose out of Nature.

But is, then, the disciple of Nature to copy everything in Nature without distinction?—and, of everything, every part? Only beautiful objects should be represented; and, even in these, only the Beautiful and Perfect.

Thus is the proposition further determined, but, at the same time, this asserted, that, in Nature, the perfect is mingled with the imperfect, the beautiful with the unbeautiful. Now, how should he who stands in no other relation to Nature than that of servile imitation, distinguish the one from the other? It is the way of imitators to appropriate the faults of their model sooner and easier than its excellences, since the former offer handles and tokens more easily grasped; and thus we see that imitators of Nature in this sense have imitated oftener, and even more affectionately, the ugly than the beautiful.

If we regard in things, not their principle, but the empty abstract form, neither will they say anything to our soul; our own heart, our own spirit we must put to it, that they answer us.

But what is the perfection of a thing? Nothing else than the creative life in it, its power to exist. Never, therefore, will he, who fancies that Nature is altogether dead, be successful in that profound process (analogous to the chemical) whence proceeds, purified as by fire, the pure gold of Beauty and Truth.

Nor was there any change in the main view of the relation of Art to Nature, even when the unsatisfactoriness of the principle began to be more generally felt; no change, even by the new views and new knowledge so nobly established by John Winckelmann. He indeed restored to the soul its full efficiency in Art, and raised it from its unworthy dependence into the realm of spiritual freedom. Powerfully moved by the beauty of form in the works of antiquity, he taught that the production of ideal Nature, of Nature elevated above the Actual, together with the expression of spiritual conceptions, is the highest aim of Art.

But if we examine in what sense this surpassing of the Actual by Art has been understood by the most, it turns out that, with this view also, the notion of Nature as mere product, of things as a lifeless result, still continued; and the idea of a living creative Nature was in no wise awakened by it. Thus these ideal forms also could be animated by no positive insight into their nature; and if the forms of the Actual were dead for the dead beholder, these were not less so. Were no independent production of the Actual possible, neither would there be of the Ideal. The object of the imitation was changed; the imitation remained. In the place of Nature were substituted the sublime works of Antiquity, whose outward forms the pupils busied themselves in imitating, but without the spirit that fills them. These forms, however, are as unapproachable, nay, more so, than the works of Nature, and leave us yet colder if we bring not to them the spiritual eye to penetrate through the veil and feel the stirring energy within.

On the other hand, artists, since that time, have indeed received a certain ideal impetus, and notions of a beauty superior to matter; but these notions were like fair words, to which the deeds do not correspond. While the previous method in Art produced bodies without soul, this view taught only the secret of the soul, but not that of the body. The theory had, as usual, passed with one hasty stride to the opposite extreme; but the vital mean it had not yet found.

Who can say that Winckelmann had not penetrated into the highest beauty? But with him it appeared in its dissevered elements only: on the one side as beauty in idea, and flowing out from the soul; on the other, as beauty of forms.

But what is the efficient link that connects the two? Or by what power is the soul created together with the body, at once and as if with one breath? If this lies not within the power of Art, as of Nature, then it can create nothing whatever. This vital connecting link, Winckelmann did not determine; he did not teach how, from the idea, forms can be produced. Thus Art went over to that method which we would call the retrograde, since it strives from the form to come at the essence. But not thus is the Unlimited reached; it is not attainable by mere enhancement of the Limited. Hence, such works as have had their beginning in form, with all elaborateness on that side, show, in token of their origin, an incurable want at the very point where we expect the consummate, the essential, the final. The miracle by which the Limited should be raised to the Unlimited, the human become divine, is wanting; the magic circle is drawn, but the spirit that it should inclose, appears not, being disobedient to the call of him who thought a creation possible through mere form.

. . .

Nature meets us everywhere, at first with reserve, and in form more or less severe. She is like that quiet and serious beauty, that excites not attention by noisy advertisement, nor attracts the vulgar gaze.

How can we, as it were, spiritually melt this apparently rigid form, so that the pure energy of things may flow together with the force of our spirit and both become one united mold? We must transcend Form, in order to gain it again as intelligible, living, and truly felt. Consider the most beautiful forms; what remains behind after you have abstracted from them the creative principle within? Nothing but mere unessential qualities, such as extension and the relations of space. Does the fact that one portion of matter exists near another, and distinct from it, contribute anything to its inner essence? or does it not rather contribute nothing? Evidently

the latter. It is not mere contiguous existence, but the manner of it, that makes form; and this can be determined only by a positive force, which is even opposed to separateness, and subordinates the manifoldness of the parts to the unity of one idea—from the force that works in the crystal to the force which, comparable to a gentle magnetic current, gives to the particles of matter in the human form that position and arrangement among themselves, through which the idea, the essential unity and beauty, can become visible.

Not only, however, as active principle, but as spirit and effective science, must the essence appear to us in the form, in order that we may truly apprehend it. For all unity must be spiritual in nature and origin; and what is the aim of all investigation of Nature but to find science therein? For that wherein there is no Understanding cannot be the object of Understanding; the Unknowing cannot be known. The science by which Nature works is not, however, like human science, connected with reflection upon itself; in it, the conception is not separate from the act, nor the design from the execution. Therefore, rude matter strives, as it were, blindly, after regular shape, and unknowingly assumes pure stereometric forms, which belong, nevertheless, to the realm of ideas, and are something spiritual in the material.

The sublimest arithmetic and geometry are innate in the stars, and unconsciously displayed by them in their motions. More distinctly, but still beyond their grasp, the living cognition appears in animals; and thus we see them, though wandering about without reflection, bring about innumerable results far more excellent than themselves: the bird that, intoxicated with music, transcends itself in soul-like tones; the little artistic creature, that, without practise or instruction, accomplishes light works of architecture; but all directed by an overpowering spirit, that lightens in them already with single flashes of knowledge, but as yet appears nowhere as the full sun, as in Man.

This formative science in Nature and Art is the link that connects idea and form, body and soul. Before everything stands an eternal idea, formed in the Infinite Understanding; but by what means does this idea pass into actuality and embodiment? Only through the creative science that is as necessarily connected with the Infinite Understanding, as in the artist the principle that seizes the idea of unsensuous Beauty is linked with that which sets it forth to the senses.

If that artist be called happy and praiseworthy before all to whom the gods have granted this creative spirit, then that work of art will appear excellent which shows to us, as in outline, this unadulterated energy of creation and activity of Nature.

It was long ago perceived that, in Art, not everything is performed with consciousness; that, with the conscious activity, an unconscious action must combine; and that it is of the perfect unity and mutual interpenetration of the two that the highest in Art is born.

Works that want this seal of unconscious science are recognized by the evident absence of life self-supported and independent of the producer; as, on the contrary, where this acts, Art imparts to its work, together with the utmost clearness to the understanding, that unfathomable reality wherein it resembles a work of Nature.

It has often been attempted to make clear the position of the artist in regard to Nature, by saying that Art, in order to be such, must first withdraw itself from Nature, and return to it only in the final perfection. The true sense of this saying, it seems to us, can be no other than this—that in all things in Nature, the living idea shows itself only blindly active; were it so also in the artist, he would be in nothing distinct from Nature. But should he attempt consciously to subordinate him-

self altogether to the Actual, and render with servile fidelity the already existing, he would produce *larvae*, but no works of Art. He must therefore withdraw himself from the product, from the creature, but only in order to raise himself to the creative energy, spiritually seizing the same. Thus he ascends into the realm of pure ideas; he forsakes the creature, to regain it with thousandfold interest, and in this sense certainly to return to Nature. This spirit of Nature working at the core of things, and speaking through form and shape as by symbols only, the artist must certainly follow with emulation; and only so far as he seizes this with genial imitation has he himself produced anything genuine. For works produced by aggregation, even of forms beautiful in themselves, would still be destitute of all beauty, since that, through which the work on the whole is truly beautiful, cannot be mere form. It is above form—it is Essence, the Universal, the look and expression of the indwelling spirit of Nature.

Now it can scarcely be doubtful what is to be thought of the so-called idealizing of Nature in Art, so universally demanded. This demand seems to arise from a way of thinking, according to which not Truth, Beauty, Goodness, but the contrary of all these, is the Actual. Were the Actual indeed opposed to Truth and Beauty, it would be necessary for the artist, not to elevate or idealize it, but to get rid of and destroy it, in order to create something true and beautiful. But how should it be possible for anything to be actual except the True; and what is Beauty, if not full complete Being?

What higher aim, therefore, could Art have, than to represent that which in Nature actually *is?* Or how should it undertake to excel so-called actual Nature, since it must always fall short of it?

For does Art impart to its works actual, sensuous life? This statue breathes not, is stirred by no pulsation, warmed by no blood.

But both the pretended excelling and the apparent falling short show themselves as the consequences of one and the same principle, as soon as we place the aim of Art in the exhibiting of that which truly is.

Only on the surface have its works the appearance of life; in Nature, life seems to reach deeper, and to be wedded entirely with matter. But does not the continued mutation of matter and the universal lot of final dissolution teach us the unessential character of this union, and that it is no intimate fusion? Art, accordingly, in the merely superficial animation of its works, but represents Nothingness as non-existing.

How comes it that, to every tolerably cultivated taste, imitations of the so-called Actual, even though carried to deception, appear in the last degree untrue—nay, produce the impression of spectres; whilst a work in which the idea is predominant strikes us with the full force of truth, conveying us then only to the genuinely actual world? Whence comes it, if not from the more or less obscure feeling which tells us that the idea alone is the living principle in things, but all else unessential and vain shadow?

On the same ground may be explained all the opposite cases which are brought up as instances of the surpassing of Nature by Art. In arresting the rapid course of human years; in uniting the energy of developed manhood with the soft charm of early youth; or exhibiting a mother of grown-up sons and daughters in the full possession of vigorous beauty—what does Art except to annul what is unessential, Time?

If, according to the remark of a discerning critic, every growth in Nature has but an instant of truly complete beauty, we may also say that it has, too, only an instant of full existence. In this instant it is what it is in all eternity; besides this, it has only a coming into and a passing out of existence. Art, in representing the thing at that instant, removes it out of Time, and sets it forth in its pure Being, in the eternity of its life.

After everything positive and essential had once been abstracted from Form, it necessarily appeared restrictive, and, as it were, hostile, to the Essence; and the same theory that had reproduced the false and powerless Ideal, necessarily tended to the formless in Art. Form would indeed be a limitation of the Essence if it existed independent of it. But if it exists with and by means of the Essence, how could this feel itself limited by that which it has itself created? Violence would indeed be done it by a form forced upon it, but never by one proceeding from itself. In this, on the contrary, it must rest contented, and feel its own existence to be perfect and complete.

Determinateness of form is in Nature never a negation, but ever an affirmation. Commonly, indeed, the shape of a body seems a confinement; but could we behold the creative energy it would reveal itself as the measure that this energy imposes upon itself, and in which it shows itself a truly intelligent force; for in everything is the power of self-rule allowed to be an excellence, and one of the highest.

In like manner most persons consider the particular in a negative manner—i. e., as that which is not the whole or all. Yet no particular exists by means of its limitation, but through the indwelling force with which it maintains itself as a particular Whole, in distinction from the Universe.

This force of particularity, and thus also of individuality, showing itself as vital character, the negative conception of it is necessarily followed by an unsatisfying and false view of the characteristic in Art. Lifeless and of intolerable hardness would be the Art that should aim to exhibit the empty shell or limitation of the Individual. Certainly we desire to see not merely the individual, but, more than this, its vital Idea. But if the artist has seized the inward creative spirit and essence of the Idea, and sets this forth, he makes the individual a world in itself, a class, an eternal prototype; and he who has grasped the essential character needs not to fear hardness and severity, for these are the conditions of life. Nature, that in her completeness appears as the utmost benignity, we see, in each particular, aiming even primarily and principally at severity, seclusion and reserve. As the whole creation is the work of the utmost externization and renunciation [*Entäusserung*], so the artist must first deny himself and descend into the Particular, without shunning isolation, nor the pain, the anguish of Form.

Nature, from her first works, is throughout characteristic; the energy of fire, the splendor of light, she shuts up in hard stone, the tender soul of melody in severe metal; even on the threshold of Life, and already meditating organic shape, she sinks back overpowered by the might of Form, into petrifaction.

The life of the plant consists in still receptivity, but in what exact and severe outline is this passive life inclosed! In the animal kingdom the strife between Life and Form seems first properly to begin; her first works Nature hides in hard shells, and, where these are laid aside, the animated world attaches itself again through its constructive impulse to the realm of crystallization. Finally she comes forward more boldly and freely, and vital, important characteristics show themselves, being the same through whole classes. Art, however, cannot begin so far down as Nature. Though Beauty is spread everywhere, yet there are various grades in the appearance and unfolding of the Essence, and thus of Beauty. But Art demands a certain fulness, and desires not to strike a single note or tone, nor even a detached accord, but at once the full symphony of Beauty.

Art, therefore, prefers to grasp immediately at the highest and most developed, the human form. For since it is not given it to embrace the immeasurable whole, and as in all other creatures only single fulgurations, in Man alone full entire Being appears without abatement, Art is not only permitted but required to see the sum of Nature in Man alone. But precisely on this account—that she here assembles all in one point—Nature repeats her whole multiformity, and pursues again in a narrower compass the same course that she had gone through in her wide circuit.

Here, therefore, arises the demand upon the artist first to be true and faithful in detail, in order to come forth complete and beautiful in the whole. Here he must wrestle with the creative spirit of Nature (which in the human world also deals out character and stamp in endless variety), not in weak and effeminate, but stout and courageous conflict.

Persevering exercise in the study of that by virtue of which the characteristic in things is a positive principle, must preserve him from emptiness, weakness, inward inanity, before he can venture to aim, by ever higher combination and final melting together of manifold forms, to reach the extremest beauty in works uniting the highest simplicity with infinite meaning.

Only though the perfection of form can Form be made to disappear; and this is certainly the final aim of Art in the Characteristic. But as the apparent harmony that is even more easily reached by the empty and frivolous than by others, is yet inwardly vain; so in Art the quickly attained harmony of the exterior, without inward fulness. And if it is the part of theory and instruction to oppose the spiritless copying of beautiful forms, especially must they oppose the tendency toward an effeminate characterless Art, which gives itself, indeed, higher names, but therewith only seeks to hide its incapacity to fulfill the fundamental conditions.

That lofty Beauty in which the fulness of form causes Form itself to disappear, was adopted by the modern theory of Art, after Winckelmann, not only as the highest, but as the only standard. But as the deep foundation upon which it rests was overlooked, it resulted that a negative conception was formed even of that which is the sum of all affirmation.

Winckelmann compares Beauty with water drawn from the bosom of the spring, which, the less taste it has, the wholesomer it is esteemed. It is true that the highest Beauty is characterless, but so we say of the Universe that it has no determinate dimension, neither length, breadth nor depth, since it has all in equal infinity; or that the Art of creative Nature is formless, because she herself is subjected to no form.

In this and in no other sense can we say that Grecian art in its highest development rises into the characterless; but it did not aim immediately at this. It was from the bonds of Nature that it struggled upward to divine freedom. From no lightly scattered seed, but only from a deeply infolded kernel, could this heroic growth spring up. Only mighty emotions, only a deep stirring of the fancy through the impressions of all-enlivening, all-commanding energies of Nature, could stamp upon Art that invincible vigor with which from the rigid, secluded earnestness of earlier productions up to the period of works overflowing with sensuous grace, it ever remained faithful to truth, and produced the highest spiritual Reality which it is given to mortals to behold.

In like manner, as their Tragedy commences with the grandest characteristicness in morals, so the beginning of their Plastic Art was the earnestness of Nature, and the stern goddess of Athens its first and only Muse.

This epoch is marked by that style which Winckelmann describes as the still harsh and severe, from which the next or lofty style was able to develop itself by the mere enhancement of the Characteristic into the Sublime and the Simple.

For in the statues of the most perfect or divine natures not only all the complexity of form of which human nature is capable had to be united, but moreover the union must be such as may be conceived to exist in the system of the Universe itself—the lower forms, or those relating to inferior attributes, being comprehended under higher, and all at last under one supreme form, in which they indeed extinguish one another as separately existing, but still continue in Essence and efficiency.

Thus, though we cannot call this high and self-sufficing Beauty characteristic, so far as herewith is connected the notion of limitation or conditionality in the manifestation, yet still the characteristic continues efficient, thought indistinguishable, within; as in the crystal, although transparent, the texture nevertheless remains; each characteristic element has its weight, however slight, and helps to bring about the sublime equipoise of Beauty.

The outer side or basis of all Beauty is beauty of form. But as Form cannot exist without Essence, wherever Form is, there also is Character, whether in visible presence or only perceptible in its effects. Characteristic Beauty, therefore, is Beauty in the root, from which alone Beauty can arise as the fruit. Essence may, indeed, outgrow Form, but even then the Characteristic remains as the still efficient groundwork of the Beautiful.

That most excellent critic, to whom the gods have given sway over Nature as well as Art, compares the Characteristic in its relation to Beauty, with the skeleton in its relation to the living form. Were we to interpret this striking simile in our sense, we should say that the skeleton, in Nature, is not, as in our thought, detached from the living whole; that the firm and the yielding, the determining and the determined, mutually presuppose each other, and can exist only together; thus that the vitally Characteristic is already the whole form, the result of the action and reaction of bone and flesh, of Active and Passive. And although Art, like Nature, in its higher developments, thrusts inward the previously visible skeleton, yet the latter can never be opposed to Shape and Beauty, since it has always a determining share in the production of the one as well as of the other.

But whether that high and independent Beauty should be the only standard in Art, as it is the highest, seems to depend on the degree of fulness and extent that belongs to the particular Art.

Nature, in her wide circumference, ever exhibits the higher with the lower; creating in Man the godlike, she elaborates in all her other productions only its material and foundation, which must exist in order that in contrast with it the Essence as such may appear. And again in the higher world of Man the great mass serves again as the basis upon which the godlike that is preserved pure in the few, manifests itself in legislation, government, and the establishment of Religion. So that wherever Art works with more of the complexity of Nature, it may and must display, together with the highest measure of Beauty, also its groundwork and raw material, as it were, in distinct appropriate forms.

Here first prominently unfolds itself the difference in Nature of the forms of Art.

Plastic Art, in the more exact sense of the term, disdains to give Space outwardly to the object, but bears it within itself. This, however, narrows its field; it is compelled, indeed, to display the beauty of the Universe almost in a single point. It must therefore aim immediately at the highest, and can attain complexity only separately and in the strictest exclusion of all conflicting elements. By isolating the purely animal in human nature it succeeds in forming inferior creations too, harmonious

and even beautiful, as we are taught by the beauty of numerous Fauns preserved from antiquity; yea, it can, parodying itself like the merry spirit of Nature, reverse its own Ideal, and, for instance, in the extravagance of the Silenic figures, by light and sportive treatment appear freed again from the pressure of matter.

But in all cases it is compelled strictly to isolate the work, in order to make it self-consistent and a world in itself; since for this form of Art there is no higher unity, in which the dissonance of particulars should be melted into harmony.

Painting, on the contrary, in the very extent of its sphere, can better measure itself with the Universe, and create with epic confusion. In an Iliad there is room even for a Thersites; and what does not find a place in the great epic of Nature and History!

Here the Particular scarcely counts anything by itself; the Universe takes it place, and that, which by itself would not be beautiful, becomes so in the harmony of the whole. If in an extensive painting, uniting forms by the allotted space, by light, by shade, by reflection, the highest measure of Beauty were everywhere employed, the result would be the most unnatural monotony; for, as Winckelmann says, the highest idea of Beauty is everywhere one and the same, and scarcely admits of variation. The detail would be preferred to the whole, where, as in every case in which the whole is formed by multiplicity, the detail must be subordinate to it.

In such a work, therefore, a gradation of Beauty must be observed, by which alone the full Beauty concentrated in the focus becomes visible; and from an exaggeration of particulars proceeds an equipoise of the whole. Here, then, the limited and characteristic finds it place; and theory at least should direct the painter, not so much to the narrow space in which the entire Beauty is concentrically collected, as to the characteristic complexity of Nature, through which alone he can impart to an extensive work the full measure of living significance.

Thus thought, among the founders of modern art, the noble Leonardo; thus Raphael, the master of high Beauty, who shunned not to exhibit it in smaller measure, rather than to appear monotonous, lifeless, and unreal—though he understood not only how to produce it, but also how to break up uniformity by variety of expression.

For, although Character can show itself also in rest and equilibrium of form, it is only in action that it becomes truly alive.

By character we understand a unity of several forces, operating constantly to produce among them a certain equipoise and determinate proportion, to which, if undisturbed, a like equipoise in the symmetry of the forms corresponds. But if this vital Unity is to display itself in act and operation, this can only be when the forces, excited by some cause to rebellion, forsake their equilibrium. Every one sees that this is the case in the Passions.

Here we are met by the well-known maxim of the theorists, which demands that Passion should be moderated as far as possible, in its actual outburst, that beauty of Form may not be injured. But we think this maxim should rather be reversed, and read thus—that Passion should be moderated by Beauty itself. For it is much to be feared that this desired moderation too may be taken in a negative sense—whereas, what is really requisite is to oppose to Passion a positive force. For as Virtue consists, not in the absence of passions, but in the mastery of the spirit over them, so Beauty is preserved, not by their removal or abatement, but by the mastery of Beauty over them.

The forces of Passion must actually show themselves—it must be seen that they are prepared to rise in mutiny, but are kept down by the power of Character, and break against the forms of firmly-founded Beauty, as the waves of a stream that just fills, but cannot overflow its banks. Otherwise, this striving after moderation would resemble only the method of those shallow moralists, who, the more readily to dispose of Man, prefer to mutilate his nature; and who have so entirely removed every positive element from actions that the people gloat over the spectacle of great crimes, in order to refresh themselves at last with the view of something positive.

In Nature and Art the Essence strives first after actualization, or exhibition of itself in the Particular. Thus in each the utmost severity is manifest at the commencement; for without bound, the boundless could not appear; without severity, gentleness could not exist; and if unity is to be perceptible, it can only be through particularity, detachment, and opposition. In the beginning, therefore, the creative spirit shows itself entirely lost in the Form, inaccessibly shut up, and even in its grandeur still harsh. But the more it succeeds in uniting its entire fulness in one product, the more it gradually relaxes from its severity; and where it has fully developed the form, so as to rest contented and self-collected in it, it seems to become cheerful and begins to move in gentle lines. This is the period of its fairest maturity and blossom, in which the pure vessel has arrived at perfection; the spirit of Nature becomes free from its bonds, and feels its relationship to the soul. By a gentle morning blush stealing over the whole form, the coming soul announces itself; it is not yet present, but everything prepares for its reception by the delicate play of gentle movements; the rigid outlines melt and temper themselves into flexibility; a lovely essence, neither sensuous nor spiritual, but which cannot be grasped, diffuses itself over the form, and intwines itself with every outline, every vibration of the frame.

This essence, not to be seized, as we have already remarked, but yet perceptible to all, is what the language of the Greeks designated by the name *Charis,* ours as Grace.

Wherever, in a fully developed form, Grace appears, the work is complete on the side of Nature; nothing more is wanting; all demands are satisfied. Here, already, soul and body are in complete harmony; Body is Form, Grace is Soul, although not Soul in itself, but the Soul of Form, or the Soul of Nature.

Art may linger, and remain stationary at this point; for already, on one side at least, its whole task is finished. The pure image of Beauty arrested at this point is the Goddess of Love.

But the beauty of the Soul in itself, joined to sensuous Grace, is the highest apotheosis of Nature.

The spirit of Nature is only in appearance opposed to the Soul; essentially, it is the instrument of its revelation; it brings about indeed the antagonism that exists in all things, but only that the one essence may come forth, as the utmost benignity, and the reconciliation of all the forces.

All other creatures are driven by the mere force of Nature, and through it maintain their individuality; in Man alone, as the central point, arises the soul, without which the world would be like the natural universe without the sun.

The Soul in Man, therefore, is not the principle of individuality, but that whereby he raises himself above all egoism, whereby he becomes capable of self-sacrifice, of disinterested love, and (which is the highest) of the contemplation and knowledge of the Essence of things, and thus of Art.

In him it is no longer concerned about Matter nor has it immediate concern with it, but with the spirit only as the life of things. Even while appearing in the body, it is yet free from the body. the consciousness of which hovers in the soul in the most beauteous shapes only as a light, undisturbing dream. It is no quality, no faculty, nor anything special of the sort; it knows not, but is Science; it is not good, but Goodness; it is not beautiful, as body even may be, but Beauty itself.

In the first instance, it is true, in a work of art, the soul of the artist is seen as invention in the detail, and in the total result as the unity that hovers over the work in serene stillness. But the Soul must be visible in objective representation, as the primeval energy of thought, in portraitures of human beings, altogether filled by an idea, by a noble contemplation; or as indwelling, essential Goodness.

Each of these finds its distinct expression even in the completest repose, but a more living one where the Soul can reveal itself in activity and antagonism; and since it is by the passions mainly that the peace of life is interrupted, it is the generally received opinion that the beauty of the Soul shows itself especially in its quiet supremacy amid the storm of the passions.

But here an important distinction is to be made. For the Soul must not be called upon to moderate those passions which are only an outbreak of the lower spirits of Nature, nor can it be displayed in antithesis with these; for where calm considerateness is still in contention with them, the Soul has not yet appeared; they must be moderated by unassisted Nature in Man, by the might of the Spirit. But there are cases of a higher sort, in which not a single force alone, but the intelligent Spirit itself breaks down all barriers—cases, indeed, where even the Soul is subjected by the bond that connects it with sensuous existence, to pain, which should be foreign to its divine nature; where Man feels himself hard fought and attacked in the root of his existence, not by mere powers of Nature, but by moral forces; where innocent error hurries him into crime, and thus into misery; where deep-felt injustice excites to rebellion the holiest feelings of humanity.

This is the case in all situations, truly, and, in a high sense, tragic, such as the Tragedy of the ancients brings before our eyes. Where blindly passionate forces are aroused, the collected Spirit is present as the guardian of Beauty; but if the Spirit itself be carried away, as by an irresistible might, what power shall watch over and protect sacred beauty? Or, if even the soul participate in the struggle, how shall it save itself from pain and from desecration?

Arbitrarily to restrain the power of pain, of feeling in revolt, would be to sin against the very meaning and aim of Art, and would betray a want of feeling and soul in the artist himself.

Already therein, that Beauty, based on grand and firmly-established forms, has become Character, Art has provided the means of displaying without injury to symmetry the whole intensity of Feeling. For where Beauty rests on mighty forms, as upon immovable pillars, even a slight change in its relations, scarcely touching the form, causes us to infer the great force that was necessary in order to provide it. Still more does Grace sanctify pain. It is the essential nature of Grace that it does not know itself; but not being wilfully acquired, it also cannot be wilfully lost. When intolerable anguish, when even madness, sent by avenging gods, takes away consciousness and reason, Grace stands as a protecting demon by the suffering person, and prevents it from manifesting anything unseemly, anything discordant to Humanity, but sees to it that, if the person falls, it falls at least a pure and unspotted victim.

Although not yet the Soul itself, but its forebodings only, Grace accomplishes by natural means what the Soul does by a divine power, in transforming pain, torpor, even death itself, into Beauty.

Yet Grace, which thus maintained itself in the extremest adversity, would be dead, without its transfiguration by the Soul. But what expression can belong to the Soul in this situation? It delivers itself from pain, and comes forth conquering, not conquered, by relinquishing its connection with sensuous existence.

It is for the natural Spirit to exert its energies for the preservation of sensuous existence; the Soul enters not into this contest, but its presence moderates even the storms of painfully-struggling life. Outward force can take away only outward goods, but not reach the Soul; it can tear asunder a temporal bond, not dissolve the eternal one of a truly divine love. Not hard and unfeeling, nor giving up love itself, on the contrary the Soul displays in pain this love alone, as the sentiment that outlasts sensuous existence, and thus raises itself above the ruins of outward life or fortune in divine glory.

It is this expression of the Soul that the creator of the Niobe has presented to us. All the means by which Art tempers even the Terrible, are here made use of. Mightiness of form, sensuous Grace, nay, even the nature of the subject-matter itself, soften the expression, through this, that Pain, transcending all expression, annihilates itself, and Beauty, which it seemed impossible to preserve from destruction when alive, is protected from injury by the commencing torpor.

But what would it all be without the Soul, and how does this manifest itself?

We see on the countenance of the mother, not grief alone for the already prostrated flower of her children; not alone deadly anxiety for the preservation of those yet remaining, and of the youngest daughter, who had fled for safety to her bosom; nor resentment against the cruel deities; least of all, as is pretended, cool defiance— all these we see, indeed, but not these alone; for, through grief, anxiety, and resentment streams, like a divine light, eternal love, as that which alone remains; and in this is preserved the mother, as one who was not, but now *is* a mother, and who remains united with the beloved ones by an eternal bond.

Every one acknowledges that greatness, purity, and goodness of Soul have also their sensuous expressions. But how is this conceivable, unless the principle that acts in Matter be itself cognate and similar to Soul?

For the representation of the Soul there are again gradations in Art, according as it is joined with the merely Characteristic, or in visible union with the Charming and Graceful.

Who perceives not already, in the tragedies of Aeschylus, the presence of that lofty morality which is predominant in the works of Sophocles? But in the former it is enveloped in a bitter rind, and passes less into the whole work, since the bond of sensuous Grace is still wanting. But out of this severity, and the still rude charms of earlier Art, could proceed the grace of Sophocles, and with it the complete fusion of the two elements, which leaves us doubtful whether it is more moral or sensuous Grace that enchants us in the works of this poet.

The same is true of the plastic productions of the early and severe style, in comparison with the gentleness of the later.

If Grace, besides being the transfiguration of the spirit of Nature, is also the medium of connection between moral Goodness and sensuous Appearance, it is evident how Art must tend from all points toward it as its centre. This Beauty, which results from the perfect inter-penetration of moral Goodness and sensuous Grace, seizes and enchants us when we meet it, with the force of a miracle. For, whilst the spirit of Nature shows itself everywhere else independent of the Soul, and, indeed, in a measure opposed to it, here, it seems, as if by voluntary accord, and the inward fire of divine love, to melt into union with it; the remembrance of the fundamental

unity of the essence of Nature and the essence of the Soul comes over the beholder with sudden clearness—the conviction that all antagonism is only apparent, that Love is the bond of all things, and pure Goodness the foundation and substance of the whole Creation.

Here Art, as it were, transcends itself, and again become means only. On this summit sensuous Grace becomes in turn only the husk and body of a higher life; what was before a whole is treated as a part, and the highest relation of Art and Nature is reached in this—that it makes Nature the medium of manifesting the soul which it contains.

But though in this blossoming of Art, as in the blossoming of the vegetable kingdom, all the previous stages are repeated, yet, on the other hand, we may see in what various directions Art can proceed from this centre. Especially does the difference in nature of the two forms of Plastic Art here show itself most strongly. For Sculpture, representing its ideas by corporeal things, seems to reach its highest point in the complete equilibrium of Soul and Matter—if it give a preponderance to the latter it sinks below its own idea—but it seems altogether impossible for it to elevate the Soul at the expense of Matter, since it must thereby transcend itself. The perfect sculptor indeed, as Winckelmann remarks apropos of the Belvedere Apollo, will use no more material than is needful to accomplish his spiritual purpose; but also, on the other hand, he will put into the Soul no more energy than is at the same time expressed in the material; for precisely upon this, fully to embody the spiritual, depends his art. Sculpture, therefore, can reach its true summit only in the representation of those natures in whose constitution it is implied that they actually embody all that is contained in their Idea or Soul; thus only in divine natures. So that Sculpture, even if no Mythology had preceded it, would of itself have come upon gods, and have invented such if it found none.

Moreover as the Spirit, on this lower platform, has again the same relation to Matter that we have ascribed to the Soul (being the principle of activity and motion, as Matter is that of rest and inaction), the law that regulates Expression and Passion must be a fundamental principle of its nature.

But this law must be applicable not only to the lower passions, but also equally to those higher and godlike passions, if it is permitted so to call them, by which the Soul is affected in rapture, in devotion, in adoration. Hence, since from these passions the gods alone are exempt, Sculpture is inclined from this side also to the imaging of divine natures.

The nature of Painting, however, seems to differ entirely from that of Sculpture. For the former represents objects, not like the latter, by corporeal things, but by light and color, through a medium therefore itself incorporeal and in a measure spiritual. Painting, moreover, gives out its productions nowise as the things themselves, but expressly as pictures. From its very nature therefore it does not lay as much stress on the material as Sculpture, and seems indeed for this reason, while exalting the material above the spirit, to degrade itself more than Sculpture in a like case; on the other hand to be so much more justified in giving a clear preponderance to the Soul.

Where it aims at the highest it will indeed ennoble the passions by Character, or moderate them by Grace, or manifest in them the power of the Soul: but on the other hand it is precisely those higher passions, depending on the relationship of the Soul with a Supreme Being, that are entirely suited to the nature of Painting. Indeed, while Sculpture maintains an exact balance between the force whereby a thing exists outwardly and acts in Nature and that by virtue of which it lives inwardly and as Soul, and excludes mere suffering

even from Matter, Painting may soften in favor of the Soul the characteristicness of the force and activity in Matter, and transform it into resignation and endurance, making it apparent that Man becomes more generally susceptible to the inspirations of the Soul, and to higher influences in general.

This diametrical difference explains of itself not only the necessary predominance of Sculpture in the ancient, and of Painting in the modern world (since in the former the tone of mind was thoroughly plastic, whereas the latter makes even the Soul the passive instrument of higher revelations); but this also is evident—that it is not enough to strive after the Plastic in form and manner of representation, but that it is requisite, before all, to think and to feel plastically, that is, antiquely.

And as the deviation of Sculpture into the picturesque is destructive to Art, so the narrowing down of Painting to the conditions and forms belonging to Sculpture is an arbitrarily imposed limitation. For while Sculpture, like gravitation, acts toward one point, it is permitted to Painting, as to light, to fill all space with its creative energy.

This unlimited universality of Painting is demonstrated by History itself, and by the examples of the greatest masters, who, without injury to the essential character of their art, have developed to perfection each particular stage by itself, so that we can find also in the history of Art the same sequence that may be pointed out in its nature—not indeed in exact order of time, but yet substantially. For thus is represented in Michelangelo the oldest and mightiest epoch of liberated Art, that in which it displays its yet uncontrolled strength in gigantic progeny; as in the fables of the symbolic Fore-world, the Earth, after the embrace of Uranus, brought forth at first Titans and heaven-storming giants before the mild reign of the serene gods began.

Thus the painting of the Last Judgment,

with which, as the sum of his art, that giant spirit filled the Sistine Chapel, seems to remind us more of the first ages of the Earth and its products, than of its last. Attracted toward the most hidden abysses of organic, particularly of the human form, he shuns not the Terrible; nay, he seeks it purposely, and startles it from its repose in the dark workshops of Nature. Want of delicacy, grace, pleasingness, he balances by the extremest energy; and if he excites horror by his representations, it is the terror that, according to fable, the ancient god Pan spreads around him when he suddenly appears in the assemblies of men.

It is the method of Nature to produce the extraordinary by isolation and the exclusion of opposed qualities. Thus, it was necessary that, in Michelangelo, earnestness and the deep significant energy of Nature should prevail, rather than a sense of the grace and sensibility that belong to the Soul, in order to display the extreme of pure plastic force in the painting of modern times.

After the earlier violence and the vehement impulse of birth is assuaged, the spirit of Nature is transfigured into Soul, and Grace is born. This point Art reached, after Leonardo da Vinci, in Correggio, in whose works the sensuous Soul is the active principle of Beauty.

. . .

As the modern fable of Psyche closes the circle of the old mythology; so Painting, by giving a preponderance to the Soul, attained a new, though not a higher step of Art.

This Guido Reni strove after, and became the proper painter of the soul. Such seems to us to be the necessary interpretation of his whole endeavor, often uncertain, and, in many of his works, losing itself in the vague.

This is shown, as, perhaps, in few, of his other pictures, in the masterpiece that is offered to the admiration of all in the great collection of our king.

In the figure of the heavenward-ascending Virgin, all harshness and sternness are effaced, even to the last trace; and, indeed, does not Painting itself seem in it to soar upward, transfigured on its own pinions, as the liberated Psyche delivered from the severity of Form?

Here nothing outward remains, with separate natural force; everything expresses receptivity and still endurance, even the perishable flesh, the character of which the Italian language designates by the term *morbidezza*, altogether unlike that with which Raphael invests the descending Queen of Heaven, as she appears to the adoring pope and a saint.

Though the remark be well-founded, that the original of Guido's female heads is the Niobe of antiquity, yet the ground of this similarity is surely no mere intentional imitation; perhaps a like aim led to like means.

As the Florentine Niobe is an extreme in Sculpture, and the representation in it of the Soul, so this well-known picture is an extreme in Painting, which here ventures to lay aside even the requisite of shade and the obscure, and to work almost with pure Light.

Even though it might be permitted to Painting, from its peculiar nature, to give a distinct preponderance to the Soul, yet theory and instruction will do best constantly to aim at that original Centre, whence alone Art may be produced ever anew; whereas, at the stage last mentioned, it must necessarily stand still, or degenerate into cramped mannerism. For even that higher passion is opposed to the idea of having reached the acme of energy, whose image and reflex Art is called upon to display.

A right intelligence will ever enjoy seeing a creature worthily, and, as far as possible, also individually, represented; yea, Deity itself would look down with pleasure on a being that, gifted with a pure soul, should stoutly assert the dignity of its nature outwardly also, and by its sensually efficient existence.

We have seen how the work of Art, springing up out of the depths of Nature, begins with determinateness and limitation, unfolds its inward plenitude and infinity, is finally transfigured in Grace, and at last attains to Soul. But we can conceive only in detail what, in the creative act of mature Art, is but one operation. No theory and no rules can give this spiritual, creative power. It is the pure gift of Nature, which here, for the second time, makes a close; for, having fully actualized herself, she invests the creature with her creative energy. But as, in the grand progress of Art, these different stages appeared successively, until, at the highest, all joined in one; so also, in particulars, sound culture can spring up only where it has unfolded itself regularly from the germ and root to the blossom.

The requirement that Art, like everything living, should commence from the first rudiments, and, to renew its youth, constantly return to them, may seem a hard doctrine to an age that has so often been assured that it has only to take from works of Art already in existence the most consummate Beauty, and thus, as at a step, to reach the final goal. Have we not already the Excellent, the Perfect? How then should we return to the rudimentary and unformed?

Had the great founders of modern Art thought thus, we should never have seen their miracles. Before them also stood the creations of the ancients, round statues and works in relief, which they might have transferred immediately to their canvas. But such an appropriation of a Beauty not self-won, and therefore unintelligible, would not satisfy an artistic instinct that aimed throughout at the fundamental, and from which the Beautiful was again to create itself with free original energy. They were not afraid, therefore, to appear simple, artless, dry, beside those exalted ancients; nor to cherish Art for a long time in the undistinguished bud, until the period of Grace had arrived.

Whence comes it that we still look upon these works of the older masters, from Giotto to the teacher of Raphael, with a sort of reverence, indeed with a certain predilection, if not that the faithfulness of their endeavor, and the grand earnestness of their serene voluntary limitation, compel our respect and admiration.

The same relation that they held to the ancients, the present generation holds to them. Their time and ours are joined by no living transmission, no link of continuous, organic growth; we must reproduce Art in the way they did, but with energy of our own, in order to be like them.

Even that Indian-summer of Art, at the end of the sixteenth and the beginning of the seventeenth centuries, could call forth only a few new blossoms on the old stem, but no productive germs, still less plant a new tree of Art. But to set aside the works of perfected Art, and to seek out its scanty and simple beginnings, as some have desired, would be a new and perhaps greater mistake; it would be no real return to the fundamental; simplicity would be affectation, and grow into hypocritical show.

But what prospect does the present time offer for an Art springing from a vigorous germ, and growing up from the root? For it is in a great measure dependent on the character of its time; and who would promise the approbation of the present time to such earnest beginnings, when Art, on the one hand, scarcely obtains equal consideration with other instruments of prodigal luxury, and, on the other, artists and amateurs, with entire want of ability to grasp Nature, praise and demand the Ideal?

Art springs only from that powerful striving of the inmost powers of the heart and the spirit, which we call Inspiration. Everything that from difficult or small beginnings has grown up to great power and height, owes its growth to Inspiration.

Thus spring empires and states, thus arts and sciences. But it is not the power of the individual that accomplishes this, but the Spirit alone, that diffuses itself over all. For Art especially is dependent on the tone of the public mind, as the more delicate plants on atmosphere and weather; it needs a general enthusiasm for Sublimity and Beauty, like that which, in the time of the Medici, as a warm breath of spring, called forth at once and together all those great spirits.

. . .

It is only when the public life is actuated by the same forces through whose energy Art is elevated, that the latter can derive any advantage from it; for Art cannot, without giving up the nobility of its nature, aim at anything outward.

Art and Science can move only on their own axes; the artist, like every spiritual laborer, can follow only the law that God and Nature have written in his heart. None can help him—he must help himself; nor can he be outwardly rewarded, since anything that he should produce for the sake of aught out of itself, would thereby become a nullity; hence, too, no one can direct him, nor prescribe the path he is to tread. Is he to be pitied if he have to contend against his time, he is deserving of contempt if he truckle to it. But how should it be even possible for him to do this? Without great general enthusiasm there are only sects—no public opinion; not an established taste, not the great ideas of a whole people, but the voices of a few arbitrarily-appointed judges, determine as to merit; and Art, which in its elevation is self-sufficing, courts favor, and serves where it should rule.

To different ages are given different inspirations. Can we expect none for this age, since the new world now forming itself, as it exists in part already outwardly, in part inwardly and in the hearts of men, can no longer be measured by any standard of previous opinion, and since everything, on the contrary, loudly demands higher standards and an entire renovation?

Should not the sense to which Nature and History have more livingly unfolded themselves, restore to Art also its great arguments? The attempt to draw sparks from the ashes of the Past, and fan them again into universal flame, is a vain endeavor. Only a revolution in the ideas themselves is able to raise Art from its exhaustion; only new Knowledge, new Faith, can inspire it for the work by which it can display, in a renewed life, a splendor like the past.

An Art in all respects the same as that of foregoing centuries, will never return; for Nature never repeats herself. Such a Raphael will never be again, but another, who shall have reached in an equally original manner the summit of Art. Only let the fundamental conditions be fulfilled, and renewed Art will show, like that which preceded it, in its first works, its aim and intent. In the production of the distinctly characteristic, if it proceed from a fresh original energy, Grace is already present, even though hidden, and in both the advent of the Soul already determined. Works produced in this manner, even in their rudimentary imperfection, are necessary and eternal.

SAMUEL TAYLOR COLERIDGE [1772–1834]

>>>>><<<<<

From *Biographia Literaria* [1817]

. . . But as it was my constant reply to authorities brought against me from later poets of great name, that no authority could avail in opposition to TRUTH, NATURE, LOGIC, and the LAWS of UNIVERSAL GRAMMAR; actuated too by my former passion for metaphysical investigations; I labored at a solid foundation, on which permanently to ground my opinions, in the component faculties of the human mind itself, and their comparative dignity and importance. According to the faculty or source, from which the pleasure given by any poem or passage was derived, I estimated the merit of such poem or passage. As the result of all my reading and meditation, I abstracted two critical aphorisms, deeming them to comprise the conditions and criteria of poetic style; first, that not the poem which we have *read*, but that to which we *return*, with the greatest pleasure, possesses the genuine power, and claims the name of *essential poetry*. Second, that whatever lines can be translated into other words of the same language, without diminution of their significance, either in sense, of association, or in any worthy feeling, are so far vicious in their diction. Be it however observed, that I excluded from the list of worthy feelings, the pleasure derived from mere novelty in the reader, and the desire of exciting wonderment at his powers in the author. Oftentimes since then, in pursuing French tragedies, I have fancied two marks of admiration at the end of each line, as hieroglyphics of the author's own admiration at his own cleverness. Our genuine admiration of a great poet is a continuous *under-current* of feeling; it is everywhere present, but seldom anywhere as a separate excitement. I was wont boldly to affirm, that it would be scarcely more difficult to push a stone out from the pyramids with the bare hand, than to alter a word, or the position of a word, in Milton or Shakespeare, (in their most important works at least,) without making the author say something else, or something worse, than he does say. One great distinction, I appeared to myself to see plainly, between, even the characteristic faults of our elder poets, and the false beauty of the moderns. In the former, from DONNE to COWLEY, we find the most fantastic out-of-the-way thoughts, but in the most pure and genuine mother English; in the latter, the most obvious thoughts, in language the most fantastic and arbitrary. Our faulty elder poets sacrificed the passion and passionate flow of poetry, to the subtleties of intellect, and to the starts of wit; the moderns to the glare and glitter of a perpetual, yet broken and heterogeneous imagery, or rather to an amphibious something, made up, half of image, and half of abstract meaning. The one sacrificed the heart to the head; the other both heart and head to point and drapery.

. . .

This excellence, which in all Mr. Wordsworth's writings is more or less predominant, and which constitutes the character of his mind, I no sooner felt, than I sought to understand. Repeated meditations led me first to suspect, (and a more intimate analysis of the human faculties, their appropriate marks, functions, and effects matured my conjecture into full conviction,) that fancy and imagination were two

From S. T. Coleridge, *Biographia Literaria,* edited, with his Aesthetical Essays, by J. Shawcross (Oxford: Oxford University Press, 1907), Vol. I, pp. 14-15, 60-62, 202; Vol. II, pp. 8-20.

distinct and widely different faculties, instead of being, according to the general belief, either two names with one meaning, or, at furthest, the lower and higher degree of one and the same power. It is not, I own, easy to conceive a more opposite translation of the Greek *Phantasia* than the Latin *Imaginatio;* but it is equally true that in all societies there exists an instinct of growth, a certain collective, unconscious good sense working progressively to desynonymize those words originally of the same meaning, which the conflux of dialects had supplied to the more homogenous languages, as the Greek and German: and which the same cause, joined with accidents of translation from original works of different countries, occasion in mixt languages like our own. The first and most important point to be proved is, that two conceptions perfectly distinct are confused under one and the same word, and (this done) to appropriate that word exclusively to one meaning, and the synonyme (should there be one) to the other. But if (as will be often the case in the arts and sciences) no synonyme exists, we must either invent or borrow a word. In the present instance the appropriation has already begun, and been legitimated in the derivative adjective: Milton had a highly *imaginative,* Cowley a very *fanciful* mind. If therefore I should succeed in establishing the actual existences of two faculties generally different, the nomenclature would be at once determined. To the faculty by which I had characterized Milton, we should confine the term *imagination;* while the other would be contra-distinguished as *fancy.* Now were it once fully ascertained, that this division is no less grounded in nature, than that of delirium from mania, or Otway's

Lutes, lobsters, seas of milk, and ships of amber,

from Shakespeare's

What! have his daughters brought him to this pass?

or from the preceding apostrophe to the elements; the theory of the fine arts, and of poetry in particular, could not, I thought, but derive some additional and important light. It would in its immediate effects furnish a torch of guidance to the philosophical critic; and ultimately to the poet himself. In energetic minds, truth soon changes by domestication into power; and from directing in the discrimination and appraisal of the product, becomes influencive in the production. To admire on principle, is the only way to imitate without loss of originality.

. . .

The IMAGINATION then, I consider either as primary, or secondary. The primary IMAGINATION I hold to be the living Power and prime Agent of all human Perception, and as a repetition in the finite mind of the eternal act of creation in the infinite I AM. The secondary Imagination I consider as an echo of the former, co-existing with the conscious will, yet still as identical with the primary in the *kind* of its agency, and differing only in *degree,* and in the *mode* of its operation. It dissolves, diffuses, dissipates, in order to recreate; or where this process is rendered impossible, yet still at all events it struggles to idealize and to unify. It is essentially *vital,* even as all objects (*as* objects) are essentially fixed and dead.

FANCY, on the contrary, has no other counters to play with, but fixities and definites. The Fancy is indeed no other than a mode of Memory emancipated from the order of time and space; while it is blended with, and modified by that empirical phenomenon of the will, which we express by the word CHOICE. But equally with the ordinary memory the Fancy must receive all its materials ready made from the law of association.

. . .

CHAPTER XIV

. . . But in order to render myself intelligible I must previously, in as few words as possible, explain my ideas, first, of a POEM; and secondly, of POETRY itself, in *kind,* and in *essence.*

The office of philosophical *disquisition* consists in just *distinction;* while it is the priviledge of the philosopher to preserve himself constantly aware, that distinction is not division. In order to obtain adequate notions of any truth, we must intellectually separate its distinguishable parts; and this is the technical *process* of philosophy. But having so done, we must then restore them in our conceptions to the unity, in which they actually co-exist; and this is the *result* of philosophy. A poem contains the same elements as a prose composition; the difference therefore must consist in a different combination of them, in consequence of a different object being proposed. According to the difference of the object will be the difference of the combination. It is possible, that the object may be merely to facilitate the recollection of any given facts or observations by artificial arrangement; and the composition will be a poem, merely because it is distinguished from prose by metre, or by rhyme, or by both conjointly. In this, the lowest sense, a man might attribute the name of a poem to the well-known enumeration of the days in the several months;

> Thirty days hath September,
> April, June, and November, etc.

and others of the same class and purpose. And as a particular pleasure is found in anticipating the recurrence of sounds and quantities, all compositions that have this charm super-added, whatever be their contents, *may* be entitled poems.

So much for the superficial *form.* A difference of object and contents supplies an additional ground of distinction. The immediate purpose may be the communication of truths; either of truth absolute and demonstrable, as in works of science; or of facts experienced and recorded, as in history. Pleasure, and that of the highest and most permanent kind, may *result* from the *attainment* of the end; but it is not itself the immediate end. In other works the communication of pleasure may be the immediate purpose; and though truth, either moral or intellectual, ought to be the *ultimate* end, yet this will distinguish the character of the author, not the class to which the work belongs. Blest indeed is that state of society, in which the immediate purpose would be baffled by the perversion of the proper ultimate end; in which no charm of diction or imagery could exempt the Bathyllus even of an Anacreon, or the Alexis of Virgil, from disgust and aversion!

But the communication of pleasure may be the immediate object of a work not metrically composed; and that object may have been in a high degree attained, as in novels and romances. Would then the mere superaddition of metre, with or without rhyme, entitle *these* to the name of poems? The answer is, that nothing can permanently please, which does not contain in itself the reason why it is so, and not otherwise. If metre be superadded, all other parts must be made consonant with it. They must be such, as to justify the perpetual and distinct attention to each part, which an exact correspondent recurrence of accent and sound are calculated to excite. The final definition then, so deduced, may be thus worded. A poem is that species of composition, which is opposed to works of science, by proposing for its *immediate* object pleasure, not truth; and from all other species (having *this* object in common with it) it is discriminated by proposing to itself such delight from the *whole,* as is compatible with a distinct gratification from each component *part.*

Controversy is not seldom excited in consequence of the disputants attaching each a different meaning to the same word; and

in few instances has this been more striking, than in disputes concerning the present subject. If a man chooses to call every
composition a poem, which is rhyme, or
measure, or both, I must leave his opinion
uncontroverted. The distinction is at least
competent to characterize the writer's intention. If it were subjoined, that the
whole is likewise entertaining or affecting,
as a tale, or as a series of interesting reflections, I of course admit this as another
fit ingredient of a poem, and an additional
merit. But if the definition sought for be
that of a *legitimate* poem, I answer, it must
be one, the parts of which mutually support and explain each other; in all their
proportion harmonizing with, and support-
ing the purpose and known influences of
metrical arrangement. The philosophic critics of all ages coincide with the ultimate
judgement of all countries, in equally denying the praises of a just poem, on the one
hand, to a series of striking lines or dis-
tiches, each of which, absorbing the whole
attention of the reader to itself, disjoins it
from its context, and makes it a separate
whole, instead of an harmonizing part;
and on the other hand, to an unsustained
composition, from which the reader collects rapidly the general result, unattracted
by the component parts. The reader should
be carried forward, not merely or chiefly
by the mechanical impulse of curiosity, or
by a restless desire to arrive at the final
solution; but by the pleasureable activity of
mind excited by the attractions of the journey itself. Like the motion of a serpent,
which the Egyptians made the emblem of
intellectual power; or like the path of
sound through the air; at every step he
pauses and half recedes, and from the ret-
rogressive movement collects the force
which again carries him onward. "Prae-
cipitandus est *liber* spiritus," says Petronius
Arbiter most happily. The epithet, *liber*,
here balances the preceding verb; and it
is not easy to conceive more meaning con-
densed in fewer words.

But if this should be admitted as a satisfactory character of a poem, we have still
to seek for a definition of poetry. The writings of PLATO, and Bishop TAYLOR, and
the "Theoria Sacra" of BURNET, furnish
undeniable proofs that poetry of the highest kind may exist without metre, and even
without the contra-distinguishing objects
of a poem. The first chapter of Isaiah (indeed a very large portion of the whole
book) is poetry in the most emphatic
sense; yet it would be not less irrational
than strange to assert, that pleasure, and
not truth, was the immediate object of the
prophet. In short, whatever *specific* import
we attach to the word, poetry, there will
be found involved in it, as a necessary
consequence, that a poem of any length
neither can be, or ought to be, all poetry.
Yet if an harmonious whole is to be produced, the remaining parts must be preserved *in keeping* with the poetry; and
this can be no otherwise effected than by
such a studied selection and artificial arrangement, as will partake of *one*, though
not a *peculiar* property of poetry. And this
again can be no other than the property
of exciting a more continuous and equal
attention than the language of prose aims
at, whether colloquial or written.

My own conclusions on the nature of
poetry, in the strictest use of the word,
have been in part anticipated in the preceding disquisition on the fancy and
imagination. What is poetry? is so nearly
the same question with, what is a poet?
that the answer to the one is involved in
the solution of the other. For it is a distinction resulting from the poetic genius
itself, which sustains and modifies the
images, thoughts, and emotions of the poet's
own mind.

The poet, described in *ideal* perfection,
brings the whole soul of man into activity,
with the subordination of its faculties to
each other, according to their relative
worth and dignity. He diffuses a tone and
spirit of unity, that blends, and (as it

were) *fuses,* each into each, by that synthetic and magical power, to which we have exclusively appropriated the name of imagination. This power, first put in action by the will and understanding, and retained under their irremissive, though gentle and unnoticed, controul [*laxis effertur habenis*] reveals itself in the balance or reconciliation of opposite or discordant qualities: of sameness, with difference; of the general, with the concrete; the idea, with the image; the individual, with the representative; the sense of novelty and freshness, with old and familiar objects; a more than usual state of emotion, with more than usual order; judgement ever awake and steady self-possession, with enthusiasm and feeling profound or vehement; and while it blends and harmonizes the natural and the artificial, still subordinates art to nature; the manner to the matter; and our admiration of the poet to our sympathy with the poetry. "Doubtless," as Sir John Davies observes of the soul (and his words may with slight alteration be applied, and even more appropriately, to the poetic IMAGINATION)

Doubtless this could not be, but that she turns
    Bodies to spirit by sublimation strange,
As fire converts to fire the things it burns,
    As we our food into our nature change.

From their gross matter she abstracts their
        forms,
    And draws a kind of quintessence from
        things;
Which to her proper nature she transforms,
    To bear them light on her celestial wings.

Thus does she, when from individual states
    She doth abstract the universal kinds;
Which then re-clothed in divers names and
        fates
    Steal access through our senses to our
        minds.

Finally, GOOD SENSE is the BODY of poetic genius, FANCY its DRAPERY, MOTION its LIFE, and IMAGINATION the SOUL that is everywhere, and in each; and forms all into one graceful and intelligent whole.

CHAPTER XV

In the application of these principles to purposes of practical criticism as employed in the appraisal of works more or less imperfect, I have endeavoured to discover what the qualities in a poem are, which may be deemed promises and specific symptoms of poetic power, as distinguished from general talent determined to poetic composition by accidental motives, by an act of the will, rather than by the inspiration of a genial and productive nature. In this investigation, I could not, I thought, do better, than keep before me the earliest work of the greatest genius, that perhaps human nature has yet produced, our *myriad-minded* Shakespeare. I mean the "Venus and Adonis," and the "Lucrece"; works which give at once strong promises of the strength, and yet obvious proofs of the immaturity, of his genius. From these I abstracted the following marks, as characteristics of original poetic genius in general.

1. In the "Venus and Adonis," the first and most obvious excellence is the perfect sweetness of the versification; its adaptation to the subject; and the power displayed in varying the march of the words without passing into a loftier and more majestic rhythm than was demanded by the thoughts, or permitted by the propriety of preserving a sense of melody predominant. The delight in richness and sweetness of sound, even to a faulty excess, if it be evidently original, and not the result of an easily imitable mechanism, I regard as a highly favourable promise in the compositions of a young man. "The man that hath not music in his soul" can indeed never be a genuine poet. Imagery (even taken from nature, much more when transplanted from books, as travels, voyages, and works of natural history); affecting incidents; just thoughts; interesting personal or domestic feelings; and with these the art of

their combination or intertexture in the form of a poem; may all by incessant effort be acquired as a trade, by a man of talents and much reading, who, as I once before observed, has mistaken an intense desire of poetic reputation for a natural poetic genius; the love of the arbitrary end for a possession of the peculiar means. But the sense of musical delight, with the power of producing it, is a gift of imagination; and this together with the power of reducing multitude into unity of effect, and modifying a series of thoughts by some one predominant thought or feeling, may be cultivated and improved, but can never be learned. It is in these that "poeta nascitur non fit."

2. A second promise of genius is the choice of subjects very remote from the private interests and circumstances of the writer himself. At least I have found, that where the subject is taken immediately from the author's personal sensations and experiences, the excellence of a particular poem is but an equivocal mark, and often a fallacious pledge, of genuine poetic power. We may perhaps remember the tale of the statuary, who had acquired considerable reputation for the legs of his goddesses, though the rest of the statue accorded but indifferently with ideal beauty; till his wife, elated by her husband's praises, modestly acknowledged that herself had been his constant model. In the "Venus and Adonis" this proof of poetic power exists even to excess. It is throughout as if a superior spirit more intuitive, more intimately conscious, even than the characters themselves, not only of every outward look and act, but of the flux and reflux of the mind in all its subtlest thoughts and feelings, were placing the whole before our view; himself meanwhile unparticipating in the passions, and actuated only by that pleasureable excitement, which had resulted from the energetic fervor of his own spirit in so vividly exhibiting, what it had so accurately and profoundly contemplated. I think, I should have conjectured from these poems, that even then the great instinct, which impelled the poet to the drama, was secretly working in him, prompting him by a series and never broken chain of imagery, always vivid and, because unbroken, often minute; by the highest effort of the picturesque in words, of which words are capable, higher perhaps than was ever realized by any other poet, even Dante not excepted; to provide a substitute for that visual language, that constant intervention and running comment by tone, look and gesture, which in his dramatic works he was entitled to expect from the players. His "Venus and Adonis" seem at once the characters themselves, and the whole representation of those characters by the most consummate actors. You seem to be told nothing, but to see and hear everything. Hence it is, that from the perpetual activity of attention required on the part of the reader; from the rapid flow, the quick change, and the playful nature of the thoughts and images; and above all from the alienation, and, if I may hazard such an expression, the utter *aloofness* of the poet's own feelings, from those of which he is at once the painter and the analyst; that though the very subject cannot but detract from the pleasure of a delicate mind, yet never was poem less dangerous on a moral account. Instead of doing as Ariosto, and as, still more offensively, Wieland has done, instead of degrading and deforming passion into appetite, the trials of love into the struggle of concupiscence; Shakespeare has here represented the animal impulse itself, so as to preclude all sympathy with it, by dissipating the reader's notice among the thousand outward images, and now beautiful, now fanciful circumstances, which form its dresses and its scenery; or by diverting our attention from the main subject by those frequent witty or profound reflections, which the poet's ever active mind has deduced from,

or connected with, the imagery and the incidents. The reader is forced into too much action to sympathize with the merely passive of our nature. As little can a mind thus roused and awakened be brooded on by mean and indistinct emotion, as the low, lazy mist can creep upon the surface of a lake, while a strong gale is driving it onward in waves and billows.

3. It has been before observed that images, however beautiful, though faithfully copied from nature, and as accurately represented in words, do not of themselves characterize the poet. They become proofs of original genius only as far as they are modified by a predominant passion; or by associated thoughts or images awakened by that passion; or when they have the effect of reducing multitude to unity, or succession to an instant; or lastly, when a human and intellectual life is transferred to them from the poet's own spirit,

Which shoots its being through earth, sea, and air.

In the two following lines for instance, there is nothing objectionable, nothing which would preclude them from forming, in their proper place, part of a descriptive poem:

Behold yon row of pines, that shorn and bow'd
Bend from the sea-blast, seen at twilight eve.

But with a small alteration of rhythm, the same words would be equally in their place in a book of topography, or in a descriptive tour. The same image will rise into semblance of poetry if thus conveyed:

Yon row of bleak and visionary pines,
By twilight glimpse discerned, mark! how they
    flee
From the fierce sea-blast, all their tresses wild
Streaming before them.

I have given this as an illustration, by no means as an instance, of that particular

excellence which I had in view, and in which Shakespeare even in his earliest, as in his latest, works surpasses all other poets. It is by this, that he still gives a dignity and a passion to the objects which he presents. Unaided by any previous excitement, they burst upon us at once in life and in power.

Full many a glorious morning have I seen
Flatter the mountain tops with sovereign eye.
                    Shakespeare, Sonnet 33rd.

Not mine own fears, nor the prophetic soul
Of the wide world dreaming on things to
    come—
    *   *   *   *   *   *
The mortal moon hath her eclipse endur'd,
And the sad augurs mock their own presage;
Incertainties now crown themselves assur'd,
And Peace proclaims olives of endless age.
Now with the drops of this most balmy time
My Love looks fresh, and DEATH to me
    subscribes!
Since spite of him, I'll live in this poor rhyme,
While he insults o'er dull and speechless
    tribes.
And thou in this shalt find thy monument,
When tyrants' crests, and tombs of brass are
    spent.
                    Sonnet 107.

As of higher worth, so doubtless still more characteristic of poetic genius does the imagery become, when it moulds and colors itself to the circumstances, passion, or character, present and foremost in the mind. For unrivalled instances of this excellence, the reader's own memory will refer him to the LEAR, OTHELLO, in short to which not of the "great, ever living, dead man's" dramatic works? "Inopem me copia fecit." How true it is to nature, he has himself finely expressed in the instance of love in Sonnet 98.

From you have I been absent in the spring,
When proud April drest in all its trim
Hath put a spirit of youth in every thing,
That heavy Saturn laugh'd and leap'd with
    him.

Yet nor the lays of birds, nor the sweet smell
Of different flowers in odour and in hue,
Could make me any summer's story tell,
Or from their proud lap pluck them, where
    they grew:
Nor did I wonder at the lilies white,
Nor praise the deep vermilion in the rose;
They were, tho' sweet, but figures of delight,
Drawn after you, you pattern of all those.
Yet seem'd it winter still, and, you away,
As with your shadow I with these did play!

Scarcely less sure, or if a less valuable,
not less indispensable mark

Γονίμου μὲν ποιητοῦ————
————ὅστις ῥῆμα γενναῖον λάκοι,

will the imagery supply, when, with more
than the power of the painter, the poet
gives us the liveliest image of succession
with the feeling of simultaneousness!

With this, he breaketh from the sweet
    embrace
Of those fair arms, that held him to her heart,
And homeward through the dark lawns runs
    apace:
Look! how a bright star shooteth from the sky,
So glides he in the night from Venus' eye.

4. The last character I shall mention,
which would prove indeed but little, except as taken conjointly with the former;
yet without which the former could scarce
exist in a high degree, and (even if this
were possible) would give promises only of
transitory flashes and a meteoric power; is
DEPTH, and ENERGY of THOUGHT. No man
was ever yet a great poet, without being
at the same time a profound philosopher.
For poetry is the blossom and the fragrancy
of all human knowledge, human thoughts,
human passions, emotions, language. In
Shakespeare's *poems* the creative power and
the intellectual energy wrestle as in a war
embrace. Each in its excess of strength
seems to threaten the extinction of the
other. At length in the DRAMA they were
reconciled, and fought each with its shield

before the breast of the other. Or like
two rapid streams, that, at their first meeting within narrow and rocky banks, mutually strive to repel each other and inter-
mix reluctantly and in tumult; but soon
finding a wider channel and more yielding
shores blend, and dilate, and flow on in
one current and with one voice. The
"Venus and Adonis" did not perhaps allow the display of the deeper passions.
But the story of Lucretia seems to favor
and even demand their intensest workings.
And yet we find in *Shakespeare's* management of the tale neither pathos, nor any
other *dramatic* quality. There is the same
minute and faithful imagery as in the former poem, in the same vivid colors, in-
spirited by the same impetuous vigor of
thought, and diverging and contracting
with the same activity of the assimilative
and of the modifying faculties; and with a
yet larger display, a yet wider range of
knowledge and reflection; and lastly, with
the same perfect dominion, often *domina-
tion,* over the whole world of language.
What then shall we say? even this; that
Shakespeare, no mere child of nature; no
automaton of genius; no passive vehicle of
inspiration possessed by the spirit, not possessing it; first studied patiently, meditated
deeply, understood minutely, till knowledge, become habitual and intuitive, wedded itself to his habitual feelings, and at
length gave birth to that stupendous
power, by which he stands alone, with no
equal or second in his own class; to that
power which seated him on one of the
two glory-smitten summits of the poetic
mountain, with Milton as his compeer,
not rival. While the former darts himself
forth, and passes into all the forms of
human character and passion, the one Proteus of the fire and the flood; the other
attracts all forms and things to himself,
into the unity of his own IDEAL. All
things and modes of action shape themselves anew in the being of MILTON;
while SHAKESPEARE becomes all things,

yet for ever remaining himself. O what great men hast thou not produced, England! my country! truly indeed—

Must *we* be free or die, who speak the tongue,
Which SHAKESPEARE spake; the faith and
    morals hold,
Which MILTON held. In every thing we are
    sprung
Of earth's first blood, have titles manifold!

WORDSWORTH.

From *On Poesy or Art*

Man communicates by articulation of sounds, and paramountly by the memory in the ear; nature by the impression of bounds and surfaces on the eye, and through the eye it gives significance and appropriation, and thus the conditions of memory, or the capability of being remembered, to sounds, smells, &c. Now Art, used collectively for painting, sculpture, architecture and music, is the mediatress between, and reconciler of, nature and man. It is, therefore, the power of humanizing nature, of infusing the thoughts and passions of man into everything which is the object of his contemplation; color, form, motion, and sound, are the elements which it combines, and it stamps them into unity in the mould of a moral idea.

The primary art is writing;—primary, if we regard the purpose abstracted from the different modes of realizing it, those steps of progression of which the instances are still visible in the lower degrees of civilization. First, there is mere gesticulation; then rosaries or *wampum;* then picture-language; then hieroglyphics, and finally alphabetic letters. These all consists of a translation of man into nature, of a substitution of the visible for the audible.

The so called music of savage tribes as little deserves the name of art for the understanding, as the ear warrants it for music. Its lowest state is a mere expression

Op. cit. pp. 253-9.

of passion by sounds which the passion itself necessitates;—the highest amounts to no more than a voluntary reproduction of these sounds in the absence of the occasioning causes, so as to give the pleasure of contrast,—for example, by the various outcries of battle in the song of security and triumph. Poetry also is purely human; for all its materials are from the mind, and all its products are for the mind. But it is the apotheosis of the former state, in which by excitement of the associative power passion itself imitates order, and the order resulting produces a pleasureable passion, and thus it elevates the mind by making its feelings the object of its reflexion. So likewise, whilst it recalls the sights and sounds that had accompanied the occasions of the original passions, poetry impregnates them with an interest not their own by means of the passions, and yet tempers the passion by the calming power which all distinct images exert on the human soul. In this way poetry is the preparation for art, inasmuch as it avails itself of the forms of nature to recall, to express, and to modify the thoughts and feelings of the mind. Still, however, poetry can only act through the intervention of articulate speech, which is so peculiarly human, that in all languages it constitutes the ordinary phrase by which man and nature are contradistinguished. It is the original force of the word "brute," and even "mute" and "dumb" do not convey the absence of sound, but the absence of articulated sounds.

As soon as the human mind is intelligibly addressed by an outward image exclusively of articulate speech, so soon does art commence. But please to observe that I have laid particular stress on the words "human mind,"—meaning to exclude thereby all results common to man and all other sentient creatures, and consequently confining myself to the effect produced by the congruity of the animal impression with the reflective powers of the mind; so that not the thing presented, but that which is re-presented by the thing, shall be the source of the pleasure. In this sense nature itself is to a religious observer the art of God; and for the same cause art itself might be defined as of a middle quality between a thought and a thing, or, as I said before, the union and reconciliation of that which is nature with that which is exclusively human. It is the figured language of thought, and is distinguished from nature by the unity of all the parts in one thought or idea. Hence nature itself would give us the impression of a work of art, if we could see the thought which is present at once in the whole and in every part; and a work of art will be just in proportion as it adequately conveys the thought, and rich in proportion to the variety of parts which it holds in unity.

If, therefore, the term "mute" be taken as opposed not to sound but to articulate speech, the old definition of painting will in fact be the true and best definition of the Fine Arts in general, that is, *muta poesis,* mute poesy, and so of course poesy. And, as all languages perfect themselves by a gradual process of desynonymizing words originally equivalent, I have cherished the wish to use the word "poesy" as the generic or common term, and to distinguish that species of poesy which is not *muta poesis* by its usual name "poetry"; while of all the other species which collectively form the Fine Arts, there would remain this as the common definition,—that they all, like poetry, are to express intellectual purposes, thoughts, conceptions, and sentiments which have their origin in the human mind,—not, however, as poetry does, by means of articulate speech, but as nature or the divine art does, by form, color, magnitude, proportion, or by sound, that is, silently or musically.

Well! it may be said—but who has ever thought otherwise? We all know that art is the imitatress of nature. And, doubtless, the truths which I hope to convey would be barren truisms, if all men meant the same by the words "imitate" and "nature."

But it would be flattering mankind at large, to presume that such is the fact. First, to imitate. The impression on the wax is not an imitation, but a copy, of the seal; the seal itself is an imitation. But, further, in order to form a philosophic conception, we must seek for the kind, as the heat in ice, invisible light, &c., whilst, for practical purposes, we must have reference to the degree. It is sufficient that philosophically we understand that in all imitation two elements must coexist, and not only coexist, but must be perceived as coexisting. These two constituent elements are likeness and unlikeness, or sameness and difference, and in all genuine creations of art there must be a union of these disparates. The artist may take his point of view where he pleases, provided that the desired effect be perceptibly produced,—that there be likeness in the difference, difference in the likeness, and a reconcilement of both in one. If there be likeness to nature without any check of difference, the result is disgusting, and the more complete the delusion, the more loathsome the effect. Why are such simulations of nature, as waxwork figures of men and women, so disagreeable? Because, not finding the motion and the life which we expected, we are shocked as by a falsehood, every circumstance of detail, which before induced us to be interested, making the distance from truth more palpable. You set out with a supposed reality and are disappointed and disgusted with the deception; whilst, in respect to a work of genuine imitation, you begin with an acknowledged total difference, and then every touch of nature gives you the pleasure of an approximation to truth. The fundamental principle of all this is undoubtedly the horror of falsehood and the love of truth inherent in the human breast. The Greek tragic dance rested on these principles, and I can deeply sympathize in imagination with the Greeks in this favorite part of their theatrical exhibitions, when I call to mind the pleasure I felt in beholding the combat to the Horatii and Curiatii most exquisitely danced in Italy to the music of Cimarosa.

Secondly, as to nature. We must imitate nature! yes, but what in nature,—all and every thing? No, the beautiful in nature. And what then is the beautiful? What is beauty? It is, in the abstract, the unity of the manifold, the coalescence of the diverse; in the concrete, it is the union of the shapely (*formosum*) with the vital. In the dead organic it depends on regularity of form, the first and lowest species of which is the triangle with all its modifications, as in crystals, architecture, &c.; in the living organic it is not mere regularity of form, which would produce a sense of formality; neither is it subservient to any thing beside itself. It may be present in a disagreeable object, in which the proportion of the parts constitutes a whole; it does not arise from association, as the agreeable does, but sometimes lies in the rupture of association; it is not different to different individuals and nations, as has been said, nor is it connected with the ideas of the good, or the fit, or the useful. The sense of beauty is intuitive, and beauty itself is all that inspires pleasure without, and aloof from, and even contrarily to, interest.

If the artist copies the mere nature, the *natura naturata,* what idle rivalry! If he proceeds only from a given form, which is supposed to answer to the notion of beauty, what an emptiness, what an unreality there always is in his productions, as in Cipriani's pictures! Believe me, you must master the essence, the *natura naturans,* which presupposes a bond between nature in the higher sense and the soul of man.

The wisdom in nature is distinguished from that in man by the co-instantaneity of the plan and the execution; the thought and the product are one, or are given at once; but there is no reflex act, and hence there is no moral responsibility. In man there is reflexion, freedom, and choice; he is, therefore, the head of the visible creation. In the objects of nature are presented, as in a mirror, all the possible elements, steps, and processes of intellect antecedent to consciousness, and therefore to the full development of the intelligential act; and man's mind is the very focus of all the rays of intellect which are scattered throughout the images of nature. Now so to place these images, totalized, and fitted to the limits of the human mind, as to elicit from, and to superinduce upon, the forms themselves the moral reflexions to which they approximate, to make the external internal, the internal external, to make nature thought, and thought nature,—this is the mystery of genius in the Fine Arts. Dare I add that the genius must act on the feeling, that body is but a striving to become mind,—that it is mind in its essence!

In every work of art there is a reconcilement of the external with the internal; the conscious is so impressed on the unconscious as to appear in it; as compare mere letters inscribed on a tomb with figures themselves constituting the tomb. He who combines the two is the man of genius; and for that reason he must partake of both. Hence there is in genius itself an unconscious activity; nay, that is the genius in the man of genius. And this is the true exposition of the rule that the artist must first eloign himself from nature in order to return to her with full effect. Why this? Because if he were to begin by mere painful copying, he would produce masks only, not forms breathing life. He must out of his own mind create forms according to the severe laws of the intellect, in order to generate in himself that co-ordination of freedom and law, that involution of obedience in the prescript, and of the prescript in the impulse to obey, which assimilates him to nature, and enables him to understand her. He merely absents himself for a season from her, that his own spirit, which has the same ground with nature, may learn her unspoken language in its main radicals, before he approaches to her endless compositions of them. Yes, not to acquire cold notions—lifeless technical rules —but living and life-producing ideas, which shall contain their own evidence, the certainty that they are essentially one with the germinal causes in nature,—his consciousness being the focus and mirror of both,—for this does the artist for a time abandon the external real in order to return to it with a complete sympathy with its internal and actual. For of all we see, hear, feel and touch the substance is and must be in ourselves; and therefore there is no alternative in reason between the dreary (and thank heaven! almost impossible) belief that every thing around us is but a phantom, or that the life which is in us is in them likewise; and that to know is to resemble, when we speak of objects out of ourselves, even as within ourselves to learn is, according to Plato, only to

recollect;—the only effective answer to which, that I have been fortunate to meet with, is that which Pope has consecrated for future use in the line—

And coxcombs vanquish Berkeley with a grin!

The artist must imitate that which is within the thing, that which is active through form and figure, and discourses to us by symbols—the *Naturgeist,* or spirit of nature, as we unconsciously imitate those whom we love; for so only can he hope to produce any work truly natural in the object and truly human in the effect. The idea which puts the form together cannot itself be the form. It is above form, and is its essence, the universal in the individual, or the individuality itself,— the glance and the exponent of the indwelling power.

ARTHUR SCHOPENHAUER [1788–1860]

>>>>><<<<<

From *The World as Will and Idea* [1818, 1844]

BOOK III

30. In the first Book the world was explained as mere *idea,* object for a subject. In the Second Book we considered it from its other side, and found that in this aspect it is *will,* which proved to be simply that which this world is besides being idea. In accordance with this knowledge we called the world as idea, both as a whole and in

From Arthur Schopenhauer, *The World as Will and Idea,* translated by R. B. Haldane and J. Kemp (New York: Charles Scribner's Sons; London: Routledge & Kegan Paul, 1883). Reprinted by permission of Routledge & Kegan Paul, Ltd.

its parts, the *objectification of will,* which therefore means the will become object, i.e. idea. Further, we remember that this objectification of will was found to have many definite grades, in which, with gradually increasing distinctness and completeness, the nature of will appears in the idea, that is to say, presents itself as object. In these grades we already recognised the Platonic Ideas, for the grades are just the determined species, or the original unchanging forms and qualities of all natural bodies, both organised and unorganised, and also the general forces which reveal themselves according to natural laws. These Ideas, then, as a whole express themselves in innumerable individuals and particulars, and are related to these as archetypes to their copies. The multiplicity of such individuals is only conceivable through time and space, their appearing and passing away through causality, and in all these forms we recognise merely the different modes of the principle of sufficient reason, which is the ultimate principle of all that is finite, of all individual existence, and the universal form of the idea as it appears in the knowledge of the individual as such. The Platonic Idea, on the other hand, does not come under this principle, and has therefore neither multiplicity nor change. While the individuals in which it expresses itself are innumerable, and unceasingly come into being and pass away, it remains unchanged as one and the same, and the principle of sufficient reason has for it no meaning. As, however, this is the form under which all knowledge of the subject comes, so far as the subject knows as an *individual,* the Ideas lie quite outside the sphere of its knowledge. If, therefore, the Ideas are to become objects of knowledge, this can only happen by transcending the individuality of the knowing subject. The more exact and detailed explanation of this is what will now occupy our attention. . . .

33. Since now, as individuals, we have no other knowledge than that which is subject to the principle of sufficient reason, and this form of knowledge excludes the Ideas, it is certain that if it is possible for us to raise ourselves from the knowledge of particular things to that of the Ideas, this can only happen by an alteration taking place in the subject which is analogous and corresponds to the great change of the whole nature of the object, and by virtue of which the subject, so far as it knows an Idea, is no more individual.

It will be remembered from the preceding book that knowledge in general belongs to the objectification of will at its higher grades, and sensibility, nerves, and brain, just like the other parts of the organised being, are the expression of the will at this stage of its objectivity, and therefore the idea which appears through them is also in the same way bound to the service of will as a means [*mēchanē*] for the attainment of its now complicated [*polytelestera*] aims for sustaining a being of manifold requirements. Thus originally and according to its nature, knowledge is completely subject to the will, and, like the immediate object, which, by means of the application of the law of causality, is its starting-point, all knowledge which proceeds in accordance with the principle of sufficient reason remains in a closer or more distant relation to the will. For the individual finds his body as an object among objects, to all of which it is related and connected according to the principle of sufficient reason. Thus all investigations of these relations and connections lead back to his body, and consequently to his will. Since it is the principle of sufficient reason which places the objects in this relation to the body, and, through it, to the will, the one endeavour of the knowledge which is subject to this principle will be to find out the relations in which objects are placed to each other through this principle, and thus to trace their innumerable connections in space, time, and causality. For only through these is the object *interesting* to the individual, i.e. related to the will. Therefore the knowledge which is subject to the will knows nothing further of objects then their relations, knows the objects only so far as they exist at this time, in this place, under these circumstances, from these causes, and with these effects—in a word, as particular things; and if all these relations were to be taken away, the objects would also have disappeared for it, because it knew nothing more about them. We must not disguise the fact that what the sciences consider in things is also in reality nothing more than this; their relations, the connections of time and space, the causes of natural changes, the resemblance of forms, the motives of actions,—

thus merely relations. What distinguishes science from ordinary knowledge is merely its systematic form, the facilitating of knowledge by the comprehension of all particulars in the universal, by means of the subordination of concepts, and the completeness of knowledge which is thereby attained. . . .

34. The transition which we have referred to as possible, but yet to be regarded as only exceptional, from the common knowledge of particular things to the knowledge of the Idea, takes place suddenly; for knowledge breaks free from the services of the will, by the subject ceasing to be merely individual, and thus becoming the pure will-less subject of knowledge, which no longer traces relations in accordance with the principle of sufficient reason, but rests in fixed contemplation of the object presented to it, out of its connection with all others, and rises into it.

A full explanation is necessary to make this clear, and the reader must suspend his surprise for a while, till he has grasped the whole thought expressed in this work, and then it will vanish of itself.

If, raised by the power of the mind, a man relinquishes the common way of looking at things, gives up tracing, under the guidance of the forms of the principle of sufficient reason, their relations to each other, the final goal of which is always a relation to his own will; if he thus ceases to consider the where, the when, the why, and the whither of things, and looks simply and solely at the *what*; if, further, he does not allow abstract thought, the concepts of the reason, to take possession of his consciousness, but, instead, of all this, gives the whole power of his mind to perception, sinks himself entirely in this, and lets his whole consciousness be filled with the quiet contemplation of the natural object actually present, whether a landscape, a tree, a mountain, a building, or whatever it may be; inasmuch as he *loses* himself in this object, i.e. forgets even his individual-

ity, his will, and only continues to exist as the pure subject, the clear mirror of the object, so that it is as if the object alone were there, without any one to perceive it, and he can no longer separate the perceiver from the perception, but both have become one, because the whole consciousness is filled and occupied with one single sensuous picture; if thus the object has to such an extent passed out of all relation to something outside it, and the subject out of all relation to the will, then that which is so known is no longer the particular thing as such; but it is the *Idea,* the eternal form, the immediate objectivity of the will at this grade; and, therefore, he who is sunk in this perception is no longer individual, for in such perception the individual has lost himself; but he is *pure,* will-less, painless, timeless *subject of knowledge. . . .* In such contemplation the particular thing becomes at once the *Idea* of its species, and the perceiving individual becomes *pure subject of knowledge.* The individual, as such, knows only particular things; the pure subject of knowledge knows only Ideas. For the individual is the subject of knowledge, in its relation to a definite particular manifestation of will, and in subjection to this. This particular manifestation of will is, as such, subordinated to the principle of sufficient reason in all its forms; therefore, all knowledge which relates itself to it also follows the principle of sufficient reason, and no other kind of knowledge is fitted to be of use to the will but this, which always consists merely of relations to the object. The knowing individual as such, and the particular things known by him, are always in some place, at some time, and are links in the chain of causes and effects. The pure subject of knowledge and his correlative, the Idea, have passed out of all these forms of the principle of sufficient reason: time, place, the individual that knows, and the individual that is known, have for them no meaning. . . . When the Platonic Idea appears, in it subject and object are no longer to be distinguished, for the Platonic Idea, the adequate objectivity of will, the true world as idea, arises only when the subject and object reciprocally fill and penetrate each other completely; and in the same way the knowing and the known individuals, as things in themselves, are not to be distinguished. For if we look entirely away from the true *world as idea,* there remains nothing but *the world as will.* The will is the "in-itself" of the Platonic Idea, which fully objectifies it; it is also the "in-itself" of the particular thing and of the individual that knows it, which objectify it incompletely. As will, outside the idea and all its forms, it is one and the same in the object contemplated and in the individual, who soars aloft in this contemplation, and becomes conscious of himself as pure subject. These two are, therefore, in themselves not different, for in themselves they are will, which here knows itself; and multiplicity and difference exist only as the way in which this knowledge comes to the will, i.e. only in the phenomenon, on account of its form, the principle of sufficient reason.

35. In order to gain a deeper insight into the nature of the world, it is absolutely necessary that we should learn to distinguish the will as thing-in-itself from its adequate objectivity, and also the different grades in which this appears more and more distinctly and fully, i.e. the Ideas themselves, from the merely phenomenal existence of these Ideas in the forms of the principle of sufficient reason, the restricted method of knowledge of the individual. We shall then agree with Plato when he attributes actual being only to the Ideas, and allows only an illusive, dream-like existence to things in space and time, the real world for the individual. Then we shall understand how one and the same Idea reveals itself in so many phenomena, and presents its nature only bit by bit to the individual, one side after another. Then we shall also distinguish the Idea itself from the way in which its manifestation appears in the observation of the individual, and recognise the former as essential and the latter as unessential. Let us consider this with the help of examples taken from the most insignificant things, and also from the greatest. When the clouds move, the figures which they form are not essential, but indifferent to them; but that as elastic vapour they are pressed together, drifted along, spread out, or torn asunder by the force of the wind: this is their nature, the essence of the forces which objectify themselves in them, the Idea; their actual forms are only for the individual observer. To the brook that flows over stones, the eddies, the waves, the foam-flakes which it forms are indifferent and unessential; but that it follows the attraction of gravity, and behaves as inelastic, perfectly mobile, formless, transparent fluid: this is its nature; this, *if known through perception,* is its Idea; these accidental forms are only for us so long as we know as individuals. . . . What appears in the clouds, the brook, and the crystal is the weakest echo of that will which appears more fully in the plant, more fully still in the beast, and most fully in man. But only the essential in all these grades of its objectification constitutes the Idea; on the other hand, its unfolding or development, because broken up in the forms of the principle of sufficient reason into a multiplicity of many-sided phenomena, is unessential to the Idea, lies merely in the kind of knowledge that belongs to the individual and has reality only for this. The same thing necessarily holds good of the unfolding of that Idea which is the completest objectivity of will. Therefore, the history of the human race, the throng of events, the change of times, the multifarious forms of human life in different lands and countries, all this is only the accidental form of the manifestation of the Idea, does not belong to the Idea itself, in which

alone lies the adequate objectivity of the will, but only to the phenomenon which appears in the knowledge of the individual, and is just as foreign, unessential, and indifferent to the Idea itself as the figures which they assume are to the clouds, the form of its eddies and foam-flakes to the brook.

To him who has thoroughly grasped this, and can distinguish between the will and the Idea, and between the Idea and its manifestation, the events of the world will have significance only so far as they are the letters out of which we may read the Idea of man, but not in and for themselves. He will not believe with the vulgar that time may produce something actually new and significant; that through it, or in it, something absolutely real may attain to existence, or indeed that it itself as a whole has beginning and end, plan and development, and in some way has for its final aim the highest perfection (according to their conception) of the last generation of man, whose life is a brief thirty years. . . . In the manifold forms of human life and in the unceasing change of events, he will regard the Idea only as the abiding and essential, in which the will to live has its fullest objectivity, and which shows its different sides in the capacities, the passions, the errors and the excellences of the human race; in self-interest, hatred, love, fear, boldness, frivolity, stupidity, slyness, wit, genius, and so forth, all of which crowding together and combining in thousands of forms (individuals), continually create the history of the great and the little world, in which it is all the same whether they are set in motion by nuts or by crowns. Finally, he will find that in the world it is the same as in the dramas of Gozzi, in all of which the same persons appear, with like intention, and with a like fate; the motives and incidents are certainly different in each piece, but the spirit of the incidents is the same; the actors in one piece know nothing of the incidents of another, al-though they performed in it themselves; therefore, after all experience of former pieces, Pantaloon has become no more agile or generous, Tartaglia no more conscientious, Brighella no more courageous, and Columbine no more modest.

36. History follows the thread of events; it is pragmatic so far as it deduces them in accordance with the law of motivation, a law that determines the self-manifesting will wherever it is enlightened by knowledge. At the lower grades of its objectivity, where it still acts without knowledge, natural science, in the form of etiology, treats of the laws of the changes of its phenomena, and, in the form of morphology, of what is permanent in them. This almost endless task is lightened by the aid of concepts, which comprehend what is general in order that we may deduce what is particular from it. Lastly, mathematics treats of the mere forms, time and space, in which the Ideas, broken up into multiplicity, appear for the knowledge of the subject as individual. All these, of which the common name is science, proceed according to the principle of sufficient reason in its different forms, and their theme is always the phenomenon, its laws, connections, and the relations which result from them. But what kind of knowledge is concerned with that which is outside and independent of all relations, that alone is really essential to the world, the true content of its phenomena, that which is subject to no change, and therefore is known with equal truth for all time, in a word, the *Ideas,* which are the direct and adequate objectivity of the thing-in-itself, the will? We answer, *Art,* the work of genius. It repeats or reproduces the eternal Ideas grasped through pure contemplation, the essential and abiding in all the phenomena of the world; and according to what the material is in which it reproduces, it is sculpture or painting, poetry or music. Its one source is the knowledge of Ideas; its one aim the communication of this

knowledge. While science, following the unresting and inconstant stream of the four-fold forms of reason and consequent, with each end attained sees further, and can never reach a final goal nor attain full satisfaction, any more than by running we can reach the place where the clouds touch the horizon; art, on the contrary, is everywhere at its goal. For it plucks the object of its contemplation out of the stream of the world's course, and has it isolated before it. And this particular thing, which in that stream was a small perishing part, becomes to art the representative of the whole, an equivalent of the endless multitude in space and time. It therefore pauses at this particular thing; the course of time stops; the relations vanish for it; only the essential, the Idea, is its object. We may, therefore, accurately define it as the *way of viewing things independent of the principle of sufficient reason,* in opposition to the way of viewing them which proceeds in accordance with that principle, and which is the method of experience and of science. This last method of considering things may be compared to a line infinitely extended in a horizontal direction, and the former to a vertical line which cuts it at any point. The method of viewing things which proceeds in accordance with the principle of sufficient reason is the rational method, and it alone is valid and of use in practical life and in science. The method which looks away from the content of this principle is the method of genius, which is only valid and of use in art. The first is the method of Aristotle; the second is, on the whole, that of Plato. The first is like the mighty storm, that rushes along without beginning and without aim, bending, agitating, and carrying away everything before it; the second is like the silent sunbeam, that pierces through the storm quite unaffected by it. The first is like the innumerable showering drops of the waterfall, which, constantly changing, never rest for an instant; the second is like

the rainbow, quietly resting on this raging torrent. Only through the pure contemplation described above, which ends entirely in the object, can Ideas be comprehended; and the nature of *genius* consists in pre-eminent capacity for such contemplation. Now, as this requires that a man should entirely forget himself and the relations of which he stands, *genius* is simply the completest *objectivity,* i.e. the objective tendency of the mind, as opposed to the subjective, which is directed to one's own self —in other words, to the will. Thus genius is the faculty of continuing in the state of pure perception, of losing oneself in perception, and of enlisting in this service the knowledge which originally existed only for the service of the will; that is to say, genius is the power of leaving one's own interests, wishes, and aims entirely out of sight, thus of entirely renouncing one's own personality for a time, so as to remain *pure knowing subject,* clear vision of the world; and this not merely at moments, but for a sufficient length of time, and with sufficient consciousness, to enable one to reproduce by deliberate art what has thus been apprehended, and "to fix in lasting thoughts the wavering images that float before the mind." It is as if, when genius appears in an individual, a far larger measure of the power of knowledge falls to his lot than is necessary for the service of an individual will; and this superfluity of knowledge, being free, now becomes subject purified from will, a clear mirror of the inner nature of the world. This explains the activity, amounting even to disquietude, of men of genius, for the present can seldom satisfy them, because it does not fill their consciousness. This gives them that restless aspiration, that unceasing desire for new things, and for the contemplation of lofty things, and also that longing that is hardly ever satisfied, for men of similar nature and of like stature, to whom they might communicate themselves; whilst the common mortal, entirely filled and satisfied by the common present, ends in it, and finding everywhere his like, enjoys that peculiar satisfaction in daily life that is denied to genius.

Imagination has rightly been recognised as an essential element of genius; it has sometimes even been regarded as identical with it; but this is a mistake. As the objects of genius are the eternal Ideas, the permanent, essential forms of the world and all its phenomena, and as the knowledge of the Idea is necessarily knowledge through perception, is not abstract, the knowledge of the genius would be limited to the Ideas of the objects actually present to his person, and dependent upon the chain of circumstances that brought these objects to him, if his imagination did not extend his horizon far beyond the limits of his actual personal existence, and thus enable him to construct the whole out of the little that comes into his own actual apperception, and so to let almost all possible scenes of life pass before him in his own consciousness. Further, the actual objects are almost always very imperfect copies of the Ideas expressed in them; therefore the man of genius requires imagination in order to see in things, not that which Nature has actually made, but that which she endeavored to make, yet could not because of that conflict of her forms among themselves which we referred to in the last book. We shall return to this farther on in treating of sculpture. The imagination then extends the intellectual horizon of the man of genius beyond the objects which actually present themselves to him, both as regards quality and quantity. Therefore extraordinary strength of imagination accompanies, and is indeed a necessary condition of genius. But the converse does not hold, for strength of imagination does not indicate genius; on the contrary, men who have no touch of genius may have much imagination. For as it is possible to consider a real object in two opposite ways, purely objectively, the way of genius grasping its Idea, or in the common way, merely in the relations in which it stands to other objects and to one's own will, in accordance with the principle of sufficient reason, it is also possible to perceive an imaginary object in both of these ways. Regarded in the first way, it is a means to the knowledge of the Idea, the communication of which is the work of art; in the second case, the imaginary object is used to build castles in the air congenial to egotism and the individual humour, and which for the moment delude and gratify; thus only the relations of the phantasies so linked together are known. The man who indulges in such an amusement is a dreamer; he will easily mingle those fancies that delight his solitude with reality, and so unfit himself for real life: perhaps he will write them down, and then we shall have the ordinary novel of every description, which entertains those who are like him and the public at large, for the readers imagine themselves in the place of the hero, and then find the story very agreeable.

The common mortal, that manufacture of Nature which she produces by the thousand every day, is, as we have said, not capable, at least not continuously so, of observation that in every sense is wholly disinterested, as sensuous contemplation, strictly so called, is. He can turn his attention to things only so far as they have some relation to his will, however indirect it may be. Since in this respect, which never demands anything but the knowledge of relations, the abstract conception of the thing is sufficient, and for the most part even better adapted for use; the ordinary man does not linger long over the mere perception, does not fix his attention long on one object, but in all that is presented to him hastily seeks merely the concept under which it is to be brought, as the lazy man seeks a chair, and then it interests him no further. This is why he is so soon done with everything, with works of art, objects of natural beauty, and indeed everywhere with the truly significant contemplation of all the scenes of life. He does not linger; only seeks to know his own way in life, together with all that might at any time become his way. Thus he makes topographical notes in the widest sense; over the consideration of life itself as such he wastes no time. The man of genius, on the other hand, whose excessive power of knowledge frees it at times from the service of will, dwells on the consideration of life itself, strives to comprehend the Idea of each thing, not its relations to other things; and in doing this he often forgets to consider his own path in life, and therefore for the most part pursues it awkwardly enough. While to the ordinary man his faculty of knowledge is a lamp to lighten his path, to the man of genius it is the sun which reveals the world. This great diversity in their way of looking at life soon becomes visible in the outward appearance both of the man of genius and of the ordinary mortal. The man in whom genius lives and works is easily distinguished by his glance, which is both keen and steady, and bears the stamp of perception, of contemplation. This is easily seen from the likenesses of the few men of genius whom Nature has produced here and there among countless millions. On the other hand, in the case of an ordinary man, the true object of his contemplation, what he is prying into, can be easily seen from his glance, if indeed it is not quite stupid and vacant, as is generally the case. Therefore the expression of genius in a face consists in this, that in it a decided predominance of knowledge over will is visible, and consequently there also shows itself in it a knowledge that is entirely devoid of relation to will, i.e. *pure knowing*. On the contrary, in ordinary countenances there is a predominant

expression of will; and we see that knowledge only comes into activity under the impulse of will, and thus is directed merely by motives.

Since the knowledge that pertains to genius, or the knowledge of Ideas, is that knowledge which does not follow the principle of sufficient reason, so, on the other hand, the knowledge, which does follow that principle is that which gives us prudence and rationality in life, and which creates the sciences. Thus men of genius are affected with the deficiencies entailed in the neglect of this latter kind of knowledge. Yet what I say in this regard is subject to the limitation that it only concerns them in so far as and while they are actually engaged in that kind of knowledge which is peculiar to genius; and this is by no means at every moment of their lives, for the great though spontaneous exertion which is demanded for the comprehension of Ideas free from will must necessarily relax, and there are long intervals during which men of genius are placed in very much the same position as ordinary mortals, both as regards advantages and deficiencies. On this account the action of genius has always been regarded as an inspiration, as indeed the name indicates, as the action of a superhuman being distinct from the individual himself, and which takes possession of him periodically. The disinclination of men of genius to direct their attention to the content of the principle of sufficient reason will first show itself, with regard to the ground of being, as dislike of mathematics; for its procedure is based upon the most universal forms of the phenomenon space and time, which are themselves merely modes of the principle of sufficient reason, and is consequently precisely the opposite of that method of thought which seeks merely the content of the phenomenon, the Idea which expresses itself in it apart from all relations. The logical method of mathematics is also antagonistic to genius, for it does not sat-isfy but obstructs true insight, and presents merely a chain of conclusions in accordance with the principle of the ground of know-ing. The mental faculty upon which it makes the greatest claim is memory, for it is necessary to recollect all the earlier propositions which are referred to. Experi-ence has also proved that men of great artistic genius have no faculty for mathe-matics; no man was ever very distinguished for both. . . . Further, as quick compre-hension of relations in accordance with the laws of causality and motivation is what specially constitutes prudence or sagacity, a prudent man, so far as and while he is so, will not be a genius, and a man of genius, so far as and while he is so, will not be a prudent man. Lastly, perceptive knowledge generally, in the province of which the Idea always lies, is directly op-posed to rational or abstract knowledge, which is guided by the principle of the ground of knowing. It is also well known that we seldom find great genius united with pre-eminent reasonableness; on the contrary, persons of genius are often sub-ject to violent emotions and irrational pas-sions. But the ground of this is not weak-ness of reason, but partly unwonted en-ergy of that whole phenomenon of will—the man of genius—which expresses itself through the violence of all his acts of will, and partly preponderance of the knowledge of perception through the senses and un-derstanding over abstract knowledge, pro-ducing a decided tendency to the percep-tible, the exceedingly lively impressions of which so far outshine colourless concepts, that they take their place in the guidance of action, which consequently becomes ir-rational. Accordingly the impression of the present moment is very strong with such persons, and carries them away into un-considered action, violent emotions and passions. Moreover, since, in general, the knowledge of persons of genius has to some extent freed itself from the service of will,

they will not in conversation think so much of the person they are addressing as of the thing they are speaking about, which is vividly present to them; and there-fore they are likely to judge or narrate things too objectively for their own inter-ests; they will not pass over in silence what would more prudently be concealed, and so forth. Finally, they are given to soliloquising, and in general may exhibit certain weaknesses which are actually akin to madness. It has often been remarked that there is a side at which genius and madness touch, and even pass over into each other, and indeed poetical inspiration has been called a kind of madness: *ama-bilis insania,* Horace calls it . . . It might seem from this that every advance of in-tellect beyond the ordinary measure, as an abnormal development, disposes to mad-ness. In the meantime, however, I will explain as briefly as possible my view of the purely intellectual ground of the rela-tion between genius and madness, for this will certainly assist the explanation of the real nature of genius, that is to say, of that mental endowment which alone can produce genuine works of art. But this necessitates a brief explanation of madness itself.

A clear and complete insight into the nature of madness, a correct distinct con-ception of what constitutes the difference between the sane and the insane, has, as far as I know, not as yet been found. Neither reason nor understanding can be denied to madmen, for they talk and un-derstand, and often draw very accurate conclusions; they also, as a rule, perceive what is present quite correctly, and appre-hend the connection between cause and effect. Visions, like the phantasies of de-lirium, are no ordinary symptom of mad-ness: delirium falsifies perception, madness the thoughts. For the most part, madmen do not err in the knowledge of what is immediately *present;* their raving always relates to what is *absent* and *past,* and only through these to their connection with what is present. Therefore it seems to me that their malady specially concerns the memory; not indeed that memory fails them entirely, for many of them know a great deal by heart, and sometimes recognise persons whom they have not seen for a long time; but rather that the thread of memory is broken, the continuity of its connection destroyed, and no uniformly connected recollection of the past is possible. Particular scenes of the past are known correctly, just like the particular present; but there are gaps in their recollection which they fill up with fictions, and these are either always the same, in which case they become fixed ideas, and the madness that results is called monomania or melancholy; or they are always different, momentary fancies, and then it is called folly, *fatuitas.* This is why it is so difficult to find out their former life from lunatics when they enter an asylum. The true and the false are always mixed up in their memory. Although the immediate present is correctly known, it becomes falsified through its fictitious connection with an imaginary past; they therefore regard themselves and others as identical with persons who exist only in their imaginary past; . . . If the madness reaches a high degree, there is complete absence of memory, so that the madman is quite incapable of any reference to what is absent or past, and is only determined by the caprice of the moment in connection with the fictions which, in his mind, fill the past. . . . The knowledge of the madman has this in common with that of the brute, both are confined to the present. What distinguishes them is that the brute has really no idea of the past as such, though the past acts upon it through the medium of custom, so that, for example, the dog recognises its former master even after years, that is to say, it receives the wonted impression at the sight of him; but of the time that has passed since it saw him it has no recollection. The

madman, on the other hand, always carries about in his reason an abstract past, but it is a false past, which exists only for him, and that either constantly, or only for the moment. The influence of this false past prevents the use of the true knowledge of the present which the brute is able to make.

We see, from what has been said, that the madman has a true knowledge of what is actually present, and also of certain particulars of the past, but that he mistakes the connection, the relations, and therefore falls into error and talks nonsense. Now this is exactly the point at which he comes into contact with the man of genius; for he also leaves out of sight the knowledge of the connection of things, since he neglects that knowledge of relations which conforms to the principle of sufficient reason, in order to see in things only their Ideas, and to seek to comprehend their true nature, which manifests itself to perception, and in regard to which *one thing* represents its whole species, in which way, as Goethe says, one case is valid for a thousand. The particular object of his contemplation, or the present which is perceived by him with extraordinary vividness, appear in so strong a light that the other links of the chain to which they belong are at once thrown into the shade, and this gives rise to phenomena which have long been recognised as resembling those of madness. That which in particular given things exists only incompletely and weakened by modifications, is raised by the man of genius, through his way of contemplating it, to the Idea of the thing, to completeness: he therefore sees everywhere extremes, and therefore his own action tends to extremes; he cannot hit the mean, he lacks soberness, and the result is what we have said. He knows the Ideas completely but not the individuals. Therefore it has been said that a poet may know mankind deeply and thoroughly, and may yet have a very imperfect knowledge of men. He is easily deceived, and is a tool in the hands of the crafty.

37. Genius, then, consists, according to our explanation, in the capacity for knowing, independently of the principle of sufficient reason, not individual things, which have their existence only in their relations, but the Ideas of such things, and of being oneself the correlative of the Idea, and thus no longer an individual, but the pure subject of knowledge. Yet this faculty must exist in all men in a smaller and different degree; for if not, they would be just as incapable of enjoying works of art as of producing them; they would have no susceptibility for the beautiful or the sublime; indeed, these words could have no meaning for them. We must therefore assume that there exists in all men this power of knowing the Ideas in things, and consequently of transcending their personality for the moment, unless indeed there are some men who are capable of no aesthetic pleasure at all. The man of genius excels ordinary men only by possessing this kind of knowledge in a far higher degree and more continuously. Thus, while under its influence he retains the presence of mind which is necessary to enable him to repeat in a voluntary and intentional work what he has learned in this manner; and this repetition is the work of art. Through this he communicates to others the Idea he has grasped. This Idea remains unchanged and the same, so that aesthetic pleasure is one and the same whether it is called forth by a work of art or directly by the contemplation of nature and life. The work of art is only a means of facilitating the knowledge in which this pleasure consists. That the Idea comes to us more easily from the work of art than directly from nature and the real world, arises from the fact that the artist, who knew only the Idea, no longer the actual, has reproduced in his work the pure Idea, has abstracted it from the actual, omitting all disturbing accidents. The artist lets us see

the world through his eyes. That he has these eyes, that he knows the inner nature of things apart from all their relations, is the gift of genius, is inborn; but that he is able to lend us this gift, to let us see with his eyes, is acquired, and is the technical side of art. Therefore, after the account which I have given in the preceding pages of the inner nature of aesthetical knowledge in its most general outlines, the following more exact philosophical treatment of the beautiful and the sublime will explain them both, in nature and in art, without separating them further. First of all we shall consider what takes place in a man when he is affected by the beautiful and the sublime; whether he derives this emotion directly from nature, from life, or partakes of it only through the medium of art, does not make any essential, but merely an external, difference.

38. In the aesthetical mode of contemplation we have found *two inseparable constituent parts*—the knowledge of the object, not as individual thing but as Platonic Idea, that is, as the enduring form of this whole species of things; and the self-consciousness of the knowing person, not as individual, but as *pure will-less subject of knowledge*. The condition under which both these constituent parts appear always united was found to be the abandonment of the method of knowing which is bound to the principle of sufficient reason, and which, on the other hand, is the only kind of knowledge that is of value for the service of the will and also for science. Moreover we shall see that the pleasure which is produced by the contemplation of the beautiful arises from these two constituent parts, sometimes more from the one, sometimes more from the other, according to what the object of the aesthetical contemplation may be.

All *willing* arises from want, therefore from deficiency, and therefore from suffering. The satisfaction of a wish ends it; yet for one wish that is satisfied there remain at least ten which are denied. Further, the desire lasts long, the demands are infinite; the satisfaction is short and scantily measured out. But even the final satisfaction is itself only apparent; every satisfied wish at once makes room for a new one; both are illusions; the one is known to be so, the other not yet. No attained object of desire can give lasting satisfaction, but merely a fleeting gratification; it is like the alms thrown to the beggar, that keeps him alive to-day that his misery may be prolonged till the morrow. Therefore, so long as our consciousness is filled by our will, so long as we are given up to the throng of desires with their constant hopes and fears, so long as we are the subject of willing, we can never have lasting happiness nor peace. It is essentially all the same whether we pursue or flee, fear injury or seek enjoyment; the care for the constant demands of the will, in whatever form it may be, continually occupies and sways the consciousness; but without peace no true well-being is possible. The subject of willing is thus constantly stretched on the revolving wheel of Ixion, pours water into the sieve of the Danaids, is the ever-longing Tantalus.

But when some external cause or inward disposition lifts us suddenly out of the endless stream of willing, delivers knowledge from the slavery of the will, the attention is no longer directed to the motives of willing, but comprehends things free from their relation to the will, and thus observes them without personal interest, without subjectivity, purely objectively, gives itself entirely up to them so far as they are ideas, but not in so far as they are motives. Then all at once the peace which we were always seeking, but which always fled from us on the former path of the desires, comes to us of its own accord, and it is well with us. It is the painless state which Epicurus prized as the highest good and as the state of the gods; for we are for the moment set free from the miser-able striving of the will; we keep the Sabbath of the penal servitude of willing; the wheel of Ixion stands still.

But this is just the state which I described above as necessary for the knowledge of the Idea, as pure contemplation, as sinking oneself in perception, losing oneself in the object, forgetting all individuality, surrendering that kind of knowledge which follows the principle of sufficient reason, and comprehends only relations; the state by means of which at once and inseparably the perceived particular thing is raised to the Idea of its whole species, and the knowing individual to the pure subject of will-less knowledge, and as such they are both taken out of the stream of time and all other relations. It is then all one whether we see the sun set from the prison or from the palace.

Inward disposition, the predominance of knowing over willing, can produce this state under any circumstances. This is shown by those admirable Dutch artists who directed this purely objective perception to the most insignificant objects, and established a lasting monument of their objectivity and spiritual peace in their pictures of *still life*, which the aesthetic beholder does not look on without emotion; for they present to him the peaceful, still, frame of mind of the artist, free from will, which was needed to contemplate such insignificant things so objectively, to observe them so attentively, and to repeat this perception so intelligently; and as the picture enables the onlooker to participate in this state, his emotion is often increased by the contrast between it and the unquiet frame of mind, disturbed by vehement willing, in which he finds himself. In the same spirit, landscape-painters, and particularly Ruisdael, have often painted very insignificant country scenes, which produce the same effect even more agreeably.

All this is accomplished by the inner power of an artistic nature alone; but that purely objective disposition is facilitated and assisted from without by suitable objects, by the abundance of natural beauty which invites contemplation, and even presses itself upon us. Whenever it discloses itself suddenly to our view, it almost always succeeds in delivering us, though it may be only for a moment, from subjectivity, from the slavery of the will, and in raising us to the state of pure knowing. This is why the man who is tormented by passion, or want, or care, is so suddenly revived, cheered, and restored by a single free glance into nature: the storm of passion, the pressure of desire and fear, and all the miseries of willing are then at once, and in a marvellous manner, calmed and appeased. For at the moment at which, freed from the will, we give ourselves up to pure will-less knowing, we pass into a world from which everything is absent that influenced our will and moved us so violently through it. This freeing of knowledge lifts us as wholly and entirely away from all that, as do sleep and dreams; happiness and unhappiness have disappeared; we are no longer individual; the individual is forgotten; we are only pure subject of knowledge; we are only that *one* eye of the world which looks out from all knowing creatures, but which can become perfectly free from the service of will in man alone. Thus all difference of individuality so entirely disappears, that it is all the same whether the perceiving eye belongs to a mighty king or to a wretched beggar; for neither joy nor complaining can pass that boundary with us. So near us always lies a sphere in which we escape from all our misery; but who has the strength to continue long in it? As soon as any single relation to our will, to our person, even of these objects of our pure contemplation, comes again into consciousness, the magic is at an end; we fall back into the knowledge which is governed by the principle of sufficient reason; we know no longer the Idea, but the particular thing, the link of a chain to which we also belong, and

we are again abandoned to all our woe. Most men remain almost always at this standpoint because they entirely lack objectivity, i.e. genius. Therefore they have no pleasure in being alone with nature; they need company, or at least a book. For their knowledge remains subject to their will; they seek, therefore, in objects, only some relation to their will, and whenever they see anything that has no such relation, there sounds within them, like a ground bass in music, the constant inconsolable cry, "It is of no use to me"; thus in solitude the most beautiful surroundings have for them a desolate, dark, strange, and hostile appearance.

Lastly, it is this blessedness of will-less perception which casts an enchanting glamour over the past and distant, and presents them to us in so fair a light by means of self-deception. For as we think of days long gone by, days in which we lived in a distant place, it is only the objects which our fancy recalls, not the subject of will, which bore about with it then its incurable sorrows just as it bears them now; but they are forgotten, because since then they have often given place to others. Now, objective perception acts with regard to what is remembered just as it would in what is present, if we let it have influence over us, if we surrendered ourselves to it free from will. Hence it arises that, especially when we are more than ordinarily disturbed by some want, the remembrance of past and distant scenes suddenly flits across our minds like a lost paradise. The fancy recalls only what was objective, not what was individually subjective, and we imagine that that objective stood before us then just as pure and undisturbed by any relation to the will as its image stands in our fancy now; while in reality the relation of the objects to our will gave us pain then just as it does now. We can deliver ourselves from all suffering just as well through present objects as through distant ones whenever we raise ourselves to a purely objective contemplation of them, and so are able to bring about the illusion that only the objects are present and not we ourselves. Then, as the pure subject of knowledge, freed from the miserable self, we become entirely one with these objects, and, for the moment, our wants are as foreign to us as they are to them. The world as idea alone remains, and the world as will has disappeared.

In all these reflections it has been my object to bring out clearly the nature and the scope of the subjective element in aesthetic pleasure; the deliverance of knowledge from the service of the will, the forgetting of self as an individual, and the raising of the consciousness to the pure will-less, timeless, subject of knowledge, independent of all relations. With this subjective side of aesthetic contemplation, there must always appear as its necessary correlative the objective side, the intuitive comprehension of the Platonic Idea. But before we turn to the closer consideration of this, and to the achievements of art in relation to it, it is better that we should pause for a little at the subjective side of aesthetic pleasure, in order to complete our treatment of this by explaining the impression of the *sublime* which depends altogether upon it, and arises from a modification of it. After that we shall complete our investigation of aesthetic pleasure by considering its objective side. . . .

39. . . . We have already remarked above that the transition to the state of pure perception takes place most easily when the objects bend themselves to it, that is, when by their manifold and yet definite and distinct form they easily become representatives of their Ideas, in which beauty, in the objective sense, consists. This quality belongs pre-eminently to natural beauty, which thus affords even to the most insensible at least a fleeting aesthetic satisfaction: . . . As long as that which raises us from the knowledge of mere relations subject to the will, to aes-

thetic contemplation, and thereby exalts us to the position of the subject of knowledge free from will, is this fittingness of nature, this significant and distinctness of its forms, on account of which the Ideas individualised in them readily present themselves to us; so long is it merely *beauty* that affects us and the sense of the *beautiful* that is excited. But if these very objects whose significant forms invite us to pure contemplation, have a hostile relation to the human will in general, as it exhibits itself in its objectivity, the human body, if they are opposed to it, so that it is menaced by the irresistible predominance of their power, or sinks into insignificance before their immeasurable greatness; if, nevertheless, the beholder does not direct his attention to this eminently hostile relation to his will, but, although perceiving and recognising it, turns consciously away from it, forcibly detaches himself from his will and its relations, and, giving himself up entirely to knowledge, quietly contemplates those very objects that are so terrible to the will, comprehends only their Idea, which is foreign to all relations, so that he lingers gladly over its contemplation, and is thereby raised above himself, his person, his will, and all will:—in that case he is filled with the sense of the *sublime,* he is in the state of spiritual exaltation, and therefore the object producing such a state is called *sublime.* Thus what distinguishes the sense of the sublime from that of the beautiful is this: in the case of the beautiful, pure knowledge has gained the upper hand without a struggle, for the beauty of the object, i.e. that property which facilitates the knowledge of its Idea, has removed from consciousness without resistance, and therefore imperceptibly, the will and the knowledge of relations which is subject to it, so that what is left is the pure subject of knowledge without even a remembrance of will. On the other hand, in the case of the sublime that state of pure knowledge is only attained by a conscious and forcible breaking away from the relations of the same object to the will, which are recognised as unfavourable, by a free and conscious transcending of the will and the knowledge related to it.

This exaltation must not only be consciously won, but also consciously retained, and it is therefore accompanied by a contant remembrance of will; yet not of a single particular volition, such as fear or desire, but of human volition in general, so far as it is universally expressed in its objectivity the human body. If a single real act of will were to come into consciousness, through actual personal pressure and danger from the object, then the individual will thus actually influenced would at once gain the upper hand, the peace of contemplation would become impossible, the impression of the sublime would be lost, because it yields to the anxiety, in which the effort of the individual to right itself has sunk every other thought. A few examples will help very much to elucidate this theory of the aesthetic sublime and remove all doubt with regard to it; at the same time they will bring out the different degrees of this sense of the sublime. It is in the main identical with that of the beautiful, with pure will-less knowing, and the knowledge, that necessarily accompanies it of Ideas out of all relation determined by the principle of sufficient reason, and it is distinguished from the sense of the beautiful only by the additional quality that it rises above the known hostile relation of the object contemplated to the will in general. Thus there come to be various degrees of the sublime, and transitions from the beautiful to the sublime, according as this additional quality is strong, bold, urgent, near, or weak, distant, and merely indicated. . . . As man is at once impetuous and blind striving of will (whose pole or focus lies in the genital organs), and eternal, free, serene subject of pure knowing (whose pole is the brain); so, corresponding to this antithesis, the sun is both the source of *light,* the condition of the most perfect kind of knowledge, and therefore of the most delightful of things— and the source of *warmth,* the first condition of life, i.e. of all phenomena of will in its higher grades. Therefore, what warmth is for the will, light is for knowledge. Light is the largest gem in the crown of beauty, and has the most marked influence on the knowledge of every beautiful object. Its presence is an indispensable condition of beauty; its favourable disposition increases the beauty of the most beautiful. Architectural beauty more than any other object is enhanced by favourable light, though even the most significant things become through its influence most beautiful. If, in the dead of winter, when all nature is frozen and stiff, we see the rays of the setting sun reflected by masses of stone, illuminating without warming, and thus favourable only to the purest kind of knowledge, not to the will; the contemplation of the beautiful effect of the light upon these masses lifts us, as does all beauty, into a state of pure knowing. But, in this case, a certain transcending of the interests of the will is needed to enable us to rise into the state of pure knowing, because there is a faint recollection of the lack of warmth from these rays, that is, an absence of the principle of life; there is a slight challenge to persist in pure knowing, and to refrain from all willing, and therefore it is an example of a transition from the sense of the beautiful to that of the sublime. It is the faintest trace of the sublime in the beautiful; and beauty itself is indeed present only in a slight degree. . . .

The following situation may occasion this feeling in a still higher degree: Nature convulsed by a storm; the sky darkened by black threatening thunder-clouds; stupendous, naked, overhanging cliffs, completely shutting out the view; rushing, foaming torrents; absolute desert; the wail of the wind sweeping through the clefts of the rocks. Our dependence, our strife with hostile nature, our will broken in the conflict, now appears visibly before our eyes. Yet, so long as the personal pressure does not gain the upper hand, but we continue in aesthetic contemplation, the pure subject of knowing gazes unshaken and unconcerned through that strife of nature, through that picture of the broken will, and quietly comprehends the Ideas even of those objects which are threatening and terrible to the will. In this contrast lies the sense of the sublime.

But the impression becomes still stronger, if, when we have before our eyes, on a large scale, the battle of the raging elements, in such a scene we are prevented from hearing the sound of our own voice by the noise of a falling stream; or, if we are abroad in the storm of tempestuous seas, where the mountainous waves rise and fall, dash themselves furiously against steep cliffs, and toss their spray high into the air; the storm howls, the sea boils, the lightning flashes from black clouds, and the peals of thunder drown the voice of storm and sea. Then, in the undismayed beholder, the two-fold nature of his consciousness reaches the highest degree of distinctness. He perceives himself, on the one hand, as an individual, as the frail phenomenon of will, which the slightest touch of these forces can utterly destroy, helpless against powerful nature, dependent, the victim of chance, a vanishing nothing in the presence of stupendous might; and, on the other hand, as the eternal, peaceful, knowing subject, the condition of the object, and, therefore, the supporter of this whole world; the terrific strife of nature only his idea; the subject itself free and apart from all desires and necessities, in the quiet comprehension of the Ideas. This is the complete impression of the sublime. Here he obtains a glimpse of a power beyond all comparison superior to the individual, threatening it with annihilation.

The impression of the sublime may be produced in quite another way, be presenting a mere immensity in space and time; immeasurable greatness dwindles the individual to nothing. Adhering to Kant's nomenclature and his accurate division, we may call the first kind the dynamical, and the second the mathematical sublime, although we entirely dissent from his explantation of the inner nature of the impression, and can allow no share in it either to moral reflections, or to hypostases from scholastic philosophy.

If we lose ourselves in the contemplation of the infinite greatness of the universe in space and time, meditate on the thousands of years that are past or to come, or if the heavens at night actually bring before our eyes innumerable worlds and so force upon our consciousness the immensity of the universe, we feel ourselves dwindle to nothing; as individuals, as living bodies, as transient phenomena of will, we feel ourselves pass away and vanish into nothing like drops in the ocean. But at once there rises against the ghost of our own nothingness, against such lying impossibility, the immediate consciousness that all these worlds exist only as our idea, only as modifications of the eternal subject of pure knowing, which we find ourselves to be as soon as we forget our individuality, and which is the necessary supporter of all worlds and all times the condition of their possibility. The vastness of the world which disquieted us before, rests now in us; our dependence upon it is annulled by its dependence upon us. All this, however, does not come at once into reflection, but shows itself merely as the felt consciousness that in some sense or other (which philosophy alone can explain) we are one with the world, and therefore not oppressed, but exalted by its immensity. . . .

40. Opposites throw light upon each other, and therefore the remark may be in place here, that the proper opposite of the

sublime is something which would not at the first glance be recognised, as such: *the charming* or *attractive*. By this, however, I understand, that which excites the will by presenting to it directly its fulfillment, its satisfaction. We saw that the feeling of the sublime arises from the fact, that something entirely unfavourable to the will, becomes the object of pure contemplation, so that such contemplation can only be maintained by persistently turning away from the will, and transcending its interests; this constitutes the sublimity of the character. The charming or attractive, on the contrary, draws the beholder away from the pure contemplation which is demanded by all apprehension of the beautiful, because it necessarily excites this will, by objects which directly appeal to it, and thus he no longer remains pure subject of knowing, but becomes the needy and dependent subject of will. . . . In historical painting and in sculpture the charming consists in naked figures, whose position, drapery, and general treatment are calculated to excite the passions of the beholder, and thus pure aesthetical contemplation is at once annihilated, and the aim of art is defeated. . . .

The ancients are almost always free from this fault in their representations of beauty and complete nakedness of form, because the artist himself created them in a purely objective spirit, filled with ideal beauty, not in the spirit of subjective, and base sensuality. The charming is thus everywhere to be avoided in art.

There is also a negative species of the charming or exciting which is even more reprehensible than the positive form which has been discussed; this is the disgusting or the loathsome. It arouses the will of the beholder, just as what is properly speaking charming, and therefore disturbs pure aesthetic contemplation. But it is an active aversion and opposition which is excited by it; it arouses the will by presenting to it objects which it abhors. Therefore it

has always been recognised that it is altogether inadmissible in art, where even what is ugly, when it is not disgusting, is allowable in its proper place, as we shall see later.

41. . . . When we say that a thing is *beautiful*, we thereby assert that it is an object of our aesthetic contemplation, and this has a double meaning; on the one hand it means that the sight of the thing makes us *objective*, that is to say, that in contemplating it we are no longer conscious of ourselves as individuals, but as pure will-less subjects of knowledge; and on the other hand it means that we recognise in the object, not the particular thing, but an Idea; and this can only happen, so far as our contemplation of it is not subordinated to the principle of sufficient reason, does not follow the relation of the object to anything outside it (which is always ultimately connected with relations to our own will), but rests in the object itself. For the Idea and the pure subject of knowledge always appear at once in consciousness as necessary correlatives, and on their appearance all distinction of time vanishes, for they are both entirely foreign to the principle of sufficient reason in all its forms, and lie outside the relations which are imposed by it; they may be compared to the rainbow and the sun, which have no part in the constant movement and succession of the falling drops. Therefore, if, for example, I contemplate a tree aesthetically, i.e. with artistic eyes, and thus recognise, not it, but its Idea, it becomes at once of no consequence whether it is this tree or its predecessor which flourished a thousand years ago, and whether the observer is this individual or any other that lived anywhere and at any time; the particular thing and the knowing individual are abolished with the principle of sufficient reason, and there remains nothing but the Idea and the pure subject of knowing, which together constitute the adequate objectivity of will at this grade. And the

Idea dispenses not only with time, but also with space, for the Idea proper is not this special form which appears before me but its expression, its pure significance, its inner being, which discloses itself to me and appeals to me, and which may be quite the same though the spatial relations of its form be very different.

Since, on the one hand, every given thing may be observed in a purely objective manner and apart from all relations; and since, on the other hand, the will manifests itself in everything at some grade of its objectivity, so that everything is the expression of an Idea; it follows that everything is also *beautiful*. That even the most insignificant things admit of pure objective and will-less contemplation, and thus prove that they are beautiful, is shown by what was said above in this reference about the Dutch pictures of still-life (section 38). But one thing is more beautiful than another, because it makes this pure objective contemplation easier, it lends itself to it, and, so to speak, even compels it, and then we call it very beautiful. This is the case sometimes because, as an individual thing, it expresses in its purity the Idea of its species by the very distinct, clearly defined and significant relation of its parts, and also fully reveals that Idea through the completeness of all the possible expressions of its species united in it, so that it makes the transition from the individual thing to the Idea, and therefore also the condition of pure contemplation, very easy for the beholder. Sometimes this possession of special beauty in an object lies in the fact that the Idea itself which appeals to us in it is a high grade of the objectivity of will, and therefore very significant and expressive. Therefore it is that man is more beautiful than all other objects, and the revelation of his nature is the highest aim of art. Human form and expression are the most important objects of plastic art, and human action the most important object of poetry.

Yet each thing has its own peculiar beauty, not only every organism which expresses itself in the unity of an individual being, but also everything unorganised and formless, and even every manufactured article. For all these reveal the Ideas through which the will objectifies itself at its lowest grades, they give, as it were, the deepest resounding bass-notes of nature. Gravity, rigidity, fluidity, light, and so forth, are the Ideas which express themselves in rocks, in buildings, in waters. Landscape-gardening or architecture can do no more than assist them to unfold their qualities distinctly, fully, and variously; they can only give them the opportunity of expressing themselves purely, so that they lend themselves to aesthetic contemplation and make it easier. Inferior buildings or ill-favoured localities, on the contrary, which nature has neglected or art has spoiled, perform this task in a very slight degree or not at all; yet even from them these universal, fundamental Ideas of nature cannot altogether disappear. To the careful observer they present themselves here also, and even bad buildings and the like are capable of being aesthetically considered; the Ideas of the most universal properties of their materials are still recognisable in them, only the artificial form which has been given them does not assist but hinders aesthetic contemplation. Manufactured articles also serve to express Ideas, only it is not the Idea of the manufactured article which speaks in them, but the Idea of the material to which this artificial form has been given. This may be very conveniently expressed in two words, in the language of the schoolmen, thus, the manufactured article expresses the Idea of its *forma substantialis*, but not that of its *forma accidentalis*; the latter leads to no Idea, but only to a human conception of which it is the result. It is needless to say that by manufactured article no work of plastic art is meant. The schoolmen understand, in fact, by *forma substantialis* that which I call the grade of the objectification of will in a thing. We shall return immediately, when we treat of architecture, to the Idea of the material. Our view, then, cannot be reconciled with that of Plato if he is of opinion that a table or a chair express the Idea of a table or a chair, but we say that they express the Ideas which are already expressed in their mere material as such. . . . We may take this opportunity of mentioning another point in which our doctrine of Ideas differs very much from that of Plato. He teaches that the object which art tries to express, the ideal of painting and poetry, is not the Idea but the particular thing. Our whole exposition hitherto has maintained exactly the opposite, and Plato's opinion is the less likely to lead us astray, inasmuch as it is the source of one of the greatest and best known errors of this great man, his depreciation and rejection of art, and especially poetry; he directly connects his false judgment in reference to this with the passage quoted. . . .

43. Matter as such cannot be the expression of an Idea. For, as we found in the first book, it is throughout nothing but causality: its being consists in its causal action. But causality is a form of the principle of sufficient reason; knowledge of the Idea, on the other hand, absolutely excludes the content of that principle. We also found, in the second book, that matter is the common substratum of all particular phenomena of the Ideas, and consequently is the connecting link between the Idea and the phenomenon, or the particular thing. Accordingly for both of these reasons it is impossible that matter can for itself express any Idea. This is confirmed *a posteriori* by the fact that it is impossible to have a perceptible idea of matter as such, but only an abstract conception; in the former, i.e. in perceptible ideas are exhibited only the forms and qualities of which matter is the supporter, and in all of which Ideas reveal themselves. This

corresponds also with the fact, that causality (the whole essence of matter) cannot for itself be presented perceptibly, but is merely a definite causal connection. On the other hand, *every phenomenon* of an Idea, because as such it has entered the form of the principle of sufficient reason, or the *principium individuationis,* must exhibit itself in matter, as one of its qualities. So far then matter is, as we have said, the connecting link between the Idea and the *principium individuationis,* which is the form of knowledge of the individual, or the principle of sufficient reason. Plato is therefore perfectly right in his enumeration, for after the Idea and the phenomenon, which include all other things in the world, he gives matter only, as a third thing which is different from both. The individual, as a phenomenon of the Idea, is always matter. Every quality of matter is also the phenomenon of an Idea, and as such it may always be an object of aesthetic contemplation, i.e. the Idea expressed in it may always be recognised. This holds good of even the most universal qualities of matter, without which it never appears, and which are the weakest objectivity of will. Such are gravity, cohesion, rigidity, fluidity, sensitiveness to light, and so forth.

If now we consider *architecture* simply as a fine art and apart from its application to useful ends, in which it serves the will and not pure knowledge, and therefore ceases to be art in our sense; we can assign to it no other aim than that of bringing to greater distinctness some of those ideas, which are the lowest grades of the objectivity of will; such as gravity, cohesion, rigidity, hardness, those universal qualities of stone, those first, simplest, most inarticulate manifestations of will; the bass notes of nature; and after these light, which in many respects is their opposite. Even at these low grades of the objectivity of will we see its nature revealing itself in discord; for properly speaking the conflict between gravity and rigidity is the sole aesthetic material of architecture; its problem is to make this conflict appear with perfect distinctness in a multitude of different ways. It solves it by depriving these indestructible forces of the shortest way to their satisfaction, and conducting them to it by a circuitous route, so that the conflict is lengthened and the inexhaustible efforts of both forces become visible in many different ways. The whole mass of the building, if left to its original tendency, would exhibit a mere heap or clump, bound as closely as possible to the earth, to which gravity, the form in which the will appears here, continually presses, while rigidity, also objectivity of will, resists. But this very tendency, this effort, is hindered by architecture from obtaining direct satisfaction, and only allowed to reach it indirectly and by roundabout ways. The roof, for example, can only press the earth through columns, the arch must support itself, and can only satisfy its tendency towards the earth through the medium of the pillars, and so forth. But just by these enforced digressions, just by these restrictions, the forces which reside in the crude mass of stone unfold themselves in the most distinct and multifarious ways; and the purely aesthetic aim of architecture can go on further than this. Therefore the beauty, at any rate, of a building lies in the obvious adaptation of every part, not to the outward arbitrary end of man (so far the work belongs to practical architecture), but directly to the stability of the whole, to which the position, dimensions, and form of every part must have so necessary a relation that, where it is possible, if any one part were taken away, the whole would fall to pieces. For just because each part bears just as much as it conveniently can, and each is supported just where it requires to be and just to the necessary extent, this opposition unfolds itself, this conflict between rigidity and gravity, which constitutes the life, the

manifestation of will, in the stone, becomes completely visible, and these lowest grades of the objectivity of will reveal themselves distinctly. In the same way the form of each part must not be determined arbitrarily, but by its end, and its relation to the whole. . . . According to what has been said, it is absolutely necessary, in order to understand the aesthetic satisfaction afforded by a work of architecture, to have immediate knowledge through perception of its matter as regards its weight, rigidity, and cohesion, and our pleasure in such a work would suddenly be very much diminished by the discovery that the material used was pumice-stone; for then it would appear to us as a kind of sham building. We would be affected in almost the same way if we were told that it was made of wood, when we had supposed it to be of stone, just because this alters and destroys the relation between rigidity and gravity, and consequently the significance and necessity of all the parts, for these natural forces reveal themselves in a far weaker degree in a wooden building. Therefore no real work of architecture as a fine art can be made of wood, although it assumes all forms so easily; this can only be explained by our theory. If we were distinctly told that a building, the sight of which gave us pleasure, was made of different kinds of material of very unequal weight and consistency, but not distinguishable to the eye, the whole building would become as utterly incapable of affording us pleasure as a poem in an unknown language. All this proves that architecture does not affect us mathematically, but also dynamically, and that what speaks to us through it, is not mere form and symmetry, but rather those fundamental forces of nature, those first Ideas, those lowest grades of the objectivity of will. The regularity of the building and its parts is partly produced by the direct adaptation of each member to the stability of the whole, partly it serves to facilitate the survey and comprehension of the whole, and finally, regular figures to some extent enhance the beauty because they reveal the constitution of space as such. But all this is of subordinate value and necessity, and by no means the chief concern; indeed, symmetry is not invariably demanded, as ruins are still beautiful.

Works of architecture have further quite a special relation to light; they gain a double beauty in the full sunshine, with the blue background, and again they have quite a different effect by moonlight. Therefore, when a beautiful work of architecture is to be erected, special attention is always paid to the effects of the light and to the climate. The reason of all this is, indeed, principally that all the parts and their relations are only made clearly visible by a bright, strong light; but besides this I am of opinion that it is the function of architecture to reveal the nature of light just as it reveals that of things so opposite to it as gravity and rigidity. For the light is intercepted, confined, and reflected by the great opaque, sharply outlined, and variously formed masses of stone, and thus it unfolds its nature and qualities in the purest and clearest way, to the great pleasure of the beholders, for light is the most joy-giving of things, as the condition and the objective correlative of the most perfect kind of knowledge of perception.

Now, because the Ideas which architecture brings to clear perception, are the lowest grades of the objectivity of will, and consequently their objective significance, which architecture reveals to us, is comparatively small; the aesthetic pleasure of looking at a beautiful building in a good light will lie, not so much in the comprehension of the Idea, as in the subjective correlative which accompanies this comprehension; it will consist pre-eminently in the fact that the beholder, set free from the kind of knowledge that belongs to the individual, and which serves the will and follows the principle of suffi-

cient reason, is raised to that of the pure subject of knowing free from will. It will consist then principally in pure contemplation itself, free from all the suffering of will and of individuality. In this respect the opposite of architecture, and the other extreme of the series of the fine arts, is the drama, which brings to knowledge the most significant Ideas. Therefore in the aesthetic pleasure afforded by the drama the objective side is throughout predominant.

Architecture has this distinction from plastic art and poetry: it does not give us a copy but the thing itself. It does not repeat, as they do, the known Idea, so that the artist lends his eyes to the beholder, but in it the artist merely presents the object of the beholder, and facilitates for him the comprehension of the Idea by bringing the actual, individual object to a distinct and complete expression of its nature. . . .

44. . . . The vegetable world offers itself everywhere for aesthetic enjoyment without the medium of art; but so far as it is an object of art, it belongs principally to landscape-painting; to the province of which all the rest of unconscious nature also belongs. In paintings of still life, and of mere architecture, ruins, interiors of churches, &c., the subjective side of aesthetic pleasure is predominant, i.e. our satisfaction does not lie principally in the direct comprehension of the represented Ideas, but rather in the subjective correlative of this comprehension, pure, will-less knowing. For, because the painter lets us see these things through his eyes, we at once receive a sympathetic and reflected sense of the deep spiritual peace and absolute silence of the will, which were necessary in order to enter with knowledge so entirely into these lifeless objects, and comprehend them with such love, i.e. in this case with such a degree of objectivity. The effect of landscape-painting proper is indeed, as a whole, of this kind; but because the Ideas expressed are more distinct and signifi-

cant, as higher grades of the objectivity of will, the objective side of aesthetic pleasure already comes more to the front and assumes as much importance as the subjective side. Pure knowing as such is no longer the paramount consideration, for we are equally affected by the known Platonic Idea, the world as idea at an important grade of the objectification of will.

But a far higher grade is revealed by animal painting and sculpture. . . . In these representations the objective side of aesthetic pleasure obtains a marked predominance over the subjective. The peace of the subject which knows these Ideas, which has silenced its own will, is indeed present, as it is in all aesthetic contemplation; but its effect is not felt, for we are occupied with the restlessness and impetuosity of the will represented. It is that very will, which constitutes our own nature, that here appears to us in forms, in which its manifestation is not, as in us, controlled and tempered by intellect, but exhibits itself in stronger traits, and with a distinctness that borders on the grotesque and monstrous. For this very reason there is no concealment; it is free, naïve, open as the day, and this is the cause of our interest in animals. . . .

45. The great problem of historical painting and sculpture is to express directly and for perception the Idea in which the will reaches the highest grade of its objectification. The objective side of the pleasure afforded by the beautiful is here always predominant, and the subjective side has retired into the background. It is further to be observed that the next grade below this, animal painting, the characteristic is entirely one with the beautiful; the most characteristic lion, wolf, horse, sheep, or ox, was always the most beautiful also. The reason of this is that animals have only the character of their species, no individual character. In the representation of men the character of the species is separated from that of the individual; the former is now

called beauty (entirely in the objective sense), but the latter retains the name, character, or expression, and the new difficulty arises of representing both, at once and completely, in the same individual.

Human beauty is an objective expression, which means the fullest objectification of will at the highest grade at which it is knowable, the Idea of man in general, completely expressed in the sensible form. But however much the objective side of the beautiful appears here, the subjective side still always accompanies it. And just because no object transports us so quickly into pure aesthetic contemplation, as the most beautiful human countenance and form, at the sight of which we are instantly filled with unspeakable satisfaction, and raised above ourselves and all that troubles us; this is only possible because this most distinct and purest knowledge of will raises us most easily and quickly to the state of pure knowing, in which our personality, our will with its constant pain, disappears, so long as the pure aesthetic pleasure lasts. Therefore it is that Goethe says: "No evil can touch him who looks on human beauty; he feels himself at one with himself and with the world." That a beautiful human form is produced by nature must be explained in this way. At this its highest grade the will objectifies itself in an individual; and therefore through circumstances and its own power it completely overcomes all the hindrances and opposition which the phenomena of the lower grades present to it. Such are the forces of nature, from which the will must always first extort and win back the matter that belongs to all its manifestations. Further, the phenomenon of will at its higher grades always has multiplicity in its form. Even the tree is only a systematic aggregate of innumerably repeated sprouting fibres. This combination assumes greater complexity in higher forms, and the human body is an exceedingly complex system of different parts, each of which has a peculiar life of its own, *vita propria,* subordinate to the whole. Now that all these parts are in the proper fashion subordinate to the whole, and co-ordinate to each other, that they all work together harmoniously for the expression of the whole, nothing superfluous, nothing restricted; all these are the rare conditions, whose result is beauty, the completely expressed character of the species. So is it in nature. But how in art? One would suppose that art achieved the beautiful by imitating nature. But how is the artist to recognise the perfect work which is to be imitated, and distinguish it from the failures, if he does not anticipate the beautiful *before experience?* . . . No knowledge of the beautiful is possible purely *a posteriori,* and from mere experience; it is always, at least in part, *a priori,* although quite different in kind, from the forms of the principle of sufficient reason, of which we are conscious, *a priori.* These concern the universal form of phenomena as such, as it constitutes the possibility of knowledge in general, the universal *how* of all phenomena, and from this knowledge proceed mathematics and pure natural science. But this other kind of knowledge *a priori,* which makes it possible to express the beautiful, concerns, not the form but the content of phenomena, not the *how* but the *what* of the phenomenon. That we all recognise human beauty when we see it, but that in the true artist this takes place with such clearness that he shows it as he has never seen it, and surpasses nature in his representation; this is only possible because *we ourselves are* the will whose adequate objectification at its highest grade is here to be judged and discovered. Thus alone have we in fact an anticipation of that which nature (which is just the will that constitutes our own being) strives to express. And in the true genius this anticipation is accompanied by so great a degree of intelligence that he recognises the Idea in the particular thing, and thus, as it were, *understands the half-uttered speech of nature,* and articulates clearly what she only stammered forth. He expresses in the hard marble that beauty of form which in a thousand attempts she failed to produce, he presents it to nature, saying, as it were, to her, "That is what you wanted to say!" And whoever is able to judge replies, "Yes, that is it." Only in this way was it possible for the genius of the Greeks to find the type of human beauty and establish it as a canon for the school of sculpture; and only by virtue of such an anticipation is it possible for all of us to recognise beauty, when it has actually been achieved by nature in the particular case. This anticipation is the *Ideal.* It is the *Idea* so far as it is known *a priori,* at least half, and it becomes practical for art, because it corresponds to and completes what is given *a posteriori* through nature. The possibility of such an anticipation of the beautiful *a priori* in the artist, and of its recognition *a posteriori* by the critic, lies in the fact that the artist and the critic are themselves the "in-itself" of nature, the will which objectifies itself. For, as Empedocles said, like can only be known by like: only nature can understand itself: only nature can fathom itself: but only spirit also can understand spirit. . . .

Human beauty was explained above as the fullest objectification of will at the highest grade at which it is knowable. It expresses itself through the form; and this lies in space alone, and has no necessary connection with time, as, for example, motion has. Thus far then we may say: the adequate objectification of will through a merely spatial phenomenon is beauty, in the objective sense. A plant is nothing but such a merely spatial phenomenon of will; for no motion, and consequently no relation to time (regarded apart from its development), belongs to the expression of its nature; its mere form expresses its whole being and displays it openly. But brutes and men require, further, for the full revelation of the will which is manifested in them, a series of actions, and thus the manifestation in them takes on a direct relation to time. As the merely spatial manifestation of will can objectify it fully or defectively at each definite grade,—and it is this which constitutes beauty or ugliness,—so the temporal objectification of will, i.e. the action, and indeed the direct action, the movement, may correspond to the will, which objectifies itself in it, purely and fully without foreign admixture, without superfluity, without defect, only expressing exactly the act of will determined in each case;—or the converse of all this may occur. In the first case the movement is made with *grace*, in the second case without it. Thus as beauty is the adequate representation of will generally, through its merely spatial manifestation; *grace* is the adequate representation of will through its temporal manifestation, that is to say, the perfectly accurate and fitting expression of each act of will, through the movement and position which objectify it. Since movement and position presuppose the body, Winckelmann's expression is very true and suitable, when he says, "Grace is the proper relation of the acting person to the action." Grace consists, according to what has been said, in every movement being performed, and every position assumed, in the easiest, most appropriate and convenient way, and therefore being the pure, adequate expression of its intention, or of the act of will, without any superfluity, which exhibits itself as aimless, meaningless bustle, or as wooden stiffness. Grace presupposes as its condition a true proportion of all the limbs, and a symmetrical, harmonious figure; for complete ease and evident appropriateness of all positions and movements are only possible by means of these. Grace is therefore never without a certain degree of beauty of person. The two, complete and united, are the most distinct manifestation of will at the highest grade of its objectification.

It was mentioned above that in order rightly to portray man, it is necessary to separate the character of the species from that of the individual, so that to a certain extent every man expresses an Idea peculiar to himself. Therefore the arts whose aim is the representation of the Idea of man, have as their problem, not only beauty, the character of the species, but also the character of the individual, which is called, *par excellence, character*. But this is only the case in so far as this character is to be regarded, not as something accidental and quite peculiar to the man as a single individual, but as a side of the Idea of humanity which is specially apparent in this individual, and the representation of which is therefore of assistance in revealing this Idea. Thus the character, although as such it is individual, must yet be Ideal, that is, its significance in relation to the Idea of humanity generally (the objectifying of which it assists in its own way) must be comprehended and expressed with special prominence. . . .

In sculpture, beauty and grace are the principal concern. The special character of the mind, appearing in emotion, passion, alternations of knowing and willing, which can only be represented by the expression of the countenance and the gestures, is the peculiar sphere of *painting*. For although eyes and colour, which lie outside the province of sculpture, contribute much to beauty, they are yet far more essential to character. Further, beauty unfolds itself more completely when it is contemplated from various points of view; but the expression, the character, can only be completely comprehended from *one* point of view. . . .

49. The truth which lies at the foundation of all that we have hitherto said about art, is that the object of art, the representation of which is the aim of the artist, and the knowledge of which must therefore precede his work as its germ and source, is an Idea in Plato's sense, and

never anything else; not the particular thing, the object of common apprehension, and not the concept, the object of rational thought and of science. Although the Idea and the concept have something in common, because both represent as unity a multiplicity of real things; yet the great difference between them has no doubt been made clear and evident enough by what we have said about concepts in the first book, and about Ideas in this book. I by no means wish to assert, however, that Plato really distinctly comprehended this difference; indeed many of his examples of Ideas, and his discussions of them, are applicable only to concepts. The *concept* is abstract, discursive, undetermined within its own sphere, only determined by its limits, attainable and comprehensible by him who has only reason, communicable by words without any other assistance, entirely exhausted by its definition. The *Idea* on the contrary, although defined as the adequate representative of the concept, is always object of perception, and although representing an infinite number of particular things, is yet thoroughly determined. It is never known by the individual as such, but only by him who has raised himself above all willing and all individuality to the pure subject of knowing. Thus it is only attainable by the man of genius, and by him who, for the most part through the assistance of the works of genius, has reached an exalted frame of mind, by increasing his power of pure knowing. It is therefore not absolutely but only conditionally communicable, because the Idea, comprehended and repeated in the work of art, appeals to every one only according to the measure of his own intellectual worth. So that just the most excellent works of every art, the noblest productions of genius, must always remain sealed books to the dull majority of men, . . . For as a rule a man must have worth in himself in order to recognise it and believe in it willingly and freely in others. On this rests the necessity

of modesty in all merit, and the disproportionately loud praise of this virtue, which alone of all its sisters is always included in the eulogy of every one who ventures to praise any distinguished man, in order to appease and quiet the wrath of the unworthy. What then is modesty but hypocritical humility, by means of which, in a world swelling with base envy, a man seeks to obtain pardon for excellences and merits from those who have none? For whoever attributes to himself no merits, because he actually has none, is not modest but merely honest.

The *Idea* is the unity that falls into multiplicity on account of the temporal and spatial form of our intuitive apprehension; the *concept,* on the contrary, is the unity reconstructed out of multiplicity by the abstraction of our reason; the latter may be defined as *unitas post rem,* the former as *unitas ante rem.* Finally, we may express the distinction between the Idea and the concept, by a comparison, thus: the *concept* is like a dead receptacle, in which, whatever has been put, actually lies side by side, but out of which no more can be taken (by analytical judgment) than was put in (by synthetical reflection); the (Platonic) *Idea,* on the other hand, develops, in him who has comprehended it, ideas which are new as regards the concept of the same name; it resembles a living organism, developing itself and possessed of the power of reproduction, which brings forth what was not put into it.

It follows from all that has been said, that the concept, useful as it is in life, and serviceable, necessary and productive as it is in science, is yet always barren and unfruitful in art. The comprehended Idea, on the contrary, is the true and only source of every work of art. In its powerful originality it is only derived from life itself, from nature, from the world, and that only by the true genius, or by him whose momentary inspiration reaches the point of genius. Genuine and immortal works of art spring only from such direct apprehension. Just because the Idea is and remains object of perception, the artist is not conscious in the abstract of the intention and aim of his work; not a concept, but an Idea floats before his mind; therefore he can give no justification of what he does. He works, as people say, from pure feeling, and unconsciously, indeed instinctively. On the contrary, imitators, mannerists, *imitatores, servum pecus,* start, in art, from the concept; they observe what pleases and affects us in true works of art; understand it clearly, fix it in a concept, and thus abstractly, and then imitate it, openly or disguisedly, with dexterity and intentionally. They suck their nourishment, like parasite plants, from the works of others, and like polypi, they become the colour of their food. . . . All imitators, all mannerists, apprehend in concepts the nature of representative works of art; but concepts can never impart inner life to a work. The age, i.e. the dull multitude of every time, knows only concepts, and sticks to them, and therefore receives mannered works of art with ready and loud applause: but after a few years these works become insipid, because the spirit of the age, i.e. the prevailing concepts, in which alone they could take root, have changed. Only true works of art, which are drawn directly from nature and life, have eternal youth and enduring power, like nature and life themselves. For they belong to no age, but to humanity, and as on that account they are coldly received by their own age, to which they disdain to link themselves closely, and because indirectly and negatively they expose the existing errors, they are slowly and unwillingly recognised; on the other hand, they cannot grow old, but appear to us ever fresh and new down to the latest ages. Then they are no longer exposed to neglect and ignorance, for they are crowned and sanctioned by the praise of the few men capable of judging, who appear singly and rarely in the course of ages, and give in their votes, whose slowly growing number constitutes the authority, which alone is the judgment-seat we mean when we appeal to posterity. . . .

50. If the aim of all art is the communication of the comprehended Idea, which through the mind of the artist appears in such a form that it is purged and isolated from all that is foreign to it, and may now be grasped by the man of weaker comprehension and no productive faculty; if further, it is forbidden in art to start from the concept, we shall not be able to consent to the intentional and avowed employment of a work of art for the expression of a concept; this is the case in the *Allegory.* An allegory is a work of art which means something different from what it represents. But the object of perception, and consequently also the Idea, expresses itself directly and completely, and does not require the medium of something else which implies or indicates it. Thus, that which in this way is indicated and represented by something entirely different, because it cannot be made object of perception, is always a concept. Therefore through the allegory a conception has always to be signified, and consequently the mind of the beholder has to be drawn away from the expressed perceptible idea to one which is entirely different, abstract and not perceptible, and which lies quite outside the work of art. The picture or statue is intended to accomplish here what is accomplished far more fully by a book. Now, what we hold is the end of art, representation of a perceivable, comprehensible Idea, is not here the end. No great completeness in the work of art is demanded for what is aimed at here. It is only necessary that we should see what the thing is meant to be, for, as soon as this has been discovered, the end is reached, and the mind is now led away to quite a different kind of idea to an abstract conception, which is the end that was in view.

If then an allegorical picture has artistic value, it is quite separate from and independent of what it accomplishes as allegory. Such a work of art serves two ends at once, the expression of a conception and the expression of an Idea. Only the latter can be an end of art; the other is a foreign end, the trifling amusement of making a picture also do service as a legend, as a hieroglyphic, invented for the pleasure of those to whom the true nature of art can never appeal.

Allegory has an entirely different relation to poetry from that which it has to plastic, and pictorial art, and although it is to be rejected in the latter, it is not only permissible, but very serviceable to the former. For in plastic and pictorial art it leads away from what is perceptibly given, the proper object of all art, to abstract thoughts; but in poetry the relation is reversed; for here what is directly given in words is the concept, and the first aim is to lead from this to the object of perception, the representation of which must be undertaken by the imagination of the hearer. If in plastic and pictorial art we are led from what is immediately given to something else, this must always be a conception, because here only the abstract cannot be given directly; but a conception must never be the source, and its communication must never be the end of a work of art. In poetry, on the contrary, the conception is the material, the immediately given, and therefore we may very well leave it, in order to call up perceptions which are quite different, and in which the end is reached. Many a conception or abstract thought may be quite indispensable to the connection of a poem, which is yet, in itself and directly, quite incapable of being perceived; and then it is often made perceptible by means of some example which is subsumed under it. This takes place in every trope, every metaphor, simile, parable, and allegory, all of which differ only in the length and completeness

of their expression. Therefore, in the arts which employ language as their medium, similes and allegories are of striking effect. . . . But in poetry, as in plastic art, the allegory passes into the symbol if there is merely an arbitrary connection between what it presented to perception and the abstract significance of it. For as all symbolism rests, at bottom, on an agreement, the symbol has this among other disadvantages, that in time its meaning is forgotten, and then it is dumb. Who would guess why the fish is a symbol of Christianity if he did not know? Only a Champollion; for it is entirely a phonetic hieroglyphic. . . .

51. If now, with the exposition which has been given of art in general, we turn from plastic and pictorial art to poetry, we shall have no doubt that its aim also is the revelation of the Ideas, the grades of the objectification of will, and the communication of them to the hearer with the distinctness and vividness with which the poetical sense comprehends them. Ideas are essentially perceptible; if, therefore, in poetry only abstract conceptions are directly communicated through words, it is yet clearly the intention to make the hearer perceive the Ideas of life in the representatives of these conceptions, and this can only take place through the assistance of his own imagination. But in order to set the imagination to work for the accomplishment of this end, the abstract conceptions, which are the immediate material of poetry as of dry prose, must be so arranged that their spheres intersect each other in such a way that none of them can remain in its abstract universality; but, instead of it, a perceptible representative appears to the imagination; and this is always further modified by the words of the poet according to what his intention may be. As the chemist obtains solid precipitates by combining perfectly clear and transparent fluids; the poet understands how to precipitate, as it were, the concrete, the individual, the per-

ceptible idea, out of the abstract and transparent universality of the concepts by the
manner in which he combines them. For
the Idea can only be known by perception;
and knowledge of the Idea is the end of
art. The skill of a master, in poetry as in
chemistry, enables us always to obtain the
precise precipitate we intended. This end
is assisted by the numerous epithets in
poetry, by means of which the universality of every concept is narrowed more
and more till we reach the perceptible.
Homer attaches to almost every substantive
an adjective, whose concept intersects and
considerably diminishes the sphere of the
concept of the substantive, which is thus
brought so much the nearer to perception:
. . .

From the general nature of the material,
that is, the concepts, which poetry uses to
communicate the Ideas, the extent of its
province is very great. The whole of nature, the Ideas of all grades, can be represented by means of it, for it proceeds according to the Idea it has to impart, so that
its representations are sometimes descriptive, sometimes narrative, and sometimes
directly dramatic. If, in the representation
of the lower grades of the objectivity of
will, plastic and pictorial art generally surpass it, because lifeless nature, and even
brute nature, reveals almost its whole being
in a single well-chosen moment; man, on
the contrary, so far as he does not express
himself by the mere form and expression
of his person, but through a series of actions and the accompanying thoughts and
emotions, is the principal object of poetry,
in which no other art can compete with it,
for here the progress or movement which
cannot be represented in plastic or pictorial
art just suits its purpose.

The revelation of the Idea, which is the
highest grade of the objectivity of will,
the representation of man in the connected
series of his efforts and actions, is thus the
great problem of poetry. It is true that
both experience and history teach us to
know man; yet oftener men than man,
i.e. they give us empirical notes of the
behaviour of men to each other, from
which we may frame rules for our own
conduct, oftener than they afford us deep
glimpses of the inner nature of men. The
latter function, however, is by no means
entirely denied them; but as often as it is
the nature of mankind itself that discloses itself to us in history or in our own
experience, we have comprehended our experience, and the historian has comprehended history, with artistic eyes, poeti-
cally, i.e. according to the Idea, not the
phenomenon, in its inner nature, not in
its relations. Our own experience is the indispensable condition of understanding
poetry as of understanding history; for it is,
so to speak, the dictionary of the language
that both speak. But history is related to
poetry as portrait-painting is related to historical painting; the one gives us the true
in the individual, the other the true in
the universal; the one has the truth of the
phenomenon, and can therefore verify it
from the phenomenal, the other has the
truth of the Idea, which can be found in
no particular phenomenon, but yet speaks
to us from them all. The poet from deliberate choice represents significant characters in significant situations; the historian
takes both as they come. Indeed, he must
regard and select the circumstances and
the persons, not with reference to their inward and true significance, which expresses
the Idea, but according to the outward, apparent, and relatively important significance with regard to the connection and
the consequences. He must consider nothing in and for itself in its essential character and expression, but must look at everything in its relations, in its connection, in
its influence upon what follows, and expe-
cially upon its own age. . . . But the poet
comprehends the Idea, the inner nature of
man apart from all relations, outside
all time, the adequate objectivity of the
thing-in-itself, at its highest grade. Even in

that method of treatment which is necessary for the historian, the inner nature and significance of the phenomena, the kernel of all these shells, can never be entirely lost. He who seeks for it, at any rate, may find it and recognise it. Yet that which is significant in itself, not in its relations, the real unfolding of the Idea, will be found far more accurately and distinctly in poetry than in history, and, therefore, however paradoxical it may sound, far more really genuine inner truth is to be attributed to poetry than to history. For the historian must accurately follow the particular event according to life, as it develops itself in time in the manifold tangled chains of causes and effects. It is, however, impossible that he can have all the data for this; he cannot have seen all and discovered all. He is forsaken at every moment by the original of his picture, or a false one substitutes itself for it, and this so constantly that I think I may assume that in all history the false outweighs the true. The poet, on the contrary, has comprehended the Idea of man from some definite side which is to be represented; thus it is the nature of his own self that objectifies itself in it for him. His knowledge, as we explained above when speaking of sculpture, is half *a priori*; his ideal stands before his mind firm, distinct, brightly illuminated, and cannot forsake him; therefore he shows us, in the mirror of his mind, the Idea pure and distinct, and his delineation of it down to the minutest particular is true as life itself. . . .

The representation of the Idea of man, which is the work of the poet, may be performed, so that what is represented is also the representer. This is the case in lyrical poetry, in songs, properly so called, in which the poet only perceives vividly his own state and describes it. Thus a certain subjectivity is essential to this kind of poetry from the nature of its object. Again, what is to be represented may be entirely different from him who represents

it, as is the case in all other kinds of poetry, in which the poet more or less conceals himself behind his representation, and at last disappears altogether. In the ballad the poet still expresses to some extent his own state through the tone and proportion of the whole; therefore, though much more objective than the lyric, it has yet something subjective. This becomes less in the idyll, still less in the romantic poem, almost entirely disappears in the true epic, and even to the last vestige in the drama, which is the most objective and, in more than one respect, the completest and most difficult form of poetry. The lyrical form of poetry is consequently the easiest, and although art, as a whole, belongs only to the true man of genius, who so rarely appears, even a man who is not in general very remarkable may produce a beautiful song if, by actual strong excitement from without, some inspiration raises his mental powers; for all that is required for this is a lively perception of his own state at a moment of emotional excitement. . . . Yet in the lyrics of true poets the inner nature of all mankind is reflected, and all that millions of past, present, and future men have found, or will find, in the same situations, which are constantly recurring, finds its exact expression in them, and because the situations, by constant recurrence, are permanent as man himself and always call up the same sensations, the lyrical productions of genuine poets remain through thousands of years true, powerful, and fresh. But if the poet is always the universal man, then all that has ever moved a human heart, all that human nature in any situation has ever produced from itself, all that dwells and broods in any human breast—is his theme and his material, and also all the rest of nature. Therefore the poet may just as well sing of voluptuousness as of mysticism, be Anacreon or Angelus Silesius, write tragedies or comedies, represent the sublime or the common mind—according to humour or vocation. And no one has the right to prescribe to the poet what he ought to be—noble and sublime, moral, pious, Christian, one thing or another, still less to reproach him because he is one thing and not another. He is the mirror of mankind, and brings to its consciousness what it feels and does. . . .

Tragedy is to be regarded, and is recognised as the summit of poetical art, both on account of the greatness of its effect and the difficulty of its achievement. It is very significant for our whole system, and well worthy of observation, that the end of this highest poetical achievement is the representation of the terrible side of life. The unspeakable pain, the wail of humanity, the triumph of evil, the scornful mastery of chance, and the irretrievable fall of the just and innocent, is here presented to us; and in this lies a significant hint of the nature of the world and of existence. It is the strife of will with itself, which here, completely unfolded at the highest grade of its objectivity, comes into fearful prominence. It becomes visible in the suffering of men, which is now introduced, partly through chance and error, which appear as the rulers of the world, personified as fate, on account of their insidiousness, which even reaches the appearance of design; partly it proceeds from man himself, through the self-mortifying efforts of a few, through the wickedness and perversity of most. It is one and the same will that lives and appears in them all, but whose phenomena fight against each other and destroy each other. In one individual it appears powerfully, in another more weakly; in one more subject to reason, and softened by the light of knowledge, in another less so, till at last, in some single case, this knowledge, purified and heightened by suffering itself, reaches the point at which the phenomenon, the veil of Maya, no longer deceives it. It sees through the form of the phenomenon, the *principum individuationis*. The egoism which rests on this perishes with it, so that now the *motives*

that were so powerful before have lost their might, and instead of them the complete knowledge of the nature of the world, which has a *quieting* effect on the will, produces resignation, the surrender not merely of life, but of the very will to live. Thus we see in tragedies the noblest men, after long conflict and suffering, at last renounce the ends they have so keenly followed, and all the pleasures of life for ever, or else freely and joyfully surrender life itself. So is it with the steadfast prince of Calderon; with Gretchen in "Faust," with Hamlet, whom his friend Horatio would willing follow, but is bade remain a while, and in this harsh world draw his breath in pain, to tell the story of Hamlet, and clear his memory; so also is it with the Maid of Orleans, the Bride of Messina; they all die purified by suffering, i.e. after the will to live which was formerly in them is dead. In the "Mohammed" of Voltaire this is actually expressed in the concluding words which the dying Palmira addresses to Mohammed: "The world is for tyrants: live!" On the other hand, the demand for so-called poetical justice rests on entire misconception of the nature of tragedy, and, indeed, on the nature of the world itself. . . .

52. Now that we have considered all the fine arts in the general way that is suitable to our point of view, beginning with architecture, the peculiar end of which is to elucidate the objectification of will at the lowest grades of its visibility, in which it shows itself as the dumb unconscious tendency of the mass in accordance with laws, and yet already reveals a breach of the unity of will with itself in a conflict between gravity and rigidity—and ending with the consideration of tragedy, which presents to us at the highest grades of the objectification of will this very conflict with itself in terrible magnitude and distinctness; we find that there is still another fine art which has been excluded from our consideration, and had to be ex-

cluded, for in the systematic connection of our exposition there was no fitting place for it—I mean *music*. It stands alone, quite cut off from all the other arts. In it we do not recognise the copy or repetition of any Idea of existence in the world. Yet it is such a great and exceedingly noble art, its effect on the inmost nature of man is so powerful, and it is so entirely and deeply understood by him in his inmost consciousness as a perfectly universal language, the distinctness of which surpasses even that of the perceptible world itself, that . . . we must attribute to music a far more serious and deep significance, connected with the inmost nature of the world and our own self, and in reference to which the arithmetical proportions, to which it may be reduced, are related, not as the thing signified, but merely as the sign. That in some sense music must be related to the world as the representation to the thing represented, as the copy to the original, we may conclude from the analogy of the other arts, all of which possess this character, and affect us on the whole in the same way as it does, only that the effect of music is stronger, quicker, more necessary and infallible. Further, its representative relation to the world must be very deep, absolutely true, and strikingly accurate, because it is instantly understood by every one, and has the appearance of a certain infallibility, because its form may be reduced to perfectly definite rules expressed in numbers, from which it cannot free itself without entirely ceasing to be music. Yet the point of comparison between music and the world, the respect in which it stands to the world in the relation of a copy or repetition, is very obscure. Men have practised music in all ages without being able to account for this; content to understand it directly, they renounced all claim to an abstract conception of this direct understanding itself.

I gave my mind entirely up to the impression of music in all its forms, and then returned to reflection and the system of thought expressed in the present work, and thus I arrived at an explanation of the inner nature of music and of the nature of its imitative relation to the world—which from analogy had necessarily to be presupposed—an explanation which is quite sufficient for myself, and satisfactory to my investigation, and which will doubtless be equally evident to any one who has followed me thus far and has agreed with my view of the world. Yet I recognise the fact that it is essentially impossible to prove this explanation, for it assumes and establishes a relation of music, as idea, to that which from its nature can never be idea, and music will have to be regarded as the copy of an original which can never be directly presented as idea.

The (Platonic) Ideas are the adequate objectification of will. To excite or suggest the knowledge of these by means of the representation of particular things (for works of art themselves are always representations of particular things) is the end of all the other arts, which can only be attained by a corresponding change in the knowing subject. Thus all these arts objectify the will indirectly only by means of the Ideas; and since our world is nothing but the manifestation of the Ideas in multiplicity, though their entrance into the *principium individuationis* (the form of the knowledge possible for the individual as such), music also, since it passes over the Ideas, is entirely independent of the phenomenal world, ignores it altogether, could to a certain extent exist if there was no world at all, which cannot be said of the other arts. Music is as *direct* an objectification and copy of the whole *will* as the world itself, nay, even as the Ideas, whose multiplied manifestation constitutes the world of individual things. Music is thus by no means like the other arts, the copy of the Ideas, but the *copy of the will itself*, whose objectivity the Ideas are. This is why the effect of music is so much more powerful and pentrating than that of the other arts, for they speak only of shadows, but it speaks of the thing itself. Since, however, it is the same will which objectifies itself both in the Ideas and in music, though in quite different ways, there must be, not indeed a direct likeness, but yet a parallel, an analogy, between music and the Ideas whose manifestation in multiplicity and incompleteness is the visible world. The establishing of this analogy will facilitate, as an illustration, the understanding of this exposition, which is so difficult on account of the obscurity of the subject.

I recognise in the deepest tones of harmony, in the bass, the lowest grades of the objectification of will, unorganised nature, the mass of the planet. It is well known that all the high notes which are easily sounded, and die away more quickly, are produced by the vibration in their vicinity of the deep bass-notes. When, also, the low notes sound, the high notes always sound faintly, and it is a law of harmony that only those high notes may accompany a bass-note which actually already sound along with it of themselves (its *sons harmoniques*) on account of its vibration. This is analogous to the fact that the whole of the bodies and organisations of nature must be regarded as having come into existence through gradual development out of the mass of the planet; that is both their supporter and their source, and the same relation subsists between the high notes and the bass. There is a limit of depth, below which no sound is audible. This corresponds to the fact that no matter can be perceived without form and quality, i.e. without the manifestation of a force which cannot be further explained, in which an Idea expresses itself, and more generally, that no matter can be entirely without will. Thus, as a certain pitch is inseparable from the note as such, so a certain grade of the manifestation of will is inseparable from matter. Bass is thus, for

us, in harmony what unorganised nature, the crudest mass, upon which all rests, and from which everything originates and develops, is in the world. Now, further, in the whole of the complemental parts which make up the harmony between the bass and the leading voice singing the melody, I recognise the whole gradation of the Ideas in which the will objectifies itself. Those nearer to the bass are the lower of these grades, the still unorganised, but yet manifold phenomenal things; the higher represent to me the world of plants and beasts. The definite intervals of the scale are parallel to the definite grades of the objectification of will, the definite species in nature. The departure from the arithmetical correctness of the intervals, through some temperament, or produced by the key selected, is analogous to the departure of the individual from the type of the species. Indeed, even the impure discords, which give no definite interval, may be compared to the monstrous abortions produced by beasts of two species, or by man and beast. But to all these bass and complemental parts which make up the *harmony* there is wanting that connected progress which belongs only to the high voice singing the melody, and it alone moves quickly and lightly in modulations and runs, while all these others have only a slower movement without a connection in each part for itself. The deep bass moves most slowly, the representative of the crudest mass. Its rising and falling occurs only by large intervals, in thirds, fourths, fifths, never by *one* tone, unless it is a bass inverted by double counterpoint. This slow movement is also physically essential to it; a quick run or shake in the low notes cannot even be imagined. The higher complemental parts, which are parallel to animal life, move more quickly, but yet without melodious connection and significant progress. The disconnected course of all the complemental parts, and their regulation by definite laws, is analogous to the fact that in the whole irrational world, from the crystal to the most perfect animal, no being has a connected consciousness of its own which would make its life into a significant whole, and none experiences a succession of mental developments, none perfects itself by culture, but everything exists always in the same way according to its kind, determined by fixed law. Lastly, in the *melody,* in the high, singing, principal voice leading the whole and progressing with unrestrained freedom, in the unbroken significant connection of *one* thought from beginning to end representing a whole, I recognise the highest grade of the objectification of will, the intellectual life and effort of man. As he alone, because endowed with reason, constantly looks before and after on the path of his actual life and its innumerable possibilities, and so achieves a course of life which is intellectual, and therefore connected as a whole; corresponding to this, I say, the *melody* has significant intentional connection from beginning to end. It records, therefore, the history of the intellectually enlightened will. This will expresses itself in the actual world as the series of its deeds; but melody says more, it records the most secret history of this intellectually-enlightened will, pictures every excitement, every effort, every movement of it, all that which the reason collects under the wide and negative concept of feeling, and which it cannot apprehend further through its abstract concepts. Therefore it has alway been said that music is the language of feeling and of passion, as words are the language of reason. . . .

But it must never be forgotten, in the investigation of all these analogies I have pointed out, that music has no direct, but merely an indirect relation to them, for it never expresses the phenomenon, but only the inner nature, the in-itself of all phenomena, the will itself. It does not therefore express this or that particular and definite joy, this or that sorrow, or pain, or horror, or delight, or merriment, or peace of mind; but joy, sorrow, pain, horror, delight, merriment, peace of mind themselves, to a certain extent in the abstract, their essential nature, without accessories, and therefore without their motives. Yet we completely understand them in this extracted quintessence. . . .

According to all this, we may regard the phenomenal world, or nature, and music as two different expressions of the same thing, which is therefore itself the only medium of their analogy, so that a knowledge of it is demanded in order to understand that analogy. Music, therefore, if regarded as an expression of the world, is in the highest degree a universal language, which is related indeed to the universality of concepts, much as they are related to the particular things. Its universality, however, is by no means that empty universality of abstraction, but quite of a different kind, and is united with thorough and distinct definiteness. In this respect it resembles geometrical figures and numbers, which are the universal forms of all possible objects of experience and applicable to them all *a priori,* and yet are not abstract but perceptible and thoroughly determined. All possible efforts, excitements, and manifestations of will, all that goes on in the heart of man and that reason includes in the wide, negative concept of feeling, may be expressed by the infinite number of possible melodies, but always in the universal, in the mere form, without the material, always according to the thing-in-itself, not the phenomenon, the inmost soul, as it were, of the phenomenon, without the body. This deep relation which music has to the true nature of all things also explains the fact that suitable music played to any scene, action, event, or surrounding seems to disclose to us its most secret meaning, and appears as the most accurate and distinct commentary upon it. This is so truly the case, that whoever gives himself up entirely to the impression of a symphony, seems to see all the possible events of life and the world take place in himself, yet if he reflects, he can find no likeness between the music and the things that passed before his mind. For, as we have said, music is distinguished from all the other arts by the fact that it is not a copy of the phenomenon, or, more accurately, the adequate objectivity of will, but is the direct copy of the will itself, and therefore exhibits itself as the metaphysical to everything physical in the world, and as the thing-in-itself to every phenomenon. We might, therefore, just as well call the world embodied music as embodied will; and this is the reason why music makes every picture, and indeed every scene of real life and of the world, at once appear with higher significance, certainly all the more in proportion as its melody is analogous to the inner spirit of the given phenomenon. It rests upon this that we are able to set a poem to music as a song, or a perceptible representation as a pantomime, or both as an opera. Such particular pictures of human life, set to the universal language of music, are never bound to it or correspond to it with stringent necessity; but they stand to it only in the relation of an example chosen at will to a general concept. In the determinateness of the real, they represent that which music expresses in the universality of mere form. For melodies are to a certain extent, like general concepts, an abstraction from the actual. This actual world, then, the world of particular things, affords the object of perception, the special and individual, the particular case, both to the universality of the concepts and to the universality of the melodies. But these two universalities are in a certain respect opposed to each other; for the concepts contain particulars only as the first forms abstracted from perception, as it were, the separated shell of

things; thus they are, strictly speaking, *abstracta*; music, on the other hand, gives the inmost kernel which precedes all forms, or the heart of things. . . .

The unutterable depth of all music by virtue of which it floats through our consciousness as the vision of a paradise firmly believed in yet ever distant from us, and by which also it is so fully understood and yet so inexplicable, rests on the fact that it restores to us all the emotions of our inmost nature, but entirely without reality and far removed from their pain. So also the seriousness which is essential to it, which excludes the absurd from its direct and peculiar province, is to be explained by the fact that its object is not the idea, with reference to which alone deception and absurdity are possible; but its object is directly the will, and this is essentially the most serious of all things, for it is that on which all depends.

In the whole of this exposition of music I have been trying to bring out clearly that it expresses in a perfectly universal language, in a homogeneous material, mere tones, and with the greatest determinateness and truth, the inner nature, the in-itself of the world, which we think under the concept of will, because will is its most distinct manifestation. Further, according to my view and contention, philosophy is nothing but a complete and accurate repetition or expression of the nature of the world in very general concepts, for only in such is it possible to get a view of that whole nature which will everywhere be adequate and applicable. Thus, whoever has followed me and entered into my mode of thought, will not think it so very paradoxical if I say, that supposing it were possible to give a perfectly accurate, complete explanation of music, extending even to particulars, that is to say, a detailed repetition in concepts of what it expresses, this would also be a sufficient repetition and explanation of the world in concepts, or at least entirely parallel to such an explanation, and thus it would be the true philosophy. . . .

. . . I have perhaps already gone too much into detail with regard to some things in this Third Book, or have dwelt too much on particulars. But my aim made it necessary, and it will be the less disapproved if the importance and high worth of art, which is seldom sufficiently recognised, be kept in mind. For if, according to our view, the whole visible world is just the objectification, the mirror, of the will, conducting it to knowledge of itself, and, indeed, as we shall soon see, to the possibility of its deliverance; and if, at the same time, the world as idea, if we regard it in isolation, and, freeing ourselves from all volition, allow it alone to take possession of our consciousness, is the most joy-giving and the only innocent side of life; we must regard art as the higher ascent, the more complete development of all this, for it achieves essentially just what is achieved by the visible world itself, only with greater concentration, more perfectly, with intention and intelligence, and therefore may be called, in the full significance of the word, the flower of life. If the whole world as idea is only the visibility of will, the work of art is to render this visibility more distinct. It is the *camera obscura* which shows the objects more purely, and enables us to survey them and comprehend them better. It is the play within the play, the stage upon the stage in "Hamlet."

The pleasure we receive from all beauty, the consolation which art affords, the enthusiasm of the artist, which enables him to forget the cares of life,—the latter an advantage of the man of genius over other men, which alone repays him for the suffering that increases in proportion to the clearness of consciousness, and for the desert loneliness among men of a different race,—all this rests on the fact that the in-itself of life, the will, existence itself, is, as we shall see farther on, a constant sor-

row, partly miserable, partly terrible; while, on the contrary, as idea alone, purely contemplated, or copied by art, free from pain, it presents to us a drama full of significance. This purely knowable side of the world, and the copy of it in any art, is the element of the artist. He is chained to the contemplation of the play, the objectification of will; he remains beside it, does not get tired of contemplating it and representing it in copies; and meanwhile he bears himself the cost of the production of that play, i.e. he himself is the will which objectifies itself, and remains in constant suffering. That pure, true, and deep knowledge of the inner nature of the world becomes now for him an end in itself: he stops there. Therefore it does not become to him a quieter of the will, as, we shall see in the next book, it does in the case of the saint who has attained to resignation; it does not deliver him for ever from life, but only at moments, and is therefore not for him a path out of life, but only an occasional consolation in it, till his power, increased by this contemplation and at last tired of the play, lays hold on the real.

SUPPLEMENT TO BOOK III

CHAPTER XXXIV

On the Inner Nature of Art

Not merely philosophy but also the fine arts work at bottom towards the solution of the problem of existence. For in every mind that once gives itself up to the purely objective contemplation of nature a desire has been excited, however concealed and unconscious it may be, to comprehend the true nature of things, of life and existence. For this alone has interest for the intellect as such, i.e. for the pure subject of knowledge which has become free from the aims of the will; as for the subject which knows as a mere individual the aims of the will alone have interest. On

this account the result of the purely objective apprehension of things is an expression more of the nature of life and
existence, more an answer to the question,
"What is life?" Every genuine and successful work of art answers this question in its
own way with perfect correctness. But all
the arts speak only the naïve and childish
language of perception, not the abstract
and serious language of *reflection;* their
answer is therefore a fleeting image: not
permanent and general knowledge. Thus
for *perception* every work of art answers
that question, every painting, every statue,
every poem, every scene upon the stage:
music also answers it; and indeed more
profoundly than all the rest, for in its
language, which is understood with absolute directness, but which is yet untrans-
latable into that of the reason, the inner
nature of all life and existence expresses
itself. Thus all the other arts hold up to
the questioner a perceptible image, and
say, "Look here, this is life." Their answer,
however correct it may be, will yet always afford merely a temporary, not a complete and final, satisfaction. For they always give merely a fragment, an example
instead of the rule, not the whole, which
can only be given in the universality of
the *conception.* For this, therefore, thus
for reflection and in the abstract, to give
an answer which just on that account
shall be permanent and suffice for always,
is the task of philosophy. However, we see
here upon what the relationship of philosophy to the fine arts rests, and can conclude from that to what extent the capacity of both, although in its direction
and in secondary matters very different, is
yet in its root the same.

Every work of art accordingly really aims
at showing us life and things as they are in
truth, but cannot be directly discerned by
every one through the mist of objective
and subjective contingencies. Art takes
away this mist.

The works of the poets, sculptors, and
representative artists in general contain an
unacknowledged treasure of profound wisdom; just because out of them the wisdom
of the nature of things itself speaks,
whose utterances they merely interpret by
illustrations and purer repetitions. On this
account, however, every one who reads the
poem or looks at the picture must certainly contribute out of his own means to
bring that wisdom to light; accordingly he
comprehends only so much of it as his
capacity and culture admit of; as in the
deep sea each sailor only lets down the lead
as far as the length of the line will allow.
Before a picture, as before a prince, every
one must stand, waiting to see whether
and what it will speak to him; and, as in
the case of a prince, so here he must not
himself address it, for then he would only
hear himself. It follows from all this that in
the works of the representative arts all
truth is certainly contained, yet only *vir-
tualiter* or *implicite;* philosophy, on the
other hand, endeavours to supply the same
truth *actualiter* and *explicite,* and therefore, in this sense, is related to art as wine
to grapes. What it promises to supply
would be, as it were, an already realised
and clear gain, a firm and abiding possession; while that which proceeds from the
achievements and works of art is one which
has constantly to be reproduced anew.
Therefore, however, it makes demands,
not only upon those who produce its works,
but also upon those who are to enjoy them
which are discouraging and hard to com-
ply with. Therefore its public remains
small, while that of art is large.

The co-operation of the beholder, which
is referred to above, as demanded for the
enjoyment of a work of art, depends partly
upon the fact that every work of art can
only produce its effect through the medium of the fancy; therefore it must excite
this, and can never allow it to be left out
of the play and remain inactive. This
is a condition of the aesthetic effect, and
therefore a fundamental law of all fine arts.

But it follows from this that through the work of art, everything must not be directly given to the senses, but rather only so much as is demanded to lead the fancy on to the right path; something, and indeed the ultimate thing, must always be left over for the fancy to do. Even the author must always leave something over for the reader to think; for Voltaire has very rightly said, *"Le secret d'être ennuyeux, c'est de tout dire."* But besides this, in art the best of all is too spiritual to be given directly to the senses; it must be born in the imagination of the beholder, although begotten by the work of art. It depends upon this that the sketches of great masters often effect more than their finished pictures; although another advantage certainly contributes to this, namely, that they are completed off-hand in the moment of conception; while the perfected painting is only produced through continued effort, by means of skilful deliberation and persistent intention, for the inspiration cannot last till it is completed. From the fundamental aesthetical law we are speaking of, it is further to be explained why wax figures never produce an aesthetic effect, and therefore are not properly works of fine art, although it is just in them that the imitation of nature is able to reach its highest grade. For they leave nothing for the imagination to do. Sculpture gives merely the form without the colour; painting gives the colour, but the mere appearance of the form; thus both appeal to the imagination of the beholder. The wax figure, on the other hand, gives all, form and colour at once; whence arises the appearance of reality, and the imagination is left out of account. Poetry, on the contrary, appeals indeed to the imagination alone, which it sets in action by means of mere words.

An arbitrary playing with the means of art without a proper knowledge of the end is, in every art, the fundamental characteristic of the dabbler. Such a man shows himself in the pillars that support nothing, aimless volutes, juttings and projections of bad architecture, in the meaningless runs and figures, together with the aimless noise of bad music, in the jingling of the rhymes of senseless poetry, &c.

It follows from the preceding chapter, and from my whole view of art, that its aim is the facilitating of the knowledge of the Ideas of the world (in the Platonic sense, the only one which I recognise for the word Idea). The Ideas, however, are essentially something perceptible, which, therefore, in its fuller determinations, is inexhaustible. The communication of such an Idea can therefore only take place on the path of perception, which is that of art. Whoever, therefore, is filled with the comprehension of an Idea is justified if he chooses art as the medium of its communication. The mere conception, on the other hand, is something completely determinable, therefore exhaustible, and distinctly thought, the whole content of which can be coldly and dryly expressed in words. Now to desire to communicate such a conception by means of a work of art is a very useless circumlocution, indeed belongs to that playing with the means of art without knowledge of its end which has just been condemned. Therefore a work of art which has proceeded from mere distinct conceptions is always ungenuine. If now, in considering a work of plastic art, or in reading a poem, or in hearing a piece of music (which aims at describing something definite), we see, through all the rich materials of art, the distinct, limited, cold, dry conception shine out, and at last come to the front, the conception which was the kernel of this work, the whole notion of which consequently consisted in the distinct thinking of it, and accordingly is absolutely exhausted by its communication, we feel disgusted and indignant, for we see ourselves deceived and cheated out of our interest and attention. We are only perfectly satisfied by the impression of a work of art when it leaves something which, with all our thinking about it, we cannot bring down to the distinctness of a conception. The mark of that hybrid origin from mere conceptions is that the author of a work of art could, before he set about it, give in distinct words what he intended to present; for then it would have been possible to attain his whole end through these words. Therefore it is an undertaking as unworthy as it is absurd if, as has often been tried at the present day, one seeks to reduce a poem of Shakespeare's or Goethe's to the abstract truth which it was its aim to communicate. Certainly the artist ought to think in the arranging of his work; but only that thought which was *perceived* before it was thought has afterwards, in its communication, the power of animating or rousing, and thereby becomes imperishable. We shall not refrain from observing here that certainly the work which is done at a stroke, like the sketches of painters already referred to, the work which is completed in the inspiration of its first conception, and as it were unconsciously dashed off, like the melody which comes entirely without reflection, and quite as if by inspiration, and finally, also the lyrical poem proper, the mere song, in which the deeply felt mood of the present, and the impression of the surroundings, as if involuntarily, pours itself forth in words, whose metre and rhyme come about of their own accord—that all these, I say, have the great advantage of being purely the work of the ecstasy of the moment, the inspiration, the free movement of genius, without any admixture of intention and reflection; hence they are through and through delightful and enjoyable, without shell and kernel, and their effect is much more inevitable than that of the greatest works of art, of slower and more deliberate execution. In all the latter, thus in great historical paintings, in long epic poems, great operas, &c., reflection, intention, and deliberate selection has had an important part; understanding, technical skill, and routine must here fill up the gaps which the conception and inspiration of genius has left, and must mix with these all kinds of necessary supplementary work as cement of the only really genuinely brilliant parts. This explains why all such works, only excepting the perfect masterpieces of the very greatest masters (as, for example, "Hamlet," "Faust," the opera of "Don Juan"), inevitably contain an admixture of something insipid and wearisome, which in some measure hinders the enjoyment of them. Proofs of this are the "Messiah," *"Gerusalemme liberata,"* even "Paradise Lost" and the "Aeneid"; and Horace already makes the bold remark, *"Quandoque dormitat bonus Homerus."* But that this is the case is the consequence of the limitation of human powers in general.

The mother of the useful arts is necessity; that of the fine arts superfluity. As their father, the former have understanding; the latter genius, which is itself a kind of superfluity, that of the powers of knowledge beyond the measure which is required for the service of the will.

GEORG WILHELM FRIEDRICH HEGEL [1770–1831]

>>>>><<<<<

From *The Philosophy of Fine Art* [1820–26]

. . . The kind of art which *we* ourselves propose to examine is one which is *free* in its aim and its means. That art in general can serve other objects, and even be merely a pastime, is a relation which it possesses in common with thought itself. From one point of view thought likewise, as science subservient to other ends, can be used in just the same way for finite purposes and means as they chance to crop up, and as such serviceable faculty of science is not self-determined, but determined by something alien to it. But, further, as distinct from such subservience to particular objects, science is raised of its own essential resources in free independence to truth, and exclusively united with its own aims in discovering the true fulfillment in that truth.

Fine art is not art in the true sense of the term until it is also thus free, and its *highest* function is only then satisfied when it has established itself in a sphere which it shares with religion and philosophy, becoming thereby merely one mode and form through which the *Divine*, the profoundest interests of mankind, and spiritual truths of widest range, art brought home to consciousness and expressed. It is in works of art that nations have deposited the richest intuitions and ideas they possess; and not infrequently fine art supplies a key of interpretation to the wisdom and religion of peoples; in the case of many it is the only one. This is an attri-

From G. W. F. Hegel, *The Philosophy of Fine Art*, Vol. I, translated by F. P. B. Osmaston (London: G. Bell & Sons, Ltd., 1920). Introduction, II, III; Part I, Chapter I.

bute which art shares in common with religion and philosophy, the peculiar distinction in the case of art being that its presentation of the most exalted subject-matter is in sensuous form, thereby bringing them nearer to Nature and her mode of envisagement, that is closer to our sensitive and emotional life. The world, into the profundity of which thought penetrates, is a supersensuous one, a world which to start with is posited as a Beyond in contrast to the immediacy of ordinary conscious life and present sensation. It is the freedom of reflecting consciousness which disengages itself from this immersion in the *"this side,"* or immediacy, in other words sensuous reality and finitude. But the mind is able, too, to heal the *fracture* which is thus created in its progression. From the wealth of its own resources it brings into being the works of fine art as the primary bond of mediation between that which is exclusively external, sensuous and transitory, and the medium of pure thought, between Nature and its finite reality, and the infinite freedom of a reason which comprehends. Now it was objected that the *element of art* was, if we view it as a whole, of an *unworthy* character, inasmuch as it consisted of appearance and deceptions inseparable from such. Such a contention would of course be justifiable, if we were entitled to assume that appearance had no *locus standi* at all. An appearance or show is, however, essential to actuality. There could be no such thing as truth if it did not appear, or, rather, let itself appear, were it not further true for some *one* thing or person, *for* itself as also *for* spirit. Consequently it cannot be appearance in general against which such an objection can be raised, but the particular mode of its manifestation under which art makes actual what is essentially real and true. If, then, the appearance, in the medium of which art gives determinate existence to its creations, be defined as *deception,* such an objection is in the first instance intelligible if we compare it with the *external world* of a phenomena, and its *immediate* relation to ourselves as material substance, or view it relatively to our own world of emotions, that is our inward sensuous life. Both these are worlds to which in our everyday life, the life, that is, of visible experience, we are accustomed to attach the worth and name of reality, actuality and truth as contrasted with that of art, which fails to possess such reality as we suppose. Now it is just this entire sphere of the empirical world, whether on its personal side or its objective side, which we ought rather to call in a stricter sense than when we apply the term to the world of art, merely a show or appearance, and an even more unyielding form of deception. It is only beyond the immediacy of emotional life and that world of external objects that we shall discover reality in any true sense of its own independent right and substance, that which is at once of the substance of Nature and of mind, which, while it is actually *here* in present and determinate existence, yet retains under such limitation of essential and self-concentrated being, and only in virtue of such is truly real. The predominance of these universal powers is precisely that which art accentuates and manifests. In the external and soul-world of ordinary experience we have also no doubt this essence of actuality, but in the chaotic congeries of particular detail, encumbered by the immediacy of sensuous envisagement, and every kind of caprice of condition, event, character, and so forth. Now it is just the show and deception of this false and evanescent world which art disengages from the veritable significance of phenomena to which we have referred,

implanting in the same a reality of more exalted rank born of mind. The phenomena of art therefore are not merely appearance and nothing more; we are justified in ascribing to them, as contrasted with the realities of our ordinary life, an actually higher reality and more veritable existence. To as little extent are the representations of art a deceptive appearance as compared with the assumed truer delineations of historical writing. For immediate existence also does not belong to historical writing. It only possesses the intellectual appearance of the same as the medium of its delineations, and its content remains charged with the entire contingent *materia* of ordinary reality and its events, developments and personalities, whereas the work of art brings us face to face with the external powers paramount in history with this incidental association of the immediate sensuous present and its unstable appearance expunged.

If, however, it is in contrast with philosophic thought and religious and ethical principles, that the mode of appearance of the shapes of art, is described as a deception, there is certainly this in support of the view that the mode of revelation attained by a content in the realm of thought is the truest reality. In comparison, nevertheless, with the appearance of immediate sensuous existence, and that of historical narration, the show of art possesses the advantage that, in its own virtue, it points beyond itself, directing us to a somewhat spiritual, which it seeks to envisage to the conceptive mind. Immediate appearance, on the contrary, does not give itself out to be thus illusive, but rather to be the true and real, though as a matter of fact such truth is contaminated and obstructed by the immediately sensuous medium. The hard rind of Nature and the everyday world offer more difficulty to the mind in breaking through to the Idea than do the products of art.

. . . What in the first instance is

known to us under current conceptions of a work of art may be subsumed under the three following determinations:

(1) A work of art is no product of Nature. It is brought into being through the agency of man.

(2) It is created essentially *for* man; and, what is more, it is to a greater or less degree delivered from a sensuous medium, and addressed to his *senses*.

(3) It contains an *end* bound up with it.

1. With regard to the first point, that a work of art is a product of human activity, an inference has been drawn from this (*a*) that such an activity, being the conscious production of an external object can also be *known* and *divulged*, and learned and reproduced by others. For that which one is able to effect, another—such is the notion—is able to effect or to imitate, when he has once simply mastered the way of doing it. In short we have merely to assume an acquaintance with the rules of art-production universally shared, and anybody may then, if he cares to do so, give effect to executive ability of the same type, and produce works of art. It is out of reasoning of this kind that the above-mentioned theories, with their provision of rules, and their prescriptions formulated for practical acceptance, have arisen. Unfortunately that which is capable of being brought into effect in accordance with suggestions of this description can only be something formally regular and mechanical. For only that which is mechanical is of so exterior a type that only an entirely empty effort of will and dexterity is required to accept it among our working conceptions, and forthwith to carry it out; an effort, in fact, which is not under the necessity to contribute out of its own resources anything concrete such as is quite outside the prescriptive power of such general rules.

This is apparent with most vividness when precepts of this kind are not limited to what is purely external and mechanical, but extend their pretensions to the activity of the artist in the sense that implies wealth of significance and intelligence. In this field our rules pass off to purely indefinite generalities, such as "the theme ought to be interesting, and each individual person must speak as is appropriate to his status, age, sex and situation." But if rules are really to suffice for such a purpose their directions ought to be formulated with such directness of detail that, without any further co-operation of mind, they could be executed precisely in the manner they are prescribed. Such rules being, in respect to this content, abstract, clearly and entirely fall short of their pretension of being able to complete the artistic consciousness. Artistic production is not a formal activity in accordance with a series of definitions; it is, as an activity of soul, constrained to work out of its own wealth, and to bring before the mind's eye a wholly other and far richer content, and a more embracing and unique creation than ever can be thus prescribed. In particular cases such rules may prove of assistance, in so far, that is, as they contain something really definite and consequently useful for practice. But even here their guidance will only apply to conditions wholly external.

(*b*) This above indicated tendency has consequently been wholly given up; but writers in doing so have only fallen as unreservedly into the opposite extreme. A work of art came to be looked upon, and so far rightly, as no longer the product of an activity *shared by all men*, but rather as a creation of a mind gifted in an extraordinary degree. A mind of this type has in this view *merely* to give free vent to its peculiar endowment, regarded as a specific natural power. It has to free itself absolutely from a pursuit of rules of universal application, as also from any admixture of conscious reflection with its creative and, as thus viewed, wholly instinctive powers, or rather it should be on its guard therefrom, the assumption being that such an exercise of conscious thought can only act on its creations as an infection and a taint. Agreeably to such a view the work of art has been heralded as the product of *talent* and *genius;* and it is mainly the aspect of natural gift inseparable from the ordinary conception of talent and genius, which has been emphasized. There is to some extent real truth in this. Talent is specific, genius universal capacity. With neither of these can a man endow himself *simply* by the exercise of his self-conscious activity. We shall consider this at greater length in a subsequent chapter.

In the present context we would merely draw attention to the false assumption in this view that in artistic production every kind of self-reflection upon the artist's own activity was regarded as not merely superfluous, but actually injurious. In such a view the process of creation by talent or genius simply is taken to be a general *state;* or we may define it more precisely as a condition of inspiration. To such a condition, it is said, genius is in some measure exalted by the subject-matter itself; it is also to some extent voluntarily able to place itself under such a condition, a process of self-inhibition in which the genial service of the champagne bottle is not forgotten. An idea of this kind was in vogue during the so-called "Epoch of Genius," which originated with the early poetical work of Goethe, receiving subsequent illustration in those of Schiller. These poets by their rejection of all rules hitherto fabricated made as it were an entirely new start; with deliberate intention they ran counter to such rules, and while doing so distanced all competitors by many lengths. I do not, however, propose to discuss with more detail the confusions which have prevailed over the conception of inspiration and genius, and the notion, which even at the present day finds advocates, that inspiration simply by itself can effect anything and everything.

The real and indeed sole point to maintain as essential is the thesis that although artistic talent and genius essentially implies an element of natural power, yet it is equally indispensable that it should be thoughtfully cultivated, that reflection should be brought to bear on the particular way it is exercised, and that it should be also kept alive with use and practice in actual work. The fact is that an important aspect of the creating process is merely facility in the use of a medium; that is to say, a work of art possesses a purely technical side, which extends to the borders of mere handicraft. This is most obviously the case in architecture and sculpture, less so in painting and music, least of all in poetry. A facility here is not assisted at all by inspiration; what solely indispensable is reflection, industry, and practice. Such technical skill an artist simply *must* possess in order that he may be master over the external material, and not be thwarted by its obstinacy.

Add to this that the more exalted the rank of an artist the more profoundly ought he to portray depths of soul and mind; and these are not to be known by flashlight, but are exclusively to be sounded if at all, by the direction of the man's own intelligence on the world of souls and the objective world. In this respect, therefore, once more *study* is the means whereby the artist brings to consciousness such a content, and appropriates the material and structure of his conceptions. At the same time no doubt one art will require such a conscious reception and cognitive mastery of the content in question more than another. Music, for example, which has exclusively to deal with the entirely undefined motion of the soul within, with the musical tones of that which is, relatively, feeling denuded of positive thought, has little or no need to bring home to consciousness the substance of intellectual conception. For this very reason musical talent declares itself as a rule in very early youth, when the head is still empty and the emotions have barely had a flutter; it has, in fact, attained real distinction at a time in the artist's life when both intelligence and life are practically without experience. And for the matter of that we often enough see very great accomplishment in musical composition and execution hung together with considerable indigence of mind and character. It is quite another matter in the case of poetry. What is of main importance here is a presentation of our humanity rich in subject-matter and reflective power, of its profounder interests, and of the forces which move it. Here at least mind and heart must themselves be richly and profoundly disciplined by life, experience, and thought before genius itself can bring into being the fruit that is ripe, the content that has substance, and is essentially consummate. The early productions of Goethe and Schiller are characterized by an immaturity, we may even call it a rawness and barbarity, which really are appalling. This phenomenon, that in the majority of those experiments we find a preponderating mass of features which are absolutely prosaic, or at least uninspired and commonplace, is a main objection to the ordinary notion that inspiration is inseparable from youth and its sirocco season. These two men of genius were the first beyond question to give our nation true works of poetry, are, in fact, our national poets; but for all that it was only their mature manhood, which made it a present of creations profound, sterling of their kind, creations of genuine inspiration, and no less technically complete in their artistic form. We naturally recall the case of the veteran Homer, who only composed and uttered his immortal songs in his old age.

(c) A third view, held relatively to the idea of a work of art as a product of human activity, concerns the position of such towards the phenomena of Nature. The natural tendency of ordinary thinking in this respect is to assume that the product of human art is of *subordinate* rank to the works of Nature. The work of art possesses no feeling of its own; it is not through and through a living thing, but, regarded as an external object, is a dead thing. It is usual to regard that which is alive of higher worth than what is dead. We may admit, of course, that the work of art is not in itself capable of movement and alive. The living natural thing is, whether looked at within or without, an organization with the life-purpose of such worked out into the minutest detail. The work of art merely attains to the show of animation on its surface. Below this it is ordinary stone, wood, or canvas, or in the case of poetry idea, the medium of such being speech and letters. But this element of external existence is not that which makes a work a creation of fine art. A work of art is only truly such in so far as originating in the human spirit, it continues to belong to the soil from which it sprang, has received, in short, the baptism of the mind and soul of man, and only presents that which is fashioned in consonance with such a sacrament. An interest vital to man, the spiritual values which the single event, one individual character, one action possesses in its devolution and final issue, is seized in the work of art and emphasized with greater purity and clarity than is possible on the ground of ordinary reality where human art is not. And for this reason the work of art is of higher rank than any product of Nature whatever, which has not submitted to this passage through the mind. In virtue of the emotion and insight, for example, in the atmosphere of which a landscape is portrayed by the art of painting, this creation of the human spirit assumes a higher rank than the purely natural landscape. Everything which partakes of spirit is better than anything begotten of mere Nature. However this may be, the fact remains that no purely natural existence is able, as art is, to represent divine ideals.

And further, all that the mind borrows from its own ideal content it is able, even in the direction of external existence, to endow with *permanence*. The individual living thing on the contrary is transitory; it vanishes and is unstable in its external aspect. The work of art persists. At the same time it is not mere continuation, but rather the form and pressure thereon of the mintage of soul-life which constitutes its true pre-eminence as contrasted with Nature's reality.

But this higher position we have thus assigned to the work of art is yet further contested by another prevalent conception of ordinary ideas. It is contended that Nature and all that proceeds from her are a work of God, created by His goodness and wisdom. The work of art is on the contrary *merely* a human product fashioned by human hands according to human design. The fallacy implied in this contrast between the products of Nature viewed as a divine creation and human activity as of wholly finite energy consists in the apparent assumption that God is not operative in and through man, but limits the sphere of His activity to Nature alone. We must place this false conception entirely on one side if we are desirous of penetrating to the true idea of art; or rather, as opposed to such a conception we ought to accept the extreme opposite thereto, namely, that God is more honoured by that which mind makes and creates than by everything brought into being and fashioned in the natural process. For not only is there a divinity in man, but it is actually effective in him in a form which is adequate to the essential nature of God in a far higher degree than in the work of Nature. God is a Spirit, and it is only in man that the medium, through which the Divine passes, possesses the form of spirit fully conscious of the activity in which it manifests its ideal presence. In Nature the medium correspondent to this is the unconscious sensuous and external *materia*, which is by many degrees inferior to consciousness in its worth. In the products of art God works precisely as He works through the phenomena of Nature. The divine substance, however, as it is asserted in the work of art has secured, being begotten of spirit life itself, a highway commensurable to its existence; determinate existence in the unconscious sensuousness of Nature is not a mode of appearance adequate to the Divine Being.

(*d*) Assuming, then, that the work of art is a creation of man in the sense that it is the offspring of mind or spirit we have still a further question in conclusion, which will help us to draw a more profound inference still from our previous discussion. That question is, "What is the human *need* which stimulates art-production?" On the one hand the artistic activity may be regarded as the mere play of accident, or human conceits, which might just as well be left alone as attempted. For, it may be urged, there are other and better means for carrying into effect the aims of art, and man bears within himself higher and more weighty interests, than art is capable of satisfying. In contrast to such a view art appears to originate in a higher impulse, and to satisfy more elevated needs, nay, at certain times, the highest and most absolute of all, being, as it has been, united to the most embracing views of entire epochs and nations upon the constitution of the world and the nature of their religion.

This inquiry, however, concerning a necessity for art which shall not be merely contingent, but absolute, we are not as yet able to answer with completeness; it demands, in fact, a concreter mode of exposition than is compatible with the form of this introduction. We must accordingly deem it sufficient for the present merely to establish the following points.

The universal and absolute want from which art on its side of essential form arises originates in the fact that man is a *thinking* consciousness, in other words that he renders explicit *to himself,* and from his own substance, what he is and all in fact that exists. The objects of Nature exist exclusively in immediacy and *once for all.* Man, on the contrary, as mind *reduplicates* himself. He is, to start with, an object of nature as other objects; but in addition to this, and no less truly, he exists *for himself;* he observes himself, makes himself present to his imagination and thought, and only in virtue of this active power of self-realization is he actually mind or spirit. This consciousness of himself man acquires in a twofold way; in the *first* instance *theoretically.* This is so in so far as he is under a constraint to bring himself in his own inner life to consciousness—all which moves in the human heart, all that surges up and strives therein—and generally, so far as he is impelled to make himself an object of perception and conception, to fix for himself definitely that which thought discovers as essential being, and in all that he summons out of himself, no less than in that which is received from without, to recognize only himself. And *secondly,* this realization is effected through a *practical* activity. In other words man possesses an impulse to assert himself in that which is presented him in immediacy, in that which is at hand as an external something to himself, and by doing so at the same time once more to recognize himself therein. This purpose he achieved by the alteration he effects in such external objects, upon which he imprints the seal of his inner life, rediscovering in them thereby the features of his own determinate nature. And man does all this, in order that he may as a free agent divest the external world of its stubborn alienation from himself—and in order that he may enjoy in the configuration of objective fact an external reality simply of himself. The very first impulse of the child implies in essentials this practical process of deliberate change in external fact. A boy throws stones into the stream, and then looks with wonder at the circles which follow in the water, regarding them as a result in which he sees something of his own doing. This human need runs through the most varied phenomena up to that particular form of self-reproduction in the external fact which is presented us in human art. And it is not merely in relation to external objects that man acts thus. He treats himself, that is, his natural form, in a similar manner: he will not permit it to remain as he finds it; he alters it deliberately. This is the rational ground of all ornament and decoration, though it may be as barbarous, tasteless, entirely disfiguring, nay, as injurious as the crushing of the feet of Chinese ladies, or the slitting of ears and lips. For it is among the really cultured alone that a change of figure, behaviour, and every mode and manner of self-expression will issue in harmony with the dictates of mental elevation.

This universal demand for artistic expression is based on the rational impulse in man's nature to exalt both the world of his soul experience and that of Nature for himself into the conscious embrace of mind as an object in which he rediscovers himself. He satisfies the demand of this spiritual freedom by making explicit to his *inner* life all that exists, no less than from the further point of view giving a realized *external* embodiment to the self made thus explicit. And by this reduplication of what is his own he places before the vision and within the cognition of himself and others what is within him. This is the free rationality of man, in which art as also all action and knowledge originates. We shall investigate at a latter stage the specific need for art as compared with that for other political and ethical action, or that for religious ideas and scientific knowledge.

2. We have hitherto considered the work of art under the aspect that it is fashioned by man; we will now pass over to the second part of our definition, that it is produced for his *sense-apprehension,* and

consequently is to a more or less degree under obligations to a sensuous medium.

(a) This reflection has been responsible for the inference that the function of fine art is to arouse feeling, more precisely the feeling which suits us—that is, pleasant feeling. From such a point of view writers have converted the investigation of fine art into a treatise on the emotions and asked what kind of feelings art ought to excite— take fear, for example, and compassion— with the further question how such can be regarded as pleasant, how, in short, the contemplation of a misfortune can bring satisfaction. This tendency of reflection dates for the most part from the times of Moses Mendelssohn, and many such trains of reasoning may be found in his writings. A discussion of this kind, however, did not carry the problem far. Feeling is the undefined obscure region of spiritual life. What is felt remains cloaked in the form of the separate personal experience under its most abstract persistence; and for this reason the distinctions of feeling are wholly abstract; they are not distinctions which apply to the subject-matter itself. To take examples— fear, anxiety, care, dread, are of course one type of emotion under various modifications; but in part they are purely quantitative degrees of intensity, and in part forms which reflect no light on their content itself, but are indifferent to it. In the case of fear, for instance, an existence is assumed, for which the individual in question possesses an interest, but sees at the same time the negative approach which threatens to destroy this existence, and thereupon discovers in immediate fusion within himself the above interest and the approach of that negative as a contradictory affection of his personal life. A fear of this sort, however, does not on its own account condition any particular content; it may associate with itself subject-matter of the most opposed and varied character. The feeling merely as such is in short a wholly empty form of a subjective state.

Such a form may no doubt in certain cases itself be essentially complex, as we find it is with hope, pain, joy, and pleasure; it may also in this very complexity appropriate various modes of content, as, for example, we have a feeling of justice, an ethical feeling, a sublime religious feeling, and so forth; but despite the fact that a content of this kind is present in different modes of feeling, no light whatever is thereby thrown on such content which will disclose its essential and definite character. The feeling throughout remains a purely subjective state which belongs to me, one in which the concrete fact vanishes, as though contracted to a vanishing point in the most abstract of all spheres. For this reason an inquiry over the nature of the emotions which art ought or ought not to arouse, comes simply to a standstill in the undefined; it is an investigation which deliberately abstracts from genuine content and its concrete substance and notion. Reflection upon feeling is satisfied with the observation of the personal emotional state and its singularity, instead of penetrating and sounding the matter for study, in other words the work of art, and in doing so bidding good-bye to the wholly subjective state and its conditions. In feeling, however, it is just this subjective state void of content which is not merely accepted, but becomes the main thing; and that is precisely why people are so proud of having emotions. And for no other reason that is why such an investigation is tedious owing to its indefinite nature and emptiness, and even repellent in its attention to trivial personal idiosyncrasies.

(b) Inasmuch, however, as the work of art is not merely concerned with exciting some kind of emotion or other—for this is an object it would share without any valid distinction with eloquence, historical composition, religious edification and much else—but is only a work of art in so far as it is beautiful, it occurred to reflective minds to discover a *specific feeling for*

beauty, and a distinct *sense-faculty* correspondent with it. In such an inquiry it
soon became clear that a sense of this kind
was no definite and mere instinct rigidly
fixed by Nature, which was able by itself
and independently to distinguish the beautiful. As a consequence the demand was
made for *culture* as a condition precedent
to such a sense, and the sense of beauty
as thus cultivated was called *taste,* which,
albeit an instructed apprehension and discovery of the beautiful, was none the less
assumed to persist in the character of immediate feeling. We have already discussed
the way in which abstract theory attempted
to form such a sense of taste, and how external and one-sided that sense remained.
While the critical sense generally of the
time when such ideas were in currency was
lacking in the *universality* of its principles,
as a *specific* critique of particular works of
art it was less concerned to substantiate a
judgment *more decisive* than hitherto—indeed the material to effectuate this was not
as yet forthcoming—than to promote in a
general way the *cultivation* of such a taste.
Consequently this educative process also
came to a halt in the region of the more
indefinite, and merely busied itself by its
reflections in the fitting out of feeling as a
sense of beauty in such a way that beauty
could immediately be discovered whenever
and wherever it might chance to appear.
The real depth of the subject-matter remained notwithstanding a closed book to
such a taste. Profundity of this kind demands not merely sensitive reception and
abstract thought, but the reason in its concrete grasp and the most sterling qualities
of soul-life. Taste on the contrary is merely
directed to the outside surfaces, which are
the playground of the feelings, and upon
one-sided principles may very well pass as
currency. But for this very reason our so-
called good taste is scared by every kind of
profounder artistic effect, and is dumb
where the ideal significance is in question,
and all mere externalities and accessories

vanish. For when great passions and the
movements of a profound soul assert themselves, we do not bother ourselves any more
with the finer distinctions of taste and its
retail traffic in trifles. It is conscious that
genius leaves such ground far behind it in
its stride; and shrinking before that power
feels on its part far more comfortable, not
knowing very well which way to turn.

(c) Thus it is the further change has
come about that critics of art-production no
longer have an eye simply to the education of taste, or are intent upon the illustration of such a sense. The *connoisseur,*
or art-scholar, has taken the place of the
man, or judge of artistic taste. The positive
side of art-scholarship, in so far as it implies a sound and exhaustive acquaintance
with the entire embrace of what is distinctive and peculiar in a given work of art,
we have already maintained to be a necessary condition of artistic research. A work
of art, owing to its nature, which, if it is
material from one point of view, is also related to a particular person, originates from
specific conditions of the most varied kind,
among which as exceptionally important we
may mention the date and place of its origins, the characteristic personality of the
artist, and, above all, the degree of executive accomplishment secured by the art. All
these points of view have to be taken into
consideration if we wish to obtain a view
and knowledge of such a work which is
clear in its outlines, and founded on a true
basis, nay, even wish to enjoy it rightly.
It is with these that our art-scholarship is
mainly occupied; and all that it can do for
us in this way should be gratefully accepted. Though it is quite true such art-
scholarship must be reckoned as of essential
importance, it ought not to be regarded as
the sole, or indeed the highest, constituent
in the relation of the contemplative spirit
to a work of art and art generally. Such
art-scholarship (this is the defective tendency) may restrict itself wholly to a knowledge of purely external characteristics,

either on the side of technique or historical condition, or in other directions; it may continue to possess the barest inkling of the true nature of a given work, or simply no knowledge at all. It may even form a depreciatory verdict on the value of profounder inquiries as compared with purely matter of fact, technical, and historical knowledge. Yet even so an art-scholarship, assuming it to be really genuine and thorough, at least proceeds upon grounds and knowledge which are definite, and an intelligent judgment; and it is association with such that our more accurate review of the distinct, if also to some extent exterior, aspects of a work of art, and our estimate of their relative significance, is secured.

(d) Following the above observations upon the modes of inquiry which were suggested by that aspect of a work of art in which, as itself an object with a material medium, it possessed an essential relation to man as himself receptive through sense, we will now examine this point of view in its more essential connection with art itself. We propose to do this partly (a) in respect to the art-product viewed as an object, partly (β) as regards the personal characteristics of the artist, his genius, talent, and so forth. We do not, however, propose to enter into matter which can in this connection exclusively proceed from the knowledge of art according to its universal concept. The truth is we are not as yet in the full sense on scientific ground; we have merely reached the province of external reflection.

(a) There is no question, then, that a work of art is presented to sensuous apprehension. It is submitted to the emotional sense, whether outer or inner, to sensuous perception and the imaged sense, precisely as the objective world is so presented around us, or as is our own inward sensitive nature. Even a speech, for example, may be addressed to the sensuous imagination and feeling. Notwithstanding this fact,

however, the work of art is not exclusively directed to the *sensuous* apprehension, viewed, that is, as an object materially conditioned. Its position is of the nature, that along with its sensuous presentation it is fundamentally addressed to the *mind*. The mind is intended to be affected by it and to receive some kind of satisfaction in it.

This function of the work of art at once makes it clear how it is that it is in no way intended to be a natural product or, on the side where it impinges on Nature, to possess the living principle of Nature. This, at least, is a fact whether the natural product is ranked lower or higher than a *mere* work of art, as people are accustomed to express themselves in the tone of depreciation.

In other words the sensuous aspect of a work of art has a right to determinate existence only in so far as it exists for the human mind, not, however, in so far as itself, as a material object, exists for itself independently.

If we examine more closely in what way the sensuous *materia* is presented to man we find that what is so can be placed under various relations to the mind.

(aa) The lowest in grade and that least compatible with relation to intelligence is purely sensuous sensation. It consists primarily in mere looking, listening, just as in times of mental overstrain it may often be a relaxation to go about without thought, and merely listen and have a look round. The mind, however, does not rest in the mere apprehension of external objects through sight and hearing; it makes them objective to its own inward nature, which thereupon is impelled itself to give effect to itself in these things as a further step under a sensuous mode, in other words, it relates itself to them as *desire*. In this appetitive relation to the external world man, as a sensuous particular thing, stands in a relation of opposition to things in general as in the same way particulars. He does not address himself to them with open mind and the universal ideas of thought; he retains an isolated position, with its personal impulses and interests, relatively to objects as fixed in their obduracy as himself, and makes himself at home in them by using them, or eating them up altogether, and, in short, gives effect to his self-satisfaction by the sacrifice he makes of them. In this negative relation desire requires for itself not merely the superficial show of external objects, but the actual things themselves in their material concrete existence. Mere pictures of the wood, which it seeks to make use of, or of the animals, which it hopes to eat up, would be of no service to desire. Just as little is it possible for desire to suffer the object to remain in its freedom; its craving is just this to force it to annihilate this self-subsistency and freedom of external facts, and to demonstrate that these things are only there to be destroyed and devoured. But at the same time the particular person is neither himself free, begirt as he is by the particular limited and transitory interests of his desires, for his definite acts do not proceed from the essential universality and rationality of his will, neither is he free relatively to the external world, for desire remains essentially determined by things and related to them.

This relation, then, of desire is not that in which man is related to the work of art. He suffers it to exist in its free independence as an object; he associates himself with it without any cravings of this kind, rather as with an object reflective of himself, which exists solely for the contemplative faculty of mind. For this reason, as we have said, the work of art, although it possesses sensuous existence, does not require sensuous concrete existence, nor yet the animated life of such objects. Or, rather, we should add, it *ought* not to remain on such a level, in so far as its true function is exclusively to satisfy spiritual interests, and to shut the door on all approach to mere desire. Hence

we can understand how it is that practical desire rates the particular works of Nature in the organic or inorganic world, which are at its service, more highly than works of art, which are obviously useless in this sense, and only contribute enjoyment to other capacities of man's spirit.

(ββ) A second mode under which the externally present comes before the conscious subject is, as contrasted with the single sensuous perception and active desire, the purely theoretical relation to the *intelligence*. The theoretic contemplation of objects has no interest in consuming the same in their particularity and satisfying or maintaining itself through the sense by their means; its object is to attain a knowledge of them in their *universality*, to seek out their ideal nature and principle, to comprehend them according to their notional idea. Consequently this contemplative interest is content to leave the particular things as they are, and stands aloof from them in their objective singularity, which is not the object of such a faculty's investigation. For the rational intelligence is not a property of the particular person in the sense that desire is so; it appertains to his singularity as being itself likewise essentially universal. So long as it persists in this relation of universality to the objects in question, it is his reason in its universal potency which is attempting to discover *itself* in Nature, and thereby the inward or essential being of the natural objects, which his sensuous existence does not present under its mode of immediacy, although such existence is founded therein. This interest of contemplation, the satisfaction of which is the lack of *science*, is, however, shared in this scientific form just as little by art as it shared in the common table of those impulses of the purely practical desire. Science can, it is true, take as its point of departure the sensuous thing in its singularity, and possess itself of some conception, how this individual thing is present in its specific colour or form. But for all that this isolated thing of sense as

GEORG WILHELM FRIEDRICH HEGEL

such possesses no further relation to mind, inasmuch as the interest of intelligence makes for the universal, the law, the thought and notion of the object, and consequently not only does it forsake it in its immediate singularity, but it actually transforms it within the region of idea, converting a concrete object of sense into an abstract subject-matter of thought, that is converting it into something other than the same object of its sensuous perception actually was. The artistic interest does not follow such a process, and is distinct from that of science for this reason. The contemplation of art restricts its interest simply in the way in which the work of art, as external object, in the directness of its definition, and in the singularity wherein it appears to sense, is manifested in all its features of colour, form, and sound, or as a single isolated vision of the whole; it does not go so far beyond the immediately received objective character as to propose, as is the case with science, the ideal or conceptive thinking of this particular objectivity under the terms of the rational and universal notion which underlies it.

The interest of art, therefore, is distinguishable from the practical interest of desire in virtue of the fact that it suffers its object to remain in its free independence, whereas desire applies it, even to the point of destruction, to its own uses. The contemplation of art, on the other hand, differs from that of a scientific intelligence in an analogous way in virtue of the fact that it cherishes an interest for the object in its isolated existence, and is not concerned to transform the same into terms of universal thought and notion.

(γγ) It follows, then, that, though the sensuous *materia* is unquestionably present in a work of art, it is only as surface or *show* of the sensuous that it is under any necessity to appear. In the sensuous appearance of the work of art it is neither the concrete material stuff, the empirically perceived completeness and extension of the internal organism which is the object of desire, nor is it the universal thought of pure ideality, which in either case the mind seeks for. Its aim is the sensuous presence, which, albeit suffered to persist in its sensuousness, is equally entitled to be delivered from the framework of its purely material substance. Consequently, as compared with the immediately envisaged and incorporated object of Nature, the sensuous presence in the work of art is transmuted to mere semblance or *show,* and the work of art occupies a midway ground with the directly perceived objective world on one side and the ideality of pure thought on the other. It is not as yet pure thought, but, despite the element of sensuousness which adheres to it, it is no longer purely material existence, in the sense at least that stones, plants, and organic life are such. The sensuous element in a work of art is rather itself somewhat of ideal intension, which, however, as not being actually the ideal medium of thought, is still externally presented at the same time as an object. This semblance of the sensuous presents itself to the mind externally as the form, visible appearance, and harmonious vibration of things. This is always assuming that it suffers the objects to remain in their freedom as objective facts, and does not seek to penetrate into their inward essence by abstract thought, for by doing so they would (as above explained) entirely cease to exist for it in their external singularity.

For this reason the sensuous aspect of art is only related to the two *theoretical* senses of *sight* and *hearing*; smell on the other hand, taste, and the feeling of touch are excluded from the springs of art's enjoyment. Smell, taste, and touch come into contact with matter simply as such, and with the immediate sensuous qualities of the same; smell with the material volatization through the air; taste with the material dissolution of substance, and touch or mere bodily feeling with qualities such as heat, coldness, smoothness, and so forth. On this account these senses cannot have to do with the objects of art, which ought to subsist in their actual and very independence, admitting of no purely sensuous or rather physical relation. The pleasant for such senses is not the beauty of art. Thus art on its sensuous side brings before us deliberately merely a shadow-world of shapes, tones, and imaged conceptions, and it is quite beside the point to maintain that it is simply a proof of the impotence and limitations of man that he can only present us with the surface of the physical world, mere *schemata,* when he calls into being his creative works. In art these sensuous shapes and tones are not offered as exclusively for themselves and their form to our direct vision. They are presented with the intent to secure in such shape satisfaction for higher and more spiritual interests, inasmuch as they are mighty to summon an echo and response in the human spirit evoked from all depths of its conscious life. In this way the sensuous is *spiritualized* in art, or, in other words, the life of *spirit* comes to dwell in it under sensuous guise.

(β) For this reason, however, a product of art is only possible in so far as it has received its passage through the mind, and has originated from the productive activity of mind. This brings us to another question we have to answer, and it is this: "How is the sensuous or material aspect, which is imperative as a condition of art, operative in the artist as conjoined to his personal productive activity?" Now this mode or manner of artistic production contains, as an activity personal to the artist, in essentials just the same determinants which we found posited in the work of art. It must be a spiritual activity, which, however, at the same time possesses in itself the element of sensuousness and immediacy. It is neither, on the one hand, purely mechanical work, such as is purely unconscious facility in sleight of hand upon physical objects; or a

stereotyped activity according to teachable rule of thumb; nor, on the other hand, is it a productive process of science, which tends to pass from sensuous things to abstract ideas and thoughts, or is active exclusively in the medium of pure thought. In contrast to these the two aspects of mental idea and sensuous material must in the artistic product be united. For example, it would be possible in the case of poetical compositions to attempt to embody what was the subject-matter in the form of prosaic thought in the first instance, and only after doing so to attach to the same imaginative ideas rhymes and so on, so that as a net result such imagery would be appendent to the abstract reflections as so much ornament and decoration. An attempt of this kind, however, could only lead us to a poor sort of poetry, for in it we should have operative a twofold kind of activity in its *separation,* which in the activity of genuine artistic work only holds good in inseparable unity. It is this true kind of creative activity which forms what is generally described as the artistic *imagination.* It is the rational element, which in its import as spirit only exists, in so far as it actively forces its way into the presence of consciousness, yet likewise, and only subject to this condition, displays all its content to itself under a sensuous form. This activity possesses therefore a spiritual content, but it clothes the same in sensuous image, and for this reason, that it is only able to come to a knowledge of the same under this sensuous garb. We may compare such a process with that of a man of experience in life, a man, shall we add, of real geniality and wit, who—while at the same time being fully conscious in what the main importance of life consists, what are the things which essentially bind men together, what moves them and is the mainspring of their lives—nevertheless has neither brought home this content in universal maxims, nor indeed is able to unfold it to others in the generalities of the reflective process, but makes these mature results of his intelligence without exception clear to himself and others in particular cases, whether real or invented, or by examples and such like which hit the mark. For in the ideas of such a man everything shapes itself into the concrete image determinate in its time and place, to which therefore the addition of names and any other detail of external condition causes no difficulty. Yet such a kind of imagination rather rests on the recollection of conditions, he has lived through, actual experience, than it is a creative power of itself. Memory preserves and renews the particularity and external fashion of such previous events with all their more distinct circumstances, but on the other hand does not suffer the universal to appear independently. The creative imagination of an artist is the imagination of a great mind and a big heart; it is the grasp and excogitation of ideas and shapes, and, in fact, nothing less than this grasp of the profoundest and most embracing human interests in the wholly definite presentations of imagery borrowed from objective experience. A consequence of this is, that imagination of this type is based in a certain sense on a natural gift, a general talent for it, as we say, because its creative power essentially implies an aspect of sense presentation. It is no doubt not unusual to speak in the same way of scientific "talent." The sciences, however, merely presuppose the general capacity for thought, which does not possess, as imagination does, together with its intellectual activity, a reference to the concrete testimony of Nature, but rather precisely abstracts from the activity that form in which we find it in Nature. It would be, therefore, truer to the mark if we said there is no specific scientific talent in the sense of a purely natural endowment. Imagination, on the other hand, combines within it a mode of instinct-like creativeness. In other words the essential plasticity and material element in a work of art is subjectively present in the artist as

part of his native disposition and impulse, and as his unconscious activity belongs in part to that which man receives straight from Nature. No doubt the entire talent and genius of an individual is not wholly exhausted by that we describe as natural capability. The creation of art is quite as much a spiritual and self-cognized process; but for all that we affirm that its spirituality contains an element of plastic or configurative facility which Nature confers on it. For this reason, though almost anybody can reach a certain point in art, yet, in order to pass beyond this—and it is here that the art in question really begins —a talent for art which is inborn and of a higher order altogether is indispensable.

Considered simply as a natural basis a talent of this kind asserts itself for the most part in early youth, and is manifested in the restless persistency, ever intent with vivacity and alertness, to create artistic shapes in some particular sensuous medium, and to make this mode of expression and utterance the unique one or the one of main importance and most suitable. And thus also a virtuosity up to a certain point in the technique of art which is arrived at with ease is a sign of inborn talent. A sculptor finds everything convertible into plastic shape, and from early days takes to modelling clay; and so on generally whatever men of such innate powers have in their minds, whatever excites and moves their souls, becomes forthwith a plastic figure, a drawing, a melody, or a poem.

(γ) Thirdly, and in conclusion: the *content* of art is also in some respects borrowed from the objective world perceived in sense, that is Nature; or, in any case, if the content is also of a spiritual character, it can only be grasped in such a way, that the spiritual element therein, as human relations, for example, are displayed in the form of phenomena which possess objective reality.

3. There is yet another question to solve, namely, what the interest or the *End* is,

which man proposes to himself in the creation of the content embodied by a work of art. This was, in fact, the third point of view, which we propounded relatively to the art-product. Its more detailed discussion will finally introduce us to the true notional concept of art itself.

If we take a glance at our ordinary ideas on this subject, one of the most prevalent is obviously

(a) The principle of the imitation of Nature. According to this view the essential aim or object of art consists in imitation, by which is understood a facility in copying natural forms as present to us in a manner which shall most fully correspond to such facts. The success of such an exact representation of Nature is assumed to afford us complete satisfaction.

(α) Now in this definition there is to start with absolutely nothing but the formal aim to bring about the bare repetition a second time by man, so far as his means will permit of this, of all that was already in the external world, precisely too in the way it is there. A repetition of this sort may at once be set down as

(aa) A *superfluous* task for the reason that everything which pictures, theatrical performances represent by way of imitation—animals, natural scenery, incidents of human life—we have already elsewhere before us in our gardens or at home, or in other examples of the more restricted or extended reaches of our personal acquaintance. Looked at, moreover, more closely, such a superfluity of energy can hardly appear otherwise than a presumptuous trifling; it is so because

(ββ) It lags so far behind Nature. In other words art is limited in its means of representation. It can only produce one-sided illusions, a semblance, to take one example, of real fact addressed exclusively to *one* sense. And, moreover, if it does wholly rely on the bare aim of *mere* imitation, instead of Nature's life all it gives us ever is the mere pretence of its sub-

stance. For some such reason the Turks, who are Mohammedans, will not put up with any pictures or copies of men and other objects. When James Bruce, in his travels through Abyssinia, showed a painted fish to a Turk, that worthy was at first astonished; but, quickly recovering himself, he made answer as follows: "If this fish shall rise up against you at the last day, and say, 'You have certainly given me a body, but no living soul,' how are you going to justify yourself against such a complaint?" . . . There are, no doubt, no less examples of completely deceptive imitation. The painted grapes of Zeuxis have been accepted from antiquity and long after as an instance of art's triumph, and also of that of the principle of imitation, because, we are told, actual doves pecked at them. . . . But if we will only reflect a moment on such and other instances we can only come to the conclusion that instead of praising works of art, because they have deceived *even* doves and monkeys, the foolish people ought to be condemned who imagine that the quality of a work of art is enhanced if they are able to proclaim an effect of the same so miserable as the supreme and last word they can say for it. In short, to sum up, we may state emphatically that in the mere business of imitation art cannot maintain its rivalry with Nature, and if it makes the attempt it must look like a worm which undertakes to crawl after an elephant.

(γγ) Having regard, then, to this invariable failure, that is, relative of human imitation as contrasted with the natural prototype, we have no end left us but the pleasure offered by sleight of hand in its effort to produce something which resembles Nature. And it is unquestionably a fact that mankind are able to derive enjoyment from the attempt to reproduce with their individual labour, skill, and industry what they find about them. But a delight and admiration of this kind also becomes, if taken alone, indeed just in proportion as the copy follows slavishly the thing copied, so much the more icily null and cold, or brings its reaction of surfeit and repugnance. There are portraits which, as has been drily remarked, are positively shameless in their likeness; and Kant brings forward a further example of this pleasure in imitation pure and simple to the effect that we are very soon tired of a man—and there really are such—who is able to imitate the nightingale's song quite perfectly; for we no sooner find that it is a man who is producing the strain than we have had enough of it. We then take it to be nothing but a clever trick, neither the free outpouring of Nature, nor yet a work of art. We expect, in short, from the free creative power of men something quite other than a music of this kind, which only retains our interest when, as in the case of the nightingale's note, it breaks forth in unpremeditated fashion, resembling in this respect the rhythmic flood of human feeling, from the native springs of its life. And as a general rule this delight we experience in the skill of imitation can only be of a restricted character; it becomes a man better to derive enjoyment from that which he brings to birth from himself. In this respect the invention of every insignificant technical product is of higher rank; and mankind may feel more proud of having invented the hammer, nail, and so forth, than in making themselves adepts as imitators. For this abstract zest in the pursuit of imitation is on the same lines as the feat of the man who had taught himself to throw lentils through a small aperture without missing. He made an exhibition of this feat to Alexander, and Alexander merely made him a present as a reward for this art, empty and useless as it was, of a bushel of lentils.

(β) Inasmuch as, moreover, the principle of imitation is purely formal, *objective beauty* itself disappears, if that principle is accepted as the end. For the question is then no longer what is the *constitution* of that which is to be imitated, but simply whether the copy is *correct* or no. The object and the content of the beautiful comes to be regarded as a matter of indifference. When, in other words, putting the principle of mere imitation on one side, we speak, in connection with animals, human beings, places, actions, and characters, of a distinction between beauty and ugliness, it remains none the less the fact that relatively to such a principle we are referring to a distinction which does not properly belong to an art for which we have appropriated this principle of imitation to the exclusion of all others. In such a case, therefore, whenever we select objects and attempt to distinguish their beauty and ugliness, owing to this absence of a standard we can apply to the infinite forms of Nature, we have in the final resort only left us the *personal taste*, which is fixed by no rule, and admits of no discussion. And, in truth, if we start, in the selection of objects for representation, from that which mankind *generally* discover as beautiful and ugly, and accept accordingly for artistic imitation, in other words, from their particular taste, there is no province in the domain of the objective world which is not open to us, and which is hardly likely to fail to secure its admirer. At any rate, among men we may assume that, though the case of every husband and his wife may be disputed, yet at least every bridegroom regards his bride as beautiful; very possibly being the only person who does so; and that an individual taste for a beauty of this kind admits of no fixed rules at all may be regarded as a bit of bad luck for both parties. If, moreover, we cast a glance wholly beyond mere individuals and their accidental taste to that of nations, this again is full of diversity and oppositions. . . . Indeed, if we consider the works of art of those extra-European peoples, their images of gods, for instance, which have been imaginatively conceived as worthy of veneration and sublime, they can only appear to us as frightful idols; their music will merely ring in our ears as an abominable noise, while, from the opposite point of view, such aliens will regard our sculptures, paintings, and musical compositions as having no meaning or actually ugly.

(γ) But even assuming that we abstract from an objective principle of art, and retain the beautiful as established on the subjective and individual taste, we shall soon discover, from the point of view of art itself, that the imitation of natural objects, which appeared to be a universal principle, and indeed one secured by important authorities, is not to be relied upon, at least under this general and wholly abstract conception of it. If we look at the particular arts we cannot fail to observe that, albeit painting and sculpture portray objects which resemble those of Nature, or the type of which is essentially borrowed from Nature, the works of architecture on the contrary—and this, too, is one of the *fine* arts—quite as little as the compositions of poetry, to the extent at least that these latter are not restricted to mere description, cannot justly be described as imitations of Nature. At any rate, if we are desirous of maintaining such a thesis with respect to the arts thus excluded, we should find ourselves forced to make important deviations from the track, in order to condition our proposition in various ways, and level down our so-called truth at least to the plane of probability. But once accept probability, and we should again be confronted with a great difficulty in determining precisely what is and what is not probable; and in the end no one could really think of or succeed, even if he did so, in excluding from poetry all compositions of an entirely capricious and completely imaginative character.

The end or object of art must therefore consist in something other than the purely formal imitation of what is given to objective sense, which invariably can merely call into being technical *legerdemain* and not *works* of art. It is no doubt an essential constituent of a work of art that it should have

natural forms as a foundation, because the mode of its representation is in external form, and thereby along with it in that of natural phenomena. In painting it is obviously an important study to learn to copy with accuracy colours in their mutual relations, such as light effects and reflections, and so forth, and, with no less accuracy, the forms and shapes of objects carried into their most subtle gradations of line. It is in this respect that in modern times more particularly the principle of the imitation of Nature and naturalism generally has come into vogue. The object has been to recall an art, which has deteriorated into weakness and nebulosity, to the strength and determinate outlines of Nature, or, in yet another direction, as against the purely arbitrary caprice and convention of a studio, which is in truth as remote from Nature as it is from art, and merely indicates the path of art's declension, to assert the claim of the legitimate, direct, and independent, no less than coherent stability of natural fact. But while admitting that from a certain point of view such an effort is reasonable enough, yet for all that the naturalism which it demands, taken by itself, is neither the substantive thing, not yet of primary importance, in the true basis of art; and although the external fact in its natural appearance constitutes an element of essential value, yet the objective fact alone does not supply the *standard* of rightness, nor is the mere imitation of external phenomena, in their external shape that is, the *end* of art.

(b) And as a consequence of this we have the further question—"What is the true *content* of art, and with what aim is that content brought before us?" On this head we are confronted by the common opinion that it is the task and object of art to bring before our sense, feeling, and power of emulation *every thing* that the spirit of man can perceive or conceive. Art has in short to realize for us the well-known saying, "*Nihil humani a me alienum puto."* Its object is therefore declared to be that of arousing and giving life to slumbering emotions, inclinations, passions of *every* description, of filling the heart up to the brim; of compelling mankind, whether cultured or the reverse, to pass through all that the human soul carries in its most intimate and mysterious chambers, all that it is able to experience and reproduce, all that the heart is able to stir and evoke in its depths and its countlessly manifold possibilities; and yet further to deliver to the domain of feeling and the delight of our vision all that the mind may possess of essential and exalted being in its thought and the Idea—that majestic hierarchy of the noble, eternal, and true; and no less to interpret for us misfortune and misery, wickedness and crime; to make the hearts of men realize through and through all that is atrocious and dreadful, no less than every kind of pleasure and blessedness; and last of all to start the imagination like a rover among the day-dream playing-fields of the fancy, there to revel in the seductive mirage of visions and emotions which captivate the senses. All this infinitely manifold content—so it is held—it is the function of art to explore, in order that by this means the experience of our external life may be repaired of its deficiencies, and yet from a further point of view that the passions we share with all men may be excited, not merely that the experiences of life may not have us unmoved, but that we ourselves may thereafter long to make ourselves open channels of a universal experience. Such a stimulus is not presented on the plane of actual experience itself, but can only come through the semblance of it, that is to say through the illusions which art, in its creations, substitutes for the actual world. And the possibility of such a deception, by means of the semblances of art, depends on the fact that all reality must for man pass through the medium of the vision and imaginative idea; and it is only after such a passage that it penetrates the emotional life

and the will. In such a process it is of no consequence whether it is immediate external reality which claims his attention, or whether the result is effected by some other way, in other words by means of images, symbols, and ideas, which contain and display the content of such actuality. Men are able to imagine things, which do not actually exist, as if they did exist. Consequently it is precisely the same thing for our emotional life, whether it is the objective world or merely the show of the same, in virtue of which a situation, a relation, or any content of life, in short, is brought home to us. Either mode is equally able to stir in us an echo to the essential secret which it carries, whether it be in grief or joy, in agitation or convulsion, and can cause to flow through us the feelings and passions of anger, hate, pity, anxiety, fear, love, reverence and admiration, honour and fame.

The awakening of every kind of emotion in us, the drawing our soul through every content of life, the realization of all these movements of soul-life by means of a presence which is only external as an illusion—this it is which, in the opinion described, is pre-eminently regarded as the peculiar and transcendent power of artistic creation.

We must not, however, overlook the fact that in this view of art as a means to imprint on the soul and the mind what is good and evil alike, to make man more strong in the pursuit of what is noblest, no less than enervate his definite course, by transporting his emotional life through the most sensuous and selfish desires, the task as yet proposed to art remains throughout of an entirely formal character; without possessing independently an assured aim all that art can offer is the empty form for every possible kind of ideal and formative content.

(c) As a matter of fact art does possess this formal side, namely, that it is able to bring before our senses and feeling and artistically adorn every possible kind of material, precisely as the thoughts of ordinary reflection elaborate every possible subject-matter and models of action, supplying the same with its equipment of reasons and vindications. In the presence, however, of such a variety of content we cannot fail to observe that these diversified emotions and ideas, which it is assumed art has to stimulate or enforce, intersect each other, contradict and mutually cancel each other. Indeed, under this aspect, the more art inspires men to emotions thus opposed, to that extent precisely it merely enlarges the cleavage in their feelings and passions, and sets them staggering about in Bacchantic riot, or passes over into sophistry and scepticism precisely as your ordinary free thinkers do. This variety of the material of art itself compels us, therefore, not to remain satisfied with so formal a determination. Our rational nature forces its way into this motley array of discord, and demands to see the resurrection of a higher and more universal purpose from these elements despite their opposition, and to be conscious of its attainment. Just in a similar manner the social life of mankind and the State are no doubt credited with the aim that in them *all* human capacities and *all* individual potencies should meet with expansion and expression in *all* their features and tendencies. But in opposition to so formal a view there very quickly crops up the question in what *unity* these manifold manifestations are to be concentrated, and what *single end* they must have for their fundamental concept and ultimate end. Just as in the case of the notional concept of the human State so too there arises in that of human art the need, as to a part thereof, for an end *common* to the particular aspects, no less than in part for one which is more exalted and *substantive* in its character.

As such a substantive end the conclusion of reflection is readily brought home to us that art possesses at once the power and function to mitigate the savagery of mere desires.

(*a*) With regard to this first conception we have merely to ascertain what characteristic peculiar to art implies this possibility of eliminating this rawness of desire, and of fettering and instructing the impulses and passions. Coarseness in general has its ground-root in an unmitigated self-seeking of sensuous impulses, which take their plunge off and are exclusively intent on the satisfaction of their concupiscence. Sensual desire is, however, all the more brutal and domineering, in proportion as, in its isolation and confinement, it appropriates the *entire man,* so that he does not retain the power to separate himself in his universal capacity from this determinacy and to maintain the conscious presence of such universality. Even if the man in such a case explains, "the passion is mightier than myself," though it is true no doubt that for that man's mind the abstract ego is separate from the particular passion, yet it is purely so in a formal way. All that such a separation amounts to is that as against the force of the passion the ego, in its universal form or competency, is of no account at all. The savageness of passion consists therefore in the fusion of the ego as such a universal with the confined content of its desire, so that a man no longer possesses volitional power outside this single passion. Such savageness and untamed force of the possibilities of passion art mitigates in the first instance to the extent that it brings home to the mind and imagination of man what he does actually feel and carry into effect in such a condition. And even if art restricts itself to this that it places before the vision of the mind pictures of passion, nay, even assuming such to be flattering pictures, yet for all that a power of amelioration is contained therein. At least we may say, that by this means is brought before a man's intelligence what apart from such presentment he merely *is.* The man in this way contemplates his impulses and inclinations; and whereas apart from this they whirl him away without giving him time to reflect, he now sees them outside himself and already, for the reason that they come before him rather as objects than a part of himself, he begins to be free from them as aliens. For this reason it may often happen that an artist, under the weight of grief, mitigates and weakens the intensity of his own emotions in their effect upon him by the artistic representation of them. Comfort, too, is to be found even in tears. The man who to start with is wholly given up to and concentrated in sorrow, is able thus, at any rate, to express that which is merely felt within in a direct way. Yet more alleviating is the utterance of such inner life in words, images, musical sound, and shapes.

It was therefore a good old custom in the case of funerals and layings-out to appoint wailing women, in order to give audible expression to grief, or generally to create an external sympathy. For manifestations of sympathy bring the content of human sorrow to the sufferer in an objective form; he is by their repetition driven to reflect upon it, and the burden is thereby made lighter. And so it has from of old been considered that to weep or to speak oneself out are equally means whereby freedom is secured from the oppressing burden, or at least the heart is appreciably lifted. Consequently the mitigation of the violence of passions admits of this general explanation that man is released from his unmediated confinement in an emotion, becomes aware of it as a thing external to himself, to which he is consequently obliged to place himself in an ideal relation. Art, while still remaining within the sphere of the senses, faces man from the might of his sensitive experience by means of its representations. No doubt we frequently hear that pet phrase of many that it is man's duty to remain in immediate union with Nature. Such union is in its unmediated purity nothing more or less than savagery

and wildness; and art, precisely in the way that it dissolves this unity for human beings, lifts them with gentle hands over this inclosure in Nature. The way men are occupied with the objects of art's creation remains throughout of a contemplative character; and albeit in the first instance it educates merely an attention to the actual facts portrayed, yet over and beyond this, and with a power no less decisive, it draws man's attention to their significance, it forces him to compare their content with that of others, and to receive without reserve the general conclusions of such a survey and all the ramifications such imply.

(β) To the characteristic above discussed adheres in natural sequence the second which has been predicated of art as its essential aim, namely, the *purification* of the passions, an instruction, that is, and a building to *moral* completeness. For the defining role that art has to bridle savage nature and educate the passions remained one wholly formal and general, so that the further question must arise as to a *specific* kind and an essential and *culminating* point of such an educative process.

($\alpha\alpha$) The doctrine of the purification of the passions shares in the defect previously noted as adhering to the mitigation of desires. It does, however, emphasize more closely the fact that the representations of art needed a standard, by means of which it would be possible to estimate their comparative worth and unworth. This standard is just their effectiveness to separate what is pure from that which is the reverse in the passions. Art, therefore, requires a content which is capable of expressing this purifying power, and in so far as the power to assert such effectiveness is assumed to constitute the substantive end of art, the purifying content will consist in asserting that effective power before consciousness in its *universality* and *essentiality*.

($\beta\beta$) It is a deduction from the point of view just described that it is the end of art to *instruct*. Thus, on the one hand, the peculiar character of art consists in the movement of the emotions and in the satisfaction which is found in this movement, even in fear, compassion, in painful agitation and shock—that is to say, in the satisfying concern of the feelings and passions, and to that extent in a complacent, delighted, or enthusiastic attitude to the objects of art and their presentation and effect: while, on the other hand, this artistic object is held to discover its higher standard exclusively in its power to instruct, in the *fabula docet,* and thereby in the usefulness, which the work of art is able to exercise on the recipient. . . .

In respect, then, to such instruction we have to ask whether the idea is that the same ought to be direct or indirect in the work of art, explicit or implicit.

Now if the question at issue is one of general importance to art about a universal rather than contingent purpose, such an ultimate end, on account of the essential spirituality of art, can only be itself of spiritual import; in other words, so far from being of accidental importance it must be true in virtue of its own nature and on its own account. An end of this kind can only apply to instruction in so far as a genuine and essentially explicit content is brought before the mind by means of the work of art. From such a point of view we are entitled to affirm that it is the function of art to accept so much the more of a content of this nature within its compass in proportion to the nobility of its rank, and that only in the verity of such a content will it discover the standard according to which the pertinency of or the reverse of what is expressed is adjudged. Art is in truth the primary *instructress* of peoples.

But, on the other hand, if the object of instruction is so entirely treated as an *end* that the universal nature of the content presented cannot fail to be asserted and rendered bluntly on its own account explicit as abstract thesis, prosaic reflection or general maxim, rather than merely in an indi-

rect way contained by implication in the concrete embodiment of art, then and in that case, by means of such a separation, the sensuous, plastic configuration, which is precisely that which makes the artistic product a *work of art,* is merely an otiose accessory, a husk, a semblance, which are expressly posited as nothing more than *shell* and semblance. Thereby the very nature of a work of art is abused. For the work of art ought not to bring before the imaginative vision a content in its universality as such, but rather this universality under the mode of individual concreteness and distinctive sensuous particularity. If the work in question does not conform to such a principle, but rather sets before us the generalization of its content with the express object of instruction pure and simple, then the imaginative no less than the material aspect of it are merely an external and superfluous ornament, and the work of art is itself a shattered thing within that ornament, a ruin wherein form and content no longer appear as a mutually adherent growth. For, in the case supposed, the particular object of the senses and the ideal content apprehended by the mind have become external to one another.

Furthermore, if the object of art is assumed to consist in utilitarian *instruction* of this kind, that other aspect of delight, entertainment, and diversion is simply abandoned on its own account as *unessential;* it has now to look for its substance to the utility of the matter of instruction, to which it is simply an accompaniment. But this amounts to saying, that art does not carry its vocation and purpose in itself, but that its fundamental conception is in something else, to which it subserves as a *means.* Art becomes, in short, merely one of the many means, which are either of use, or may be employed to secure, the aim of instruction. This brings us to the boundary line where art can only cease to be an end on its own independent account; it is deliberately deposed either to the mere plaything of entertainment, or a mere means of instruction.

(γγ) The line of this limit is most emphasized when the question is raised as to the end or object of highest rank for the sake of which the passions have to be purified or men have to be instructed. This goal has frequently in modern times been identified with *moral improvement,* and the end of art is assumed to consist in this that its function is to prepare our inclinations and impulses, and generally to conduct us to the supreme goal of moral perfection. In this view we find instruction and purification combined. The notion is that art by the insight it gives us of genuine moral goodness, in other words, through its instruction, at the same time summons us to the process of purification, and in this way alone can and ought to bring about the improvement of mankind as the right use they can make of it and its supreme object.

With reference to the relation in which art stands to the end of improvement, we may practically say the same thing as we did about the didactic end. It may readily be admitted that art as its principle ought not to make the immoral and its advance its end. But it is one thing deliberately to make immorality the aim of its presentation and another not expressly to do so in the case of morality. It is possible to deduce an excellent moral from any work of art whatever; but such depends, of course, on a particular interpretation and consequently on the individual who draws the moral. The defence is made of the most immoral representations on the ground that people ought to become acquainted with evil and sin in order to act morally. Conversely, it has been maintained that the portrayal of Mary Magdalene, the fair sinner, who afterwards repented, has seduced many into sin, because art makes repentance look so beautiful, and you must first sin before you can repent. The doctrine of moral improvement, however logically carried out, is not merely satisfied that a moral

should be conceivably deducible from a work of art through interpretation; on the contrary, it would have the moral instruction clearly made to emerge as the substantive aim of the work; nay, further, it would deliberately exclude from art's products all subjects, characters, actions, and events which fail to be moral in its own sense. For art, in distinction from history and the sciences, which have their subject-matter determined for them, has a choice in the selection of its subjects.

In order that we may be in a position to estimate this view of the moral end of art on the basis of principle, we ought above all to raise the question as to the precise standpoint of the morality which is recommended for our reception by this view. If we examine more closely the standpoint of morality such as is submitted us to-day under an enlightened interpretation, we soon discover that its conception does not immediately coincide with that which we describe in a general way as virtue, respectability, uprightness, and so forth. To be a respectable honest man is not sufficient to make a man moral in the sense under discussion, for morality in this sense implies *reflection* and the definite consciousness of what is consonant with duty, and the acts which issue from such a consciousness. Now duty is itself the law of the will, which man, however, freely establishes out of himself, and thereon is taken to determine himself to this duty for duty's sake and its fulfillment's sake; in other words he only does good as acting under the conviction already secured that it is the good. This law—the duty which is selected and carried into effect for duty's sake to be the rule of conduct out of free conviction and the inner conscience—is, on its own account, the abstract universal of the will, which is the absolute antithesis to Nature, the impulses of sense, selfish interests, the passions and all that is commonly described collectively as emotional life and heart. In this opposition the one side is regarded as *ne-*

gating the other; and for the reason that both are present in the individual in their opposition, he is compelled, as determining himself from his own identity, to adopt the choice of one to the rejection of the other. Such a decision and the act carried out in accordance with it merely become moral from the standpoint now considered on the one hand in virtue of the free conviction of duty, and on the other by reason of the victory secured not only over the particular will, the natural motives, inclinations, passions and so on, but also in virtue of the noble feelings and higher impulses. For the modern ethic starts from the fixed opposition between the will in its spiritual universality and its sensuous natural particularity; it does not consist in the perfected mediation of these opposed aspects, but in their mutual conflict as opposed to one another, which carries with it the demand, that the impulses in their antagonism to duty ought to yield to it.

An opposition of this nature is not merely present to mind in the restricted confines of moral action; it asserts itself as a fundamental severance and antithesis between that which is actual essentially, and on its own account, and that which is external reality and existence. Apprehended in entirely formal terms it is the contrast exposed by the universal, in so far as it is fixed in its substantive independence over against the particular, as the latter is also on its part rigidly exterior to it. In more concrete form it appears in Nature as the opposition of the abstract law to the wealth of particular phenomena, each of which possesses its specific characteristics. It appears in mind as that between the sensuous and spiritual in man, as the conflict of spirit with the flesh; it is that of duty for duty's sake; of the cold imperative with particular impulses, the warm heart, the sensuous inclinations and impulses, in a word with man simply as individual. Or it appears as the harsh antagonism between the inward freedom and the external necessity of natural condition, and, lastly, as the contra-

diction of the dead, essentially emptied, concept, when confronted with the fulness of concrete life, in other words, of theory and subjective thought as contrasted with objective existence and experience.

Such are antithetical points of view, the discovery of which is not to be ascribed either to the ingenuity of reflective minds, or the pedantry of a philosophical cult. They have in all ages, if in manifold guise, occupied and disquieted the human consciousness, although it is our more modern culture which has emphasized their opposition most deliberately, and forced it in each case to the keenest edge of contradiction. Intellectual culture, or rather the rapier edge of the modern understanding, creates in man this contrast, which converts him into some amphibious animal. He is compelled to live in two worlds mutually contradictory; and in this divided house consciousness, too, wanders aimlessly; tossed over from one side to the other it is unable to discover permanent satisfaction for itself in either one side or the other. For, on the one hand, we see mankind confined within common reality and earthly temporal condition, oppressed by necessity and want, in Nature's toils, entangled in matter, in sensuous aims and their enjoyment, dominated and whirled away by impulse and passion. On the other hand he lifts himself up to eternal ideas, to a realm of thought and freedom. As Will he legislates for himself universal laws and destinations, he disrobes the world of the life and blossom of its reality; he dissolves it in abstractions, that the mind may vindicate its right and intrinsic worth by this very dissolution of Nature's rights and such maltreatment, a process in which he brings home to her again the necessity and violence he has experienced at her hands. Such a cleavage of life and mind is, however, accompanied for modern culture with the demand that a contradiction so deep-seated should be dissolved. The mere understanding of abstract reflection is unable to disengage itself from the obstinacy of such contradictions. The solution consequently remains here for consciousness a mere *ought,* and the present and reality is merely moved within the continuous unrest of a to and fro, which seeks for that reconciliation it is unable to find. The problem therefore arises whether such a many-sided and fundamental antagonism, which is unable to pass beyond the mere ought and postulate of its solution, can be the essential and wholly expressed truth, and, indeed, the final and supreme consummation. If the culture of the civilized world has fallen into such a contradiction it becomes the task of philosophy to dissolve the same, in other words to demonstrate that neither the one side or the other, in its onesided abstractness, should be held to possess truth, but that they contain within themselves the principle of their dissolution. The truth only *then* comes before us in the reconciliation and mediation of both; and this mediation is no mere postulate, but is, in its essential nature, and in its actual presence the at the same time accomplished and self-accomplishing. And, in fact, this view agrees directly with unwitting faith and will, which always has before its conscious life this contradiction in its resolution, and in action accepts it as its aim and carries it into effect. All that philosophy achieves is to contribute the insight of thought into the essence of such cleavage. It demonstrates, or seeks to demonstrate, how that which truth really is is simply the resolution of the fracture, and, be it added, not in the sense that this antagonism and its alternative aspects in any way *are not,* but in the sense that they are *there* in reconciliation.

(*d*) When discussing moral improvement as the ultimate end accepted for art it was found that its principle pointed to a higher standpoint. It will be necessary also to vindicate this standpoint for art.

Thereby the false position to which we have already directed attention vanishes, namely, that art has to serve as a means for moral ends and the moral end of the world generally by means of its didactive and ameliorating influence, and by doing so has its essential aim not in itself, but in something else. If we therefore continue still to speak of an end or goal of art, we must at once remove the perverse idea, which in the question, "What is the end?" will still make it include the supplemental query, "What is the use?" The perverseness consists in this that the work of art would then have to be regarded as related to something else, which is presented to us as what is essential and ought to be. A work of art would in that case be merely a useful instrument in the realization of an end which possessed real and independent importance outside the realm of art. As opposed to this we must maintain that it is art's function to reveal *truth* under the mode of art's sensuous or material configuration, to display the reconciled antithesis previously described, and by this means to prove that it possesses its final aim in itself, in this representation in short and self-revelation. For other ends such as instruction, purification, improvement, procuring of wealth, struggle after fame and honour have nothing whatever to do with this work of art as such, still less do they determine the fundamental idea of it.

It is then from this point of view, into which the reflective consideration of our subject-matter finally issues, that we have to grasp the fundamental idea of art in terms of its ideal or inward necessity, as it is also from this point of view that historically regarded the true appreciation and acquaintance with art took its origin. For that antithesis, to which we have drawn attention, did not merely assert its presence within the general thought of educated men, but equally in philosophy as such. It was only after philosophy was in a position to overcome this opposition absolutely that it grasped the fundamental notion of its own content, and, to the extent it did so, the idea of Nature and of art.

For this reason, as this point of view implies the re-awakening of philosophy in the widest connotation of the term, so also it is the re-awakening of the science of art. We may go further and affirm that aesthetic as a science is in a real sense primarily indebted to this re-awakening for its true origination, and art for its higher estimation.

. . .

2. All that exists, then, has only truth in so far as it is a definite existence of the Idea. For the Idea is alone the truly real. The truth of the phenomenal is not derived from the fact that its particular existence is of an inward or external character, and as such is in a general sense reality; it is so wholly in virtue of the fact that such reality is adequate to the notion. Then alone is determinate existence real and true. And the truth, to which we here refer, is not a *subjective* interpretation of it, namely, that a particular existence is accordant with my own conception of it. It is truth in the objective sense that the reality of the Ego, or of any external object, action, or circumstance actually contributes to the realization of the notion. If this identity is not established the existence remains purely phenomenal. Instead of the objectification of the notion in its completeness what obtains is purely a detached aspect of it; and with regard to this, whatever self-subsistence it may appear to have in opposition to the unity and universality of the notion, such can only work to its final confusion by setting it in hostility to the true notion itself. Our conclusion, therefore, is that only the reality which adequately expresses the notion is truly reality, and the reason it is so is that therein the Idea manifests itself as existence.

3. We have maintained that beauty is *Idea*. It follows that *beauty* and *truth* are, in one aspect of them, *identical*. In other words, beauty must itself in its intrinsic being be true. A closer investigation will further show to us that truth must be *distinguished* from beauty.

The idea is true in the sense that it is so by virtue of its essential being and according to its fundamental principle, and as such truth it is thought. It is not its sensuous and external existence, but the *universal* Idea of thought as present in this. At the same time the Idea is driven to seek its realization in external and objectively determined existence, both in the sphere of Nature and that of Mind. The true, in the absolute sense, also exists. And in so far as, in this its external existence, it is immediately apprehended by consciousness, and the notion rests in immediate unity with its external appearance, the Idea is not only true, but is also *beautiful*. The *beautiful* may therefore be defined as the *sensuous semblance* of the Idea. For the sensuous condition and the object world generally maintain no real self-subsistence in beauty, but have merely to surrender the immediacy of their *being*. In beauty such are posited simply as the determinate existence and externality of the notion, and as a form of reality, which itself manifests the *notion* in unity with its external appearance in this its particular objective existence. For this reason it can only pass as the semblance of the notion.

(*a*) Accordantly with this it is impossible for the understanding alone to grasp the significance of beauty. For inasmuch as objective reality is apprehended by this faculty as something at least quite other than ideality, sensuous perception, as something very different from the notion, the external object as something that is anywhere rather than within world of the conscious self, to that extent it cannot fail to emphasize the contradictions implied in such separation, rather than penetrate to the ideal unity we have above described. The understanding remains rooted in the finite, the incomplete and untrue abstraction. The beautiful is on the contrary itself essentially *infinite* and free.

. . .

We may say, then, that the aesthetic contemplation of the beautiful is a liberal education, a portrayal of the object in its free and infinite being, with no detracting consideration of its use or employment for finite wants and purposes. Further, the *object* as a *thing of beauty* is neither under force or compulsion at our hands, nor is it in conflict with and overcome by other things outside it. It is of the essence of beauty that the notion, end and soul thereof, no less than its existent form, and variety generally, manifest themselves out of their own intrinsic wealth rather than through the energy of something outside them. The reason of this lies in the fact, already insisted upon, that their truth consists solely in the unity and harmony of their notion with their objective existence. And inasmuch as the notion is itself concrete totality, its objective reality also appears as a manifestation of the same, homogeneous in all its parts, which, as thus imbedded in the notion, appear to fall into such ideal unity and animation. For this harmony of the notion and its envisagement is nothing less than perfected suffusion. Accordingly the exterior form and shape is manifested, not as such by its separation from other material, or as an impression mechanically related to aims which are foreign to it, but as the form of reality wherein the notion accommodates itself out of its own stuff and substance. Finally, however much the particular aspects, parts or articulations of the beautiful object are presented in the ideal unity of the notion and its unified envisagement, that harmony must be so rendered visible to sense,

that in relation to one another they preserve the semblance of self-subsistent freedom; in other words they must not only possess the ideal unity of the *notion as such*, but must reflect back the side of a reality which is substantially objective also. Both aspects, in short, must be present in beautiful objects; for these are, on the one hand, the *necessity* posited through the notion and discovered in the harmonious conclusion of these particular aspects, and on the other, the envisagement of their freedom as essentially one with the whole, and *not merely* that of the *unity* which exists between the parts. Necessity in its full definition means the just relation of the two aspects, which coalesce so completely that to posit one is to posit the other. Such a necessity must unquestionably be present in beautiful objects. It is not, however, under the mode of necessity that it appears; rather it should conceal itself beneath the semblance of unintentional accident. Otherwise the particular parts of such a real presence lose the position they should occupy according to their own real existence, and only appear in the service of their ideal unity, to which they therefore remain in abstract subordination.

In virtue of the freedom and infinitude above analysed, which is inherent in the notion of beauty, whether we view it in its objective presence as a thing of beauty, or under its aesthetic contemplation, we disengage the province of the beautiful from the relations of finite condition, to exalt it into that of the Idea and its truth.

ALEXANDER SMITH [?–1851]

>>>><<<<

The Philosophy of Poetry (1835)

Few questions have more frequently been asked, than that—"wherein does *poetry* differ from *prose?*" and few questions have been less satisfactorily answered. Those who have little taste for poetry, have seldom troubled themselves about this matter at all, while those who regard the art with enthusiasm, have seemed to shrink from too narrow an examination of the object of their adoration, as if they felt that they might thereby dissipate a charming illusion, and increase their knowledge at the expense of their enjoyment. For my own part, I confess myself one of those who are not so much dazzled with the charms of poetry, as to be unable to examine them steadily, or describe them coolly. My interest in it is such as to incline me to speculate upon the nature of its attractions, while I am yet sufficiently *insensible* to those attractions to be able to pursue my speculations with the most philosophical composure.

The term *prose*, is used in two significations; in one of which it stands opposed to *poetry*—in the other, to *verse*. It being admitted, however, that verse is not essential to poetry, it follows that *prose*, in the sense in which it is merely opposed to *verse*, may be *poetry*—and, in the sense in which it is merely opposed to *poetry*, may be *verse*. What is to be inquired here, is, what is the nature, not of *verse*, but of *poetry*, as opposed to prose. So strong,

From *Blackwood's Edinburgh Magazine*, Vol. XXXVIII (1835), pp. 827-39. The article was published anonymously; both the article and its author remained completely unknown until rediscovered by M. H. Abrams and discussed in his *The Mirror and the Lamp* (New York: Oxford University Press, 1953).

however, is the connexion between poetry and verse, that this subject would be but very indifferently treated should that connexion fail to be properly accounted for; and I shall, in the sequel, have occasion to point out how it happens that *verse* must, generally speaking, always be *poetry*.

It seems to me that a clear line of demarcation exists between poetry and prose, and one which admits of being plainly and accurately pointed out.

No distinction is more familiarly apprehended by those who have considered the different states in which the mind exists, or acts which it performs, than that which subsists between acts or states of *intelligence*, and acts or states of *emotion*. Acts or states of intelligence are those in which the mind perceives, believes, comprehends, infers, remembers. Acts or states of emotion are those in which it hopes, fears, rejoices, sorrows, loves, hates, admires, or dislikes. The essential distinction between poetry and prose is this:— prose is the language of *intelligence*, poetry of *emotion*. In prose, we communicate our *knowledge* of the objects of sense or thought—in poetry, we express how these objects *affect* us.

In order, however, to appreciate the justice of the definition of poetry now given, the term *feeling*, or *emotion*, must be taken in a somewhat wider, but more logical or philosophical, sense, than its ordinary acceptation warrants. In common discourse, if I mistake not, we apply the word *emotion* more exclusively to mental affections of a more violent kind, or at least only to high degrees of mental affection in general. Except in philosophical writings, the perception of the *beautiful* is not designated as a state of emotion. A man who is tranquilly admiring a soft and pleasing landscape, is not, in common language, said to be in a state of emotion; neither are curiosity, cheerfulness, elation, reckoned emotions. A man is said to be under emotion, who is strongly agitated with grief, anger, fear. At present, however, we include, in the term *emotion*, every species of mental (as distinct from bodily) pleasure or pain, desire or aversion, and all degrees of these states.

It will be asked, does every expression of emotion then constitute poetry? I answer it does, as regards the specific character of poetry, and that which distinguishes it from prose. Every expression of emotion is poetry, in the same way, but only in the same way, as every succession of sounds, at musical intervals, every single chord, is *music*. In one sense, we call such successions or harmonies *music*, only when they are combined into rhythmical pieces of a certain length; so we only call the expression of emotion *poetry*, when it expands itself to a certain extent, and assumes a peculiar defined form—of which more afterwards. But as even two or three notes, succeeding one another, or struck together at certain intervals, are *music*, as distinct from any other succession or combinations of sounds—such as the noise of machinery, of water, of firearms, so is the shortest exclamation expressive of emotion *poetry*, as distinct from the expression of any intellectual act, such as that of belief, comprehension, knowledge. To which it is to be added, that though looking to the specific essence of poetry, every expression of feeling is poetry, yet that expression may always be more or less true and successful; and, as we sometimes say of a dull or insipid air, that there is *no music* in it —so we say, that a composition, in its essential character, poetical, is not *poetry*— as meaning, that it is not good poetry—i.e. though an expression of feeling, yet not of a refined feeling, or not a faithful, an affecting, or a striking expression of it.

By the *language of emotion*, however, I mean the language in which that emotion vents itself—not the description of the emotion, or the affirmation that it is felt. Such description or affirmation is the mere communication of a fact—the affirmation that I feel something. This is prose. Between such and the expression of emotion, there is much the same difference as that which exists between the information a person might give us of his feeling bodily pain, and the exclamations or groans which his suffering might extort from him.

But by expressions of feeling or emotion, it is not, of course, to be supposed that I mean mere *exclamation*. Feeling can only be expressed so as to excite the sympathy of others—(being the end for which it is expressed)—with reference to a cause or object moving that feeling. Such cause or object, in order to be comprehended, may require to be stated in the form of a proposition or propositions (whether general or particular), as in a narrative, a description or a series of moral truths. The essential character, however, of a poetical narrative or description, and that which distinguishes it from a merely prosaic one, is this—that its direct object is not to convey information, but to intimate a subject of feeling, and transmit that feeling from one mind to another. In prose, the main purpose of the writer or speaker is to inform, or exhibit truth. The information may excite emotion, but this is only as accidental effect. In poetry, on the other hand, the information furnished is merely subsidiary to the conveyance of the emotion. The particulars of the information are not so properly stated or told, as appealed or referred to by the speaker for the purpose of discovering and justifying his emotion, and creating a sympathetic participation of it in the mind of the hearer.

The description of a scene or an incident may be highly picturesque, striking, or even affecting, and yet not in the slightest degree poetical, merely because it is communicated as information, not referred to as an object creating emotion; because the writer states the fact accurately and distinctly as it is, but does not exhibit himself as affected or moved by it. Take the following extract, for instance:—

The Torch was lying at anchor in Bluefields' Bay. It was between eight and nine in the morning. The land wind had died away, and the sea breeze had not set in—there was not a breath stirring. The pennant from the mast-head fell sluggishly down, and clung amongst the rigging like a dead snake; whilst the folds of the St. George's ensign that hung from the mizen peak were as motionless, as if they had been carved in marble.

The anchorage was one unbroken mirror, except where its glass-like surface was shivered into sparkling ripples by the gambols of a skip jack, or the flashing stoop of his enemy the pelican; and the reflection of the vessel was so clear and steady, that at the distance of a cable's length you could not distinguish the water line, nor tell where the substance ended and shadow began, until the casual dashing of a bucket overboard for a few moments broke up the phantom ship; but the wavering fragments soon re-united, and she again floated double, like the swan of the poet. The heat was so intense, that the iron stancheons of the awning could not be grasped with the hand; and where the decks were not screened by it, the pitch boiled out from the seams. The swell rolled in from the offing, in long shining undulations, like a sea of quicksilver, whilst every now and then a flying fish would spark out from the unruffled bosom of the heaving water, and shoot away like a silver arrow, until it dropped with a flash into the sea again. There was not a cloud in the heavens; but a quivering blue haze hung over the land, through which the white sugar works and overseers' houses on the distant estates appeared to twinkle like objects seen through a thin smoke, whilst each of the tall stems of the cocoa-nut trees on the beach, when looked at steadfastly, seemed to be turning round with a small spiral motion, like so many endless screws. There was a dreamy indistinctness about the outlines of the hills, even in the im-

mediate vicinity, which increased as they receded, until the blue mountains in the horizon melted into sky.

It would seem to me impossible for words to convey a more vivid picture than is here presented; yet there is not, I think, more *poetry* in it than in the specification of a patent.

To illustrate the distinction between poetry and prose, we may remark, that words of precisely the same grammatical and verbal import, nay, the *same words,* may be either prose or poetry, according as they are pronounced, without, or with *feeling;* according as they are uttered, merely to inform or to express and communicate emotion. "The sun is set," merely taken as stating a fact, and uttered with the enunciation, and in the tone in which we communicate a fact, is just as truly prose as "it is a quarter past nine o'clock." "The sun is set," uttered as an expression of the emotions which the contemplation of that event excites in a mind of sensibility, is poetry; and, simple as are the words, would, with unexceptionable propriety, find place in a poetical composition. "My son Absalom" is an expression of precisely similar import to "my brother Dick," or "my uncle Toby," not a whit more poetical than either of these, in which there is assuredly no poetry. It would be difficult to say that "oh! Absalom, my son, my son," is not poetry; yet the grammatical and verbal import of the words is exactly the same in both cases. The interjection "oh," and the repetition of the words "my son," add nothing whatever to the meaning; but they have the effect of making words which are otherwise but the intimation of a fact, the expression of an *emotion* of exceeding depth and interest, and thus render them eminently poetical.

The poem of *Unimore,* published sometime ago by Professor Wilson in Blackwood's Magazine, commences with these words:

"Morven, and morn, and spring, and solitude."

Suppose these to be the explanatory words at the beginning of a dramatic piece, and stated thus: "Scene, Morven, a solitary tract in the Highlands—season, spring—time, the morning," it would be absurd to say that the import conveyed is not precisely the same. Why is the second mode of expression prose? Simply because it informs. Why is the first poetry? (and who, in entering on the perusal of the composition, the commencement of which it forms, would deny it to be poetry?) because it conveys not information, but emotion; or at least what information it contains is not offered as such, being only an indirect intimation of the objects in regard to which the emotion is felt. The words, pronounced in a certain rhythm and tone, are those of a person placed in the situation described, and in the state of feeling which that situation would excite, the feeling, namely, of *sublimity, inspired by solitude* and mountainous or romantic scenery; of *beauty*,[1] by the brilliant hues of the morning sky, the splendour of the rising sun, and the bright green of the new leaves yet sparkling with dew; the feeling of *tenderness*, which we experience in regard to the infancy, not less of the vegetable, than of the animal world; the feeling, lastly, of complacent delight with which we compare the now passed desolation and coldness of winter, with the warmth and animation of the present and the approaching period. These are the feelings, joined per-

haps with various legendary associations connected with the scene, that would be conveyed by the words we are considering. Pronouncing these words in the tone and manner which disposes us to sympathize with the feelings with which they were uttered, and exerting our imagination to promote that sympathy, we experience a peculiar delight which no words, conveying mere information, could create; we attribute that delight to the poetical character of the composition.

So much for what may be called the soul of poetry. Let us next consider the peculiarities of its bodily form, and outward appearance.

It is well known that emotions express themselves in different *tones* and *inflections* of voice from those that are used to communicate mere processes of thought, properly so called; and also that, in the former case, the words of the speaker fall into more smooth and rhythmical combinations than in the latter. Our feelings are conveyed in a melodious succession of tones, and in a measured flow of words; our thoughts (and in a greater degree the less they are accompanied with feeling) are conveyed in irregular periods, and at harsh intervals of tone. Blank verse and rhyme are *but more artificial dispositions of the natural expressions of feeling*. They are adapted to the expression of feeling, i.e., suitable for poetry—but not necessary to it. They do not constitute poetry when they do not express feeling. The propositions of Euclid, the laws of Justinian, the narratives of Hume, might be thrown into as elaborate verse as ever Pope or Darwin composed; but they would never, even in that shape, be taken for poetry, unless so far as a certain structure of words is a natural indication of *feeling*. Indeed, when there is a possibility, from the nature of the subject, that feeling may be excited, the use of a measured structure of words, and a harmonious inflection of tones, implies that the speaker is in a *state of feel-*

[1] The philosophical reader will sufficiently understand what I mean by the *feelings* of sublimity and beauty, taken as distinct from certain *qualities* in outward objects supposed to be the cause of those feelings; to which qualities, however, and not the feelings, the terms *sublimity* and *beauty* are, in common discourse, more exclusively applied. The word *heat* either means something in the fire, or something in the sentient body affected by the fire. It is in a sense resembling the latter, that I here use sublimity and beauty.

ing; and hence what he utters we should denominate poetry.

And in this behold the true reason why verse and poetry pass in common discourse for synonymous terms—verse, especially when recited in the modulations of voice requisite to give it its proper effect, possessing *necessarily* the peculiar qualities which distinguish an *expression of feeling.* Hence it may perhaps be truly said, that though all poetry is not verse, all serious verse is poetry—poetry in its kind, at least, if not of the degree of excellence to which we may choose to limit the designation. I say, all *serious* verse—because a great part of the amusement we find in humourous and burlesque poetry, arises from the incongruity observed between the language —that of feeling—and the subject, which may not only have no tendency to excite such feeling, but to excite a feeling of an opposite kind. But that—although verse, generally speaking, is poetry—poetry may exist without verse (although never without rhythmical language), is evident from a reference, for example, to the compositions ascribed to Ossian, which none would deny to be poetry.

These considerations explain how that which, in its original language, is poetry, becomes, in a translation, however exactly and properly conveying the meaning, the merest prose. The following translation of Horace, by Smart, conveys the exact meaning of the original. Why, then, is it not poetry? (For who would ever take it for poetry?) Simply, because it is not formed into the rhythmical periods, and thence does not suggest the melodious inflections in which we convey emotion. And it is yet in our power, by speaking it in a feeling manner, to give it the character of poetry:—

The royal edifices will, in a short time, leave but a few acres for the plough. Ponds of wider extent than the Lucrine lake, will be every where to be seen; and the barren plane-tree will supplant the elms. Then banks of violets, and myrtle groves, and all the tribe of nosegays, shall diffuse their odours in the olive plantations, which were fruitful to their preceding master. Then the dense boughs of the laurel shall exclude the burning beams. It was not so prescribed by the institutes of Romulus, and the unshaven Cato, and ancient custom. Their private revenue was contracted, while that of the community was great. No private men were then possessed of ten-foot galleries, which collected the shady northern breezes; nor did the laws permit them to reject the casual turf for their own huts, though at the same time they obliged them to ornament, in the most sumptuous manner, with new stone, the buildings of the public, and the temples of the gods, at a common expense.

But although verse, however highly adapted to poetry, is not essential to it, it is found very materially to heighten the intrinsic charms of poetical composition. There is a pleasure derived from the reading of harmonious[2] verse, whether blank or rhymed, altogether distinct from any that is conveyed by the mere sense or meaning of a composition, and which indeed is capable of being excited by the verse of an unknown language. Of the cause of this pleasure we can (so far as I am aware)

[2] It may not be superfluous to observe, that such words as *melodious, harmonious,* or *musical,* applied to verse, are purely figurative, possessing nothing whatever of the kind to which these terms are applied in music. The only thing that verse and music possess in common, is rhythmical measure. The musical qualities applied to verse have regard to mere articulations of sound, not to intervals or combinations of it. In the audible reading of verse, however, and even of poetical prose, there is room for the introduction of musical intervals; and, so far as my own observation goes, the inflections of a good speaker are not, as is usually stated, performed by chromatic or imperceptible slides, but by real diatonic intervals, and these generally of the larger kinds, such as fifths, sixths, and octaves—bearing a considerable resemblance, in fact, to the movements of a fundamental bass—the difference, if I mistake not, being mostly in the nature of the rhythm and the cadences. So intimate is the connexion between a musical sound and its concords (3d, 5th, and 8th), so natural and easy the transition, that any but a practised ear is apt to take for an imperceptible slide what is in reality a *large* interval.

give no other account than that such is our constitution; although there is no doubt that our perception of contrivance and ingenuity—of difficulty overcome (and apparently no slight difficulty)—enters largely into the delight which we feel; a delight too which admits of receiving great increase from the infinite varieties of form and combination which verses and rhymes are capable of assuming. The same observation holds with regard to music; the pleasure derived from the different varieties of musical rhythm being distinct from—though eminently auxiliary to—that excited by the melody and harmony. Music, however, is far more dependent for its full effect upon rhythmical division, than poetry is upon verse. In the former, as well as in the latter, the observation of contrivance adds very materially to the gratification. Hence the use of musical fugues, canons, &c. And I would observe, by the way, that a censure frequently passed in regard to musical compositions of a more elaborate cast, by persons whose ear is not sufficiently exercised to discern the merits of such—namely, that a taste for such composition is an unnatural and false taste—is by no means a reasonable one; or at least it is no more reasonable than a similar censure would be on our permitting ourselves to be gratified by the varieties of verse and rhyme in poetry. I am not sure, indeed, but there have been persons of so etherealized a taste, as even to profess a squeamishness in regard to the use of rhyme.

Nor is verse merely adapted, in a general way, to the expression of emotion. The infinite variety of particular measures and rhymes—some swift and lively, some slow and melancholy—are available by the poet for the purpose of heightening every expression of sentiment. Hence, while he ministers to the physical delight of the ear, and gratifies us by the perception of the art displayed in his easy and correct versification, he humours the character or the caprices of his subject, by causing his verses sometimes to glide on in a smooth unmurmuring stream—sometimes to dash away with a noisy and startling vehemence.

But farther—the language of *emotion* is generally *figurative* or *imaginative* language. It is of the nature of emotion to express itself in the most forcible manner —in the manner most adapted to justify itself, and light up a kindred flame in the breast of the auditor. Hence the poet flies from the use of literal phraseology as unfit for his purpose; and the eye of his fancy darts hither and thither, until it lights on the figures or images that will most vividly and rapidly convey the sentiment that fills his soul. The mind, anxious to convey not the truth or fact with regard to the object of its contemplation, but its own feelings as excited by the object, pours forth the stream of its associations as they rise from their source. Our perceptions of external events and objects are distinct, fixed, and particular. The feelings which such objects excite are dim, fluctuating, general. Our language is correspondent in each case. Hence many expressions highly poetical, that is, eminently fitted for conveying a *feeling* from one mind to another, would be, if taken in reference to the object, and considered in their grammatical meaning, absolutely nonsensical. Washington Irving speaks of the "dusty splendour" of Westminster Abbey—an expression deservedly admired for the vividness of the impression it conveys. Taken as conveying a specific matter of information, it is absolute nonsense. *Splendour* is not a subject of which *dusty* could be an attribute; a space or a body might be dusty; but the splendour of an object might, in strict propriety of language, as well be spoken of as long, or loud, or square. So in the line,

"The starry Galileo and his woes,"

the literal inapplicability of the epithet "starry" to an astronomer is obvious. The expression is one, not of a truth that is *perceived,* but of an association that is *felt.*

No epithet, signifying the mere addiction of Galileo to astronomical pursuits, could have struck us like that which thus suggests the visible glories that belong to the field of his speculations. From the consideration now illustrated, it results also, that the imagery, having often no essential connexion with the object, but merely an accidental connexion in the mind of the poet, strikes one class of readers in the most forcible manner, and fails of all effect with others. The expression of Milton—"smoothing the raven plume of darkness till it smiled," is greatly admired, or at least often quoted. I must confess, that, to my mind, it is like a parcel of words set down at random. I may observe, indeed, that many persons of an imaginative frame of mind, and who, in consequence, take a great delight in the mere exercise of imagination (and who at the same time possess a delicate ear for verse), find any poetry exquisite, however destitute of meaning, which merely suggests ideas or images that may serve as the germs of fancy in their own minds. There are many passages in Byron—Wordsworth—Young—and these enthusiastically admired, which, I must confess, are to me utterly unintelligible; or at least, the understanding of which (where that is possible) I find to require as great in exercise of thought as would be required by so much of Burtler's Analogy, or Euclid's Demonstrations.

Lastly—as regards the peculiar character of the *language* of poetry—it is important to observe, that a principal cause of the boldness and variety that may be remarked to belong to poetical expression, is one which would, at first sight, seem to produce an effect directly the reverse; this is —*the fetters imposed by the verse.* The expression which would be the most obvious, and even the most exact (if exactitude were what was most required), is often not the one that will suit the verse. The consequence is, that a new one must be coined for the purpose; and I believe every poet would admit that some of his happiest epithets and most adorned expressions have been lighted upon in the course of a search for terms of a certain *metrical dimension.* The necessity of obeying the laws of the verse, leads also to a peculiar latitude in the application of terms; and as the impression of this necessity is also present to the mind of the reader, he readily grants the poetical license to the composer, and admits of verbal combinations, which, in prose, would seem far-fetched and affected. Thus the verse, then, instead of contracting, extends the choice of expression. The aptitude of a term or an epithet to fill the verse, becomes part of its aptitude in general; and what is first tolerated from its necessity, is next applauded for its novelty.

Behold now the whole character of poetry. It is *essentially* the *expression of emotion;* but the expression of emotion *takes place* by measured language (it may be verse, or it may not)—harmonious tones— and figurative phraseology. And it will, I think, invariably be found, that wherever a passage, line, or phrase of a poetical composition, is censured as being of a *prosaic* character, it is from its conveying some matter of mere *information,* not subsidiary to the prevailing emotion, and breaking the continuity of that emotion.

It might perhaps be thought a more accurate statement, if, instead of defining poetry to be in its essence the *language of emotion,* and representing the imaginative character of poetry as merely resulting from its essential nature as thus defined, I had included its imaginative character in the definition, and made that character part of the essence of poetry. It will seem that the *"language of imagination"* would be to the full as just a definition of poetry as the *"language of emotion";* or, at least, that these are respectively the definitions of two different species of poetry, each alike entitled to the denomination. I shall assign the reasons why I consider the statement I have adopted to be a more true and philosophical one than that now supposed.

In the first place, the conveyance, by language, of an imaginative mental process, needs not be in the slightest degree poetical. A novel is entirely a work of imagination—it is not therefore a poem. The description of an imagined scene or event, needs not indeed differ in the least from that of a real one; it may therefore be purely prosaical. It is not the imaginative process by itself, and merely as such, but the feelings that attend it, the expression of which constitutes poetry. So much as regards the subject of a composition. As regards style, in like manner, there may be a great deal of imagery or figurative phraseology in a composition, without entitling it to be reckoned poetical; or, so far as entitled to be called poetical, it will be found to be expressive of emotion. On the other hand, the expression of emotion, even in relation to an actual scene or event (if it is merely the language of emotion and not that of persuasion—which, as elsewhere remarked, is the definition of eloquence) is, in every case, poetical, and notwithstanding that the style may be perfectly free from imagery or figure; nor again, without implying emotion on the part of the writer or speaker, will any language, or any subject, be poetical. It is then essential to poetry to be of an emotive—not essential to it to be of an imaginative character. But this imaginative character, though not of the essence of poetry, results from that essence. It is in a moved or excited state of mind, and only, I might say, in a moved or excited state, that we resort to the use of figure or imagery. The exercise of imagination is pleasurable chiefly as an indulgence of emotion. Do we usually exercise imagination on uninteresting subjects?—or what does *interesting* or *uninteresting* mean, but exciting or not exciting emotion? What else is it but our craving desire to admire—to be awed—to sympathize—to love—to regret—to hope; in one word, to feel or to be moved, that

leads us to picture in the mind, scenes, or forms, or characters of beauty or grandeur; or states of enjoyment or distress; or situations of agony or rapture; or incidents of horror or delight; or deeds of heroism, or tenderness, or mercy, or cruelty? Why do we recall the joys or the sorrows that are past? why do we dwell on hopes that have been blighted—affections that have been crushed—delusions that have been dispelled? Why do we summon up the scenes and the companions of our childhood and youth? It is because such images or pictures *move* us—and poetry is the expression of our emotions.

So intimate is the connexion between *emotion* and *fancy*, that it is often not very easy to say whether the feeling is the parent of the image by which it expresses itself, or whether, on the contrary, the image is the parent of the feeling. The truth seems to be, that they produce and reproduce one another. Feeling generates fancy; and fancy, in its turn, upholds and nourishes feeling. If, as Mr. Alison has maintained, and as most people seem disposed to grant, the pleasures of taste are resolvable in a great measure into a certain delight which we experience in pursuing a train of images and associations—the intimate connexion between emotion and fancy, and the consequent tendency to express emotion (or at least the emotions of taste) by figures and imagery, will be at once apparent. It is however sufficient for my present purpose to exhibit the fact of the connexion.

We may, in one or two familiar instances, exemplify the nature of the poetical character, and the intimacy of the union that subsists between fancy and emotion.

"The curfew tolls the knell of parting day."

The vital character of this line, as constituting it poetry, is, that it is not the mere *fact* or *truth*—(namely, that the tolling of the bell is a sign of the ending of the day) —that the words of the poet aim at communicating, but his *emotion* in regard to the fact; and, filled as his mind is with this emotion, his fancy first flies away to the origin of the evening bell, and, as we may imagine, rapidly wanders amid the associations of antiquity and romance, which link themselves to the name of the *curfew*. The sound of the bell, intimating the close of day, he invests, for the moment, with the import of the death knell summoning a soul from life; and the epithet "parting," bespeaks the similitude of his present frame of mind to that excited by the interruption of a cherished intercourse with an animated being—with a companion, a friend, a lover.

"How sweet the moonlight sleeps upon this bank."

The obvious purpose of these words is to express a feeling, not to furnish a matter of information; and the feeling cannot be adequately expressed by literal, or without figurative phraseology. "To represent the tranquillity of moonlight is the object of this line; and the *sleep* is beautiful, because it gives *a more intense and living form of the same idea;* the rhythm falls beautifully in with this, and just lets the cadence of the emphasis dwell upon the sound and sense of the sweet word 'sleep,' and the alliteration assimilates the rest of the line into one harmonious symmetry."

And here I may distinguish two different exercises of the imagination in poetry. The first of these is where a figure of speech—a trope or metaphor—is used for the mere purpose of giving strength or illustration to some expression of feeling.[3] The other—and what is more properly called imagery in poetry—is where the

recollection or imagination of a sensible impression is that itself which moves the feeling. In many cases—as in the instance just quoted—the two operations are blended. And as sensible objects are so often the exciting causes of feeling, the happy conveyance of the impressions they create is one of the chief arts of the poet. Hence the *picturesque* character of poetical language—its aptitude to present a picture or image of an actual object calculated to affect us.

We may now see that a poetical genius —a poetical taste—may be said to consist essentially of *sensibility* (or aptitude to feel emotion), and, by consequence, of *imagination* (or aptitude to place ourselves in situations exciting emotion). The poet—the reader of poetry—seeks not to know truth as distinct from falsehood or error—to reason or draw inferences—to generalize—to classify—to distinguish; he seeks for what may move his awe- admiration—pity—tenderness; scenes of sublimity and beauty; incidents exciting fear, suspense, grief—joy —surprise—cheerfulness—regret. Whether these scenes or these incidents are real or fictitious, he cares not. It is enough to him that he can imagine them. Behold the compressed lips—the knitted brows—the fixed and sharpened eye of the philosophical enquirer, whose aim it is to *know*—to discover and communicate truth. The character of his countenance is that of keen penetration, as if he would dart his glances into the innermost recesses of science. Compare with this the open forehead—the rolling eye—the flexible mouth—the changing features of the poet, whose aim it is to feel, and convey his feelings. His countenance has been moulded to the expression of feeling, and is a constant record of that succession of emotions which passes through his breast.

Let us not suppose, however, that the pleasure derived from poetical composition is simply a pleasure arising from being in a state of emotion. Many emotions are

---

[3] And it is because a figure may also be used to strengthen or illustrate a mere truth or the expression of an intellectual process, that *figurative language* is not necessarily *poetical*.

themselves far from pleasant; but we take pleasure in the skilful expression of these emotions, for the same reason that we are often delighted with the picture of an object which would itself attract no notice, or be positively offensive or painful.

A survey of the different species of poetical composition will serve to illustrate and strengthen the preceding statements.

In an epic or narrative poem, some event, or connected chain of events, is narrated with the various feelings which arise from the view of such event or events, and in a manner calculated to excite a sympathetic participation of these feelings in the mind of the hearer or reader. The historian of such transactions merely speaks for our information. He arranges his subjects so as to give us the clearest understanding of the dates, course, and connexion of the incidents. The poet seeks not to inform us, or, at least, this is not his ultimate or principal object, but merely subsidiary to the expression of his own emotions, and the excitement of similar emotions in the breasts of others. Hence, instead of a methodical introduction such as a historian would adopt, he plunges at once *in medias res*—places before us some scene, strongly calculated, both from its own character and the apparent feelings with which he describes it, to excite our interest. Our curiosity once raised, he continues at once to gratify and keep alive, by the presentation of a succession of circumstances, or rather the indirect intimation of a succession of circumstances, filling, as his language testifies, his own mind with grief, joy, indignation, pity, tenderness, fear, hope, awe, admiration, and all the other passions of the soul, and awakening the like passions in ours. From the nature and ends of epic poetry arises the necessity of preserving what is called the *unity* of the poem; which means the presenting of one object to the mind of the reader of sufficient interest to absorb his continued attention, and in reference to which the subordinate incidents may acquire a degree of importance not perhaps intrinsically belonging to such incidents themselves.

Similar remarks will apply to the tragic drama—with only this difference, that here the actors of the scene are made to express directly the emotions which their several situations excite.

Descriptive poetry conveys an expression of the feelings excited by *the view of the scenes and operations of nature and the works of art,* whether grand, or simply beautiful. The rugged precipice, the vast mountain, the fierce torrent, the sombre forest, the hurricane, the thunder, the earthquake, the storm; or, on the other hand, the variegated plain, the glittering stream, the gracefully undulating surface, the luxuriant foliage, the hedge-row, the shrub, the flower, the rising and setting sun, the refreshing shower, the lively breeze, the glowing stars; or, again, the proud feudal fortress; the melancholy abbey, the splendid villa, the awful cathedral, with the associations connected with each; or, lastly, the appearance of animated nature, the peaceful labours of the husbandmen, the groups of flocks and herds, the bright plumage, the exhilarating song of the feathered tribes, or the mazy dance and mingled hum of the fluttering insects:—all these objects excite, in the mind of sensibility, the emotions of sublimity, or beauty, or tenderness, or melancholy, or cheerfulness; and the aim of descriptive poetry is the expression and communication of these feelings.

Didactic or sentimental poetry expresses the emotions produced by the *contemplation of general truths regarding subjects of human interest,* the shortness of life, the vanity of youthful expectations, the ravages of the passions, the miseries of human existence, the passage of time, the terrors of death, the hopes and fears of immortality.

Satirical and humorous poetry is the expression of emotions which arise at *the view of human vice, folly, and weakness;* the expression, namely, of indignation, scorn, contempt, derision.

Of all the emotions which arise in the human breast, none are either so universally and intensely felt, or so readily sympathized with, as the *affections which take place between the sexes;* nor perhaps are there any which are capable of being so much varied and modified by the situations in which they are excited, and the individual character of the parties. Hence the innumerable aspects of the passion—its hopes and fears—its headlong ardour, and moving tenderness—its ebbs, and flows, and changes, and caprices—the torments of jealousy—the bitterness of absence, the exultation of success—"the pang of despised love"—constitute a class of subjects which has ever, above all others, been consecrated to poetry. To be a lover, indeed, is a part of the poet's profession; not to have loved is never to have been truly inspired with the poetical flame.

The difference between *eloquence* and *poetry* seems to me to consist in this, that, while the sole object of poetry is to transmit the *feelings* of the speaker or writer, that of eloquence is to convey the *persuasion* of some *truth*—whether with a view to excite to action or not. And in proportion as the writer, in enforcing any particular truth, exhibits himself as affected by such truth, i.e. as feeling emotion at the contemplation of it; or, which is the index of emotion, expresses himself in a figurative or imaginative style—in such proportion the composition, though in a prose form, becomes in reality, and is felt to be, poetical. Hence poetry may be eloquent, and eloquence poetical—which is only saying, in other words, that the expression of emotion may contain an impressive statement of some truth which excites the emotion; or, vice versa, that the enforcement of a truth may be attended with a striking display of emotion excited by the contemplation of that truth. The line that separates poetry and eloquence, then, is sometimes altogether imperceptible. Indeed, for rea-

sons which we have seen, the same proposition which *not* in verse, will be *prose*—in verse will be *poetry.*

The reasons already assigned to show why verse must generally possess the poetical character, have occasioned the term poetry to be almost exclusively confined to verse: so that though a composition, not in verse, may be essentially poetical, as being the expression of emotion, we do not call it poetical unless eminently so—that is, distinguished by a peculiarly imaginative and refined cast of thought.[4]

And now, having attempted to assign the *essential distinction* that subsists between poetical and prosaic composition, I cannot help expressing my opinion that compositions in *verse* are, *as such,* and as distinct from the degree of merit they may individually possess, usually rated at a value far disproportionate to their real importance.

The expression of an *emotive* does not seem to possess any intrinsic superiority over that of an *intellectual* mental process. The interest attending it is different, but not necessarily greater. In one important respect it is inferior. Feelings associate among themselves, and are capable of being presented in connexion; but they will gradually connect in one order as well, or nearly so, as in another. Hence the want in poetry (that is, in what is *nothing but poetry*)[5] of progressive interest—of that sort of interest which belongs to chains of fact

[4] A prayer to the Deity is essentially poetical, as being the expression of awe, admiration, gratitude, contrition, entreaty. Hence good taste, as well as just religious feeling, is shocked by the introduction, in a prayer, of any mere *proposition* (such as the affirmation of a doctrine) not in its nature exciting emotion. But *verse,* however generally suitable to the expression of emotion, would be inconsistent with the simplicity that ought to belong to prayer.

[5] I say *what is nothing but poetry,* because the interest derived from story, incident, and character, can be equally well conveyed in prose composition, nay, infinitely better, from a variety of causes, and chiefly from the inadmissibility, in poetry, of the mention of any fact not calculated to be spoken of *with emotion.* Hence, at once, the comparative meagreness and obscurity of poetical narratives.

or reasoning—interest kept alive by the expectation of, and gratified by the arrival at, a result. The mathematician's famous query in regard to the Aeneid, "What does all this prove?" is more faulty in regard to its applicability to the particular case, and to the narrowness of the idea it expresses, than as being destitute of a general foundation in truth. Take up any sentimental poem, that is, a composition which is poetry alone, poetry left to its own resources, "the Seasons," "the Pleasures of Hope"— your enjoyment in reading will be much the same whether you dip into a page here and there, or go directly on from the commencement. Here then is one essential inferiority attaching to the poetical as compared with the prosaic character—to the expression of *emotive,* as compared with that of *intellectual* processes. But, waving this comparison, *verse* is not indispensable to the expression of feeling. What is prose in form, is often poetry in substance. Our question regards the value generally attached to verse, as verse. Is verse then never employed but in the conveyance of sentiments of a *more valuable* kind than are ever to be found in the prose form? In answer, I take upon me to affirm, that in any ordinary book of serious or tasteful reflection, there are sentiments to be found, which, extracted from the connexion in which they are presented, no one would think of looking at twice, which are to the full as important, as striking, as touching, as vividly and elegantly expressed, as any thing which one may please to signify the value of a sentiment by, as are the subjects of many a "sonnet," or set of "stanzas," or "verses" which will yet be copied, translated, criticised, and the date and occasion of its composition settled with as much precision as if it were the commencement of an era. Is it the mere versification then that confers the value? Now without doubt there is a peculiar pleasure in verse as such, a pleasure which is the effect of positive constitution, and about which, therefore, there can be no dispute. But the

pleasure arising from versification merely, will only, I think, be ranked among the more insignificant of our gratifications. It is not an enjoyment of a vivid, considerable kind. It is at most agreeable. But so is elegant penmanship—so may be the pattern of a carpet, a room paper, or a chimney ornament. There is that trifling sort of gratification which one will rather meet than the contrary, but not what we should go far out of our way to find. Then, again, the perception of ingenuity and contrivance, is no doubt pleasing; but a pleasure of that kind which inevitably loses its value as we become familiarized to it. We give our tribute to the talent and ingenuity of the workman, but we derive little pleasure from the work. It is trite to observe that many things which cost a vast deal of skill and labour to do, are felt of very little value when done. But farther, I must allow, in addition to the sort of pleasure which we take in verse, as such, the additional intensity which it is capable of giving to the expression of the sentiment. But here the difference between verse and prose is but in degree, and the degree sometimes but very slight. *A sentiment, which expressed in prose would be of little value, cannot be of much when expressed in verse.* Is there not, then, I again ask, a degree of interest and importance generally attached to "verses," "lines," "stanzas," utterly disproportionate to what is in justice due?

One will be apt to say here, all this is disputing about a matter of *taste,* which is universally allowed to be idle. To a person destitute of a taste for poetry, it is as impossible to prove its value, as to prove the value of music to one who has no musical ear. Now all this would be very well if verse were something essentially different from anything else, and, in its distinctive nature, the object of a *specific taste,* distinguishable from other tastes. This cannot be pretended to be the case. The difference between a thought expressed in prose, and the same thought expressed in verse, is obviously too trifling to make the former the object of a distinct constitutional faculty. The musician can, *with mathematical precision,* state the intervals, and the chords, and the successions of sounds, which, and which alone, delight his ear. Musical successions or harmonies can never be mixed or confounded with other species of sounds, nor with any thing else whatever, as poetry may be mixed or confounded with prose. Again, there is no one who fails of receiving a strong delight from music who has the mere organic perception of musical intervals (who has an ear). To every man who can merely take up or remember an air—who can hum, whistle, or sing it, *in tune,* music is not merely pleasing, but a substantial, material enjoyment. The love of music, then, is universal among those who have merely a certain physical capacity, and whoever does not relish it, can be shown to want a physical capacity. Not so with poetry. A man who is extremely callous to its charms shall detect a flaw in versification as accurately as the keenest poetical enthusiast—shall do verse as much justice in the reading (in proportion to what he could do to prose composition)—shall even (I do not say he could do so without difficulty) compose faultless verses. He shall be—with the reservation we are supposing, if a reservation it must be—a man of sense, feeing, taste; nay, generally addicted to literary pursuits. Here, then, is one having all the physical and mental requisites for enjoying poetry, and who, though without in any considerable degree enjoying, may even be able to distinguish its beauties. If such a person fails in deriving any lively enjoyment from poetry—and numerous cases of this kind I believe exist—must not the fair inference be, not that he wants a peculiar faculty, but that, to the object of this supposed faculty there is attached a somewhat fictitious and imaginary value?

The comparison now made between poetry and music may not, it is true, seem a fair one, inasmuch as a love of music is so indisputably dependent on a certain physical organization. There are many cases, it will be urged, in which *taste* is allowed to be the *sole arbiter,* without appeal to any other tribunal, where yet there is no particular independent faculty such as an ear for music, and where yet the degree of taste for particular species of beauty differs remarkably in different individuals—as taste for painting, sculpture, architecture, natural scenery. Now I say, in the first place, that each of these objects of taste differ from every other thing in a way that *poetry* does not differ from *prose,* and may claim to be amenable to taste in a way that poetry, *simply as distinguished from prose,* cannot; and, next, that I believe there is no person of cultivated mind who is so indifferent to the objects of taste now enumerated, as many persons of cultivated mind are to poetry.

What then do I aim at showing? That all poetry is worthless? that the pleasure derived from poetry is altogether factitious and imaginary? no more than I should aim at showing that prose is worthless; that the pleasure derived from prose is factitious and imaginary. But I contend that poetry, *as poetry,* has no more claim to have value attached to it than prose has *as prose.* I object not to the estimation that is made of numerous individuals of the species, but to that mode of the species itself. I complain, not that many compositions that are poetical are placed in the highest rank of literary merit; not even that their being poetical is conceived greatly to heighten their value, and to display a peculiar and additional talent in the authors of them; but that many others have this value assigned to them, *simply because they are poetical, and for nothing else.* But, after all, what is there here, it will be asked, that any body disputes? Who desires, on the one hand, that worthless poetry should be preserved or valued? Who would deny, on the other, that worthless poetry is, in fact, despised and allowed to perish?

Now I acknowledge the difficulty, without specific proofs, which my present limits would not admit, of satisfying any one who should object to the justice of the opinions now offered. These opinions undoubtedly relate to a question of degree. I do not affirm that all poetry is rated above its value. I do not deny that some poetry is rejected. But I affirm, that much of what is allowed a place as poetry *of value,* poetry worth preserving and reading, is intrinsically worthless, worthless at least as regards any *pleasure to be derived from the perusal of it.* The truth of this position, with merely the general reasons on which it is founded, I must leave to be determined by the experience and reflection of individual readers.

AUGUSTE COMTE [1798–1857]

→→→→←←←←

From *A General View of Positivism* [1848]

. . . [We] may now proceed to consider the aesthetic character of Positivism. In the first place, it furnishes us with a satisfactory theory of Art; a subject which has never been systematically explained; all previous attempts to do so, whatever their value, having viewed the subject incompletely. The theory here offered is based on the subjective principle of the new philosophy, on its objective dogma, and on its social purpose; as set forward in the two first chapters of this work.

Art may be defined as an ideal representation of Fact; and its object is to cultivate our sense of perfection. Its sphere therefore is co-extensive with that of Science. Both deal in their own way with the world of Fact; the one explains it, the other beautifies it. The contemplations of the artist and of the man of science follow the same encyclopaedic law; they begin with the simple objects of the external world; they gradually rise to the complicated facts of human nature. I pointed out

From Auguste Comte, *A General View of Positivism,* translated by J. H. Bridges (London: G. Routledge & Sons, 1908), Chapter V.

in the second chapter that the scientific scale, the scale, that is, of the True, coincided with that of the Good: we now see that it coincides with that of the Beautiful. Thus between these three great creations of Humanity, Philosophy, Polity, and Poetry, there is the most perfect harmony. The first elements of Beauty, that is to say, Order and Magnitude, are visible in the inorganic world, especially in the heavens; and they are there perceived with greater distinctness than where the phenomena are more complex and less uniform. The higher degrees of Beauty will hardly be recognized by those who are insensible to this its simplest phase. But as in Philosophy we only study the inorganic world as a preliminary to the study of Man; so, but to a still greater extent, is it with Poetry. In Polity the tendency is similar but less apparent. Here we begin with material progress; we proceed to physical and subsequently to intellectual progress; but it is long before we arrive at the ultimate goal, moral progress. Poetry passes more rapidly over the three preliminary stages, and rises with less difficulty to the contemplation of moral beauty. Feeling, then, is essentially the sphere of Poetry. And it supplies not the end only, but the means.

Of all the phenomena which relate to man, human affections are the most modifiable, and therefore the most susceptible of idealization. Being more imperfect than any other, by virtue of their higher complexity, they allow greater scope for improvement. Now the act of expression, however imperfect, reacts powerfully upon these functions, which from their nature are always seeking some external vent. Every one recognizes the influence of language upon thoughts: and surely it cannot be less upon feelings, since in them the need of expression is greater. Consequently all aesthetic study, even if purely imitative, may become a useful moral exercise, by calling sympathies and antipathies into healthy play. The effect is far greater when the representation, passing the limits of strict accuracy, is suitably idealized. This indeed is the characteristic mission of Art. Its function is to construct types of the noblest kind, by the contemplation of which our feelings and thoughts may be elevated. That the portraiture should be exaggerated follows from the definition of Art; it should surpass realities so as to stimulate us to amend them. Great as the influence is of these poetic emotions on individuals, they are far more efficacious when brought to bear upon public life: not only from the greater importance of the subject matter, but because each individual impression is rendered more intense by combination.

Thus Positivism explains and confirms the view ordinarily taken of Poetry, by placing it midway between Philosophy and Polity; issuing from the first, and preparing the way for the second.

Even Feeling itself, the highest principle of our existence, accepts the objective dogma of Philosophy, that Humanity is subject to the order of the external world. And Imagination on still stronger grounds must accept the same law. The ideal must always be subordinate to the real; otherwise feebleness as well as extravagance is the consequence. The statesman who endeavours to improve the existing order, must first study it as it exists. And the poet, although his improvements are but imagined, and are not supposed capable of realization, must do likewise. True in his fictions he will transcend the limits of the possible, while the statesman will keep within those limits; but both have the same point of departure; both begin by studying the actual facts with which they deal. In our artificial improvements we should never aim at anything more than wise modification of the natural order; we should never attempt to subvert it. And though Imagination has a wider range for its pictures, they are yet subject to the same fundamental law, imposed by Philosophy upon Polity and Poetry alike. Even in the most poetic ages this law has always been recognized, only the external world was interpreted then in a way very differently from now. We see the same thing every day in the mental growth of the child. As his notions of fact change, his fictions are modified in conformity with these changes.

But while Poetry depends upon Philosophy for the principles on which its types are constructed, it influences Polity by the direction which it gives to those types. In every operation that man undertakes, he must imagine before he executes, as he must observe before he imagines. He can never produce a result which he has not conceived first in his own mind. In the simplest application of mechanics or geometry he finds it necessary to form a mental type, which is always more perfect than the reality which it precedes and prepares. Now none but those who confound poetry with verse-making can fail to see that this conception of a type is the same thing as aesthetic imagination, under its simplest and most general aspect. Its application to social phenomena, which constitute the chief sphere both of Art and Science, is very imperfectly understood as yet, and can hardly be said to have begun, owing to the want of any true theory of society. The real object of so applying it is, that it should regulate the formation of social Utopias; subordinating them to the laws of social development as revealed by history. Utopias are to the Art of social life what geometrical and mechanical types are to their respective arts. In these their necessity is universally recognized; and surely the necessity can not be less in problems of such far greater intricacy. Accordingly we see that, notwithstanding the empirical condition in which political art has hitherto existed, every great change has been ushered in, one or two centuries beforehand, by an Utopia bearing some analogy to it. It was the product of the aesthetic genius of Humanity working under an imperfect sense of its conditions and requirements. Positivism, far from laying an interdict on Utopias, tends rather to facilitate their employment and their influence, as a normal element in society. Only, as in the case of all other products of imagination, they must always remain subordinated to the actual laws of social existence. And thus by giving a systematic sanction to this the Poetry, as it may be called, of Politics, most of the dangers which now surround it will disappear. Its present extravagances arise simply from the absence of some philosophical principle to control it, and therefore there is no reason for regarding them with great severity.

The whole of this theory may be summed up in the double meaning of the word so admirably chosen to designate our aesthetic functions. The word *Art* is a remarkable instance of the popular instinct from which language proceeds, and which is far more enlightened than educated persons are apt to suppose. It indicates, however vaguely, a sense of the true position of Poetry, midway between Philosophy and Polity, but with a closer relation to the latter. True, in the case of the technical arts the improvements proposed are practically realized

while those of the fine arts remain imaginary. Poetry, however, does produce one result of an indirect but most essential kind; it does actually modify our moral nature. If we include oratory, which is only Poetry in a simpler phase, though often worthless enough, we find its influence exerted in a most difficult and critical task, that of arousing or calming our passions; and this not arbitrarily, but in accordance with the fixed laws of their action. Here it has always been recognized as a moral agency of great power. On every ground, then, Poetry seems more closely related to practical than to speculative life. For its practical results are of the most important and comprehensive nature. Whatever the utility of other parts, material, physical, or intellectual, they are only subsidiary or preparatory to that which in Poetry is the direct aim, moral improvement. In the Middle Ages it was common in all Western languages to speak of it as a Science, the proper meaning of the word Science being then very imperfectly understood. But as soon as both artistic and scientific genius had become more fully developed, their distinctive features were more clearly recognized, and finally the name of Art was appropriated to the whole class of poetic functions. The fact is, at all events, an argument in favour of the Positive theory of idealization, as standing midway between theoretical inquiry and practical result.

Evidently, then, it is in Art that the unity of human natures finds its most complete and most natural representation. For Art is in direct relation with the three orders of phenomena by which human nature is characterized; Feelings, Thoughts, and Actions. It originates in Feeling; the proof of this is even more obvious than in the case of Philosophy and Polity. It has its basis in Thought, and its end is Action. Hence its power of exerting an influence for good alike on every phase of our existence, whether personal or social.

Hence too its peculiar attribute of giving equal pleasure to all ranks and ages. Art invites the thinker to leave his abstractions for the study of real life; it elevates the practical man into a region of thought where self-love has no place. By its intermediate position it promotes the mutual reaction of Affection and Reason. It stimulates feeling in those who are too much engrossed with intellectual questions: it strengthens the contemplative faculty in natures where sympathy predominates. It has been said of Art that its province is to hold a mirror to nature. The saying is usually applied to social life where its truth is most apparent. But it is no less true of every aspect of our existence; for under every aspect it may be a source of Art, and may be represented and modified by it. Turning to Biology for the cause of this sociological relation, we find it in the relation of the muscular and nervous systems. Our motions, involuntary at first, and then voluntary, indicate internal impressions, moral impressions more especially; and as they proceed from them, so they react upon them. Here we find the first germ of a true theory of Art. Throughout the animal kingdom language is simply gesticulation of a more or less expressive kind. And with man aesthetic development begins in the same spontaneous way.

With this primary principle we may now complete our statical theory of Art, by indicating in it three distinct degrees or phases. The fine arts have been divided into imitative and inventive; but this distinction has no real foundation. Art always imitates, and always idealizes. True, as the real is in every case the source of the ideal, art begins at first with simple Imitation. In the childhood, whether of men or of the race, as also with the lower animals, servile imitation, and that of the most insignificant actions, is the only symptom of aesthetic capacity. No representation, however, has at present any claim to the title of Art (although from motives of puerile vanity the name is often given to it), except so far as it is made more beautiful, that is to say, more perfect. The representation thus becomes in reality more faithful, because the principal features are brought prominently forward, instead of being obscured by a mass of unmeaning detail. This it is which constitutes Idealization; and from the time of the great masterpieces of antiquity, it has become more and more the characteristic feature of aesthetic productions. But in recognizing the superiority of Idealization as the second stage of Art, we must not forget the necessity of its first stage, Imitation. Without it neither the origin nor the nature of Art could be correctly understood.

In addition to the creative process, which is the chief characteristic of Art, there is a third function which, though not absolutely necessary in its imitative stage, becomes so in its ideal stage. I mean the function of Expression strictly so called, without which the product of imagination could not be communicated to others. Language, whether it be the Language of sound or form, is the last stage of the aesthetic operation, and it does not always bear a due proportion to the inventive faculty. When it is too defective, the sublimest creations may be ranked lower than they deserve, owing to the failure of the poet to communicate his thought completely. Great powers of style may, on the other hand, confer unmerited reputation, which however does not endure. An instance of this is the preference that was given for so long a time to Racine over Corneille.

So long as Art is confined to Imitation, no special language is required; imitation is itself the substitute for language. But as soon as the representation has become idealized by heightening some features and suppressing or altering others, it corresponds to something which exists only in the mind of the composer; and its communication to the world requires additional labour devoted exclusively to Expression. In this final process so necessary to the complete success of his work, the poet moulds his signs upon his inward type; just as he began at first by adapting them to external facts. So far there is some truth in Grétry's principle that song is derived from speech by the intermediate stage of declamation. The same principle has been applied to all the special arts; it might also be applied to Poetry, oratory being the link between verse and prose. These views, however, are somewhat modified by the historical spirit of Positive Philosophy. We must invert Grétry's relation of cause and effect; at least when we are considering those primitive times, when Art and Language first arose together.

The origin of all our faculties of expression is invariably aesthetic; for we do not express till after we have felt strongly. Feeling had, in primitive times at all events, far more to do with these faculties than Thought, being a far stronger stimulant to external demonstration. Even in the most highly wrought languages, where, in consequence of social requirements, reason has to a great extent encroached upon emotion, we see evidence of this truth. There is a musical element in the most ordinary conversation. Listening carefully to a lecture on the most abstruse mathematical problem, we shall hear intonations which proceed obviously from the heart rather than the head, and which are indications of character even in the most unimpassioned speaker. Biology at once explains this law, by teaching that the stimulus to the muscles used in expression, whether vocal or gesticulatory, comes principally from the affective region of the brain; the specu-region being too inert to produce muscular contraction for which

there is no absolute necessity. Accordingly, Sociology regards every language as containing in its primitive elements all that is spontaneous and universal in the aesthetic development of Humanity; enough, that is, to satisfy the general need of communicating emotion. In this common field the special arts commence, and they ultimately widen it. But the operation is the same in its nature, whether carried on by popular instinct or by individuals. The final result is always more dependent on feeling than on reason, even in times like these, when the intellect has risen in revolt against the heart. Song, therefore, comes before Speech; Painting before Writing; because the first things we express are those which move our feelings most. Subsequently the necessities of social life oblige us to employ more frequently, and ultimately to develop, those elements in painting or in song, which relate to our practical wants and to our speculative faculties so far as they are required for supplying them; these forming the topics of ordinary communication. Thus the emotion from which the sign had originally proceeded becomes gradually effaced; the practical object is alone thought of, and expression becomes more rapid and less emphatic. The process goes on until at last the sign is supposed to have originated in arbitrary convention; though, if this were the case, its universal and spontaneous adoption would be inexplicable. Such, then, is the sociological theory of Language, on which I shall afterwards dwell more fully. I connect it with the whole class of aesthetic functions, from which in the lower animals it is not distinguished. For no animal idealizes its song or gesture so far as to rise to anything that can properly be called Art.

HIPPOLYTE TAINE [1828–93]

→→→→×←←←←

From *The Philosophy of Art* [1865]

I.

The principal point of this method consists in recognizing that a work of art is not isolated, and, consequently, that it is necessary to study the conditions out of which it proceeds and by which it is explained.

At first and evidently, a work of art . . . belongs to a certain whole, that is to say, to the entire work of the artist producing it. It is well known that the different works of an artist bear a family likeness, . . . a certain resemblance to each other. We know that every artist has his own style, a style recognized in all his productions. . . .

This is the first whole to which we must refer a work of art. And here is the second. The artist himself, considered in connection with his productions, is not isolated; he also belongs to a whole, one greater than himself, comprising the school or family of artists of the time and country to which he belongs. . . .

Rubens apparently stands alone, without either predecessor or successor. On going to Belgium, however, . . . you find a group of painters with genius resembling his. . . . At the present day they seem to be obscured by the glory of their great contemporary; but it is not the less true that to comprehend him it is necessary to study him amidst this cluster of brilliants of which he is the brightest gem. . . .

This being the second step, there now

From Hippolyte Taine, *The Philosophy of Art,* translated by J. Durand (New York: Holt & Williams, 1873).

remains the third. This family of artists is itself comprehended in another whole more vast, which is the world surrounding it and whose taste is similar. The social and intellectual condition is the same for the public as for the artists; they are not isolated men; it is their voice alone that we hear at this moment, through the space of centuries, but beneath this living voice which comes vibrating to us, we distinguish a murmur, and, as it were, a vast low sound, the great infinite and varied voice of the people, chanting in unison with them. . . .

Everywhere may be found similar examples of the alliance, the intimate harmony existing between an artist and his contemporaries; . . . if we desire to comprehend the taste or genius of an artist, the reasons leading him to choose a particular style of painting or drama, to prefer this or that character of color, and to represent particular sentiments, we must seek for them in the social and intellectual conditions of the community in the midst of which he lived.

We have, therefore, to lay down this rule: that in order to comprehend a work of art, an artist, or a group of artists, we must clearly comprehend the general social and intellectual condition of the times to which they belong. Herein is to be found the final explanation; herein resides the primitive cause determining all that follows it. . . .

Just as there is a physical temperature, which by its variations determines the appearance of this or that species of plant, so there is a moral temperature, which by its variations determines the appearance of this or that species of art. And as we study the physical temperature in order to comprehend the advent of this or that species of plant . . . so it is necessary to study the moral temperature in order to comprehend the advent of various phases of art, whether pagan sculpture or realistic painting, mystic architecture or classical literature, voluptuous music or ideal poetry. The productions of the human mind, like those of animated nature, are only to be explained by their milieu. . . .

Suppose now we should succeed . . . and should be able to mark clearly and precisely the various intellectual conditions which have lead to the birth of Italian painting—its development, its bloom, its varieties and decline. Suppose the same undertaking succeeded with other countries, and other ages, and with the different branches of art, architecture, sculpture, painting, poetry and music. Suppose, that through the effect of all these discoveries, we succeed in defining the nature and in marking the conditions of existence of each art, we shall then have a complete explanation of the Fine Arts and of art in general; that is to say, a Philosophy of the Fine Arts—which is called an aesthetic system. This is what we aim at and nothing else. Ours is modern, and differs from the ancient, inasmuch as it is historic and not dogmatic; that is to say, it imposes no precepts, but ascertains and verifies laws. Ancient aesthetics gave, at first, a definition of beauty . . . ; then starting hence, as from an article of a code, they absolved, condemned, admonished and directed. It is my good fortune not to have such a formidable task to meet. . . . My sole duty is to offer you facts and show you how these facts are produced. The modern method . . . consists in considering human products, and particularly works of art, as facts and productions of which it is essential to mark the characteristics and seek the causes, and nothing more. Thus understood, science neither pardons nor prescribes; it verifies and explains. . . .

V.

. . . We have now arrived at a definition of the work of art. . . . We have by degrees arrived at a conception of art more and more elevated, and consequently more and more exact. At first we thought that the object of art was to imitate sensible appearances. Then separating material from intellectual imitation, we found that what it desired to produce in sensible appearances is the *relationships of parts*. Finally, remarking that relationships are, and ought to be, modified in order to obtain the highest reaches of art, we proved that if we study the relationship of parts it is to *make predominant an essential character*. . . . [T]hus to sum up the result of our labor:—"The end of a work of art is to manifest some essential or salient character, consequently some important idea, clearer and more completely than is attainable from real objects. Art accomplishes this end by employing a group of connected parts, the relationships of which it systematically modifies. . . ."

VII.

Now that we know the nature of art, we can comprehend its importance. . . . Our admiration for art can now be justified, and we can mark its place in the order of life.

Man, in many respects, is an animal endeavoring to protect himself against nature and against other men. He is obliged to provide himself with food, clothing and shelter, and to defend himself against climate, want and disease. To do this he tills the ground, navigates the sea . . . he forms families and states, and establishes magistracies, functionaries, constitutions, laws and armies. After so many inventions and such labor, he is not yet emancipated from his original condition. . . . At this moment a superior life dawns on him— that of contemplation, by which he is lead to interest himself in the creative and permanent causes on which his own being and that of his fellows depends, in the leading and essential characters which rule each aggregate, and impress their marks on the minutest details. Two ways are open to him for this purpose. The first is Science, by which, analyzing these causes and these fundamental laws, he expresses them in abstract terms and precise formulae; the second is Art, by which he manifests these causes and these fundamental laws no longer through definitions, inaccessible to the multitude, and only intelligible to a favored few, but in a sensible way, appealing not alone to reason, but also to the heart and senses of the humblest individual. Art has this peculiarity, that it is at once *noble* and *popular,* manifesting whatever is most exalted, and manifesting it to all.

WALTER PATER [1839–94]

→→→→←←←←

From *The Renaissance* [1868–73]

PREFACE

Many attempts have been made by writers on art and poetry to define beauty in the abstract, to express it in the most general terms, to find some universal formula for it. The value of these attempts has most often been in the suggestive and penetrating things said by the way. Such discussions help us very little to enjoy what has been well done in art or poetry, to discriminate between what is more and what is less excellent in them, or to use words like beauty, excellence, art, poetry, with a more precise meaning than they would otherwise have. Beauty, like all other qualities presented to human experience, is relative, and the definition of it becomes unmeaning and useless in proportion to its abstractness. To define beauty, not in the most abstract but in the most concrete terms possible, to find not its universal formula, but the formula which expresses most adequately this or that special manifestation of it, is the aim of the true student of aesthetics.

"To see the object as in itself it really is,"

From Walter Pater, *The Renaissance* (New York: Random House, n.d.), pp. xxv-xxviii, 194-9.

has been justly said to be the aim of all true criticism whatever; and in aesthetic criticism the first step towards seeing one's object as it really is, is to know one's own impression as it really is, to discriminate it, to realise it distinctly. The objects with which aesthetic criticism deals—music, poetry, artistic and accomplished forms of human life—are indeed receptacles of so many powers or forces: they possess, like the products of nature, so many virtues or qualities. What is this song or picture, this engaging personality presented in life or in a book, to *me?* What effect does it really produce on me? Does it give me pleasure? and if so, what sort or degree of pleasure? How is my nature modified by its presence, and under its influence? The answers to these questions are the original facts with which the aesthetic critic has to do; and, as in the study of light, of morals, of number, one must realise such primary data for one's self, or not at all. And he who experiences these impressions strongly, and drives directly at the discrimination and analysis of them, has no need to trouble himself with the abstract question what beauty is in itself, or what its exact relation to truth or experience—metaphysical questions, as unprofitable as metaphysical questions elsewhere. He may pass them all by as being, answerable or not, of no interest to him.

The aesthetic critic, then, regards all the objects with which he has to do, all works of art, and the fairer forms of nature and human life, as powers or forces producing pleasurable sensations, each of a more or less peculiar or unique kind. This influence he feels, and wishes to explain, by analysing and reducing it to its elements. To him, the picture, the landscape, the engaging personality in life or in a book, *La Gioconda*, the hills of Carrara, Pico of Mirandola, are valuable for their virtues, as we say, in speaking of a herb, a wine, a gem; for the property each has of affecting one with a special, a unique, impression of pleasure. Our education becomes complete in proportion as our susceptibility to these impressions increases in depth and variety. And the function of the aesthetic critic is to distinguish, to analyse, and separate from its adjuncts, the virtue by which a picture, a landscape, a fair personality in life or in a book, produces this special impression of beauty or pleasure, to indicate what the source of that impression is, and under what conditions it is experienced. His end is reached when he has disengaged that virtue, and noted it, as a chemist notes some natural element, for himself and others; and the rule for those who would reach this end is stated with great exactness in the words of a recent critic of Sainte-Beuve:—*De se borner à connaître de près les belles choses, et à s'en nourrir en exquis amateurs, en humanistes accomplis.*

What is important, then, is not that the critic should possess a correct abstract definition of beauty for the intellect, but a certain kind of temperament, the power of being deeply moved by the presence of beautiful objects. He will remember always that beauty exists in many forms. To him all periods, types, schools of taste, are in themselves equal. In all ages there have been some excellent workmen, and some

excellent work done. The question he asks is always:—In whom did the stir, the genius, the sentiment of the period find itself? where was the receptacle of its refinement, its elevation, its taste? "The ages are all equal," says William Blake, "but genius is always above its age."

Often it will require great nicety to disengage this virtue from the commoner elements with which it may be found in combination. Few artists, not Goethe or Byron even, work quite cleanly, casting off all *débris,* and leaving us only what the heat of their imagination has wholly fused and transformed. Take, for instance, the writings of Wordsworth. The heat of his genius, entering into the substance of his work, has crystallised a part, but only a part, of it; and in that great mass of verse there is much which might well be forgotten. But scattered up and down it, sometimes fusing and transforming entire compositions, like the Stanzas on *Resolution and Independence,* or the *Ode on the Recollections of Childhood,* sometimes, as if at random, depositing a fine crystal here or there, in a matter it does not wholly search through and transmute, we trace the action of his unique, incommunicable faculty, that strange, mystical sense of a life in natural things, and of man's life as a part of nature, drawing strength and color and character from local influences, from the hills and streams, and from natural sights and sounds. Well! that is the *virtue,* the active principle, in Wordsworth's poetry; and then the function of the critic of Wordsworth is to follow up that active principle, to disengage it, to mark the degree in which it penetrates his verse. . . .

. . .

CONCLUSION

To regard all things and principles of things as inconstant modes or fashions has more and more become the tendency of modern thought. Let us begin with that which is without—our physical life. Fix upon it in one of its more exquisite intervals, the moment, for instance, of delicious recoil from the flood of water in summer heat. What is the whole physical life in that moment but a combination of natural elements to which science gives their names? But those elements, phosphorus and lime and delicate fibres, are present not in the human body alone: we detect them in places most remote from it. Our physical life is a perpetual motion of them—the passage of the blood, the waste and repairing of the lenses of the eye, the modification of the tissues of the brain under every ray of light and sound—processes which science reduces to simpler and more elementary forces. Like the elements of which we are composed, the action of these forces extends beyond us: it rusts iron and ripens corn. Far out on every side of us those elements are broadcast, driven in many currents; birth and gesture and death and the springing of violets from the grave are but a few out of ten thousand resultant combinations. That clear, perpetual outline of face and limb is but an image of ours, under which we group them—a design in a web, the actual threads of which pass out beyond it. This at least of flame-like our life has, that it is but the concurrence, renewed from moment to moment, of forces parting sooner or later on their ways.

Or, if we begin with the inward world of thought and feeling, the whirlpool is still more rapid, the flame more eager and devouring. There it is no longer the gradual darkening of the eye, the gradual fading of colour from the wall—movements of the shore-side, where the water flows down indeed, though in apparent rest—but the race of the mid-stream, a drift of momentary acts of sight and passion and thought. At first sight experience seems to bury us under a flood of external objects, pressing upon us with a sharp and importunate reality, calling us out of ourselves in a thousand forms of action. But when reflexion begins to play upon those objects they are dissipated under its influence; the cohesive force seems suspended like some trick of magic; each object is loosed into a group of impressions—colour, odour, texture—in the mind of the observer. And if we continue to dwell in thought on this world, not of objects in the solidity with which language invests them, but of impressions, unstable, flickering, inconsistent, which burn and are extinguished with our consciousness of them, it contracts still further: the whole scope of observation is dwarfed into the narrow chamber of the individual mind. Experience, already reduced to a group of impressions, is ringed round for each one of us by that thick wall of personality through which no real voice has ever pieced on its way to us, or from us to that which we can only conjecture to be without. Every one of those impressions is the impression of the individual in his isolation, each mind keeping as a solitary prisoner its own dream of a world. Analysis goes a step farther still, and assures us that those impressions of the individual mind to which, for each one of us, experience dwindles down, are in perpetual flight; that each of them is limited by time, and that as time is infinitely divisible, each of them is infinitely divisible also; all that is actual in it being a single moment, gone while we try to apprehend it, of which it may ever be more truly said that it has ceased to be than that it is. To such a tremulous wisp constantly re-forming itself on the stream, to a single sharp impression, with a sense in it, a relic more or less fleeting, of such moments gone by, what is real in our life fines itself down. It is with this movement with the passage and dissolution of impressions, images, sensations, that analysis leaves off —that continual vanishing away, that strange, perpetual weaving and unweaving of ourselves.

Philosophieren, says Novalis, *ist dephlegmatisieren, vivificieren.* The service of philosophy, of speculative culture, towards the human spirit, is to rouse, to startle it to a life of constant and eager observation. Every moment some form grows perfect in hand or face; some tone on the hills or the sea is choicer than the rest; some mood of passion or insight or intellectual excitement is irresistibly real and attractive to us, —for that moment only. Not the fruit of experience, but experience itself is the end. A counted number of pulses only is given to us of a variegated, dramatic life. How may we see in them all that is to be seen in them by the finest senses? How shall we pass most swiftly from point to point, and be present always at the focus where the greatest number of vital forces unite in their purest energy?

To burn always with this hard, gemlike flame, to maintain this ecstasy, is success in life. In a sense it might even be said that our failure is to form habits: for after all, habit is relative to a stereotyped world, and meantime it is only the roughness of the eye that makes any two persons, things, situations, seem alike. While all melts under our feet, we may well grasp at any exquisite passion, or any contribution to knowledge that seems by a lifted horizon to set the spirit free for a moment, or any stirring of the senses, strange dyes, strange colours, and curious odours, or work of the artist's hands, or the face of one's friend. Not to discriminate every moment some passionate attitude to those about us, and in the very brilliancy of their gifts some tragic dividing of forces on their ways, is, on this short day of frost and sun, to sleep before evening. With this sense of the splendor of our experience and of its awful brevity, gathering all we are into one desperate effort to see and touch, we shall hardly have time to make theories about the things we see and touch. What we have to do is to be for ever curiously testing new opinions and courting new impressions, never acquiescing in a facile orthodoxy of Comte, or of Hegel, or of our own. Philosophical theories or ideas, as points of view, instruments of criticism,

may help us to gather up what might otherwise pass unregarded by us. "Philosophy is the microscope of thought." The theory or idea or system which requires of us the sacrifice of any part of this experience, in consideration of some interest into which we cannot enter, or some abstract theory we have not identified with ourselves, or of what is only conventional, has no real claim upon us.

One of the most beautiful passages of Rousseau is that in the sixth book of the *Confessions*, where he describes the awakening in him of the literary sense. An undefinable taint of death had clung always about him, and now in early manhood he believed himself smitten by mortal disease. He asked himself how he might make as much as possible of the interval that remained; and he was not biassed by anything in his previous life when he decided that it must be by intellectual excitement, which he found just then in the clear, fresh writings of Voltaire. Well! we are all *condamnés* as Victor Hugo says: we are all under sentence of death but with a sort of indefinite reprieve—*les hommes sont tous condamnés à mort avec des sursis indéfinis:* we have an interval, and then our place knows us no more. Some spend this interval in listlessness, some in high passions, the wisest, at least among "the children of this world," in art and song. For our one chance lies in expanding that interval, in getting as many pulsations as possible into the given time. Great passions may give us this quickened sense of life, ecstasy and sorrow of love, the various forms of enthusiastic activity, disinterested or otherwise, which come naturally to many of us. Only be sure it is passion—that it does yield you this fruit of a quickened, multiplied consciousness. Of such wisdom, the poetic passion, the desire of beauty, the love of art for its own sake, has most. For art comes to you proposing frankly to give nothing but the highest quality to your moments as they pass, and simply for those moments' sake.

FRIEDRICH NIETZSCHE [1844–1900]

>>>>><<<<<

From *The Birth of Tragedy* [1872]

We shall do a great deal for the science of aesthetics, once we perceive not merely by logical inference, but with the immediate certainty of intuition, that the continuous development of art is bound up with the *Apollonian* and *Dionysian* duality: just as procreation depends on the duality of the sexes, involving perpetual strife with only periodically intervening reconciliations. The terms Dionysian and Apollonian we borrow from the Greeks, who disclose to the discerning mind the profound mysteries of their view of art, not, to be sure, in concepts, but in the impressively clear figures of their gods. Through Apollo and Dionysus, the two art-deities of the Greeks, we come to recognize that in the Greek world there existed a sharp opposition, in origin and aims, between the Apollonian art of sculpture, and the non-plastic, Dionysian, art of music. These two distinct tendencies run parallel to each other, for the most part openly at variance; and they continually incite each other to new and more powerful births, which perpetuate an antogonism, only superficially reconciled by the common term "Art"; till at last, by a metaphysical miracle of the Hellenic will, they appear coupled with each other, and through this coupling eventually generate the art-product, equally Dionysian and Apollonian, of Attic tragedy.

In order to grasp these two tendencies, let us first conceive of them as the separate art-worlds of *dreams* and *drunkenness*.

From Friedrich Nietzsche, *The Birth of Tragedy,* translated by Clifton P. Fadiman, Sections 1, 16, 21. Copyright 1927 and renewed 1954 by The Modern Library, Inc. Reprinted from *The Philosophy of Nietzsche,* by permission of Random House, Inc.

These physiological phenomena present a contrast analogous to that existing between the Apollonian and the Dionysian. It was in dreams, says Lucretius, that the glorious divine figures first appeared to the souls of men; in dreams the great shaper beheld the splendid corporeal structure of superhuman beings; and the Hellenic poet, if questioned about the mysteries of poetic inspiration, would likewise have suggested dreams. . . .

The beautiful appearance of the dreamworlds, in creating which every man is a perfect artist, is the prerequisite of all plastic art, and in fact, as we shall see, of an important part of poetry also. In our dreams we delight in the immediate apprehension of form; all forms speak to us; none are unimportant, none are superfluous. But, when this dream-reality is most intense, we also have, glimmering through it, the sensation of its appearance: at least this is my experience, as to whose frequency, aye, normality, I could adduce many proofs, in addition to the sayings of the poets. Indeed, the man of philosophic mind has a presentiment that underneath this reality in which we live and have our being, is concealed another and quite different reality, which, like the first, is an appearance; and Schopenhauer actually indicates as the criterion of philosophical ability the occasional ability to view men and things as mere phantoms or dream-pictures. Thus the aesthetically sensitive man stands in the same relation to the reality of dreams as the philosopher does to the reality of existence; he is a close and willing observer, for these pictures afford him an interpretation of life, and it is by these processes that he trains himself for life. And it is not only the agreeable and friendly pictures that he experiences in himself with such perfect understanding: but the serious, the troubled, the sad, the gloomy, the sudden restraints, the tricks of fate, the uneasy presentiments, in short, the whole Divine Comedy of life, and the Inferno, also pass before him, not like mere shadows on the wall—for in these scenes he lives and suffers—and yet not without that fleeting sensation of appearance. And perhaps many will, like myself, recall that amid the dangers and terrors of dream-life they would at times, cry out in self-encouragement, and not without success. "It is only a dream! I will dream on!" I have likewise heard of persons capable of continuing one and the same dream for three and even more successive nights: facts which indicate clearly that our innermost beings, our common subconscious experiences, express themselves in dreams because they must do so and because they take profound delight in so doing.

This joyful necessity of the dream-experience has been embodied by the Greeks in their Apollo: for Apollo, the god of all plastic energies, is at the same time the soothsaying god. He, who (as the etymology of the name indicates) is the "shining one," the deity of light, is also ruler over the fair appearance of the inner world of fantasy. The higher truth, the perfection of these states in contrast to the incompletely intelligible everyday world, this deep consciousness of nature, healing and helping in sleep and dreams, is at the same time the symbolical analogue of the soothsaying faculty and of the arts generally, which make life possible and worth living. But we must also include in our picture of Apollo that delicate boundary, which the dream-picture must not overstep—lest it act pathologically (in which case appearance would impose upon us as pure reality). We must keep in mind that measured restraint, that freedom from the wilder emotions, that philosophical calm of the sculptor-god. . . . We might apply to Apollo the

words of Schopenhauer when he speaks of the man wrapped in the veil of Mâyâ: *Welt als Wille und Vorstellung*, I. p. 416: "Just as in a stormy sea, unbounded in every direction, rising and falling with howling mountainous waves, a sailor sits in a boat and trusts in his frail barque: so in the midst of a world of sorrows the individual sits quietly, supported by and trusting in his *principium individuationis*." In fact, we might say of Apollo, that in him the unshaken faith in this *principium* and the calm repose of the man wrapped therein receive their sublimest expression; and we might consider Apollo himself as the glorious divine image of the *principium individuationis*, whose gestures and expression tell us of all the joy and wisdom of "appearance," together with its beauty.

In the same work Schopenhauer has depicted for us the terrible *awe* which seizes upon man, when he is suddenly unable to account for the cognitive forms of a phenomenon, when the principle of reason, in some one of its manifestations, seems to admit of an exception. If we add to this awe the blissful ecstasy which rises from the innermost depths of man, aye, of nature, at this very collapse of the *principium individuationis*, we shall gain an insight into the nature of the *Dionysian*, which is brought home to us most intimately perhaps by the analogy of *drunkenness*. It is either under the influence of the narcotic draught, which we hear of in the songs of all primitive men and peoples, or with the potent coming of spring penetrating all nature with joy, that these Dionysian emotions awake, which, as they intensify, cause the subjective to vanish into complete self-forgetfulness. . . .

Under the charm of the Dionysian not only is the union between man and man reaffirmed, but Nature which has become estranged, hostile, or subjugated, celebrates once more her reconciliation with her prodigal son, man. Freely earth proffers her gifts, and peacefully the beasts of prey approach from desert and mountain. The chariot of Dionysus is bedecked with flowers and garlands; panthers and tigers pass beneath his yoke. . . . Now the slave is free; now all the stubborn, hostile barriers, which necessity, caprice or "shameless fashion" have erected between man and man, are broken down. Now, with the gospel of universal harmony, each one feels himself not only united, reconciled, blended with his neighbor, but as one with him; he feels as if the veil of Mâyâ had been torn aside and were now merely fluttering in tatters before the mysterious Primordial Unity. In song and in dance man expresses himself as a member of a higher community; he has forgotten how to walk and speak; he is about to take a dancing flight into the air. His very gestures bespeak enchantment. Just as the animals now talk, just as the earth yields milk and honey, so from him emanates supernatural sounds. He feels himself a god, he himself now walks about enchanted, in ecstasy, like to the gods whom he saw walking about in his dreams. He is no longer an artist, he has become a work of art: in these paroxysms of intoxication the artistic power of all nature reveals itself to the highest gratification of the Primordial Unity. The noblest clay, the most costly marble, man, is here kneaded and cut, and to the sound of the chisel strokes of the Dionysian world-artist rings out the cry of the Eleusinian mysteries: "Do ye bow in the dust, O millions? Do you divine your creator, O world?"

. . .

. . . In contrast to all those who are intent on deriving the arts from one exclusive principle, as the necessary vital source of every work of art, I shall keep my eyes fixed on the two artistic deities of the Greeks, Apollo and Dionysus, and recognise in them the living and conspicuous representatives of *two* worlds of art differing in their intrinsic essence and in their highest aims. I see Apollo as the transfig-

uring genius of the *principium individuationis* through which alone the redemption in appearance is truly to be obtained; while by the mystical triumphant cry of Dionysus the spell of individuation is broken, and the way lies open to the Mothers of Being, to the innermost heart of things. This extraordinary antithesis, which stretches like a yawning gulf between plastic art as the Apollonian, and music as the Dionysian art, has revealed itself to only one of the great thinkers, to such an extent that, even without this clue to the symbolism of the Hellenic divinities, he conceded to music a character different from, and an origin anterior to, all the other arts, because, unlike them, it is not a copy of the phenomenon, but an immediate copy of the will itself, and therefore represents *the metaphysical of everything physical in the world,* the thing-in-itself of every phenomenon. (Schopenhauer, *Welt als Wille und Vorstellung,* I. 310.) . . .

Perhaps we may lead up to this fundamental problem by asking: what aesthetic effect results when the essentially separate art-forces, the Apollonian and the Dionysian, enter into simultaneous activity? Or more briefly: how is music related to image and concept? . . .

According to the doctrine of Schopenhauer . . . we may understand music as the immediate language of the will, and we feel our fancy stimulated to give form to this invisible and yet so actively stirred spirit-world which speaks to us, and we feel prompted to embody it in an analogous example. On the other hand, image and concept, under the influence of a truly corresponding music, acquire a higher significance. Dionysian art therefore is wont to exercise two kinds of influences on the Apollonian art-faculty: music incites to the *symbolic-intuition* of Dionysian universality, and music allows the symbolic image to emerge *in its highest significance.* From these facts, intelligible in themselves and not inaccessible to a more penetrating examination, I infer the capacity of music to give birth to *myth* (the most significant exemplar), and particularly the *tragic myth*: the myth which expresses Dionysian knowledge in symbols. In the phenomenon of the lyrist, I have shown how music strives to express its nature in Apollonian images. If now we reflect that music at its greatest intensity must seek to attain also to its highest symbolization, we must deem it possible that it also knows how to find the symbolic expression for its unique Dionysian wisdom; and where shall we seek for this expression if not in tragedy and, in general, in the conception of the tragic?

From the nature of art as it is usually conceived according to the single category of appearance and beauty, the tragic cannot honestly be deduced at all; it is only through the spirit of music that we can understand the joy involved in the annihilation of the individual. For only by the particular examples of such annihilation are we made clear as to the eternal phenomenon of Dionysian art, which gives expression to the will in its omnipotence, as it were, behind the *principium individuationis,* the eternal life beyond all phenomena, and despite all annihilation. The metaphysical joy in the tragic is a translation of the instinctive unconscious Dionysian wisdom into the language of the scene: the hero, the highest manifestation of the will, is disavowed for our pleasure, because he is only phenomenon, and because the eternal life of the will is not affected by his annihilation. "We believe in eternal life," exclaims tragedy; while music is the immediate idea of this life. Plastic art has an altogether different aim: here Apollo dispels the suffering of the individual by the radiant glorification of the *eternity of the phenomenon*: here beauty triumphs over the suffering inherent in life; pain is in a sense obliterated from the features of nature. In Dionysian art and its tragic symbolism the same na-

ture cries to us with its true, undissembled voice: "Be as I am! Amidst the ceaseless flux of phenomena I am the eternally creative primordial mother, eternally impelling to existence, eternally self-sufficient amid this flux of phenomena!"

. . .

. . . But if we ask what medicinal means enabled the Greeks, in their best period, despite the fury of their Dionysian and political impulses, neither to exhaust themselves in ecstatic brooding, nor in a consuming scramble for empire and worldly honor, but on the contrary to achieve the splendid mixture which we find in a noble, inflaming, and contemplatively disposing wine, we must remember the enormous power of *tragedy,* exciting, purifying, and releasing the entire life of a people; the highest value of which we shall divine only when, as with the Greeks, it presents itself as the essence of all the prophylactic healing forces, as the mediator arbitrating between the strongest and most inherently fateful characteristics of a people.

Tragedy absorbs into itself the highest musical ecstasy so that it absolutely brings music to perfection among the Greeks, as among ourselves; but it then places beside it tragic myth and the tragic hero. The latter, like a mighty Titan, takes the entire Dionysian world on his shoulders and relieves us of the burden; while, on the other hand, by means of this same tragic myth, tragedy is able through the tragic hero, to deliver us from the intense longing for this existence, and to remind us with warning hand of another existence and a higher joy, for which the struggling hero prepares himself presentiently by his destruction, not by his victories. Tragedy sets a sublime symbol, the myth, between the universal authority of its music and the receptive Dionysian hearer, and produces in him the illusion that music is only the most effective means for the animating, the plastic world of myth. Relying upon this noble illusion, she may now move her limbs for the dithyrambic dance, and abandon herself unhesitatingly to an orgiastic feeling of freedom, in which, as music itself, without this illusion, she could not venture to indulge. The myth, while protecting us from the music, on the other hand, affords it the highest freedom. By way of return, music imparts to tragic myth an impressive and convincing metaphysical significance such as could never be attained by word and image, without this unique aid; and the tragic spectator in particular experiences thereby the sure presentment of supreme joy to which the path through destruction and negation leads; so that he imagines he hears the innermost abyss of things speaking audibly to him. . . .

Here between our highest excitement and the music in question are interposed the tragic myth and the tragic hero—in reality only as symbols of the most universal facts, of which only music can speak directly. If, however, we felt as purely Dionysian beings, myth as a symbol would stand by us absolutely ineffective and unnoticed, and would never for a moment prevent us from giving ear to the re-echo of the *universalia ante rem*. Here, however, the *Apollonian* power, with a view to the restoration of the almost shattered individuals, bursts forth with the healing balm of the blissful illusion: all of a sudden we imagine we see only Tristan, motionless, asking himself dully: "The old tune, why does it wake me?" And what once moved us like a hollow sigh from the heart of being now seems to tell us only how "waste and empty is the sea." And whereas, breathless, we once thought to expire by a convulsive distention of all our feelings, and only a slender tie bound us to our present existence, we now hear and see only the hero wounded to death, yet not dying, with his despairing cry: "Longing! Longing! In death still longing! for very

longing not dying!" And whereas, formerly after such an excess and superabundance of consuming agonies, the jubilation of the horn rent our hearts almost like the very extreme of agony, the rejoicing Kurwenal now stands between us and this "jubilation as such," his face turned toward the ship which carries Isolde. However powerfully we are touched by fellow-suffering, it nevertheless delivers us in a manner from the primordial suffering of the world, just as the symbol-image of the myth delivers us from the immediate perception of the highest world-idea, just as the thought and the word deliver us from the unchecked effusion of the unconscious will. The glorious Apollonian illusion makes it appear as if the very tone-world presented itself to us as a plastic cosmos, as if even the fate of Tristan and Isolde had been merely formed and molded therein as out of some most soft and yielding material.

Thus does the Apollonian tear us away from Dionysian universality and make us delight in individuals; to these it attaches our sympathetic emotion; through these it satisfies our sense of beauty which longs for great and sublime forms; it presents us with biographical portraits, and incites us to a thoughtful comprehension of the essence of life dwelling within them. With the immense combined power of the image, the concept, the ethical teaching and the sympathetic emotion—the Apollonian influence uplifts man from his orgiastic self-annihilation and deceives him concerning the universality of the Dionysian process into the belief that he is seeing a detached picture of the world (Tristan and Isolde for instance), and that, *through music,* he will be enabled to *see* it with still more essential clearness. What can the healing magic of Apollo not accomplish when it can even excite in us the illusion that the Dionysian is actually in the service of the Apollonian and is capable of enhancing its effects, in fact, that music is essentially the representative art for an Apollonian content?

By means of the pre-established harmony obtaining between perfected drama and its music, the drama attains the highest degree of conspicuousness, such as is usually unattainable in mere spoken drama. As all the animated figures of the scene in the independently evolved lines of melody simplify themselves before us to the distinctness of a single curved line, the co-existence of these lines is also audible in the harmonic change which sympathizes in a most delicate manner as the process evolves: through which change the relations of things become immediately perceptible to us in a sensible and not at all abstract manner, as we likewise perceive that it is only in these relations that the essence of a character and of a melodic line manifests itself clearly. And while music thus compels us to a broader and more intensive vision than usual, and makes us spread out the curtain of the scene before our eyes like a delicate texture, the world of the stage is as infinitely expanded for our spiritualized, introspective eye as it is illumined outwardly from within. How can the word-poet furnish anything analogous, who strives to attain this internal expansion and illumination of the visible stage-world by a much more imperfect mechanism and by an indirect method, proceeding as he does from word and concept? Although musical tragedy also avails itself of the word, it can at the same time place beside it its basis and origin, and can make clear to us the development of the word, from within outwards.

Concerning the process just described, however, we may still make the definite statement that it is only a glorious appearance, namely, the aforementioned Appollonian *illusion,* through whose influence we are to be delivered from the Dionysian obtrusion and excess. For, at bottom, the relation of music to drama is precisely the reverse; music is the essential idea of of the world, drama is but the reflection of this idea, a detached adumbration of it. The identity between the melody and the living form, between the harmony and the character-relations of that form, is true in a sense opposite to what one would suppose on the contemplation of musical tragedy. We may agitate and enliven the form in the most conspicuous manner, and illuminate it from within, but it still remains merely a phenomenon, from which there is no bridge to lead us to the true reality, to the heart of the world. But out of this heart speaks music; and though countless phenomena of the kind might be passing manifestations of this music, they could never exhaust its essence, but would always be merely its externalized copies. Of course, as regards the intricate relation of music and drama, nothing can be explained, while everything may be confused by the popular and thoroughly false antithesis of soul and body; but the unphilosophical crudeness of this antithesis seems to have become—who knows for what reasons —a readily accepted Article of Faith with our aestheticians, while they have learned nothing concerning an antithesis of the phenomenon and the thing-in-itself—or perhaps for equally unknown reasons they have not cared to learn anything about it.

Should our analysis have established the point that the Apollonian element in tragedy has by means of its illusion gained a complete victory over the Dionysian primordial element of music, and has made music itself subservient to its end, namely, the clearest possible elucidation of the drama, it would certainly be necessary to add a very important restriction: that at the most essential point this Apollonian illusion is dissolved and annihilated. The drama, which, aided by music, unfolds itself before us with such inwardly illumined distinctness in all its movements and figures, that we imagine we see the texture unfolding on the loom as the shuttle flies to and fro—this drama attains as a whole an effect which *transcends all Apollonian artistic effects*. In the collective effect of tragedy, the Dionysian once again dominates. Tragedy closes with a sound which could never emanate from the realm of Apollonian art. And the Apollonian illusion thereby reveals itself as what it really is— the assiduous veiling during the performance of the tragedy of the intrinsically Dionysian effect: which, however, is so powerful, that it ends by forcing the Apollonian drama itself into a sphere where it begins to talk with Dionysian wisdom, and even denies itself and its Apollonian conspicuousness. So that the intricate relation of the Apollonian and the Dionysian in tragedy may really be symbolized by a fraternal union of the two deities: Dionysus speaks the language of Apollo; Apollo, however, finally speaks the language of Dionysus; and so the highest goal of tragedy and of art in general is attained.

From *The Will to Power*

Apollonian, Dionysian. There are two conditions in which art manifests itself in man even as a force of nature, and disposes of him whether he consent or not: it may be as a constraint to visionary states, or it may be an orgiastic impulse. Both conditions are to be seen in normal life, but they are then somewhat weaker: in dreams and in moments of elation or intoxication.

But the same contrast exists between the dream state and the state of intoxication: both of these states let loose all manner of artistic powers within us, but each unfetters powers of a different kind. Dream-

From Friedrich Nietzsche, *The Will to Power*, translated by A. M. Ludovici (London: T. N. Foulis, 1910), Part IV. Reprinted by permission of George Allen & Unwin, Ltd.

land gives us the power of vision, of association, of poetry: intoxication gives us the power of grand attitudes of passion, of song, and of dance.

Sexuality and voluptuousness belong to the Dionysiac intoxication: but neither of them is lacking in the Apollonian state. There is also a difference of tempo between the states. . . . *The extreme peace of certain feelings of intoxication* (or, more strictly, the slackening of the feeling of time, and the reduction of the feeling of space) is wont to reflect itself in the vision of the most restful attitudes and states of the soul. The classical style essentially represents repose, simplification, foreshortening, and concentration—the *highest feeling of power* is concentrated in the classical type. To react with difficulty: great consciousness: no feeling of strife.

The feeling of intoxication is, as a matter of fact, equivalent to a sensation of *surplus power*: it is strongest in seasons of rut: new organs, new accomplishments, new colours, new forms. Embellishment is an outcome of *increased power*. Embellishment is merely an expression of a triumphant will, of an increased state of co-ordination, of a harmony of all the strong desires, of an infallible and perpendicular equilibrium. Logical and geometrical simplification is the result of an increase of power: conversely, the mere aspect of such a simplification increases the sense of power in the beholder. . . . The zenith of development: the grand style.

Ugliness signifies *the decadence of a type*: contradiction and faulty co-ordination among the inmost desires—this means a decline in the *organising* power, or, psychologically speaking, in the "will."

The condition of pleasure which is called intoxication is really an exalted feeling of power. . . . Sensations of space and time are altered; inordinate distances are traversed by the eye, and only then become visible; the extension of the vision over greater masses and expanses; the refinement of the organ which apprehends the smallest and most elusive things; divination, the power of understanding at the slightest hint, at the smallest suggestion; intelligent sensitiveness; *strength* as a feeling of dominion in the muscles, as agility and love of movement, as dance, as levity and quick time; strength as the love of proving strength, as bravado, adventurousness, fearlessness, indifference in regard to life and death. . . . All these elated moments of life stimulate each other; the world of images and of imagination of the one suffices as a suggestion for the other: in this way states finally merge into each other which might do better to keep apart, e.g. the feeling of religious intoxication and sexual irritability (two very profound feelings, always wonderfully co-ordinated. What is it that pleases almost all pious women, old or young? Answer: a saint with beautiful legs, still young, still innocent). Cruelty in tragedy and pity (likewise normally correlated). Spring-time, dancing, music, —all these things are but the display of one sex before the other—as also that "infinite yearning of the heart" peculiar to Faust.

Artists when they are worth anything at all are men of strong propensities (even physically), with surplus energy, powerful animals, sensual; without a certain overheating of the sexual system a man like Raphael is unthinkable. . . . To produce music is also in a sense to produce children; chastity is merely the economy of the artist, and in all creative artists productiveness certainly ceases with sexual potency. . . . Artists should not see things as they are; they should see them fuller, simpler, stronger: to this end, however, a kind of youthfulness, of vernality, a sort of perpetual elation, must be peculiar to their lives.

The states in which we transfigure things and make them fuller, and rhapsodise about them, until they reflect our own fulness and love of life back upon us: sexuality, intoxication, post-prandial states, spring, triumph over our enemies, scorn, bravado, cruelty, the ecstasy of religious feeling. But three elements above all are active: *sexuality, intoxication, cruelty;* all these belong to the oldest *festal joys* of mankind, they also preponderate in budding artists.

Conversely: there are things with which we meet which already show us this transfiguration and fulness, and the animal world's response thereto is a state of excitement in the spheres where these states of happiness originate. A blending of these very delicate shades of animal well-being and desires is the *aesthetic state.* The latter only manifests itself in those natures which are capable of that spendthrift and overflowing fulness of bodily vigour; the latter is always the *primum mobile.* The sober-minded man, the tired man, the exhausted and dried-up man (e.g. the scholar), can have no feeling for art, because he does not possess the primitive force of art, which is the tyranny of inner riches: he who cannot give anything away cannot feel anything either.

"Perfection."—In these states (more particularly in the case of sexual love) there is an ingenuous betrayal of what the profoundest instinct regards as the highest, the most desirable, the most valuable, the ascending movement of its type; also of the condition towards which it is actually striving. Perfection: the extraordinary expansion of this instinct's feeling of power, its riches, its necessary overflowing of all banks.

Art reminds us of states of physical vigour: it may be the overflow and bursting forth of blooming life in the world of pictures and desires; on the other hand, it may be an excitation of the physical functions by means of pictures and desires of exalted life—an enhancement of the feeling of life, the latter's stimulant.

To what extent can ugliness exercise this power? In so far as it may communicate something of the triumphant energy of the artist who has become master of the ugly and the repulsive; or in so far as it gently excites our lust of cruelty (in some circumstances even the lust of doing harm to ourselves, self-violence, and therewith the feeling of power over ourselves).

"Beauty" therefore is, to the artist, something which is above all order of rank, because in beauty contrasts are overcome, the highest sign of power thus manifesting itself in the conquest of opposites; and achieved without a feeling of tension: violence being no longer necessary, everything submitting and obeying so easily, and doing so with good grace; this is what delights the powerful will of the artist.

The biological value of *beauty* and *ugliness*. That which we feel instinctively opposed to us aesthetically is, according to the longest experience of mankind, felt to be harmful, dangerous, and worthy of suspicion: the sudden utterance of the aesthetic instinct, e.g. in the case of loathing, implies an act of judgment. To this extent beauty lies within the general category of the biological values, useful, beneficent, and life-promoting: thus, a host of stimuli which for ages have been associated with, and remind us of, useful things and conditions, give us the feeling of beauty, i.e. the increase of the feeling of power (not only things, therefore, but the sensations which are associated with such things or their symbols).

In this way beauty and ugliness are recognised as determined by our most fundamental self-preservative values. Apart from this, it is nonsense to postulate anything as beautiful or ugly. Absolute beauty exists just as little as absolute goodness and truth. In a particular case it is a matter of the self-preservative conditions of a certain type of man: thus the gregarious man will have quite a different feeling for beauty from the exceptional or super-man.

It is the optics of things in the foreground which only consider immediate consequences, from which the value beauty (also goodness and truth) arises.

All instinctive judgments are shortsighted in regard to the concatenation of consequences: they merely advise what must be done forthwith. Reason is essentially an obstructing apparatus preventing the immediate response to instinctive judgments: it halts, it calculates, it traces the chain of consequences further.

Judgments concerning beauty and ugliness are short-sighted (reason is always opposed to them): but they are convincing in the highest degree; they appeal to our instincts in that quarter where the latter decide most quickly and say yes or no with least hesitation, even before reason can interpose.

The most common affirmations of beauty stimulate each other reciprocally; where the aesthetic impulse once begins to work, a whole host of other and foreign perfections crystallise around the "particular form of beauty." It is impossible to remain objective, it is certainly impossible to dispense with the interpreting, bestowing, transfiguring, and poetising power (the latter is a stringing together of affirmations concerning beauty itself). The sight of a beautiful woman. . . .

Thus (1) judgment concerning beauty is short-sighted; it sees only the immediate consequences.

(2) It smothers the object which gives rise to it with a charm that is determined by the association of various judgments concerning beauty, which, however, are quite alien to the *essence of the particular object*. To regard a thing as beautiful is necessarily to regard it falsely (that is why incidentally love marriages are from the social point of view the most unreasonable form of matrimony).

Concerning the genesis of Art.—That making perfect and seeing perfect, which is peculiar to the cerebral system overladen with sexual energy (a lover alone with his sweetheart at eventide transfigures the smallest details: life is a chain of sublime things, "the misfortune of an unhappy love affair is more valuable than anything else"); on the other hand, everything perfect and beautiful operates like an unconscious recollection of that amorous condition and of the point of view peculiar to it—all perfection, and the whole of the beauty of things, through contiguity, revives aphrodisiac bliss. (Physiologically it is the creative instinct of the artist and the distribution of his semen in his blood.) The desire for art and beauty is an indirect longing for the ecstasy of sexual desire, which gets communicated to the brain. The world become perfect through "love."

. . .

All art works like a suggestion on the muscles and the senses which were originally active in the ingenuous artistic man; its voice is only heard by artists—it speaks to this kind of man, whose constitution is attuned to such subtlety in sensitiveness. The concept "layman" is a misnomer. The deaf man is not a subdivision of the class whose ears are sound. All art works as a *tonic*; it increases strength, it kindles desire (i.e. the feeling of strength), it excites all the more subtle recollections of intoxication; there is actually a special kind of memory which underlies such states—a distant fitful world of sensations here returns to being.

Ugliness is the contradiction of art. It is that which art *excludes*, the *negation* of art: wherever decline, impoverishment of life, impotence, decomposition, dissolution, are felt, however remotely, the aesthetic man reacts with his No. Ugliness *depresses*: it is the sign of depression. It *robs* strength, it impoverishes, it weighs down. . . . Ugliness *suggests* repulsive things. From one's states of health one can test how an indisposition may increase one's power of fancying ugly things. One's

selection of things, interests, and questions becomes different. Logic provides a state which is next to kin to ugliness: heaviness, bluntness. In the presence of ugliness equilibrium is lacking in a mechanical sense: ugliness limps and stumbles—the direct opposite of the godly agility of the dancer.

The aesthetic state represents an overflow *of means of communication* as well as a condition of extreme sensibility to stimuli and signs. It is the zenith of communion and transmission between living creatures it is the source of languages. In it, languages, whether of signs, sounds, or glances, have their birthplace. The richer phenomenon is always the beginning: our abilities are subtilised forms of richer abilities. But even to-day we still listen with our muscles, we even read with our muscles.

Every mature art possesses a host of conventions as a basis: in so far as it is a language. Convention is a condition of great art, *not* an obstacle to it. . . . Every elevation of life likewise elevates the power of communication, as also the understanding of man. *The power of living in other people's souls* originally had nothing to do with morality, but with a physiological irritability of suggestion: "sympathy," or what is called "altruism," is merely a product of that psycho-motor relationship which is reckoned as spirituality (psycho-motor induction, says Charles Féré). People never communicate a thought to one another: they communicate a movement, an imitative sign which is then interpreted as a thought.

Compared with music, communication by means of words is a shameless mode of procedure; words reduce and stultify; words make impersonal; words make common that which is uncommon.

It is exceptional states that determine the artist—such states as are all intimately related and entwined with morbid symptoms, so that it would seem almost impossible to be an artist without being ill.

The physiological conditions which in the artist become moulded into a "personality," and which, to a certain degree, may attach themselves to any man:—

(1) Intoxication, the feeling of enhanced power; the inner compulsion to make things a mirror of one's own fulness and perfection.

(2) The extreme sharpness of certain senses, so that they are capable of understanding a totally different language of signs—and to create such a language (this is a condition which manifests itself in some nervous diseases); extreme susceptibility out of which great powers of communion are developed; the desire to speak on the part of everything that is capable of making signs; a need of being rid of one's self by means of gestures and attitudes; the ability of speaking about one's self in a hundred different languages—in fact, a state of *explosion*.

One must first imagine this condition as one in which there is a pressing and compulsory desire of ridding one's self of the ecstasy of a state of tension, by all kinds of muscular work and movement; also as an involuntary *co-ordination* of these movements with inner processes (images, thoughts, desires)—as a kind of automatism of the whole muscular system under the compulsion of strong stimuli acting from within; the inability to resist reaction; the apparatus of resistance is also suspended. Every inner movement (feeling, thought, emotion) is accompanied by *vascular changes,* and consequently by changes in colour, temperature, and secretion. The suggestive power of music, its *"suggestion mentale."*

(3) *The compulsion to imitate:* extreme irritability, by means of which a certain example becomes contagious—a condition is guessed and represented merely by means of a few signs. . . . A complete picture is visualised by one's inner consciousness,

and its effect soon shows itself in the movement of the limbs,—in a certain suspension of the *will* (Schopenhauer !!!!). A sort of blindness and deafness towards the external world,—the realm of admitted stimuli is sharply defined.

This differentiates the artist from the layman (from the spectator of art): the latter reaches the height of his excitement in the mere act of apprehending: the former in giving—and in such a way that the antagonism between these two gifts is not only natural but even desirable. Each of these states has an opposite standpoint —to demand of the artist that he should have the point of view of the spectator (of the critic) is equivalent to asking him to impoverish his creative power. . . . In this respect the same difference holds good as that which exists between the sexes: one should not ask the artist who gives to become a woman—to *"receive."*

Our aesthetics have hitherto been women's aesthetics, inasmuch as they have only formulated the experiences of what is beautiful, from the point of view of the receivers in art. In the whole of philosophy hitherto the artist has been lacking . . . i.e. as we have already suggested, a necessary fault: for the artist who would begin to understand himself would therewith begin to mistake himself—he must not look backwards, he must not look at all; he must give.—It is an honour for an artist to have no critical faculty; if he can criticise he is mediocre, he is modern.

. . .

A romanticist is an artist whose great dissatisfaction with himself makes him productive—who looks away from himself and his fellows, and sometimes, therefore, looks backwards.

Is art the result of dissatisfaction with reality? or is it the expression of gratitude for happiness experienced? In the first case, it is romanticism; in the second, it is glorification and dithyramb (in short, apotheosis art): even Raphael belongs to this, except for the fact that he was guilty of the duplicity of having deified the Christian view of the world. He was thankful for life precisely where it was not exactly Christian. . . .

Romanticism and its opposite. In regard to all aesthetic values I now avail myself of this fundamental distinction: in every individual case I ask myself has hunger or has superabundance been creative here? At first another distinction might perhaps seem preferable,—it is far more obvious,— e.g. the distinction which decides whether a desire for stability, for eternity, for Being, or whether a desire for instruction, for change, for Becoming, has been the cause of creation. But both kinds of desire, when examined more closely, prove to be ambiguous, and as a matter of fact are only susceptible of interpretation in the light of the scheme which I think I was right to place foremost.

The desire for destruction, for change, for Becoming, may be the expression of an overflowing power pregnant with promises for the future (my term for this, as is well known, is Dionysian); it may, however, also be the hate of the ill-constituted, of the needy and of the physiologically botched, that destroys, and must destroy, because such creatures are indignant at, and annoyed by, everything lasting and stable.

The act of immortalising can, on the other hand, be the outcome of gratitude and love: an art which has this origin is always an apotheosis art; dithyrambic, as perhaps with Rubens; happy, as perhaps with Hafiz; bright and gracious, and shedding a ray of glory over all things, as in Goethe. But creation may also, however, be the outcome of the tyrannical will of the great sufferer who would make the most personal, individual, and narrow trait about him, the actual idiosyncrasy of his pain—in fact, into a binding law and imposition,

and who thus wreaks his revenge upon all things by stamping, branding, and violating them with the image of his torment. The latter case is romantic pessimism in its highest form, whether this be Schopenhauerian voluntarism or Wagnerian music.

. . .

What is tragic?—Again and again I have pointed to the great misunderstanding of Aristotle in maintaining that the tragic emotions were the two depressing emotions —fear and pity. Had he been right, tragedy would be an art unfriendly to life: it would have been necessary to caution people against it as against something generally harmful and suspicious. Art, otherwise the great stimulus of life, the great intoxicant of life, the great will to life, here became a tool of decadence, the handmaiden of pessimism and ill-health (for to suppose, as Aristotle supposed, that by exciting these emotions we thereby purged people of them, is simply an error). Something which habitually excites fear or pity, disorganises, weakens, and discourages: and supposing Schopenhauer were right in thinking that tragedy taught resignation (i.e. a meek renunciation of happiness, hope, and of the will to live), this would presuppose an art in which art itself was denied. Tragedy would then constitute a process of dissolution; the instinct of life would destroy itself in the instinct of art. Christianity, Nihilism, tragic art, physiological decadence; these things were supposed to be linked, they were supposed to preponderate together and to assist each other onwards—downwards. . . . Tragedy would thus be a symptom of decline.

This theory may be refuted in the most cold-blooded way, namely, by measuring the effect of a tragic emotion by means of a dynamometer. The result would be a fact which only the bottomless falsity of a doctrinaire could misunderstand: that tragedy is a tonic. If Schopenhauer refuses to see the truth here, if he regards general depression as a tragic condition, if he would have informed the Greeks that they did not firmly possess the highest principles of life: it is only owing to his *parti pris,* to the need of consistency in his system, to the dishonesty of the doctrinaire—that dreadful dishonesty which step by step corrupted the whole psychology of Schopenhauer (he who had arbitrarily and almost violently misunderstood genius, art itself, morality, pagan religion, beauty, knowledge, and almost everything).

The tragic artist.—Whether, and in regard to what, the judgment "beautiful" is established is a question of an individual's or of a people's strength. The feeling of plenitude, of overflowing strength (which gaily and courageously meets many an obstacle before which the weakling shudders) —the feeling of power utters the judgment "beautiful" concerning things and conditions which the instinct of impotence can only value as hateful and ugly. The *flair* which enables us to decide whether the objects we encounter are dangerous, problematic, or alluring, likewise determines our aesthetic Yea. ("This is beautiful," is an affirmation).

From this we see that, generally speaking, a preference for questionable and terrible things is a symptom of strength; whereas the taste for pretty and charming trifles is characteristic of the weak and the delicate. The love of tragedy is typical of strong ages and characters: its *non plus ultra* is perhaps the *Divina Commedia.* It is the heroic spirits which in tragic cruelty say Yea unto themselves: they are hard enough to feel pain as a pleasure.

On the other hand, supposing weaklings desire to get pleasure from an art which was not designed for them, what interpretation must we suppose they would like to give tragedy in order to make it suit their taste? They would interpret their own feelings of value into it: e.g. the "triumph of the moral order of things," or the teaching

of the "uselessness of existence," or the incitement to "resignation" (or also half-medicinal and half-moral outpourings, *à la* Aristotle). Finally, the art of terrible natures, in so far as it may excite the nerves, may be regarded by the weak and exhausted as a stimulus: this is now taking place, for instance, in the case of the admiration meted out to Wagner's art. A test of man's well-being and consciousness of power is the extent to which he can acknowledge the terrible and questionable character of things, and whether he is in any need of a faith at the end.

This kind of artistic pessimism is precisely the reverse of that religio-moral pessimism which suffers from the corruption of man and the enigmatic character of existence: the latter insists upon deliverance, or at least upon the hope of deliverance. Those who suffer, doubt, and distrust themselves, —the sick, in other words,—have in all ages required the transporting influence of visions in order to be able to exist at all (the notion "blessedness" arose in this way). A similar case would be that of the artists of decadence, who at bottom maintain a Nihilistic attitude to life, and take refuge in the beauty of form,—in those select cases in which Nature is perfect, in which she is indifferently great and indifferently beautiful. (The "love of the beautiful" may thus be something very different: it may be the expression of impotence in this respect.) The most convincing artists are those who make harmony ring out of every discord, and who benefit all things by the gift of their power and inner harmony: in every work of art they merely reveal the symbol of their inmost experiences—their creation is gratitude for their life.

The depth of the tragic artist consists in the fact that his aesthetic instinct surveys the more remote results, that he does not halt shortsightedly at the thing that is nearest, that he says Yea to the whole cosmic economy, and that he justifies the terrible, the evil, and the questionable; that he more than justifies it.

WILLIAM MORRIS [1834–96]

>>>>><<<<

From *Art and the People: A Socialist's Protest against Capitalist Brutality* [1883]

The words Popular Art, or Art of the People, have a meaning, you may be sure; the thing which they mean has really existed, or you would have little to look at when you stray into the National Gallery and the British Museum: the Art of the People has in many places and in many times solaced and sustained the people amidst their griefs and troubles.

And a great gift such an art seems to me; an art made intelligently by the whole body of those who live by their labour: instinct with their thoughts and aspirations, moving whither they are moving, changing as they change, the genuine expression of their sense of the beauty and mystery of life: an art born of their joy and outliving their sorrow, though tinged by it: an art leaving to future ages living witness of the existence of deft hands and eager minds not too proud to tell us of their imperfect thoughts and their glimpses of insight into wonders and terrors, as they passed amid the hurry of their daily work through the sunshine and the shadow of their lives.

This, I say, is the Art of the People, and on this is founded all Art which is worth anything. I do not believe that Art worthy of the name can long exist, unless it rests on such a foundation: . . .

And one thing I must tell you before I go further, that this art is not a mere dream of something which might have been; as I have said it has in many times

From *William Morris*, Vol. II., "Morris as a Socialist," edited by May Morris (Oxford: Basil Blackwell, 1936), pp. 382-405. Reprinted by permission of Basil Blackwell.

and places solaced the lives of toiling men; and this I have noticed of the times and places where it has flourished, that it has always been in advance of the apparent progress of the times that produced it. I have been astonished when I have looked into the popular art of past ages to find work so refined and elegant done in times so rude and rough: work bearing so many tokens of quick wit and invention done in times so ignorant and superstitious; works showing so many signs of freedom of thought and pleasure in life and external nature in days which seem to us to have been so full of oppression, gloom and turmoil; all these, mind you, qualities of hand and soul which could not have been produced to the order of rich men; for such qualities are spontaneous and cannot be bought with money or compelled by power; in short it is not easy to exaggerate the contrast between the beauty and thoughtfulness of the handicrafts of certain periods, and the folly and disgrace of their history as otherwise told. . . .

Now the fine arts must be divided into two classes or kinds: the first what we may call the intellectual Arts, represented by painting and sculpture, address themselves wholly to the mind of man; they have no necessary connexion with any articles of material use, I mean. . . .[B]ut besides these strictly intellectual Arts, there is a large body of art (or the pretence of it) which forms part of the matters of our daily life; our houses, our furniture, our utensils for eating and drinking, and our clothes are ornamented by this lesser kind of art, which cannot be dissociated from the things which we use every day: and this is commonly called decorative or ornamental art. . . . [W]hile nations and times (though not many) have lacked the purely intellectual art, no nation or time has ever consented to do without the ornamental art; and lastly I must tell you that in all times when the Arts were in a healthy condition there was an intimate connexion between these two kinds of art; nay moreover that in those times when art flourished most, the higher and the lower kinds of art were divided from one another by no hard and fast lines; the highest of the intellectual art had ornamental character in it and appealed to all men, and to all the faculties of a man; while the humblest of the ornamental art shared in the meaning and deep feeling of the intellectual; one melted into the other by scarce perceptible gradations: or to put it in other words, the best artist was a workman, the humblest workman was an artist.

Well, let us see how it fares with art today: . . . as a body the whole public, Upper, Middle and Lower classes, is ignorant of art: apart from the artists themselves and those very few persons who have special gifts of sympathy with them, there is no real knowledge of what art means; nothing at the best save certain vague prepossessions, which are but the phantoms of that Tradition I have spoken of, which once bound artist and public together. Therefore the artists are obliged to express themselves, as it were, in a language "not understood of the people": nor is this their fault; if they were to try, as some think they should, to meet the public halfway, and work in such a manner as to satisfy only those prepossessions of men ignorant of art, they would be casting aside their special gifts, and would become traitors to that cause of art which it is their duty and glory to serve: they have no choice save to do their own personal work without any hope of being understood as things now are; to stand apart as possessors of some sacred mystery, which, whatever happens, they must at least do their best to guard: and by this isolation their loss is great; great both to their own minds and to the work they produce; and as to our loss, the loss of the public, it is not easy to measure: for, you see, it comes to this, if we are to consider the distribution of the great and elevating intellectual pleasure of the enjoyment of the higher arts, that only a very few among the most cultivated classes can share in it.

But . . . what is likely to be the state of that other side of the fine arts which is commonly called decorative art; art which is to be found on nearly every piece of goods which is offered for sale? How is it likely to be with this art which above all other depends on the co-operation of men with each other?

. . . I will simply assert that under the system I have been speaking of it is impossible to turn out art: you must take an artist's word for that.

Let us look at the system again and summarize its beautiful arrangements: I am supposing it, mind you, to be a system for the production of art as it verily professes to be in some degree in all cases, while sometimes it is supposed to be employed making wares which are pure works of art. This in short is the system: at the head is a man who is absolutely master of the production, who is forced by his position not to heed whether what he produces is good or bad so long as it sells at a profit: his will is carried one step further by subordinates who have to take care that the wares shall sell at a profit and of nothing else; and finally the "hands" who accomplish the will of the "captain of labour" have one thing only to do, to make their labour profitable—to their master.

What place can art have in such a system? How much can people care about art who will put up with the products of such a system? . . .

Therefore the sad truth is that there is no popular art today, no art which represents the feelings and aspirations of the people at large, as for example the buildings of the Middle Ages represented the feelings and aspirations of the people, gentle and simple, lay and clerk, of that period. . . .

. . . [O]f what used to be popular art there remains but a ghastly pretence of ornament which is nothing but a commercial imposture, or at best but a foolish survival of a half-remembered habit. . . .

Popular art is a thing the world once had and has now lost: is the loss grievous or trivial?

I answer first by another question: Is it right that the most of civilized men, all town-dwellers at least, should be deprived of the sight of beautiful things? is it right that they should, except on rare occasions, have to look on mere squalid ugliness?

I do not think we can seriously argue that question: consider what it means; loss of the sense of beauty. Indeed you may say that people will get used to it and will not feel it: alas! that is too true of this loss as of others. Think then what follows! We shall no longer be able to understand the meaning of the poets and great writers of the world; their language will be dead to us. What would be left to us indeed of all that makes life worth living? What! shall man go on generation after generation gaining fresh command over the powers of nature, gaining more and more luxurious appliances for the comfort of the body yet generation after generation losing some portion of his natural senses: that is, of his life and soul? Think of a race of men whose eyes are only of use to serve them to carry their food to their mouths without spilling it! . . .

I can easily suppose that it seems strange to most of you to hear that there can be pleasure in labour: and truly to most men nowadays . . . there is no pleasure in it; yet there are still a few men whose life is spent in creating beauty for the sake of beauty, that is to say that their work may give pleasure to themselves and others.

Now consider such work, think of the pleasure that lies in a great piece of intellectual art, a picture, a poem or a piece of music; the pleasure and elevation of soul which you receive from it as you look or read or listen: think of this I say, and I believe it will be as inconceivable to you as it is to me that such work can be done without pleasure, that what it has rejoiced you so to receive has been no joy, nothing but weariness for the author, the inventor, to give. . . .

Now further I assert that some portion of this pleasure of creation is felt by every man who duly makes anything for the benefit of mankind: in which sentence you see there lie two important claims for labour: the first that such labour must be *duly* done; the second that it must be done for the benefit of the commonwealth.

It must be duly done; there must be in it some of the keen interest which every healthy man takes in healthy life; and in order that there may be such interest, it must have in it variety and hope besides that mysterious bodily pleasure which goes with the deft exercise of the bodily powers: the variety and hope that should go with all labour are intimately connected with each other: for the hope means hope of excellence, the hope of doing something different from day to day; nay in the end, of doing something which no other man but the workman has yet thought of in some respects at least: a piece of work so done, you understand, is a work of art, and he who does it is an artist, and only so done can any work that has any endurance in it be done duly.

But also not only must the work be done duly, but it must be done for the benefit of the commonwealth: when done it must be worth the trouble and labour spent on it, and when this claim is satisfied there is added self-respect to the hope and variety which I have just claimed as due to worthy labour: so that the pleasure which an artist, that is a free workman, feels in his labour, is made up of these three things, variety, hope of excellence and self-respect: and the feelings of those who receive his work with due sympathy may be expressed by the corresponding words, surprise, pleasure and gratitude: and, believe me, the knowledge that one's work will be so received is a reward which the greatest man cannot afford to fall short of, and which the humblest cannot be deprived of without suffering grievous wrong.

But the workman of today is not free:

he is during his working hours at least the slave of a system of labour which does not in the least concern itself with his pleasure in the work: instead of the incitement of the hope of excellence and the amusement of variety, it uses one goad to labour, the fear of ruin and starvation: . . .

Who can wonder that all work which can be ill done is ill done nowadays? it would be more reasonable hope to expect to find figs on thistles than to find art growing from such a system.

LEO TOLSTOY [1828–1910]

What Is Art? [1898]

CHAPTER II

. . . What is this art, which is considered so important and necessary for humanity that for its sake these sacrifices of labour, of human life, and even of goodness may be made?

"What is art? What a question! Art is architecture, sculpture, painting, music and poetry in all its forms," usually replies the ordinary man, the art amateur, or even the artist himself, imagining the matter about which he is talking to be perfectly clear, and uniformly understood by everybody. But in architecture, one inquires further, are there not simple buildings which are not objects of art, and buildings with artistic pretensions which are unsuccessful and ugly and therefore cannot be considered as works of art?

It is the same in sculpture, in music and in poetry. Art, in all its forms, is bounded on one side by the practically useful and

From Tolstoy, *What Is Art? and Essays on Art*, translated by Aylmer Maude (London: Oxford University Press, 1930). Selections are from Chapters II, IV, V, VI, XV, XVI. Reprinted by permission of Oxford University Press.

on the other by unsuccessful attempts at art. How is art to be marked off from each of these? The ordinary educated man of our circle, and even the artist who has not occupied himself especially with aesthetics, will not hesitate at this question either. He thinks the solution has been found long ago, and is well known to everyone.

"Art is such an activity as produces beauty," says such a man. . . .

CHAPTER IV

What then is this conception of beauty, so stubbornly held to by people of our circle and day as furnishing a definition of art?

In the subjective aspect, we call beauty that which supplies us with a particular kind of pleasure.

In the objective aspect, we call beauty something absolutely perfect, and we acknowledge it to be so only because we receive, from the manifestation of this absolute perfection, a certain kind of pleasure; so that this objective definition is nothing but the subjective conception differently expressed. In reality both conceptions of beauty amount to one and the same thing, namely, the reception by us of a certain kind of pleasure, i.e. we call "beauty" that which pleases us without evoking in us desire.

Such being the position of affairs, it would seem only natural that the science of art should decline to content itself with a definition of art based on beauty (i.e. on that which pleases), and seek a general definition, which should apply to all artistic productions, and by reference to which we might decide whether a certain article belonged to the realm of art or not. But no such definition is supplied, as the reader may see from those summaries of the aesthetic theories which I have given, and as he may discover even more clearly from the original aesthetic works, if he will be at the pains to read them. All attempts to define absolute beauty in itself—whether as an imitation of nature, or as suitability to its object, or as a correspondence of parts, or as symmetry, or as harmony, or as unity in variety, etc.—either define nothing at all, or define only some traits of some artistic productions, and are far from including all that everybody has always held, and still holds, to be art.

There is no objective definition of beauty. The existing definitions (both the metaphysical and the experimental), amount only to one and the same subjective definition which (strange as it seems to say so) is, that art is that which makes beauty manifest, and beauty is that which pleases (without exciting desire). Many aestheticians have felt the insufficiency and instability of such a definition, and, in order to give it a firm basis, have asked themselves why a thing pleases. And they have converted the discussion on beauty into a question concerning taste, as did Hutcheson, Voltaire, Diderot, and others. But all attempts to define what taste is must lead to nothing, as the reader may see both from the history of aesthetics and experimentally. There is and can be no explanation of why one thing pleases one man and displeases another, or vice

versa. So that the whole existing science of aesthetics fails to do what we might expect from it, being a mental activity calling itself a science, namely, it does not define the qualities and laws of art, or of the beautiful (if that be the content of art), or the nature of taste (if taste decides the question of art and its merit), and then, on the basis of such definitions, acknowledge as art those productions which correspond to these laws, and reject those which do not come under them. But this science of aesthetics consists in first acknowledging a certain set of productions to be art (because they please us), and then framing such a theory of art that all those productions which please a certain circle of people should fit into it. There exists an art canon, according to which certain productions favoured by our circle are acknowledged as being art,—Phidias, Sophocles, Homer, Titian, Raphael, Bach, Beethoven, Dante, Shakespeare, Goethe, and others,—and the aesthetic laws must be such as to embrace all these productions. In aesthetic literature you will incessantly meet with opinions on the merit and importance of art, founded not on any certain laws by which this or that is held to be good or bad, but merely on the consideration whether this art tallies with the art canon we have drawn up. . . .

All the existing aesthetic standards are built on this plan. Instead of giving a definition of true art, and then deciding what is and what is not good art by judging whether a work conforms or does not conform to the definition, a certain class of works, which for some reason please a certain circle of people, is accepted as being art, and a definition of art is then devised to cover all these productions. I recently came upon a remarkable instance of this method in a very good German work, *The History of Art in the Nineteenth Century*, by Muther. Describing the pre-Raphaelites, the Decadents and the Symbolists (who are already included in the canon of art), he not only does not venture to blame their tendency, but earnestly endeavours to widen his standard so that it may include them all, they appearing to him to represent a legitimate reaction from the excesses of realism. No matter what insanities appear in art, when once they find acceptance among the upper classes of our society a theory is quickly invented to explain and sanction them; just as if there had never been periods in history when certain special circles of people recognised and approved false, deformed, and insensate art which subsequently left no trace and has been utterly forgotten. And to what lengths the insanity and deformity of art may go, especially when, as in our days, it knows that it is considered infallible, may be seen by what is being done in the art of our circle to-day.

So that the theory of art, founded on beauty, expounded by aesthetics, and, in dim outline, professed by the public, is nothing but the setting up as good, of that which has pleased and pleases us, i.e. pleases a certain class of people.

In order to define any human activity, it is necessary to understand its sense and importance. And, in order to do that, it is primarily necessary to examine that activity in itself, in its dependence on its causes, and in connection with its effects, and not merely in relation to the pleasure we can get from it.

If we say that the aim of any activity is merely our pleasure, and define it solely by that pleasure, our definition will evidently be a false one. But this is precisely what has occurred in the efforts to define art. Now, if we consider the food question, it will not occur to anyone to affirm that the importance of food consists in the pleasure we receive when eating it. Everyone understands that the satisfaction of our taste cannot serve as a basis for our definition of the merits of food, and that we have therefore no right to presuppose that the

dinners with cayenne pepper, Limburg cheese, alcohol, etc., to which we are accustomed and which please us, form the very best human food.

And in the same way, beauty, or that which pleases us, can in no sense serve as the basis for the definition of art; nor can a series of objects which afford us pleasure serve as the model of what art should be.

To see the aim and purpose of art in the pleasure we get from it, is like assuming (as is done by people of the lowest moral development, e.g. by savages) that the purpose and aim of food is the pleasure derived when consuming it.

Just as people who conceive the aim and purpose of food to be pleasure cannot recognise the real meaning of eating, so people who consider the aim of art to be pleasure cannot realise its true meaning and purpose, because they attribute to an activity, the meaning of which lies in its connection with other phenomena of life, the false and exceptional aim of pleasure. People come to understand that the meaning of eating lies in the nourishment of the body only when they cease to consider that the object of that activity is pleasure. And it is the same with regard to art. People will come to understand the meaning of art only when they cease to consider that the aim of that activity is beauty, i.e. pleasure. The acknowledgment of beauty (i.e. of a certain kind of pleasure received from art) as being the aim of art, not only fails to assist us in finding a definition of what art is, but, on the contrary, by transferring the question into a region quite foreign to art (into metaphysical, psychological, and even historical discussions as to why such a production pleases one person, and such another displeases or pleases someone else), it renders such definition impossible. And since discussions as to why one man likes pears and another prefers meat do not help towards finding a definition of what is essential in nourishment, so the solution of questions of taste in art (to which the discussions on art involuntarily come) not only does not help to make clear what this particular human activity which we call art really consists in, but renders such elucidation quite impossible, until we rid ourselves of a conception which justifies every kind of art, at the cost of confusing the whole matter.

To the question, What is this art, to which is offered up the labour of millions, the very lives of men, and even morality itself? we have extracted replies from the existing aesthetics, which all amount to this: that the aim of art is beauty, that beauty is recognised by the enjoyment it gives, and that artistic enjoyment is a good and important thing, because it *is* enjoyment. In a word, that enjoyment is good because it is enjoyment. Thus, what is considered the definition of art is no definition at all, but only a shuffle to justify existing art. Therefore, however strange it may seem to say so, in spite of the mountains of books written about art, no exact definition of art has been constructed. And the reason of this is that the conception of art has been based on the conception of beauty.

CHAPTER V

What is art, if we put aside the conception of beauty, which confuses the whole matter? The latest and most comprehensible definitions of art, apart from the conception of beauty, are the following:—(1 *a*) Art is an activity arising even in the animal kingdom, and springing from sexual desire and the propensity to play (Schiller, Darwin, Spencer), and (1 *b*) accompanied by a pleasurable excitement of the nervous system (Grant Allen). This is the physiological-evolutionary definition. (2) Art is the external manifestation, by means of lines, colours, movements, sounds, or words, of emotions felt by man (Véron). This is the experimental definition. According to the very latest definition (Sully), (3) Art

is "the production of some permanent object, or passing action, which is fitted not only to supply an active enjoyment to the producer, but to convey a pleasurable impression to a number of spectators or listeners, quite apart from any personal advantage to be derived from it."

Notwithstanding the superiority of these definitions to the metaphysical definitions which depended on the conception of beauty, they are yet far from exact. (1 *a*) The first, the physiological-evolutionary definition, is inexact, because, instead of speaking about the artistic activity itself, which is the real matter in hand, it treats of the derivation of art. The modification of it (1 *b*), based on the physiological effects on the human organism, is inexact, because within the limits of such definition many other human activities can be included, as has occurred in the neo-aesthetic theories, which reckon as art the preparation of handsome clothes, pleasant scents, and even of victuals.

The experimental definition (2), which makes art consist in the expression of emotions, is inexact, because a man may express his emotions by means of lines, colours, sounds, or words, and yet may not act on others by such expression; and then the manifestation of his emotions is not art.

The third definition (that of Sully) is inexact, because in the production of objects or actions affording pleasure to the producer and a pleasant emotion to the spectators or hearers apart from personal advantage, may be included the showing of conjuring tricks or gymnastic exercises, and other activities which are not art. And, further, many things, the production of which does not afford pleasure to the producer, and the sensation received from which is unpleasant, such as gloomy, heart-rending scenes in a poetic description or a play, may nevertheless be undoubted works of art.

The inaccuracy of all these definitions

arises from the fact that in them all (as also in the metaphysical definitions) the object considered is the pleasure art may give, and not the purpose it may serve in the life of man and of humanity.

In order correctly to define art, it is necessary, first of all, to cease to consider it as a means to pleasure, and to consider it as one of the conditions of human life. Viewing it in this way, we cannot fail to observe that art is one of the means of intercourse between man and man.

Every work of art causes the receiver to enter into a certain kind of relationship both with him who produced, or is producing, the art, and with all those who, simultaneously, previously or subsequently, receive the same artistic impression.

Speech, transmitting the thoughts and experiences of men, serves as a means of union among them, and art acts in a similar manner. The peculiarity of this latter means of intercourse, distinguishing it from intercourse by means of words, consists in this, that whereas by words a man transmits his thoughts to another, by means of art he transmits his feelings.

The activity of art is based on the fact that a man, receiving through his sense of hearing or sight another man's expression of feeling, is capable of experiencing the emotion which moved the man who expressed it. To take the simplest example: one man laughs, and another, who hears, becomes merry; or a man weeps, and another, who hears, feels sorrow. A man is excited or irritated, and another man, seeing him, comes to a similar state of mind. By his movements, or by the sounds of his voice, a man expresses courage and determination, or sadness and calmness, and this state of mind passes on to others. A man suffers, expressing his sufferings by groans and spasms, and this suffering transmits itself to the other people; a man expresses his feeling of admiration, devotion, fear, respect, or love to certain objects, persons, or phenomena, and others are infected by the same feelings of admiration, devotion, fear, respect, or love to the same objects, persons, and phenomena.

And it is on this capacity of man to receive another man's expression of feeling, and experience those feelings himself, that the activity of art is based.

If a man infects another or others, directly, immediately, by his appearance, or by the sounds he gives vent to at the very time he experiences the feeling; if he causes another man to yawn when he himself cannot help yawning, or to laugh or cry when he himself is obliged to laugh or cry, or to suffer when he himself is suffering—that does not amount to art.

Art begins when one person, with the object of joining another or others to himself in one and the same feeling, expresses that feeling by certain external indications. To take the simplest example: a boy, having experienced, let us say, fear on encountering a wolf, relates that encounter; and, in order to evoke in others the feeling he had experienced, describes himself, his condition before the encounter, and surroundings, the wood, his own lightheartedness, and then the wolf's appearance, its movements, the distance between himself and the wolf, etc. All this, if only the boy when telling the story, again experiences the feelings he had lived through and infects the hearers and compels them to feel what the narrator had experienced, is art. If even the boy had not seen a wolf but had frequently been afraid of one, and if, wishing to evoke in others the fear he had felt, he invented an encounter with a wolf, and recounted it so as to make his hearers share the feelings he experienced when he feared the wolf, that also would be art. And just in the same way it is art if a man, having experienced either the fear of suffering or the attraction of enjoyment (whether in reality or in imagination), expresses these feelings on canvas or in marble so that others are infected by them. And it is also art if a man feels or imagines to himself feelings of delight, gladness, sorrow, despair, courage, or despondency, and the transition from one to another of these feelings, and expresses these feelings by sounds, so that the hearers are infected by them, and experience them as they were experienced by the composer.

The feelings with which the artist infects others may be most various—very strong or very weak, very important or very insignificant, very bad or very good: feelings of love for native land, self-devotion and submission to fate or to God expressed in a drama, raptures of lovers described in a novel, feelings of voluptuousness expressed in a picture, courage expressed in a triumphal march, merriment evoked by a dance, humour evoked by a funny story, the feeling of quietness transmitted by an evening landscape or by a lullaby, or the feeling of admiration evoked by a beautiful arabesque—it is all art.

If only the spectators or auditors are infected by the feelings which the author has felt, it is art.

To evoke in oneself a feeling one has once experienced, and having evoked it in oneself, then, by means of movements, lines, colours, sounds, or forms expressed in words, so to transmit that feeling that others may experience the same feeling— this is the activity of art.

Art is a human activity, consisting in this, that one man consciously, by means of certain external signs, hands on to others feelings he has lived through, and that other people are infected by these feelings, and also experience them.

Art is not, as the metaphysicians say, the manifestation of some mysterious Idea of beauty, or God; it is not, as the aesthetical physiologists say, a game in which man lets off his excess of stored-up energy; it is not the expression of man's emotions by external signs; it is not the production of pleasing objects; and, above all, it is not pleasure; but it is a means of union among men, joining them together in the same

feelings, and indispensable for the life and progress towards well-being of individuals and of humanity.

As, thanks to man's capacity to express thoughts by words, every man may know all that has been done for him in the realms of thought by all humanity before his day, and can, in the present, thanks to this capacity to understand the thoughts of others, become a sharer in their activity, and can himself hand on to his contemporaries and descendants the thoughts he has assimilated from others, as well as those which have arisen within himself; so, thanks to man's capacity to be infected with the feelings of others by means of art, all that is being lived through by his contemporaries is accessible to him, as well as the feelings experienced by men thousands of years ago, and he has also the possibility of transmitting his own feelings to others.

If people lacked this capacity to receive the thoughts conceived by the men who preceded them, and to pass on to others their own thoughts, men would be like wild beasts, or like Kaspar Hauser.

And if men lacked this other capacity of being infected by art, people might be almost more savage still, and, above all, more separated from, and more hostile to, one another.

And therefore the activity of art is a most important one, as important as the activity of speech itself, and as generally diffused.

We are accustomed to understand art to be only what we hear and see in theatres, concerts, and exhibitions; together with buildings, statues, poems, novels. . . . But all this is but the smallest part of the art by which we communicate with each other in life. All human life is filled with works of art of every kind—from cradle-song, jest, mimicry, the ornamentation of houses, dress and utensils, up to church services, buildings, monuments, and triumphal processions. It is all artistic activity. So that by art, in the limited sense of the word, we do not mean all human activity transmitting feelings, but only that part which we for some reason select from it and to which we attach special importance.

This special importance has always been given by all men to that part of this activity which transmits feelings flowing from their religious perception, and this small part of art they have specifically called art, attaching to it the full meaning of the word.

That was how men of old—Socrates, Plato, and Aristotle—looked on art. Thus did the Hebrew prophets and the ancient Christians regard art; thus it was, and still is, understood by the Mohammedans, and thus is it still understood by religious folk among our own peasantry.

Some teachers of mankind—as Plato in his *Republic,* and people such as the primitive Christians, the strict Mohammedans, and the Buddhists—have gone so far as to repudiate all art.

People viewing art in this way (in contradiction to the prevalent view of to-day, which regards any art as good if only it affords pleasure) considered, and consider, that art (as contrasted with speech, which need not be listened to) is so highly dangerous in its power to infect people against their wills, that mankind will lose far less by banishing all art than by tolerating each and every art.

Evidently such people were wrong in repudiating all art, for they denied that which cannot be denied—one of the indispensable means of communication, without which mankind could not exist. But not less wrong are the people of civilised European society of our class and day, in favouring any art if it but serves beauty, i.e. gives people pleasure.

Formerly, people feared lest among the works of art there might chance to be some causing corruption, and they prohibited art altogether. Now, they only fear lest they should be deprived of any enjoy-ment art can afford, and patronise any art. And I think the last error is much grosser than the first, and that its consequences are far more harmful.

CHAPTER VI

But how could it happen that the very art, which in ancient times was merely tolerated (if tolerated at all), should have come, in our times, to be invariably considered a good thing if only it affords pleasure?

It has resulted from the following causes. The estimation of the value of art (i.e. of the feelings it transmits) depends on men's perception of the meaning of life; depends on what they consider to be the good and the evil of life. And what is good and what is evil is defined by what are termed religions.

Humanity unceasingly moves forward from a lower, more partial, and obscure understanding of life, to one more general and more lucid. And in this, as in every movement, there are leaders,—those who have understood the meaning of life more clearly than others,—and of these advanced men there is always one who has, in his words and by his life, expressed this meaning more clearly, accessibly, and strongly than others. This man's expression of the meaning of life, together with those superstitions, traditions, and ceremonies which usually form themselves round the memory of such a man, is what is called a religion. Religions are the exponents of the highest comprehension of life accessible to the best and foremost men at a given time in a given society; a comprehension towards which, inevitably and irresistibly, all the rest of that society must advance. And therefore only religions have always served, and still serve, as bases for the valuation of human sentiments. If feelings bring men nearer the ideal their religion indicates, if they are in harmony with it and do not contradict it, they are good; if they estrange men from it and oppose it, they are bad.

If the religion places the meaning of life in worshipping one God and fulfilling what is regarded as His will, as was the case among the Jews, then the feelings flowing from love to that God, and to His law, successfully transmitted through the art of poetry by the prophets, by the psalms, or by the epic of the book of Genesis, is good, high art. All opposing that, as for instance the transmission of feelings of devotion to strange gods, or of feelings incompatible with the law of God, would be considered bad art. Or if, as was the case among the Greeks, the religion places the meaning of life in earthly happiness, in beauty and in strength, then art successfully transmitting the joy and energy of life would be considered good art, but art which transmitted feelings of effeminacy or despondency would be bad art. If the meaning of life is seen in the well-being of one's nation, or in honouring one's ancestors and continuing the mode of life led by them, as was the case among the Romans and the Chinese respectively, then art transmitting feelings of joy at sacrificing one's personal well-being for the common weal, or at exalting one's ancestors and maintaining their traditions, would be considered good art; but art expressing feelings contrary to this would be regarded as bad. If the meaning of life is seen in freeing oneself from the yoke of animalism, as is the case among the Buddhists, then art successfully transmitting feelings that elevate the soul and humble the flesh will be good art, and all that transmits feelings strengthening the bodily passions will be bad art.

In every age, and in every human society, there exists a religious sense, common to that whole society, of what it good and what is bad, and it is this religious conception that decides the value of the feelings transmitted by art. And therefore, among all nations, art which transmitted feelings considered to be good by this general religious sense was recognised as being good and was encouraged; but art which transmitted feelings considered to be bad by this general religious conception, was recognised as being bad, and was rejected. All the rest of the immense field of art by means of which people communicate one with another, was not esteemed at all, and was only noticed when it ran counter to the religious conception of its age, and then merely to be repudiated. . . .

. . .

CHAPTER XV

Art, in our society, has been so perverted that not only has bad art come to be considered good, but even the very perception of what art really is has been lost. In order to be able to speak about the art of our society, it is, therefore, first of all necessary to distinguish art from counterfeit art.

There is one indubitable indication distinguishing real art from its counterfeit, namely, the infectiousness of art. If a man, without exercising effort, or seeing another man's work, experiences a mental condition which unites him with that man and with other people who also partake of that work of art, then the object evoking that condition is a work of art. And however poetical, realistic, effectual, or interesting a work may be, it is not a work of art if it does not evoke that feeling (quite distinct from all other feelings) of joy, and of spiritual union with another (the author) and with others (those who are also infected by it).

It is true that this indication is an *internal* one, and that there are people who have forgotten what the action of real art is, who expect something else from art (in our society the great majority are in this state), and that therefore such people may mistake for this aesthetic feeling the feeling of divertisement and a certain excitement which they receive from counterfeits of art. But though it is impossible to undeceive these people, just as it is impossible to convince a man suffering from "Daltonism" that green is not red, yet, for all that, this indication remains perfectly definite to those whose feeling for art is neither perverted nor atrophied, and it clearly distinguishes the feeling produced by art from all other feelings.

The chief peculiarity of this feeling is that the receiver of a true artistic impression is so united to the artist that he feels as if the work were his own and not someone else's—as if what it expresses were just what he had long been wishing to express. A real work of art destroys, in the consciousness of the receiver, the separation between himself and the artist, nor that alone, but also between himself and all whose minds receive the work of art. In this freeing of our personality from its separation and isolation, in this uniting of it with others, lies the chief characteristic and the great attractive force of art.

If a man is infected by the author's condition of soul, if he feels this emotion and this union with others, then the object which has effected this is art; but if there be no such infection, if there be not this union with the author and with others who are moved by the same work—then it is not art. And not only is infection a sure sign of art, but the degree of infectiousness is also the sole measure of excellence in art.

The stronger the infection the better is the art, as art, speaking now apart from its subject-matter, i.e. not considering the quality of the feelings it transmits.

And the degree of the infectiousness of art depends on three conditions:—

(1) On the greater or lesser individuality of the feeling transmitted; (2) on the greater or lesser clearness with which the feeling is transmitted; (3) on the sincerity of the artist, i.e. on the greater or lesser force with which the artist himself feels the emotion he transmits.

The more individual the feeling transmitted the more strongly does it act on the receiver; the more individual the state of soul into which he is transferred the more pleasure does the receiver obtain, and therefore the more readily and strongly does he join in it.

The clearness of expression assists infection, because the receiver, who mingles in consciousness with the author, is the better satisfied the more clearly the feeling is transmitted, which, as it seems to him, he has long known and felt, and for which he has only now found expression.

But most of all is the degree of infectiousness of art increased by the degree of sincerity in the artist. As soon as the spectator, hearer, or reader feels that the artist is infected by his own production, and writes, sings, or plays for himself and not merely to act on others, this mental condition of the artist infects the receiver; and, contrariwise, as soon as the spectator, reader, or hearer feels that the author is not writing, singing, or playing for his own satisfaction,—does not himself feel what he wishes to express,—but is doing it for him, the receiver, a resistance immediately springs up, and the most individual and the newest feelings and the cleverest technique not only fail to produce any infection but actually repel.

I have mentioned three conditions of contagiousness in art, but they may all be summed up into one, the last, sincerity, i.e. that the artist should be impelled by an inner need to express his feeling. That condition includes the first; for if the artist is sincere he will express the feeling as he experienced it. And as each man is different from everyone else, his feeling will be individual for everyone else; and the more individual it is,—the more the artist has drawn it from the depths of his nature,—the more sympathetic and sincere will it be. And this same sincerity will impel the artist to find a clear expression of the feeling which he wishes to transmit.

Therefore this third condition—sincerity—is the most important of the three. It is always complied with in peasant art, and this explains why such art always acts so powerfully; but it is a condition almost entirely absent from our upper-class art, which is continually produced by artists actuated by personal aims of covetousness or vanity.

Such are the three conditions which divide art from its counterfeits, and which also decide the quality of every work of art apart from its subject-matter.

The absence of any one of these conditions excludes a work from the category of art and relegates it to that of art's counterfeits. If the work does not transmit the artist's peculiarity of feeling, and is therefore not individual, if it is unintelligibly expressed, or if it has not proceeded from the author's inner need for expression—it is not a work of art. If all these conditions are present, even in the smallest degree, then the work, even if a weak one, is yet a work of art.

The presence in various degrees of these three conditions: individuality, clearness, and sincerity, decides the merit of a work of art, as art, apart from subject-matter. All works of art take rank of merit according to the degree in which they fulfill the first, the second, and the third of these conditions. In one the individuality of the feeling transmitted may predominate; in another, clearness of expression; in a third, sincerity; while a fourth may have sincerity and individuality but be deficient in clearness; a fifth, individuality and clearness, but less sincerity; and so forth, in all possible degrees and combinations.

Thus is art divided from not art, and thus is the quality of art, as art, decided, independently of its subject-matter, i.e. apart from whether the feelings it transmits are good or bad.

But how are we to define good and bad with reference to its subject-matter.

CHAPTER XVI

How in art are we to decide what is good and what is bad in subject-matter?

Art, like speech, is a means of communication, and therefore of progress, i.e. of the movement of humanity forward towards perfection. Speech renders accessible to men of the latest generations, all the knowledge discovered by the experience and reflection, both of preceding generations and of the best and foremost men of their own times; art renders accessible to men of the latest generations all the feelings experienced by their predecessors, and those also which are being felt by their best and foremost contemporaries. And as the evolution of knowledge proceeds by truer and more necessary knowledge dislodging and replacing what is mistaken and unnecessary, so the evolution of feeling proceeds through art—feelings less kind and less needful for the well-being of mankind are replaced by others kinder and more needful for that end. That is the purpose of art. And, speaking now of its subject-matter, the more art fulfills that purpose the better the art, and the less it fulfills it the worse the art.

And the appraisement of feelings (i.e. the acknowledgment of these or those feelings as being more or less good, more or less necessary for the well-being of mankind) is made by the religious perception of the age.

In every period of history, and in every human society, there exists an understanding of the meaning of life which represents the highest level to which men of that society have attained—an understanding defining the highest good at which that society aims. And this understanding is the religious perception of the given time and society. And this religious perception is always clearly expressed by some advanced men, and more or less vividly perceived by all the members of the society. Such a religious perception and its corresponding expression exists always in every society. If it appears to us that in our society there is no religious perception, this is not because there really is none, but only because we do not want to see it. And we often wish not to see it because it exposes the fact that our life is inconsistent with that religious perception.

Religious perception in a society is like the direction of a flowing river. If the river flows at all, it must have a direction. If a society lives, there must be a religious perception indicating the direction in which, more or less consciously, all its members tend.

And so there always has been, and there is, a religious perception in every society. And it is by the standard of this religious perception that the feelings transmitted by art have always been estimated. Only on the basis of this religious perception of their age have men always chosen from the endlessly varied spheres of art that which transmitted feeling making religious perception operative in actual life. And such art has always been highly valued and encouraged; while art transmitting feelings already outlived, flowing from the antiquated religious perceptions of a former age, has always been condemned and despised. All the rest of art, transmitting those most diverse feelings by means of which people commune together, was not condemned, and was tolerated, if only it did not transmit feelings contrary to religious perception. Thus, for instance, among the Greeks, art transmitting the feeling of beauty, strength, and courage (Hesiod, Homer, Phidias) was chosen, approved, and encouraged; while art transmitting feelings of rude sensuality, despondency, and effeminacy was condemned and despised. Among the Jews, art transmitting feelings of devotion and submission to the God of the Hebrews and to His will (the epic of Genesis, the prophets, the Psalms) was chosen and encouraged, while art transmitting feelings of idolatry (the golden calf) was condemned and despised. All the rest of art—stories, songs, dances, ornamentation of houses, of utensils, and of clothes —which was not contrary to religious perception, was neither distinguished nor discussed. Thus, in regard to its subject-matter, has art been appraised always and everywhere, and thus it should be appraised, for this attitude towards art proceeds from the fundamental characteristics of human nature, and those characteristics do not change.

I know that according to an opinion current in our times, religion is a superstition, which humanity has outgrown, and that it is therefore assumed that no such thing exists as a religious perception common to us all by which art, in our time, can be estimated. I know that this is the opinion current in the pseudo-cultured circles of to-day. People who do not acknowledge Christianity in its true meaning because it undermines all their social privileges, and who, therefore, invent all kinds of philosophic and aesthetic theories to hide from themselves the meaninglessness and wrongness of their lives, cannot think otherwise. These people intentionally, or sometimes unintentionally, confusing the conception of a religious cult with the conception of religious perception, think that by denying the cult they get rid of religious perception. But even the very attacks on religion, and the attempts to establish a life-conception contrary to the religious perception of our times, most clearly demonstrate the existence of that religious perception condemning the lives that are not in harmony with it.

If humanity progresses, i.e. moves forward, there must inevitably be a guide to the direction of that movement. And religions have always furnished that guide. All history shows that the progress of humanity is accomplished not otherwise than under the guidance of religion. But if the race cannot progress without the guidance of religion—and progress is always going on, and consequently also in our own times— then there must be a religion of our times. So that, whether it pleases or displeases the so-called cultured people of to-day, they must admit the existence of religion—not of a religious cult, Catholic, Protestant, or another, but of religious perception—which, even in our times, is the guide always present where there is any progress. And if a religious perception exists amongst us, then our art should be appraised on the basis of that religious perception; and, as has always and everywhere been the case, art transmitting feelings flowing from the religious perception of our time should be chosen from all the indifferent art, should be acknowledged, highly esteemed, and encouraged; while art running counter to that perception should be condemned and despised, and all the remaining indifferent art should neither be distinguished nor encouraged.

The religious perception of our time, in its widest and most practical application, is the consciousness that our well-being, both material and spiritual, individual and collective, temporal and eternal, lies in the growth of brotherhood among all men—in their loving harmony with one another. This perception is not only expressed by Christ and all the best men of past ages, it is not only repeated in the most varied forms and from most diverse sides by the best men of our own times, but it already serves as a clue to all the complex labour of humanity, consisting as this labour does, on the one hand, in the destruction of physical and moral obstacles to the union of men, and, on the other hand, in establishing the principles common to all men which can and should unite them into one universal brotherhood. And it is on the basis of this perception that we should appraise all the phenomena of our life, and, among the rest, our art also; choosing from all its realms whatever transmits feelings flowing from this religious perception, highly prizing and encouraging such art, rejecting whatever is contrary to this perception, and not attributing to the rest of art an importance not properly pertaining to it.

The chief mistake made by people of the upper classes of the time of the so-called Renaissance,—a mistake which we still perpetuate,—was not that they ceased to value and to attach importance to religious art (people of that period could not attach importance to it, because, like our own upper classes, they could not believe in what the majority considered to be religion), but their mistake was that they set up in place of religious art which was lacking, an insignificant art which aimed only at giving pleasure, i.e. they began to choose, to value, and to encourage, in place of religious art, something which, in any case, did not deserve such esteem and encouragement.

One of the Fathers of the Church said that the great evil is not that men do not know God, but that they have set up, instead of God, that which is not God. So also with art. The great misfortune of the people of the upper classes of our time is not so much that they are without a religious art, as that, instead of a supreme religious art, chosen from all the rest as being specially important and valuable, they have chosen a most insignificant and, usually, harmful art, which aims at pleasing certain people, and which, therefore, if only by its exclusive nature, stands in contradiction to that Christian principle of universal union which forms the religious perception of our time. Instead of religious art, an empty and often vicious art is set up, and this hides from men's notice the need of that true religious art which should be present in life in order to improve it.

It is true that art which satisfies the demands of the religious perception of our time is quite unlike former art, but, notwithstanding this dissimilarity, to a man who does not intentionally hide the truth from himself, it is very clear and definite what does form the religious art of our age. In former times, when the highest religious perception united only some people (who, even if they formed a large society, were yet but one society surrounded by others—

Jews, or Athenian or Roman citizens), the feelings transmitted by the art of that time flowed from a desire for the might, greatness, glory, and prosperity of that society, and the heroes of art might be people who contributed to that prosperity by strength, by craft, by fraud, or by cruelty (Ulysses, Jacob, David, Samson, Hercules, and all the heroes). But the religious perception of our times does not select any one society of men; on the contrary, it demands the union of all—absolutely of all people without exception—and above every other virtue it sets brotherly love to all men. And, therefore, the feelings transmitted by the art of our time not only cannot coincide with the feelings transmitted by former art, but must run counter to them.

BIBLIOGRAPHY

>>>>>><<<<<<

Though the principles of order applied in organizing this bibliography are not readily apparent to the naked eye, the arrangement is deliberate and not random; and it is intended to maximize the usefulness of the material gathered here. The obvious division into major categories needs no explanation: the first category is of general works whose contents cover, or range over, the whole of the history of Western aesthetics; this is followed by four groups of limited chronological range—ancient, medieval and Renaissance, early modern, nineteenth century. The items within each major category are then divided into subgroups; each subgroup being ordered alphabetically. In the first category (General) there are two subgroups: the first six items are histories of aesthetics; the remaining ten are more limited or specialized works which nevertheless range over the whole of the period covered in this book. In the remaining four categories the arrangement of subgroups is primarily chronological. Each begins with a group, or groups, of general works covering the period, where there are any such; followed by a set of subgroups which progress chronologically through the period. Within each chronological subgroup I have separated primary from secondary works, and books from articles. Thus the reader will find within the second category (The Classical Tradition) a list of recent editions of Plato's works, followed by an alphabetized list of books on Plato's philosophy and an alphabetized list of articles on Plato's aesthetics. I have deemed it more useful to have all the critical writings on Plato, or Kant, grouped together, than to have them scattered through an alphabetized list of writings covering a major period in aesthetics.

Where the name of a periodical appears frequently I have used an abbreviation after the first appearance. Thus *Harvard Studies in Classical Philology* is listed as *HSCP* after its initial citation.

1. GENERAL

Beardsley, M. *A Short History of Aesthetics.* New York, 1965. (The most recent and most readable history of Aesthetics in English.)

Bosanquet, B. *A History of Aesthetic.* London, 1904.

Croce, B. *Aesthetic, Part II: History of Aesthetic,* trans. by D. Ainslie. New York, 1909.

Gilbert, K., and H. Kuhn. *A History of Esthetics.* Bloomington, 1953.

Listowel, William, Earl of. *A Critical History of Modern Aesthetics.* London, 1933.

McKeon, R. "Imitation and Poetry," in *Thought, Action and Passion.* Chicago, 1954.

→

Carritt, E. F. *Philosophies of Beauty.* New York, 1931.

Carritt, E. F. *The Theory of Beauty.* London, 1928.

Clark, B. (ed.). *European Theories of the Drama.* New York, 1930.

Cooper, L. *Theories of Style in Literature.* New York, 1907.

Crane, R. S. (ed.). *Critics and Criticism.* Chicago, 1952.

Hauser, A. *The Social History of Art.* New York, 1951.

Saintsbury, G. *A History of Criticism and Literary Taste in Europe.* Edinburgh, 1901-4.

Smith, J. H., and E. W. Parks (eds.). *The Great Critics.* New York, 1939.

Strunk, O. (ed.). *Source Readings in Music History.* New York, 1950.

Venturi, L. *History of Art Criticism.* New York, 1936.

2. THE CLASSICAL TRADITION

Atkins, J. W. H. *Literary Criticism in Antiquity.* Cambridge, 1934.

Gilbert, A. H. (ed.). *Literary Criticism from Plato to Dryden.* Detroit, 1962.

Panofsky, E. *Idea.* Leipzig, 1924.

Roberts, W. R. *Greek Rhetoric and Literary Criticism.* New York, 1928.

Sikes, E. E. *The Greek View of Poetry.* New York, 1931.

→

Bowra, C. M. *The Greek Experience*. Cleveland, 1957.

Cooper, L. (ed.). *The Greek Genius and Its Influence*. New Haven, 1917.

Dodds, E. R. *The Greeks and the Irrational*. Berkeley, 1956.

Guthrie, W. K. C. *The Greeks and Their Gods*. London, 1950.

Jaeger, W. *Phaideia*, 2nd ed., trans. by Gilbert Highet. New York, 1939-44.

Snell, B. *The Discovery of the Mind*, trans. by T. Rosenmeyer. Cambridge, 1953.

→

Else, G. F. "Imitation in the Fifth Century," *Classical Philology* 53 (1958).

Sperduti, A. "The Divine Nature of Poetry in Antiquity," *Transactions and Proceedings of the American Philological Association* [*TAPA*] 81 (1950).

→

Plato. *Dialogues*, 4th ed., trans. by B. Jowett. Oxford, 1953.

Plato. *The Collected Dialogues*, E. Hamilton and H. Cairns (eds.). New York, 1961.

→

Cornford, F. M. *The Republic of Plato*. New York, 1945.

Ferguson, J. *Republic, Book Ten*. London, 1957.

Friedlander, P. *Plato*, trans. by H. Meyerhoff. New York, 1958.

Gadamer, H. G. *Plato und die Dichter*. Frankfurt, 1934.

Grube, G. M. A. *Plato's Thought*. London, 1935.

Havelock, E. *Preface to Plato*. Oxford, 1963.

Lodge, R. C. *Plato's Theory of Art*. London, 1953.

Nettleship, R. L. *Lectures on the Republic of Plato*. London, 1890.

Schuhl, P. M. *Platon et l'art de son temps*. Paris, 1933.

Taylor, A. E. *Plato*. London, 1929.

Verdenius, W. J. *Mimesis*. Leiden, 1949.

→

Broos, H. F. M. "Plato and Art," *Mnemosyne* 4 (1951).

Collingwood, R. G. "Plato's Theory of Art," *Mind* 34 (1925).

Gilbert, A. H. "Did Plato Banish the Poets or the Critics?" *Studies in Philology* 36 (1934).

Gilbert, K. "The Relation of the Moral to the Aesthetic Standard in Plato," *Philosophical Review* 43 (1934).

Greene, W. C. "Plato's View of Poetry," *Harvard Studies in Classical Philology* [*HSCP*] 29 (1918).

Grube, G. M. A. "Plato's Theory of Beauty," *Monist* 37 (1927).

Kuhn, H. "The True Tragedy," *HSCP* 52-53 (1941-42).

→

Ross, W. D. (ed.). *The Works of Aristotle*. Oxford, 1910-52.

→

Butcher, H. S. *Aristotle's Theory of Poetry and Fine Art*. New York, 1923.

Bywater, I. *Aristotle on the Art of Poetry*. Oxford, 1909.

Cooper, L. *The Poetics of Aristotle*. Boston, 1923.

Else, G. F. *Aristotle's Poetics: The Argument*. Cambridge, 1957.

House, H. *Aristotle's Poetics*. London, 1956.

Potts, L. J. *Aristotle on the Art of Fiction*. Cambridge, 1959.

Telford, K. *Aristotle's Poetics*. Chicago, 1961.

→

Cooper, L., and A. Gudeman. *A Bibliography of the Poetics of Aristotle*. New Haven, 1928.

Cooper, L. *An Aristotelian Theory of Comedy*. New York, 1922.

Cooper, L. *On the Art of Poetry*. Boston, 1913.

Jaeger, W. *Aristotle*. Oxford, 1948.

Ross, W. D. *Aristotle*. London, 1923.

→

Bradley, A. C. *Shakespearean Tragedy*. London, 1951.

Dixon, W. M. *Tragedy*. London, 1925.

Kitto, H. D. F. *Form and Meaning in Drama*. London, 1956.

Kitto, H. D. F. *Greek Tragedy*. London, 1939.

Lucas, F. L. *Tragedy in Relation to Aristotle's Poetics*. New York, 1928.

Matthei, L. E. *Studies in Greek Tragedy*. Cambridge, 1918.

Thompson, J. A. K. *Irony*. Cambridge, 1927.

→

Friedlander, P. "Die griechische Tragödie und das Tragische," *Antike* 1-2 (1925-26).

Else, G. F. "Aristotle on the Beauty of Tragedy," *HSCP* 49 (1938).

Gilbert, A. H. "The Aristotelian Catharsis," *Philosophical Review* 35 (1926).

Gilbert, K. "Aesthetic Imitation and Imitators in Aristotle," *Philosophical Review* 45 (1936).

Ingarden, R. "A Marginal Commentary on Aristotle's Poetics," *Philosophy and Phenomenological Research* 21 (1961).

Langbaum, R. "Aristotle and Modern Literature," *Journal of Aesthetics and Art Criticism* [*JAAC*] 15 (1955).

Post, L. A. "Aristotle and Menander," *TAPA* 69 (1938).

Trench, W. F. "The Function of Poetry According to Aristotle," *Studies* (Dublin) 19 (1930).

Will, W. F. "Aristotle and the Question of Character in Literature," *Review of Metaphysics* 14 (1960).

→

Theophrastus. *Characters*, R. C. Jebb and J. E. Sandys (eds.). London, 1909.

→

Oates, W. J. (ed.). *The Stoic and Epicurean Philosophers.* New York, 1940.
→

DeLacy, P. "Stoic Views of Poetry," *American Journal of Philology* 69 (1948).
Wilkinson, L. P. "Philodemus and Poetry," *Greece and Rome* 2 (1932).
Wilkinson, L. P. "Philodemus on *Ethos* in Music," *Classical Quarterly* 33 (1939).
→

Blakeney, E. H. *Horace on the Art of Poetry.* London, 1928.
Fiske, G. *Lucilius and Horace.* Madison, 1920.
Fiske, G. *Cicero's "De Oratore" and Horace's "Ars Poetica."* Madison, 1929.
Padelford, F. M. *Essays on the Study and Use of Poetry by Plutarch and Basil the Great.* New York, 1902.
→

Plutarch. *Moralia,* trans. by F. C. Babbitt. New York, 1927.
→

Fyfe, W. H., and W. R. Roberts (trs.). *Aristotle: The Poetics, Longinus: On the Sublime, Demetrius: On Style.* New York, 1927.
Henn, T. R. *Longinus and English Criticism.* Cambridge, 1934.
Longinus. *On the Sublime,* trans. by W. R. Roberts. Cambridge, 1907.
Longinus. *On Elevation of Style,* trans. by T. G. Tucker. Melbourne, 1935.
Plotinus. *Enneads,* trans. by S. McKenna. London, 1926.
→

Brehier, E. *The Philosophy of Plotinus,* trans. by J. Thomas. Chicago, 1958.
Inge, W. R. *The Philosophy of Plotinus.* London, 1918.
Keyser, E. de. *La Signification de l'art dans les Enneades de Plotin.* Louvain, 1955.
Rieff, P. F. "Plotin und die deutsche Romantik," *Euphorion* 19 (1912).
→

Bundy, M. W. "The Theory of Imagination in Classical and Medieval Thought," *Univ. Illinois Studies in Language and Literature* 12 (1927).
→

Augustine. *Earlier Writings,* trans. by J. H. S. Burleigh. Philadelphia, 1953.
Augustine. *Basic Writings,* W. J. Oates (ed.). New York, 1948.
Chapman, E. *Saint Augustine's Philosophy of Beauty.* New York, 1939.
Gilson, E. *Introduction à l'étude de saint Augustin.* Paris, 1943.
Svoboda, K. *L'Esthétique de St. Augustin et ses sources.* Brno, 1933.
→

Abercrombie, N. *St. Augustine and French Classical Thought.* Oxford, 1938.

Mazzeo, J. A. "The Augustinian Conception of Beauty and Dante's Convivio," *JAAC* 11 (1953).

3. THE MIDDLE AGES AND THE RENAISSANCE

Baldwin, C. S. *Medieval Rhetoric and Poetic.* New York, 1928.
Bruyne, E. de. *Etudes d'esthétique médiévale.* Bruges, 1946.
Coulton, G. C. *Life in the Middle Ages.* Cambridge, 1930.
Coulton, G. C. *Art and the Reformation.* Oxford, 1928.
Gilson, E. *The Spirit of Medieval Philosophy.* London, 1936.
Huppe, B. F. *Doctrine and Poetry.* New York, 1959.
Huizinga, J. *The Waning of the Middle Ages.* London, 1924.
Ker, W. P. *The Dark Ages.* New York, 1904.
Male, E. *The Gothic Image.* New York, 1958.
Maritain, J. *Art and Scholasticism.* New York, 1930.
Seznec, J. *The Survival of the Pagan Gods.* New York, 1953.
Taylor, H. O. *The Classical Heritage of the Middle Ages.* New York, 1903.
→

McKeon, R. "Rhetoric in the Middle Ages," *Speculum* 17 (1942).
→

Dionysius. *Treatise on the Divine Names,* trans. by J. Parker. London, 1897.
Holt, E. G. *Literary Sources of Art History.* Princeton, 1947.
Panofsky, E. *Abbot Suger, on the Abbey-Church of St. Denis.* Princeton, 1946.
→

Thomas Aquinas. *Basic Writings,* A. C. Pegis (ed.). New York, 1945.
Bourke, V. J. (ed.). *The Pocket Aquinas.* New York, 1960.
→

Callahan, L. *A Theory of Esthetic according to the Principles of St. Thomas Aquinas.* Washington, D.C., 1927.
de Wulf, M. *Etudes historiques sur l'esthétique de St. Thomas d'Aquin.* Louvain, 1896.
Duffy, J. *A Philosophy of Poetry Based on Thomistic Principles.* Washington, 1945.
Kovach, F. J. *Die Ästhetik des Thomas von Aquin.* Berlin, 1961.
→

Gilson, E. *The Philosophy of St. Bonaventure,* trans. by T. Sheed. New York, 1938.
→

Jackson, W. W. *Dante's Convivio.* Oxford, 1909.
Osgood, C. G. *Boccaccio on Poetry.* Princeton, 1930.
Panofsky, E. *Gothic Architecture and Scholasticism.* New York, 1957.

Panofsky, E. *Studies in Iconology.* New York, 1939.
Panofsky, E. *Renaissance and Renascences in Western Art.* Stockholm, 1960.
→
Chastel, A. *Marsile Ficin et l'art.* Geneva and Lille, 1954.
Kristeller, P. *The Philosophy of Marsilio Ficino.* New York, 1943.
Nelson, J. C. *Renaissance Theory of Love.* New York, 1958.
→
Bruno, Giordano. *The Heroic Enthusiasts,* trans. by L. Williams. London, 1887-89.
→
Alberti, L. B. *On Painting,* trans. by J. Spencer. New Haven, 1956.
Alberti, L. B. *On Architecture,* trans. by J. Leoni. London, 1955.
Cennini, C. *The Craftsman's Handbook,* trans. by D. Thompson. New Haven, 1933.
Dürer, A. *Writings,* W. M. Conway (ed.). New York, 1958.
Vasari, G. *The Lives of the Painters, Sculptors and Architects.* London, 1927.
Vinci, Leonardo da. *Treatise on Painting,* trans. by A. P. McMahon. Princeton, 1956.
→
Clark, K. *Leonardo da Vinci.* Cambridge, 1940.
Clements, R. J. *Michelangelo's Art Theory.* New York, 1961.
Panofsky, E. *The Codex Huygens and Leonardo da Vinci's Art Theory.* London, 1940.
Panofsky, E. *The Life and Art of Albrecht Dürer.* Princeton, 1955.
→
Blunt, A. *Artistic Theory in Italy, 1450-1600.* Oxford, 1940.
Smith, G. (ed.). *Elizabethan Critical Essays.* Oxford, 1904.
Spingarn, J. E. *History of Literary Criticism in the Renaissance.* New York, 1899.
Wittkower, R. *Architectural Principles in Age of Humanism.* London, 1949.
→
Charlton, H. B. *Castelvetro's Theory of Poetry.* Manchester, 1913.
Hathaway, B. *The Age of Criticism: The Late Renaissance in Italy.* Ithaca, 1961.
Vida, M. G. *The Art of Poetry,* trans. by C. Pitt. Boston, 1892.
→
Lowinsky, E. E. "Music in the Culture of the Renaissance," *Journal of the History of Ideas* [*JHI*] 15 (1954).
Mahon, D. "Studies in Seicento Art and Theory," *Studies of the Warburg Institute* 16 (1947).
Nahm, M. "Leonardo da Vinci's Philosophy of Originality," *Bucknell Review* 8 (1958).
Wilson, H. S. "Some Meanings of 'Nature' in Renaissance Literary Theory," *JHI* 2 (1941).

Wittkower, R. "Individualism in Art and Artists: A Renaissance Problem," *JHI* 22 (1961).

4. THE DEVELOPMENT OF MODERN AESTHETICS

Padelford, F. M. (tr.). *Scaliger's Poetics.* New York, 1905.
Sidney, Sir Philip. *An Apologie for Poetry.* Oxford, 1907.
→
Elledge, S., and D. Schier (eds.). *The Continental Model: Selected French Critical Essays of the Seventeenth Century.* Minneapolis, 1960.
Fontaine, A. *Les Doctrines d'art en France.* Paris, 1909.
Soreil, A. *Introduction à l'histoire de l'esthétique française.* Brussels, 1955.
→
Boileau-Despréaux, N. *L'Art poétique.* Paris, 1674.
Brody, J. *Boileau and Longinus.* Geneva, 1958.
Haley, M. P. *Racine and the Art poétique of Boileau.* Baltimore, 1938.
Smith, D. N. (ed.). *Boileau: L'Art poétique.* Cambridge, 1898.
Moore, W. G. "Boileau and Longinus," *French Studies* 14 (1960).
→
Krantz, E. *Essai sur l'esthétique des Descartes.* Paris, 1882.
Lemaître, J. *Corneille et le poétique d'Aristote.* Paris, 1888.
→
Davis, C. "Ut pictura poesis," *Modern Language Review* 30 (1935).
Howard, W. G. "Ut pictura poesis," *PMLA* 24 (1909).
Lee, R. W. "Ut pictura poesis: The Humanistic Theory of Painting," *Art Bulletin* 22 (1940).
Saisselin, R. G. "Ut pictura poesis: Du Bos to Diderot," *JAAC* 20 (1961).
Saisselin, R. G. "The Origins of Modern Aesthetics," *British Journal of Aesthetics* 4 (1964).
→
Bacon, Francis. *Works.* London, 1819.
Hobbes, T. *English Works,* W. Molesworth (ed.). London, 1839-45.
Locke, J. *An Essay Concerning Human Understanding,* A. C. Fraser (ed.). Oxford, 1894.
→
Spingarn, J. E. (ed.). *Critical Essays of the Seventeenth Century.* Oxford, 1908.
Thorpe, C. D. *The Aesthetic Theory of Thomas Hobbes.* Ann Arbor, 1940.
Willey, B. *The Seventeenth Century Background.* London, 1934.
→

Langdon, I. *Milton's Theory of Poetry and Fine Art.* New Haven, 1924.
→

Bond, D. F. " 'Distrust' of Imagination in English Neo-classicism," *Philological Quarterly* 14 (1935).

Bundy, M. W. "Bacon's True Opinion of Poetry," *Studies in Philology* 27 (1930).

Elledge, S. "The Background and Development in English Criticism of the Theories of Generality and Particularity," *PMLA* 62 (1947).

Jones, R. F. "Science and Criticism in the Neo-classical Age of English Literature," *JHI* 1 (1940).

Kallich, M. "The Association of Ideas and Critical Theory: Hobbes, Locke, and Addison," *Journal of English Literary History* [*ELH*] 12 (1945).

Lovejoy, A. O. " 'Nature' as Aesthetic Norm," *Modern Language Notes* 42 (1927).

Rogerson, Brewster. "The Art of Painting the Passions," *JHI* 14 (1953).

Stolnitz, J. "Locke and the Categories of Value in Eighteenth-Century British Aesthetic Theory," *Philosophy* 38 (1963).

Trowbridge, H. "The Place of Rules in Dryden's Criticism," *Modern Philology* 44 (1946).

Williamson, G. "The Restoration Revolt against Enthusiasm," *Studies in Philology* 30 (1933).
→

Addison, J. *Works.* London, 1888.

Akenside, M. *The Pleasures of Imagination.* London, 1744.

Alison, A. *Essays on the Nature and Principles of Taste.* Edinburgh, 1815.

Baillie, J. *An Essay on the Sublime.* London, 1747.

Beattie, J. *Essays on Poetry and Music.* London, 1776.

Blair, H. *A Critical Dissertation on the Poems of Ossian.* London, 1790.

Blair, H. *Lectures on Rhetoric and Belles Lettres.* London, 1790.

Burke, E. *A Philosophical Inquiry into the Origin of Our Ideas of the Sublime and Beautiful,* J. T. Boulton (ed.) New York, 1958.

Dennis, J. *Critical Works,* E. N. Hooker (ed.). Baltimore, 1939-43.

Gerard, A. *An Essay on Genius.* London, 1774.

Gerard, A. *An Essay on Taste.* Edinburgh, 1780.

Gilpin, W. *Three Essays.* London, 1794.

Harris, J. *Three Treatises.* London, 1803.

Hogarth, W. *The Analysis of Beauty,* J. Burke (ed.). Oxford, 1955.

Hume, D. *Essays, Moral, Political and Literary.* London, 1875.

Hume, D. *A Treatise of Human Nature.* London, 1882.

Hutcheson, F. *An Essay on the Nature and Conduct of the Passions.* London, 1728.

Hutcheson, F. *An Inquiry into the Original of Our Ideas of Beauty and Virtue.* London, 1725.

Jeffrey, F. "Review of Alison's Essays," *The Edinburgh Review* 18 (1811).

Kames, H. H. *Elements of Criticism.* Edinburgh, 1765.

Knight, R. P. *An Analytical Inquiry into the Principles of Taste.* London, 1806.

Lauder, T. D. (ed.). *Sir Uvedale Price on the Picturesque.* Edinburgh, 1842.

Olson, E. (ed.). *Longinus, "On the Sublime," and Sir Joshua Reynolds' Discourses on Art.* Chicago, 1945.

Reid, T. *Works,* Sir W. Hamilton (ed.). Edinburgh, 1880.

Repton, H. *The Art of Landscape Gardening,* J. Nolen (ed.). Boston, 1907.

Reynolds, Sir J. *Literary Works,* E. Malone (ed.). London, 1819.

Shaftesbury. *Characteristics,* J. M. Robertson (ed.). London, 1900.

Smith, Adam. *Essays Philosophical and Literary.* London, 1880.

Stewart, D. *Collected Works,* Sir W. Hamilton (ed.). Edinburgh, 1877.

Young, E. *Conjectures on Original Composition,* in *Works,* Vol. 5. London, 1783.
→

Elledge, S. *Eighteenth Century Critical Essays.* Ithaca, 1961.
→

Bate, W. J. *From Classic to Romantic: Premises of Taste in Eighteenth Century England.* Cambridge, Mass., 1949.

Brett, R. L. *The Third Earl of Shaftesbury.* London, 1951.

Brunius, T. *David Hume on Criticism.* Stockholm, 1952.

Burke, J. *Hogarth and Reynolds.* Oxford, 1943.

Cassirer, E. *The Philosophy of the Enlightenment.* Princeton, 1951.

Fowler, T. *Shaftesbury and Hutcheson.* London, 1882.

Hipple, W. J. *The Beautiful, the Sublime and the Picturesque in Eighteenth Century British Aesthetic Theory.* Carbondale, 1957.

Jessop, T. E. *A Bibliography of David Hume and of Scottish Philosophy.* London, 1938.

McCosh, J. *The Scottish Philosophy.* New York, 1890.

McKenzie, G. *Critical Responsiveness.* Berkeley, 1949.

Monk, S. *The Sublime.* New York, 1935.

Needham, H. A. *Taste and Criticism in the Eighteenth Century.* London, 1952.

Randall, H. W. *The Critical Theory of Lord Kames.* Northampton, Mass., 1944.

Scott, W. R. *Francis Hutcheson.* Cambridge, 1900.

Smith, N. K. *The Philosophy of David Hume.* London, 1941.

Tuveson, E. L. *The Imagination as a Means of Grace.* Berkeley, 1960.

Essays and Studies by members of the English
Association. Oxford, 1937.
→

Bredvold, L. "The Tendency towards Platonism
in Neo-classical Esthetics," ELH 1 (1934).

Brett, R. L. "The Aesthetic Sense and Taste in
the Literary Criticism of the Early Eighteenth
Century," Review of English Studies 20
(1944).

Brown, S. G. "Observations on Hume's Theory
of Taste," English Studies 20 (1938).

Clough, W. O. "Reason and Genius—An Eighteenth Century Dilemma," Philological Quarterly 23 (1944).

Crane, R. S. "On Writing the History of English Criticism, 1650-1800," University of Toronto Quarterly 22 (1953).

De Wolfe, I. "Townscape: A Plea for an English Visual Philosophy Founded on the True
Rock of Sir Uvedale Price," Architectural Review 106 (1949).

Goodman, P. "Neo-Classicism, Platonism and
Romanticism," Journal of Philosophy 31
(1934).

Grene, M. "Gerard's Essay on Taste," Modern
Philology 41 (1943).

Hipple, W. J. "The Aesthetics of Dugal Stewart: Culmination of a Tradition," JAAC 14
(1955).

Hipple, W. J. "General and Particular in the
Discourses of Sir Joshua Reynolds; A Study in
Method," JAAC 11 (1953).

Hipple, W. J. "The Logic of Hume's Essay 'Of
Tragedy,'" Philosophical Quarterly 6 (1956).

Howard, W. G. "Burke among the Forerunners
of Lessing," PMLA 22 (1907).

Kallich, M. "The Associationist Criticism of
Francis Hutcheson and David Hume," Studies
in Philology 43 (1946).

Kallich, M. "The Meaning of Archibald Alison's Essays on Taste," Philological Quarterly
27 (1948).

Kallich, M. "The Argument Against the Association of Ideas in Eighteenth-Century Aesthetics," Modern Language Quarterly 15
(1954).

Macklem, M. "Reynolds and the Ambiguities
of Neo-Classical Criticism," Philological Quarterly 31 (1952).

McCutchen, R. P. "Eighteenth Century Aesthetics: A Search for Surviving Values," Harvard Library Bulletin 10 (1959).

Pevsner, N. "Richard Payne Knight," Art Bulletin 31 (1949).

Robbins, D. O. "The Aesthetics of Thomas
Reid," JAAC 2 (1942).

Stolnitz, J. "Beauty: Some Stages in the History of an Idea," JHI 22 (1961).

Stolnitz, J. "On the Origins of 'Aesthetic Dis-
interestedness,'" JAAC 20 (1961).

Stolnitz, J. "On the Significance of Lord
Shaftesbury in Modern Aesthetic Theory,"
Philosophical Quarterly 11 (1961).

Thompson, E. "The Discourses of Sir Joshua
Reynolds," PMLA 32 (1917).

Thorp, C. D. "Addison and Hutcheson on the
Imagination," ELH 2 (1935).

Thorp, C. D. "Addison's Contribution to Criticism," in The Seventeenth Century, by R. F.
Jones et al. Stanford, 1951.

Tuveson, E. "Space, Deity and the 'Natural
Sublime,'" Modern Language Quarterly 12
(1951).

Voitle, R. B. "Shaftesbury's Moral Sense,"
Studies in Philology 52 (1955).

Wasserman, E. R. "The Pleasures of Tragedy,"
ELH 14 (1947).

Wecter, D. "Burke's Theory of Words, Images
and Emotion," PMLA 60 (1940).

Whitney, L. "English Primitivistic Theories of
Epic Origins," Modern Philology 21 (1924).
→

Vico, G. La Scienza Nuova. Naples, 1725.
The New Science, trans. by T. Bergin and M.
Fisch. Ithaca, 1948.

Vico, G. Opera. Milan, 1852-54.
→

Batteux, C. Les Beaux Arts réduits à un même
principe. Paris, 1746.

Diderot, D. Oeuvres complètes. Paris, 1876.

Dubos, L'Abbé. Réflexions critiques sur la
poésie et sur la peinture. Paris, 1719. Dubos, L'Abbé. Critical Reflections on Poetry
and Painting, trans. by T. Nugent. London,
1748.
→

Adams, H. P. The Life and Writings of Giambattista Vico. London, 1935.

Croce, B. The Philosophy of Giambattista Vico,
trans. by R. G. Collingwood. London, 1913.

De Sanctis, F. History of Italian Literature.
New York, 1931.

Flint, R. Vico. Edinburgh, 1884.
→

Belaval, Y. L'Esthétique sans paradoxe de Diderot. Paris, 1950.

Fellows, O., and N. Torrey (eds.). Diderot
Studies II. Syracuse, 1952.

Folkierski, W. Entre le classicisme et le romantisme. Paris, 1925.

Gilman, M. The Idea of Poetry in France.
Cambridge, 1958.
→

Boas, G. "The Arts in the 'Encyclopédie,'"
JAAC 23 (1964).

Durkin, T. J. "Three Notes to Diderot's Aesthetic," JAAC 15 (1957).

Gilman, M. "The Poet according to Diderot,"
Romanic Review 37 (1946).

Kristeller, P. "The Modern System of the
Arts," JHI 12-13 (1951-52).

Kubota, J. "Diderot's Idea of 'Imitation of Nature,'" Bigaku 8 (1957).

Walker, E. M. "Towards an Understanding of
Diderot's Aesthetic Theory," Romanic Review 35 (1944).

→

Baumgarten, A. G. *Reflections on Poetry*, trans. by K. Aschenbrenner and W. Holther. Berkeley, 1954.

Baumgarten, A. G. *Aesthetica*. Frankfurt, 1758.

Herder, J. G. *Werke*, B. Suphan (ed.). Berlin, 1878.

Lessing, G. E. *Laokoon*, trans. by E. A. McCormick. New York, 1962.

Lessing, G. E. *Prose Works*, trans. by E. Beasley and H. Zimmern. London, 1890.

Mendelssohn, M. *Briefe über die Empfindungen*. Berlin, 1755.

Winckelmann, J. J. *Reflections on the Painting and Sculpture of the Greeks*, trans. by H. Fuseli. London, 1767.

→

Hamann, A. *Lessing's Laokoon*. Oxford, 1878.

Howard, W. G. *Laokoon*. New York, 1910.

Nolte, F. O. *Lessing's Laokoon*. Lancaster, 1940.

Robertson, J. G. *Lessing's Dramatic Theory*. Cambridge, 1939.

Schmidt, J. *Leibniz und Baumgarten*. Halle, 1875.

→

Kant, I. *Observations on the Feeling of the Beautiful and Sublime*, trans. by R. Goldthwait. Berkeley, 1960.

Kant, I. *Werke*, E. Cassirer (ed.). Berlin, 1914-22.

Kant, I. *Critique of Judgement*, trans. by J. H. Bernard. London, 1892.

Kant, I. *Critique of Judgement*, trans. by J. C. Meredith. Oxford, 1928.

Kant, I. *Analytic of the Beautiful*, trans. by W. Cerf. New York, 1963.

→

Basch, V. *Essai critique sur l'esthétique de Kant*. Paris, 1927.

Caird, E. *The Critical Philosophy of Immanuel Kant*. Glasgow, 1909.

Cassirer, H. W. *Commentary on Kant's Critique of Judgment*. London, 1938.

Cohen, H. *Kants Begründung der Aesthetik*. Berlin, 1889.

Dunham, B. *A Study in Kant's Aesthetics*. Lancaster, 1934.

Hendel, C. W. (ed.). *The Philosophy of Kant and Our Modern World*. New York, 1957.

Jacoby, G. *Herders und Kants Aesthetik*. Leipzig, 1907.

Knox, I. *The Aesthetic Theories of Kant, Hegel and Schopenhauer*. New York, 1936.

Lindsay, A. D. *Kant*. London, 1934.

MacMillan, R. *The Crowning Phase of the Critical Philosophy*. London, 1912.

Menzer, P. *Kants Aesthetik in ihrer Entwicklung*. Berlin, 1952.

Nivelle, A. *Les Théories esthétiques en Allemagne de Baumgarten à Kant*. Paris, 1956.

Schlapp, O. *Kants Lehre vom Genie*. Göttingen, 1901.

Simmel, G. *Kant und Goethe*. Berlin, 1906.

Whitney, G. T., and D. F. Bowers (eds.). *The Heritage of Kant*. Princeton, 1939.

Will, F. *Intelligible Beauty in Aesthetic Thought from Winckelmann to Victor Cousin*. Tübingen, 1958.

→

Cassirer, E. *Rousseau, Kant and Goethe*. Princeton, 1945.

Cassirer, E. *Idee und Gestalt*. Berlin, 1921.

Carritt, E. F. "The Sources and Effects in England of Kant's Philosophy of Beauty," *Monist* 35 (1925).

Lee, H. N. "Kant's Theory of Aesthetics," *Philosophical Review* 40 (1931).

Schueller, H. M. "Immanuel Kant and the Aesthetics of Music," *JAAC* 14 (1955).

Zimmerman, R. L. "Kant: The Aesthetic Judgment," *JAAC* 21 (1963).

5. POST-KANTIAN AESTHETICS

Goethe, J. W. *Werke*. Weimar, 1887 ff.

Schiller, F. *Aesthetical and Philosophical Essays*, N. H. Dole (ed.). New York, 1902.

Schiller, F. *Letters on the Aesthetic Education of Man*, trans. by R. Snell. New Haven, 1954.

Ungar, F. *Friedrich Schiller: An Anthology for Our Time*. New York, 1959.

→

Carlyle, T. *Essays on Goethe*. London, 1828-32.

Carlyle, T. *Life of Schiller*. London, 1846.

Kerry, S. *Schiller's Writings on Aesthetics*. Manchester, 1961.

Lewes, G. H. *The Life and Works of Goethe*. New York, 1930.

Miller, R. D. *Schiller and the Idea of Freedom*. Harrogate, 1959.

Rosalewski, W. *Schillers Aesthetik*. Heidelberg, 1912.

Spingarn, J. E. (ed.). *Goethe's Literary Essays*. New York, 1921.

Usinger, F. *Friedrich Schiller und die Idee des Schönen*. Wiesbaden, 1955.

→

Coleridge, S. T. *Biographia Literaria*, J. Shawcross (ed.). Oxford, 1907.

Coleridge, S. T. *Shakespearean Criticism*, T. M. Raysor (ed.). London, 1930.

Shelley, P. B. *Literary and Philosophical Criticism*, J. Shawcross (ed.). London, 1909.

Wordsworth, W. *Literary Criticism*, N. C. Smith (ed.). London, 1905.

Wordsworth, W. *Prefaces and Essays on Poetry*, A. J. George (ed.). Boston, 1892.

→

Baker, J. V. *The Sacred River*. Baton Rouge, 1957.

Coburn, K. (ed.). *Coleridge's Philosophical Lectures*. New York, 1949.

Coburn, K. (ed.). *Inquiring Spirit*. London, 1951.

Fogle, R. H. *The Idea of Coleridge's Criticism*. Berkeley, 1962.

Hirsch, E. D. *Wordsworth and Schelling*. New Haven, 1960.

Mackail, J. W. *Coleridge's Literary Criticism*. London, 1908.

McKenzie, G. *Organic Unity in Coleridge*. Berkeley, 1939.

Mill, J. S. *Mill and Bentham on Coleridge*. London, 1950.

Notopoulos, J. A. *The Platonism of Shelley*. Durham, 1949.

Peacock, M. L. *The Critical Opinions of William Wordsworth*. Baltimore, 1950.

Richards, I. A. *Coleridge on Imagination*. London, 1950.

Shairp, J. C. *Studies in Poetry and Philosophy*. Boston, 1887.

Stallknecht, N. *Strange Seas of Thought*. Bloomington, 1958.

Verkoren, L. *A Study of Shelley's "Defence of Poetry."* Amsterdam, 1937.

→

Benziger, J. "Organic Unity: Leibniz to Coleridge," *PMLA* 64 (1951).

Brett, R. "Coleridge's Theory of Imagination," *English Studies* 2 (1949).

McElderry, J. "Common Elements in Wordsworth's 'Preface' and Shelley's 'Defence of Poetry,'" *Modern Language Quarterly* 5 (1944).

Thorpe, C. D. "Coleridge as Aesthetician and Critic," *JHI* 5 (1944).

→

Hegel, G. W. F. *Philosophy of Fine Art*, trans. by F. P. B. Osmaston. London, 1920.

Hegel, G. W. F. *Introduction to the Philosophy of Fine Art*, trans. by B. Bosanquet. London, 1905.

Schelling, F. *Sämtliche Werke*. Stuttgart, 1856-61.

Schelling, F. *Philosophie der Kunst*. Munich, 1927.

Schopenhauer, A. *The World as Will and Idea*, trans. by R. B. Haldane and J. Kemp. London, 1883.

Schopenhauer, A. *The World as Will and Representation*, trans. by E. F. J. Payne. Indian Hills, Colo., 1958.

Schopenhauer, A. *Complete Essays*, trans. by B. Saunders. New York, 1923.

Schleiermacher, F. D. E. *Ästhetik*, R. Odebrecht (ed.). Berlin, 1931.

→

Lotze, H. *Geschichte der Ästhetik*. Munich, 1868.

→

Adams, J. S. *The Aesthetics of Pessimism*. Philadelphia, 1940.

Fauconnet, A. *L'Esthétique de Schopenhauer*. Paris, 1913.

Findlay, J. N. *Hegel*. London, 1958.

Gardner, P. *Schopenhauer*. Baltimore, 1963.

Gibelin, J. *L'Esthétique de Schelling*. Paris, 1934.

Kedney, J. S. *Hegel's Aesthetic*. Chicago, 1897.

Paolucci, H., and A. Paolucci. *Hegel on Tragedy*. New York, 1960.

Stace, W. T. *The Philosophy of Hegel*. London, 1924.

Tessèdre, B. *L'Esthétique de Hegel*. Paris, 1958.

Vecchi, C. *L'Estetica di Hegel*. Milan, 1956.

→

Bradley, A. C. "Hegel's Theory of Tragedy," in *Oxford Lectures on Poetry*. London, 1909.

Fackenheim, E. L. "Schelling's Philosophy of the Literary Arts," *Philosophical Quarterly* 4 (1954).

Mundt, E. K. "Three Aspects of German Aesthetic Theory," *JAAC* 17 (1959).

Schueller, H. M. "Schelling's Theory of the Metaphysics of Music," *JAAC* 15 (1957).

→

Blake, W. *Poetry and Prose*, G. Keynes (ed.). New York, 1939.

Carlyle, T. *Heroes and Hero Worship*. London, 1888.

Emerson, R. W. *Essays*. New York, 1941.

Hazlitt, W. *Complete Works*, P. P. Howe (ed.). London, 1930-34.

Hunt, L. *Imagination and Fancy*. New York, 1848.

Keats, J. *Letters*, M. B. Forman (ed.). Oxford, 1948.

Keble, J. *Lectures on Poetry*. Oxford, 1912.

Mill, S. J. *Early Essays*, J. W. M. Gibbs (ed.). London, 1897.

Nietzsche, F. *Complete Works*, O. Levy (ed.). New York, 1962.

Novalis. *Romantische Welt*. Leipzig, 1939.

Poe, E. A. *Representative Selections*, M. Alterton and H. Craig (eds.). New York, 1935.

Schlegel, A. W. *Vorlesungen über philosophische Kunstlehre*. Leipzig, 1911.

Schlegel, F. *Prosaische Jugendschriften*. Vienna, 1882.

Usher, J. *Clio: or A Discourse on Taste*. London, 1769.

→

Abrams, M. H. *The Mirror and the Lamp*. New York, 1953.

Babbitt, I. *Masters of Modern French Criticism*. New York, 1912.

Babbitt, I. *The New Laokoon*. New York, 1910.

Babbitt, I. *Rousseau and Romanticism*. New York, 1919.

Bowra, C. M. *The Romantic Imagination*. Cambridge, Mass., 1949.

Brandes, G. *Main Currents in Nineteenth Century Literature*. New York, 1923.

Flaccus, L. W. *Artists and Thinkers*. New York, 1916.

Heller, E. *The Disinherited Mind.* New York, 1959.

Lovejoy, A. O. *Essays in the History of Ideas.* Baltimore, 1948.

Powell, A. E. *The Romantic Theory of Poetry.* London, 1926.

Praz, M. *The Romantic Agony.* London, 1933.

Rouge, I. F. *Schlegel et la genèse du romantisme allemand.* Paris, 1904.

Schneider, E. *The Aesthetics of William Hazlitt.* Philadelphia, 1933.

Shroder, M. *Icarus: The Image of the Artist in French Romanticism.* Cambridge, 1961.

Walzel, O. *German Romanticism,* trans. by A. Lussky. New York, 1932.

Wellek, R. *History of Modern Criticism.* New Haven, 1955.
→

Adams, H. "The Blakean Aesthetic," *JAAC* 13 (1954).

Eichner, H. "Friedrich Schlegel's Theory of Romantic Poetry," *PMLA* 71 (1955).

Kaufmann, W. "Nietzsche and Rilke," *Kenyon Review* 17 (1955).

Robson, J. M. "Mill's Theory of Poetry," *Univ. of Toronto Quarterly* 29 (1960).

Schutze, M. "Studies in the Mind of Romanticism," *Modern Philology* 16-17 (1918-19).

Wellek, R. "The Concept of 'Romanticism' in Literary History," *Comparative Literature* 1 (1949).
→

Kaufmann, W. *Nietzsche.* Princeton, 1950.

Knight, A. *Some Aspects of the Life and Works of Nietzsche.* Cambridge, 1933.

Lea, F. *The Tragic Philosopher.* London, 1957.

Ludovici, A. M. *Nietzsche and Art.* London, 1912.

Morgan, G. A. *What Nietzsche Means.* Cambridge, 1941.
→

Hopkins, V. C. *Spires of Form: A Study of Emerson's Aesthetic Theory.* Cambridge, 1951.

Metzger, C. R. *Emerson and Greenough.* Berkeley, 1954.

Metzger, C. R. *Thoreau and Whitman.* Seattle, 1961.
→

Adams, P. R. "Emerson and the Organic Metaphor," *PMLA* 69 (1954).

Brown, T. M. "Greenough, Paine, Emerson and the Organic Aesthetic," *JAAC* 14 (1956).
→

Comte, A. *A General View of Positivism,* trans. by J. H. Bridges. London, 1880.

Cousin, V. *Lectures on the True, the Beautiful and the Good,* trans. by O. Wright. New York, 1858.

Guyau, M. *L'Art au point de vue sociologique.* Paris, 1895.

Marshall, H. R. *Pain, Pleasure and Aesthetics.* London, 1894.

Morris, W. *Collected Works.* London, 1910-15.

Morris, M. (ed.). *William Morris.* Oxford, 1936.

Pater, W. *Appreciations.* New York, 1905.

Pater, W. *The Renaissance.* London, 1873.

Pater, W. *Marius the Epicurean.* New York, 1921.

Proudhon, J. *Du Principe de l'art et de sa destination sociale.* Paris, 1939.

Ruskin, J. *Works,* Cook and Wedderburn (eds.). London, 1903-12.

Taine, H. *The Philosophy of Art,* trans. by J. Durand. New York, 1875.

Tolstoy, L. *What Is Art? and Essays on Art,* trans. by A. Maude. London, 1930.

Véron, E. *Aesthetics.* London, 1879.

Zola, E. *The Experimental Novel,* trans. by B. Sherman. New York, 1893.
→

Hardison, O. B. (ed.). *Modern Continental Literary Criticism.* New York, 1962.

Levin, M. (ed.). *Perspectives in Criticism.* Cambridge, 1950.

Peters, R. L. (ed.). *Victorians on Literature and Art.* New York, 1961.

Weber, E. (ed.). *Paths to the Present: European Thought from Romanticism to Existentialism.* New York, 1962.
→

Becker, G. *Documents of Modern Literary Realism.* Princeton, 1963.

Cassagne, A. *La Théorie de l'art pour l'art en France.* Paris, 1906.

Ciari, J. *Symbolism from Poe to Mallarmé.* London, 1956.

Kallen, H. *Art and Freedom.* New York, 1942.

Weinberg, B. *French Realism: The Critical Reaction.* London, 1937.
→

Child, R. C. *The Aesthetic of Walter Pater.* New York, 1940.

Ferran, A. *L'Esthétique de Baudelaire.* Paris, 1933.

Fishman, S. *The Interpretation of Art.* Berkeley, 1963.

Ladd, H. *The Victorian Morality of Art: An Analysis of Ruskin's Esthetic.* New York, 1932.
→

Egan, R. F. "The Genesis of the Theory of 'Art for Art's Sake' in Germany and in England," *Smith Coll. Studies in Modern Language,* 2, 5 (1921, 1924).

Hannay, A. H. "The Concept of Art for Art's Sake," *Philosophy* 29 (1954).

Morawski, S. "The Problem of Value and Criteria in Taine's Aesthetics," *JAAC* 21 (1963).

Morris, B. "Ruskin on the Pathetic Fallacy," *JAAC* 14 (1955).

Singer, I. "The Aesthetics of 'Art for Art's Sake,'" *JAAC* 12 (1954).

Wellek, R.   "Taine's Literary Theory and Criticism," *Criticism* 1 (1959).

Wellek, R.   "Walter Pater's Literary Theory and Criticism," *Victorian Studies* 1 (1957).

Wilcox, J.   "The Beginnings of l'art pour l'art," *JAAC* 11 (1953).

Yamakawa, K.   "Coleridge and Pater as Aestheticians," *Erbungaku Kenkyu* 33 (1956).

→

Garrod, H. W.   *Tolstoi's Theory of Art.*   Oxford, 1935.

Kvito, D.   *A Philosophical Study of Tolstoy.*   New York, 1927.

Redpath, T.   *Tolstoy.*   New York, 1960.